The Christology
of the Fourth Gospel

The Christology
of the Fourth Gospel

Its Unity and Disunity in the Light of John 6

Paul N. Anderson

TRINITY PRESS INTERNATIONAL
VALLEY FORGE, PENNSYLVANIA

First U.S. edition published 1997 by Trinity Press International, P.O. Box 851, Valley Forge, PA 19482-0851. Trinity Press International is a division of the Morehouse Group. Originally published 1996 by J.C.B. Mohr (Paul Siebeck), Tübingen, Germany.

Anderson, Paul N., 1956-
The christology of the Fourth Gospel : its unity and disunity in the light of John 6 / by Paul N. Anderson.
       p.   cm.
A revision of the author's thesis (doctoral)— University of Glasgow, 1988.
Originally published: Tübingen : Mohr, 1996, in series:
Wissenschaftliche Untersuchungen zum Neuen Testament. 2. Reihe.
Includes bibliographical references and indexes.
ISBN 1-56338-199-0 (pbk. : alk. paper)
1. Bible. N.T. John—Criticism, interpretation, etc. 2. Jesus Christ—Person and Offices. 3. Bible. N.T. John VI—Criticism, interpretation, etc. I. Title.
BS2615.2.A53 1997
226.5'06—dc21   97-7838
                                                                 CIP

Printed in the United States of America

97 98 99 00 01 02 03 04 05   3 2 1

Contents

Foreword

Paul N. Anderson's Glasgow doctoral dissertation is at once one of the most concentrated and intensive exegetical studies and one of the most wide-ranging and suggestive essays on Johannine christology that I have seen. As the author himself states it, his purpose is "to gain clearer insight into the christological tensions of the Fourth Gospel by means of seeking a deeper understanding of the dialectical process of thought by which the evangelist has come to embrace such a distinctively unitive *and* disunitive christology." In pursuing this goal Anderson concentrates on chapter 6, the Feeding of the Five Thousand and subsequent events and discourses, in which the tensions and dialectical character of John's thought become apparent.

The identification of tensions is credited to Rudolf Bultmann, although his efforts to resolve them by source and rearrangement theories are rejected, and C.K. Barrett's suggestions about the dialectical character of John's thought then become seminal in their resolution. Anderson's exegesis of John 6 is itself a major contribution. In my opinion both his appreciation of Bultmann's interpretation and and his refusal to accept his literary-critical resolution of exegetical problems are well-founded. Also like Bultmann, he cannot regard the narrative and discourse of chapter 6 as simply derivative from the Synoptic Gospels or Mark. At the same time the relationship is clear. Rather than regard it as a problem amenable to source and redaction criticism, whether of the Synoptic Gospels or other documents, Anderson seeks to understand the Johannine version of this material as an independent development of, and reflection upon, the same events that are somewhat differently recounted in the Synoptics.

This mode of understanding leads Anderson to some of his most stimulating suggestions, which, however, might make him seem vulnerable to the charge of psychologizing the text. And yet, by using the research and categories of the American theologians Fowler and Loder, who have undertaken to analyze and describe the experience and development of faith on the basis of empirical investigation, Anderson applies their insights and results to the Gospel of John. The proposal that something like what they describe lies at the root of the tensions of Johannine thought is provocative and will doubtless raise questions. Just at this point, however, Anderson's positive theological relationship to Bultmann's hermeneutic becomes evident. Like Bultmann, Anderson believes that the basic structures of human existence and experience are universal through time and space, so that the analysis of the nature of faith among twentieth century Westerners has relevance to what is enshrined in a first-century text. Moreover, he also believes, again with Bultmann, that the nature of Christian faith, if it is genuinely faith, cannot be different in a Christian of the first century and one of the twentieth. By contrast, however, in his appeal to empirical evidence and experience rather than the structures of human existence, Anderson is typically Anglo-Saxon.

One of the most remarkable aspects of Anderson's research and proposals is the way he is able to take into account the perspectives of recent major contributions to Johannine research. Aside from Bultmann and Barrett, there is C.H. Dodd, whose work on the historical tradition of the Fourth Gospel as oral tradition with a historical basis Anderson obviously finds congenial. J.L. Martyn's (and Raymond E. Brown's) position on the Jewish-Christian, originally inner-synagogal, dynamic behind the Fourth Gospel is basically accepted, although Anderson believes it antedates the *birkat ha-minim.* At the level of the present text, or the most recent environment of the Fourth Gospel, Anderson finds considerable room to agree with Käsemann: the Johannine version of Christian faith and the Johannine conception of the nature of the church and churchly authority stand consciously over against the Petrine. Anderson would, however, nuance this tension more in the fashion of Brown than of Käsemann himself. John represents a view of gospel and church in tension and dialogue with the Petrine, rather than a sectarian version of Christianity that is, so to speak, beyond the pale.

In holding open the possibility that the Gospel of John represents an original, independent, eyewitness source, Anderson's work will doubtless appeal to certain conservative and evangelical interests. It would, however, be misleading to characterize his work as conservative. It is, rather, bold and imaginative. Doubtless any scholar will find reason to take exception to some parts or aspects of it. Nevertheless, by putting old and important issues in a fresh perspective and attempting to apply new methods, Anderson stimulates us to reappraise our own solutions to the Johannine riddles. In doing so, he will have also set an agenda for his own career, if he undertakes to address all the counterquestions his proposals will doubtless engender.

D. Moody Smith

Preface

This work is a revision of and considerable expansion upon my doctoral thesis submitted to the University of Glasgow in December of 1988. Much appreciation is felt for D. Moody Smith's contributing such a complimentary Foreword, and for Martin Hengel's generous inclusion of this work in the WUNT 2 monograph series. Much appreciation is also felt for the helpfulness of Siebeck/Mohr publishers on the production end of the project.

A bit of explanation is due regarding the reader's use of the footnotes. Simple, bibliographical references are usually made in the text itself, but fuller discussions of points and multiple bibliographic references are reserved for the footnotes. Because this work is often critical of majority and minority views within the guild, judgments in the main text at times require substantiation, which one hopes does not digress too far afield. Where end notes in the original thesis were overly lengthy, these have either been shortened, reconfigured or included as separate appendices at the end of the book. Tables and charts have also been added and crafted to clarify points made within the text, and Greek has been adapted for accessibility.

While significant monographs by J. Ashton, J. Neyrey, J. Painter, W.R.G. Loader, U. von Wahlde, F. Segovia and others, produced recently, as well as significant works by Synoptic scholars, receive little explicit mention, this does not imply their being overlooked. They will, one hopes, be engaged in future discussions.

Paul N. Anderson

Acknowledgments

In many ways scholarship is a parasitic venture. The scholar draws his or her 'life' from the vitality of those whose work has preceded theirs, and from the support of many others. Continuing the analogy, where the parasite simply feeds off the host, offering nothing in return, both host and parasite are soon diminished. However, where the parasite offers back another contribution in exchange for sustenance received, not only is the relationship between parasite and host mutually beneficial, but the biosphere is strengthened and ecosystems sustained. Therefore, this work represents the contributing side of a symbiotic relationship; it is but a small beginning of that which is offered in return for that which I have received so generously from so many others.

First, I should like to thank the faculties of Malone College in Canton, Ohio and the Earlham School of Religion in Richmond, Indiana for my undergraduate and graduate introductions to the pursuit of truth: to Roger Barrett, Alvin Anderson and Miriam Burke, for their training in the fields of cognitive and developmental studies; and to Elton Trueblood and Alan Kolp for their encouragement to write and stimulation of my interest in the Gospel of John, respectively. I am also deeply grateful to Otto Betz and Martin Hengel for their tutorial guidance during my research in Tübingen over the summer of 1987, to the communities of Tyndale House in Cambridge, and Woodbrooke College in Selley Oak, England, for their assisting my research over the summer and autumn of 1988, and to the faculty of George Fox University for providing the 1991 summer research grant which facilitated preparing the thesis for publication.

Second, I should like to thank members of the Faculty of Divinity at the University of Glasgow for their guidance and support. Guidance has been enriching, ranging from the course on the history of biblical interpretation, taught by Robert Davidson and Ernest Best, and the provocative seminar on the Gospel of John, taught by Christopher Evans, to the Glasgow New Testament Seminar, hosted by John Barclay and John Riches. I am also grateful to the university for being 'liberated' to give myself to full-time study by receiving the Overseas Research Scholarship and the Divinity Postgraduate Fellowship from 1986-1988, as well as to the John Sarrin Trust in America for their support. To my fellow researchers, Leslie Milton and Hugh Pyper I say a hearty 'thanks', for endless cups of coffee and discussions about 'things Johannine' — not necessarily in that order — and to Wendy Sproston and the British New Testament Conference Johannine Seminar, to Robert Kysar and the National SBL Johannine Literature Section, to Jeff Staley and Michael Cosby and the Pacific Northwest Region SBL New

Testament and Hellenistic Religions Section, to Wayne Rollins and the National SBL Psychology and Biblical Studies Group, to John Painter and Alan Culpepper and the SNTS Johannine Literature Seminar, to Vernon Robbins and the Rhetoric and to the New Testament Section of the National SBL meetings, to Irv Brendlinger and the Center for Christian Studies in Portland, Oregon and to my students and colleagues at George Fox University for allowing me the opportunity to test some of these ideas within the 'oral tradition' before expressing them in the written. This allowed the work to mature considerably since my doctoral research. I also appreciate Raymond Brown's helpful comments on Table 21 and Appendix VIII. Most of all, however, I am truly grateful to my adviser, John Riches, for his knowledgeable guidance and incisive judgments over my years of research at the University of Glasgow. If an adviser may be considered anything like a 'duelling-partner', challenging an advisee to excellence by both example and exercise, I am indeed fortunate to have had such a rigorous — and yet profitable — experience.

There are many others who have proof-read, typed, responded to ideas, and been engaged in correspondence and discussion, who know my appreciation apart from having been mentioned here. But finally, I must reserve my deepest thanks for those family and friends who have made our two years in Scotland possible, and who supported the extensive revision process in the meantime. To our parents, brothers and sisters, and their families we say 'thanks', but especially to Carla, Sarah, Della and Olivia is my appreciation most profoundly felt, for their enduring the throes of 'research-related widowhood and orphandom'. To them this book is dedicated. My only hope is that I should be able to return but a portion of the loving support and contributions I have received so liberally from others.

May, 1995   *Paul N. Anderson*

Abbreviations

1. Journals and Periodicals

ATR	*Anglican Theological Review.*
ABR	*Australian Biblical Review.*
Bib	*Biblica.*
BJRL	*Bulletin of the John Rylands Library.*
BK	*Bibel und Kirche.*
BR	*Biblical Research.*
BTB	*Biblical Theology Bulletin.*
BZ	*Biblische Zeitschrift*
CBQ	*Catholic Biblical Quarterly.*
CTM	*Currents in Theology and Mission.*
DownR	*Downside Review.*
EQ	*Evangelical Quarterly.*
EstBib	*Estudios Bíblicos.*
ET	*Expository Times.*
ETR	*Etudes théologiques et religieuses.*
EvTh	*Evangelische Theologie.*
HTR	*Harvard Theological Review.*
HeyJ	*Heythrop Journal.*
Int	*Interpretation.*
JBL	*Journal of Biblical Literature.*
JSNT	*Journal for the Study of the New Testament.*
JTS	*Journal of Theological Studies.*
LV	*Lumière et Vie.*
Neot	*Neotestamentica.*
NKZ	*Neue kirchliche Zeitschrift.*
NovT	*Novum Testamentum.*
NTS	*New Testament Studies.*
QRT	*Quaker Religious Thought.*
RB	*Revue biblique.*
RGG	*Religion in Geschichte und Gegenwart.*
RHPR	*Revue d'histoire et de philosophie religieuses.*
RivB	*Rivista biblica.*
RSR	*Recherches de science religieuse.*
RTP	*Revue de théologie et de philosophie.*
SJT	*Scottish Journal of Theology.*
ThD	*Theological Digest.*
ThR	*Theologische Rundschau.*
TS	*Theological Studies.*
TTKi	*Tiddsskrift for Teologi og Kirche.*
TTZ	*Trierer theologische Zeitschrift.*

TynB	*Tyndale Bulletin.*
VigChr	*Vigiliae christianae.*
ZNW	*Zeitschrift für die neutestamentliche Wissenschaft und die Kunde der älteren Kirche.*
ZTK	*Zeitschrift für Theologie und Kirche.*

2. *Series and Collections*

AnBib	Analecta Biblica.
ConBNT	Coniectanea biblica, New Testament.
IDB	*Interpreter's Dictionary of the Bible*, 5 vols., ed., G. Buttrick et. al., Nashville, 1962–1976.
IRT	Issues in Religion and Theology.
JSNTS	Journal for the Study of the New Testament Supplement Series.
LCL	Loeb Classical Library, Cambridge, Mass.
LTPM	Louvain Theological & Pastoral Monographs.
NovTSup	Novum Testamentum, Supplements.
PTMS	Pittsburgh Theological Monograph Series.
SBB	Stuttgarter biblische Beiträge.
SBLASP	Society of Biblical Literature Abstracts and Seminar Papers.
SBLDS	Society of Biblical Literature Dissertation Series.
SBLMS	Society of Biblical Literature Monograph Series.
SNTSMS	Society for New Testament Studies Monograph Series.
SNTW	Studies of the New Testament and its World.
SE	Studia Evangelica, ed., F.L. Cross, Berlin.
TDNT	*Theological Dictionary of the New Testament*, 10 vols., ed. G. Kittel and G. Bromiley, Grand Rapids, 1964–1976.
UNT	Untersuchungen zum Neuen Testament.
WBC	Word Biblical Commentary.
WMANT	Wissenschaftliche Monographien zum Alten und Neuen Testament.
WUNT	Wissenschaftliche Untersuchungen zum Neuen Testament.

3. *Works Often Cited* (by name or key-word)

Ashton	*The Interpretation of John*, ed. J. Ashton, IRT, Philadelphia/London, 1986.
Barrett	*The Gospel According to St. John*, Philadelphia, 1978.
	(Dialectical): 'The Dialectical Theology of St. John', in his *New Testament Essays*, London, 1972, pp. 49–69.
Borgen	(*Bread*): *Bread from Heaven*, Leiden, 1965.
Brown	*The Gospel According to John (I—XII)*, New York, 1966.
	(*Community*): *The Community of the Beloved Disciple*, New York, 1979.
	(*NTE*): *New Testament Essays*, Milwaukee, 1965.
Bultmann	*The Gospel of John*, Philadelphia, 1971.
Culpepper	*The Anatomy of the Fourth Gospel*, Philadelphia, 1983.
Fortna	*The Gospel of Signs*, Cambridge, 1970.
Fowler	*Stages of Faith Development*, San Francisco, 1981.
Käsemann	*The Testament of Jesus*, Philadelphia, 1968.
Lindars	*The Gospel of John*, Grand Rapids/London, 1972.
Loder	*The Transforming Moment*, San Francisco, 1981.
Martyn	*History and Theology in the Fourth Gospel*, Nashville, 1979.

Meeks   *The Prophet-King: Moses Traditions and the Johannine Christology*, Leiden, 1967.

Schnackenburg   *The Gospel According to St. John* Vols. 1–3, London/New York, 1980, 1982, 1983.

Smith   *The Composition and Order of the Fourth Gospel*, New Haven, 1965.

4. Besides the standard abbreviations for books of the Bible

Philo:
Leg. all.	Allegorical Interpretation.
Congr.	The Preliminary Studies.
Mut.	On The Change of Names.
Mos.	On Moses.

Ignatius of Antioch:
Eph.	his letter to the Ephesians.
Ro.	his letter to the Romans.
Magn.	his letter to the Magnesians.
Phil.	his letter to the Philadelphians.

List of Tables

Introduction

John's Christological Unity and Disunity:
Identifying The Options

To consult the Fourth Gospel is to be confronted with the classic issues of christology, and to do christology is to be drawn back time and again to the christological interpretation of the Fourth Gospel. This is due, in part, to the struggles faced in Western Christianity's attempt to assimilate John's christology into its thought. Indeed, many of the key debates of the seven ecumenical councils hinged upon the distinctive portrayal of Christ in the Fourth Gospel.[1] What is even more amazing, however, is that in several of the christological debates opposing parties *both* drew from the Fourth Gospel to substantiate their positions. As T.E. Pollard observed:[2]

> At the turn of this century, F.C. Conybeare, in a review of Alfred Loisy's *Le quartrième évangile,* wrote: "If Athanasius had not had the Fourth Gospel to draw texts from, Arius would never have been confuted." [*HJ*, VII (1903), 620] That is however only part of the

---

1 Consider, for instance, John's influence upon such issues as pre-existence versus subordinationism, *homoousia*, hypostatic union, monotheletism, and *filioque* debates. Had it not been for the Gospel of John the events leading up to and during the seven ecumenical councils would certainly have had a different history (cf. M.F. Wiles, *The Spiritual Gospel,* Cambridge, 1960, esp. pp. 112–128, for patristic interpretations of John; and T.E. Pollard, *Johannine Christology and the Early Church,* Cambridge, 1970; who identifies at least four strands of Johannine christological debates). Pollard is also so convinced of the formative influence of Johannine christology upon the christological development of the early church in general that he is able to say:

> I am not unaware that other books and key passages of scripture (e.g. Philipppians 2:6ff., Colossians 1:15ff., Proverbs 8:22ff.) also played an important role. Nevertheless, I believe that it was St John's Gospel, with its Logos-concept in the Prologue and its emphasis on the Father-Son relationship, that raised in a most acute way the problems which led the church to formulate her doctrines of the trinity and the person of Christ. (*Ibid, p. xi*)

2 *Ibid.,* p. 3. One can identify an impressive similarity of function between the theological debates of the early church Fathers and the literary-composition theories of modern scholars. While there is little connection between their approaches to biblical texts, they have addressed a common set of issues: namely, how the multifaceted presentation of Christ in the New Testament — and John in particular — might be understood clearly and coherently. While early christological discussions assimilated the assets and limitations of a Platonic world-view, the Fathers were primarily concerned with doing sound exegesis of the scriptures. M.F. Wiles suggests that:

truth, for it would also be true to say that if Arius had not the Fourth Gospel to draw texts from, he would not have needed confuting.

The obvious question following such an observation is: 'What is the origin of John's distinctive christology?' Only as this question is addressed can one acquire an adequate understanding of what John is saying about Christ, and just as importantly, what John is not.

There are basically three possible approaches to the tensions within John's christology. One may diminish their existence, one may locate one of the poles of the tensions as external to the thinking and writing of the evangelist, or one may identify them as internal to the thinking and writing of the evangelist. Any of these approaches must also include an explanation of how such a phenomenon may have occurred; thus, christological tensions cannot simply be discussed in isolation from historical, literary, and theological issues. The solving of one set of problems often creates a new set of problems to be addressed. The primary focus of this study, however, is John's christological unity and disunity, which calls for an introductory discussion of the three basic options concerning one's approach to the christological tensions in the Fourth Gospel.

1. The first option is to diminish or ignore the apparent contradictions, attempting to harmonize the christological tensions (or to stay with the metaphor, attempting to 'harmonize the discord') in John. This had been the primary approach to interpreting the Fourth Gospel until the beginning of the 19th century.[3] Rather than coming to grips with the problems inherent to John's unitive and disunitive

---

There is no title that the Fathers would have coveted more for themselves than that of Biblical theologians. Later scholars may point with justice to the influence of Greek metaphysical thought upon their writings and their understanding of the Gospel, but in conscious aim and intention their overriding purpose was to interpret the message of the Bible. (*op. cit.*, p. 158)

Where many of their efforts went into reconciling apparent contradictions dogmatically, modern scholars have attempted to address these issues using the tools and critical methodologies of the modern age. Such theological giants as Wellhausen, Loisy, and Bultmann are but a few examples of modern scholars who have sought to address these and other perplexities by devising literary/composition theories to resolve them. While their tools and methodologies have been different, biblical scholars — both modern and patristic — have been driven by a common interest: to account for the christological tensions in the Fourth Gospel.

3 The issue of authorship, for instance, had not been questioned seriously until the beginning of the 19th century. As an example of the turning of the tide among scholars, consider K.G. Bretschneider's *Probabilia de Evangelii et Epistolarum Johannis Apostoli indole et origine eruditorum iudiciis modeste subiecit* (Leipzig, 1820). Translated by E. Haenchen and R.W. Funk, the title is, 'Probable conclusions about the type and origin of the Gospel and Epistles of the Apostle John, modestly submitted to the judgment of the scholarly world'. (E. Haenchen, *A Commentary on the Gospel John* vol. 1, E.t. by R.W. Funk, Philadelphia, 1984, p. 24). 'This book, intended for the professional world', says Haenchen, 'nevertheless contained sentences like this:

thought, the traditional approach to John's unitive and disunitive christology has sought to make sense of its tensions by means of metaphysical speculation or dogmatic postulation. However, to ascribe John's christological tensions to representations of metaphysical mysteries misses the intriguing issue of *how* John's christology came to incorporate such tensions and diminishes one's appreciation of the Fourth Gospel's richness and distinctive presentation of Christ.

On one hand, the Word was with God and the Word was God (1:1).[4] On the other hand, the Son can do nothing on his own authority (5:30), but *only* what he sees the Father doing (5:19).[5] This seems to imply that there are both elevated and subordinationist christologies in John. Regarding the signs, on one hand, they are used apologetically, to evoke a believing response from the reader (20:31).[6] On the other hand, the evangelist highlights not the miraculous value of the signs, but their existential significance. In fact, the second of the two macarisms[7] in John even blesses that faith which is independent of the need to see miraculous signs (20:29). And, what of the contrast between present and futuristic eschatologies in John? On one hand, the one hearing the word of Jesus and believing in God has already passed from judgment into life (5:24).[8] On the other hand, the one 'eating the flesh' and

---

It is not possible that both the Jesus of the first three Gospels and the Jesus of the Fourth Gospel are historically true at the same time, since the greatest differences obtain between them not only in the mode of speech, but also in the way evidence is adduced and in the kind of activity; it is also not possible that the first three Evangelists invented Jesus' teachings, morals, and way of teaching; the author of the Fourth Gospel could quite possibly have concocted his Jesus. (*Ibid.*, Bretschneider, p. vii; *Ibid.*, Haenchen, p. 24.) While this book was not immediately accepted, the questions it raised regarding the relationship between John and the Synoptics are still with us today. The simplistically dichotomous evaluation of the Synoptics' value as 'historical' and John's value as 'spiritual' is still evidenced today by the fact that there is little, if any, place for the Fourth Gospel in current investigations of the life of Jesus. (See R.E. Brown, 'After Bultmann, What?', *CBQ* 26, 1964, pp. 28–30; and also 'The Problem of Historicity in John', *CBQ* 24, 1962, pp. 1–14; and *NTE*, 187–217. Also, see n. 33, below.)

It was not until some time after Bretschneider's earlier contribution, however, that the problems *within* the Fourth Gospel began to be addressed with the tools of literary criticism. In 1907 J. Wellhausen published his *Erweiterungen und Änderungen im vierten Evangelium* (Berlin), and in 1908 he published his commentary (*Das Evangelium Johannis*, Berlin). Then, in four issues of *Nachrichten der Gesellschaft der Wissenschaften in Göttingen*, from 1907–1908, E. Schwartz produced articles regarding '*Aporien im vierten Evangelium*'. From that time on, criticism of the Fourth Gospel has not only focused upon John/Synoptic comparison/contrasts. It has also sought to explain the perplexities (aporias) within the Fourth Gospel itself.

4 See Appendix I, "John's Exalted Christology".
5 See Appendix II, "John's Subordinated Christology".
6 See Appendix III, "Johannine Signs as Facilitators of Belief".
7 See Appendix IV, "Johannine Signs and the Existentializing Work of the Evangelist".
8 See Appendix V, "Realized Eschatology in John".

'drinking the blood' of Jesus will be raised up in the last day (6:54).[9] It could be that the evangelist was not concerned with being consistent, and that it is only to a modern audience that these appear to be contradictory sets of propositions.[10] However, if the christological thought of John is found to be genuinely self-contradictory, then at best the Gospel is a self-negating witness to be disbelieved; or at worst we have the confused musings of a schizophrenic to be patronizingly disregarded.[11] Therefore, to overlook the tensions in John without addressing the problems they present is not an option for contemporary and serious study of the Fourth Gospel.

2. A second option is to acknowledge John's christological tensions, but to ascribe them to literary sources *external* to the thinking of the evangelist.[12] This approach preserves a certain singularity of perspective and non-contradiction of thought, as differences are explained by the evangelist's use of earlier sources or by later interpolations added to his work. Therefore, the tensions are explained by the existence of multiple contributors, and even multiple christologies in

---

9 See Appendix VI, "Futuristic Eschatology in John". Consider also John's tensions between determinism/free will, true Israelites/the Jews, universalistic/particularistic soteriology, and its apparent ambivalence toward the sacraments.

10 Questions raised by scholars often say as much about the era of the scholar as the epoch being discussed. What appear to us to be 'contradictions' may not have seemed to be such to the evangelist. Thus, R. Kysar's criticism of modern scholars' analyses of Johannine christology is well taken. Says Kysar:

Contemporary interpreters are too often inclined, it seems to me, to analyze the christology of this early Christian document by means of categories which are in all probability not those of the FE. Did the evangelist operate within the conceptual framework of such polarities as faith and history, human and divine, or person and function? In all likelihood he did not consciously use such categories. The understanding of the FE's view of Christ will gain ground when we are able to grasp those modes of thought in which the evangelist, and not necessarily the interpreter, is at home.

(R. Kysar, 'The Fourth Gospel. A Report on Recent Research', *Aufstieg und Niedergang der römischen Welt*: ii Principat, Bd. 25, 3, ed. by H. Temporini and W. Haase, Berlin, 1985, pp. 2448f.).

11 While 'schizophrenic' may not be the best way to talk about the apparent contradictions in John's christology, it nonetheless describes the sense of disjointedness some scholars have detected within John's thought. Alluding to J. Behm's article ('Der gegenwärtige Stand der Erforschung des Johannesevangeliums', *TLZ* 73, 1948, pp. 21–30), R.T. Fortna says about Johannine aporias: 'At times it has been suggested that these phenomena are to be attributed to some defect in the evangelist, such as carelessness, unconcern for consistency, or senility.' (pp. 2–3)

12 In saying the tensions were external to the thinking of the evangelist, one must devise a literary theory of how this could have happened. Simplistically put, the evangelist may have incorporated material into his Gospel with which he disagreed at least slightly. Or, he may have been critical of the way a particular story or tradition was slanted, so he 'corrected' its nuance. It is almost certain that his work was edited for publication by another hand (Jn. 21:24f.), and it is possible that during this stage of composition further material may have been added, or existing material altered. This is what is meant by 'influences external to the thinking of the Fourth Evangelist'.

John. This view is articulated by E. Haenchen in an essay introducing his commentary ('Various Christologies in the Gospel of John', pp. 91–97):

> There is a great deal to be said for the view that we are hearing the voices of two theologically diverging evangelists in the Fourth Gospel. ... In the underlying tradition Jesus is pictured as a great miracle-worker, whose mighty deeds demonstrate and authenticate his divinity. John corrects this perspective embedded in the tradition in a fundamental way, without having to deny the miracles reported by the tradition. For him, their value lies elsewhere. (pp. 94–95)

In this paragraph Haenchen represents the views of many scholars[13] who maintain in somewhat modified forms the most widely accepted aspect of Bultmann's composition theory pertaining to the literary origins of John.[14] While D. Carson is correct, that Johannine source criticism has moved beyond the work of Bultmann,[15] one nonetheless continually finds the source of many current discussions traced back to Bultmann's epoch-making contribution to the issue: his commentary on John.[16]

One of the key contributions — and scandals — of Bultmann's work for modern interpreters is that it ascribes what appear to be irreconcilable tensions to

---

13 For instance, see R.T. Fortna, 1970; and W. Nicol, *The Sēmeia in the Fourth Gospel*, Leiden, 1972; as well as J. Becker, 'Wunder und Christologie: Zum literarkritischen und christologischen Problem der Wunder im Johannesevangelium', *NTS* 16, 1969–70, pp. 130–48.

14 While Bultmann's former pupil, H. Becker, expanded upon the gnostic origin of the *Offenbarungsreden* in his doctoral dissertation, *Die Reden des Johannesevangeliums und der Stil der gnostischen Offenbarungsreden*, Göttingen, 1956; and while S. Temple's book, *The Core of the Fourth Gospel*, London/Oxford, 1975, attempts to demonstrate the process by which the Fourth Gospel had been expanded upon an earlier 'core' of discourse material, Bultmann's *Offenbarungsreden* hypothesis has left most scholars finally unconvinced. On the other hand, scholars have generally been more receptive to Bultmann's *sēmeia* source theory. The probable reason for this difference in reception is that Bultmann is able to produce more convincing stylistic, contextual, and theological (and especially, *christological*) evidence for his *sēmeia* source hypothesis. The *theios anēr christology* of the *sēmeia* source is quite distinguishable from the more reflective *Tendenz* of the evangelist, according to Bultmann. Thus, any appreciation of his literary/composition theories *must deal centrally with his treatment of the christological tensions of the Fourth Gospel.*

15 On one occasion, D.A. Carson says that some ' ... writers are still engaging in detailed polemics against Bultmann's source criticism — unfortunately ignoring the fact that the debate has moved on somewhat during the last forty years.' ('Recent Literature on the Fourth Gospel: Some Reflections', *Themelios* 9, 1983, p. 11). Perhaps this is because, as Carson states elsewhere, the ' ... seminal work behind all modern attempts to reconstruct a literary source, or literary sources, for the fourth gospel, is, of course, the *magnum opus* of Rudolph Bultmann' ('Current Source Criticism of the Fourth Gospel: Some Methodological Questions', *JBL* 97, 1978, p. 414).

16 D.M. Smith, for instance, considers three prevalent trends in Johannine studies to be directly or indirectly a reflection of scholars' attempts to address issues raised by Bultmann. These include a) the search for a Johannine tradition which is independent from the Synoptic gospels, b) studies of the relationship between the kerygmatic character of the Johannine discourses and their pre-gospel homiletic function and form, and c) inquiries into the socio-

various literary sources. According to Bultmann, underlying the Fourth Gospel are at least three main written sources, and the evangelist has woven these into an 'historicized drama'.[17] By means of intricate linguistic analysis and the consistent assignment of theological motifs to their credited sources, Bultmann believes he is able to distinguish these sources on stylistic, contextual, and theological grounds. Therefore, according to Bultmann, there are at least *four separate christologies* interwoven within the Fourth Gospel, and each of these may be attributed to a separate source. a) The christology of the *Offenbarungsreden* source is that of the Gnostic Redeemer-myth, which portrays a redeemer figure who comes down from heaven and enlightens the elect with secret, divine knowledge, thus sealing their salvation. b) The christology of the *sēmeia* source is that of the *theios anēr*, who, through mighty acts of power, convinces his Jewish audience to believe in him. c) The christology of the evangelist is more creative and developed. While incorporating the other christological emphases, he believes that the existential significance of Jesus' words and works is the

---

religious context out of which John emerged. (See D.M. Smith, 'The Sources of the Gospel of John: An Assessment of the Present State of the Problem', *NTS* 10, 1964, pp. 336–351.)

Of course, Bultmann cannot be given total credit for these developments, as his work and the later work of others was influenced by such contributions as those of J. Wellhausen (*op. cit.*); B. Bauer (*Kritik der evangelischen Geschichte des Johannes*, Bremen, 1840); F.C. Baur (*Kritische Untersuchungen über die kanonischen Evangelien, ihr Verhältniß zu einander, ihren Charakter und Ursprung*, Tübingen, 1847); F. Spitta (*Das Johannes-Evangelium als Quelle der Geschichte Jesu*, Göttingen, 1910); H. Wendt (*Die Schichten im vierten Evangelium*, Göttingen, 1911); E. Hirsch (*Das vierte Evangelium in seiner ursprünglichen Gestalt verdeutscht und erklärt*, Tübingen, 1936); and W. Bousset (esp. 'Ist das vierte Evangelium eine literarische Einheit?', *TR* 12, 1909, pp. 1–12, 39–64). Nevertheless, Bultmann's mastery as a theologian, a researcher of ancient religions, and a linguistic analyst was demonstrated in his ability to synthesize earlier theories into a coherent whole. This had not been done at such a level of sustained and exhaustive argumentation before. Thus, the observation of E. Haenchen is correct that:

> The impression of the unity of this work helped to give his commentary the influence it came to have: like a mighty tree, it appeared not to permit anything strong and important to prosper in its shadow. This effect did not set in immediately, but once it began, it became clear that Bultmann's commentary on the Gospel of John decisively dominated an entire generation. (p. 34)

17 This is the converse of a 'dramatized history'. In the former, places, dates and other history-type (*historisch*) information is included for the purpose of making the drama more believable — an approach employed widely by writers of historical fiction or novels. A dramatized history, however, is concerned with presenting an account of a significant event or series of events in ways that are instructive for later audiences. Here, the outer details of places, dates and sequence form the main structure. The 'historian' then adds to the narrative dialogues, interactions with other people, and other 'human' factors which make the plot come alive. There is some license for paraphrase, but it is only done as an effort to elucidate the author's understanding of the events being described (cf. Bultmann, p. 210). He understands and portrays the events of Jesus' ministry as scenarios of the saving and revealing 'discourse' between God and humanity.

priority for faith. For him, to believe in Jesus is to enter into a spiritual relationship whereby all human and religious endeavours must eventually give way to complete faith in God's revelation in Jesus. d) The christology of the redactor is bound up with his ecclesiastical concerns. He prepares the Gospel to be received by the church of his day and therefore adds sacramental and futuristic themes, restores the image of Peter, and attributes to the Gospel apostolic authorship.

The clearest context in which these four christologies can be seen is in John 6, where they all occur together.[18] From the *sēmeia* source we have the feeding of the 5,000 (6:1–13) and Jesus' walking on the water (6:16–21, 25); from the *Offenbarungsreden* source we have the Bread of Life discourses and other material (6:27a, 33, 35, 37b, 44a, 45c, 47b, and 48); and from the redactor we have the so-called 'eucharistic interpolation' and a few other additions (6:1c, 18, 23c, 27b, 39c, 40c, 44b, and 51c–58). For this reason, ch. 6 has often been considered the 'showpiece' of Johannine source theories as well as for theories of multiple christologies in John.[19] John 6 may thus be termed *the 'Grand Central Station' of Johannine historical, literary and theological issues.*

Bultmann's source theory appears to have several other assets, as well as weaknesses. Historically, John's disagreement with the Synoptics is no longer an issue as the Fourth Gospel contains virtually no historical information, according to Bultmann. The historicizing details were included by the evangelist to make his drama come to life and thus enhance its impact. This would also account for the large quantity of symbolic content in John. One problem with such a view, however, is that there is still a great deal of historical-type detail in John which does not appear to be used symbolically. To say that such details are simply historicizing touches added to enhance the narrative effect does not do them justice. Also, the once widely-held view, that the Synoptics are intended to be understood more historically and John to be understood more spiritually,[20] is simplistic and inadequate. This is especially clear where the Johannine

---

18 This accounts for the vast number of critical and interpretive articles which have recently been written on John 6. Other than the Passion narratives, it is here that John may be most adequately compared with the Synoptics (consider the feeding of the multitude, 6:1–15; the sea crossing, 6:16–21; and Peter's confession, 6:68f.). It is also in ch. 6 that the literary characteristics of supposed sources may be analyzed, and it is here that the unity and/or disunity of the theological (and especially the christological) content of John may be evaluated.

19 Consider for instance, R. Kysar's article entitled, 'The Source Analysis of the Fourth Gospel — A Growing Consensus?' *NovT* 15, 1973, pp. 134–152. In this essay, Kysar attempts to demonstrate a 'growing consensus' among scholars regarding the existence of sources and redactions in John. In doing so, he charts the results of nine scholars' source-critical analyses of John 6. More will be said about this article below, in Chapter 3.

20 This was certainly the issue C.H. Dodd wanted to raise with Bultmann and others who had come to regard the Fourth Gospel as patently non-historical. In his *Historical Tradition in the Fourth Gospel*, Cambridge, 1965, Dodd sought not to 'prove' the historicity of the Fourth Gospel, but to explore 'what kind of history' it was intended to convey. In doing so, he recognized that the old Johannine/Synoptic comparison was obsolete. Says Dodd:

tradition appears to be earlier and more reliable than that of the Synoptics. It is also becoming increasingly recognized among scholars that much of Mark's editorial work is motivated by theological purposes as well as historical ones. Likewise, Matthew and Luke. Thus, all four gospels are motivated by *both* theological and historical interests. The basic issue, however, is whether Bultmann has incorrectly inferred the purpose of the Fourth Evangelist and the literary history of his work. While the question of John's historicity may be left open for now, to say that the evangelist was not seeking to provide an historical, or at least a 'meta-historical'[21] witness to the earthly ministry of Jesus is forced.

The comparison between the Fourth Gospel and the Synoptics has been placed in a fresh light. That there is a real difference between them is a fact which has been manifest to clear-sighted readers of the gospels ever since the time when Clement wrote that "John, observing that the bodily facts had been made clear in the [earlier] gospels ... composed a spiritual gospel". [Eusebius, *EH*, 6, 14, 7.] But the difference was exaggerated by nineteenth-century criticism, as if the Synoptic Gospels were entirely 'somatic' and John was nothing but 'pneumatic'; as if, in other words, the Synoptics gave us nothing but plain, brute facts of history and John nothing but abstract theology in symbolic guise. (pp. 4–5)
This presupposition was challenged by Dodd in his examination of the content and character of the Fourth Gospel. Not only did he find a great deal of historically reliable detail unique to John, but he also attempted to show the form of the material underlying the Fourth Gospel was based upon *oral* rather than written traditions. His work has been followed and built upon by such scholars as M. Hengel, (*The Johannine Question*, London/Philadelphia, 1989); J.A.T. Robinson (*The Priority of John*, London, 1985); R.E. Brown (*New Testament Essays*, Milwaukee, 1965); B. Lindars (*Behind the Fourth Gospel*, London, 1971); and L.L. Morris (*Studies in the Fourth Gospel*, Exeter/Grand Rapids, 1969). Curiously, Dodd's work has yet to be satisfactorily challenged — or heeded — by the guild. (Cf. D.A. Carson, 'Historical Tradition in the Fourth Gospel: After Dodd, What?', *Gospel Perspectives* II, ed. R.T. France and D. Wenham, Sheffield, 1981, pp. 84–145).
   Thus, while Bultmann's source-hypotheses may account for the presence of historical content in John (as some of the sources contained apparently historical information), it did not analyze critically basic assumptions regarding 'historicity' — as such — especially with relation to the evangelist's reasons for writing (see also F. Mussner, *The Historical Jesus in the Gospel of St John*, E.t. by W.J. O'Hara, New York, 1967; for an insightful explanation of the Fourth Gospel's interpretive portrayal of the history of Jesus as one who speaks to the needs of the early church, *using Johannine language*).
21 The descriptive term, 'metahistorical', is used by D.M. Smith in his essay (reprinted from *Int*, 31, 1977), 'The Presentation of Jesus in the Fourth Gospel', *Interpreting the Gospels*, Philadelphia, 1981, pp. 278–290. The point that deserves to be taken seriously by Johannine scholars is that actual events are not historic, in and of themselves. Only when they are interpreted as 'significant' do they acquire 'historical' value for the present and the future. This may happen negatively as well as positively, and W. Pauck has described this phenomenon well ('The Significance of Adolf von Harnack's *Interpretation of Church History*', *Union Seminary Quarterly review*, 1954, p. 15):
   We study history in order to intervene in the course of history and we have a right to do so. ... To intervene in history — this means that we must reject the past when it reaches into the present only in order to block us.

In other words, to say that the evangelist was writing an historicized drama misrepresents the apparent purpose of the evangelist. He was more likely writing a dramatized history.[22] This is not to say that the redactor did not 'publish' it for rhetorical reasons. A related historical issue has to do with how well Bultmann's interpretation fits in with what was happening within the context of Johannine Christianity, but that discussion will be saved for later.

Bultmann's literary solutions are not without their problems either. While some literary problems are solved (i.e., the order of John 5 and 6, the abrupt ending of ch. 14, the origin of ch. 21, etc.), other problems emerge — not the least of which includes the disordering of numerous texts and fragments which just happened to break between complete phrases and sentences. This sort of thing could indeed have happened with an ancient codex or scroll, but it seems very improbable that it could have happened to such a degree within the middle of the text, leaving a redactor with so many disconnected-yet-complete phrases and sentences to be reordered incorrectly.[23] Another series of criticisms has come from scholars who have tested the linguistic unity and disunity of the Fourth Gospel and have questioned the possibility of detecting underlying sources on the basis of literary analysis alone.[24] These and other problems cause one to sympathize with R.E. Brown's criticism of Bultmann's elaborate literary scheme.

> In summary, the theory of accidental displacement seems to create almost as many problems as it solves. The solution to our problem would appear to lie in the direction of a more deliberate procedure. (p. XXVIII)

The theological grounds for Bultmann's theory of composition are the strongest, and the most widely accepted aspects of his hypotheses (his identification of a *sēmeia* source and the additions of a redactor) have found agreement primarily

---

In other words, Harnack's work as a historian was *not* simply to find out 'what actually happened', but to challenge conventional interpretations of what happened in order to provide a new interpretive foundation for the future. His intention was (according to Pauck) ' ... to overcome history by history ... and transform it into something better' (p. 16). The function of the adjective, 'historical', is always a rhetorical one.

22 Therefore, history and theology must be considered on two levels: the level of the reported event and the level of its reporting. The epoch-making monograph of this topic has been J.L. Martyn's *History and Theology in the Fourth Gospel* (1968, revised and enlarged 1979), which J. Ashton refers to as ' ... probably the most important monograph on the Gospel since Bultmann's commentary' (p. 5).

23 See also R.E. Brown's criticisms along these lines (pp. XXVI–XXVIII) and B.S. Easton's 'Bultmann's RQ Source', *JBL* 65, 1946, pp. 143–156.

24 For thorough discussions of the literary unity of John, (especially in reaction to Bultmann's commentary) see D.M. Smith's analyses in *Composition*, pp. 64–79; and in 'The Sources of the Gospel of John: An Assessment of the Present State of the Problem', *NTS* 10, 1963/4, pp. 336–351. See also R.T. Fortna, pp. 203–218.

because of their theological, and more specifically, their *christological* foundation.[25]
The weakness of assuming distinct literary sources on the basis of theological
judgments, however, is obvious. It rests upon at least three layers of judgment:
a) a correct and singular interpretation of what the text both says and means, b)
an accurate assessment that meanings are genuinely incompatible with each
other within the text as they stand, and c) a superior reassignment of material to
other sources which creates fewer problems — or at least preferable ones. If any
of these layers of judgment be flawed, *in any way*, the validity of one's
interpretation is correspondingly weakened.[26] For this reason, the counsel of
C.K. Barrett is well taken.

> I take it that if the gospel makes sense as it stands it can generally be assumed that this is
> the sense it was intended to make. ... *Someone* published it substantially as it now stands;
> and I continue to make the assumption that he knew his business, and that it is the first duty
> of a commentator to bring out this person's meaning. (p. 22)

3. A third possibility in approaching John's christological tensions is to treat
them as tensions *internal* to the thinking and writing of the evangelist. The problem,
of course, is to find a way of taking seriously these theological, literary, and
historical tensions as well as 'letting John be John'.[27] A crucial issue regarding an
adequate understanding of John's christological unity and disunity is whether
or not to see them as a reflection of a dialectical form of thought which underlies

---

25 Again, the christological approach to the Fourth Gospel of many scholars has been based
    upon the work of Bultmann, especially regarding the theory that multiple christologies
    underlay John's distinctive presentation of Jesus. One may detect a certain continuity
    between Bultmann's detection of various christologies underlying the Marcan tradition, and
    he appears to be making similar moves in analyzing John.
    It is also significant that due to the criticism of Bultmann's literary hypotheses by such
    scholars as E. Schweizer (1939), E. Ruckstuhl (1951), and B. Noack (1954), those aspects
    of his theories which have depended chiefly on literary or theological analyses alone have
    fallen by the wayside. An example of this is his *Offenbarungsreden* source theory.

26 The primary target for critics of John's disunity has been the claim that John contains various
    sources, detectable on the basis of stylistic analysis. The contributions of three of these
    scholars may be summarized as follows: while Schweizer's work was being written around
    the same time as Bultmann's commentary, he nevertheless addressed some of the same
    issues. By applying thirty-three linguistic analyses of Johannine language and style, he
    concluded that while source-criticism may be a useful tool and that John probably used
    sources, it would be difficult to discover these on the basis of linguistic analysis alone.
    Ruckstuhl was more sweeping in his criticism. He argued that not only were sources
    impossible to identify, but all source criticism of the Fourth Gospel should be abandoned.
    Noack took a different stance. By analyzing John's use of the Old Testament, Noack
    demonstrated that the Fourth Evangelist probably did not quote this source but cited it loosely
    from memory. He concluded that if John treated his only known source so loosely, it would
    be impossible to infer with certainty John's use of hypothetical sources.

27 For an extended arguing of this point, see J.D.G. Dunn, 'Let John be John: A Gospel for its
    Time', in P. Stuhlmacher (ed.), *Das Evangelium und die Evangelien: Vorträge vom Tübinger
    Symposium 1982*, Tübingen, 1983, pp. 309–339.

the compositional process.[28] While not all dialectic is dialogue, all dialogue is dialectical. May the christological tensions in the Fourth Gospel be attributable to at least three levels on which some form of dialogue is taking place? These include *theological and ecclesiological dialogues* within the historical situation of the evangelist and his community; the *intended literary dialogue* between the evangelist and the implied reader — reflecting the rhetorical purpose behind the composition and circulation of the Gospel; and the *reflective dialogue* within the thinking of the evangelist himself, as he ponders these issues and ultimately the significance of the incarnation. Assessing these inquiries requires at least three major tasks inherent to addressing John's christological tensions as being internal to the thinking of the evangelist: a) One involves investigating the kinds of issues the evangelist and his community would have faced over an extended period of time. b) The second involves trying to make sense of the Gospel as a complete literary composition, seeking to interpret the tensions as clues to the intentionality of the writer whenever a part, or the whole, may have been written. c) The third involves addressing the ways people think reflectively — a kind of 'cognitive criticism', by which the epistemological origins of John's unitive and disunitive content are explored.

a) One of the fastest-growing trends in Johannine research has been the inquiry into the socio-religious situation of Johannine Christianity, and these studies contribute significantly to one's understanding of some of the issues faced by the evangelist. Of particular interest is the relationship between John's historical situation and its christology. Research into the nature of the community of the Beloved Disciple has been carried out notably by such scholars as J.L. Martyn, R.E. Brown, W. Meeks and D. Rensberger.[29] Martyn's contribution has been to investigate the impact of the *Birkat ha-Minim*, as Christians were excommunicated from the Synagogue around the turn of the first century. While the Fourth Gospel narrates the story of Jesus' ministry, the more telling historical content has to do with how these traditions were valued and understood by Johannine Christians. Therefore, while John 9:22 may have had some connection to the time of the actual ministry of Jesus, it (and 16:2) more accurately portrays the

---

28 R. Kysar (*Report, op. cit.*) suggests that Johannine christological studies in the future should involve historical, literary and theological studies. 'The FE seems to have formulated his view of Christ within a tension between several poles.' (p. 2449) One of the most significant essays in recent years is C.K. Barrett's exploration of the 'dialectical' style of thinking underlying John 6, based on the Socratic model of *thinking* being 'the soul's dialogue with herself' (Dialectical). This model has the tandem advantages of clear historical precedence and epistemological suitability.

29 See J.L. Martyn, 1979, and *The Gospel of John in Christian History*, New York, 1978; R.E. Brown, *Community*, and *The Epistles of John*, New York, 1982; W. Meeks, 'The Man from Heaven in Johannine Sectarianism' *JBL* 91, 1972, pp. 44–72; and D. Rensberger, *Johannine Faith and Liberating Community*, Philadelphia, 1988.

feelings of late first-century Christians who were being expelled from the Synagogue. Meeks ('Man from Heaven') describes this process as follows:

> The group had to distinguish itself over against the sect of John the Baptist and even more passionately over against a rather strong Jewish community, with which highly ambivalent relationships had existed. It suffered defections, conflicts of leadership, and schisms. ... More precisely, there must have been a continuing dialectic between the group's historical experience and the symbolic world which served both to explain that experience and to motivate and form the reaction of the group members to the experience. (Ashton, p. 145)

Therefore, the christological disunity of the Fourth Gospel may at least be partially attributed to the dialectical relationships within the Johannine community and between it and other contemporary groups. Brown suggests that there were actually four phases of development through which the Johannine community had come (*Community*, pp. 22–24). At first, in the pre-Gospel era, Johannine Christians worshipped within the Synagogue, and they would have been indistinguishable from other forms of Jewish Christianity. It was not until anti-Temple and anti-Davidic Samaritan converts entered the community, however, that the upheaval began. The acceptance of the second group catalyzed the development of a high, pre-existence christology, which threatened Jewish monotheistic values. This led to the expulsion of Christians from the Synagogue, which was followed by the conversion of Gentiles and their addition to the Johannine community.

Phase two was the phase in which the Gospel was written. During this time Johannine Christians were being excommunicated from the Synagogue, and this accounts for the Fourth Gospel's acrimonious portrayal of 'the Jews'. Thus the second phase in the history of the Johannine community involved the transition from being 'Christian Jews' to being 'Jewish Christians'.

Phase three involved the situation of division within the Johannine community, and this was about the time that the Johannine Epistles were written (*Community*, p. 23). During this time, the author of 1 John seems bothered by the numerical growth of the secessionists (1 John 4:5), and he seeks to bolster the faith of believers against false teachers (1 John 2:27; 2 John 10f.). It is during this time that the Johannine community faced the threat of docetism, and this is reflected by emphases on the fleshly incarnation of Jesus. The fourth phase, according to Brown:

> ... saw the dissolution of the two Johannine groups after the Epistles were written. The secessionists, no longer in communion with the more conservative side of the Johannine community, probably moved rapidly in the second century toward docetism, gnosticism, Certinthianism, and Montanism. This explains why the Fourth Gospel, which they brought with them, is cited earlier and more frequently by heterodox writers than by orthodox writers. (*Ibid.*, p. 24)

While Brown owes much to his former colleague, J.L. Martyn, and vice versa, his work has nonetheless been one of the most formative influences upon emerging theories of what the Johannine community may have looked like. The advantage of such a scenario is that by understanding the situation out of which the Fourth

Gospel emerged, one's understanding of the evangelist's message is greatly enhanced. There may even be detectable layers, or strata, which the interpreter may investigate, as an archaeologist would excavate an ancient tel. The problem with such an endeavour, however, is that virtually all of the stratification must be somewhat assumed by the scholar. Even the sequence between the production of the Gospel and the Epistles is not without question, let alone the christological content within the Fourth Gospel itself.[30]

b) Another recent trend within Johannine scholarship has been to analyze the literary purpose and construction of the Fourth Gospel, especially as they relate to its intended function: that of evoking a response from the reader. The advantage of reader-response criticism is that the scholar is concerned primarily with understanding the intended message of the writer, and this liberates him or her from some historical and dogmatic conundrums. Issues of history and theology do come into consideration, but it is more in the interest of understanding the socio-religious context out of which such ideas developed that the reader-response critic studies the setting of Johannine Christianity. According to J. Staley:[31]

> By raising the issue of the rhetorical impact of narrative medium upon narrative audience, the anachronistic quality of texts comes to the forefront and raises all kinds of hermeneutical and historical questions for the New Testament narrative critic. ... But at the same time the narrative critic's task has a peculiar bent to it; a synchronic twist, occasioned by the text's various media transformations in the course of its two thousand year preservation.

Such scholars as R.A. Culpepper, D. Wead, P. Duke, G. O'Day and J. Staley have built upon the work of reader-response critics and W. Booth's two books, *The Rhetoric of Fiction* (Chicago, 1961) and *A Rhetoric of Irony* (Chicago, 1974). The weakness of such approaches, as argued in the 1988 Nottingham Ph.D. thesis of M. Stibbe,[32] is that historical and theological issues tend to be too easily brushed aside.

---

30 This point is made by J. Lieu in her book *The Second and Third Epistles of John: History and Background*, Edinburgh, 1986. In this book she argues that the Johannine Epistles could just as easily have preceded the Gospel as have followed it. Says Lieu:
    > We should not too easily seek to uncover layers of redaction supposedly reflecting stages in a development which can be reconstructed as if the Gospel and Epistles constituted an archaeological site; originality in concept and originality in time are not coterminous, while the "later" ideas of the Epistles may reflect the original or continuing ideas of the community or any part of it. The Gospel as we have it reflects a variety of responses to the idea of tradition and faithfulness to the past ... . (p. 180)

31 *The Print's First Kiss: A Rhetorical Investigation of the Implied Reader in the Fourth Gospel*, Atlanta, 1988, pp. 121f. Also, cf. Staley's article, 'The Structure of John's Prologue: Its Implications for the Gospel's Narrative Structure', *CBQ* 48, 1986, pp. 241–263; R.A. Culpepper, 1983; D. Wead, *The Literary Devices of John's Gospel*, Basel, 1970; P. Duke, *Irony in the Fourth Gospel*, Atlanta, 1985; G.R. O'Day, *Revelation in the Fourth Gospel: Narrative Mode and Theological Claim*, Philadelphia, 1986.

32 Developed especially in pp. 120–157, and illustrated using John 18–19 as the central text (pp. 158–307), M. Stibbe ('The Artistry of John; The Fourth Gospel as Narrative Christology', Ph.D. thesis, University of Nottingham, submitted August, 1988) has argued:

John is not written as a fictional drama,[33] even though the evangelist uses a variety of dramatic techniques in constructing his narrative. Rather, John's compiler claims the work (or at least significant portions of it) to have been an interpretive witness to the life and ministry of Jesus, and therefore it demands to be considered, at least preliminarily, within this genre of literature.

c) However, not only is it important to consider the christological content of the Fourth Gospel, but it is equally vital to investigate the means by which John's distinctive understanding of Christ may have emerged.[34] Whether or not the evangelist was addressing contemporary threats within or from without Johannine Christianity, and whether or not the christology of the Fourth Gospel owes its structure and form to the rhetorical purposes of the evangelist, these developments were taking place presumably within the mind of someone — say, the evangelist. Therefore, any attempt to address the christological tensions of the Fourth Gospel

---

Narrative criticism has advocated a text-immanent study of the final form of NT narratives and has rejected any consideration of their life-history prior to textualisation. ... Narrative critics have justified this omission on the grounds that historical criticism of the Bible has peeled away the skin and flesh of NT narratives and left us with a mere core of Jesus's sayings and actions. Historical criticism has been so preoccupied with what lies BEHIND NT narrative that it has destroyed what lies IN FRONT of it. The question I want to ask is this: even if traditional methods of biblical study have indeed distracted us from the literary qualities of NT narrative, is it right to omit historical questions and to treat NT narratives as self-contained narrative worlds with no reference to the real world? (p. 3)

33 The false dichotomy is to assume the author of John must be *either* a dramatist *or* an historian (versus R.H. Strachan, *The Fourth Evangelist: Dramatist or Historian?*, London, 1925, esp. pp. 11–40). The notion that John 13–19 represents an a-historical 'cultic drama' of the Passion narrative has been called 'an anachronism without parallel' by A.L. MacPherson, and challenged successfully in his 'The Interpretation of the Fourth Gospel', Ph.D. Dissertation, Trinity College, Cambridge, 1940 (citation p. 45).

34 Of course, there may be other explanations (or combinations of factors) to account for John's christological unity and disunity which must be taken into consideration. Such possibilities include the following: a) The Son's being sent from — and yet returning to — the Father may reflect a typological schema (incorporating movement from high to low, to high again) which the evangelist has assimilated into his portrayal of Jesus. b) The combination of present and future eschatologies may not have been as exceptional (and therefore, not as problematic) as some scholars have assumed. This would be especially true if contemporary examples can be found that combine present and future eschatologies together. c) What appear to be predestinarian views, in tension with the 'free will' of the responder to God's saving initiative, may not actually be as 'contradictory' as some have argued. Thus, a combination of explanations may eventually have to be posed in order to do justice to the various kinds of tensions in John. However, the ambivalent attitude of the evangelist to the signs, and the apparent contradiction between the flesh and humanity of Jesus are genuinely problematic, and therefore, the foundational question for interpretation still persists: 'May these apparent contradictions be ascribed to tensions *internal* or *external* to the thinking and writing of the evangelist?' Such is the central interest of the present study.

must ultimately consider the dialectical character of the evangelist's christology, as it may have developed within his experience and thought.

The first difficulty with such an endeavour begins with understanding the kinds of christological categories with which the evangelist is at home (see R. Kysar's perceptive observation above, p. 4, note 10). On the other hand, if a legitimate attempt can be made to 'crack the thinking' of the Fourth Evangelist, the christological interpretation of John would be enhanced significantly. A serious deficiency in biblical studies is the failure to consider the cognitive and epistemological origins of theological motifs. While no approach is foolproof, the application of appropriate cognitive models may provide a way forward here. One of course must always guard against 'psychologizing the text', but given the rise of research-based cognitive and developmental studies over the last three decades, cognitive analyses of the epistemological origins of New Testament motifs may be where sociological investigations of the same were thirty years ago. Therefore, a primary focus of this study will be an attempt to gain clearer insight into the christological tensions of the Fourth Gospel by means of seeking a deeper understanding of the dialectical process of thought by which the evangelist has come to embrace such a distinctively unitive *and* disunitive christology.

In doing so, John 6 will serve as the *locus argumenti*, as it is within this chapter that so many theological, literary, and historical issues converge. Conclusions from this analysis will be extended then to christological tensions elsewhere in the Gospel. Some exploration will also be made into the kind of Christianity reflected by the Fourth Gospel. Therefore, Part I of this study will survey the field of current literature on John's christology, with a special interest in ways its unitive and disunitive features have been treated. Connections will also be made with John 6. Part II will focus on Bultmann's treatment of John 6, seeking to evaluate his stylistic, contextual and theological judgments. Some of his insights will then be developed by means of applying them to cognitive models which inform one as to the character and origin of dialectical thinking — especially as it relates to John's christology. Part III will provide a translation and exegesis of John 6, as well as discussions of various kinds of dialogues implied by the text. A conclusion will then draw the findings together and seek to make a contribution toward understanding the origin, character and significance of the christological unity and disunity of the Fourth Gospel, in the light of John 6.

Part I

Three Relevant Surveys

Nowhere else in the New Testament
do we find ourselves in a greater dilemma than in John,
even though everywhere in the New Testament
we encounter such riddles that
introductions to the New Testament could,
to a great extent,
be placed into the literary genre of fairy tales,
their dry tone
or their pretence of factual reporting notwithstanding.
The Evangelist whom we call John
appears to be a man without definite contours.

Ernst Käsemann
The Testament of Jesus

In the introduction the scope of this study was narrowed down to the question: 'Is the christological unity and disunity of John attributable to tensions internal or external to the thinking and writing of the evangelist?' Part I will survey recent literature with the purpose of seeking to evaluate various approaches to this issue by Johannine scholars. Because this particular topic has not been approached in the same way until now,[1] a survey of the field of literature must be somewhat indirect, gathering relevant information along related topics, in order to provide an assessment of current approaches to the issue.

The strategy of Part I is first to locate the christological unity/disunity issue within the spectrum of recent approaches to John's christology (Ch. 1); to examine five major commentaries in order to identify the relationship between a scholar's understanding of the christological unity/disunity issue, the theory of composition within which he accommodates such a view, and the way in which his approach is illustrated in his treatment of John 6 (Ch. 2); and, to consider the approaches of three scholars to unity/disunity issues related to John 6 (Ch. 3). These surveys will be primarily descriptive, and yet they will also be somewhat evaluative, as judgments made in Part I will be foundational for the constructive work of Parts II and III. Throughout Part I the dilemma alluded to by Käsemann above will surface repeatedly as the conflicting views of scholars, on a multiplicity of issues, are considered. Not only is the Fourth Evangelist a 'man without contours', but seemingly, so is his (or their) christology (or christologies).

Chapter 1

Recent Approaches to the
Christology of the Fourth Gospel

Recent approaches to the christology of the Fourth Gospel have been many and diverse. Therefore, it is hoped this survey will shed some light on what J.L. Price calls 'the complex labyrinth of "the Johannine problem"',[2] and perhaps, even open some doors through the 'complex labyrinth' of recent literature concerned with John's distinctive christology. However, the delineation of such approaches is only possible in part, as many scholars approach John's christology from several angles at the same time. This is especially the case for studies which are more comprehensive and thus cover several of the categories mentioned. Often these are among the most salient contributions, and yet, even within these portrayals of John's christology, a variety of approaches can be detected. For instance, R. Kysar has detected three clusters of issues which continue to play central roles in the analysis of John's christology. They include the history/faith, flesh/glory, and person/function of Christ.[3]

---

1 While constituent elements of John's christological unity and disunity have been approached from many different angles, this is the first full-length and direct treatment of this topic, to the author's knowledge. Nevertheless, significant contributions to the topic include, C.K. Barrett, 'The Dialectical Theology of St. John', in his *New Testament Essays*, London, 1972, pp. 49–69; M. de Jonge, 'Variety and Development in Johannine Christology', in his *Jesus: Stranger from Heaven and Son of God*, Missoula, 1977, pp. 193–222; E. Liebert, 'That You May Believe: The Fourth Gospel and Structural Development Theory', *BTB* 14:2, 1984, pp. 67–73; J. Lieu, *The Second and Third Epistles of John*, Edinburgh, 1986, pp. 198–216; B. Lindars, 'The Fourth Gospel: An Act of Contemplation', in *Studies in the Fourth Gospel*, ed. F.L. Cross, London, 1961, pp. 23–35. See also below, p. 31, n. 32.

2 J.L. Price, 'The Search for the Theology of the Fourth Gospel', in *New Testament Issues*, ed., R. Batey, London, 1970, pp. 226–241. In this excellent survey of recent investigations of John's theology (and thus, christology) Price identifies four 'doors into the Johannine labyrinth' (pp. 228ff.). These include comparisons between John and the Synoptics, 'redaction criticism' (sources — evangelist — redactor, etc.), history-of-religions research, and what Price calls 'theme research'.

3 Kysar describes these briefly (*The Fourth Evangelist and His Gospel*, Minneapolis, 1975, p. 179), as follows:

Today the issues involved in the quest for the key to understanding the christology of John seem to be three in number: First, there is the issue of the relationship between history and faith. ... The second issue which is articulated in the contemporary literature on this subject

While the findings of this survey will be somewhat parallel to the studies of Price, Kysar and others, its focus will be different. Rather than simply to categorize the vast number of recent essays, articles and books addressing John's christology, this survey will attempt to identify major approaches to John's christology for the purpose of locating the place of the unity/disunity issue within each approach. Briefly, there have been five major kinds of approaches to John's christology: comprehensive overviews, text-centred christological approaches, theological-christological approaches, literary-christological approaches, and historical-christological approaches. While the christological unity/disunity issue is treated differently within each approach, this survey will clarify the extent to which this issue is central within each approach, although it is hardly treated directly in any of them. The scope of this survey will not be exhaustive, but at most representative in summary form. Broad categories will be sketched in order to illuminate the central issue at hand: to identify how recent approaches to John's christology have treated John's christological unity and disunity, and to consider the implications for a direct study of this topic.

A. *Comprehensive Overviews of John's Christology*

Comprehensive overviews of John's christology normally gather information regarding John's distinctive presentation of Jesus into some manageable form. The strength of this approach is that it can provide a terse and helpful digest of some of John's main christological themes; but this is also its weakness. Because general surveys are usually concerned to provide an overview, they can seldom go any deeper than a superficial sketch. Nonetheless, the treatment of any issue must begin somewhere, and thus the comprehensive overview plays an introductory though limited role.

Not surprisingly, some of the better examples of comprehensive overviews of John's christology may be found among some of the better-known texts of New Testament theology, studies in christology of the New Testament, and special treatments of John's christology. These include works by Conzelmann, Schillebeeckx, Davey and others.[4] Even a quick perusal of these and other studies

---

is the relationship of flesh (*sarx*) and glory (*doxa*) in the johannine Christ. ... Finally, still another relationship has been posed as the key in grasping the evangelist's thought, namely, that between the person and function of Christ.

4 For an excellent example of a New Testament theology text which treats John's christology thoughtfully, see H. Conzelmann, *An Outline of the Theology of the New Testament*, E.t. by J. Bowden, London, 1969, where he discusses such themes as the Johannine Logos, christological titles and their significance, the revelational connection between the Father and the Son, the sending of the Son by the Father and the characteristics of the divine Emissary, and Jesus' account of himself, including the 'I am' sayings (pp. 321–358). For an example of a text on New Testament christology which treats John's distinctive christology

suggests two conclusions: a) John's christological unity/disunity has not been treated directly within recent scholarship; and yet, b) nearly every study addresses the component elements of this issue, identifying such problems as John's high/low christology, the evangelist's apparent ambivalence toward the signs, and the puzzling relationship of the Father to the Son. Therefore, an attempt must be made to isolate the issue more clearly and to treat it more directly. The implications of such a task are described by D.L. Mealand ('The Christology of the Fourth Gospel', *SJT* 31, 1978, pp. 449–467):

> Much modern theology has reinterpreted theology in the light of Christology. It has rethought the nature of deity in the light of Christology and Christian revelation. Such a procedure shows how influential within Christian theology the contribution of the Christology of the Fourth Gospel continues to be, though the success of such reconstructions is of necessity subject to evaluation from the perspectives of philosophy and systematic theology as well as that of New Testament studies. (p. 467)

B. *Text-Centred Approaches*

A second method of approaching John's christology has been to examine a particular word, phrase, theme or section within the text itself in order to apply one's findings to an understanding of John's overall portrayal of Christ. This text-centered approach includes the analysis of such aspects as christological titles, christological motifs, passages which may represent the 'central structure' of John's christology, and christological schemas. While the christological unity/disunity issue has not been a direct focus of such studies, one can nevertheless identify central connections.

1. The study of John's *christological titles* has been primarily concerned with analyzing a particular title of, or reference to, Jesus in order to assess its contribution

---

particularly well, see also E. Schillebeeckx, *Christ; The Christian Experience for the Modern World*, E.t., J. Bowden, London, 1980, pp. 305–432. Most central to the present study, however, are his five 'keys' for understanding the Gospel of John, which include the following: Jesus as eschatological prophet greater than Moses (pp. 309–321), the Johannine descent-ascent model of understanding salvific revelation (pp. 321–331), the existential confrontation with the decision to believe or not to believe (pp. 331–343), the historical character of the Johannine tradition (pp. 343–349), and the structure of the Gospel itself as it relates to John's distinctive presentation of Jesus (pp. 349–351). For a good example of a scholar's attempt to analyze the various aspects of John's christology within a single monograph, see J.E. Davey, *The Jesus of St. John; Historical and Christological Studies in the Fourth Gospel*, London, 1958. Many more excellent treatments may be cited, but these are simply a few of the best.

5   The distinctiveness of such titles and references to Jesus in John relates to their occurrence and use. For instance, christological titles occurring distinctively (some uniquely) in John include the Aramaism, *Messias* (1:41; 4:25; most of the following citations of authors and dates of publications [in the largely bibliographical notes 5–9] may be found in Bibliography

to an appreciation of John's christology. Such 'titles' as 'Messiah', *logos*, 'the prophet' or prophet/king, 'the Son', 'God', *monogenēs*, 'Holy One of God,' etc. are distinctively Johannine in their occurrence;[5] while 'Son of God', 'Christ' and 'Son of Man' are distinctively Johannine in their usage.[6] However, their relationship to the unity/disunity issue is often couched in high/low analyses, and this tension is often dealt with by means of emphasizing the high *or* low elements, or by assuming multiple authorship.[7]

2. Likewise, the ways that various *christological motifs* (a particular theme or formula which contributes to John's presentation of Jesus) have been investigated suggest that the unity/disunity issue has been central to these interests as well. For instance, Old Testament typologies have been investigated in the interest of understanding the ways in which Jesus was perceived within Johannine Christianity. If he is considered the fulfilment of an Abraham, Elijah or Moses typology, or if Jesus is portrayed as the initiator of a 'new Exodus', these *typological* motifs suggest a Jewish/Christian christology. Likewise, such *thematic* motifs, such as

---

I: de Jonge/1972; Moloney/1977), and the Hellenistic, *logos* (1:1_, 14; cf. Borgen/1972; Cahill/1976; McNamara/1968; Miller/1981, 1983; Richter/1972), as well as 'the prophet' and 'prophet-king' (4:19, 44; 6:14f.; 7:40, 52; 9:17; cf. de Jonge/1973; Johnson/1969; Meeks/1967; cf. also 'King of Israel/the Jews', 'King' [1:49; 12:13, 15; 18:33, 37_, 39; 19:3, 12, 14, 15, 19, 21_]), 'the Son' (3:35, 36_; 5:19_, 20, 21, 22, 23, 26, 6:40; 8:35, 36; 14:13; 17:1_. In *every one* of these instances 'the Son' is used in connection with 'the Father'.), *Theos* (1:1, 18; 20:28; cf. Boobyer/1967–8; Mastin/1975; Miller/1981; Reim/1984), *monogenēs* (1:14, 18; 3:16, 18; Fennema/1985), and 'Holy One of God' (6:69 — a rather odd reference to Jesus — elsewhere in the NT used only by the demoniac in Mk. 1:24; Lk. 4:34; cf. Joubert/1968).

6 Alternatively, some titles in John are not primarily distinctive regarding their occurrence, but regarding their usage. For instance, 'Son of God' carries distinctively confessional overtones in John, as it is often used of others to refer to Jesus (Jn. 1:34, 49; 19:7). In 11:27 and 20:31 it is used as part of the Johannine pistic formula (cf. Howton/1964; de Jonge/1978). Also, the Johannine use of 'Christ' is clearly bound up with prevalent expectations regarding the coming redeemer of Israel (1:20, 25, 41; 3:28; 4:25, 29; 7:26, 27, 31, 41_, 42; 9:22; 10:24; 11:27; 12:34; the only exceptions being 1:17; 17:3; and 20:31). Also, even though the 'Son of Man' is used only a dozen times in John (1:51; 3:13, 14; 5:27; 6:27, 53, 62; 8:28; 12:23, 34_; 13:31), its distinctive use, as contrasted with its use in the Synoptic tradition, has attracted the greatest amount of attention (among studies concerned with Johannine christological titles) within recent years (cf. Borgen/1977; Coppens/1977; Dion/1967; Freed/1967; Kinniburgh/1968; Lindars/1970; Moloney/1979; Pamment/1985; de la Potterie/1968; Ruckstuhl/1972; Schnackenburg/1965; Schulz/1957; Smalley/1968–9; Trémel/1962–3).

7 For instance, some titles in John seem to be references to Jesus' exaltation (*logos*, 'God', *monogenēs*, 'Son of God', 'Holy One of God', etc.), while others appear to be references to the humanity of Jesus ('Son of Man', 'prophet', etc. Also, cf. 'Son of Joseph' [1:45; 6:42]; 'Jesus of Nazareth' [1:45; 18:5, 7; 19:19]; '*Rabbi*' [1:38, 49; 3:2, 26; 4:31; 6:25; 9:2; 11:8; '*Rabboni*', 20:16]; etc.). As even the titles of the above essays and books will suggest, a frequent interest of approaches to John's christology via christological titles is to emphasize either the *exalted or the fleshly* aspect of a particular title.

doxa, phos/skotia, and *gnosis* etc. have also been explored, normally with the result that something of John's Hellenistic background is illuminated.[8]

More controversial, however, have been John's *egō eimi* sayings of Jesus. These sayings fall into two categories linguistically and theologically. Some occur with a predicate nominative (I am the bread of life/living bread, the light of the world, the sheep gate, the good shepherd, etc.), while others occur in the 'absolute', having no predicate (4:26; 6:20; 8:24, 28, 58; 13:19; 18:5, 6, 8). There has been relatively little dispute about the metaphorical function of the passages which include the predicate nominative, but scholars have been quite divided about the meaning of the so-called 'absolute' *egō eimi* passages. The main part of the issue is whether or not these passages are theophanic, going back to Exodus 3:14 where the name of God is 'I AM', or whether they are an everyday formula for recognition, 'I am he'. In the latter case the phrase may have its roots in the LXX rendition of Deutero-Isaiah (43:25; 51:12; 52:6, etc.) where the Hebrew *ani hu* is translated *egō eimi*. P. Harner has argued that 8:58 and 13:19 are the only instances in which *egō eimi* is used exclusively as an absolute phrase, whereas in 4:26; 6:20; 8:24, 28; 18:5, 6, 8, the phrase may have a 'double meaning', suggesting both possibilities of the theophanic and everyday meanings of the term.[9] Overall, however, the use of *egō eimi* is distinctively Johannine, an expression employed by the evangelist to reveal something about Christ. It is reminiscent of the revealing and saving work of Yahweh, as well as images used to describe the true calling of Israel.[10]

---

8 Old Testament typological studies have analyzed ways that Jesus is portrayed as fulfilling the roles of Moses (1:17, 45; 3:14f.; 5:45f.; 6:32f.; cf. Glasson/1963) or Abraham (8:58; cf. Freed/1983), the Exodus typology (R.H. Smith/1962), and even the Archangel, Michael (14:14–18, 25–27; 15:26f.; 16:5–11, 12–16; cf. O. Betz/1963) in John.

9 P.B. Harner, *The "I Am" of the Fourth Gospel*, Philadelphia, 1970. Harner believes that the absolute use of the term 'expresses primarily the unity between the Father and the Son ... to be appropriated by Jesus' followers through faith ...' (p. 51). He also concludes that:

The usage of this phrase corresponds to the use of titles such as "lord" and "christ" with reference to Jesus. ... In a similar way the *egō eimi* represents an attempt to formulate and express the significance in Christian faith. (p. 65)

Other treatments of the *egō eimi* in John include special attention to the phrase in recent commentaries (cf. Brown, pp. 533–538; Bultmann, pp. 225f. n. 3; Schnackenburg, Vol. II, pp. 79–89) and other works (Feuillet/1966; Freed/1979; Schweizer/1939; Stevens/1977).

10 Just as Jesus as the Johannine Son of Man draws attention to his 'representative humanity' (cf. M. Pamment, 'The Son of Man in the Fourth Gospel', *JTS* 36, p. 58), so each of the 'I Am' metaphors of John (bread, shepherd, vine, light, truth, etc.) may be said to represent the spiritual calling of *Israel*, being a channel of God's blessing in the world. This is even more evident regarding the absolute use of the term, and this connection is certainly recognized by Schnackenburg (Vol. II, p. 88):

After the exclusive ring of the Old Testament revelation formula in the mouth of Yahweh, there can be no doubt that ... its transfer to Jesus meant the attribution to him of what was to Jewish ears an unprecedented status. ... Jesus is God's eschatological revealer in whom God utters himself. However, his self-revelation is, as we see in the Old Testament

3. The *central structure of John's christology*, a third text-centered approach to John's christology, involves the identification of a particularly terse and pregnant passage which is thought to contain a summary of John's christology. Borrowing from W.R.G. Loader's 1984 article, texts which may be referred to as portraying the 'central structure' of John's christology include such passages as John 1:1–18; 3:31–36; ch. 17; and 20:30–31.[11] For various reasons the Prologue has been analyzed most extensively among 'central structure' passages, especially regarding such questions as its relationship to the Gospel as a whole, the cultural background of its thought, and its hymnic-strophic structure. The main interest regarding an interpretation of the Prologue, however, has tended to orbit around its function as an 'interpretive fulcrum' (1:14), especially as it relates to the flesh/pre-existence

---

passages which describe God's call to Israel, his affection and his promise, a revelation of salvation for those who believe in him.

11 Loader's significant essay ('The Central Structure of Johannine Christology', *NTS* 30, 1984, pp. 188–216) outlines some of the key christological motifs in John in a clear and helpful way. Thus, based upon an outline on *John 3:31–36*, one may infer the following christological 'structure':

   (i)   The Reference to Jesus and God as Son and Father.
   (ii) That the Son comes from and returns to the Father.
   (iii) That the Father has sent the Son.
   (iv) That the Father has given all things into the Son's hands.
   (v)   That the Son says and does what the Father has told him (existing in many variants).
          He makes the Father known. (p. 191f.)

Works which find something like a 'central structure' in the *Prologue* (emphasizing both the literary and the theological connections) include C.K. Barrett, 'The Prologue of St. John' in his *New Testament Essays*, London, 1972, pp. 27–48; D. Deeks, 'The Structure of the Fourth Gospel', *NTS* 15, 1968, pp. 107–129; A. von Harnack, 'Über das Verhältnis des Prologs des vierten Evangeliums zum ganzen Werk', *ZTK* 2, 1892, pp. 189–231; H. Ridderbos, 'The Structure and Scope of the Prologue to the Gospel of John', *NovT* 8, 1966, pp. 180–201; J.A.T. Robinson, 'The Relation of the Prologue to the Gospel of St. John', *NTS* 9, 1962, pp. 120–129; S. Schulz, 'Die Komposition des Johannesprologs und die Zusammensetzung des 4. Evangeliums', *SE* I, Berlin, 1959, pp. 351–361; J. Staley, 'The Structure of John's Prologue: Its Implications for the Gospel's Narrative Structure', *CBQ* 48, 1986, pp. 241–263.

Works which find in *Jesus' prayer* (ch. 17) something like an outline of the Gospel's christology include: S. Agourides, 'The "High Priestly Prayer" of Jesus', *SE* IV, Berlin, 1968, pp. 137–145; and E. Käsemann, *The Testmament of Jesus*, London, 1968.

Works which identify *John 20:31* as the clearest outline of the Gospel's purpose include the following: de Jonge, 'The Fourth Gospel: The Book of the Disciples', in *Jesus: Stranger from Heaven and Son of God*, Missoula, 1977, pp. 1–27; E.P. Groenwald, 'The Christological Meaning of John 20:31', *Neot* 2, 1968, pp. 131–140; S.P. Kealy, *That You May Believe*, Slough, 1978; and M. Tenney, *John: The Gospel of Belief*, Grand Rapids, 1948. What is interesting about most of these studies is that even though they approach John's christological structure or outline from various vantage points there is a high degree of complementarity between them. Thus, many of Loader's conclusions are applicable for most of the other 'central structure' passages as well (p. 209).

of Jesus.[12] This illustrates again that one of the central interests of Johannine christological studies continues to be intertwined with making sense of John's christological tensions.

4. A fourth text-centred approach to John's christology involves *christological schemas*. In other words, because the structure of John's christology may not be static, but apparently involves movement (descent/ascent, being sent from/ returning to the Father, etc.), various attempts have been made to understand John's christology within an envoy, or an agency, schema. A pivotal contribution has been the 1983 monograph by G.C. Nicholson, in which he argues that the descent-ascent schema in John provides the key to understanding the plot of the Gospel.[13] A primary advantage of such *katabasis/anabasis* schemas and sending/returning analyses has been recognized by R. Kysar (*op. cit.*, p. 196), in that they allow '... one to formulate the johannine insistence upon both the reality of the flesh and the reality of the glory in the person of Jesus'. Thus, christological schemas also offer an interpretive structure within which several of John's unitive *and* disunitive christological motifs might be embraced simultaneously.

C. *Theological-Christological Approaches*

As a contrast to text-centred approaches, theological-christological approaches to John begin with a particular theological problem emerging from apparent contradictions in the text, or theological difficulties resulting from interpretations of John. Some of these studies evaluate the history of Johannine interpretation,[14] but most

---

12 A suitable survey of the flesh/glory debate in recent years may be found in R. Kysar's *The Fourth Evangelist and His Gospel*, Minneapolis, 1975, pp. 185–199. Having identified basically three positions taken by recent scholars, emphasizing a) the dominance of glory, b) the dominance of flesh, and c) the indivisibility of flesh and glory, Kysar appropriately points to John 1:14 as the pivotal text, and his discussion of the Bultmann/Käsemann debate is helpful (p. 185).

13 Nicholson's monograph (*Death as Departure*, Chico, 1983) is but one of several recent texts using a dynamic, rather than a static, christological model to describe Jesus' divine origin, his being sent into the world, and his returning to the Father. See also, J.-A. Bühner, *Der Gesandte und sein Weg im virten Evangelium*, Tübingen, 1977; E. Haenchen, ' "Der Vater, der mich gesandt hat" ', *NTS* 9, 1963, pp. 208–216; J. Kuhl, *Die Sendung Jesu Christi und der Kirche nach dem Johannesevangelium*, Sieburg, 1967; J.P. Miranda, *Der Vater, der mich gesandt hat*, Bern/Frankfurt, 1972 (cf. also *Sendung*, 1977).

14 Any rethinking of the incarnation must take into account the history of Johannine interpretation, especially as it relates to John's christology (cf. as just one example, R.H. Fuller, *ATR* Supplementary Series 7, 1976, pp. 57–66). At times, scholars have sought to reinterpret orthodox views in the light of new understandings of John's christology. Two examples are C.K. Barrett, ' "The Father is Greater than I"(Joh 14:28): Subordinationist Christology in the New Testament', in his *Essays on John*, London, 1982, pp. 19–36; and F. Watson, 'Is John's Christology Adoptionist?' in *The Glory of Christ in the New Testament*, Caird Festschrift,

of them tend to deal with such current (and long-standing) interpretive problems as the humanity/divinity of Jesus, the relationship of the Son to the Father, or the relationship between Jesus' signs and faith.

1. Regarding *Jesus' humanity/divinity* (flesh/glory), scholars have tended to interpret John from the perspective of one pole or the other. For instance, within two years of each other, J. O'Grady and J. Neyrey[15] presented studies arguing opposite interpretations of John's presentation of Jesus' humanity and divinity. As the titles suggest, the former argues that the fleshly humanity of Jesus in John has been underrated by scholars, while the latter argues that the ethos of John's high christology may be summed up by John 6:63: 'the flesh profits nothing'. The classic example of this debate in recent years, however, is the argument between Bultmann and Käsemann regarding the interpretation of John 1:14 (the 'fulcrum' of the Prologue, suggesting the christological inclination of the Gospel). Succinctly, Bultmann interprets the emphasis of John 1:14 to be vs. 14a, 'the Word became *flesh*'; while Käsemann interprets vs. 14c, 'and we beheld his *glory*' to be the interpretive fulcrum of the Prologue.[16] The implication is that depending on one's identification of Jesus' 'flesh' or 'glory' as the pivotal emphasis of the Prologue, one might also assume the same to be the theological inclination of the evangelist. The implications of the Bultmann/Käsemann debate over John 1:14 for the christological unity/disunity issue is that *both* scholars are attempting to alleviate one of the key tensions in John's christology (the high/low tension), but by employing different means. Bultmann removes the tension by arguing that only one of the poles (the fleshly emphasis) is internal to the thinking of the evangelist. The other pole has its origin in another literary source. On the other hand, Käsemann eliminates the tension by denying the existence of the 'fleshly' pole altogether. He argues that the 'docetising' christology of the evangelist embraced but one view of Jesus — that of God striding over the earth in all his glory. However, in both cases a great deal of explaining must be done in order to 'eliminate' the other pole.

2. A twin issue is *the Son's relationship to the Father* in John. Since the debates of the second and third centuries CE, John's presentation of Jesus as subordinate to the Father, equal to the Father, or both, has attracted a great deal of attention. In recent years, some Johannine scholars have gravitated toward a subordinationist

---

Oxford, 1987, pp. 113–124. Cf. also, H. Schneider, ' "The Word Was Made Flesh" (An Analysis of the Theology of Revelation in the Fourth Gospel)', *CBQ* 31, 1969, pp. 344–356.

15 J. O'Grady, 'The Human Jesus in the Fourth Gospel', *BTB* 14:2, 1984, pp. 63–66; J. Neyrey, ' "My Lord and My God": The Divinity of Jesus in John's Gospel', *SBL, 1986 Seminar Paper Series* 25, Atlanta, pp. 152–171.

16 A further discussion of this debate may be found in the Introduction (above) and in Chapter 7 (below). For the meanwhile, see M. Meye Thompson, *The Humanity of Jesus in the Fourth Gospel*, Philadelphia, 1988, for a significant contribution to the Bultmann/Käsemann debate and an extensive development of John's incarnational christology.

interpretation,[17] but this has created a problem: what to do with John's high christological material. Two articles by A.C. Sundberg[18] have sought to provide a way forward. The thesis of the first (1970) is that because the *isos tō Theō* christology of John 5:21, 26 'differs radically from the subordination christology that is so dominant in the Fourth Gospel' (p. 24), it must be attributed to a source other than the writing of the evangelist. This thesis is developed further in Sundberg's 1976 article, where he describes the subordination/egalitarian issue as 'the christological nettle of the Fourth Gospel' (p. 36). His conclusion is that:

> Two christologies are at work in the Fourth Gospel. One is the older, though developed in terms of intimacy, christology of the subordinate agent of God who does his will in obedience. The other is a new christology in which the Son has reached his majority and has been granted like rank, position and power with the Father that, perhaps, should be called binitarian theology rather than christology. It professes that the Son is a god like the Father is God. In this the accusation of the Jews and the confession of Thomas agree. (p. 37)

3. A third theological-christological Johannine issue is *the evangelist's apparent ambivalence toward the signs of Jesus*. On one hand, the signs appear to be central to the rhetorical thrust of the Gospel (20:30f.); on the other hand, the evangelist appears to devalue the role of the signs regarding faith (20:29). This has led scholars such as Bultmann, Fortna and others[19] to suggest that the evangelist has made use of a 'non-reflective' signs source, which he includes in the Gospel in a somewhat critical way.

Even more obvious in the third approach to John's christology is the interest of theological-christological studies in John's apparent contradictions and unitive/disunitive tensions. And, as suggested by the above examples, one's approach to John's theological unity and disunity has definite literary and historical implications — and vice versa.

---

17 For instance, in his monograph (*The Jesus of St. John*, London, 1958), J.E. Davey, after establishing that the christology of John is one of *dependence* upon the Father (pp. 73–89), develops in the next chapter 15 ways in which the Johannine Jesus is portrayed as dependent (pp. 90–158). Likewise, E.M. Sidebottom (*The Christ of the Fourth Gospel in the Light of First-Century Thought*, London, 1961) assumes that John's christology is subordinationist.

18 A.C. Sundberg, '*Isos tō Theō* Christology in John 5:17–30', *BR* 15, 1970, pp. 19–31; and 'Christology in the Fourth Gospel', 1976, *BR* 21, pp. 29–37. Regarding the second article, the title is printed in the table of contents in an incorrect, but telling, way: 'Christolog*ies* of the Fourth Gospel', suggesting Sundberg's view that the christological disunity of John can be explained on the basis of *multiple christologies within it*.

19 Even such scholars as J.L. Martyn and P. Borgen have been willing to accept that John may have been composed around an earlier signs source of some sort or another. Fortna's analyses continue to be the most thoughtful and extensive treatments of what this source may have looked like (pp. 221–234). Fortna argues that this unreflective source was not so concerned with the implications of Jesus' Messiahship, nor with reflecting upon its meaning, 'but as a textbook for potential Jewish converts the Gospel of Signs sought to prove one thing, and one thing only: that Jesus was the Messiah in whom men should believe' (p. 234).

D. *Literary-Christological Approaches*

Approaches to John's christology from a literary vantage point generally have tended to focus on one of three interests: the destination and purpose of John, diachronic theories of composition, or synchronic analyses of the evangelist's literary artistry.

1. The *destination and purpose* of John debate has often gravitated around interpretations of 20:31,[20] and views have ranged from John's literary purpose being a strictly evangelistic one, to an apology against the followers of John the Baptist, to an argument with the Jews or a local Synagogue, to a dispute with Christian heretics, to an attempt to provide encouragement for believing Christians — both Gentile and Jewish. With the identification of a primary literary thrust, the christological unity *and disunity* of John falls into place more easily. In other words, once John's primary 'destination and purpose' has been identified, other themes which seem disunitive may be assigned places of 'secondary' importance.

2. *Diachronic literary theories* have sought to explain John's literary and theological perplexities by means of postulating several stages in the composition of the Gospel, involving multiple authorship and a conflation of literary sources. Such obvious transitional problems as the odd sequence of chs. 4–7, the abrupt ending of ch. 14, and the apparent full stop of 20:31 have led scholars to offer various explanations for these and other difficulties. It is obvious, however, that Bultmann's composition theory has attempted to solve some theological and historical problems as well (cf. Chapters 2, 4, 5 and 6 below). In Fortna's redaction-critical analysis one may also infer the centrality of theological interests within his diachronic approach:

> John's interest in de-emphasizing the source's christological concentration on the *miracles* as in themselves the basis for understanding Jesus is clearly a movement away from one very common way of portraying divine men.
>
> Form-critical considerations seem to support this. The signs of Jesus are far more purely *novelistic* in their pre-Johannine than in their Johannine form; in particular, the source

---

20 Borrowing from the title and inspiration of J.A.T. Robinson's, 'The Destination and Purpose of St. John's Gospel' (*NTS* 6, 1959, pp. 117–131), subsequent essays such as A. Wind's 'Destination and Purpose of the Gospel of John', *NovT* 14, 1972, pp. 26–69; W.C. Van Unnik, 'The Purpose of St. John's Gospel', in *Sparsa Collecta; The Collected Essays of W.C. Van Unnik*, Leiden, 1973, pp. 37–63; J.W. Bowker, 'The Origin and Purpose of St. John's Gospel', NTS 11, 1965, pp. 398–408; and J.C. Fenton, 'Towards an Understanding of John', SE IV, Berlin, 1968, pp. 28–37 (cf. also R.E. Brown, in the introduction to his commentary, 'The Destination and Purpose of the Fourth Gospel', pp. LXVII–LXXIX); scholars have recently sought to discover the central message of John, and such endeavours have had significant implications for christological interpretation. These and other studies have normally sought to interpret the setting out of which John emerged, as well as the audience to which it was addressed, applying, then, some interpretation of vs. 20:31 to the evangelist's overall purpose.

displays a thaumaturgic interest that the evangelist nowhere develops. While he frequently reproduces the older story intact, with only an occasional insertion, he rarely lets it stand on its own ... but instead makes of the miraculous event only an occasion for the revelatory discourse that he attaches to it. Attention is partially shifted away from the deed as such, and especially from Jesus as the author of the deed, to its *theo*logical significance, namely, the Father's presence in all the Son does.

Along with Fortna,[21] several leading Johannine scholars have followed Bultmann's example and have also employed diachronic methodologies in assessing the origins of various parts of John. It is also true, however, that ever since the 1939 work of E. Schweizer, refutations of diachronic theories have almost matched the number and vigour of such studies, themselves.[22] Despite Ruckstuhl's largely successful demonstration of John's *literarische Einheit*,[23] however, a division still exists between those who advocate a diachronic approach to John and those who do not. At least one contributing factor in this interpretive *impasse* is the intrinsic connection between theological and literary interests. Because neither Bultmann, Teeple, nor Fortna has begun by setting forth the christological unitive and disunitive features of John as the central interest for their studies,[24] Schweizer,

---

21 Cf. R. Fortna, 'Christology in the Fourth Gospel: Redaction-Critical Perspectives', *NTS* 21, 1975, pp. 489–504; citation, p. 491. Including the eight other scholars surveyed by R. Kysar, 'The Source Analysis of the Fourth Gospel — A Growing Consensus?', *NovT* 15, 1973, pp. 134–152 (cf. discussion below in Chapter 3), perhaps the closest parallel to Bultmann's diachronic approach to John's composition is the approach taken by H. Teeple, *The Literary Origin of the Gospel of John*, Evanston, 1974. See also U. von Walde, *The Earliest Version of John's Gospel: Recovering the Gospel of Signs*, Wilmington, 1989.

22 The contribution of E. Schweizer, (*Egō Eimi*, Göttingen, 1939), E. Ruckstuhl (*Die literarische Einheit des Johannesevangeliums*, Freiburg, 1951), and B. Noack (*Zur johanneischen Tradition*, Copenhagen, 1954), and the two 1984 articles by V.S. Poythress ('The Use of the Intersentence Conjunctions *De, Oun, Kai*, and Asyndeton in the Gospel of John', *NovT* 26, 1984, pp. 312–340; and 'Testing for Johannine Authorship by Examining the Use of Conjunctions', *Westminster Journal of Theology* 46, 1984, pp. 350–369) have confirmed Schweizer's original conclusion, that, 'Im grossen und ganzen ist also das Johannes-Evangelium ein einheitliches Werk, dessen Verfasser benutztes Material selbständig mit seinem Stil und Geist prägt' (p. 108f.).

23 The battle in which Ruckstuhl challenged Bultmann, several years after the production of his commentary, has since been taken up between Ruckstuhl and Fortna (cf. Ruckstuhl's 'Johannine Language and Style; The Question of their Unity', in de Jonge's *L'Evangile*, pp. 124–147, where most of his essay is given to challenging Fortna, pp. 129–145). In this article nearly three decades hence, Ruckstuhl admits somewhat sheepishly, though not undecidedly, that:

> With respect to my criticism of Bultmann's literary divisions in Jn, I am now not afraid to confess that in those days I was a rather young fellow, ready for a fight, and that my writer's tone was somewhat aggressive. Since then much water has flowed down the Rhine, pluralism and ecumenism have grown strong, and I have come to understand more and more that Bultmann is a great man. ... I am nevertheless still confident that my criticism of his position was substantially correct. (p. 126f.)

24 It is with the publication of Fortna's second monograph on his subject that the extensive and

Ruckstuhl and others have often missed the theological value of diachronic studies. Therefore, when they have attacked claims that the Gospel is a literary disunity, they have missed one of the central points being made by scholars using diachronic approaches, and this may also explain why diachronic advocates have not found their criticisms necessarily convincing. The major interpretive function of diachronic approaches has been to identify and distribute various theological strands into their respective, hypothetical sources, and thereby to address some of the central problems of John's christological disunity.

3. *Synchronic* approaches have reacted against this sort of move and have tended to focus on John's message as communicated by means of literary rhetoric, regardless of its content or the tensions inherent to it.[25] A weakness with such approaches, however, is that their advocates have often overlooked the problems addressed by diachronic studies, so that theological and historical problems seem to fade away into the evangelist's bag of literary techniques, or into the hypothesizing of reader-response factors.[26] If diachronic studies have minimized John's *unity*, synchronic studies have minimized John's *disunity*, and thus the conjunction, 'and' is the aggravation of diachronic and synchronic approaches alike. John's christology is unitive *and* disunitive, and this conjunctive element must be addressed if scholars are to make further headway in understanding the character and origins of its distinctiveness.

---

rich implications for Johannine interpretation are outlined clearly. In this exceptionally clear and lucid book (*The Fourth Gospel and its Predecessor; From Narrative Source to Present Gospel*, Philadelphia/Edinburgh, 1988) Fortna seeks to account for 'the Johannine riddle' (i.e. the spiritualizing of 'outward facts', pp. 1–10) by developing in greater detail a reconstruction of how the evangelist-as-redactor may have co-opted his narrative source. The interpretive significance of this theory is most clearly developed in Fortna's six appended excurses (pp. 205–314) in which he develops such themes as: the source's 'genre' as a missionary tract, the relationship between seeing and believing, the soteriological aspect of the source's Messianism, differing treatments of the death of Jesus and eschatology between source and evangelist, and the symbolic use of 'locale' and characters (individuals and groups) by the evangelist. The obvious implication of these essays is that Fortna's interest is highly *theological* as well as literary (cf. p. 213), and thus far debates over John's style and composition have largely understated this important matter.

25 See discussion above in introduction (notes 32, 33), in Ashton's discussion (pp. 13–16), and P.N. Anderson, 'The *Sitz im Leben* of the Johannine Bread of Life Discourse and its Evolving Context' (SNTS Johannine Literature Seminar paper, 1993, p. 22 n. 33).

26 Indeed, some of John's disunitive features must be due to the evangelist's use of irony, the audiences he intends to convince, the changing situation in which his part of the church finds itself, and simply the way a first-century writer may have told his story. These possibilities, however, still do not diminish the fact that regarding many themes, and throughout the Gospel, this writer *seems* to contradict himself, and such a problem affects one's appreciation of the veracity — let alone one's ability to grasp the intended meaning — of the Gospel's christocentric message.

E. *Historical-Christological Approaches*

'Historical' approaches to John's christology have taken various paths, depending upon the interest of the scholar. Despite its appeal to objectivity, the very word, 'historical', is always used rhetorically. It implies a contrast to that which is not 'true'. Therefore, one may infer at least three interests pertaining to history, as they relate to John's distinctive portrayal of Jesus.

1. *'Historicity' interests* have related to the historical authenticity of the Johannine witness to Jesus, especially in the light of its disagreement with the Synoptic portrayals of Jesus' ministry. Central aspects of this debate include comparison/contrasts with the Synoptics, John's internal claims and evidence regarding 'eye-witness' material, and the witness of the Early Fathers regarding John's origin. The christological tensions addressed within this debate have been the apparent contradiction between the compiler's claim that the authorial source of John was an 'eye-witness' (Jn. 21:24f.) and follower of Jesus, while this individual is not named, nor is his account sufficiently harmonious with Synoptic portrayals of Jesus' ministry[27] to be considered the authentic work of an eye-witness.

2. The *History of Religions* approach to John's christology has compared John's christology with contemporary mythologies, seeking to illuminate the origins of some of John's distinctive christological motifs. Especially notable have been such constructs as the Gnostic Redeemer-myth and the *theios anēr* (God-man) typology.[28] Despite the fact that in recent years some scholars have raised serious

---

27 Some of the more thoughtful recent treatments of John and the Synoptics include C.K. Barrett, 'John and the Synoptic Gospels' *ET* 85, 1973/4, pp. 228–233; R.E. Brown, 'John and the Synoptic Gospels: A Comparison', in his *New Testament Essays*, pp. 246–271; B. Lindars, 'John and the Synoptics: A Test Case', *NTS* 27, 1981, pp. 287–294; F. Neirynk, 'John and the Synoptics', in de Jonge's *L'Evangile*, pp. 73–106; D.M. Smith, 'John and the Synoptics', *Bib* 63, 1982, pp. 102–113, and 'John and the Synoptics: Some Dimensions of the Problem', *NTS* 26, 1980, pp. 425–444. See especially D.M. Smith's unprecedented monograph, *John Among the Gospels*, Minneapolis, 1992.

28 A variety of critical analyses over the last three decades or so have posed serious challenges to various mythological constructs, hitherto accepted as representative of views prevalent within the culture in which John must have been written. Specifically, these include the 'Gnostic Redeemer-myth' and the '*theios anēr*' messianic concept. G. MacRae and his Harvard Seminar on Gnosticism have provided one of the most enduring sources of such challenges, and his two 1970 articles are instructive. In 'The Jewish Background of the Gnostic Sophia Myth', *NovT* 12, 1970, pp. 86–101, MacRae identifies no fewer than 15 parallels between earlier Jewish and later gnostic wisdom mythologies. The implication for Johannine studies is that parallels between John and later gnostic writings may *both* have their origins in Judaism. In his 'The Fourth Gospel and *Religionsgeschichte*', *CBQ* 32, 1970, pp. 12–24, MacRae argues that to see the evangelist as co-opting a signs source with a *theios anēr* christology is too simplistic. The Johannine Jesus is portrayed as fulfilling both Jewish and Hellenistic expectations, but ultimately, he stands beyond these (p. 23f.).

questions regarding the historical adequacy of such constructs,[29] they have served a significant interpretive function for those who have used them. Primarily, the Gnostic Redeemer-myth has been used to explain the descending/ascending movement of Jesus, while the *theios anēr* motif has been used to explain the problem of Jesus' embellished miracles in John — given the evangelist's apparent de-emphasizing of their miraculous value. In both cases, *religionsgeschichtliche* approaches have been adopted as a means of addressing John's christological unity and disunity. Such constructs have often been employed by diachronic studies, implying tensions between alien christologies and the christology of the evangelist.[30]

. 3. A third historical interest has been *the history of Johannine Christianity*. While diachronic in terms of time, these studies have been largely synchronic in terms of authorship or authorial group. Over the last three decades the historical interest of Johannine scholars has shifted from the search for the historical Jesus

---

29 Other critiques of mythological constructs include E.M. Yamauchi's *Pre-Christian Gnosticism*, Grand Rapids/London, 1973; 'Jewish Gnosticism? The Prologue of John, Mandean Parallels and the Trimorphic Protenoia' (in Festschrift for G. Quispel), Leiden, 1981, pp. 467–497; and 'The Descent of Ishtar, the Fall of Sophia, and the Roots of Jewish Gnosticism', *TB* 29, 1978, pp. 143–175; P. Perkins, 'Gnostic Christologies and the New Testament', *CBQ* 43, 1981, pp. 590–606; H.C. Kee, *Miracle in the Early Christian World*, New Haven/London, 1983; and especially, C.R. Holladay, *Theios Anēr in Hellenistic Judaism: A Critique of the Use of this Category in New Testament Christology*, Missoula, 1977. In this extensive and thorough investigation of the entire corpus of contemporary Jewish and Greek literature, Holladay finds *only four references* to anything like a *theios anēr*, and each of these references uses the term *differently*. Therefore, while such a concept may have genuine value for debates among 20th century scholars, to assume that it was ever a unified and coherent mythological construct, used meaningfully by first-century Hellenistic Jews, is unfounded. Thus, his conclusion is remarkably close to that of O. Betz, 'The Concept of the So-Called "Divine Man" in Mark's Christology', in *Studies in New Testament and Early Christian Literature* (ess. hon. Allen P. Wikgren) ed. D.E. Aune, Leiden, 1972, pp. 229–240, who says:

> Finally, I do not think that there is such a complicated Christology in Mark, resulting from two opposing views and a rejected heresy. ... There are attempts to explain the Christology of John's Gospel in a way similar to the Divine Man analysis of Mark. We are told that there is a rather primitive *Theios anēr* presentation of Jesus in the Johannine Sēmeia-Source which had been corrected by the sophisticated Revealer Christology of the evangelist. I must confess that the existence of such a Sēmeia-Source seems to me no less questionable than that of the so-called Divine Man concept. (p. 240)

30 Whether those advocating the use of 'mythological constructs' or their critics actually win the day is not as significant as an understanding of the interpretive functions of such constructs. The Gnostic Redeemer-myth has offered at least a partial explanation of the movement of Jesus (esp. in John) from above to below, and back to above again, while the *theios anēr* construct has sought to provide a partner in dialogue with the evangelist, as it relates to his apparent ambivalence to Jesus' signs. *Both* of these aspects are central to John's christolgoical unity and disunity, and it behooves the holder and the challenger of views using such constructs to integrate their positions with their interpretive implications.

to the search for the historical Johannine community.[31] The current interest in the socio-religious setting of Johannine Christianity is a corrective to the tendency of previous studies to focus on religious *ideas* alone, to the exclusion of considering their *function* within a religious group. According to R.E. Brown (*Community*, p. 166–169), the following christological characteristics may be attributed to the following socio-religious developments: a) John's Prophet-like-Moses and anti-Temple christology was the result of Samaritan converts entering the Johannine community in the middle first century, thus challenging the original Davidic Messianism which would have been quite similar to the type of christology represented by Mark. b) The acceptance of this second group led to the development of a high, pre-existent christology, which was catalyzed in debates with the Jewish leaders over the divine mission (and identity) of Jesus. c) Over this debate ('di-theism' versus Jewish monotheism) Johannine Christian Jews were forced to leave the Synagogue and to become Jewish Christians. With the addition of Gentile converts, Johannine christology assimilated more Hellenistic ways of describing the exalted Christ — which led to docetising tendencies among Gentile Christians. d) This led to a split within Johannine Christianity, and by the time 1 John was written, those who refused to confess that Jesus had come in the flesh were labelled as the 'antichrists'.

Something like this may indeed have occurred, but there are two major problems regarding such constructs as they relate to John's christological unity and disunity. First, they must be based upon a high degree of speculation. An oversight regarding one 'layer' of community reconstruction may jeopardize the accuracy of other layers built upon it. Second, even within the passages attributed to various phases of the 'community's' history, there is still a great amount of christological unity and disunity. Thus, even if christological movement (lower to higher, to lower, etc.) can be accurately inferred within different 'strata' of community development, a unifying aspect (and problem!) of John's christology is its pervasive *disunity*. Therefore, John's christological unity and disunity demands to be addressed as a separate issue, in and of itself. Such a venture will include the best insights and solid findings of the above approaches, but it may also call for new venues of analysis to be explored.

---

31 The recent trend within Johannine studies is not so much a quest for the 'historical Jesus', but a quest for the 'historical evangelist' and his socio-religious context (cf. Ashton, p. 5). One of the finest examples of these is D. Rensberger's *Johannine Faith and Liberating Community*, Philadelphia, 1988. Other contributions to this area of interest may be found in Bibliography IV, below.

Findings

A survey of recent approaches to John's christology illustrates the extent to which unitive/disunitive interests have pervaded recent christological studies, but it also betrays a puzzling phenomenon: while John's christological unity and disunity is of central interest to most recent approaches to John's christology, attempts to analyze the problem directly are remarkably few.[32] There may indeed be multiple components of its origin, but more of a direct investigation into the epistemological origin and character of John's christological unity and disunity is needed. While an analysis (cursory, though it has been) of recent approaches to John's christology facilitates a better understanding of the unitive/disunitive tensions within it, the converse is also true. Greater clarity as to the origin and character of John's christological unity and disunity will also enhance one's understanding of most other interests pertaining to John's distinctive christology. Such are some of the primary implications of the present study.

---

32 Although see E.D. Freed, 'Variations in the Language and Thought of John', *ZNW* 55, 1964, pp. 167–197; M. de Jonge, 'Variety and Development in Johannine Christology', in his *Stranger*, 1977, pp. 193–222; S. Smalley, 'Diversity and Development in John', *NTS* 17, 1970–1971, pp. 276–292; and C.F.D. Moule, 'The Individualism of the Fourth Gospel', *NovT* 5, 1962, pp. 171–190. See also above, p. 17, n. 1.

Chapter 2

A Survey of Significant Commentaries

While John's christological unity and disunity has been of central interest to most recent approaches to John's christology, few scholars have treated the topic directly as an isolated problem. Nonetheless, theological, literary and historical interests have often been motivated by attempts to address John's christological tensions, but the relationship between these three areas of interest is seldom articulated clearly. Therefore, the purpose of this chapter is to identify the correlation between three aspects of five recent and major commentaries on John.[1] These aspects include: the authors' assessments of John's christological unity and disunity, their theories of composition, and their treatments of John 6. Correlation does not imply causation, but it does serve to suggest implications one's approach to John's christological unity and disunity may have for one's theory of how John came into being — and vice versa.

A. *Rudolf Bultmann, 1941 (1971)*

Bultmann's approach to the christological unity and disunity of John is to isolate the existentialist christology of the evangelist as central, and to assign diverging christological motifs to other literary sources. This preserves a certain degree of non-contradiction of thought for the evangelist, while explaining the presence of disparate christological material in John as originating elsewhere. Thus, Bultmann approaches John's unitive *and* disunitive christological themes by setting *both*

---

1 Of course, several other recent commentaries deserve consideration, but space does not allow treatment of all of these in Chapter 2. For instance, two other outstanding commentaries by German scholars include J. Becker's *Das Evangelium nach Johannes*, Gütersloh, Vol. 1, 1979; Vol. 2, 1981; and E. Haenchen, *A Commentary on the Gospel of John* 2 Vols., E.T., R.W. Funk, eds. R.W. Funk and U. Busse, Philadelphia, 1984. Noteworthy commentaries by British scholars include E.C. Hoskyns, *The Fourth Gospel*, ed. F.N. Davey, London, 2nd ed. 1947; C.H. Dodd, *The Interpretation of the Fourth Gospel*, Cambridge, 1953; and G.R. Beasley-Murray, *John*, Waco, 1987. Of course, many others still deserve to be mentioned (see Bibliography II), but two points suffice: a) comments from these and other scholars will be drawn into the discussion elsewhere, and b) the correlation between a scholar's approach to John's christological unity and disunity, theory of composition, and treatment of John 6 may be noted in these commentaries and in others.

aspects in sharp relief. The result is that he infers at least five literary sources, each of which has its own distinctive christological perspective, and these inferences are argued on the basis of stylistic, contextual and theological corroboration. The key to Bultmann's analysis, however, lies in his understanding of the evangelist's perspective as the central concern of John's christology. Against this interpretation other themes and literary forms are evaluated and ascribed to other literary sources accordingly.

According to Bultmann, the orientation of the evangelist is determined by his conviction that Jesus is the true Revealer, as opposed to John the Baptist (p. 17f.). The Baptist is portrayed as one who repeatedly witnesses to the superiority of Jesus over himself, and the evangelist also incorporates several gnostic motifs which had been assimilated by the Baptist's community. Thus, such motifs as the Gnostic Redeemer-myth and parts of revelation discourses are interwoven into the evangelist's presentation of Jesus. However, this does not happen uncritically, and the main concern of the evangelist differs from his gnostic orientation in a very significant way. Rather than perceiving the agent of God's salvation as a superhuman being, the evangelist is convinced that Jesus comes to humanity requiring belief, not on the basis of attesting miracles or some other divine manifestation, but solely on the basis of accepting that he is who he says he is. This is the *offense of the incarnation*: that people are confronted with the Word of God, which goes against the conventions of human-made (both gnostic and Jewish) religion. It calls for humanity to believe in God's salvation, calling for the abandonment of all temporal forms of religious security (p. 62f.). On the other hand, the paradox of the incarnation is that the glory of God is revealed in the *humanity* of the Son.[2] It calls the world to believe in God's Son in a way that is beyond the need for attesting miracles, beyond dependence upon institutional sacraments, and beyond the need for the eye-witness 'proof' before trusting in his saving revelation. The incarnation meets people at the very centre of their existence, and this theme runs throughout the entire Gospel. Thus, the *disunity* of John's christology is the result of the tension between the evangelist's central christological concern and the somewhat deflective ones of his sources and subsequent redactor. The apparent *unity* of John is the literary result of the evangelist and the redactor imitating the styles of their respective sources.

---

2 Bultmann's understanding of the offense of the incarnation is also well articulated in his *Theology of the New Testament* Vol. 2, E.t. by K. Grobel, New York, 1955:

   In all these misunderstandings of the offense of the assertion, "the word became flesh" finds expression. This offense lies in the fact that the Revealer appears as a man whose claim to be the Son of God is one which he cannot, indeed, must not, prove to the world. For the Revelation is judgment upon the world and is necessarily felt as an attack upon it and an offense to it, so long as the world refuses to give up its norms. Until it does so, the world inevitably misunderstands the words and deeds of the Revealer, or they remain a riddle for it (10:6; 16:25, 29), even though Jesus has said everything openly all along (18:20). (p. 46)

Bultmann's understanding of the christological unity/disunity issue is reflected very clearly in his composition theory.[3] The sources used by the evangelist include a collection of revelation discourses, a *sēmeia* source, a Passion-narrative source and the evangelist-himself as a source. From the *Offenbarungsreden* source was gathered the Prologue, which had been an early hymn of the Baptist community, and many of the discourses attributed to Jesus. The *sēmeia* source provides the basis for the miracles attributed to Jesus, and the pre-Marcan Passion source provides much of the basis for John's Passion narrative. Apparent breaks in chronological, geographic and thematic sequence are explained by the theory that due to external circumstances the original text had fallen into disorder. Therefore, the editor attempted (unsuccessfully) to reconstruct the original order, and he also added various portions and themes to make the Gospel more palatable for a Christian audience around the turn of the first century.

These literary sources account for the diversity of christological content in John. According to Bultmann, John's christological affinities with the Gnostic Redeemer-myth, in which God sends an agent from heaven to impart salvific knowledge to humans, is explicable on the basis that the evangelist made use of an *Offenbarungsreden* source, similar in style and content to the Odes of Solomon. The portrayal of Jesus in the Hellenistic *theios anthropos* mould, as he does miraculous signs and sees into the hearts of strangers and is all-knowing about the future, results from the evangelist's critical incorporation of a non-reflective *sēmeia* source. The somewhat historically reliable, yet independent (from the Synoptics) source of John's Passion narrative is the Passion source. Finally, such themes as pietistic sacramentology, futuristic eschatology, and claims of John's apostolic origin have been added by the 'churchly' redactor. By means of his largely critical acceptance of the christological perspectives of his sources, the evangelist

---

3 Although Bultmann never clearly describes his composition theory in a systematic way (however, cf. the introduction to the 1971 Westminster Press English edition, where W. Schmithals has contributed a helpful introduction [pp. 3–12]; and cf. D.M. Smith), one may certainly detect some of the theological assumptions underlying his construct. Especially in his *New Testament Theology* (*op. cit.*), three aspects of his composition theory are given interpretive significance: a) Although the descending and ascending Jesus in John represents the evangelist's use of the Gnostic Redeemer-myth (pp. 12–14), the evangelist has altered its otherwise dualistic outlook and interpreted the story of the Revealer as a 'dualism of decision' (p. 21). b) Although Jesus is portrayed in the mould of a Hellenistic *theios anēr*, who has miraculous knowledge at his command and who does miraculous signs, the evangelist has transformed these stories into ' ... symbolic pictures which indicate that the believer feels himself searched and known by God and that his own existence is exposed by the encounter with the Revealer' (p. 42). c) While the evangelist's attitude toward the sacraments is 'critical or at least reserved' (p. 59), an 'ecclesiastical redactor' has added sacramental motifs at 19:34b; 6:51b–58; and ch. 21, differing from the evangelist's christology and eschatology. Thus, in each of these cases Bultmann's composition theory accounts for how such a motif, or section, may have become a part of the Gospel, and yet also how the evangelist's christological stance is ideologically other.

has been able to construct a Gospel which confronts humanity with the reality of God's saving activity and leads to a crisis. Each must decide whether or not to accept the Revealer through faith. This introduces a dualistic frame of reality, which unlike more developed gnostic dualism is neither cosmological nor metaphysical. It is a crisis of *existence*: a *dualism of decision*.

These composition theories can be observed by considering Bultmann's treatment of John 6, and in doing so several issues come to the surface. First, the order of chs. 5 and 6 is not correct, as the original order was 4, 6, 5, 7. This order keeps Jesus in Galilee (4 and 6), and it unifies the Jerusalem feasts mentioned in chs. 5 and 7. Thematically, this reordering is also called for, as ch. 6 shows that the revelation is the 'crisis' of humanity's natural desire for life, while ch. 5 portrays the 'crisis' of his religion. A second issue involves the sources underlying the chapter. For 6:1–26 the evangelist cannot have used Mark, and since the material must have originated from a source other than himself, he must have used the *sēmeia* source. Likewise, vss. 27–59 reflect a combination of the revelation-sayings source and the contribution of the evangelist. Into the Bread of Life discourse was inserted a eucharistic passage by an ecclesiastical redactor, which raises a third issue, the unity of the chapter.

At this point Bultmann proposes that vss. 51b–58 represent a secondary interpretation of the Bread of Life discourse in terms of the Lord's Supper. They have been added by the redactor because he has felt the lack of any eucharistic theme in the Gospel. Thus, he has set out to correct the evangelist's position which is critical of cultic, sacramental piety. This raises a fourth issue which regards the theological stance of the Fourth Evangelist. According to Bultmann, the central importance of the Fourth Gospel's presentation of Jesus is the existential enlightenment which comes from believing in the Christ of faith. The Fourth Gospel is of little historical value, claims Bultmann, as its purpose was not to outline the career of the Jesus of history. Rather, its purpose was to communicate the salvific and revelational mission of Jesus in terms of an historicized drama. Thus, in the evangelist's portrayal of the words and works of Jesus, his revelatory mission is furthered. Jesus not only performs enlightening and nourishing functions (as do light and bread), but in response to the questions, 'Who is the true Light of the world?' and 'What is the true Bread from heaven?', the Johannine Jesus declares, *egō eimi*: 'It is I!'

B. *C.K. Barrett, 1955, 1978*

In 1955 the first edition of C.K. Barrett's commentary was published, and on many major issues Barrett disagreed with Bultmann. According to Barrett, the peculiar character of John's christological unity and disunity may be attributed to the view that the evangelist was a highly creative theologian, who did not have just one view on each topic. Rather, he was one who constantly found himself engaged in dialogue with various understandings of the gospel, to which he responded with his own perspective on each matter. This was especially the case regarding christology and such related themes as belief on the basis of miracles, sacramentalism, and eschatological views which were too limited. Thus, John represents a literary unity, and its christological disunity is simply a reflection of the evangelist's creative mind, able to consider an issue first from one angle and then another.

The theological development of the Fourth Gospel revolves around its christology, which in turn illuminates its theology, as the Son points to the Father. John's christology is more systematic and thought through than that of the Synoptics. For John, 'Jesus *is* the Gospel, and the Gospel *is* Jesus' (p. 70). He reveals God's self-communication to the world as the ontological mediator between God and humanity. Thus, he also mediates true knowledge and salvation, and these come as a result of believing in Jesus as the Christ, the Son of God (17:3). John's eschatology holds various dangers in check. The subjective dangers of mysticism are held in tension with the intellectual content of Christianity, and the twin dangers of perfectionism and antinomianism are held in check by the mediation of Christ and the ethical expression of Christianity.

Miracles in the Fourth Gospel are also a function of its christology. They are signs pointing to the identity and divine origin of Jesus. In contrast to the Synoptics, there are no ordinances to baptize or to establish the eucharist, and yet John is very 'sacramental'. 'The incarnation was itself sacramental in that it visibly represented truth and at the same time conveyed that which it represented.' (p. 82) The Holy Spirit bears witness to Christ and makes operative what Christ has already effected, and John's pneumatology lays the foundation for a co-equal trinity. Thus, Barrett attributes the unitive and disunitive features of John's christology to the evangelist's being a creative theologian,[4] able to hold truth in tension.

This perspective may also be identified in his treatment of the composition and authorship of John. The evangelist was probably a disciple of John the Apostle, and this accounts for the sizeable quantity of eye-witness material as well as the

---

4 Some of the most thoughtful essays developing an image of the Fourth Evangelist-as-theologian have been written by C.K. Barrett, and may be found in his three volumes of collected essays: *New Testament Essays,* London, 1972; *The Gospel of John and Judaism,* E.t., D.M. Smith, Philadelphia, 1975; and *Essays on John,* London, 1982. His section on 'The Theology of the Gospel' (pp. 67–99) in his commentary is especially suggestive, and it opens with this statement:

> The theology of the Fourth Gospel, though cast in the form of a miscellaneous account of the life and teaching of Jesus of Nazareth, is the result of a serious attempt to evaluate and restate the apostolic faith in a situation differing, in some respects considerably, from that in which it was first grasped and proclaimed. John was not a theologian who worked from hand to mouth, reassessing and adapting this or that doctrine as occasion arose; he seized upon the earlier tradition as a whole, and refashioned it as a whole (see pp. 97ff.). The result of this is that any attempt to itemize his theology and present it in neat compartments is bound to misrepresent it. (p. 67)

reflective and theological tone in which the Gospel was written. According to Barrett, this bold and creative theologian was '... widely read both in Judaism and Hellenism ...' (p. 133), and he used the Gospel of Mark as his primary written source. This accounts for the basic chronological and linguistic similarities between Mark and John, as well as interpretive differences between them. He died before his Gospel was published, and the final edition was produced around 100 CE by another disciple who at least partially misunderstood the connection between John the Apostle and the Beloved Disciple. The Beloved Disciple was correctly understood to have referred to John the Apostle, but wrongly understood to be saying that John was the writer of the Gospel. Thus, '21:24 was now composed in the model of 19:35, and the book was sent out on its long career as the work of John, foe of the heretics and beloved of his Lord' (p. 134). Therefore, John should be regarded as a literary unity, and problems of interpretation should be struggled with as part of the existing text — as we have it — and not 'solved' by introducing multiple authors and sources as means of dealing with primarily interpretive problems.

As in the case of Bultmann, Barrett's approach to chapter 6 also reflects his approach to John's christological unity and disunity as well as his composition theory: the view that the Gospel is a literary whole. While agreeing with Bultmann that some chronological and geographical problems would be resolved by the translocation of chapters 5 and 6, Barrett retains the present order. Feeling that the author was more interested in theological progression than the recording of an itinerary, Barrett looks for the theological meaning behind the intentional ordering of ch. 6 after ch. 5. The primary sources underlying ch. 6 are Mark and the Jewish scriptures, as John 6:1–15 reflects a combination of Mark 6:35–44 and 8:1–9, and John 6:16–21 was probably derived from Mark 6:45–54. The fact that Luke's scene seems a bit out of place increases the probability of John's literary dependence upon Mark. Thus, the evangelist included the lake scene because it was firmly fixed in tradition, and he used it in order to move the scene back to Capernaum where the Bread of Life discourse was given (p. 279). This discourse (6:22–59) could be viewed as an extended exegesis of Psalms 78:24, developing the theme that 'Jesus is the Son of Man, and it is in communion with him that men have eternal life' (p. 282).

This leads us to the question of the unity of John 6. While Bultmann regards 6:51–58 as the addition of a redactor, Barrett maintains the unity of the chapter:

> John was not an anti-sacramentalist, whose work was interpolated by an orthodox sacramentalist, but a profound theologian, capable of acceptance, but of highly critical acceptance, of the sacraments. ... He had not abandoned futurist eschatology in the interests of a purely present Christian experience, but was a profound theologian, capable of holding present and future together in unity. (p. 25)

According to Barrett, if these suppositions hold true, the case for extensive redaction falls to the ground, leaving only a few instances in which additions were made. Therefore, while 'flesh' and 'blood' may refer to the eucharist, they more emphatically point to the *incarnation* (the 'flesh-and-bloodness' of Jesus). Thus, the feeding *and* the discourse build up to a climactic description of what the reciprocal indwelling between Christ and the believer is like. The flesh and blood of Jesus 'really are what true food and drink should be, to fulfil the ideal, archetypal function of food and drink, that is in giving eternal life to those who receive them' (p. 299).

C. *Raymond E. Brown, 1966 and 1970*

While Brown believes John's christological tensions are internal to the evangelist's thinking and writing, his approach is 'diachronic' in the sense that acute concerns — at different times in the 'history' of Johannine Christianity — are responsible for a fair amount of the Gospel's christological disunity. Rather than assume an earlier written source like Mark, or a *sēmeia* source, Brown believes the Gospel's content and its interpretation are intrinsic to the evangelist's interpretation of his experience as an apostle and follower of Jesus. Thus, the christological unity of John is based upon its single authorship, while its disunity is largely a reflection of the evangelist's various stages of maturation, as well as his varied responses to christological issues faced within Johannine Christianity. Therefore, even though the other evangelists must be considered theologians in their own rights, 'it is still true that the fourth evangelist is the theologian par excellence' (p. XLIX). This may be seen in his theory of composition.

Brown's theory of composition consists of five stages. The *first stage* involved the 'existence of a body of traditional material pertaining to the words and works of Jesus — material similar to what has gone into the Synoptic Gospels, but material whose origins were independent of the Synoptic tradition' (p. XXXIV).

The *second stage* involved 'the development of this material in Johannine patterns ... through oral preaching and teaching'. These patterns and units were moulded over several decades by a 'principal preacher'. He was responsible for most of the content of the Gospel, although he was not the only source (p. XXXIV–XXXV).

The *third stage* of composition involved 'the organization of this material from stage 2 into a consecutive Gospel. This would be the first edition of the Fourth Gospel as a distinct work.' It was the dominant preacher who probably organized this, the first written edition of the Gospel. Its linguistic and thematic coherence reflect this likelihood (p. XXXV–XXXVI).

The *fourth stage* involved the evangelist's editing of his first draft. He may have done so more than once, but his purpose was to improve the Gospel by answering objections and solving problems arising out of the earlier edition (p. XXXVI).

The *fifth stage* was a final editing, and according to Brown, it was done by 'someone other than the evangelist and whom we shall call the redactor' (p. XXXVI). He was a close friend of the evangelist and a part of the Johannine 'school'. He included material which had not been previously inserted into the Gospel, but which had been composed in stage two. This explains the uneven and somewhat awkward appearance of material which seems to duplicate existing content. Because the evangelist had died by then, his more developed editing skills are absent, and even material not due directly to his influence (ch. 21) is included by the redactor.

Parallel to Brown's theory of composition are the following observations about the tradition behind the Fourth Gospel. John neither depends on the Synoptics nor their sources for its information. A few linguistic details may have been borrowed from Mark at stage five, but even this Brown doubts. From the accuracy of socio-religious and geographical details in the material unique to John, it may be said that 'the Fourth Gospel reflects a knowledge of Palestine as it was before its destruction in A.D. 70, when some of its landmarks perished' (XLII). Thus, the setting is authentic, and the value of the information found only in John must be elevated as having more merit than it was thought to have had over the last two centuries. John does reflect a general chronology, but stage five has made its reconstruction and harmonization with the Synoptics nearly impossible. Agreeing with J.N. Sanders, 'John is deeply historical — historical in the sense in which history is concerned not only with what happened but also with the deepest meaning of what happened' (p. XLIX).

The principal background for Johannine thought was Palestinian Judaism, and the Hellenistic influence on the Gospel was due simply to its presence in the thought and speech of Palestine. Thus, the theory of dependence on early Oriental Gnosticism, though not entirely disproven, is unnecessary. The same milieu out of which gnostic thought emerged was the context in which the evangelist lived and ministered. Therefore, it is not surprising that his Gospel account should reflect this world view.

Brown approaches John 6 as a chapter which includes a great deal of early, traditional material. This explains its similarities to the Synoptic accounts of the feeding miracle(s) and the walking on the water, and it also accounts for the uniqueness of the Johannine material. While theories of rearrangement offer some geographical and chronological solutions, reversing chapters 5 and 6 creates new problems which are just as bad, if not worse. Thus, rearrangement theories are not compelling, according to Brown. There is no manuscript evidence for them, and the bread-water sequence of chapters 6 and 7 'seems to be a deliberate reference to Old Testament passages with the same sequence' (p. 236).

The Fourth Evangelist's correct selection of details between the two feeding accounts in Mark is not a result of his astute choosing of Marcan material. Rather, it reflects drawing upon 'an independent tradition which had the same general sequence as precanonical Mark' (p. 239). The final redactor may have added Marcan details and wording, but 'it is just as possible that such details were part of the Johannine tradition from its earliest traceable stage' (p. 244). Likewise, regarding the sea crossing, 'John's brevity and lack of emphasis on the miraculous are almost impossible to explain in terms of a deliberate alteration of the Marcan narrative' (p. 254). Thus, John's account of the walking on the water reflects a relatively undeveloped form of the story and should be considered more primitive than Mark's account. The theological function of the scene prepares the way for the Bread of Life discourse. As the crossing of the Red Sea led to God's provision of manna in the wilderness, so the crossing of the Sea of Galilee prepares the way for the homiletical portrayal of Jesus as the Bread of Life.

While there is little agreement between scholars as to the divisions of the discourse, Brown agrees with the general aproach of P. Borgen, that the discourse reflects a midrashic development of an Old Testament theme. Brown disagrees with Borgen, however, in that he believes 6:35–58 reflects not a single discourse but two parallel ones. Similarities between the progression of themes between 6:35–50 and 6:51–58, and differences in their vocabulary, support the view that they are parallel discourses. Brown also feels that the theological orientation of 6:35–50 is primarily sapiential and secondarily sacramental. In other words, the true 'bread', or nourishment of humanity, is being taught by God, and Jesus as the Revealer has become the source of this nourishment. Eucharistic themes carry over between the former sapiential rendition of the feeding in 6:35–50 and the more fully developed eucharistic interpretation of the discourse in 6:51–58.

Borrowing some ideas from Borgen and Guilding, Brown proposes the possibility that 'behind John 6:35–50 we have a homily preached by Jesus on a text selected from a *seder* read in the Capernaum synagogue at Passover time' (p. 280). To this section 6:51–58 has been added, and Brown proposes that 'the backbone of vss. 51–58 is made up of material from the Johannine narrative of the institution of the Eucharist which originally was located in the Last Supper scene and that this material has been recast into a duplicate of the Bread of Life Discourse' (p. 287). Therefore, 6:59–71 originally followed 6:35–50, and the flesh/spirit dualism of 6:36 referred to the sapiential Moses/Jesus contrast, not to the eucharist. The turning away of disciples (vs. 66) reflects the rejection of Wisdom personified versus offence at either the coarse description of the eucharist or the anti-docetic reference to flesh and blood. The confession of Peter (6:67–71) is parallel to the Synoptic scene at Caesarea Philippi (Mk. 8:27–33, etc.). It is closest to Matthew's account (Matt. 16:16–19) but is probably earlier.

D. *Rudolf Schnackenburg, 1965, 1971 and 1975*

Having been composed roughly over the same period of time as Brown's two-volume commentary and sharing some similarities of perspective, it is interesting to note the somewhat parallel, yet distinct, development of Schnackenburg's appraisal of John's christology and composition history. For Schnackenburg, John's christology is bound up with the 'main interest' (p. 153–172) of the Gospel, which is articulated in the evangelist's 'concluding statement' found in John 20:31. Therefore:

> The Johannine Christology is essentially ordained to soteriology. Everything that the Johannine Jesus says and does, all that he reveals and all that he accomplishes as "signs",

takes place in view of man's attaining salvation, in view of his gaining divine life. And since this salvation is inextricably linked with himself, since he reveals himself in word and deed, all his work is interpreted "Christologically" by the evangelist. Thus the concluding statement really provides us with the key to understanding the presentation according to the mind of the evangelist. (p. 155)

While Schnackenburg does not deal explicitly with the problem of John's christological unity and disunity, he nevertheless comments upon the 'tensions' within John's content and attributes them to the style of the evangelist's thinking. Thus, as opposed to agreeing with Boismard, that John's differing eschatological viewpoints suggest two different 'strata' in the Gospel (p. 70f.), Schnackenburg believes that these tensions within John's eschatology 'grow out of the Johannine Christology, which is as fully aware of the contrast between the Son and the Father, and of the Son's obedience, as of his perfect inner unity with the Father' (p. 71). Similar tensions may also be detected in the evangelist's treatment of such relationships as faith and signs (p. 517), predestination and personal responsibility (Vol. 2, pp. 259–274) and the exaltation and glorification of Jesus (Vol. 2, pp. 398–410). The presentation of these and other themes in dynamic tension represents 'a literary work which matured in a long process of meditation and preaching, embodying many interests and traditions' (p. 153). Therefore, John's christological unity and disunity may be attributed to the reflective thinking of the evangelist, having matured within different settings over a long period of time.

The means by which such views are accommodated within a composition theory involves Schnackenburg's following assumptions: a) The Gospel is 'essentially the work of the evangelist, who relied, however, on diverse traditions, and allowed his gospel to grow and mature slowly, but did not finish it completely' (p. 72).

b) He may have had some knowledge of the Synoptic traditions, although direct use of them cannot be demonstrated. Also, the 'use of a written "*sēmeia*-source" may be maintained with some probability' (p. 72).

c) Oral traditions and logia may also have been incorporated by the evangelist, as well as liturgical or kerygmatic material (1:1–18; 6:31–58), but he was 'unable to give his work final form' (p. 73).

d) Therefore, the redactors added ch. 21, rearranged chs. 5 and 6, moved 7:15–17 (from just after 5:47) to its present place, added the evangelist's later material (3:31–36, 13–21; chs. 15–17; and perhaps 12:44–50), and otherwise 'confined themselves to brief glosses and additions (4:2 or 4:1f.; 4:44; 6:22f.; 7:39b; 11:2; perhaps 12:16)' (p. 73). Although his opinion has shifted a bit by the time the third volume of his commentary was written,[5] Schnackenburg's original hypothesis

---

5 While the commentaries of Brown and Schnackenburg share several commonalities, an interesting parallel has transpired regarding a common (though independent) changing of their minds about the authorship of John. While Schnackenburg had in his first volume outlined his understanding of the evangelist as the spokesman and transmitter of the

was that the evangelist was 'both the spokesman who transmitted the tradition and the preaching of the Apostle John, and a theologian in his own right and teacher of readers of whom he addressed' (p. 102).

John's uniformity of style and language is impressive, and the movement of thought combines a steady linear progression with a concentric mode of thinking, 'which progresses in new circles: a meditative way of thought which uses few arguments but goes deeper and deeper into the subject to gain better and higher understanding of it' (p. 117). The spiritual setting and origin of the Fourth Gospel combine the worlds of Judaism and Hellenism, and the interpretation of the Old Testament is remarkably christological. Gnostic affinities may be explained by the hypothesis that the Johannine tradition began in Palestine, was subjected to Syrian (gnostic) influences, and it ultimately reached Asia Minor (Ephesus) where it was fixed and edited (p. 152).

In Schnackenburg's treatment of John 6 he reverses the order of chs. 5 and 6, as he feels that internal tensions cannot be explained in any better way. As a literary unit, however, John 6 is self-contained. It serves as 'the climax and turning point' of Jesus' Galilean ministry (Vol. 2, p. 10), as the systematic development of Jesus as the Bread and Life calls for a decisive response to God's salvation in Jesus. According to Schnackenburg:

> The evangelist deliberately used the traditional account to portray Jesus' revelation of himself as the bread of life come down from heaven. He regarded the feeding as a "sign" to be matched by the revelatory discourse on the following day, to be given its deepest meaning by the words of Jesus himself. He also used the reactions of the crowd to prepare his readers for the theme of faith and unbelief. This is also introduced in the "midrash" (36–47) and becomes central in the subsequent crisis of faith among the disciples (6:60–71). (p. 24)

While some of the language of the feeding narrative is remarkably similar to that of Mark, this does not imply dependence, nor does it explain the uniqueness of the Johannine account. The lake scene provides even further evidence suggesting John used early sources which were parallel to, but independent from, those of the Synoptics. The form of the discourse is that of a Jewish, midrashic sermon. Based on Ps. 78:24 and other Old Testament themes, 6:31 forms the scriptural starting point of the sermon. From thence is developed the revelatory discourse on Jesus as the Bread of Life, which forms the climax of ch. 6. The unity of vss. 51c–58 with

---

preaching of the Apostle John (p. 102), by his third volume he has extended this opinion, distancing the Johannine tradition even further from the Apostle John (Vol. III, pp. 375–388). Brown has taken note of this (although he seems to have exaggerated the transition, as Schnackenburg appears to be asserting his *continuity* with his 1970 opinion, cf. Vol. III, p. 385), and Brown has tied it to his own inclination to see the connecting of John the Apostle and the Beloved Disciple as considerably later. Says Brown, 'Parenthetically, I am inclined to change my mind (as R. Schnackenburg has also done) from the position that I took in the first volume of my AB commentary identifying the Beloved Disciple as one of the Twelve, viz., John son of Zebedee' (*Community*, p. 33).

the rest of the chapter is a difficult issue, with problems inherent to every solution. While many scholars are of the opinion that the section is a eucharistic one which was added by a later editor, Schnackenburg maintains that it is easier to account for if the whole section is considered the work of one author. He believes that while there is eucharistic language in the section, it is not pointing to the sacramental necessity of the eucharist. Rather, it is pointing to the sacramental nature of the incarnation, wherein all worship, fellowship and rituals have their origin.

E. *Barnabas Lindars, 1972*

Like Schnackenburg, Lindars recognizes the importance of interpreting the Fourth Gospel in the light of its central message: 'The Gospel according to John is a book with a message. The author wants to bring the reader to a point of decision.' (p. 24) As described in 20:30f. and 3:16, the crucial factor of this decision is one's believing attitude toward Jesus Christ. It is in this sense that light is separated from darkness and life is separated from death. However, Lindars is also aware of some of John's theological inconsistencies, and he attempts to offer at least the foundation for an explanation:

> There can be no doubt that John himself was absolutely convinced that his presentation of Jesus — his Christology — is true. Whether we can agree with him depends largely on our own religious presuppositions. There is a magisterial quality about John's writing which appears to admit of no contradiction; but we should not be completely tricked by this into supposing that his thought is completely homogeneous and systematized. To some extent he is still groping. ... Very often the statements are so ambivalent that it is not clear whether John means by the Father-Son relationship the spiritual relation of any devout person with his God, or the metaphysical relation which applies solely to Christ as the Man from Heaven. ... There are moments when he appears to contradict himself flatly — e.g. 10.30: "I and the Father are one" and 14.28: "the Father is greater than I".
>
> ... The inconsistencies suggest that his idea of the meaning of Jesus stands midway between the original experiences of the disciples and the beginnings of a formal system of thought, containing both a measure of truth and a measure of distortion. The fact remains that it is still possible to claim, as has been done many times through the centuries, that no one has grasped the meaning of Jesus better than John. (p. 55f.)

Therefore, John is not to be considered an historical record of an 'eye-witness' (p. 54f.), but a reflective meditation upon the significance of the words and works of Jesus.[6] These thoughts have been developed homiletically, and they often reflect a common sequence: a sign, followed by a transitional dialogue, discourse and a closing dialogue (pp. 51–54). One of the acute issues addressed by the evangelist

---

6 Lindars develops this insight even further in his 'The Fourth Gospel: an Act of Contemplation', in *Studies in the Fourth Gospel*, ed. F.L. Cross, London, 1961, pp. 23–35. See also his thoughtful essay, 'The Theology of the Fourth Gospel', in his *Behind the Fourth Gospel*, London, 1971, pp. 61–79.

was the threat of docetism (pp. 61–63), and this concern is illuminated by Lindars' theory of composition.

Lindars believes that the Gospel was based on two kinds of material. One was closely parallel to the sources of the stories found in the Synoptic Gospels, and the other involved 'Synoptic-type sayings of Jesus', which have been highlighted by the Johannine double *amēn* (p. 47f.). Various rearrangements may have been made by the evangelist's editing of his own work, but overall, Lindars advocates a minimalist hypothesis of diachronic composition, and this is the strength of his approach. Lindars infers the Gospel was written in what may be considered roughly two editions, as it appears that such passages as 1:1–18; ch. 6; 11:1–46; 12:9–11; chs. 15–17; and 21:1–23 were added to one corpus of material at a later time (p. 50f.). Their style and content certainly appear to be Johannine, and this makes theories of multiple authorship superfluous. On the other hand, one can detect several new themes emerging in the 'supplementary material' (such as emphases upon the 'flesh' of Jesus),[7] and thus the intention of the evangelist varied over the course of composing earlier and later Gospel material.

In his treatment of John 6, several of Lindars' literary-critical opinions may be identified. Thus, he says:

> The whole chapter has such a clear internal unity and self-consistency, it is so well balanced and articulated, that it ranks as one of the finest products of John's pen. But at the same time it bears so little relation to the progress of the Gospel as a whole that it seems best to take it as an independent composition, inserted by John into the second edition of his work. (p. 234)

---

7 It is unclear whether or not Lindars' adding discussions of John 6 and 13–20 to his essays in *Behind the Fourth Gospel* (p. 9) reflects a broadening of his perspective, or whether it mainly suggests an inclusion of specific examples which illustrate the implications of his views. What *is* delightfully clear about Lindars' treatment of Johannine critical issues, however, is that he has begun with evidence that is most certain and has moved from thence to make interpretive observations. This is most clearly observed between his first and last chapters of the above collection of essays. In 'The Riddle of the Fourth Gospel' (pp. 11–26), Lindars analyzes the main aporias (geographical, temporal, thematic, pp. 14–16) and form-critical problems (editorial connections, Synoptic-type narrative, sustained discourses, and the passion/resurrection narrative, p. 16f.) without trying to offer an interpretively integrated solution too soon. After considering the evidence for sources underlying John (pp. 27–42), Lindars explains his theory as to how the Gospel may have been composed (pp. 43–60).

While such a theory is not devoid of theological interpretation — and indeed, no theory can be — one does not find the theological implications developed until the last chapter, 'The Theology of the Fourth Gospel' (pp. 61–79). This is the appropriate sequence. The interpretive significance for the present study is that John's literary aporias can be treated as genuinely problematic, and yet accommodated within an adequate and relatively simple theory of composition (in this case, two editions of John by the same author) without hypothesizing an unduly complex, diachronic history of composition. This minimally-speculative approach cannot but enhance the validity of one's interpretation.

This explains the break between chs. 5 and 7, as well as the continuity of theme inherent to its current order. According to Lindars, ch. 6 is a 'full-scale example, and the only one which John has given us, of the important assertion that Moses "wrote of" Jesus (5:46). It is a chapter which is concerned with the witness of scripture to Christ to a degree far greater than is generally recognized' (p. 208f.). It also serves as a lucid illustration of the claim attributed to Jesus (5:39), that it is to him the scriptures point.

In the feeding narrative, John makes use of an independent collection of traditional material which Mark has also used as a source. Likewise, John's account of the lake scene reflects the using of a source at an even more primitive stage in the history of transmission than the form(s) used by Matthew and Mark, and the origin of the discourse can be inferred by its literary form. Upon the foundation of the feeding, John 6:26–58 develops a homiletical discourse as a Christian equivalent to a Jewish midrash which has been adopted for the purposes of the written Gospel. Building on Borgen's contribution, it contains three expositions of the proemical text: 'He gave them bread from heaven.' Verses 41–51 develop the theme 'bread from heaven to eat', which is essentially a sapiential theme, and 6:52–58 is an exposition of 'to eat' (p. 253). Therefore, '... the eucharistic interpretation is latent beneath the sapiential section (35–50), and the sapiential continues without any diminution in the eucharistic section (51–8)' (p. 251). Thus, 6:52–58 is not to be regarded as a later addition. It is the conclusion of the discourse which explains what it means to partake of the living Bread, Jesus, in eucharistic terms.

The departure of disciples (vss. 60ff.) reflects the desire for unity articulated in the Gospel and especially in 1 John. It is likely that these represent Christians who were lapsing into docetism. Their reaction is not a mere objection to the 'fleshly' language of 6:52ff. Rather, 'the real heresy of the Docetists is the denial of the Incarnation of Jesus, and so also of the reality of his death, and thus cuts at the heart of the entire discourse' (p. 271). The flesh/spirit dualism of 6:63 refers to one's inability/ability to understand Jesus' spiritual words, and Peter's confession is based on the same tradition as that used by the Synoptics, although it is less developed. Even so, Peter concludes the chapter with the crowning touch, combining revelational and sapiential themes together: 'You alone have the words of eternal life.' (p. 275) Thus, John 6 should be considered as a single, well-developed unit, which presents Jesus as the true 'Bread of Life'.

Findings

Despite the fact that the authors of five recent and major commentaries disagree about the means by which John was composed and the best interpretation of ch. 6, all five scholars have a significant amount of interest in the Gospel's christological unity and disunity, and each theory of composition accommodates these tensions in its own way. This observation involves *no* attempt to assess whether or not theories of composition have been designed in accordance with the scholar's understanding of John's christological unity and disunity, or whether the reverse is true. It does, however, suggest the relationship is a significant one, and that findings related to John's composition will affect one's understanding of its christological unity and disunity — *and* vice versa. This means that John's christological unity and disunity, while being treated directly as an independent issue, must be considered in the light of theories pertaining to the means by which the Fourth Gospel has come into being. This relationship may be explored further by considering recent approaches to the unity and disunity of John 6.

Chapter 3

A Survey of Three Approaches
to the Unity and Disunity of John 6

Given that a relationship may be inferred between recent scholars' treatments of John's christological unity and disunity and their approaches to its composition, a survey of three differing treatments of John 6 will serve to bring the central questions and assumptions of this study into sharpest focus. As mentioned in the introduction, John 6 has recently been considered the showcase for diachronic theories. It contains material attributed to four out of the five major literary contributors, as analyzed by Bultmann, and thus should provide a testing-ground to demonstrate the veracity of diachronic composition theories — with conclusions being applicable to the rest of the Gospel as well.[1]

The implications for John's christological unity and disunity are: a) If John 6 does indeed demonstrate itself to contain material from various literary sources, each of which assumes a distinctive christological posture, then it may reasonably be assumed that John's christological unity and disunity is the result (at least in part) of a 'literary dialogue' between authors, redactors and their sources. b) If, however, John 6 is found to be a literary unity, having (basically) only one author, then the christological tensions of John 6 and beyond must be regarded as *internal* to the thinking and writing of the evangelist. c) Whatever conclusion one comes to, *some* hypothesis must be offered in order to explain the origin of the dialectical tensions within John 6 and the rest of the Gospel, as these comprise the most distinguishing characteristic of the christology of the Fourth Gospel. These findings will then be explored and tested in Part II.

---

1 R. Kysar has stated this assumption clearly in his 1973 article ('The Source Analysis of the Fourth Gospel — A Growing Consensus?', *NovT* 15, pp. 134–152):

> Chapter six has been selected for a number of reasons, but primarily because it offers a single chapter in which both narrative and discourse material appear. Moreover, the chapter offers Johannine material which in some cases has obvious synoptic contacts and in other cases drastically non-synoptic pericopes. ... It is the assumption that such a sampling of the degree of consensus among the theories might be suggestive of the sort of consensus to be found should the theories as applied to the entire gospel be compared as they have been here in the case of chapter six. (p. 135f.)

A. *Robert Kysar*

Feeling that D.M. Smith did not go far enough in his 1963/4 *NTS* article (Vol. 10, 'The Sources of the Gospel of John: An Assessment of the Present State of the Problem', pp. 336–351) when he suggested three areas of consensus were emerging regarding source criticism in John, Robert Kysar seeks to demonstrate a fourth aspect of the 'growing consensus' among source-critical scholars. The significance of Kysar's analysis is that if a clear consensus or basic agreement is emerging between scholars who claim to have identified multiple literary sources underlying John 6, then even their preliminary agreements should provide the solid scaffolding for an eventual demonstration of John's diachronic composition — an interest having far-reaching implications for Johannine interpretation. In Kysar's words:

> It is the proposal of this paper that we attempt to go further in seeking ... a consensus, at least of a preliminary kind, among the critics with regard to the passages they isolate. Such an effort appears necessary, if the critical study of John is to proceed. (p. 135)

As a means of illustrating his thesis, Kysar samples the work of nine scholars who employ source-critical means of analysis, different though they be from each other.[2] After plotting these scholars' assignments of words and sections in John 6:1–53 with reference to their respective sources (pp. 140–150), Kysar emerges with the following conclusions (pp. 150–151): 'First, there is obviously an area of general agreement among the theories . . .' To summarize, they are:

> 1. Verses 1–15, 16–21, and 22–25 'are generally agreed to be evidence for the use of a signs or miracle source'.
> 2. Verses 27a, 35b, 37b, 44a,b, 45b, 47b–48 'are commonly claimed to be from some sort of Vorlage'.
> 3. Verses 1, 24, 52–59 (except vs. 53), 60–65, and 66–71 are generally agreed to be 'passages where the evangelist has inserted his own material'.
> 4. 'Generally, it is obvious that there is much greater agreement on the narrative portion of the chapter than the discourse passages, and it would appear that our critics agree that the method of the evangelist was to insert short sayings from a source (e.g., vs. 27, 35b, 37b, 44, 48, 46b–48, and 53) into larger and more complex discourses of his own composition.'

A second observation of Kysar's is that considerable agreement has been emerging on two further points: 'First, that a source(s) has been utilized at ... 28b–

---

2 These scholars include R. Bultmann (*Das Evangelium des Johannes*, Göttingen, 1941 [1962; E.t. 1971]; and D.M. Smith (*The Composition and Order of the Fourth Gospel*, New Haven, 1965); H. Becker (*Die Reden des Johannesevangeliums und der Stil der gnostischen Offenbarungsreden*, Göttingen, 1956); R. Fortna (*The Gospel of Signs*, Cambridge, 1970); W. Wilkens (*Die Entstehungsgeschichte des vierten Evangeliums*, Zollikon, 1958); W. Hartke (*Vier urchristliche Parteien und ihre Vereinigung zur apostolischen Kirche*, Berlin, 1961); E.C. Broome, Jr. ('The Sources of the Fourth Gospel', *JBL* 63, 1944, pp. 107–121); O. Merlier (*Le quatrième Évangile: La question Johannique*, Paris, 1961); S. Schulz (*Komposition und Herkunft der johanneischen Reden*, Stuttgart, 1960); and M.-E. Boismard ('L'évolution du thème eschatologique dans les traditions johanniques', *RB* 68, 1961, pp. 507–524).

31, 46, [45?], and 52. Second, that v. 6 was not part of the original signs source seems to have notable support. (p. 151) Kysar then concludes his study with a restatement of his thesis and a plea for source analysis to move forward despite 'the circle which stands opposed to the entire enterprise' (p. 152, n. 1). Says Kysar:

> The evidence obtained from this survey is sufficient to suggest that a substantial agreement might indeed exist among the critics with regard to the entire gospel and that such a consensus needs to be examined and utilized in further johannine studies. It is imperative that the critical study of this gospel attempt to employ the work of others upon which there can be some concurrence, lest our work become hopelessly mired down in repetitive research. (p. 152)

Despite Kysar's contribution, however, a number of scholars have yet to be convinced (cf. Barrett, *John*, p. 15), and thus an examination of Kysar's conclusions may be helpful. First, though, a major objection should be stated as to the general premise under which Kysar has operated. A central weakness of Kysar's study is that he has failed to acknowledge *the role of Bultmann's contribution* regarding the recent employment of source-critical approaches to John. While Bultmann's work simply appears alongside those of the others, it is particularly significant that of the eight others, all contributions have been published after (and in some ways as responses to) Bultmann's commentary, published in 1941. Thus, the latter eight scholars were all (to varying degrees) following the lead of, or reacting against, Bultmann. This is especially the case for J. Becker, for whom Bultmann was his *Doktorvater*, and for R. Fortna, who sought to re-design Bultmann's *sēmeia* source into what he called a 'Signs Gospel'. Also, it is 'instructive' (to use Kysar's term) to note that the three trends mentioned in D.M. Smith's article were listed specifically as trends which reflected the influence of Bultmann's contribution, assessing whether or not scholars have agreed with his findings (pp. 349–351). Rather than simply looking for a correlation between eight or nine scholars' detections of potential sources underlying John 6, the more telling questions are: 'How have scholars responded to Bultmann's detection of sources?'; 'What explanations might there be for their agreement?'; and, 'What explanations might there be for their disagreement?'.

Regarding the first question, if Kysar's sample is reviewed in search of *how often the lead of Bultmann is followed*, one cannot really say that there is much of a consensus emerging at all — even among the *convinced*. Providing Kysar's data are correct, a reappraisal of his findings shows the following:[3]

---

3 Kysar's failure to acknowledge the degree of scholars' agreement with Bultmann is reflected in his rubrical means of displaying his findings. Even though there are nine scholars surveyed, there are only *five* lines on which to display such findings, and the first of these is occupied by Bultmann's analysis. The second line is occupied by Fortna's Signs Gospel and Becker's *Offenbarungsreden*, the third by Wilkens' *Grundevangelium* and expansionary *Reden* source, the fourth by Hartke's signs and ur-gospel sources, and the fifth is taken by 'a conglomerate representation of the theories of Broome, Merlier, Schulz, and Boismard' (p.

a) For 6:1–15 only in verses 3, 8, and 9 is there total agreement with Bultmann about the use of an earlier source by a later writer.

b) For 6:16–21 there is more agreement. Scholars agree with Bultmann totally in all of verses 16, 19, 20, and 21.

c) Agreement for 6:22–25 is minimal, at best. The only place in which all four scholars mentioned agree with Bultmann is vs. 25a.

d) In the rest of the chapter, agreement is even less. From 6:26–71, Bultmann identifies at least eight passages attributable to his *Offenbarungsreden*. They are 27a–b, 33, 35b–d, 37c–d, 44a–b, 45c, 47b, and 48.

Unfortunately, of the seven other scholars listed, the only works comparable with Bultmann's are those of Becker and Hartke. Becker agrees with Bultmann 75% of the time, and Hartke agrees with him *none* of the time. The percentages of agreement between the source assignments of the other five and those of Bultmann are roughly as follows: Schulz 18%, Merlier 23%, Broome 25%, Wilkens 32%, and Boismard 35%. Thus, of seven source-critical scholars surveyed, the only one to agree with Bultmann's findings more than 35% of the time in 6:26ff. is H. Becker, Bultmann's doctoral student, whose work was later introduced and published by Bultmann, himself.

Thus, in 6:1–25, 50% or more of the scholars listed disagree with Bultmann in at least twelve of the verses (1, 2, 4, 6, 7, 12, 14, 15, 22, 23, 24, 25), and agreement is far less for 6:26–53. The only two verses in which anything like a consensus may be acknowledged in vss. 26–53 are 35b–c, where 6 of the 7 other scholars mentioned agree with Bultmann that an earlier source was used, and vs. 52, where 6 of the 7 other scholars agreed with Bultmann that no source was used. If a consensus is emerging, it is indeed limited to a very few verses. Therefore, in response to our first question, rather than saying that a consensus is emerging regarding source-critical approaches to John, it would be more accurate to say that Bultmann's contribution has been responsible for a growing interest in, and a growing use of, source-critical methodologies by scholars investigating the underlying traditions of John. There is some consensus in at least parts of approximately 16 verses of John 6:1–53, but there is a wide discrepancy for most of the remaining verses.

Regarding the second and third questions above, explanations for these scholars' agreement and disagreement may be considered as follows: *agreement* may be attributed to the opinion that the source and redaction criticism, so successful for Synoptic studies, may also be applicable for John. If a narrative-source such as Mark, and a sayings-source such as Q, may be assumed to underlie John, then attempts to isolate John's narratives and discourses from the evangelist's interpretive material may be attempted with good reason. Thus, if scholars were

---

139). The statistical vulnerability of his graphic representation is that even when *all five* lines are filled, it may only mean that four out of the other seven agree with Bultmann. It is also true that some sources (such as Fortna's narrative source and Becker's sayings source) appear to be comprised of mutually exclusive literary forms of material. Even so, the other four lines vary greatly when compared and contrasted to Bultmann's analysis. For the specifics, see Glasgow thesis, P.N. Anderson (1988), p. 420f. n. 3.

going to identify Synoptic-like narrative material in John they would obviously turn to 6:1–15 and 16–21, where these two miracles alone are to be found also in the Synoptics. And, if scholars were to look for pithy sayings in John 6 they might begin with the Son of Man sayings (vss. 27, 53, 62), the *egō eimi* sayings (vss. 35, 48, 51), or the *amēn amēn* sayings (vss. 26, 32, 47, 53), which is exactly what scholars have done.

On the other hand, *disagreement* must be due to scholars' basic lack of consensus regarding the best criteria for identifying John's underlying sources. Bultmann, for instance, supposes that most of the 'historicizing' detail is the added work of the evangelist. Therefore, details of places and times, etc., were supposedly not part of the original source (6:1–4, 6, etc.). Fortna, on the other hand, feels that the proper names and the use of *oun, hina*, etc., reflect later additions; so in 6:5, 7, 11, 12, 14, etc., he disagrees with Bultmann. Otherwise, his judgments would be almost identical. It is also obvious, even by the names given to various sayings sources, that scholars have looked for different 'markers' of source material. For example, it is not surprising to find a discrepancy between Broome's collection of *egō eimi* sayings and *amēn amēn* sayings, and Schulz's 'Son of Man' tradition. Thus, disagreement in the detection of source material has to do primarily with the lack of agreement between source-critical scholars regarding meaningful criteria for the detection of sources, and a central problem is the dearth of contemporary parallels for comparison.

In conclusion, Kysar's sample shows some agreement between source-critical scholars, but it is nowhere near an 'emerging consensus'. Even for the scholar wishing to be convinced, Kysar's study does little more than illustrate the fact that one recent approach to investigating the underlying traditional material in John has been to use source-critical methodologies. Agreement has been highest where the material is most compact and appears to be earliest (6:3, 5, 8–11, 16–21, 27, 35, 45–48, 53, etc.), but scholars are by no means agreed even on the means by which sources should be identified. This trend is definitely in response to Bultmann's contribution; and therefore, any serious source-critical work must wrestle with his judgments.

B. *Peder Borgen*

In his 1965 monograph (*Bread*), Peder Borgen has made the most significant contribution to the study of John 6 in recent years, and its implications for the present study are central. Using a form-critical analysis and comparisons between John 6:31–58 and Philonic and Palestinian midrashic developments of the manna tradition, Borgen argues that the Bread of Life discourse in John 6 is a literary unity. By means of demonstrating a 'common homiletical pattern', Borgen's targeted contribution within Philonic and Johannine research is to challenge the diachronic approaches of Bousset and Bultmann, respectively. In other words, rather than to take the approach of Schweizer and Ruckstuhl, arguing the linguistic and stylistic uniformity of John, and rather than using Noack's 'oral tradition' approach, Borgen's goal is to compare John's treatment of the manna theme with its parallels in contemporary literature in order to assess the unity of John 6:31–58 (pp. 16). The interpretive significance of such a study is that if this section is a literary unity, then one must re-evaluate the hypothesis of the evangelist's use of an *Offenbarungsreden* source and subsequent disordering and reordering of the text. One must also interpret the so-called 'eucharistic interpolation' (vss. 51c–58) as intrinsic to the manna homily. The successful arguing of such a thesis would thus mean that the christological tensions inherent to John 6:31–58 must be regarded as *internal* to the thinking and writing of the evangelist and dealt with accordingly.

The broad outline of Borgen's study is as follows: a) both Philo (*Mut.* 258–260; *Leg. all. III* 162, 168; and *Congr.* 170, 173–174) and John (6:31–58) employ fragments from the haggadic manna tradition, along with other Old Testament motifs, as an 'exegetical paraphrase' of an Old Testament text (pp. 7–27). b) A 'common homiletic pattern' may be identified within Philo's (*Leg. all. III* 162–168; *Mut.* 253–263) and John's (6:31–58) use of the manna tradition, but their uses are more creative and less 'wooden' than later Palestinian developments of the manna motif (pp. 28–58). c) This common homiletical pattern is followed more closely in John (pp. 59–98), but in both Philo and in John, it

> ... consists of the following points: (1) The Old Testament quotation. (2) The interpretation. (3) The objection to the interpretation. (4) Point (2), the interpretation, freely repeated and questioned. (5) The answer which can conclude with a reference to point (2), the interpretation (p. 85).

d) In Philo's interpretation of the manna tradition (*Mut.* 253–263) he addresses the socio-religious needs of his Alexandrian audience, by using 'manna' as a symbol for Jewish wisdom from the Torah, thus making a distinction between the 'heavenly philosophy of the synagogue' and the pagan encyclical educational system of the dominant culture (pp. 99–121). e) In the homily of *Leg. all. III* 162–168 an interesting conflation may be inferred: Philo assimilates Platonic thought patterns regarding views of the universe, heaven and earth, while retaining a Jewish concept of a personal God, to be trusted by humanity (pp. 122–146).

f) The homily of John also betrays the adaptation of Old Testament themes to be relevant within a Platonic culture in response to the acute needs of the author's community of faith. Thus: 'In John the bread from heaven has been given the life-giving functions of Torah and wisdom. The presence of the bread is pictured with features from the theophany at Sinai and the invitation to eat and drink extended by wisdom.' (p. 157) Another association is of bread with the 'commissioned agent', whereby according to halakhic understandings of early Merkabah mysticism, the sender sends forth his agent and through the agent accomplishes his transactions by means of a representative who is *like the sender in all ways*. 'Thus, not only his authority and function are derived from the sender, but also his qualities.' (p. 162) The situation faced by the evangelist is one in which docetism is becoming a problem, and in vss. 51–58 the Docetists are proved to be 'externalists', thus using their own arguments against them (pp. 183–192). Therefore, John 6:31–58 is a homiletical development of the manna tradition found in Exodus 16:4, and it represents a literary unity, parallel to contemporary midrashic developments of the manna tradition.

Responses to Borgen's monograph have generally been quite positive. Lindars, for instance, correctly recognizes a central implication of this contribution: 'If John is using a Jewish method of exegesis, it affects our estimate not only of the background, but the destination of his work.'[4] Not surprisingly, Martyn disagrees with Borgen and argues that the inferred 'Christian Docetist' might instead be leaders of the Synagogue who, '... lodge a demand based on orthodox typology'.[5] One of the most sustained disagreements with Borgen comes from G. Richter (1969), who, while agreeing that John 6:31–58 reflects a midrashic exposition of an Old Testament text, believes that vss. 51b–58 betray a different authorship. According to Richter, vss. 31–51a hold closer to the 'homiletical pattern' described by Borgen, while the contrast between the incarnational thrust of these verses and the eucharistic emphasis of vss. 51b–58 suggests a difference in *thematische Identität*. Applying the motif of 'belief in Jesus' (20:31) as the central interest of the evangelist, Richter argues that because the thrust of vss. 51b–58 is eucharistic, Borgen has actually demonstrated the opposite of his thesis, and that vss. 31–51a and 51b–58 are separate homiletic units. In a response to Richter, Borgen defends his work successfully against this and several other criticisms. He

---

4   See Lindars' review in *JTS* 18, 1967, pp. 192–194; and see also Lindars' profitable
    incorporation of Borgen's midrashic outline in his commentary (pp. 253–270). Lindars'
    midrashic outline is especially close to the midrashic style of Exodus Mekilta (Tractate
    Vayassa, chs. III and IV), where each phrase is interpreted individually and expanded upon;
    although Ex. 16:4 is there being developed as the primary text, rather than a secondary one
    (cf. below, notes 9–11 for distinction).

5   Martyn's review is also positive about Borgen's contribution (*JBL* 86, 1967, pp. 244f.; cf.
    also, his *History and Theology*, p. 127, n. 188), but he is more critical of Borgen's analysis
    of the socio-religious situation underlying John. While Martyn agrees that there is much
    value in interpreting Philo's content in light of his addressing the needs of Alexandrian Jews
    faced with the pursuit of pagan careers, he questions how far the situation reflected in 1 John
    may enlighten the situation faced by the Fourth Evangelist, and in particular, to what extent
    a docetising threat may be inferred. On this point, however, one may object that Martyn's
    own interpretive interests and understandings must be taken into consideration. While
    Martyn is probably correct in his analysis of Jewish-Christian tensions in the late first century
    and in his assumption that these are reflected in various places in John to have been acute
    concerns of the evangelist, these tensions *did not only begin in the 80's –90's* (cf. Ac. 6:9ff.;
    8:1ff.; 17:1ff.; and esp. chs. 19–21), and they are not necessarily the only — nor the most
    acute — tensions faced by the evangelist at the time that John 6 was written (cf. below,
    Chapter 10). Therefore, it is entirely possible that at least two (possibly three or four) debates
    are depicted within John 6:25–66, including the reflection upon external debates with Jewish
    leaders *and* a more urgent appeal to those facing the threat of docetising tendencies.

also re-emphasizes a central implication of his study regarding a contrast between the exegesis of Philo and John and later rabbinic midrashim:[6]

> Our analysis suggests that one significant aspect of this development is that a fresh, creative paraphrase of words from the Old Testament text together with fragments from the tradition has changed into a text being followed by [a] compilation of fixed units from the tradition. In many cases, therefore, philological exegesis, harmonization of contradiction, etc. ("pure exegesis") in the earlier stage formed [an] integral part of the creative and contemporizing paraphrase, while they later were preserved mechanically as separate units of tradition.
>
>   In this way Philo and John throw light upon earlier stages of the kind of exposition of which the rabbinic midrashim represent a later stage.

In evaluating the strengths and weaknesses of Borgen's work, it must be said again that his has probably been the most significant contribution to recent studies of John 6, as well as to form-critical analyses of the Fourth Gospel. Therefore, some of its strengths include the following: 1. Borgen has demonstrated convincingly that, based upon a 'common homiletical pattern' between the use of the manna tradition in the writings of Philo, John, and Palestinian midrashim, the diachronic approaches of Bousset and Bultmann to Philo and John must be called into serious question. The implications for Johannine studies are most significant. Based upon contemporary parallels and a thorough analysis of John 6:31–58, the section may be considered a thematic and formal unity, having a coherent thrust and homiletical form. This means that hypothesizing a 'revelation-sayings source' as the probable origin of the Bread of Life discourses, and a redactional interpolation as the best explanation for the so-called 'eucharistic section' in John 6, are unnecessary. The success of this aspect of Borgen's analysis is reflected by the fact that recent scholars have all but abandoned Bultmann's *Offenbarungsreden* source hypothesis, and other explanations have been sought to explain the meaning and origin of vss. 51–58.

2. A second strength of Borgen's work has been to identify the literary form of John 6:31–58, and so to illuminate the context of its original use and purpose. If this section were indeed a homily, preached within the setting of Johannine cultic life, one can detect a transition within Johannine Christianity from the 'bread of God' being Torah and wisdom to the bread ultimately embodied in Jesus (p. 157). The theophanic presentations of Yahweh in the days of Moses have now been eclipsed by the incarnation, which becomes for Johannine Christians the ultimate theophany. The exhortative thrust of the homily calls for the hearers of the sermon

---

6 The debate between Richter and Borgen is one of the more significant ones in recent years, especially as it relates to an understanding of the formal and thematic unity of John 6. In his 1969 essay ('Zur Formgeschichte und literarische Einheit von Joh IV, 31–58', *ZNW* 60, 1969 p. 21–55; also in his *Studien zum Johannesevangelium*, pp. 88–119) Richter has raised several objections with Borgen, which he answers rather effectively in his counter-reply ('*Bread From Heaven*; Aspects of Debates on Expository Method and Form', in his *Logos Was the True Light — and Other Essays on the Gospel of John*, Trondheim, 1983, pp. 32–45; citation, p. 41).

to become 'seers' of the spiritual meaning of the scriptures, the manna, and finally the ministry of Jesus (pp. 177–180). To look for the inward and spiritual meaning of the scriptures is to fulfil the etymological meaning of 'Israel' (being a 'nation of vision'). This applies to members of the Johannine audience as well, who are called to *see* in Jesus' words and works their spiritual significance. The clear emphasis upon ingesting the 'flesh and blood' of Jesus in vss. 53–58 is directed toward correcting exaggerated expressions of such spiritualization, and the evangelist does so by accusing the Docetists of being *externalists* (vs. 63; p. 183). Therefore, as a midrashic homily, the destination and meaning of John 6:31–58 is illuminated, and some of its inconsistencies are explained (p. 184). The evangelist was addressing groups with *different needs* in his audience, and this accounts for some of the changes of emphasis (sapiential/eucharistic) within the section.

3. A third strength of Borgen's contribution has to do with the *religionsgeschichtliche* background of John 6. While Borgen acknowledges that John's world-view is closer to gnosticism than those of Philo and the Palestinian midrashim, to say that Mandean gnosticism is the only — let alone the best — explanation for the origin for John's *logos* christology and ethical dualism no longer holds (p. 164). In fact, John's concept of Jesus as the bread of God has as its closest parallel the concept of *agency* within the Jewish halakhic tradition, later developed more fully within juridical and Merkabah forms of mysticism. This concept of agency also accounts for some of the unitive and disunitive christological content of John. Because Jesus is God's representative agent he can say *nothing* except what he has been commissioned to say, and because he represents the Father completely, he is *to be equated with the Father in all ways*. According to the halakhic rules of agency, 'the sender had to authorize the agent by transferring his own rights and the property concerned to the agent' (p. 160; cf. Jn. 6:39). The underlying assumption is that 'the agent is like the one who sent him' (p. 162), and therefore, the one who has seen the Son has seen the Father (Jn. 14:9) — the result being that one's response to the agent is equated with responding to the sender (p. 163). To believe in Jesus is to trust the Father who sent him, and as the apostolic representative of God, Jesus reveals the Father's saving love with ambassadorial finality.

As well as strengths, Borgen's contribution has several weaknesses. 1. The first has to do with the imprecise meaning of the word, 'midrash'. In recent years scholars' interest in the forms and functions of midrashic literature has grown to the extent that 'midrash-criticism' is nearly becoming an autonomous field of study. Conspicuous within this development, however, is the growing reluctance of scholars to ascribe a precise, exclusive meaning to the term.[7] Thus, it is difficult to see how the identification of John 6:31–58 as a 'midrash' is any more significant

---

7 One of the clearest definitions of 'midrash' is given by G. Porton ('Defining Midrash' in J. Neusner's *The Study of Ancient Judaism I; Mishnah, Midrash, Sidur*, U.S.A., 1981, pp. 55–92):

than regarding the section as an 'exegetical paraphrase'[8] or simply a scriptural allusion.

In brief, I would define *midrash* as a type of literature, oral or written, which stands in direct relationship to a fixed, canonical text, considered to be the authoritative and revealed word of God by the midrashist and his audience, and in which this canonical text is explicitly cited or clearly alluded to. (p. 62)

The origin of midrashic exegesis goes back to the Old Testament, as much of its content is a commentary upon earlier writings and traditions. As an identifiable discipline, however, midrash may be traced to Ezra, who in 444 BCE began to study and exposit the Torah (Ez. 7:10; Neh. 8:2–18; cf. M.P. Miller, IDB, *Supplementary Volume* V, pp. 593–597). Thus, a transition in Judaism may be identified between being a 'people of the land' and becoming a 'people of the book'. This transition may be observed in its classic development from the third–twelfth centuries CE, which is the period over which the Rabbinic midrashim were written. As the discipline evolved, however, various types of content (legal, historical, prophetic, apocalyptic, allegorical, mystical, etc.) and various literary forms (narrative, anthological, *pesher*, homiletic, targumic, etc.) emerged (*Ibid.*, p. 596). This has led to a problem most acutely felt by recent midrashic scholars, having to do with the delimitation of *what is not a midrash*. Thus, Miller concludes:

The more recent tendency to associate midrash with the whole phenomenon of the use of scripture in early Judaism, and thus with groups, traditions, and literature which differ markedly from the rabbinic, has raised the problem of what is properly denoted by the term. ... At present, there appears to be no wholly satisfactory way to resolve this problem. ... The term tends to lose its descriptive power when applied to a variety of uses of scripture in early Judaism, especially where the task is to discern the distinctive traditions of biblical interpretation. (p. 596f.)

8 While R. Le Déaut believes that the term may be used meaningfully if limited to 'the two essential marks of midrash (scriptural context — adaptation)' ('Apropos a Definition of Midrash', *Int* 25, 1971, pp. 259–282, cit., p. 282, n. 5), other scholars are not so confident. Porton, for example, (*op. cit.,* p. 77f.) agrees with Miller and believes that even the 'standard division between *midrash halakah* and *midrash hagadah* is meaningless. ... The so-called *halakic midrashim* contain a good deal of *hagadic* material, and the so-called *hagadic midrashim* contain a fair amount of explicit *halakic* details and a large amount of implied *halakah*'. This being the case, it is all the more instructive to take note of Neusner's agreement with Porton on this matter:

Since I find these statements [Porton's] accurate I cannot here use the word *midrash* at all. For we address the genre of writing and thinking known as *midrash* only in the context, namely, that of Rabbinic Judaism. We take up only one question, one aspect of the activity of *midrash*, namely, why people compiled (1) *midrashim* = exegesis of various verses of Scripture into (2) *midrashim* = systematic units of discourse made up mainly of exegeses of various verses of Scripture into (3) *midrashim* = whole books, that is compilations of compositions (discourses) constituted by exegeses of verses of Scripture. Since we are able to use the same word for three things, and since, moreover, that same word is made to serve by others for many more things, I shall generally avoid use of the word *midrash*. (Citation from J. Neusner, *Midrash in Context, Exegesis in Formative Judaism,* Philadelphia, 1983, p. xvii. See also G. Porton, *Understanding Rabbinic Midrash; Text and Commentary,* Hoboken, N.J., 1985; R.T. France and D. Wenham, eds., *Studies in Midrash and Historiography,* Sheffield, 1983; and I. Chernus, *Mysticism in Rabbinic Judaism; Studies in the History of Midrash,* Berlin/New York, 1982.)

2. A more serious objection has to do with the likelihood that Borgen has misidentified the homiletical 'form' of the way the manna tradition is used in Philo, John, Exodus Mekilta and Midrash Rabbah. Borgen's 'homiletical pattern' works well for the midrashim in which Exodus 16:4 is the *primary* text being developed (Exodus Rabbah 25:1–8), but *not* for the rest of the midrashim in which the manna motif is used *nearly always as a secondary text*.[9] This is true for the uses of the manna motif in Philo, Midrash Rabbah, Exodus Mekilka *and* John 6 (see Appendix VII below). Apart from the eight midrashic developments of various meanings of 'Then the Lord said to Moses: Behold I will cause to rain bread from heaven for you.' (Ex. 16:4), the 'common midrashic pattern' identified by Borgen does not work for other treatments of the manna motif. In virtually all the other cases in which the manna motif is used midrashically within ancient Jewish or Christian literature, manna is used as a 'rhetorical trump' to make a dualistic contrast between that which is of earthly origin and that which is of heavenly origin.[10] John 6:31 is

---

9 In other words, Borgen argues the existence of a 'common homiletical pattern' on the basis that the citation and interpretation of the manna motif in John 6:31 is similar to other midrashic developments of a biblical text. The problem is that while the midrashic developments of the manna tradition are quite similar to the homiletical pattern cited by Borgen when Ex. 16:4 is the *primary* text being developed, the literary form is quite different when the manna motif is used as a *secondary* text.

   The evidence for such a distinction is as follows: a) When the manna motif is developed as the primary text of a midrash (Ex. 16:4), a form similar (not always identical) to the one developed by Borgen (p. 85) is used (see Exodus Rabbah 25:1–8 and Exodus Mekilta, Tractate Vayassa III–IV). b) However, Philo *never* interprets the manna motif (Ex. 16:4, or any other manna text) as the 'primary text' of a midrash, nor is the reference to 'spiritual food' in 1 Cor. 10:4 a primary text being developed exegetically. c) In this 'midrashic' literature, though, manna also is used (even more frequently) as a *secondary text*, and having an even more unified rhetorical form (Philo, *Leg. all. III* 162–168, *Fug.* 137–142, *Mut.* 253–263, *Congr.* 158–174, *Mos. I* 196–205, *Mos. II* 258–274; Midrash Rabbah, Genesis XLVIII.10, LI.2, LXVI.3; Exodus V.9, XXIV.3, XXXIII.8, XXXVIII.4, XLI.1; Deuteronomy X.4; and Exodus Mekilta, Tractate Beshallah I.201). d) The form of the use of the manna motif as a *secondary text* may be considered roughly as follows: a point, or exhortation, is made; objections may be raised (assuming the role of this-worldly perspective) to increase the tension; the manna motif is mentioned, usually in connection with God's provision (and God's way), which is obviously superior to any 'earthly' alternative; the theme is further developed, often along with other texts and added motifs; and the original appeal is made again, calling for some sort of response to the *true* way of God. e) It appears that the use of the manna motif in John 6 is more closely parallel to this outline than to the one posed by Borgen.

10 Other than in the case of Ex. 16, one may observe the interpretive significance of the manna tradition growing along with its evolving use, until it eventually becomes employed as a 'rhetorical trump'. As the monograph of B. Malina (*The Palestinian Manna Tradition*, Leiden, 1968) has demonstrated, the development of the manna motif within the Palestinian midrashic tradition (Ex. 16; Nu. 11:6–9; 21:5; Deut. 8:3, 16; Josh. 5:12; Neh. 9:15, 20; Ps. 78:23–25; Ps. 105:40; Cant. 4:5; 1 Cor. 10:3; Rev. 2:17; Jn. 6:31ff.) betrays the transition from the etiological account of the receiving of manna — a food hitherto unknown (Ex. 16),

no exception. It is with other uses of the manna motif as a *rhetorical trump* that John's 'Bread of Life' dialogues and discourses have their closest formal affinity, *rather than* Exodus Rabbah 25:1–8. In other words, John 6:31 is *not* the 'opening text' for a sermon which follows on through vs. 58. It is presented as a *rhetorical challenge to Jesus*, 'tempting' him to produce more bread (cf. Matt. 4:1–11; Lk. 4:1–13) by those who did not 'see' (perceive) his signs (vs. 26). Thus, the 'haggadic' narrative in John 6 may be considered the story of God's deliverance through Jesus' words and works (vss. 1–24), and the 'halakhic' exhortation (the 'primary text' of the homily) is vs. 27 (a conflation of Deut. 8:2f. and Is. 55:1f.). The introduction of the manna motif in vs. 31, then, is entirely parallel with the more common rhetorical use of manna as a *secondary text* within ancient Jewish literature.[11] Contrary to Borgen's 'homiletical pattern' above, the manna motif in ancient Jewish midrashic literature *nearly always* (except for Exodus Rabbah 25:1–8, etc.) appears something like the following structure:

Table 1:
'The Rhetorical Use of Manna Pattern in Ancient Jewish Literature'

(A) A point of argument, exhortation or Proem text to be developed is stated by an author, who calls for a particular action on behalf of his or her audience.

(B) This point (or the meaning of the text) is discussed, usually posing two options: one favourable and the other unfavourable.

(C) The manna motif is introduced and associated with the main point being made by the writer, 'proving' its superiority (heavenly origin).

(D) The discussion continues, and alternative responses to the author's exhortation are negatively associated with earthly bread (or the 'flesh' of quail), in contrast to heavenly 'bread', which is clearly superior.

(E) The original appeal (or text) is reiterated, often with some reference to the life-producing effect of manna and/or the death-producing effect of earthly (inferior) bread.

---

to its haggadic amplification in Nu. 11:6–9 — the interpretation of the manna as 'testing' (Nu. 21:5), to its eventual rhetorical use as a part of covenant preaching of Psalms and Nehemiah (p. 31). Thus, Malina summarizes his findings:

This development begins from the prosaic aetiological account of the name "manna," an account amplified somewhat in Nb. 11:6, 7–9, and then used as a springboard for homiletic ends. In the process the manna takes on admirable traits, ending up as heavenly food, the food of angels, rained down by God upon Israel to test and teach the desert generation (pp. 39–41)

Malina basically agrees with Borgen regarding his treatment of the manna tradition in John 6:31–58 (pp. 102–106) that the section is a literary unity (p. 106), but like Borgen mistakenly assumes the section begins with vs. 31. Rather than being a 'Christian midrash on the manna tradition, a meditation on this tradition in the light of Jesus' (p. 106), the section is more accurately *a reflection upon the significance of Jesus' works and words* — in light of the manna tradition — which they surpass.

11 See below, Appendix VII, 'Philo's Use of Manna as a *Secondary* Text'. See developments of implications below in Ch. 9.

This is clearly the rhetorical strategy of Jesus' discussants in John 6, but it is Jesus' association of manna with death-producing food which is so striking — and indeed *unique*. For the first time in the history of the use of the manna motif within Jewish/Christian writings is manna regarded as *inferior* to another kind of bread.[12] In effect, what the evangelist has done is to portray a situation in which the manna motif is used rhetorically by Jesus' discussants, but which the Johannine Jesus reformulates in the form of a threefold christocentric exhortation, using the imagery of the 'bread of life' being given by God, received by believers, and ingested by those who would be his disciples. In doing so, John's reformulation of the manna-rhetoric is highly significant. Whereas the crowd employs the manna motif as a rhetorical trump (C) in order to persuade Jesus to provide them with more bread (A), the evangelist has moved the manna motif (vs. 31) to the place of the first and primary objection (B) and has placed Jesus as the life-producing bread (vs. 35) in the pivotal position (C), formerly occupied by the manna from heaven (cf. below, Table 17). Thus, the rhetorical form of the exhortation in John 6 is as follows:

Table 2:
'The Rhetorical Structure of the Christocentric Exhortation in John 6'

(A) The main point is the exhortation to work not for the food which spoils, but for the food which endures eternally, given by the Son of Man (vs. 27; cf. Deut. 8:2f. and Is. 55:1f.).

(B) The objections are threefold: 'Our fathers ate manna in the wilderness.' (vs. 31); 'How can he say he came down from heaven?' (vs. 41f.); 'How can this one give us his flesh to eat?' (vs. 52). (The *first* objection (vss. 25–34) employs the standard rhetorical use of manna pattern (Table 1, above), using the manna scripture as a secondary proof-text.)

(C) The christocentric development of the life-producing bread is also threefold: 'I am the bread of life. He who comes to me will never go hungry ...' (vs. 35); 'I am the bread of life ... coming down from heaven, which one may eat and not die.' (vss. 48, 50f.); and, 'Whoever eats my flesh and drinks my blood has eternal life, and I will raise him up on the last day'. (vs. 54).

(D) The death-producing results of the objections are also described: 'Your forefathers ate manna in the wilderness, and yet they died.' (vss. 49, 58); '... the flesh profits nothing.' (vs. 63).

(E) The basis for the main exhortation is summed up: 'This is the bread which came down from heaven; not like that which the fathers ate, and died. Whoever eats this bread will live eternally.' (vs. 58); and, 'My words are spirit and life.' (vs. 63).

Therefore, Borgen's form-critical analysis remains lacking in two ways. First, he fails to see that the use of the manna motif in John 6:31 is less like the exegetical midrashim of Exodus Rabbah 25:1–8, and more like the more prevalent use of the

---

12 In *none* of the references to manna listed in notes 9 and 10 is manna ever referred to as *anything but superior to* other kinds of 'bread'. While one is not inclined to argue that uniqueness of occurrence implies the *ipsissima verba* of Jesus (cf. J. Jeremias, *New Testament Theology* I, E.t., J. Bowden, London, 1971, pp. 29–37), one deserves at least to ponder the creativity of the evangelist, or whoever was responsible for such a transformation of an otherwise standard Jewish concept (cf. J.K. Riches, *Jesus and the Transformation of Judaism*, Edinburgh, 1980).

manna motif in the rest of ancient Jewish literature, which is as a *rhetorical trump* (or whatever one calls the use of the manna motif as a proof-text). Second, he consequently misses the means by which the evangelist has reformed the manna rhetoric and co-opted its form christologically. The result is that we have in John 6:25–66 a christocentric exhortation, which introduces the manna motif in vs. 31 as the prototypical objection (B), and which associates the request for loaves with Israel's desire for the *flesh of quail* (Nu. 11:33; Ps. 78:24–32) as contrasted to the life-producing 'bread' which Jesus gives and is (C).

3. A third question with Borgen's analysis has to do with the sense in which John 6:31–58 is — and is not — a homily. While Borgen is correct in identifying the exhortative character of John 6:31–58, this is not to say that its content had ever assumed the form of a midrashic sermon, as such, being solely an exposition of a biblical text. The literary form of John 6 involves both narrative and dialogue, as well as discourse, and the key exhortative (halakhic) thrust is found in vs. 27, and developed in the following verses. Furthermore, vss. 31–58 occur within a larger unit (John 6:1–71), which from a literary point of view, falls into three main sections: vss. 1–24, the narration of Jesus' signs and their results; vss. 25–66, the interpretation of the signs by means of dialogues and discourses; and vss. 67–71, the narration of Peter's confession. Therefore, if there is a homily in John 6, it begins *before* the Old Testament citation (of Ps. 78:24f.) in vs. 31. The 'main haggadic text' for the sermon must thus be considered vss. 1–24, as the dialogues and discourses of vss. 25–66 comprise the Johannine interpretation of the feeding (cf. Mk. 8:11–21). This means that the 'homily' of John 6 consists *not* of an Old Testament text which is developed christologically, but the *works and words of Jesus,* which are interpreted by means of introducing scriptural citations as objections to (vs. 31) and confirmations of (vs. 45) the central, exhortative thrust of the chapter (vs. 27).

C. C.K. Barrett

While Borgen is willing to accommodate the use of a *sēmeia* source within the first part of John 6, the approach of C.K. Barrett (Dialectical) is to assume that unless there are compelling reasons to do otherwise, John 6 should be treated and interpreted as a basic unity. However, in doing so, Barrett does not try to diminish the tensions or to 'harmonize the discord' in the chapter prematurely. Rather, he attempts to provide an explanation for how such apparently contradictory styles of thinking may have occurred. Therefore, in this very significant, yet somewhat overlooked essay, Barrett interprets the theological tensions within John 6 as primarily a function of the dialectical method of thinking employed by the evangelist, and he associates this method of reflective thinking with Socratic dialectic.[13] Says Barrett:

---

13 Barrett is certainly justified in looking to the Socratic theory and method of dialectic for clues

For myself I suspect that the roots are to be found if not in Socratic theory at least in the Socratic practice. In Socratic dialogue — and dialogue (*dialegesthai*) is dialectic — concepts are looked at first from one side then from another, definitions are proposed, attacked, defended, abandoned, or improved, opposite points of view are canvassed and, sometimes at least, combined. And the process of thought itself is conceived as fundamentally unspoken dialogue.

> *Socrates:* Do you mean by "thinking" the same which I mean?
> *Theatetus:* What is that?
> *Socrates:* I mean the conversation which the soul holds with herself in considering anything ... . (pp. 49–50)

As a means of illustrating the apparent contradictions in John 6, Barrett identifies two major tensions having to do with eschatology and soteriology (p. 52f.). On one hand, the believer *has* eternal life (6:47, 50f., 58); on the other hand, the believer *will be raised up on the last day* (6:39, 40, 44, 54). And, on one hand, the means by which this life is received is simply through *coming to* and *believing in* the Son (6:29, 35, 40, 47, 63); on the other hand, 6:53–58 has been interpreted to mean that eternal life may *only* be realized through the eucharist. In response to these and other tensions in the Gospel, Barrett rejects the diachronic approach as the best means of explaining John's tensions, as they seem inherent to the thinking of the evangelist. John is both pro-Jewish and anti-Jewish; pro-gnostic and anti-gnostic. 'Here ... we have an antimony that is written into the stuff of the Gospel ...' (p. 55), says Barrett:

> These observations mean that, when we turn to the particular problems of chapter 6, we shall at any rate not leap to the conclusion that the expression of differing points of view must needs betray the hand of an interpolator, inserting his own thoughts into an existing text without regard for consistency and continuity, but consider rather that the author may have elected to express his theme in dialectical fashion, looking at it now from this side, now from

---

to the sort of forward-moving — and yet cyclical — style of progression represented by John 6 (for an excellent example of the Socratic theory of dialectic see Plato's *Phaedrus*, and for an excellent example of the Socratic dialectical method in practice, see Plato's *Theatetus*). This is especially significant regarding the literary form of John 6. The discourses in John 6 *arise out of dialogues*, which are themselves interpretive developments upon the works and words of Jesus (vss. 1–24). Therefore, the literary form out of which the exhortation of John 6 emerges (vss. 27ff.) is the dialogue which begins with the question of the crowd (vs. 25), and which continues until the reaction of the disciples in vs. 66. Thus, the epistemological method of dialectical inquiry within Jewish and Christian circles is of central interest to understanding the form *and* content of John 6. According to D. Daube (*New Testament and Rabbinic Judaism*, London, 1956, p. 154):

> In general, Socrates cultivated this interrogation for the purpose, not of meeting an attack, but of working out a thesis. In other words, his scheme would not be (1) question by an ill-wisher, (2) counter-question, (3) answer and (4) the refutation made possible by the answer; but part (1) would normally be absent. He would start interrogating a person — part (2); that person would give an answer by which he became vulnerable — part (3); and Socrates would draw the inference — part (4). The inference might indeed take the form of a new interrogation, a new part (2), bringing about a new part (3), and so on.

that. Indeed, it is possible that it was not so much the author who imposed this form upon his material, as the material that imposed the form upon him. (p. 55f.)

As a means of building a foundation to support such a statement, Barrett addresses two literary issues and five thematic ones. 1. The first *literary issue* has to do with a review of *Johannine characteristics and vocabulary*. With the crucial passage being 6:51–58, Barrett analyzes its vocabulary and concludes that: 'Only the meaning of verses 51–8, and their relation, or lack of relation, with the context, can justify the removal of these verses as a redactional gloss.' (p. 56) Citing another example, Barrett argues that just because vs. 44 introduces a new thought, it does not mean that it was necessarily written by another author. It would indeed be a strange literary world in which one author were delimited to only one theme per composition.

2. A second literary issue has to do with the *order and rearrangement of verses*. Barrett agrees with Borgen against Bultmann, that the Bread of Life discourse represents a development of the Exodus 16 manna motif and a commentary on Ps. 78:24. Providing Borgen's analysis is basically correct, which Barrett believes is the case, it may be assumed that, '... the dislocation and redaction theory is not the only means of explaining the material in this chapter, and the case for examining the chapter as it stands ... is correspondingly strengthened' (p. 58).

Barrett therefore turns to several *thematic issue* which are treated dialectically in John. 1. John 6 opens with a reference to Jesus' signs, and then the miraculous feeding of the multitude and the crossing of the sea are referred to as signs (6:26). The reaction of the crowd, however, is to see the outward events without perceiving that which they signify. Thus, *the relationship between seeing and believing* is juxtaposed *dialectically*:

> The signs are, as it were, an externalization of the significance of Jesus himself, and both seeing and not seeing him are complex and ambiguous things. To see is not necessarily to believe (36); and yet to see is a necessary concomitant, perhaps a presupposition, of faith (40). (p. 59)

Barrett thus contends that the relation between signs and faith has to do with the tension between visibility and invisibility — which pervades not only John 6, but the entire Gospel as well (esp. 20:29): 'The dialectic that begins with the tension between seeing and believing is used further to analyse the meaning of Faith itself.' (p. 60)

2. Another word that relates to faith dialectically in John 6 is '*work*'. The Johannine use of the word, *ergon*, does not simply mean 'act' or 'deed' as in the Synoptics, but when used with reference to Jesus' activity, 'work' may be taken to be virtually synonymous with 'sign'. The only work which is required by God is faith (vs. 29), and yet this statement evokes a demand for a sign (29f.).

> Here is a genuine piece of dialectic, in which the theme of "work" is thrown backwards and forwards, and is shaped and reshaped in the process. Jesus himself introduces the theme; it is wrongly taken, in a legalistic sense; Jesus replies that working is to be understood in terms of faith; and the crowd in turn replies, asking for a sign, and implying that if "works" are

to be replaced by faith, he, as the one in whom faith is to rest, must perform a work significant enough to support the faith of others who have no works of their own but only faith in him. Jesus' answer is found in the ensuing discourse on the Bread of Life. This discussion thus has the effect of bringing out another dialectical aspect of the meaning of faith. Faith is, and is not, sight; faith is, and is not, work ... faith is the theological term that expresses the dialectic of seeing and not seeing, of working and not working. (p. 61)

3. A third dialectical treatment of a theme in John 6 involves *the way the evangelist regards the Old Testament*, which in 6:32–35 is essentially a theocentric witness to the saving activity of God in the world. Life is not found *in* the scriptures (5:39), but *through* them, as they point centrally to Jesus, who points ultimately to the Father. The main characters in the unfolding drama of the biblical witness (Moses, Abraham, etc.) are not the ones who deserve attention, but God alone, who was working through them. 'It is not Moses who has given you the bread from heaven, but it is my Father ...' (6:32), says the Johannine Jesus. Thus, because the scriptures witness to Christ, who witnesses to the Father, '6:32 is ... a dialectical statement and summary of John's understanding of the Old Testament' (p. 62).

4. The theme of '*coming*' *to Jesus* is also presented dialectically in John 6. On one hand, the crowd comes to Jesus (literally, 6:15, 24) and Jesus invites people to come to him metaphorically (6:35, 37); and yet, 'coming' to Jesus is only made possible through the Father's enablement (6:37, 44, 45, 64–5). Says Barrett:

> The fact is that this chapter (and it would be possible to expand the discussion to cover the whole Gospel) contains material that suggests that it lies within the competence of man freely to make up his mind to come to Jesus and thus to receive at his hand the gift of life that he offers without distinction or reservation and that equally it contains material that suggests that this coming lies wholly within the freedom of God who alone determines who shall come to Jesus. (p. 64)

This theme is climactically illustrated in Jesus' dialogue with Peter (66–70). To Jesus' query about whether or not the twelve will abandon him, Peter replies as though the disciples had chosen to follow Jesus of their own volition. Jesus corrects this notion and emphasizes that it is *he* who has chosen them, not vice versa (vs. 70). Says Barrett, '... John approaches the doctrine of predestination in the only tolerable way; and that way is dialectical. ... Predestination is in fact a dialogue between God and man ...' (p. 64). To see is not necessarily to believe, and to come physically is not necessarily to come relationally, as coming to and believing in Jesus involve human responses to God's saving initiative revealed through the incarnation.

5. The fifth dialectical theme in John 6 treated by Barrett is the *dialectical christology of John*. In John 6 the tide of the Gospel's narrative turns. Even some of Jesus' disciples begin to leave him. Therefore, the main import of the word made flesh (1:14) is not that the incarnation should be understood only in terms of metaphysical natures, or some mechanistic portrayal of God become man. The central thrust of the *logos* christology is that it involves *God's discourse with humanity*. 'A dialectical Christology, such as John's, is not a dissection of a static Christ, but the analysis of a living, moving, speaking Christ ... .' (p. 65) If John's

christology is rightly understood as being dialectical, then two other theological tensions in John 6 are resolved: the *eschatological* and the *sacramental*.

The evangelist's treatment of eschatology is dialectical in that not only are the present and futuristic elements of eschatology placed side by side (4:23; 5:25), but 'in chapter 6 he allows them to appear in dialogue — in dialectic' (p. 66f.). A similar perspective applies to the treatment of the eucharist in John 6. Barrett agrees with Bultmann (more so than Borgen) that the coincidence of the eucharistic and futuristic eschatological references in 6:51–8 is conspicuous, but he does not agree that the redactional solution is the best one: 'They do belong together, not, however, as a corruption but as an example of the Johannine reinterpretation of Christian theology.' (p. 67) John's sacramental perspective is vastly different from the somewhat instrumental function of the Ignatian *pharmakon athanasias* (p. 67).

In concluding, Barrett also makes brief reference to the *dialectical situation* in which the evangelist lived. It was not simply the external circumstances, nor was it simply the dialogue within the mind of the evangelist himself, which must have given rise to such a Gospel. The tensions of 'life and death, truth and error, light and darkness, flesh and spirit, sight and blindness, love and hate' (p. 69) betray the creative workings of a 'Socratic mind that is capable of asking itself questions, and arguing with itself ...' (p. 68). Concludes Barrett:

> Whatever Johannine theology is, it is neither bald historicism nor unbridled gnosis. It represents rather a creative and perceptive handling of the earlier tradition, free in that it addresses to the basic Christian conviction whatever new questions a new age might suggest, obedient in that it is bound to the original apostolic witness to Jesus. The "dialectical theology of St. John" is not a novel invention, but an authentic insight into the meaning of Christian origins. (p. 68)

Several strengths and weaknesses of Barrett's essay are worthy of note. 1. The first strength of his essay is that it takes seriously the creativity and integrity of the Fourth Evangelist's exploratory style of thinking. Too often biblical scholars reduce an evangelist, source, or redactor to a caricature of some theological position, without appreciating the theological creativity and vitality of an earlier author. What Barrett has done is to demonstrate the method by which an early theologian argued with, agreed with, and yet distilled and reinterpreted the central paradox of the incarnation. In the Fourth Evangelist we have no mere uncritical purveyor of tradition. We have a highly creative theologian, who is thoroughly engaged in dialogue — not only with other groups and individuals — but within himself as well, seeking to understand *how* the signs and works of Jesus, the scriptures, the sacraments, and ultimately the incarnation itself may be responded to as a believing response to God's saving initiative. This is explored by Barrett by means of using the most basic meaning of Socratic 'dialectic', that which involves *dialogue* as an external *and* internal method of epistemological exploration.

2. A second strength of Barrett's essay is that it contributes significantly to the christological unity/disunity issue. Because of the stylistic and linguistic unity of John 6, Barrett observes correctly that diachronic distinctions must be made on the

basis of theological rather than literary judgments alone. Therefore, Barrett believes that John 6 — and the rest of the Gospel — deserves to be interpreted as it stands. The disunity of John 6 is primarily ideological, but this still poses a difficulty: how to understand the *meaning* of content which is presented dialectically. Not only is the christological content of John 6 presented dialectically, but so is its presentation of eschatology, soteriology, Jesus' signs and works, the Son's relationship to the ·Father, and the predestination of believers. However, the dialectical juxtaposition of statements and counterstatements does not suggest the evangelist is indecisive or confused. It more accurately reflects the creative and critical thinking of a first-century theologian who is more tolerant of ambiguity than of incomplete, monodimensional attempts to define the truth embodied in Jesus. For John, 'truth' has to do with the christocentric revelation of God. To believe *that* Jesus is truly the Son of God is to abide *in* him as 'the truth'. This implies that John's is a *living christology*, still in the process of being explored and formulated reflectively, rather than being a more fixed set of christological tenets. Therefore, if the evangelist was a creative theologian, able to consider an idea from one angle, and then another, the christological unity and disunity of John may be attributed largely to tensions *internal* to his thinking and writing. Barrett's demonstrating how the evangelist may have thought dialectically comprises the major contribution of this significant essay.

The limitations of Barrett's essay are twofold. 1. The first is that, while Barrett has shown convincingly that the evangelist (or whoever composed John) must have been a dialectical thinker and a creative theologian, he makes no attempt to explain *how this individual may have come to think dialectically*. In other words, while the other gospels are by no means free from ideological tensions — within each and between the three — John's christological content is even more pronouncedly unitive *and* disunitive. This phenomenon demands an investigation into the origin and character of its epistemological structure. Relevant issues include such interests as the evangelist's proximity to, or distance from, the actual ministry of Jesus, and what sort of cognitive processes he might have gone through in coming to such a reflective appreciation of it. In order to address these and other interests, the citing of contemporary parallels alone does not suffice. One must also investigate the cognitive and developmental factors which contribute to dialectical modes of thinking.[14] Given the recent advances of cognitive and developmental studies,

---

14 To say the evangelist thought about the significance of Jesus' ministry dialectically is one thing, but to investigate *how it is* he may have come to think about the earthly ministry of Jesus dialectically is another. The implications of this second area of investigation are considerably rich in their potential importance. One recent study which points the way forward is the innovative essay by E. Liebert, 'That You May Believe: The Fourth Gospel and Structural Development Theory', *BTB* 14:2, 1984, pp. 67–73. In this essay Liebert demonstrates several parallels between John's facilitation of belief for the reader (from unbelief, to developing belief, to normative belief) and ways that recent developmental theorists have understood the process of faith development. Of special interest is the work

interdisciplinary insights may illumine one's understanding of the factors contributing to theological reflection, and these insights may contribute to one's appreciation of the evangelist's unitive and disunitive christology.

2. A second limitation of Barrett's essay is that it does not develop sufficiently *the socio-religious context* within which John 6 was composed. In other words, while his study provides a refreshing consideration of the evangelist as a *thinker*, rather than a mere responder to current issues, one may also expect that the crises faced by contemporary Christians, within and outside to Johannine Christianity, must have influenced the *internal* dialogues within the evangelist's thinking. Therefore, Barrett's analysis of the evangelist's dialectical patterns of thought must be combined with an assessment of the *dialectical situation* in which he lived and ministered. A further kind of dialectic to be considered is the *literary means* by which the evangelist seeks to engage the reader in dialogue by producing a written gospel. If the evangelist is himself a dialectical thinker, one's analysis of the means by which he presents his material to his audience is of central importance for understanding the content of his christocentric message. Therefore, these three levels of dialectic, or dialogue, must be considered if one is to grasp the meaning of John's christocentric message, and they will also illumine one's understanding of its unitive and disunitive tensions.

Findings

While R. Kysar has attempted to demonstrate a 'growing consensus' among recent diachronic approaches to John 6, his study actually reveals the opposite. Source-critical scholars do not agree with each other in their assessments of literary sources thought to underlie John 6:1–53 enough to demonstrate anything more than the fact that such studies have been undertaken, assuming a narrative source, a sayings source, and/or a foundational gospel. More significantly, however, Kysar's study accentuates the significance of Bultmann's contribution, and both diachronic and synchronic studies must wrestle centrally with his treatment of John 6.

The primary contribution of Borgen's monograph is to demonstrate, on the bases of form-analysis and comparisons with contemporary midrashim upon the manna tradition, that John 6:31–58 may indeed be considered a formal and thematic unity. The implication is that Bultmann's postulation of an *Offenbarungsreden* source, a disordering and reordering of the text, and the addition of the so-called 'eucharistic interpolation' by a redactor are unnecessary. The Bread of Life discourse is developed coherently along the lines of a homiletical pattern, which reformulates the common rhetorical use of the manna motif christologically. Thus, attempts to provide an alternative sequence and to postulate underlying sources and

---

of J. Fowler (*Stages of Faith: The Psychology of Human Development and the Quest for Meaning*, New York, 1981), and his contribution will be considered below in Chapter 7.

interpolated redactions are superfluous, given the formal unity and the thematic coherence of the section. Nonetheless, some of the christological unity and disunity may be attributable to two factors: the agency christology of the evangelist, and the various needs of groups within Johannine Christianity addressed by the evangelist.

Barrett's essay makes a valuable contribution to Johannine studies in that it attempts to explore the means by which the evangelist, as a creative theologian, may have thought dialectically. Disagreeing with Bultmann, that theological tensions in John may be ascribed to multiple sources and redactors, Barrett has demonstrated that the evangelist treats over a half-dozen topics dialectically — within John 6 alone. Therefore, an attempt must be made to understand how such an individual may have come to think in such ways, and within what context. Barrett's essay makes one of the most significant contributions to the study of John's christological unity and disunity. If these tensions may be considered internal to the thinking and writing of the evangelist, interpreters must come to grips with his christology being a living exploration of the truth embodied in Jesus as the Christ, and such an insight would have interpretive implications extending to the classic issues of Christian theology — and beyond.

Summary of Part I

A survey of five recent approaches to John's christology reveals that its unitive and disunitive features have been central to most kinds of christological studies, and yet remarkably few attempts have been made to explore these tensions directly. How such a piece of writing could contain such apparently contradictory content has been explored indirectly by means of text-centred, theological, literary, and historical approaches to John's christology, and the most significant studies often combine several of these approaches. Problems have arisen, however, due to scholars' lack of clarity about the place of the christological unity/disunity issue, as it relates to the central interest(s) of their studies. This has led scholars using diachronic theories of composition to understate the christological implications of their studies, with the result that responses defending John's literary unity have often missed the underlying (central?) motivation for such studies, often leading to an unfortunate *impasse* in the discussion.

Surveys of five major and recent commentaries betray a significant correlation between each scholar's approach to John's christological unity and disunity, his theory of composition, and his treatment of John 6. Therefore, while correlation does not imply causation, this observation suggests that one's evaluation of John's christological unity and disunity will have implications for one's theory of John's composition, and vice versa. Furthermore, John 6 may be considered an adequate *locus argumenti* for exploring John's unity and disunity, literarily and christologically, with the results being applicable to the rest of the Gospel, at least in a preliminary way.

Recent analyses of John 6 have suggested the following insights regarding John's christological unity and disunity: a) While recent diachronic treatments of John 6 do not betray a 'growing consensus' about the precise identification of underlying sources, they do suggest a common conclusion — that analyses of the unity and disunity of John 6 must wrestle centrally with Bultmann's treatment of it. b) The homiletical form and exhortative thrust of John 6 may account for at least two aspects of John's christological unity and disunity. The presence of different groups within the Johannine audience often accounts for shifts in theme — especially high/low tensions in John's presentation of Jesus; and, the evangelist's agency christology largely accounts for the apparent contradiction regarding the Son's relationship to the Father. c) Ultimately, however, the tensions within John's christology must be explored as internal to the dialectical thought of the evangelist. These and other interests will be explored in Part II.

Part II

The Unity and Disunity of John 6

It was my intention
when I embarked upon this study
to introduce not the bare reference to Dr Bultmann
that I have just given,
but a much fuller account
of those who have attacked the literary
and theological unity of this chapter,
and of those who have defended it.
It has now become clear to me
that this would be
a bibliographical luxury
which I cannot allow myself —
possibly a bibliographical boredom
which I may well spare my readers.

C.K. Barrett
'The Dialectical Theology of St. John'

The purpose of Part II is to explore further the unity and disunity of John 6 in order to acquire a clearer understanding of the literary and christological unity and disunity of the Gospel. As Bultmann's commentary on John has been the most influential contribution to Johannine studies this century, both for scholars who agree *and* who disagree with him, his treatment of John 6 will be used to set the agenda for the next three chapters (4–6). Along the way, various critical issues will be raised, and the contributions of other scholars will be considered. Whether this is experienced as a bibliographical luxury or as a bibliographical boredom may depend upon the interest and disposition of the reader. However, the hope is that such discussions will facilitate a better understanding of unitive and disunitive aspects of John's composition *and* christology.

Objections may be raised as to why Bultmann's treatment of John 6 should be given such preferential consideration, given the fact that few aspects of his theories have endured the test of time. With the Nag Hammadi and Qumran finds, Bultmann's *religionsgeschichtliche* research on the gnostic background of John is no longer as compelling; with the literary-unity studies by the likes of Schweizer, Ruckstuhl and Noack, Bultmann's diachronic theory of composition has lost much of its credibility; and, with the socio-religious studies of Käsemann, Martyn, Brown and Meeks, new answers have been posed to some of the theological issues which Bultmann sought to address by means of his diachronic theory of composition. Thus, it might seem that to discuss Bultmann's treatment of John 6 may be considered antiquated and superfluous. However, the fact still remains that most major Johannine debates can still be traced to Bultmann's commentary; and no other work has combined the same rigour of literary, historical and theological criticism into such a formidable and well-reasoned argument. Therefore, the stylistic, contextual and theological[1] grounds for Bultmann's treatment of John 6 will be evaluated in the next three chapters (4–6), and in Chapter 7 an attempt will be made to explore the origin of the dialectical character of the evangelist's thought. The goal of each chapter will be to evaluate the extent to which Bultmann's arguments are convincing — to build upon them when they are — and to see if their insights may be applied otherwise where they are not.

Chapter 4

The Stylistic Unity and Disunity of John 6

One of the most convincing aspects of Bultmann's analysis is his ability to combine literary and theological criteria in the identification of John's sources. Thus, the intricate and tightly-woven character of his composition theory has been one of the most significant factors contributing to the longevity of its influence.[2] For this reason a singly stylistic, contextual, or theological analysis of Bultmann's treatment of John 6 will not suffice. These three aspects of his contribution must be considered *together* if they are to be understood properly and evaluated adequately. Therefore, the focus of this chapter is to evaluate the *stylistic and linguistic evidence* which Bultmann presents in his identification of literary sources thought to comprise John 6. If this evidence is convincing, then the literary disunity of ch. 6 will inform one's understanding of the christological unity and disunity of the Gospel. However, even if it is not, such an analysis will still facilitate a clearer understanding of the emphases and content of the evangelist's christocentric message.

---

1   The three criteria for source analysis according to R. Fortna (pp. 16–22) are 'ideological' (i.e. theological, a matter of slant or *Tendenz*), 'stylistic' (i.e. special sentence-constructions, vocabulary and use of connectives) and 'contextual' (i.e. aporias and rough transitions, parenthetical comments, catch-words or phrases, and clues from textual criticism), as well as lateral comparisons with Synoptic parallels. Thus, an entire chapter will be given to each of these three 'criteria' for a source-critical analysis of John 6.

   As will become evident, the stylistic analysis of Chapter 4 will also encompass various aspects of linguistic analysis, form-critical analysis, an evaluation of Bultmann's disordering and reordering scheme, and an assessment of the significance of his style-critical treatment of John 6. The contextual analysis of Chapter 5 will seek to evaluate the relationship between sign and discourse in John 6. It will also encompass form-critical analyses of the Johannine misunderstanding motif and comparisons with Mark 6 and 8. Chapter 6 will then seek to evaluate Bultmann's treatment of the theological tensions in John 6, with primary attention given to the ideological tensions between the incarnationalist ideology of the evangelist and the apparently contradictory slant of the so-called 'eucharistic interpolation'. Thus, Chapters 4, 5 and 6 will address the stylistic, contextual and ideological unity and disunity of John 6 — respectively — using Bultmann's analysis as a springboard.

2   This may be the greatest significance of D.M. Smith's comprehensive analysis of Bultmann's commentary (*Composition*, 1965). It is worthy to note that few other analyses have taken into consideration ideological, stylistic, *and* contextual aspects of Bultmann's theory, which may also explain why monodimensional critiques of it have neither convinced Bultmann nor many of his followers. By contrast, Smith's treatment is comprehensive, and thus its value is distinguished.

At the outset it should be acknowledged that Bultmann never claims to base his judgments upon stylistic factors alone. In fact, rather than consider the stylistic and linguistic bases for his identification of sources as 'criteria', Bultmann regards them as corroborative evidence, not necessarily convincing individually, but confirming of contextual and theological evidence as well.[3] Thus, the validity of Bultmann's proposals cannot be judged adequately until his contextual and theological arguments are also considered. Nonetheless, analysis must begin somewhere, and moving from the most objective to the most subjective of the three factors is the surest way to proceed. Thus, we begin with assessing the stylistic unity and disunity of John 6.

Briefly, the corroboration of literary sources by distinguishable stylistic and linguistic evidence in John 6 is as follows: 1. The *sēmeia* source is supposedly written in a 'Semitising Greek' style of composition, which coincides with its Jewish-Christian origin as a collection of miracle stories designed to convince a Jewish audience to believe in Jesus as God's Son (20:31). 2. On the other hand, the *Offenbarungsreden* source is supposedly a Hellenized form of Aramaic, and its original structure was that of a strophic and rhythmic composition, designed for cultic use within a gnostic community (1:1–5, 9–12, 14, 16, etc.). 3. The evangelist's purpose and style are quite different from these, according to Bultmann. His goal is to weave these (and other) sources together into a literary whole, whereby miracle stories are interpreted in light of revelation discourses, emphasizing the existential meaning of Jesus' ministry. Therefore, most clarifying statements, connecting phrases and paragraphs, time and place designations, and otherwise narratological insertions may be ascribed to the evangelist. By contrast, the identification of the redactor's contribution is based upon theological grounds (he *imitated* the style of the evangelist, p. 234). Thus, according to Bultmann, the literary origin of the material in John is as follows:

Table 3:
'The Literary Origins of the Material in John 6 According to R. Bultmann'

Sēmeia source	Offenbarungsreden	Evangelist	Redactor
1–2a	27a	2b	1 (*tēs Tiberiados*)
3	[33]	4	18
5	35b	6	23 (*eucharistēsantos*
7–13	37b	14–15	*tou kuriou*)
16–17	44a–b	23	27b
19-22	45c	24	39c
25	47b	26	40c

(*Continued on pg. 74*)

---

3 Notice Bultmann's response (*TL* 80, 1955, pp. 521–526) to B. Noack's critique (*Zur johanneischen Tradition*, Copenhagen, 1954) of his work. According to Smith:

> Against Noack's criticism, Bultmann attempts to stand his ground by asserting that while Noack tests his criteria individually (e.g., *ekeinos*) he, Bultmann, always uses them together in such a way that they offer mutual support and confirmation. (p. 78)

Table 3 (Continued from pg. 73)

Sēmeia source	Offenbarungsreden	Evangelist	Redactor
48		27c–32	44c
		34–35a	51c–58
		36–37a	
		38–39b	
		40a–b	
		41–43	
		45a–b	
		46–47a	
		49–51b	
		59–71	

Again, rather than to argue for or against the literary unity of John 6, the interest of this study is simply to evaluate the degree to which Bultmann's distinguishing of the *sēmeia* source, *Offenbarungsreden* source, and evangelist's material is convincing—on the basis of the stylistic and linguistic evidence he has marshalled.

A. *Stylistic and Linguistic Evidence for the Sēmeia Source*

In his coverage of the 'Miracle of the Epiphany' (2:1–12), Bultmann lays out in clear terms what he believes to be the beginnings of literary criteria to be used in distinguishing the style of the *sēmeia* source from that of the evangelist. The style of the source is that of a 'Semitising Greek', and according to Bultmann:

> There can be no doubt that the Evangelist has again taken a story from the tradition as the basis of his account here. Manifestly he has taken it from a source which contains a collection of miracles, and which he uses for the following miracle stories. It is the *sēmeia*-source, which in its style is clearly distinguishable from the language of the Evangelist or of the discourse-source ... . (p. 113)

While it may be argued that the evidence for distinguishing source material on the basis of stylistic criteria alone is not distributed evenly throughout the Gospel,[4] Bultmann nevertheless continues to use stylistic evidence to bolster his judgments at every turn. The main passage in John 6 in which he delineates his understanding of the style of the *sēmeia* source may be found in an extended note on his treatment of 6:1–26 (p. 211, n. 1):

---

4 For instance, there is far more stylistic and formal evidence for assuming a conflation of strophic and prosaic material in John 1:1–18 than there is in John 6:25–58, and there is more stylistic and formal evidence for assuming a miracle source underlying John 2:1–11 and 4:46–54 (complete with enumeration and a distinctive, thaumaturgic ideology) than there is for John 6:1–24. Nevertheless, Bultmann proceeds on the assumption that if a sayings and a narrative source may be inferred in these places, they may also be found elsewhere in the Gospel.

Stylistically the source shows the same characteristics as the sections which we have already attributed to the *sēmeia*-source. The style is a "Semitising" Greek, but it does not seem possible to discern in the story a translation from a literary Semitic source. The passage is characterised by the placing of the verb at the beginning of the sentence; also by the lack (in vv. 7, 8, 10, where K pl have *de*), or very simple form of connection between the sentences (*de* and *oun*). *Poiēsate* (in Greek we would expect *keleusate*) ... *anapesein* v. 10 corresponds to the Semitic causative. ... The constantly repeated *autou* also is not Greek (it corresponds to the Semitic suffix) after the different forms of *mathētai* vv. 3, 8, 12, 16 ... .

According to this analysis, the 'Semitising Greek' style of the *sēmeia* source should be distinguishable by at least three linguistic characteristics: 1. the verb at the beginning of the sentence; 2. simple connections (*de, oun,* etc., or the lack of any connection at all) between sentences; and 3. the use of various Semitic constructions versus Greek ones, especially the use of *autou* after *mathētai*. Therefore, these stylistic and linguistic 'criteria' will be tested within the rest of John 6 in order to evaluate the extent to which they may be said to corroborate the identification of distinctive literary sources.

1. The verb at the beginning of the sentence could suggest the author had learned Greek as his second language, as this *is* a Semitic style of sentence construction. Thus, the detection of a syntactic difference between material assigned to respective sources could be meaningful, but no such difference is to be found. When the entirety of John 6 is tested for the verb-first construction, the results are as follows: the verb is at the beginning of the sentence in 6:1, 2, 3, 4, 6, 7, 8, 10_, 11, 13, 20, 21, 23, 24, 26, 27, 28, 29, 30, 32, 34, 35, 36, 38, 41, 43, 45, 47, 52, 53, 57, 61, 62, 64_, 65, 67, 68, 70, 71. Therefore, *nearly two thirds* (41/64) of the sentences in John 6 begin with the main verb, while in the verses attributed to the *sēmeia* source by Bultmann, the ratio is *nearly 67%* (12/18). Bultmann's first criterion for the distinctive style of the *sēmeia* source in John 6 is absolutely non-indicative and is thus unconvincing. Verb-first construction is characteristic of two thirds of all of John 6.

2. An analysis of Bultmann's second criterion for distinguishing the 'Semitising Greek' style of the *sēmeia* source yields similar results. While it is fairly clear what Bultmann means by a lack of connection (such as *de* and *oun*) between sentences, it is less clear what the alternatives would be. Nonetheless, *de* occurs at the beginning of a sentence in vss. 2, 3, 4, 6, 10, 12, 16, 20, 39, 61, 71. Most of these (6/11) occur within material assigned to the *sēmeia* source, so this finding could be significant. However, *oun* occurs at the beginning of a sentence in vss. 5, 11, 13, 14, 15, 19, 21, 24, 28, 30, 32, 41, 52, 53, 60, 67. Most of these (11/16) are found in material *not* assigned to the *sēmeia* source. Verses which begin with no connection (other than a verb — to save from duplicating the first criterion) include vss. 17, 25, 31, 37, 40, 44, 48, 49, 54, 56, 58, 63, 66. Only 2 of 14 of these could be from the *sēmeia* source, so this result is disappointing as well.

One wonders just how convincing Bultmann's criteria for Semitic sentence construction could be. There are *only two sentences* in John 6 which do not meet one of his criteria: vss. 22 and 59. They neither begin with a verb, nor a 'simple' construction such as *de* or *oun* (*tē epaurion*; *tauta eipen*). Perhaps these are examples of connectives between sentences which are *not* 'simple' ones, or perhaps they qualify as sentences *without* a connective. Either way, one of these is ascribed to the *sēmeia* source, and the other is not! *All* the other sentences in John 6 exhibit one or more of the above features. Therefore, the question is not whether or not vss. 1–25 (roughly) betray a 'Semitising' style of Greek, as a contrast to the other material in John 6. The question is whether or not there is *any* part of John 6 (or the Gospel, for that matter) which does *not* betray such a style.

3. The Semitic vocabulary suggested by Bultmann reinforces the same conclusion. More specifically, if indeed the following of *mathētai* by *autou* is a Semitic construction, the Semitic style of the evangelist as well as the *sēmeia* source is confirmed by analyzing its occurrence in John 6 (p. 443, n. 3). As well as being found in vss. 3, 8, 12, 16, 22_, it also occurs in vss. 24, 60, 61 and 66. Therefore, *every time* some form of *mathētai* occurs in John 6 it is accompanied by *autou*, both in the *sēmeia* source material and elsewhere. The occurrence of *poiēsate* ... *anapesein* in vs. 10 merely confirms that this is a Semitic construction. The more Hellenistic *keleusate* ... *anapesein* does not occur anywhere else in the Gospel. Therefore, on the basis of the Semitic expressions, syntactic constructions and vocabulary put forth by Bultmann, the *sēmeia* source *cannot* be distinguished from the rest of the material in John 6.

One of the overall problems with Bultmann's source assignments made on the basis of stylistic criteria is that John's style is *basically uniform.*[5] Not only is the style of the *sēmeia* source 'Semitising Greek' (p. 211, n. 1), but the style of the evangelist is *also* 'Semitising' (p. 204, n. 1), as is (to a lesser degree) that of the *Offenbarungsreden.* Furthermore, the redactor has imitated the style of the evangelist (p. 234, n. 4). Therefore, one may conclude that the stylistic grounds for identifying the *sēmeia* source in John 6 are individually and cumulatively unconvincing. The traits identified as significant for the distinguishing of the *sēmeia* source are distributed equally throughout the rest of the entire chapter. Another fact is that the criteria chosen to demarcate Semitic style also characterize action narrative, while those indicating Hellenistic style are also found predictably in discourse material proper. Thus, even real differences may be source-critically non-significant.

---

5 Bultmann himself acknowledges the fact of John's overall stylistic unity in an article published nearly two decades after his commentary ('Johannesevangelium', *RGG* 3, 1959, pp. 840–850; and cf. n. 10, below), but since then other scholars have pressed the same point even beyond the work of Schweizer and Ruckstuhl. In his two 1984 essays ('Testing for Johannine Authorship by Examining the Use of Conjunctions', *Westminster Theological Journal* 46, pp. 350–369; and 'The Use of the Intersentence Conjunctions *de, oun, kai,* and Asyndeton in the Gospel of John', *NovT* 26, pp. 312–340) V. Poythress, for example, has concluded that John is a basic stylistic unity (even 21:1–23), but that 7:53–8:11 demonstrates itself to be of a significantly different style, enough so, as to emphasize the rest of the Gospel's literary unity.

However, lest it be assumed that it is only stylistic evidence upon which Bultmann bases his identification of *sēmeia* source material, it should also be acknowledged that he uses *formal* criteria as well. Believing that the literary form of this source is narrative prose, written to convince a Jewish audience that Jesus is the Messiah, Bultmann also identifies some Synoptic-like, narrative material as belonging to the source. Thus, it is not surprising that the material attributed to this source (vss. 1–25) should have a remarkably close resemblance to the Marcan account of parallel events. According to Bultmann, the *sēmeia* source material in John 6 is:[6]

Table 4:
'Bultmann's Reconstruction of the *Sēmeia* Source Material Underlying John 6:1–25'

(6:1) After these things Jesus went to the other side of Galilee ... (2a) and a large crowd followed him. ... (3) So Jesus went up into the mountain and there sat down with his disciples. ... (5) Therefore, lifting up his eyes and beholding that a large crowd was coming toward him, Jesus says to Philip,

"Whence shall we buy loaves that these may eat?" ...

(7) Philip answered him,

"Two hundred denarii would not be enough for each of them to take [even] a little."

(8) One of his disciples, Andrew, the brother of Simon Peter, says to him,

(9) "There is a lad here who has five barley loaves and two fishes; but what are these among so many?"

(10) Jesus said,

"Have the people recline."

Now there was much grass there; therefore the men reclined, their number being about five thousand. (11) Then Jesus took the loaves, and having given thanks distributed to those reclining, and likewise of the fish, as much as they wished. (12) Now when they were filled, he tells his disciples,

"Gather up the left-over fragments, that nothing may be wasted."

(13) Therefore, they gathered and filled twelve baskets with the fragments of five barley loaves which were left over by those who had eaten. ...

(16) And when evening came his disciples went down to the sea, (17) and embarking in a boat came across the sea to Capernaum. And darkness now had come and Jesus had not yet come to them. ... (19) Therefore, having rowed about twenty-five or thirty *stadia* [furlongs] they behold Jesus walking on the sea and coming toward the boat, and they were frightened. (20) But he said to them,

"It is I! Do not fear!"

(21) Therefore, they wished to take him into the boat, and immediately the boat was at the land to which they were going. (22) On the next day the crowd, standing across the sea, saw that there had been only one boat there, and that Jesus did not enter the boat with his disciples but had departed alone. ... (25) And finding him across the sea they said to him, "Rabbi, when did you get here?"

---

6 This rendition of the *sēmeia* source account underlying John 6:1–25 is a translation of D.M. Smith's reproduction of the same material in Greek (p. 40f.).

Such a sequence certainly appears to represent a basic framework of narrated events, free from interpretive comments (6:4, 6, 14f., 18, 23f.; p. 210), but this is where elements of style and form give way to judgments based upon assumed notions of how the evangelist's work must have differed from his sources. For instance, other narrative sections in John 6, which seem stylistically indistinguishable from vss. 1–25, are assigned to the evangelist (vss. 26–34; 59–71, etc.). Thus, Bultmann must base his distinctions upon ideological assumptions, such as the notion that Jesus' signs were thaumaturgic in their pre-Johannine existence, while the theological posture of the evangelist is existentializing and incarnational (pp. 113–119). Thus, the narrative section of vss. 60–71 is identified as a 'composition of the Evangelist's with the aid of the synoptic tradition ...' (p. 443, n. 3), and this judgment is based upon theological-interpretive grounds. According to Bultmann, vss. 60–71 portray the defection of disciples because the offence of the incarnation (cf. pp. 60–76) is that it leads to the 'way of the cross' (pp. 443–451). Therefore, Bultmann's decision to ascribe vss. 1–25 to a *sēmeia* source, and vss. 60–71 to the evangelist's reworking of the Synoptic tradition, hangs upon the assumptions that the christologies of the former and latter are thaumaturgic and incarnational, respectively, and that these ideologies would have been incompatible within the thinking of a single, first-century writer. This illustrates the thorough interwovenness between literary style, form, and ideology within Bultmann's source-critical methodology.

B. *The Style of the Offenbarungsreden Material and the Reordering of the Text*

The literary evidence supporting Bultmann's detection of *Offenbarungsreden* material in John 6 is based less on stylistic and linguistic criteria, and more on his identification of metric/strophic material underlying the Prologue. The original language of this source is thought to have been Aramaic (p. 18), reflecting the form and character of Semitic poetry (p. 15). Although the distinction seems obtuse, rather than being a kind of 'Semitising Greek', 'Hellenised Aramaic' — the *Offenbarungsreden* is supposedly the Greek transposition of a Semitic (Aramaic) collection of revelation sayings. Furthermore, as in the Prologue, Bultmann believes that this distinctively poetic and rhythmic structure can be detected throughout selected portions in the rest of the Gospel as well. The stylistic criteria of this source as defined by Bultmann are as follows:

> The *form* of the Prologue is not loose or haphazard, but rigid and even minor details are governed by strict rules. The construction is similar to that of the Odes of Solomon; each couplet is made up of two short sentences. Sometimes both parts of the couplet express one thought (vv. 9, 12, 14b); sometimes the second completes and develops the first (vv. 1, 4, 14a, 16); sometimes the two parts stand together in parallelism (v. 3), or in antithesis (vv. 5, 10, 11). This form is not foreign to Semitic poetry, and recurs often in the discourses of the Gospel. (p. 15)

As in the case of the identification of *sēmeia*-source material, the stylistic evidence for the *Offenbarungsreden* material in John 6 in the form of rhythmic/ strophic poetry certainly could be significant. If there should be found within the discourses of John 6 a series of couplets, set in distinctive, rhythmic stanzas within a larger body of prose, this could provide telling clues as to the material's literary origin. However, as Ruckstuhl has pointed out, a conspicuous problem is that Bultmann has not selected all of the metric/strophic material that he could have.[7] In fact, there is a great deal of material in John 6 which may well have qualified for the hypothetical *Offenbarungsreden* source, but which has not been selected (cf. vss. 26b, 29b, 32, 37a, 38–40, 46, 50f., 53–58, 63, etc.).

This demands an explanation. It indeed seems odd that, having described the stylistic character of the *Offenbarungsreden*, Bultmann does not, in his treatment of John 6, comment upon the poetic/rhythmic style of this source except in vs. 27(ab). While this sentence ' ... is probably based on a saying taken from the source ... it is doubtful whether it is quoted word for word, since the style of the source would lead us to expect a verb in the second half [of the] verse as well' (p. 222, n. 5). This is not to say, however, that Bultmann has left the rhythmic character of the verses he assigns to the source undemonstrated. He simply places selected texts in clear relief, and allows the profile of their rhythmic character to be self-evident. These are as follows:[8]

Table 5:
'Bultmann's Reconstruction of the *Offenbarungsreden* Material Underlying John 6:27–48'

(6:27) Work not for food which perishes,
    But for food which remains into eternal life,
    [   ].
(35) I am the bread of life;
    The one coming to me by no means hungers,
    And the one coming to me will by no means
        ever thirst.
[(33)
    For the bread of God is that which comes
    down from heaven and gives life to the world.]
(48) I am the bread of life.
    (47) The one believing has (in me) eternal life.
    (44) No one can come to me
        unless the Father [who sent me] draws him.
    (45) Everyone hearing from the Father and learning
    comes to me.
    (37) And the one coming to me
    I will by no means cast out.

---

7 In his *Die literarische Einheit des Johannesevangeliums* (pp. 43–54) Ruckstuhl has pressed Bultmann rather intensely regarding his inconsistencies in the ascribing of material to the *Offenbarungsreden*. On one hand, he raises several stophic/metric problems with the

While these verses display a certain progression of thought and rhythmic character, their obvious reordering and exclusive selectively require compelling explanations. The statistical probability that there should have been no fewer than 10 disorderings within John 6, precisely in between sentences (let alone, *only* within the discourse material) is slightly less than 1:10 quintillion.[9] Given also the fact that many potentially suitable (from a rhythmic/strophic standpoint) verses have *not* been ascribed to the source, it may be assumed that there are other factors at work: a) As in the case of the *sēmeia* source, Bultmann must depend upon his inference that a discernible difference exists between the ideology of the *Offenbarungsreden* source and that of the evangelist. Therefore, believing that the *logos* christology of the Prologue is couched in the mythology of the Gnostic Redeemer-myth (pp. 19–36), Bultmann identifies various enlightenment and revelational themes as pertaining to the source, rather than the evangelist. After these themes have been 'selected' from the corpus of John 6, they must be (re)ordered into a coherent sequence, and the disordering-reordering work serves this function. b) A second factor calling for the reordering of the text in John 6 is that, having excised vss. 51b(c)–58 as a redactional interpolation, Bultmann is left with a section ending at vs. 51a (actually b) which cannot be left to stand on its own. Bultmann's solution is to offer a restored order of the 'original' text:

> But even when we have made these omissions we have still by no means established a clear line of argument. Rather the present text is in a state of disorder, or at least of very poor order, which I can only explain by suggesting that it is the work of an editor who, having found a text which for external reasons has been completely destroyed and so disordered, attempted himself to reconstruct the original order. (p. 220)

As the evidence given by Bultmann to support this proposal is rather compact and difficult to adduce (pp. 220–221), a summary of his judgments is as follows:

---

material Bultmann has assigned to the source, but more significantly, he claims to have identified some 80 instances in which '*Zweizeilern im OR-Rhythmus*' passages are assigned to the evangelist and *not* the source (p. 48, esp. 4:32, 38; 8:48; 9:41; 13:20, etc.). Ruckstuhl is justified in calling attention to this discrepancy, as it suggests ideological (and contextual) factors underlying Bultmann's 'stylistic' analysis.

8 This rendition of the *Offenbarungsreden* material thought to be underlying John 6:27–48 is a translation of D.M. Smith's reproduction of the same material in Greek (p. 25).

9 This is not an exaggeration. The average number of Greek characters per sentence in John 6 is 80, and Bultmann has hypothesized *ten* breaks of sequence in John 6, precisely in between sentences (conspicuously, *all* of them, except for the beginning and end of the chapter, being in the discourse section). Providing the rational scholar can accept the *dis*ordering hypothesis, he or she must then also ascribe to a *re*ordering scheme by which these fragments came to be in their present order. While Bultmann is willing to admit that some of the material may have been lost in this process (p. 437, n. 3), the probability that this material should have fallen into disorder (and into fragments of *unequal lengths*), precisely in between sentences is *1 to 80 to the tenth power*; in other words, a probability of 1:10,737,418,240,000,000,000. Thus, it is not only the evangelist who brings his readers to a dualism of decision, but one of his most insightful interpreters, as well.

a) The people's question in vs. 28, 'What may we do to do the works of God?' is 'unmotivated' after Jesus' statement in vs. 27, and thus it must be considered a 'detached fragment' (p. 220f.). Bultmann's assumption is that 'In order to show that there is a connection between v. 28 and v. 27, it would have to be assumed that they understand Jesus' words in v. 27 correctly (even if they only half understand them) .... Rather v. 34 shows that they have not understood' (p. 220, n. 3). Thus, this is out of character with the misunderstanding/ understanding sequence of the standard Johannine dialogue and would therefore be unlikely.

b) 'V. 34 cannot really be taken as a continuation of vv. 32f. For the request: "Give us this bread always" (cf. 4:15), assumes that the people think of the bread of life as a miraculous bread, and not, as had been stated in vv. 32f. as the one *katabainōn ek t. our.* Vv. 34–35, by contrast, form a unit in themselves' (p. 220). In other words, to allow vss. 30–33 to stand between vss. 27 and 34f. is to assume that Jesus has been requested to perform a sign — such as providing manna from heaven (vss. 30–31) — in order for them to believe and receive the bread which comes down from heaven (vs. 34). Thus it is a 'meaningless tautology' (n. 4), especially with vss. 28–29 excised.

c) Thus, the unbelieving crowd is given the answer that 'the nature of the bread has been completely misunderstood, ... the Revealer is the bread of life, and that life is promised to faith' (vs. 35, p. 220f.).

d) 'Vv. 36–40 again strike one as somewhat strange; for v. 36 upbraids people for their unbelief. This is uncalled for at the beginning of the discussion, before the question of the believers' assurance of salvation has been discussed in vv. 37–40. But even then vv. 36–40 can hardly be considered the organic and necessary continuation of vv. 34, 35.' Also, vs. 41 is 'quite unmotivated as a direct continuation of vv. 37–40' (p. 221). The murmuring of the Jews must refer back to vs. 33, or better yet, to vs. 51a.

e) As vss. 41–46 form a 'closely-knit unit', and 'as "coming to Jesus" gives the theme of "coming" its organic place within the dialogue, ... vv. 36–40 would doubtless most appropriately follow on vv. 41–46. Even if vv. 47–51a, which characterise the Revealer as the bread of life, are not impossible as they now stand, they still have come post festum; a more suitable place for them would be, for example, after v. 33' (p. 221).

As is obvious from the above reasons for reordering, Bultmann's judgments are neither based upon stylistic *nor* ideological grounds. They may be considered 'contextual', but they are largely subjective ('unmotivated' sequence, 'meaningless tautology', and verses striking one as 'somewhat strange' are not exactly objective criteria devoid of interpretive bias). They are simply presented as evidence for the need of rearrangement, without offering any literary precedent, Johannine or otherwise. While some allowance for disordering and reordering is certainly tenable, the more complex the process the less convincing the theory becomes. Therefore, Bultmann's new set of solutions also has its own set of new problems.

1. The first problem with Bultmann's new (original) sequence is that it assumes vs. 34f. follows vs. 27 *better* than vs. 28f. Actually, there is a very high degree of continuity between vss. 33 and 34f., and between vss. 27 and 28f. The injunction, 'Work (*ergazesthe*) ... for the food (*brōsin*) which endures unto eternal life ...' (vs. 27) is followed quite appropriately by the question, 'What must we do in order to work (*ergazōmetha*) the works of God?' (vs. 28). Similarly, it is not at all unreasonable that vs. 33, 'For the bread (*artos*) of God is that which comes (the one coming) down from heaven.' should be followed by the request, 'Lord, give us this bread (*arton*) always' (vs. 34). *Arton* (vs. 34) follows *brōsin* (vs. 27) less well than

it follows *artos* (vs. 33), and *ergazōmetha* (vs. 28) follows *ergazesthe* (vs. 27) with clear continuity. Therefore, neither in the reconstructed *Offenbarungsreden* (above) nor in the 'restored' order proposed by Bultmann, is the following of vs. 27 by vss. 34f. a superior choice thematically *or* linguistically.

2. It cannot be claimed with such certainty that people *have* understood Jesus correctly and are willing to believe in him in vs. 28, while in vs. 34 they do not understand. This sequence would be illogical. It is likely, and indeed probable, that in *both* vss. 28 and 34 those reported to have been fed by Jesus the day before are now being portrayed as seeking bread, the supply of which supposedly lasts forever (vs. 27) and comes down from the sky (vs. 33) like manna from heaven (vss. 31–32). Even though people are willing to do what they must in order to acquire this 'heavenly' bread, they *have not understood* that 'what they are looking for is present in his person' (p. 225). Thus, rather than a 'meaningless tautology' (p. 220, n. 4) we have in John 6:26–35 a clear example of *the Johannine misunderstanding motif*. The people desire bread, but have difficulty seeing that Jesus is the *true* Bread. This misunderstanding is confirmed by vs. 36 (*heōrakate [me] kai ou pisteuete*), and it is a portrayal of the 'paradox' of revelation and its hiddenness (p. 227). Humanity sees the outward vehicle of revelation but fails to perceive its content. The passage is laced with irony through and through.

3. Bultmann is quite right to point out that 'the bread come down from heaven' alludes most directly to vss. 33 and 35. However, the '*kata apo tou ouranou*' theme is brought out again in vs. 38 and developed further in vss. 39–40. In his correct summation of the christological content of vs. 35, Bultmann obliterates most of the thematic evidence marshalled in support of his restored order theory:

> The whole paradox of the revelation is contained in this reply. Whoever wants something from him must know that he has to receive Jesus *himself.* Whoever approaches him with the desire for the gift of life must learn that Jesus is *himself* the gift he really wants. Jesus *gives* the bread of life in that he *is* the bread of life. ... Whoever wishes to receive life from him must therefore believe in him — or, as it is figuratively expressed must "come to him". (p. 227)

As Bultmann has interpreted the meaning of vs. 35 correctly, this statement must also be considered a summary of what appears to be the thematic progression of the very order of the verses he tries to correct. a) Those who have had their stomachs filled by Jesus the day before (6:1–15) come after him, seeking another feeding (22–25). b) Jesus explains the true nature and origin of that bread which nourishes unto eternal life (26–35). c) Because people still do not believe in him (as the living Bread from heaven), Jesus declares the absolute need for divine assistance if humanity is to be enabled to come to and believe in Jesus (36–47). d) Ultimately, however, each person must decide individually to receive the revelation of God in Jesus, and this is referred to as 'eating' the bread which is Jesus' flesh, given for the life of the world (48–51 and 'drinking' his blood, in vss. 53ff.). For this reason, it is difficult to understand the need for Bultmann's disordering/reordering work. There are no unduly troublesome literary breaks in sequence or aporias in 6:26–51, and thematically, the progression seems preferable to, or at least as good as, the one offered by Bultmann. Ironically, Bultmann's interpretation of vs. 35 confirms *not* the presence of an alien source, but the integrity of the discourse as a *unitive* construction. Thus, based upon stylistic, formal, linguistic, and thematic evidence, Bultmann's attempt to restore the 'original' order to John 6:27–71 is entirely unconvincing. As D.M. Smith (*Composition*, p. 152) concludes about John 6:

> I ... do not claim to have solved all of the problems of this perplexing chapter, but I think I have shown that Bultmann's attempts to solve them through rearrangement and excision involve him in problems of equal, if not greater difficulty. It is my view that the text may be interpreted with sufficient clarity and coherence to warrant leaving it as it is. Its incongruities or inconsistencies may be attributed to the evangelist as easily as to the redactor. They are perhaps a sign of the gulf that separates our ways of thinking from his.

The remaining factor to be considered is Bultmann's identification of the evangelist's editorial contributions. These *are* distinguishable stylistically and linguistically, and Bultmann has tailored his argument in such a way that the '... distinct characteristics of the evangelist's hand become the negative criteria for the identification of the sources' (Smith, p. 9). Therefore, before a final attempt can be made to evaluate Bultmann's literary criteria upon which his source assignments have been made, one must first consider his treatment of the evangelist's contribution.

C. *The Contribution of the Evangelist*

According to D.M. Smith (p. 9), Bultmann's belief that the sources underlying John can be identified is 'logically prior to his gathering of stylistic characteristics'. This explains at least part of the reason for his style-critical approach to John 6, despite the apparent unity of the chapter. Bultmann's wrestling with the implications of unitive and disunitive issues may be observed in his earlier treatment of the Prologue (1923, cf. Ashton, pp. 18–35) and in his consideration of A. Faure's work on Jesus' signs (*ZNW* 21, 1922, pp. 99–121; cf. esp. Jn. 2:1–11; 4:46–54; etc.; Bultmann, p. 113, n. 2; also pp. 204–209). His work on the Synoptic tradition, in which Mark serves as a narrative source, and Q serves as a sayings source for Matthew and Luke, also has been formative in Bultmann's diachronic approach to John's composition. Therefore, even though it cannot be said that all of the literary 'problems' addressed by Bultmann in his treatment of John 6 are as glaring as the sharp relief into which he casts them, his methodology is conceptually sound. If stylistic and linguistic evidence should be gathered in ways which corroborate other source-critical assignments, such evidence could be suggestive of multiple origins of the material. This also explains how Bultmann is able to approach his task *in full awareness* of the literary unity of John, as described in an article written after the publication of his commentary:[10]

---

10 This statement is from Bultmann's 1959 article ('Johannesevangelium', *RGG* 3, pp. 840–

The question about the sources [of John] is ... so difficult to answer because the speech of John seems to be so unified as to give no occasion for partitioning. The unity of speech, however, could have resulted from the evangelist's thorough editing. Close observation also shows considerable differences of speech in different sections, above all between the narrative reports and the speeches and discussions. Furthermore, certain expressions and passages may be recognized which are obviously to be traced back to the evangelist — transitions and explanations which stand out more or less clearly from the sources used.

Therefore, Smith is also correct to assume that any attempt to understand Bultmann's source-critical assignments must begin with an analysis of his identification of the narratological contribution of the evangelist (p. 9). In general terms, the evangelist's contribution is: a) *in prose*, as a contrast to the metric/strophic style of the *Offenbarungsreden*; b) *interpretive and explanatory*, as a contrast to the straightforward narration of the *sēmeia* source; c) *connective*, in the sense of providing transitional, introductory and concluding passages ('bridges') using specialized words and phrases; d) *historicizing*, in the sense that dialogues in the Rabbinic style of debate are constructed from the *Offenbarungsreden* content; e) *supplementary of illustrative chronological and geographical detail*; and f) at times *misunderstanding* the source at hand (6:22–26; 8:44).[11] These are, in Bultmann's opinion, the primary clues suggesting the evangelist's contribution to John 6.

1. The adding of *historicizing detail* in John 6 may be inferred from the editorial comments which accompany the signs narratives and the discussion which follows. Says Bultmann: 'That the Evangelist in 6:1–26 has again used part of a literary source, is shown by his own editorial insertions in v. 4, v. 6, vv. 14f., vv. 23f., and by the not entirely organic relationship of 6:27–59 ... to 6:1–26.' (p. 210) Therefore, the evangelist's 'historicizing' style of connective prose is indicated by such characteristics in John 6 as:

Table 6:
'Bultmann's Identification of the Evangelist's "Connective Prose" in John 6'

1. The reference to ... *to pascha* ... , vs. 4 (p. 211f.)
2. *touto de elegen*, vs. 6 (p. 212, n. 4)
3. *autos gar*, vss. 6, 64 (p. 212, n. 4)
4. The *alla* clause in which the verb follows immediately, vss. 24, 64 (p. 217, n. 4)
5. *hote oun* clause, vs. 24 (p. 217, n. 5)
6. *touto estin ... hina*, vs. 28f. (p. 222, n. 1)
7. The *hina* clause, vss. 30, 50 (pp. 227, n. 5; 229, n. 1)
8. *houtos*, vs. 50 (p. 229, n. 1)
9. Prose style, vss. 49–50 (p. 229, n. 1)
10. The use of *houtos* and *hina* together, vs. 50 (p. 229, n. 2)
11. *estin gegr.*, vs. 45 (p. 231, n. 3)

---

850), in which he offers a terse summary of this composition theory and theological interpretation of John. The citation is from p. 848f. and represents D.M. Smith's fitting translation (p. 3f.).

12. The 'prefatory negative', vss. 46, 38 (pp. 232, n. 3; 233, n. 3)
13. The neuter *pan* (versus vs. 45a), (p. 233, n. 2)
14. *hina echein zōēn aiōnion*, vs. 40 (p. 233, n. 6)
15. The mention of the setting at the end of a scene (Capernaum), vs. 59 (p. 234, n. 1)

While Bultmann contends that these indicators of style distinguish the evangelist's writing from other literary sources in John (p. 212, n. 4), such a claim is problematic. On one hand, he *has* identified correctly the narratological contributions of an author who makes connections between the topic at hand and similar themes elsewhere (vss. 28f., 31, 45, 50) and who makes interpretive references to the intentions of actants and the outcomes of events (vss. 6, 13f., 30, 40, 50 etc.). However, this does not prove that these were the evangelist's redactional interpolations into, or connections between, earlier written sources. They could just as easily have been the evangelist's commentary upon his own stories, intrinsic to his way of recounting the gospel narrative. Nor does the identification of the narrator's style and contribution say anything about whence he acquired his narrative content or the material underlying the dialogues and discourses of John 6.

It may be assumed that the First and Third Evangelists have also intended to be graphic and convincing, but in their redactions of Mark 6 and 8 they actually include *less* non-symbolic, illustrative ('historicizing') detail (cf. discussion below in Chapter 8) than does Mark, and far less than John 6. Therefore, the closest literary parallels (Matthew and Luke) argue *against* Bultmann's notion that the 'historicizing' and interpretive detail in John 6 represents the interpolative work of the evangelist. In both Mark and John these details appear to be carry-overs from the oral stages of their traditions.

2. Regarding the *interpretive* sections (vss. 6, 14f., 23f., 66, etc.) there is nothing *a priori* problematic with these comments being intrinsic to an earlier tradition, or at least to a singular source. The suggestion that Jesus left the crowd to get away from their designs on his future sounds even more reasonable than the somewhat pietistic Synoptic version, that he went off into the mountains to pray. And, vss. 23f. could be an obvious reference to the confusion of members of the crowd, who were anxious to see Jesus, *especially* if they were perceiving him as a king or even a prophet like Moses.[12] If this were the case, their difficulty with letting go of their

---

11 Cf. D.M. Smith (p. 7f., and esp. notes 26–34). While Smith has identified at least 63 stylistic characteristics of the evangelist's work (pp. 9–11), and at least 13 theological motifs and kinds of terminology employed by the evangelist (p. 11f.), the following discussion in the text will only involve three of the main stylistic characteristics ascribed to the evangelist: the presence of 'historicizing' detail, the adding of interpretive comments, and various theological motifs suggesting the evangelist's authorship.

12 Given Bultmann's analysis that, 'V. 15 shows that the "prophet who comes into the world" is not a forerunner of salvation but the bringer of salvation himself, for the people believe that the "prophet" must be king. ... Windisch ... thinks that the judgment of the people is based on the old belief in the magic powers of the king' (p. 213f., n. 7), it seems that the evangelist

manna-type expectations would be perfectly understandable, and the abandonment of Jesus by *even* some of his 'followers' may reflect the insights of one who was closer to the original events than Bultmann allows. These verses are not necessarily bridges between two otherwise unrelated pieces of literature. They could just as easily have been germane to the Johannine tradition itself, even at a fairly early stage of its development.

It is thus hard to imagine how a narrative *sēmeia* source could have been so innocent of reflective and interpretive material as Bultmann, Fortna and others argue. Whether the content of a story is historical or fictional in its origin, the main function of telling a story is to interpret it in a way which adds meaning to the present and a prospect for the future. Virtually all narration serves this function, and this implies the accompaniment of interpretive commentary. It is also hard to imagine how the Fourth Evangelist would have written his own story *without* inserting interpretive comments along the way. The interpretive process begins *as soon as* (or bettter yet, *because*) *an event or a narrative image is perceived to have been significant.* Therefore, to say that interpretive comments must have been added by a third hand is *non-sequitur*. Interpretive additions could have been made quite late in the tradition, or they could represent earlier commentaries on the perceived significance of events. Either way, the comments deserve to be considered intrinsically germane to the Johannine tradition unless the converse is convincingly demonstrable. To identify a comment as 'interpretive' says nothing about its authorship. All it suggests is that the comment betrays the fact that a narrator has attributed meaning to an event, and this could just as easily represent the running commentary of the evangelist upon his own story or tradition.

3. The *theological* interests of the evangelist in John 6, as suggested by Bultmann, provide the strongest evidence for distinguishing the évangelist's contributions from the material of his sources. For instance, Bultmann *is* correct to identify the evangelist's work in such passages as vss. 6, 14f., 26 and 34 (pp. 212–214). In vs. 6 the evangelist exposes his interpretation of the feeding as being a sign which will 'test' Jesus' followers, and this is confirmed in vss. 26 and 34. These interpretive comments pivot around the evangelist's understanding of the significance of the feeding. It is a *sign*, intended to reveal something about God through the one whom he has sent, and it is not just a wondrous, thaumaturgic feeding (vs. 26). Thus:

> In John ... the miracles are closely related to the history of the Revealer. They are *sēmeia* in a special sense (see v. 26) and so compel men to take their stand for or against the Revealer. Vv. 14f. therefore have been added by the Evangelist. Now we see clearly, what had only been hinted at in 2:24: the crowd misunderstand the *sēmeion*, as Jesus expressly tells them (v. 26); they want to make Jesus a Messianic king. ... Just as in vv. 26, 34 the crowd expect the bringer of salvation to fulfil their natural desires and longings, so too in vv. 14f. they see

---

stands over and against this messianic interpretation of a prophet-king (cf. H. Montefiore, 'Revolt in the Desert?', *NTS* 8, 1962, pp. 135–141). This being the case, vss. 60–66 stand *with* the other interpretive verses (6, 14f. and 23), and these reflect primitive interpretations within a unitive tradition.

him as a king whose kingdom is "of this world" (18:36); indeed they themselves want to "make" him king. Jesus resists such pressure. (p. 213f.)

As in the cases of the other means of identifying the evangelist's style of editorial commenting upon the narrative of John 6, Bultmann is entirely correct to judge these comments as central to the evangelist's theological slant. It does not follow, however, that this implies different authorship by a later writer. Indeed, if the tradition underlying John 6 is independent from, and yet parallel to, the tradition underlying Mark (p. 210, esp. n. 4), such a tradition must have had its own interpretive *and* theological slant. Put conversely, given that underlying John 6 and Mark 6 are two parallel, yet independent, traditions, both reporting what appear to have been a roughly common set of events, it would be highly unlikely that there was *ever* a time when these traditions were identically parallel, or even uniform.[13]

Therefore, while Bultmann has identified correctly the style and contribution of the evangelist, the question is whether or not these findings are significant. This implies nothing about the tradition being alien to the evangelist's contribution, as opposed to his own material which he interprets in his own way. At most, the identification of the evangelist's nuance points to his central concerns and facilitates a better understanding of how the content of the Gospel is communicated by means of its literary structure and form. At least, it *belabours the obvious*: John was written by a narrator who interpreted the works and words of Jesus existentially, and thus contrastingly to the more thaumaturgic tradition underlying Mark.

Findings

This analysis of Bultmann's treatment of the stylistic and literary unity of John 6, makes several things clear: 1. The stylistic and linguistic character of John 6 is fundamentally uniform. Not only is the *sēmeia* source material in 'Semitising Greek', but so is the rest of the chapter ... *and* the rest of the Gospel for that matter. Also, the style of the *Offenbarungsreden* source is virtually non-distinguishable

---

13 Despite the current popularity of various source and redaction hypotheses, the burden of proof still rests upon the diachronic theorist. A cardinal weakness of the *sēmeia* source hypothesis has to do with its 'double independence'. It assumes (in both Bultmann's and Fortna's renditions) that not only is the basic narrative independent from Mark, but so is the interpretation — which had to have been added by a different author. It is the necessity of the latter assumption which poses the greatest obstacle for the long-term credibility of the source hypothesis. In other words, if John contains a great deal of historically authentic-yet-independent tradition (as the largely unanswered *magnum opus* of C.H. Dodd, *Historical Tradition in the Fourth Gospel*, Cambridge, 1965, has argued), and if John's interpretation also differs significantly from that of the pre-Synoptic tradition, the posing of an independent source becomes superfluous. A more tenable hypothesis assumes that the four Gospels are 'bi-optic', with two based upon Mark, and with John standing alone. The implications of such a possibility will be explored briefly in Chapters 8–10.

from the discourse material of the evangelist. Therefore, Bultmann's assignments to this source are often based upon negative criteria, assuming the presence of the evangelist's redactional work, which is itself a flawed assumption. As D.M. Smith has observed, 'the identification or separation of sources is the obverse of the identification of the work of the evangelist' (p. 15). Thus, the stylistic and linguistic evidence for two sources underlying John 6 is imperceptible.

2. There are still good reasons for seeking to identify underlying sources in John, however, and the Synoptic hypothesis is the closest parallel for two redactional conflations of a narrative source (Mark) and a sayings source (Q) into gospel forms (Matthew and Luke). Thus, form-critical analysis is rightly used by Bultmann in his attempt to identify John's sources. However, the metric/strophic character of the material underlying the Prologue seems more difficult to identify in John 6, and an elaborate disordering and speculative reordering scheme must be hypothesized in order to 'get' the *Offenbarungsreden* material into a meaningful sequence. Source-critical distinctions are aided by the inference of mutually exclusive ideological postures for each source, and this allows much of the discourse content to be attributable to the evangelist, rather than the source. Likewise, the narrative section 6:60–71 is distinguished from the *sēmeia* source on the assumption that while its form may be similar (identical?) to 6:1–13, its ideology stresses the 'way of the cross', rather than the 'wonder of the signs'. Such a judgment can only be made, however, if the testing motif central to vss. 1–26 be excised.

3. The one certain contribution identified by Bultmann is that of the evangelist, but the question is whether or not this is significant. To say that John 6 was composed by an author using interpretive comments and connective phrases says nothing about the origin of his material, especially when its style is so uniform. If the *sēmeia* source represents a tradition parallel to Mark, there is nothing to be gained by assuming that the bulk of its 'interpretive colour' was added later, and by another author. John's may have been a later, yet 'bi-optic', account, parallel to Mark's gospel. Thus, the one *certain* source identified by Bultmann on the basis of style is the contribution of the evangelist, but this does little more than belabour the obvious: John 6 was written by an author who interpreted the gospel narrative independently from the Synoptic tradition.

4. While a close scrutiny of Bultmann's literary approach to John 6 seems to produce largely negative results, this is not entirely the case. Too often, scholars have treated Bultmann's work deconstructively but have failed to benefit from his incisive, critical work. Therefore, even if one does not find his stylistic analysis convincing, one may still employ some of his insights for future constructions: a) Bultmann is entirely correct in his observation that vss. 6, 14f., 26, 34, and 66 represent the interpretive work of the evangelist, and an exploration of the ideological inclination of these (and other) verses will contribute key insights to a genuine understanding of the evangelist's intention, even if it be found that John 6 is more of a literary unity than Bultmann assumes. b) The insight that vs. 27 is

the starting-point of the 'Bread of Life' discourse may also yield rich interpretive rewards. This would especially be the case if it were found that Borgen's identification of vs. 31 as the opening 'text' for the 'homily' may be an inferior choice to the 'exhortation of the two ways' (life and death), beginning with vs. 27, and closing with the unfortunate choice of *even* some of Jesus' followers (vs. 66).

c) Bultmann's form-critical judgments regarding the literary functions of the narrative sections and the dialogue/discourse sections of John 6 will also contribute to a better understanding of the intended reader-response of the Johannine audience. The narration of story calls for all hearers/readers to respond with openness to the essential truth conveyed by the narrative, while the form of the stylized Rabbinic debate/discourse is always designed to convince a particular audience of a more specific point rhetorically. These and other gleanings from Bultmann's contribution will be explored in the exegesis of John 6 in Part III.

Chapter 5

The Relationship Between
Sign and Discourse in John 6

Lest it be concluded that a critique of Bultmann's stylistic analysis of the material in John 6 is convincing on its own, it should be remembered that Bultmann never claimed to base his judgments on stylistic criteria alone. Rather, his judgments are based upon contextual and theological evidence as well, and critiques of his stylistic analyses have often missed some of the more significant foundation stones supporting his literary constructs. Thus, rather than base his composition theory upon a single mode of analysis, Bultmann uses various criteria in ways which offer 'mutual support and confirmation' (Smith, p. 78).[1] Therefore, the focus of this chapter will be to analyze Bultmann's *contextual bases* for his diachronic approach to John 6.

The main implication of Bultmann's contextual evidence marshalled in John 6 is his contention that there is no traditional connection between sign and discourse in John, but that the feeding and the 'Bread of Life' discourses have been woven together by the synthesizing work of the evangelist. Thus, the interpretation of the feeding did *not* accompany the earlier tradition, but was added by the evangelist in its later stages. According to Bultmann:

> It must now be clear in what sense the events in 6:1–25 were *sēmeia*. Of course the way v. 26 is related to v. 25 has already shown that the transition to the dialogue is artificial, so that the dialogue has no real bearing on the situation produced by 6:1–25. Indeed the way the Evangelist links vv. 27ff. with the previous events is most awkward, inasmuch as it is difficult to see why, after what has already happened, the crowd in vv. 30f. should ask for a miracle (and [at] that a feeding miracle!) as a proof of his authority, when the feeding miracle which occurred in vv. 14f. would have served that purpose. Clearly the Evangelist ignores the external situation and uses the feeding miracle, which he takes from the source,

---

1 The interwoven relationship between Bultmann's use of stylistic, contextual and ideological criteria is described nicely by Smith. The entire passage is as follows:

> While Bultmann's insight into the separation of sources from the work of the evangelist on the basis of the study of the relation of elements in the same context to one another is logically prior to his gathering of stylistic characteristics, the latter, when assembled, confirm the initial findings and in turn become independent criteria. With the development of stylistic criteria for the evangelist, portions of the gospel which are not original with him become more easily discernible. The distinct characteristics of the evangelist's hand become negative criteria for the identification of the sources. (p. 9)

as a symbolic picture for the main idea of the revelation discourse, namely that Jesus gives the bread of life. (p. 218)

In this paragraph so characteristically terse and pregnant with implications, Bultmann describes some of the most important contextual evidence for distinguishing between the material of the evangelist and that of his sources. A digest of this paragraph suggests three main points: a) It is quite odd that Jesus should accuse the crowd of seeking him not because they have seen the signs, but because they have had their fill of the loaves, in response to the crowd's question, '*When* did you get here?'. b) It also seems odd that the very day after witnessing a sign (the feeding) the crowd should ask for *another* sign as a proof of Jesus' identity (indeed the *same* sign, vs. 30) before committing themselves to believing in him. c) And, it seems that the 'Bread of Life' discourses may have 'no real bearing' on the feeding narrative, according to Bultmann, but address humanity's need for spiritual nourishment, which takes the narrative in a completely different direction, in contrast to vss. 1–25. Therefore, these three 'contextual' problems will be addressed in the remainder of this chapter.

A. *The Problem of Jesus' Answer*

It does seem odd that in response to the question, '*When* did you get here?' Jesus seems to have completely ignored the question and answered another one instead. Bultmann's solution is to suggest it betrays an uneasy relationship between the evangelist and his source, thus indicating an *editorial seam*. Says Bultmann:

> Thus by one means or another we get the situation of v. 25 as it was given in the source, and the question *pote hōde gegonas*? can now be asked.
>
> It is most unlikely that the account in the source ended with this question. But the Evangelist has left out the original conclusion and replaced it by v. 26. Jesus' reply gives no answer to the question, but accuses the crowd of seeking him because they experienced the miraculous feeding, and — as is obviously implied — because they hope to experience more such miracles from him. (p. 217)

Bultmann obviously believes the original ending to the sign narrative (vss. 1–25; the feeding and sea crossing should be taken as one sign, cf. p. 112, n. 1) must have contained a more fitting response by Jesus, and perhaps some attestation that the crowd believed in him because of his signs (Jn. 2:11; 4:51–53; cf. pp. 113, 208f.). Therefore, 'Like the unsuspecting *architriklinos* of 2:9f., or the uninformed servants of 4:51f., so here the *ochlos* which had been elsewhere at the time of the miracle must be called as witnesses to it' (p. 217; see also Bultmann's *The History of the Synoptic Tradition*, Oxford, 1963, pp. 224ff.). The original ending of the story, therefore, was probably in keeping with the attestation-emphasis of the typical miracle narratives, which served as the main body of the *sēmeia* source. And yet, vs. 26 corrects this perspective. Rather than following the *theios anēr* christological inclination of the source, the evangelist has steered the emerging discussion in another direction, in keeping with his distinctive theological slant.

So far so good. Bultmann's argument makes sense, and its implications also make it rather appealing: the 'problem of Jesus' answer' actually betrays an editorial seam, which also reflects an ideological shift between the christology of the evangelist and that of his source. Therefore, contextual 'evidence' supports Bultmann's diachronic theory of composition. However, there are two serious problems with this view.

1. The first problem is that it makes the evangelist seem like an overly-poor editor. If he was already replacing the conclusion, why not also replace the crowd's question with a better one? If he had wanted to stress an ideological difference more clearly, he could have added something like, 'Who is this, that even the wind and the waves should obey him?' (Mk. 4:41); or, 'Yes, Lord, we believe and know that you can feed multitudes — with more to spare — if you should only choose to!' (Mk. 8:17–21). Then the Johannine Jesus could have given a clinching repartee, such as, 'Is it not enough that I *calm my followers* in the troubled waters of life, and yet you would have me command authority over nature as well?'; or, 'Have you not understood the meaning of the loaves? It is not food for your stomachs that matters, but nourishment for your souls that counts for eternity!'. Or, if the evangelist had wanted to make his point more subtly, he simply could have omitted vs. 25 altogether and followed ... *zētountes ton Iēsoun.* (vs. 24) with ... *zēteite me ouch hoti eidete sēmeia, all'* ... (vs. 26). This would have followed much more smoothly and directly. If the evangelist were really trying to do what Bultmann is arguing — in the way he suggests — he certainly could have done a better job of it.

2. The second problem is that Bultmann's inference of this aporia is totally dependent upon the assumption that vss. 25–26 are meant to be taken purely in a straightforward, literalistic way. However, if the evangelist has been able to make a 'play on words' with *sēmeia* as 'miracles' and *sēmeion* as a *vehicle of revelation* (p. 218), one must ponder whether the evangelist might also have employed the crowd's question and Jesus' answer as an *ironic conversation* in order to make *the same ideological point suggested by Bultmann.*

It indeed seems entirely ironic that the crowd, after having been fed the day before, should ask 'how long' Jesus had been there. The Johannine audience would most certainly have understood the implicit question: 'How long have you been here? ... And, *how long* will it be *till lunch?*' Even if the note of amazement at Jesus' arrival (vs. 25) is in reference to the sea crossing, this detail adds emphasis to the crowd's anticipation of Jesus' *next* 'sign'. It is likely that John's audience would have understood the uneven transition as follows: 'The crowd say they are astonished at Jesus' arrival, but you and I know that they are most impressed with *what they might get out of* their next meeting with Jesus.' Their motivation for seeking Jesus is reminiscent of Dr. Johnson's definition of 'gratitude'. It is 'a lively sense of favours still to come' (cited by W. Barclay, *John* Vol. 1, Edinburgh, 1955, p. 209).

Thus, it is entirely likely that the uneasy transition of vs. 25 to vs. 26 reflects the use of *apparent lack of continuity* in order to emphasize the *continuous underlying motif*: that despite the crowd's seeking another handout, such is not the *bread* which truly satisfies. It is *Jesus himself* who is the 'Bread of Life'. The subtle irony of the transition would thus alert the attentive hearer/reader to the main message of the story. It is not only in 6:25f. that this device is used by the evangelist. P. Duke has detected many examples of 'local irony' in John,[2] through which ' the author of the Fourth Gospel creates his power out of the silence. In the hush that follows the ironic word is the invitation to ponder and leap to new dimensions of meaning' (p. 91). Explaining some of the characteristics of John's use of local irony, Duke concludes:

> The author quite often gets at his irony by way of *questions*. No less than twenty of the texts considered contain questions, five of them intentionally ironic by Jesus (3:10; 7:23; 10:32; 13:38; 16:31), fifteen of them unintentionally ironic by others (1:46; 4:12; 6:42; 7:15, 26, 35–36, 41b–42, 47, 48, 52a; 8:22, 53, 58; 9:27; 16:17–18). As is irony's way, these questions tend to be left *unanswered*. Only five of the twenty questions receive direct reply (7:15; 8:58; 9:27; 10:32; 16:17–18). Furthermore, of the ironic remarks made in declarative form, eleven (of nineteen) receive no specific response (2:10; 7:20, 28, 52b; 8:48, 52; 11:16, 48; 12:19; 16:29; 18:30). (pp. 90–91)

While Duke has missed the ironic character of the question in 6:25f., he has identified the ironic character of the question asked by the Samaritan woman in 4:15 (pp. 102, 183 n.14) as well as the ironic exclamation of the steward in 2:10 (pp. 83–84) — both being incidents to which Bultmann connects 6:25f. It is highly ironic that the crowd should ask how long Jesus had been on the other shore, even if they were also impressed with his mode of transport. Their reason for seeking him was obviously that they wanted a second feeding. They may even have identified him as a new Moses or Joshua who would provide another feeding in the wilderness and/ or lead them in holy war against the Romans. The fact that Jesus has understood their unspoken intention is reflected in his knowing response. Jesus' corrective is then used to further the main interest of the narrative, which is revelational, and christocentrically so.

Another possibility is that Bultmann has treated the evangelist's uses of irony elsewhere in John as contextual aporias, to be understood as indications of other editorial seams. A survey of Bultmann's treatment of the passages in which P. Duke has detected the presence of local irony, however, reveals that this is not the case. With the exception of 11:16, where the evangelist is to have inserted Thomas'

---

2 Duke's monograph (*Irony in the Fourth Gospel*, Atlanta, 1985; cf. pp. 63–94, for examples of 'local irony') is the first full-length treatment on the use of irony in John. Nevertheless, see also excellent treatments of the subject by R.A. Culpepper, *The Anatomy of the Fourth Gospel*, Philadelphia, 1983; D. Wead, 'The Literary Devices in John's Gospel', Dissertation, Basel, 1970; and G. MacRae, 'Theology and Irony in the Fourth Gospel', in *The Word and the World*, ed. R.J. Clifford and G.W. MacRae, Cambridge, Mass., 1973, pp. 83–96.

fatalistic words (Bultmann, p. 400), nowhere in the other 31 passages cited by Duke (pp. 90–91) is an ironic passage in the *sēmeia* source followed by an editorial insertion by the evangelist, according to Bultmann's analysis. Of the 15 ironic questions cited by Duke (*Ibid.*), what is most common is that Bultmann tolerates these as part of the source in which they occur. The ironic question (asked by someone other than Jesus) occurs twice in the *sēmeia* source (1:46; 9:27), and within the work of the evangelist it occurs eight times (6:42; 7:15, 26, 41b–42, 47, 48, 52a; 8:58). Less commonly, Bultmann believes the evangelist has introduced a saying from the *Offenbarungsreden* by means of an ironic question (4:12/13f.; 7:15/16ff.; 8:22/23, 53/54f.) and that in one case he has used an ironic question to follow another one (7:33–34/35–36). Thus, it may not be concluded that Bultmann's treatment of 6:25/26 as a contextual aporia is simply characteristic of his treatment of ironic questions in the text. It should also be said, however, that he seldom recognizes the evangelist's use of irony as a literary technique. Therefore, it is not surprising that he is bothered by such contextual difficulties. The very function of irony is to make a point by *disturbing* the reader with an apparent contradiction, and this was clearly the case in 6:25f. Irony always dislocates one's thought in order to relocate it along another path. Because the evangelist uses both local and extended irony throughout the Gospel, it is entirely probable that the problem of the crowd's question and Jesus' somewhat disjointed answer reflects his use of it in vss. 25–26. If this is so, the contextual evidence of John 6:25f. does not point to an editorial seam between an editor and his source, but to the evangelist's use of irony as a means of engaging the reader in a forward-moving dialogue. As R.A. Culpepper has suggested:

> The "silent" communication between author and reader assumes its most intriguing form in the ironies of the gospel. The implied author smiles, winks and raises his eyebrows as the story is told. The reader who sees as well as hears understands that the narrator means more than he says and that the characters do not understand what is happening or what they are saying. (*Anatomy*, p. 165f.)

B. *The Problem of the Redundant Request*

The second contextual difficulty identified by Bultmann in the transitional passage of 6:25ff. is the problem of the redundant request. It indeed seems odd that the same people who had received bread the day before should not count it as a *sēmeion* worthy of their belief, but they request another sign the very next day. As a contrast to his treatment of the disjointed character of the evangelist's work in vss. 25f., Bultmann asserts that in vss. 27ff., the evangelist would *not* have been the author of such 'poor order' (p. 220). Rather, it must be attributed to the work of a redactor, as the question in vs. 28 is 'unmotivated', and the connection of vs. 30 to the preceding passage is 'only in appearance' (p. 220). Therefore, Bultmann believes that the request for a sign (vss. 30f.) follows best after vs. 35, and he is willing to assume a rather complex history of textual disordering and incorrect rearrangement in order to hold to his interpretive preference that vss. 30ff. should follow vs. 35 *rather than* vs. 29. Thus, he interprets vs. 30 as follows:

> Yet the world when challenged to believe in him demands a *sēmeion* as proof of his authority (v. 30); it wants to see in order to be able to believe (see 4:48; 20:29). By asking *ti ergazē?* it shows its folly to the full. For the work of the Revealer is never a *ti*, a particular *ergon* by which one might recognise him and so believe in him. The Jews demand a miracle, similar to the miracle performed by Moses ... and so they show that they have not understood his words, but still vainly imagine that life is given by physical food (p. 227). This shows the artificiality of the connection between vv. 27ff. and the preceding feeding narrative. (p. 277, n. 6)

Therefore, Bultmann assumes that moving vss. 30–33 *after* vs. 35 removes the difficulty of the redundant request. In this case, the request for a sign would not have been a response to the means of acquiring 'the bread which abides into the age' (vs. 27b), nor to the invitation of Jesus to 'believe in the one he [God] has sent' (vs. 29). Rather, Bultmann argues that the best (only?) way to interpret the crowd's request for a sign is as a response to Jesus' invitation, ' ... the one coming to me will in no way hunger...' (vs. 35b). This sequence portrays the natural reluctance of the world to believe in the Revealer, as opposed to exercising faith, which is itself enabled by God.

Again, Bultmann has identified a contextual difficulty, and has dealt with it in a way that is both appealing and coherent. However, his approach also has its own problems. Aside from the statistical improbability (see above, Chapter 4) that a text should have been disordered in the way Bultmann suggests — let alone reordered so 'incorrectly' — two further problems deserve consideration.

1. The first problem is that vss. 28–29 must be excised if the contextual problem identified by Bultmann is to be considered as problematic as he claims it is.[3] In order to 'create' this contextual difficulty, he claims that vss. 28f. are a 'detached fragment added by the editor after vs. 27 by association with the word *ergazesthai*' (p. 221). Although the question of vs. 28 'has the characteristically Johannine ring of a misunderstanding or failure to understand' (p. 221f.), Bultmann refuses to believe that this could have been its original position in the Gospel. Thus, the editor must have moved vss. 28f. to their present location, and appended vss. 34f. so that 'it was now possible to fit in here the question about Jesus' authority and his answer to it in vv. 30–33' (p. 221 n. 3). The basis for Bultmann's perception of this

---

3 Smith is highly critical of Bultmann's excising of vss. 27bc as redactional, and thus considering 28f. as a displaced fragment:

> As we have noted, Bultmann regards verse 27bc as redactional mainly because of the way the Son of Man title is used. But is this a sufficient reason for excising verse 27bc? The contention that the differing conceptions of the Son of Man indicate different writers is in itself questionable, and Bultmann's arguments are not overwhelming. If there is not sufficient reason for excising verse 27bc as redactional, Bultmann's arguments against verses 51c–58 are dealt a serious blow. (p. 142f.)

particular problem is his questionable assumption that the crowd's query of vs. 28, 'What must we do ... ?' is an indication of the crowd's *willingness* to believe in Jesus (cf. vs. 36!). If the evangelist has indeed crafted the request of the crowd to make an ironic statement in vs. 25, he obviously has done so in vs. 34 (cf. 3:2, 4; 4:11, 15, etc.). Thus, the ironic questions and statements of the crowd in vss. 25, 28, 31f., and 34 point to the *extended* use of irony by the evangelist in the form of the Johannine misunderstanding motif. In doing so they confirm the section's unity, rather than its disunity. Furthermore, it is highly doubtful that Bultmann is correct in assuming that vs. 29 is *not* intended by the evangelist to be an invitation to believe in Jesus, unlike vs. 35, which is. They both seem to be variant expressions of the same theme. Therefore, the 'redundant request' of vs. 28 is not as 'unmotivated after Jesus' injunction in v. 27' as Bultmann believes (p. 220). It bears all the characteristics of the Johannine misunderstanding motif,[4] which the evangelist uses in all the dialogue sections of John 6 in order to prepare the way for the christological interpretation of Jesus as the true 'Bread of Life'.

---

4 It indeed seems odd that, while Bultmann says on p. 127, n. 1, 'The device of the misunderstanding occurs again and again throughout the Gospel: 2:20; 3:3f.; 4:10ff., 32f.; 6:32ff.; 7:34ff.; 14:4f., 7ff., 22ff.; 16:17f. ... ', he disallows its inference in 6:25–31. This is particularly odd, given his citation of parallels between John 6:26ff. and John 3:1ff. (p. 230, n. 1) and 4:3ff. (p. 219f.). The above note betrays Bultmann's failure to make a distinction between people's *failure to understand* (2:20; 7:34ff.; 14:4f., 7ff., 22ff.; and 16:17f., etc.) and the *Johannine misunderstanding dialogue* (see the six examples below). While the simple failure to understand plays a facilitative role in the progression of the narrative, the extended dialogues in which Jesus' discussants misunderstand a particular aspect of his teaching or mission all lead into a climactic statement by Jesus, which serves a distinctively rhetorical function. Thus, the typical form of a Johannine misunderstanding dialogue is as follows:

a) *The setting is described* (3:1–2a; 4:1–8, 27–30; 6:22–24; 13:1–5; 18:28–32).

b) *Individuals or groups ask Jesus a question* or *make a request or statement*, revealing a subtle clue to the discussants' misunderstanding (3:2b; 4:9, 31; 6:25; 13:6; 18:33).

c) *Jesus responds*, making some *corrective remark* about the true character of the Kingdom, his mission, God's work, etc. (3:3; 4:10, 32; 6:26f.; 13:7; 18:34).

d) *The discussants make further comments* which betray their continued lack of understanding more clearly, building the ironic tension in the narrative (3:4, 9; 4:11f., 15, 17, 19f., 33; 6:28, 30f., 34; 13:8a, 9; 18:35, 37a).

e) *Jesus' final response launches into a discourse*, clarifying the spiritual meaning of the topic under discussion — usually a christocentric elaboration upon the 'true' character of the Kingdom, his mission, God's work, life in the Spirit, etc. (3:5–8, 10–21; 4:21–24, 34–38; 6:35–40; 13:8b–20; 18:37bc).

See also, D.A. Carson, 'Understanding Misunderstandings in the Fourth Gospel', *TB* 33, 1982, pp. 59–91; M. de Jonge, 'Nicodemus and Jesus: Some Observations on Misunderstanding and Understanding in the Fourth Gospel', *BJRL* 53, 1971, pp. 337–359; J. Becker, *Das Evangelium nach Johannes* Vol. 1, Gütersloh, 1979, p. 135f.; Brown, p. 136f.; E. Richard, 'Expressions of Double Meaning and their Function in the Gospel of John', *NTS* 31, 1985, pp. 96–112. For the rhetorical significance of this literary form see Ch. 9, below.

2. A second problem with Bultmann's solution to the contextual difficulty of the redundant request is that it assumes too readily that vss. 30f. follow vs. 35 rather than vs. 29. In other words, as vss. 30ff. represent the world's demand for a sign before they believe in Jesus (p. 227), Bultmann contends that the challenge, 'What sign do you show, that we might see and believe?' follows Jesus' invitation to 'come to' and 'believe in' him (vs. 35) rather than following vs. 29, where Jesus also invites them to believe in him. Again, this is only possible if vss. 28f. have been excised as a redactional insertion. If, however, the section is written in the form of a Johannine misunderstanding dialogue/discourse, in which the crowd's request for *another* sign (vs. 30) is portrayed as even more ironic than their deflective question in vs. 25, then there is no justification for excising vss. 28f., and vs. 30 follows vs. 29 perfectly well. That Bultmann *recognizes* the irony of vs. 30 is confirmed by his remark that, 'By asking *ti ergazē*? it [the world] shows its folly to the full' (p. 227). Therefore, the crowd's request for a sign is portrayed as a challenge to Jesus, designed to 'tempt' him into providing more bread (cf. Matt. 4:1–11; Lk 4:1–13). It need not, therefore, be considered redundant, and thus superfluous. Rather, it follows very compatibly with their perception of him as a prophet like Moses (vs. 14f.). It is motivated by their reason for seeking him — the receiving of more loaves (vss. 22–26; cf. Mk. 6:25; 8:11–14). As a means of motivating Jesus to do another miracle, they challenge him with the story of Moses (vs. 30f.). There is a high degree of logical continuity in this progression, and Bultmann's claim that the transition is 'most awkward' (p. 218) does not provide convincing contextual evidence to require the high degree of textual disruption he advocates.

It is also interesting that Bultmann's means of gathering evidence for his diachronic scheme in these two instances (vss. 25f., 28f.) is inconsistent. In vs. 25f. the evangelist's rough transition must be explained as his editing of a source. However, in vss. 27ff. the order of an otherwise fluent text must be altered (vss. 28f. *excised*) in order to illuminate a problem, which supposedly calls for the reordering of vss. 30f., 32f., and 34f. Whether contextual difficulties are suggested by rough transitions, or glossed over by smooth ones, Bultmann is very happy to propose a diachronic solution to *his* detection of a contextual difficulty. Such moves weaken the validity of his results.

C. *The Discontinuity between Sign and Discourse*

While Bultmann's treatments of the above contextual difficulties are hardly arguable by bringing into sharp relief the rough transitions of 6:25/26 and 6:28f./30f., Bultmann's third objection is even more difficult to sustain on the basis of a single, contextual transition. In the paragraph quoted at the beginning of this chapter, Bultmann has asserted that:

> The dialogue has no real bearing on the situation produced in 6:1–25. ... Clearly the Evangelist ignores the external situation and uses the feeding miracle, which he takes from

the source, as a symbolic picture for the main idea of the revelation discourse, namely that Jesus gives the bread of life. (p. 218)

In other words, while 6:1–25 have their literary origin in the record of the *sēmeia* source, vss. 26–71 have theirs in the creative work of the evangelist (co-opting the 'Bread of Life' discourse within the *Offenbarungsreden* source) and the redactor. Bultmann is obviously correct in saying that vss. 26ff. reflect discourses which interpret and develop the meaning of the events in vss. 1–25. However, this observation alone says nothing about the literary character of vss. 1–25, let alone the conflation of literary sources. What Bultmann is arguing, however, is that the relationship of the Johannine signs and their interpretation must have come late in the history of the tradition, and that it must reflect an external, literary dialogue between a source and the evangelist. This is problematic for two reasons: a) It assumes that the *sēmeia* source material underlying John 6 had no, or very little, interpretive material along with it. b) It assumes that the rest of John 6 is merely a later reflection upon the events of 6:1–25, having no intrinsic relationship to vss. 1–25, other than the synthesizing work of the evangelist. Both of these assumptions are highly problematic.

1. The first problem is that the *sēmeia* source should be so similar to the Synoptic accounts — and especially Mark 6 and 8 — and yet so abrupt and non-reflective in its ending. According to Bultmann:

> The tradition used here is the same as in Mk. 6:30–51, which also combines the miracles of the feeding of the multitude and the walking on the sea, whereas in Mk. 8:1–10 a variant of the feeding story appears on its own. In fact the agreement between Jn. 6:1–26 and Mk. 6:30–51, both in the construction of the narrative and in matters of detail, is very considerable. Yet even here we find characteristic divergences. ... Since these divergences should be attributed to the source, rather than to the Evangelist himself, he cannot have used Mk. as his source [Quite certainly he did not use Mt. or Lk. (n. 4)]. This becomes much clearer in the story of the walking on the lake. The source used by John seems to come from an earlier stage in the tradition, since the motifs of the stilling of the storm and of the disciples' lack of understanding (Mk. 6:52) are missing. ... The most obvious inference to draw is that the Evangelist has taken the section from the *sēmeia*-source. (210f.)

Bultmann is indeed correct to identify the similarities between John 6:1–25 and Mark 6:30–51 (and surrounding contexts) as being parallel traditional accounts of the same 'events' which have developed along different lines. However, the traditions themselves are not 'the same', as suggested by the significant divergences *at every turn*. Similarities and divergences (/ indicates differences between the Marcan and Johannine accounts; — indicates similarities) between Mark's and John's accounts are as follows:

Table 7:
'Similarities *and* Divergences Between John 6 and Mark 6'

    a) Having crossed the sea — to a solitary place/to ascend a mountain (Mk. 6:32; Jn. 6:1, 3),

    b) Jesus and his disciples are — met by/followed by — a large crowd (Mk. 6:33; Jn. 6:2);

    c) Jesus — is moved with pity because they are as 'sheep without a shepherd', and he begins to teach them/lifts up his eyes to see the great crowd coming to him (Mk. 6:34; Jn. 6:5a).

d) Jesus speaks to — his disciples/Philip (Mk. 6:37a; Jn. 6:5b)

e) ... about providing — something to eat/loaves for the crowd to eat (Mk. 6:37b; Jn. 6:5c).

f) The disciples ask if they should buy 200 denarii-worth of loaves to feed them/Philip exclaims that 200 denarii would not buy enough loaves for each to have even a little (Mk. 6:37c; Jn. 6:7).

g) Five loaves and two fishes are — produced/contributed by a lad and brought to Jesus (Mk. 6:38; Jn. 6:8f.).

h) Jesus has them sit down in the — green/plentiful — grass, being about 5,000 men (Mk. 6:39, 44; Jn. 6:10).

i) Jesus takes the loaves (and fishes), — blesses them/gives thanks (Mk. 6:41a; Jn. 6:11a),

j) ... and — gives them to his disciples to distribute/distributes them — to the crowd (Mk. 6:41b; Jn. 6:11b).

k) The crowd — 'ate and were satisfied'/(omitted here, but central to Jesus' later *rebuke*) 'ate the loaves and were satisfied' (Mk. 6:42; Jn. 6.26).

l) After the crowd had eaten, the disciples gather 12 full baskets — of fragments and of the fishes/of the five barley loaves (Mk. 6:42f.; Jn. 6:12f.).

m) Jesus — withdraws/flees (Mk. 6:46b; Jn. 6:15b)

n) ... to the mountain — to pray/to escape the crowd (Mk. 6:46c; Jn. 6:15c).

o) It was evening and the disciples were in a boat, headed across the sea to Bethsaida/Capernaum (Mk. 6:45, 47; Jn. 6:16f.).

p) The wind was — against them/blowing (Mk. 6:48b; Jn. 6:18),

q) ... and they — were in the midst of the sea/had rowed about 25–30 stadia (Mk. 6:48c; Jn. 6:19a).

r) The disciples — beheld Jesus walking on the sea, and he intended to go by them/beheld Jesus walking on the sea and coming near the boat (Mk. 6:48d; Jn. 6:19b).

s) Seeing him walking on the sea, — they thought he was a phantom and shouted out. All saw him and were frightened./they were frightened (Mk. 6:49f.; Jn. 6:19c).

t) But immediately, Jesus speaks to them and says, 'Cheer up; it is I! Do not fear.'/But he declares to them, 'I AM! Do not fear.' (Mk. 6:50; Jn. 6:20).

u) He enters the boat and the wind ceases./They wanted to take him into the boat, and (but?) the boat came at once to the land to which they were going (Mk. 6:51; Jn. 6:21).

v) They are met by a crowd in search of—healing miracles/another feeding (Mk. 6:53–56; Jn. 6:22–26).

w) An(a) — indirect/direct — reference to faith based upon miraculous signs, as it relates to an interpretation of the feeding, is made (Mk. 6:52, possibly alluding to 8:17?; and Jn. 6:26f.).

x) This is followed by a discussion — between the Pharisees and teachers of the law and Jesus about the Sabbath and purity laws/between the crowd (and 'the Jews') and Jesus about the true meaning of bread from heaven (Mk. 7:1–23; Jn. 6:31–58).

The above combination of similar events and progression of narrative, yet with a significant disagreement regarding details *at every turn*, vindicates Bultmann's opinion that the Johannine and Marcan traditions here are parallel; but against Bultmann, the traditions are *clearly independent*. This has also been argued by P. Gardner-Smith. In his classic monograph (*Saint John and the Synoptic Gospels*,

Cambridge, 1938) Gardner-Smith identifies four ways in which John 6:1–15 differs from the feeding in Mark 6: a) Their introductions differ significantly. b) The motivation for the feeding is different. c) The activity and dialogues of Jesus are reported in completely different ways. d) The breaking, distributing, and gathering of the food is reported in different ways, culminating in completely distinctive outcomes (pp. 27–33). Gardner-Smith thus concludes:

> A close study of the four Gospels suggests that John knew a popular story, a story probably familiar to all Christians at the time when he wrote, but there is no evidence to prove that he had read it in Mark or Luke and considerable reason for concluding that he had not. (p. 33)

Bultmann's solution to John's independence from Mark 6 is to suggest that he must have acquired his material from another written source, the *sēmeia* source. However, this is not the only possibility, and the high degree of correlation between John 6 and the events in Mark 8 suggests an alternative hypothesis. While Bultmann is probably also correct in assuming that Mark 8:1ff. is a variation on the tradition represented by Mark 6:31ff. (p. 210, n. 1), this is *not* to say that the latter is an editorial expansion on the former. In fact, 8:19–21 suggests that Mark received two independent traditions, which are likely to have been variant interpretations of the same event. While some numbers are different (4,000 men versus 5,000; 7 loaves versus 5; 7 basketfuls versus 12, etc.), at least sixteen other elements in the story follow an identical sequence. Therefore, it seems likely that the stories in Mark 6 and 8 do not represent two distinct events but are two parallel accounts of the same event.[5] Likewise, a third is John 6. While acknowledging the relationship to Mark 6, however, Bultmann has overlooked the similarities between John 6 and Mark 8. These are highly significant regarding an understanding of the connection between sign and discourse in John 6. Thus, the similarities between Mark 8 and John 6 (and surrounding contexts) are as follows (/ indicates differences between the Marcan and Johannine accounts; — indicates similarities):

---

5 It is indeed possible that Jesus could have fed a crowd of four thousand just as easily as a crowd of five thousand, but the amazingly parallel structure of the narratives in Mark 6 and 8 make it appear likely that these represent two variant traditions, reporting the same event. Adding John 6 to the comparison/contrast between the two Marcan narratives confirms this inference, as events from both Mark 6 and 8 can be identified in John's report, independent though it be. Thus, as F.F. Bruce has acknowledged, ' ... the feeding of the 5,000 symbolizes the Lord's self-communication to the Jews, as his feeding of the 4,000 symbolizes his self-communication to the Gentiles' (1984, p. 167 n. 3). Whether or not the feeding of the 4,000 may have been a version of the original story which circulated among the seven Gentile churches (Rev. 2–3, i.e. symbolized by the *seven* loaves), and whether or not the seven baskets represent the seven elders who were ordained to care for the Gentile churches (Ac. 6:3; Luke *certainly* connects the twelve baskets with the *twelve* disciples, Lk. 9:17) is open for speculation. See also U. Schnelle (pp. 114–130) for his excellent treatment of the similarities — and yet dissimilarities — between John 6 and *both* Marcan accounts.

Table 8:

'Similarities *and* Divergences Between John 6 and Mark 8'

a) People — are amazed at/follow after — Jesus because of his miraculous healings (Mk. 7:37; Jn. 6:2).

b) A large crowd — gathers/comes toward him (Mk. 8:1; Jn. 6:5a).

c) Jesus has pity on the crowd and speaks of their need (having been with him 3 days) to be fed./Lifting up his eyes, and seeing the great crowd coming toward him, Jesus says to Philip, 'Where shall we buy bread for these people to eat?' (Mk. 8:2f.; Jn. 6:5).

d) His disciples answer that there is no place in the wilderness to acquire bread./Philip says, '200 denarii would not buy enough loaves for each to have even a little' (Mk. 8:4; Jn. 6:7).

e) The disciples produce seven loaves./Andrew finds a lad who contributes five barley loaves and two fishes (Mk. 8:5; Jn. 6:8f.).

f) Jesus — has the crowd sit down, takes the loaves, gives thanks, and has the disciples distribute them; and likewise with a few fishes/tells the disciples to have the crowd sit down, takes the loaves, gives thanks and distributes ample loaves to those who were seated; and likewise with the fishes (Mk. 8:6f.; Jn. 6:10f.).

g) The crowd 'ate and were satisfied'./(omitted here, but central to Jesus' later *rebuke*) The crowd 'ate the loaves and were satisfied' (Mk. 8:8; Jn. 6:26).

h) Afterwards, the disciples — pick up seven baskets full of left-over pieces/gather twelve baskets full of left-over pieces from the five barley loaves they had eaten (Mk. 8:8; Jn. 6:13).

i) There were about — 4,000 people there/5,000 men present (Mk. 8:9; Jn. 6:10).

j) Jesus — sends the crowd away/flees the crowd to get away from them (Mk. 8:9; Jn. 6:14),

k) ... and gets into a boat with his disciples, heading for Dalmanutha/and his disciples get into a boat (without him) and set off across the lake to Capernaum (Mk. 8:10; Jn. 6:17).

l) The Pharisees come and begin to question Jesus, 'tempting' him, and ask for a sign from heaven./The crowd comes seeking after him the next day and asks 'What sign do you do so that we may believe you?', playing the role of the 'tempter' (cf. Matt. 4:1–11; Lk. 4:1–13) (Mk. 8:11; Jn. 6:22, 24, 30f.).

m) Jesus — sighs and asks why this generation seeks a sign/responds that it was not Moses who gave the bread, but his Father who gives it (Mk.8:12a; Jn. 6.32),

n) ... and — promises that a 'sign' will be given it/says that God's bread is the one coming down from heaven, giving life for the world (Mk. 8:12b, cf. Matt. 16:4; Jn. 6:33, cf. vss. 27, 32, 51c, 62).

o) Jesus discusses the events with his disciples and warns them to beware of the yeast (teaching) of the Pharisees and Herod./Some of Jesus' disciples say, 'This is a hard saying. Who can accept it?' Jesus explains that no one can come to him unless enabled by the Father (Mk. 8:15; Jn. 6:60, 65, cf. vs. 45).

p) As the disciples were discussing the fact that they had forgotten to bring any bread, Jesus asks if their hearts had been hardened and if they did not remember the two previous feeding miracles. He then asks 'Do you still not understand?'/Aware of their grumbling, Jesus asks 'Does this offend you? What if you see the Son of Man ascending to where he was before!', whereupon even some of his disciples abandon him (Mk. 8:14, 16–21; Jn. 6:61f., 66).

q) Hardness of heart is equated with the lack of belief in Jesus' ability to produce bread./ The death-producing bread is equated with the desire for a sign, misguided allegiance to Moses and the Torah, and the reluctance to participate in Jesus' giving his flesh for the life of the world (Mk. 8:17c; Jn. 6:26f., 32f., 51–58).

r) Jesus—asks the disciples, 'Who do you say that I am?'/asks the twelve, 'Do you want to leave too?' (Mk. 8:29; Jn. 6:67).

s) Peter answers, 'You are the Christ.'/Simon Peter answers, 'Lord, to whom shall we go? You have the words of eternal life. We believe and know that you are the Holy One of God.' (Mk. 8:29; Jn. 6:68f.).

t) Jesus speaks of the suffering, betrayal and death of the Son of Man./Jesus alludes to his suffering and death, 'This bread is my flesh which I will give for the life of the world.' (Mk. 8:31; Jn. 6:51c).

u) Jesus rebukes Peter (after Peter's chiding) and says 'Get behind me, Satan! You do not have in mind the things of God, but the things of men!'/Jesus replies (after Peter's confession) 'Have I not chosen you, the twelve, and yet one of you is a devil?' And after the disciples' grumbling (vs. 61), 'The spirit gives life; the flesh profits nothing ...' (Mk. 8:33; Jn. 6:63).

Again, the above comparisons and contrasts between Mark 8 and John 6 display a high degree of similarity regarding general events and progression of narrative, and yet with major differences of detail at every step of the way. The question is, 'How might these *similarities, and yet differences*, be explained?' Bultmann's theory that John's agreement with Mark 6 is explicable on the basis of a *sēmeia* source underlying vss. 1–25 only covers some of the similarities between the Johannine and the Marcan traditions. The fact is, however, there are at least *eleven* reportings of events and themes of discussion which are common to John 6 and Mark 8 (and 7:37), but *not* to John 6 and Mark 6 (a, and l–u in the second list above), and Bultmann's *sēmeia* source theory does not account for this agreement. It could be that the evangelist has added the dialogues and discourses and that the redactor has harmonized the material to follow the Synoptic development of events. However, such a reordering theory presumes one's acceptance of a *dis*ordering theory, and the most tenable assumption is that the signs, discourses, and events of vss. 60ff. were all within the same literary context *before* the final redaction.

Another possibility is to assume that John's account is actually a conflation of Mark 6 and 8, but the main problem with this view is that John 6 differs from Mark *at nearly every turn*. The four major differences reported by P. Gardner-Smith between John 6 and Mark 6 have yet to be accounted for adequately — let alone the *forty-five differences noted above*. Thus, Marcan dependence is highly improbable — nay, absolutely so. Barrett is correct to point out the large number of linguistic agreements between the Marcan and Johannine traditions (pp. 42–54, 271ff.), but Gardner-Smith is also correct to assess that these would have been precisely the sort of graphic detail most easily remembered and passed on within the oral tradition (*op. cit.*), so this says nothing of John's literary dependence upon Mark. R.E. Brown believes that John was probably aware of Mark but used his own material (p. 238f.). B. Lindars believes that Mark 6, 8 and John 8 represent three independent traditions (pp. 236ff.). R. Fortna has correctly described the difficulty of Synoptic dependence as follows:

> The argument against literary dependence can best be illustrated as follows: the verbal relationship between the two feeding stories in Mk 6 and 8 is in every way analogous to that

between Jn's story and any one of the synoptic versions, yet obviously no one suggests that Mk 6 is literarily dependent on Mk 8, or *vice versa*; rather the relationship between them is held to lie somewhere behind the extant texts. (p. 63)

In other words, Mark 6, 8 and John 6 represent three parallel — yet independent — traditions. Just as one may assume that the sea crossing was grouped together quite early with the feeding because of the connections between Mark 6:31–52 and John 6:1–24, one may also assume an early connection between the feeding and a discussion of the meaning of the loaves, followed by Peter's confession, because of the close parallels between Mark 8:1–33 and John 6:1–71. This means that while at least some of John's interpretation of the feeding must have come later, it is doubtful that the earlier stages of the Johannine tradition were completely devoid of interpretive content. Therefore, to assume that John 6:25–71 must have been written by someone other than the author of John 6:1–24 goes against the two *closest* literary parallels (Mk. 6 and 8), and one cannot assume that the Johannine interpretation of the meaning of the feeding had to have been late, and only late. It contains early traditional material and probably evolved over several generations of homiletical interpretation.

One further point may be made regarding the apparent integrity of John 6 when considered in the light of its Synoptic counterparts. As the above lists of parallels illustrate, there are about half again as many parallels between John 6 and Mark 6, and between John 6 and Mark 8, as there are between Mark 6 and 8. While Mark 6 and 8 definitely come from the same ideological slant, the interesting fact is that they each agree most with the outline and inclusion of events in John 6, though in different ways. Because John did not copy Mark, this may suggest that while John's work is of course interpretive, rather than historical-as-such, it may have more historical integrity than is commonly assumed by critical scholars.[6]

---

6 In 1961 a *CBQ* article by R.E. Brown was published entitled, 'Incidents that are Units in the Synoptic Gospels but Dispersed in St. John' (reprinted in Brown's *NTE* under the title, 'John and the Synoptic Gospels: A Comparison', pp. 246–271). In this essay, Brown argues quite convincingly that the Johannine and Synoptic accounts represent two traditions which have 'narrated the same basic historic incidents in very dissimilar ways' (p. 246, *NTE*). Therefore, Brown concludes:

> When the two traditions differ, we are not always to assume facilely that the Synoptic Gospels are recording the historic fact and that Jn has theologically reorganized the data. In the cases we have studied, an interesting case can be made out for the basic historicity of the Johannine picture and for theological reorganization on the part of the Synoptic Gospels. We are coming to realize more and more that the critics have played us false in their minimal estimate of the historicity of the Fourth Gospel. (p. 271, *NTE*)

While Brown develops this thesis on the basis of exploring four texts in the Synoptics and identifying their corollaries in John, the reverse may also be done, starting with John 6. In other words, when the various themes in John 6 are explored in Mark ([Jn. 6:1–4/Mk. 6:31–36; 8:13]; [Jn. 6:3/Mk. 6:33f.; 8:1]; [Jn. 6:5–13/Mk. 6:37–44; 8:3–9]; [Jn. 6:14/Mk. 8:28]; [Jn. 6:15/Mk. 8:30]; [Jn. 6:16–21/Mk. 4:35–41; 6:45–51]; [Jn. 6:22–25/Mk. 8:16]; [Jn. 6:26–

This is also confirmed by Luke's and Matthew's redactions of Mark. Luke has obviously decided that there was just one feeding (Lk. 9:10–17; as well as just one sea crossing: Lk. 8:22–25) and opts for the version in Mark 6 as the preferable one. However, he follows it *not* with accounts of miracles (Mk. 7:24–27), but with Peter's confession based on Mk. 8:27–31! Thus, his redaction here departs from Mark and *agrees with the sequence and content of John 6*. Matthew stays closer to Mark's accounts and includes and expands upon both reports (Mt. 14:13–33; 15:29–16:23). It is also significant that Matthew's redaction of Mark 8 has kept the interpretation of the feeding together with the miracle and (in typical Matthean fashion) has expanded upon the discussions with the Jewish leaders and with the disciples about signs (16:1–4) and bread (16:5–12). Thus, the integrity of John's account is corroborated by both Matthew's and Luke's redactions of Mark 6 and 8. Matthew has kept the demand for a sign and the discussion following the feeding together and has even expanded upon it. Luke has agreed with (followed?) the Johannine tradition, *against* Mark (see below, Appendix VIII), keeping the confession of Peter together with the feeding of the *five* thousand. Thus, not only is the interpretation to be considered as integral to the Johannine narration of the signs, but the integrity of John 6 as a whole is corroborated by its parallels in the Synoptics.

2. The second problem with Bultmann's assertion that the evangelist 'ignored' the external events is that the thematic development within John 6 itself suggests the opposite. The discussions of the sign and the 'Bread of Life' discourses seem to be reflective developments upon 'external events', but *interpreting* is far different from *ignoring* them. The form of vss. 25ff. may indeed have been homiletical, as Borgen, Brown and Lindars have argued (not that vss. 1–24 weren't), but rather than being a midrashic homily on Ps. 78:24 (vs. 31), John 6:25–66 seems to be more of an exhortation calling for a christocentric response to God's revealing/ saving activity in Jesus as the life-producing Bread. Thus, the pivotal verse is:

Work not for food that perishes,
but for food that endures to eternal life,
which the Son of Man will give you.
On him God has placed
his seal of approval. (6:27)

29/Mk. 8:17–21]; [Jn. 6:30f./Mk. 8:11]; [Jn. 6:32–40/Mk. 8:12]; [Jn. 6:41f./Mk 6:3]; [Jn. 6:43–50/Mk. 6:4; 8:51?]; [Jn. 6:51–58/Mk. 8:34–38]; [Jn. 6:60–65/Mk. 8:31–33]; [Jn. 6:66/ Mk. 8:38]; [Jn. 6:67/Mk. 8:29a]; [Jn. 6:68f./Mk. 8:29b]; [Jn. 6:70/Mk. 8:33a]), John's narrative seems *far more unified and coherent* than Mark's. Of course, not all of these connections between John and Mark are entirely parallel, but the above comparisons simply illustrate that the opinion among scholars that John is fragmented — in contrast to the Synoptics — reflects one's using the Synoptics as the norm, rather than John. Therefore, as well as the essay written by Brown, another case might just as well be argued entitled, 'Incidents Which Are *a Unity in John 6*, but Which Are *Dispersed in the Synoptics*'.

Fundamentally, this seeking is characterized as a believing response to God's 'saving dialogue' with humanity. In many ways, humanity's response within the divine-human dialectic is the central theme of the entire Gospel (1:1–14; 3:31–36; 4:21–24; 6:35; 7:37f.; 11:25f.; 15:1–17; 20:30f.), and this may be identified as the unifying theme throughout John 6 as well. Within this dialogical framework John's narrative makes it clear that humanity is called to respond to the *present* workings of God, not just those in times past (in the Torah, the way of Moses, etc.), which for the evangelist is the eschatological Word of God, present in the man Jesus, as the Christ. Therefore, the Word of God has become flesh in order to communicate God's saving love to the world, and ultimately to *be* that communication. This *revelational* pattern occurs in John 6:1–21 and 67–71 (see below, Table 18). Conversely, where the initiative shifts to Jesus' discussants (Jn. 6:25–66) the literary form is *rhetorical* (see below, Table 19; vss. 22–24 are transitional). God's saving communication with the world calls for a believing response from it, and this 'dialogue' may be seen throughout the narrative and discourses of John 6 (* indicates a *shift* in the initiator from God or God's agent, to humans, and vice versa):

Table 9:
'Divine Initiative Versus Human Initiative in the Narration of John 6'

*a) *God's action*: to feed the crowd through Jesus' multiplication of the loaves and fishes (vss. 1–13).

> *Response*: people overlook the spiritual 'significance' of God's provision and want to make Jesus a human king (vss. 14–15).

b) *God's action*: to rescue/come to the disciples in the sea in Jesus (vss. 16–20).

> *Response*: They were stricken with awe at Jesus' appearance and words, stopped being afraid, and were willing to take him into the boat (vs. 21).

*c) (The initiative is reversed.) *The crowd's seeking*: after the feeding and the sea crossing, the crowd has come seeking more food (implied) from Jesus (vss. 22–26).

> *Jesus' response*: 'Work not for food which perishes, but for food which lasts forever.' (vs. 27).

d) *A request for clarification*: 'What must we do to do ('work' = '*get*'?) God's works?' (vs. 28).

> *Jesus' response*: 'The work of God is to believe in the one he has sent.' (vs. 29).

e) *The crowd's 'tempting' of Jesus*: They request a sign and cite Ps. 78:24 as a precedent (vs. 30f.). Here the crowd uses manna as a rhetorical trump.

> *Jesus' response*: to point out their misinterpretation of the manna story (and the eschatological initiative of God); it was not Moses who *gave*, but *Jesus' Father* who *gives* the *true bread*, which is the *one coming down from heaven*, giving life to the world (vs. 32f.).

f) *The crowd's request*: they still do not understand the kind of bread Jesus is referring to, but request to receive 'this bread all the time' (vs. 34).

> *Jesus' first discourse*: 'I am the bread of life. He who comes to me will never hunger, and he who believes in me will never thirst ...' (vss. 35–40).

g) *The 'grumbling' of the Jews*: 'How can he be the bread come down from heaven? Is this not Jesus, the son of Joseph, whose father and mother we know? ...' (vs. 41f.).

> *Jesus' second discourse*: 'No one can "come" to me unless the Father ... draws him. I . . . am the living bread that came down from heaven. If anyone eats of this bread, he

will live forever. This bread is *my flesh* which I will give for the life of the world.'
(vss. 43–51).

h) *The Jews now 'fight' among themselves*: 'How can this man give us his flesh to eat?' they ask (vs. 52).

Jesus' third discourse: 'Truly, truly, unless you eat the flesh of the Son of Man and drink his blood, you have no life in you ... ' (vss. 53–59).

i) *The disciples' reaction*: in response to this, many of Jesus' disciples grumble and say, 'This is a hard saying! Who can accept it?' (vs. 60).

Jesus' response to the disciples and reiteration of the central theme: 'Does this offend you?... The spirit gives life; the flesh avails nothing. The words I have spoken to you [above?] are spirit and they are life.' (vss. 61–65).

(Narration of result) Even some of Jesus' disciples abandon him and walk with him no longer (vs. 66).

*j) (The initiative is again reversed.) *Jesus questions 'The Twelve'*: 'Do you wish to leave as well?' (vs. 67).

Simon Peter confesses: 'Lord, to whom shall we go? You have the words of eternal life.'
*k) (Possible shift of initiative within Peter's confession — suggested by Jesus' abrupt response.) 'We believe and know that you are the Holy One of God' (vs. 68f.).

Jesus responds: 'Have I not chosen you, the Twelve? Yet one of you is a devil?' (vs. 70).
(Editorial Clarification: He meant *Judas* son of Simon Iscariot, *not* Simon *Peter*; vs. 71).

The thematic continuity in the above verses is clear. Both sign and discourse are portrayed as vehicles of God's dialogue with humanity, which calls for a believing response to God's saving initiative. This initiative is most clearly visible in the narrative sections of John 6 (vss. 1–24, 67–71), as humanity is 'tested' regarding their response to it. The evangelist's understanding of the divine/human dialectic assumes that God's 'Word' has long been at work in the creation of the world, the redemptive history of Israel, the law of Moses and the scriptures — but that it is ultimately embodied in the coming/sentness of Jesus himself. Thus, the only appropriate response to these events is to consider their divine origin and respond not simply to the agents themselves, but to God, who is, and has been, working through them.

However, this dialogue bears with it an inherent problem. The human tendency is to respond to God's activity on the level of its manifestation alone and to fail to see the spiritual dimension beyond it. Thus, 'bread' is sought rather than Bread, 'life' is valued over Life, and 'our Fathers ate ...' is confused with 'it was/is *God* who gave/gives'. When confronted with the discrepancy between God's 'Word' and human understandings of it, humanity is faced with the most difficult decision of all: to forsake even one's creaturely understanding of the spiritual, in order to be responsive to God's spiritual 'Word' in the present. This is perhaps the greatest paradox of revelation (cf. Bultmann, p. 227). Ways God has acted/communicated before can no longer be embraced as guarantees of how God will act in the future. Thus, it is one's preconceptions of 'that which is spiritual' which are the most difficult aspects of 'the flesh' to identify, and thus to relinquish (cf. vss. 27, 63). John 6 shows the reader that this was the case for the crowd (in search of bread), the Jews (seeking to be loyal to Moses and the scriptures), and even some of Jesus' disciples (who were called to forfeit their preconceptions of what 'life' in him involved). Thus, the 'testing' motif *runs throughout the entire chapter.* Not only is it Philip who is tested in verse 6, but the crowd, the Jews, and *even* some of the disciples are tested as to whether they will seek the Nourishment which Jesus gives and is, or whether they will be satisfied with something less (vs. 66). This comprises the overall thematic unity of John 6.

What is also impressive about John 6 is that in the interpretation of both sign and discourse, a singular christocentric understanding of God's interaction with humanity comes through with absolute clarity. In the evangelist we have not only ·a creative theologian, but also a radical interpreter of the gospel tradition: 'radical' in the sense that he gets to the 'root' of the significance of Jesus' ministry and then reinterprets these insights in ways which challenge his contemporaries towards life-changing experiences of faith. Therefore, in the interpretation of sign and discourse, .John 6 is not an ignoring of 'external events', but an integral employment of them in a unified way, casting new light on the immediate situation of the Johannine audience in a manner which builds for the future and is continuous with the past. In doing so, the witness of the Gospel itself becomes an ongoing means of God's communication within the divine/human dialogue (20:31). Says D.M. Smith:

> In the finished gospel, the signs and discourses have the same purpose and effect, different as they are in origin and substance. They do not afford external legitimation of the revelation of God in Jesus. Rather, they are used by the evangelist to express a purified idea of revelation, and, in the preaching of the Fourth Gospel, they become the vehicle of the event in which revelation occurs again and again. In function they are fundamentally and essentially the same, for neither has any meaning for the evangelist except as it speaks to man's actual (existential) situation and places him in the moment of decision. (p. 13)

Findings

While the contextual problems discussed above are by no means the only ones identified by Bultmann in his treatment of John 6, they are certainly pivotal ones. Upon them hang his contextual bases for distinguishing the evangelist's contribution from the conclusion of the *sēmeia* source narrative, and his assertion that the connection between the sign and its interpretation in John 6 has been added by the later work of the evangelist. The problem is that Bultmann's contextual evidence rests upon interpretive judgments which are not the only, nor necessarily the best, means of addressing specific difficulties within the text. Therefore, the findings of this chapter are as follows:

1. Regarding the perplexing transition between vss. 25 and 26ff., to say this uneasy transition represents an editorial seam between the evangelist's work and the material of his source is itself problematic. If the evangelist was intending to co-opt an earlier source, he certainly could have done a better job of dove-tailing the transition. Furthermore, Bultmann's explanation assumes that vss. 25f. must be taken in a straightforward and literal sense, while he assumes that the question of

the crowd in vs. 30 demonstrates the 'folly' of the world. What is more likely is that the odd combination of the crowd's question and Jesus' answer are meant to disturb the reader by employing subtle irony. The crowd asks 'how long' Jesus had been there, but the Johannine Jesus exposes their real intent, which is to ask, 'how long' might it be until they receive another feeding. The humorous irony of the crowd's question would undoubtedly have been recognized by the original hearer/reader, and the use of such a literary device enhances the rhetorical effectiveness of the narrative as it stands.

2. On the other hand, Bultmann asserts that vss. 28f. must be excised in order for the difficulty of transition between vss. 27 and 30f. to be fully exposed. A strange means of identifying a contextual problem! The request for a sign (vs. 30) follows vs. 29 every bit as well as it follows vs. 35, if not better. Furthermore, Bultmann has missed the more obvious use of extended irony in vss. 22–36. In this context, the request for a sign is not portrayed as the demand for proof as a prerequisite for faith, but it is portrayed as an attempt for the crowd to 'tempt' Jesus into providing more bread by means of using standard Jewish Palestinian manna rhetoric. Their lack of understanding throughout this entire section would have seemed clear to the reader/hearer, and it is confirmed explicitly in vs. 36. Therefore, neither on the basis of Jesus' odd response to the crowd (vs. 26), nor on the basis of the crowd's redundant request for a sign (vs. 30f.) is a diachronic solution required. These 'contextual difficulties' more probably reflect the evangelist's use of local and sustained irony to further the central christological thrust of John 6. As a contrast to other kinds of 'bread', it is Jesus himself who is the *true* Bread of Life.

3. There is also a high degree of continuity between the interpretations of the feeding sign and the following discussion of it in John 6, and it is likely that this connection was earlier in the Johannine tradition than Bultmann is willing to allow. This is corroborated by comparing John 6 with Mark 6, and especially with Mark 8. These represent three independent developments of a common cluster of reported events, and John's account is the most complete and thematically unified of the three. Furthermore, the integrity of John's tradition is supported by the redactions of Mark 6 and 8 and by Luke and Matthew (see further discussions in Ch. 8 below, and esp. Tables 10–15.). Therefore, it is highly unlikely that the connection between sign and discourse in John 6 was exclusively as late in the tradition as Bultmann believes. John 6:22–71 represents a Johannine development of what may have been an actual debate, which followed a feeding and a lake scene in the ministry of Jesus and which culminated in the testing of the disciples. The multiple attestation of Mark 6 and 8 and John 6, while being clearly independent, make this a likely judgment. Throughout all of John 6, a central theme unifies each scene. In Jesus, God engages humanity in a saving/revealing dialogue, which calls for believing responsiveness to God's initiative. Responding, however, is not portrayed as simply following the way of the Torah or Moses, nor even one's expectations of what/who Jesus ought to be for the world. Coming to Jesus involves trusting in him, while at the same time, exercising the willingness to release one's

expectations of how God ought to be acting on one's behalf. It involves a believing response to the divine initiative made manifest in the incarnation, which is characterized as an abiding immersion in, as well as an internalization of, God's saving work through the flesh-and-bloodness of Jesus. This is the unifying theme of *all of John 6* — and the rest of the Gospel as well.

4. Even though Bultmann's contextual evidence is finally insufficient to make his diachronic theory of composition convincing, one may still identify several aspects of his analysis which serve as solid material for further constructs. a) His identification of odd transitions between the comments of Jesus' discussants and Jesus' replies points to the extended use of irony in the dialogue section of John 6. What we have in vss. 25–66 is a series of dialogues with Jesus, each of which makes some point about inappropriate ways of coming to, or believing in, Jesus. Thus, the misunderstanding of the crowd sets the stage for the misunderstanding of the Jews, and then the disciples. These fallacious notions, thus exposed, are then corrected by Jesus' discourses. b) Bultmann's identification of the spiritualizing link between the 'external events' of the feeding in the following discourses is also highly significant. While the sequence and general reporting of events in John (as compared with Mark 6 and 8) is quite close, what is more suggestive is the interpretive difference between the Johannine and Synoptic traditions. Exploring this interest will lead to an analysis of the Fourth Evangelist's distinctive ideological slant, as well as to an investigation of the theological unity and disunity of John 6.

Chapter 6

The 'Eucharistic Interpolation'

As well as stylistic and contextual grounds for assuming John's composition-history was a diachronic one, Bultmann also believes there are convincing theological grounds to support this theory. Therefore, this chapter will focus upon the *theological unity and disunity of John 6*. While the shift in ideological perspective between the narration of Jesus' sign and the christological interpretation of its meaning in John 6 may be attributable to the evangelist's own reflection upon his tradition and thus does not require a separate *sēmeia* source to explain such a development, the so-called 'eucharistic interpolation' is another matter. Indeed, it appears that vss. 51c–58 betray an ideological slant which is in direct contradiction to the evangelist's christology. Thus, Bultmann believes these verses must represent a later addition by another writer. In other words, these verses appear to contain an instrumentalistic view of the eucharist, which opposes diametrically the evangelist's belief that faith in Jesus Christ alone is, in and of itself, efficacious. Rather, one must 'eat his flesh' and 'drink his blood' in order to receive eternal life according to John 6:53–55, and this appears to be an unmistakable reference to the indispensability of the eucharist for salvation.[1] Therefore, it would seem that vss. 51c–58 betray a later interpolation. Says Bultmann:

---

1 This is certainly the meaning which E.J. Siedlecki has sought to 'prove' in his extensive dissertation on the subject (*A Patristic Synthesis of John VI, 54–55*, Mundelin, IL, 1956). After exploring the range of patristic interpretation regarding John 6:54f., Siedlecki concludes that the Fathers taught that 'the Eucharist was absolutely necessary for salvation'. According to Siedlecki:
> *Certainly*, they taught such a doctrine because of Christ's words in John VI, 54–55; they also taught this doctrine, *probably*, because they considered both Baptism and the Eucharist to be *efficient* causes of the initial union by which one became a living member of the Mystery Body, the Church. (p. 260)
This interpretation is echoed by A. Richardson (*The Gospel According to Saint John*, London, 1959) and many others (cf. P.J. Temple, 'The Eucharist in St. John 6', *CBQ* 9, 1947, pp. 442–452). According to Richardson's interpretation of John 6:53:
> This verse asserts clearly that participation in the liturgical worship of the Christian community is the indispensable means of attaining the life of the world to come. The words EXCEPT YE EAT ... AND DRINK ... cannot refer to anything but participation in the Church's Eucharist. (p. 104)
However, Bultmann's correct judgment is that *if* the above interpretations are the best and only meanings of Jn. 6:51c–58, *then they must* be regarded as contradictory to the very heart of the evangelist's christocentric soteriology. Thus, J. Dunn ('John VI — A Eucharist Dis-

> These verses [6:51c–58] refer without any doubt to the sacramental meal of the Eucharist, where the flesh and blood of the "Son of Man" are consumed, with the result that this food gives "eternal life", in the sense that the participants in the meal can be assured of the future resurrection. Thus the Lord's Supper is here seen as the *pharmakon athanasias* or *tēs zōēs* [Ign. Eph. 20.2; Act. Thom.135 p.242,1 (note 2)]. This not only strikes one as strange in relation to the Evangelist's thought in general, and specifically to his eschatology, but it also stands in contradiction to what has been said just before. ... Thus, we must inevitably conclude that vv. 51b–58 have been added by an ecclesiastical editor. (pp. 218–219)

This paragraph is one of Bultmann's clearest arguments for a diachronic solution to the problem of John's christological unity and disunity. While the style of vss. 51c–58 is nearly identical to that of the preceding verses (the redactor 'imitated' the style of the evangelist; p. 234, n. 4), attributing this passage to the redactor must be done on the basis of theological interpretation alone. Bultmann's reasoning makes good hypothetical sense, but the soundness of any valid syllogism rests solely upon the veracity of its premises. The tenability of the interpolation hypothesis assumes: a) that Bultmann's analysis of the evangelist's christology is correct; b) that his analysis of the sacramentalistic christology of 6:51ff. is correct; and c) that the christological views of 6:51c–58 *cannot* have been embraced by the author of 6:26–51b. Upon the correctness of *all three* of these assumptions hangs the soundness of Bultmann's attribution of vss. 51c–58 to the redactor, his rearrangement of vss. 27–51b into a 'better' order (vss. 36–40 serve as a better ending to the discourse section than vss. 47–51b), and the moving of vss. 60–71 to just after 8:30–40 (pp. 443–451), as they make 'no sense' following 6:40 or 6:51b. However, these interpretive/compositional moves are extremely tenuous. The successful challenging of *any one* of Bultmann's assumptions would jeopardize his entire hypothetical construct. Furthermore, if vss. 51cff. may be allowed to follow the section leading up to vs. 51b, as Borgen argues, then the places of vss. 36–40 and 47–51b need not be exchanged, and vss. 60–71 may stay within ch. 6. Thus, implications extend to Bultmann's disordering and reordering theories, which in turn impact his reconstruction of a hypothetical *Offenbarungsreden* source.

Despite the overall persuasiveness of Borgen's argument, however, a real tension still exists between the christocentric soteriology of the evangelist and what

---

course?', *NTS* 17, pp. 328–338) has even taken Bultmann's interpretation a step further and argues that not only is the evangelist critical of the sacraments, but his allusion to them in Jn. 6 is designed to stress their ultimate *inefficacy* as means of grace. Concludes Dunn:

> At most we can say then that John uses eucharistic language for its metaphorical value, and that he adds v. 63 to underline its figurative nature in case the metaphor should be mis-understood and interpreted literally. Eating and drinking the elements of the Lord's Supper vividly represents the act of coming to and believing in Jesus and the resulting eternal life through union with him, but in the actual reception of that life the eucharistic elements are of no avail — they play no part; in the event it is the Spirit who gives life, and he does so primarily through the words of Jesus. (p. 335)

appears to be the instrumentalistic sacramentology of vss. 51c–58.[2] Granted, Borgen may still be correct in assuming that the shift in emphasis in this section marks the addressing of an acute (docetising?) need within Johannine Christianity. But insisting upon the eucharist as the only credited means by which faith in Christ is expressed and salvation is obtained is far different from exposing docetising Christians as 'externalists', and Borgen does not treat this contradictory tension clearly enough. Aware of this genuine theological problem, Brown treats vss. 51–58 as a eucharistic 'doublet', expanding upon the 'sapiential' discourse on the bread of life in vss. 35–50 (pp. 268–294). Thus, it must be acknowledged that even if vss. 51–58 are thought to have followed the preceding verses, but as a eucharistic development of the 'Bread of Life' theme, this may still suggest a diachronic history of the text. Therefore, Bultmann's analysis still demands to be addressed, especially as it relates to the apparent contradiction between the christology of the evangelist and the sort of sacramentality represented by vss. 51c–58. The purpose of this chapter will thus be to assess the central concern of the evangelist's christology as it relates to his attitude toward sacramental issues, to examine the sacramental character of vss. 51c–58, and to offer a possible explanation for the relationship of vss. 51c–58 to the rest of John 6. Before doing so, however, a clarification of terminology may facilitate the discussion.

Excursus: *What Is Meant by 'Sacrament'?*

At times scholars disagree with each other because they vary as to their evaluations of evidence and its implications, and at times scholars fail to come to unity because of their failure to define clearly the issues being discussed. The impasse over John 6:51c–58 reflects more of the latter problem than the former. Therefore, an attempt must be made to clarify one's terms, especially as they relate to the so-called 'sacramentalist interpolation' of John 6. Working definitions of such terms as 'sacrament/sacramental', 'institutional sacrament', 'ordinance', and 'sacramental instrumentalism' will help to clarify what is and is not meant by the word 'sacrament' within this discussion.

---

2 While Borgen is probably correct in assuming that Jn. 6:51c–58 is targeted towards docetising Christians, he does not treat satisfactorily the theological point made by Bultmann regarding the contradiction between an evangelist who believes that faith in Christ is enough and the evangelist's apparent stress upon the indispensability of the eucharist for salvation. Therefore, even though Richter's critique (1969) is flawed in its assumption that the employment of eucharistic imagery implies an emphasis upon itself — as a ritual — instead of the belief in Christ which it represents, he is justified in calling for greater clarity from Borgen regarding this apparent contradiction. Even such works as otherwise excellent as D. Rensberger, *Johannine Faith and Liberating Community*, Philadelphia, 1988, pp. 64–86; and L. Schenke (1980, 1983, 1985; Bib II) fail to take seriously the real contradiction between believing in Christ being *enough*, in and of itself, and views which prescribe *any* external action as necessarily expressive of inward trust and mediatory of divine grace. On this theological problem, Bultmann is correct.

A *sacrament*, in the broadest use of the term, may be taken to mean (in the classic Augustinian sense) a physical and outward sign of a spiritual and inward reality. Therefore, in the general sense, a sacrament would be any means by which God's divine presence and activity are actualized within the sphere of human perceptibility.

While the word 'sacrament' is a Latinized form of the Greek, *mustērion*, John portrays many aspects of God's saving and revealing initiative in ways which may be considered *sacramental*. In other words, they convey God's power and presence in ways that direct humanity towards God. The Torah, Moses, Abraham, the scriptures, the ministry of John the Baptist, and the words and works of Jesus are portrayed in John as sacramental witnesses to the 'ultimate sacrament': the *incarnation*. In this sense, John is thoroughly sacramental. In fact, this 'sacramental principle' may be said to be the thematic core of the entire Gospel. Says C.J. Wright:[3]

> What is this principle? It is, that the physical can be the vehicle of the spiritual, the visible of the invisible. So understood, this principle runs through the whole of the Fourth Gospel. "The Word," says the Evangelist, "became flesh, and dwelt among us ... " The God whom no one has ever seen was manifest in Jesus. This is the central theme of the Gospel.

Therefore, in the broad sense of the term, the 'sacramental' is anything which conveys God's spiritual power and presence by physical means. Penultimately, that which witnesses to the Son is sacramental, in that the incarnation is the ultimate of sacramental possibilities. Through the Son, the Father's character and presence are conveyed to the world with Christomorphic clarity.

An *institutional sacrament* is a subset of that which is sacramental, but it is determined by the church. The number of institutional sacraments has varied significantly within the church, and in the Middle Ages there were as many as 30 sacraments, until P. Lombard reduced the number to seven.[4] With the Reformation the number of institutional sacraments was reduced to two: baptism and the eucharist, as these are the two most clearly described in the New Testament. Largely based on interpretations of John 3:5 and 6:53ff., the value of baptism and the eucharist has been debated among scholars for centuries, and the key issue has been the tension between the efficacy of the Christ Event and the function of the institutional sacraments of the church. It is primarily this question which Bultmann has addressed in his treatment of 6:51ff. Is inward belief in Christ efficacious, in and of itself, or is it contingent upon using the right words or participating in any external rite or form 'correctly'? Wars have been fought, and ecclesial divisions have been leveraged, because of divergent answers to this question.

Another related word is *ordinance*. An ordinance is to be understood as a sacramental ritual which is carried out by Christians who believe that doing so is following the instructions of Jesus. In other words, some traditions have interpreted baptism to be an ordinance based on the 'great commission' of Matt. 28:19f., and the eucharist to be an ordinance based on 1 Cor. 11:25f. The only ordinance in John, however, is neither baptismal nor eucharistic. This injunction is to wash one another's feet (13:14ff.), a symbolic act of

---

3 See C.J. Wright, *Jesus, the Revelation of God; His Mission and Message According to St. John*, London, 1950; citation, p. 81f. Also, 'Physical symbols, and physical contacts *occasion* spiritual experience; but they do not *necessarily* convey it' (p. 82).

4 See P. Lombard's *Sentences* IV, i.2. It should be noted that the 'classical' definition alluded to is Augustinian, rather than Lombardian. Lombard would have considered sacraments to be equated with blessed institutional rituals or practices as determined by the Church.

mutual servanthood. What is peculiar in the Gospel of John is that while it does contain baptismal and eucharistic allusions, these are *not* portrayed as ordinances, nor is Jesus portrayed as initiating such practices. The point of clarification in John 4:2 flatly denies that Jesus ever did any baptizing, and eucharistic motifs have been totally omitted from the Johannine account of the last supper (ch. 13). Thus, it is quite strange that John's central concern should be so sacramental — in the broad sense of the term — and yet so devoid of any explicit reference to the institution of baptismal and eucharistic rites by Jesus. Does this imply a first-century opinion that ecclesial sacramental rites were innovations, primarily attributable to Jesus' followers rather than his original intention?

A final term to be considered involves the central aspect of Bultmann's objection to vss. 27 and 51c–58 belonging within the evangelist's theology. According to Bultmann, vs. 27 'represents the idea of a *sacramental meal* at which the initiates into the mysteries are given the food which endows them with eternal life' (p. 224). Thus, the eating of the 'bread of God' which comes down from heaven has its origin in the *Offenbarungsreden*, which reflects the conception of Iranian Gnosticism that life comes through living bread, living water, and the tree of life (p. 224, n. 2). As a contrast, 6:51c–58 represents the Ignatian *pharmakon athanasias* conception of the eucharist, which is based on the theophagic traditions of the Hellenistic Mystery Religions (*Ibid.*). Either way, Bultmann is highly dubious of the evangelist embracing either of these 'magical', or instrumentalist, approaches to religious rites (p. 223). They betray a misapprehension of true sacramentality and replace it with human-made forms designed to produce a spiritual effect as a result of ritualistic activity. Such instrumentalism is the diametric opposite of authentic belief in God, as revealed through the incarnation. It is precisely the bankruptcy of human devices and attempts to acquire divine grace to which the incarnation is the ultimate challenge and affront. Therefore, such instrumentalistic approaches to God, the sacramental, and indeed human-made religion itself, is what the Word-made-flesh scandalizes. According to Barrett:

> The Word became flesh; flesh became the vehicle of spiritual life and truth, and history became charged with supra-historical meaning. The incarnation was itself sacramental in that it visibly represented truth and at the same time conveyed that which it represented. (John, p. 82)

Therefore, when discussing John's sacramentology one must clarify which of the above meanings are attributed to the words 'sacrament' and 'sacramental'. In the broad sense of the term, John's christology may certainly be considered 'sacramental'. Through the 'flesh-and-bloodness' of Jesus, God has spoken to humanity, and this communication demands a response from the world. It is also clear that John contains no ritual 'ordinances' and even seems to de-emphasize the value of such sacramental rites as water baptism and the eucharist. Given this perspective, the kind of sacramentality represented by John 6:51c–58 demands to be investigated, and this brings us to Bultmann's treatment of this passage.

Bultmann contends that 6:51c–58 represents an *instrumentalist* view of the sacraments, and he believes that the redactor has added this section because he has misunderstood the incarnational thrust of vss. 60–70 and has assumed that the 'scandal' must have been the Lord's reference to his flesh and blood as food. Bultmann also believes that the original 'scandal' to which vss. 60f. refers is 'the Word made flesh', and that here ' ... it has been reduced to the idea that the hearers cannot understand that Jesus is speaking of the Lord's Supper' (p. 237). Therefore, as greater clarity is gained regarding John's sacramentology in the light of 6:51c–58, clearer insight into the unity and disunity of the Gospel will be achieved as well.

A. *Was the Evangelist an Anti-sacramentalist?*

To say that Bultmann believes the evangelist is strictly an 'anti-sacramentalist' is to overstate Bultmann's opinion. Yet, in his discussion of John 3:5 (p. 138, n. 3) he asserts that 'The originality of the words *hudatos kai*, which link the rebirth with the sacrament of baptism, is at the least very doubtful. ... Similarly in ch. 6 and ch. 13 ... the Evangelist consciously rejects the sacramentalism of ecclesiastical piety'. Bultmann's theory is strengthened on the bases that John 4:2 appears to be a flat denial of Jesus' involvement in the water-baptism ministry of John, and that the omission of an institution of the eucharist in the supper narrative is intentional. This makes the transition from the clearly christological section of John 6 to the apparently eucharistic section of vss. 51c–58 seem conspicuous, given the understanding that it 'stands in contradiction to what has been said just before' (p. 219).

Responses to Bultmann have been varied,[5] and factors contributing to the widespread disagreement among scholars include genuine differences of understanding regarding the implications of sacramental views and practices, let alone the confusion over terminology, as mentioned above. A parallel difficulty has to do with the easy confusability between later sacramental debates and the situation of the first-century church, and especially the place of Johannine faith and practice within it. For this reason, identifying the evangelist as an anti-sacramentalist is probably anachronistic. In other words, 'sacramental piety' may have been a problem in the post-Reformation age, but applying this criticism to the historical Johannine situation seems forced. Also, the assumption that instrumental sacramentality had become a problem before the turn of the first century must be based upon speculation rather than historical evidence. Thus, according to B. Lindars ('Word and Sacrament in the Fourth Gospel', *SJT* 29, 1976, pp. 49–63):

> The eucharistic words have not yet acquired the status of sacramental "form", effecting a hidden change of substance in the sacred elements. But they define the act of breaking bread and sharing the cup in relation to the central act of redemption, the sacrifice of Christ. (p. 62f.) ... [Therefore,] it is an anachronism to suggest that antisacramentalism was a factor at this time. Nowhere in the New Testament is the eucharist classed among the human ordinances, like the Jewish food laws, which the spiritual man can treat with contempt. (p. 59)

At least three other studies[6] have reached similar conclusions, although they have approached the issue from different angles. For instance, D.E. Aune (1972),

---

5 The vast number of articles and contributions on the topic of John's sacramentology listed in Bibliography III cannot be catalogued here, with regard to the opinion of each author, but see H. Klos, *Die Sakramente im Johannesevangelium*, Stuttgart, 1970, pp. 11–44, for an excellent survey of opinions.

6 These studies include: D.E. Aune, 'The Phenomenon of Early Christian "Anti-Sacramentalism" ', in *Studies in New Testament and Early Christian Literature, Essays in*

in failing to find anti-sacramentalistic themes in early Christianity, has concluded that such a 'theological posture was remarkably rare in the broad early Christian Movement' (p. 212). Therefore, Aune suggests five implications which relate to Bultmann's inference of anti-sacramentalism in John (p. 212f.): 1. There are no other cases in which anti-sacramentalist attitudes are reported within an early Jewish-Christian sect. 2. Baptism and the Eucharist 'became such polyvalent rites' that they could have been easily altered, rather than needing to have been rejected by a group. 3. There is no other evidence of an early Christian group rejecting sacraments because they were critical of their 'misuse' or an 'excessive value' attributed to them. 4. Those few groups which did reject the use of sacraments 'were not silent on the subject, as Bultmann supposes the Fourth Evangelist to be, but were aggressively vocal in their denial of the validity of Christian rites'. 5. 'To make the "word" the antithesis of "sacraments" is therefore to introduce an element into the thought of early Christians which is completely foreign to their way of thinking.'

One shortcoming with Aune's work has to do with his lack of defining the specific kind of anti-sacramentalism that may have existed in the first two Christian centuries. Hence, the value of the above excursus. In other words, while later aspects of sacramental debates are obviously anachronistic, there still appear to have been some real tensions reflected in the letters of Ignatius and the Gospel of John, and the nature of these tensions still begs an explanation. Nevertheless, Aune concludes:

> While it cannot be said that Bultmann's theory of the anti-sacramental posture of the Fourth Evangelist is a theoretical impossibility, the absence of any clear polemic against sacramentalism within the Gospel together with the total absence of early Christian anti-sacramentalism motivated by reaction to the "misuse" or "over-emphasis" of the sacraments, makes his theory, in the opinion of the present writer, improbable in the extreme. (p. 214)

A second attempt to refute the anti-sacramentalist appraisal of the Fourth Evangelist's posture is the 1981 study by K. Matsunaga, in which he seeks to take into account the internal situation of Johannine Christianity. In this study the 'historical situation' which forced the evangelist to omit explicit sacramental motifs and to engage in the '*Spiritualisierung*' of institutional sacraments is examined. According to Matsunaga, it is the presence of 'drop-outs' in the Johannine church (reflected by 6:66), which:

> ... nullified the practice of the sacraments in John's church. The receiving of Baptism or participating in the Communion did not authenticate the true discipleship of Jesus. Then, it was no longer meaningful for members of John's church to be told how these sacraments became established — the historical origin of the sacraments. It was more important and urgent for the Evangelist to clarify what the sacraments signified — in other words, what

---

Honor of A.P. Wikgren, ed. D.E. Aune, Leiden, 1972, pp. 194–214; K. Matsunaga, 'Is John's Gospel Anti-Sacramental? — A New Solution in Light of the Evangelist's Milieu', *NTS* 27, 1981, pp. 516–525; and W. Marxsen, *The Lord's Supper as a Christological Problem*, E.t., L. Nieting, Philadelphia, 1970.

made the sacraments really sacramental (cf. 6:63), — and to give new qualifications of the true discipleship. (p. 521)

Matsunaga here argues that the evangelist is not an anti-sacramentalist, but that he has a very high regard for the sacraments, which is why he spiritualizes their significance. The way he supposedly does this is to introduce social and spiritual implications of the 'Institution of Holy Communion' (p. 522) with a narrative and a discourse. As a means of emphasizing the horizontal implications of the eucharist, he includes the ordinance of the foot-washing and the command to love one another (chs. 13, 14). And, as a means of emphasizing its spiritual implications, the parable of the vine and its branches (ch. 15) is introduced. Thus, according to Matsunaga, it is the presence of 'drop-outs' in the Johannine church which has forced the evangelist to exchange historical references to Jesus' institution of the ordinances for spiritualized expositions of the horizontal and vertical implications of the sacraments. Despite the creativity of Matsunaga's study, two of its foundational assumptions are speculative. a) It must assume that the 'drop-outs' of vs. 66 have *dropped back into* the Johannine church. b) It must also assume that the 'spiritualizing' of the sacraments *followed* a more formal set of eucharistic rituals, rather than seeing the trend moving toward formalization, to which the evangelist objects. Nonetheless, Matsunaga is entirely correct to consider vss. 60–66 as reflecting at least part of the Johannine situation being addressed. He is also on the right track in considering the relation between perception and experience in the evangelist's dialectical appraisal of the sacraments, but both assumptions above are questionable at best.

A third relevant study is the 1970 essay by W. Marxsen, which examines the institutional development of the Lord's Supper within first-century Christianity at large. While this study is not concerned primarily with the Johannine situation, nor with Bultmann's treatment of the evangelist's sacramental stance, its implications are nevertheless central to the present discussion. According to Marxsen:

> In Christology one can show development from an "implicit" to an "explicit" Christology, from a "Christology in action" to a considered Christology. Exactly the same development can be shown when one traces the early history of the Lord's Supper. Such is our thesis. (p. 1)

The methodology followed by Marxsen is to trace the apparent development between earlier and later institution narratives in the Synoptics and Paul, and more specifically, the transition between Mark 14:22–24 and 1 Corinthians 11:23–25. In this thoughtful analysis, Marxsen notices that there are several differences between these two texts, suggesting the evolution of first-century eucharistic practices. a) For Mark, the drinking of the cup follows the blessing and eating of the bread, both of which happen 'as they were eating', and the drinking of the cup happens '*after supper*' (p. 6). b) Regarding the secondary 'word of interpretation' (*Deutewort*), Mark emphasizes the *contents* of the cup: the blood of Jesus, which is poured out for many as the 'blood of the covenant'. For Paul, though, it is *the cup* which is identified as the *new* covenant to be drunk in remembrance of Jesus (pp.

6–8). c) A similar development may be inferred regarding the use of bread between the situations of 1 Corinthians 10 and 11. While the emphasis in 1 Corinthians 10:16f. is upon the corporate unity, symbolized by the eating of *one* loaf (set within a 'meal' context), that which is eaten in 1 Corinthians 11:24f. is Jesus 'body', to be eaten 'in remembrance of' him (pp. 8–13). Thus, the transition from a real, fellowship meal to a symbolic, ritual one is clear. Similar developments can be traced between Matthew's co-opting of Mark and Luke's adaptation of both Mark and Paul. In other words, Marxsen is arguing that the institution of the eucharist may not be attributed directly to the historical Jesus. It must be seen a function of the formal evolution of the eucharist from a fellowship meal to a cultic service of remembrance within the institutionalizing church. Based on the criterion of dissimilarity as a marker of historical probability, this judgment is a sound one. This is not to say that Jesus would have objected to the meaningful practice of eucharistic rites, according to Marxsen, but it does make a distinction between earlier and later stages of developing eucharistic traditions in order to gain a clearer appreciation of their origins and significance.

The implications of these studies for Bultmann's identification of the evangelist as an anti-sacramentalist are as follows: a) While it is anachronistic to superimpose later sacramental debates over the hypothesized situation of Johannine Christianity, two facts remain: John denies that Jesus baptized (implying that he also *did not ordain it*), and John omits the institution of the eucharist at the supper. b) John 4:2 may simply reflect the evangelist's concern to put forward his own historical view (in contradistinction to emerging 'ordinance' motifs), and his omission of the institution of the eucharist in ch. 13 may simply reflect the evangelist's innocence of later connections between the Last Supper and covenantal rites.[7] Then again, he

---

7   See also, J. Jeremias' treatment of the transition from a fellowship meal to a more formalized cultic rite of remembrance (*The Eucharistic Words of Jesus*, E.t., N. Perrin, London, 1966, pp. 106–137). Thus, while Bultmann is correct in saying (*New Testament Theology* Vol. 2, E.t., K. Grobel, New York, 1955, p. 59) 'It is therefore permissible to say that though in John there is no direct polemic against the sacraments, his attitude toward them is nevertheless critical or at least reserved.', this does not mean that the evangelist's criticism has anything to do with 'the sacramentalism of ecclesiastical piety' (p. 219). Therefore, Jn. 4:2 may have had something to do with 3:5–8 and 22, as a matter of clarifying two things about baptism: a) While Jesus did not object to it, neither did he practice nor ordain it; and, b) while there may be nothing inherently wrong with water baptism, it must be accompanied by an immersion in, and filling with, the Holy Spirit.

The evangelist may have been addressing such tendencies as those represented by the Ephesian followers of Apollos (Ac. 18:24–19:10), who knew the 'baptism of John', but not the 'baptism of the Holy Spirit'. Therefore, the stress in John 3:5 is not upon '*water* and the Spirit', but upon '*water and the Spirit*' (cf. vss. 6–8). Likewise, if the eucharist were becoming increasingly 'ritualized' by institutionalizing Christianity, the evangelist's objection may not have been so much against the 'magical' views of 'mystery theophagy', but against the centralizing forces which may have been utilizing such rites for religio-political reasons. Thus, the question is not, 'Why does John omit the institution of the eucharist?'; but rather,

may be making a corrective point subtly, precisely through his *silence* on the words of institution. c) The events of John 6 were probably narrated within a meal setting, but the tradition still seems unaffected by institution narratives. Like 1 Corinthians 10:3 and 16, the manna tradition is used in conjunction with what appears to be more of a fellowship meal than a symbolic rite, and the emphasis is upon corporate solidarity (Jn. 6:35, 51–66). Perhaps Johannine Christianity had not yet made the transition from a real, corporate meal to a symbolic, ritual one as the *topos* in which the presence of the risen Lord was celebrated sacramentally.

B. *Ignatius of Antioch and the 'Medicine of Immortality'*

As evidence for his contention that John 6:51c–58 is a redactional interpolation,[8] Bultmann (p. 219) cites Ignatius' mention of *pharmakon athanasias* ('the medicine of immortality', *Eph.* 20:2) as a contemporary equivalent of an instrumentalistic and magical view of the sacraments.[9] This means that John 6:51c–58 appears to

---

'Why do the Synoptics *include* one?'. The Fourth Evangelist may have addressed the same needs in *other* ways, such as calling for unity, love and submission to one another, rather than emphasizing submission to the 'one bishop — as to the Lord', as reflected a few years later in the epistles of Ignatius. Therefore, after a thoughtful survey of the literature (pp. 249–259), R. Kysar is entirely justified in stating his opinion and raising the implicit query (*The Fourth Evangelist and His Gospel*, Minneapolis, 1975, p. 259):

> I believe that the early form of the gospel ... had no sacramental reference because the johannine community at that time was essentially non-sacramental. Could it be that the absence of the institution of the lord's supper from the fourth gospel is due to the fact that that narrative was not part of the johannine tradition and that the johannine community did not know the institution narratives in any form?

8 Two abuses of the *religionsgeschichtliche* method include the over-simplifying 'x = y' fallacy, and the often-conspicuous 'because x = y, and y is obviously gnostic/docetic/thaumaturgic/pietistic (or representing some other 'unacceptable' notion), x *must have come from* an earlier source or a later redactor. The uncritical comparison between John 6:51c–58 and the 'medicine of immortality' motif of Ignatius (*Eph.* 20:2) is a classic example of both of these abuses. For the *religionsgeschichtliche* method to be truly profitable, it must identify precisely *in what ways* x is like y, and just as significantly, in what ways x is *not* like y. Then, even if canonical text (x) be found to be ideologically problematic for a modern audience (y), a distillation of the core truth may still have hermeneutical value for the modern interpreter. Otherwise, the tendency to excise problematic ideologies from the text, in favour of retaining the ones that preach well, diminishes the integrity of the discipline. Nonetheless, *if* Jn. 6:51c–58 does indeed represent the same kind of magical approach to the eucharist that Ignatius' *Eph.* 20:2 is thought to reflect, this would indeed be contradictory to John's christological core and would thus demand an explanation. This calls for an extensive investigation into the parallels between Ignatius' letters and John 6.

9 While there certainly appear to be parallels between John 6:51c–58 and Ignatius' *Eph.* 20:2, Bultmann does not identify clearly what those parallels are, and even more importantly, how they differ. He also offers no attempt to demonstrate his judgment regarding Ignatius' view of the eucharist but simply assumes that:

be insisting on the absolute necessity of the eucharist for salvation, which would be obviously in clear contradiction to the christocentric soteriology of the evangelist. Put negatively, unless one participates in the eucharist one does not receive eternal life. If Bultmann and others are correct, that such an instrumentalist view of the eucharist indeed represents the view of Ignatius and vss. 51c–58, the interpolation theory becomes more compelling. This calls for a critical investigation of Ignatius' sacramental theology, which the Bultmanian school has not done effectively. When the Ignatian phrase is considered in its context it reveals a rather different meaning, and this applies directly to a better understanding of the Johannine situation. The full text of *Eph.* 20:1–2 is as follows (C.C. Richardson, *Early Christian Fathers*, New York, 1978 edition, p. 93):

> If Jesus Christ allows me, in answer to your prayers, and if it is his will, I will explain to you more about [God's] plan in a second letter I intend to write. I have only touched on this plan in reference to the New Man Jesus Christ, and how it involves believing in him and loving him, and entails his Passion and resurrection. I will do this especially if the Lord shows me that you are all, every one of you, meeting together under the influence of the grace that we owe to the Name ("Christian"), in one faith and in union with Christ, who was "descended from David according to the flesh" and is Son of man and Son of God. At these meetings you should heed the bishop and presbytery attentively, and break one loaf, which is the medicine of immortality, and the antidote which wards off death but yields continuous life in union with Jesus Christ.

When the phrases 'medicine of immortality' and 'the antidote which wards off death' are considered in their context, it is clear that the central issue is one of *corporate unity and solidarity*. It is in union with Jesus Christ (his suffering and resurrection) that the Christian receives eternal life, and it is in solidarity with the bishop and the presbytery that the individual has his or her well-being. Thus, it is the corporate unity of the church which is Ignatius' primary concern. Therefore, rightly understood within its context, the 'medicine of immortality' refers not to the breaking of *a loaf,* but the breaking of *one* loaf (cf. the clear connection to 1 Cor. 11:16), as opposed to holding separate eucharistic meals and dividing the fellowship. Whereas Paul addressed selfish disorderliness in Corinth, Ignatius addressed schismatic divisiveness in the Ephesian church. It is thus a reference to Christian solidarity with one another, living in obedience to the singular bishop as though to Christ which he advocates, and this emphasis can be seen throughout the rest of Ignatius' epistles as well.

Those who do not eat the Lord's Supper are thus denied all claim to life; the Lord's Supper, as v. 54 shows more clearly, is understood as the *pharmakon athanasias.* ... Those who participate in the sacramental meal bear with them the power which guarantees their resurrection [cf. Ign. *Ro.* 8:1]. (p. 235f.)

For John 6:51c–58 to be considered contradictory enough to be worthy of excision at least two aspects of the *religionsgeschichtliche* comparison must be established: a) that Ignatius' insistence on the necessity of participation in the eucharist is primarily a reflection of a 'magical' appraisal of its value; and b) that John's view is identical (not just parallel) to this view. Neither, however, is the case.

It is clear from the outset that a central concern for Ignatius is that the Ephesian church should be loyal and responsive to their bishop, Onesimus, and the presbytery. 'My prayer is that you should love him in the spirit of Jesus Christ and all be like him' (*Eph.* 1:3). And, 'Thus, united in your submission, and subject to the bishop and the presbytery, you will be real saints' (*Eph.* 2:2). Ignatius' underlying assumption has to do with his conviction that the bishops, 'appointed the world over, reflect the mind of Jesus Christ' (*Eph.* 3:2). Furthermore, 'It is clear, then, that we should regard the bishop as the Lord himself' (*Eph.* 6:1). Therefore, within the broader context of the letter, it becomes evident that a central concern of Ignatius is for the church to be united under the bishop and the presbytery and to submit to their leadership as though obeying the Lord himself.[10] John's tradition, however, manages centrifugal tendencies otherwise (cf. Ch. 9, below).

The occasion for Ignatius' concern is that there is within the community a sectarian faction which threatens the unity of the group and the character of their beliefs.[11] These schismatics flaunt the Name ('Christian') about (*Eph.* 7:1), but their behaviour is 'unworthy of God'. Ignatius warns his flock to stay away from them and offers a confessional statement for encouragement:

---

10 Thus, the primary parallel between the author of John 6 and Ignatius is the acute concern of how to *preserve corporate unity* within a centrifugal ecclesiastical situation. One may take note of Ignatius' awareness of this need in the introduction to his letter to Ephesian Christians: 'The source of your unity and election is genuine suffering which you undergo by the will of the Father and of Jesus Christ, our God.' Therefore, he addresses the need for *unity* from several vantage points: a) He first of all *appeals directly for unity* (*Eph.* 2:2; 12:2; 14:1; 20:1). b) Second, he *uses various metaphorical images* to bolster his appeal for unity (be like strings of a harp or a choir, so that your 'music' will be 'in tune' and 'harmonious' [4:1–2]; and, dissension is like the bite of 'mad dogs' which requires the healing [medicine] of the one physician, Jesus Christ — 'of flesh, yet spiritual ...' [7:1–2]). c) Most centrally, Ignatius *calls for unity under the single and chosen bishop*, through whom Ignatius believes the church is united with Christ (1:3; 2:2; 3:2; 5:1; 6:1). d) Ignatius *appeals for schismatics not to split off* and have their own meetings for worship, but to demonstrate their solidarity with the group — and therefore, with the bishop, and with Christ — by breaking only 'one loaf', which is 'God's bread' (5:2; 13:1; 20:2). Similar conclusions may be drawn from Ignatius' other letters. Cf. parallels between John and Ignatius below, Table 21.

11 Having identified more clearly the motivation behind Ignatius' reference to the 'breaking of one loaf' as the 'medicine of immortality', the *religionsgeschichtliche* comparison/contrast with John may be conducted with greater profitability. Bultmann is entirely correct in pointing to Ignatius' letters as offering a close parallel, in that one of the evangelist's most acute concerns is also to appeal for *unity*, against centrifugal pressures (this is even clearer in 1 and 2 John), which may have been precipitated by external threats of persecution. Furthermore, the evangelist re-tells the gospel narrative in a way which bolsters his concern for unity: a) He cites *Jesus as calling his followers to oneness with one another* — as he and the Father are one (17:21–23). b) Second, the evangelist *uses several metaphors to describe this unity with Christ and with one another* (the sheep, united under the true Shepherd [10:14–16, 27–30]; the branches 'abiding in' the vine [15:1–8], etc.). c) As a significant contrast to Ignatius, *no appeal is made to unity with a bishop or elder*, but *directly* to Christ himself, whose active leadership is thought to be present in the form of the pneumatic *Paraklētos*

You must avoid them like wild beasts. For they are mad dogs which bite on the sly. You must be on your guard against them, for it is hard to heal their bite. There is only one physician — of flesh yet spiritual, born yet unbegotten, God incarnate, genuine life in the midst of death, sprung from Mary as well as God, first subject to suffering then beyond it — Jesus Christ our Lord. (*Eph.* 7:1–2)

In this particular context, it is unclear whether these schismatics are Judaizers or Docetists, or even whether they represent some other threat.[12] It is clear, however, that Ignatius is advocating *cultic solidarity* as an antidote to the schismatic, 'rabid bite' of these 'mad dogs'.[13] Such frequent meetings for praise and the celebration

---

(1:12f.; 3:16, 34–36; 6:35, 51; 14:26; 20:31, etc.). d) Finally, the evangelist *employs eucharistic imagery to call for solidarity with Christ and with one another* in the face of impending suffering (6:53–56, 66; 15:18–27).

   The result of the comparison/contrast is that there are two ways in which the parallels between Ignatius and John converge and two ways in which they diverge. They converge in their *direct appeals for unity* and their *use of metaphorical imagery* to bolster their appeals. They diverge in that while Ignatius calls for loyalty to *the one bishop* — as to Christ, the Fourth Evangelist calls for adherence to *Christ himself* — through an abiding immersion in his present Spirit. And, while Ignatius calls for participation in the *one* eucharistic service of the worship community (co-opting the theophagic imagery of 'the mysteries' and Paul, cf. 1 Corinthians), the author of Jn. 6:51–58 calls for *solidarity with Jesus and his followers*, using eucharistic imagery to do so. In *both* Ignatius and John, to be willing to die with Christ is to be able to be raised with him. This is entirely different from incipient sacramental piety which is supposedly instrumentalistic or theophagic.

12   While in some passages it appears that the Judaizers and the Docetists are the same group, C.C. Richardson ('The Evidence for Two Separate Heresies', in his *The Christianity of Ignatius of Antioch*, New York, 1967 [1935], pp. 81–85) marshals convincing evidence to suggest that there were actually *two* heretical threats addressed by Ignatius. The first was an external one, arising from travelling *Judaizers*, who emphasized the oneness of God and Jewish customs, and who accused Christians of being ditheists. The second threat was more of an internal one, which seemed to involve *Gentile Christians* who denied Jesus' humanity, and who were as a consequence not prepared to undergo suffering themselves.

   The same two kinds of threats may be inferred in the Johannine Epistles. In 1 Jn. 2:18–25 the antichristic heretics have already 'gone out from us' (vs. 19), and they deny that Jesus is the Christ in their allegiance to 'the Father' (vs. 22f.). This group was obviously Jewish, and its seceding parties probably rejoined the local Synagogue. In 1 Jn. 4:1–3 a second antichristic threat seems to be emerging, which is characterized by the refusal to believe that Jesus Christ has 'come in the flesh' (vs. 2f.). This group was obviously docetising, and its seceding members were probably Gentiles who forfeited Christian fellowship to escape Roman persecution. By the time of 2 Jn. 7 this group has also 'gone out into the world' (cf. also C.C. Richardson, *Early Christian Fathers*, New York, 1970, p. 77; and C.K. Barrett, 'Jews and Judaizers in the Epistles of Ignatius', in his *Essays on John*, pp, 133–158).

13   Ignatius is fond of using graphic imagery to make his points. In this case, the unsalutary effects of those who act in ways unworthy of God are like wounds incurred from 'wild beasts' and 'mad dogs who bite on the sly' *(Eph.* 7:2). The remedial imagery used is also appropriate to the metaphor: 'There is only one *physician* ... Jesus Christ our Lord' *(Eph.* 7:2). The parallel is also clear in *Eph.* 19–20, regarding matters of ultimate concern. God's victory over the power of the 'prince of this world' is described as 'the destruction of death' (19:1, 3); and

of the eucharist overthrow Satan's threats, 'and his destructiveness is undone by the unity of your faith', declares the bishop of Smyrna (*Eph.* 13:1). Into this scheme fits God's plan for the bishop to be representative of the One who sent him (*Eph.* 6:1). Intimacy with the bishop is the means by which the church achieves intimacy with Christ (*Eph.* 5:1), and it is for this reason that corporate worship and communion are both salvific and salutary. Building on a Johannine phrase, perhaps from John 6:33, Ignatius again expresses his concern for solidarity:

> Make no mistake about it. If anyone is not inside the sanctuary, he lacks *God's bread*. And if the prayer of one or two has great avail, how much more that of the bishop and total Church. He who fails to join in your worship shows his arrogance by the very fact of becoming a schismatic. It is written moreover, "God resists the proud." Let us then heartily avoid resisting the bishop so that we may be subject to God. (*Eph.* 5:2–3)

On this point, recent Ignatian studies are in agreement[14] that in the *pharmakon athanasias* of *Eph.* 20:2 Ignatius does *not* represent an instrumentalistic or a magical view of the eucharist. Rather, it is *unity in Christ* that is central, and this unity is mediated through solidarity with the bishop and the presbytery (against the schismatics) and is participated in by the breaking of *one* loaf (not several) and meeting together in harmonious unity. Says J. Zizioulas (*Being as Communion*, London, 1985, p. 82, n. 55):

> A careful study of Ignatius' thought as a whole ... reveals that the eucharist for him is not *pharmakon athanasias* by virtue of possessing in its "nature" a potential for life or a possibility of life, in the sense suggested by the Greek idea of *phusis*. The eucharist as defined by Ignatius is above all a communion expressed by the assembly of the community around the bishop. The "immortality" of the eucharist is to be sought in this communion-event and not in the "nature" of eucharist as such.

'meeting together ... in one faith and union with Christ ... is the medicine of immortality, and the antidote which wards off death but yields continuous life in union with Jesus Christ' (20:1–2). Such graphic imagery for Ignatius is rarely literalistic.

14   Except for S.M. Gibbard ('The Eucharist in the Ignatius Epistles', *Studia Patristica* 8:2, 1966, pp. 214–218) whose article is more unquestioning than critical, recent Ignatian scholars have objected to the notion that Ignatius' sacramentality is 'magical' or instrumentalist. About the cited passage, C.C. Richardson says (n. 99):

> If they are outside the Church they lack the bread of God (*Eph.* 5:2); it is perhaps noteworthy that they do not lack the flesh of Christ, which we would expect if the idea of the ... Eucharist were uppermost in the mind of Ignatius. This is further borne out by Tral. 7:2, where being outside the Church is connected, not with the Eucharist, but with the bishop. ... To Ignatius, religious purity is dependent upon right relations with the bishop.

Agreeing with Richardson about this passage and about *Eph.* 20:2, W.R. Schoedel (*Ignatius of Antioch; A Commentary on the Letters of Ignatius of Antioch*, Philadelphia, 1985, pp. 54–56) also says that:

> Two conclusions may be drawn: (a) The description of the eucharist here is to be taken no more literally than the medical language of *Eph.* 7 (or of *Tr.* 6:2). (b) The fame of the drug called *athanasia* accounts for the reference to it in a variety of non-medical contexts ... [but] here the emphasis is on the unity under bishop and presbytery which provides the context within which the Ephesians "break bread". (p. 97f.)

The same conclusion must be drawn when considering references to the eucharist in other letters by Ignatius. His letter to the Philadelphians makes it clear that he believes a schismatic will not inherit God's Kingdom, and that to walk the way of heresy is to become 'out of sympathy with the Passion' (*Phil.* 3:3). A further problem is that the schismatics are holding their own eucharistic services. Thus, he says, 'Be careful, then to observe a single Eucharist. For there is one flesh of our Lord, Jesus Christ, and one cup of his blood that makes *us* one ...' (*Phil.* 4:1). Theological reasons for the schismatics' objections in Smyrna include their refusal to believe Jesus came in the flesh (*Smyrn.* 5:2). Neither do they 'accept Christ's blood', and apparently this is basis for their abstention from the eucharist.

> They hold aloof from the Eucharist and from services of prayer, because they refuse to admit that the Eucharist is the flesh of our Saviour Jesus Christ, which suffered for our sins and which, in his goodness, the Father raised [from the dead]. (*Smyrn.* 7:1)

In *Smyrn.* 7:2 it becomes clear that the reason believing in the death and suffering of Jesus is so important to Ignatius is that he accepts the Pauline notion that one only rises with Christ if one is prepared to die with him. If the Docetist does not believe that Jesus suffered, it would also be unlikely that such a person would feel compelled to undergo suffering for the Christian cause. Embracing the Passion (and suffering) of Christ is, for Ignatius, not primarily a matter of doctrine, but of *praxis*. To embrace the suffering of Jesus is to be willing also to suffer as his follower. This is an especially acute issue for Ignatius, as he prepares for his own martyrdom and finds courage in identifying with the tradition of the martyrs and the suffering of Christ (*Ro.* 4–8). Again alluding to John 6 and 7, it is this preparation for martyrdom to which Ignatius refers when he employs eucharistic imagery in *Ro.* 7:2–3:

> For though alive, it is with a passion for death that I am writing to you. My Desire has been crucified and there burns in me no passion for material things. There is living water in me, which speaks and says inside me, "Come to the Father." I take no delight in corruptible food or in the dainties of this life. What I want is God's bread, which is the flesh of Christ, who came from David's line; and for drink I want his blood: an immortal love feast indeed!

Even though this passage refers to eucharistic elements, Ignatius is *not* simply talking about how he loves the spiritual food of the eucharist over other meals. He is speaking of *his own solidarity with the suffering and death of Jesus* (cf. also *Eph.* 20:1). This is the existential 'nourishment' of ingesting Christ's 'flesh' and 'blood'. As Ignatius reaches the end of his life, he grows more and more aware of his impending martyrdom. His solidarity with the suffering, and *therefore* the resurrection, of his Lord must have been for him personally a key factor in his urgent feelings about the eucharist. It is sharing in the *suffering of Jesus* — 'the ingesting of his flesh and blood' — which is increasingly understood by Ignatius as 'God's bread' and which leads to a hope in the life to come.

Therefore, neither in Ignatius' use of the term '*pharmakon athanasias*' nor in any other reference to the sacraments in his epistles, does he betray a baldly magical or instrumental view of the eucharist. It is true that he believes in the Pauline idea that to include oneself in the death of Jesus leads to being included also in his resurrection, but even though he refers to this as partaking of the flesh and blood of Christ, this hardly constitutes an exact parallel with theophagic Mystery Religions. A key motivation behind his urgent appeals for participation in the eucharist of the church is that Docetists had been denying the physicality of Jesus' suffering. Thus, they also abstained from eucharistic services, refusing to believe that the elements are actually the flesh and blood of Jesus. They held their own meetings for worship, in which their own modes of eucharistic ritual may have been employed. This threat to the monepiscopacy provided Ignatius the fuel for his anti-schismatic fire, and thus, he called for unity under one bishop — as loyalty unto one Lord. Therefore, the question of *which* eucharistic meal is the efficacious one evokes a definitive response from Ignatius that the only true sacrament is that which has been administered properly, and this can only be done by one who is Christ's designated representative within the assembly.

At this point, a further connection between the Ignatian and Johannine approaches to schismatic tendencies deserves consideration. The fact that some of the seceding party's ethos in Ignatius' situation were both docetising and reluctant to partake of the eucharist is intriguing. U. Schnelle (*Antidoketische Christologie im Johannesevangelium*, Göttingen, 1987, pp. 114ff.) argues that as the Johannine secessionists were clearly docetising (by 2 Jn. 7), the evangelist has called for 'eating the flesh' and 'drinking the blood' of Jesus (i.e. participation in the eucharist) as a confrontational way of challenging their schismatic and docetising tendencies. The question here, though, is whether John 6:53–58 calls for adhering to the *cross of Jesus* (vs. 51c) and *maintaining corporate solidarity* in the face of persecution by means of employing eucharist imagery, or whether it requires cultic participation in the formal eucharist as a facilitator of non-docetic (incarnational) faith and an outward measure of faithfulness.

Another creative approach to the issue is D. Rensberger's chapter on 'Sacraments and Boundary: The Social Significance of Baptism and Eucharist' (*Johannine Faith and Liberating Community*, Philadelphia, 1988, pp. 64–86), where he argues that 'the "sacraments" of baptism and eucharist ... are closely linked to the christological and communal issues that were paramount among his [the Fourth Evangelist's] concerns' (p. 81). Building on W. Meeks' *The First Urban Christians* (New Haven, 1983, pp. 153–160), Rensberger concludes (p. 81):

> Baptism represents the threshold between the world and the community for John, and also the risk of crossing that threshold. The eucharist reinforces this boundary, too, and is linked to the maintenance of solidarity within the community of those who faithfully abide in Jesus and remain faithful in love to one another.

However, these approaches fail to distinguish between the use of eucharistic imagery to instill corporate solidarity and the advocating of eucharistic ritual participation as the sole means to the same goal. They may represent Ignatius' view but do not represent the Fourth Evangelist's. Given the absence of sacramental institutions and ordinances in John, as well as the clear incompatibility between

John's christocentric soteriology and later instrumentalism, John 6:53–58 must be considered in the light of vs. 51. The appeal is to adhere to the cross (vs. 51c), not to engage in a symbolic meal. The 'real thing' for the evangelist is full and loving participation in the community of faith (Jn. 13:34f.), not a ritualized symbol of that reality. In this way he was *like* Ignatius, but also very *different* from him.

From this discussion it is clear that even though John 6:51ff. may be considered parallel to the eucharistic inclination of Ignatius, one must reach a conclusion other than the one reached by Bultmann. Neither of these represents a magical or an instrumentalistic approach to the eucharist. Both convey the understanding that to ingest the 'flesh and blood' of Jesus is to share in the gift of eternal life, which God provides through him. In the face of persecution, this clearly involves solidarity with Jesus in his suffering and death if one hopes to share in his resurrection. For Ignatius, participation in the eucharist is an outward confirmation of this solidarity, while for John, eucharistic imagery is employed, perhaps in order to appeal for solidarity more vividly. Such a view is entirely at home within the theology of the Fourth Evangelist, and it requires no theory of interpolation.

Actually, it is entirely probable that there was a derivative relationship between Ignatius' use of eucharistic motifs and the concerns underlying John 6:51ff. Such issues as sharing in Christ's suffering, unity within the fellowship, and emphasizing a spirit-based, form of 'christocracy' may very well have been a part of the situation within Johannine Christianity which called for, in such pressing terms, ingesting the 'flesh and blood' of Jesus. Ignatius seems to have expressed these communal themes in institutional and cultic forms. Even in the Synoptic tradition, being baptized and drinking 'the cup' of Jesus refer explicitly to martyrdom and suffering (cf. Mk. 10:34–35). Therefore, for nascent Christianity in general, the eucharist had more import than simply to commemorate the Passion. It had to do with identification with Jesus in ways which affected *praxis*: the ethical fibre of everyday life. Thus, says, C.C. Richardson (*The Christianity of Ignatius of Antioch*, New York, 1967 (1935), p. 56):

> If indeed the sixth chapter of John's Gospel has reference to the Eucharist, the same connection of the elements with life is to be found there as in Ignatius. Moreover, in both John and Ignatius this concept of life is highly ethical. It is not ... the immortality of the cults, although Ignatius happens to use a phrase that is found in the literature of the mystery religions (*Eph. 20:2*). Life to him is the undying fellowship with Jesus Christ, which is conditioned on faith and love, and the Eucharist comes to be the pledge of this present life and future hope, not so much by virtue of any mystical efficacy in the elements, as by the believer's inseparable connection with the Christian brotherhood. It binds the believer to the Church, as obedience binds the Church to God. The Eucharist indeed is the testimony and assurance of the Christian's obedient faith and Christlike love.

If something like this were the case, Bultmann's theological reasons for excising vss. 51c–58 are totally undermined. The semeiological use of eucharistic imagery in order to make a christocentric appeal for corporate solidarity in the face of persecution is entirely at home with the theology at the core of the evangelist's concerns, even as understood by Bultmann. Thus, an analysis of Ignatian sacramentology from a socio-religious perspective suggests the *authenticity* of John 6:51c–58 rather than its incongruence with the surrounding context. Bultmann's appeal to one final piece of *contextual* evidence still deserves consideration, as vs. 51b comes to a full stop, and vs. 51c begins an entirely new theme which is incongruous with that which it follows ... or does it?

C. John 6:51c: Opening Sentence, or Concluding Clause?

A third element in Bultmann's theory that John 6:51c–58 is an interpolation is the contextual assessment that the literary 'seams' of the passage are vss. 51b/c and 58/59. While it is clear that vs. 58 marks the end of that which precedes it and sets the stage for that which follows, it is less clear that the previous section concludes at vs. 51b and that vs. 51c marks the beginning of the section leading up to vs. 58. The implications regarding the 'contextual problem' of vs. 51b/c are these: if it be demonstrated that vs. 51c (' ... and the bread which I shall give is my flesh, for the life of the world') is indeed the opening sentence of vss. 52–58, then the theme of this section is, according to Bultmann, the eucharistic 'flesh' of Jesus, given for the life of the world. If, on the other hand, vs. 51c is found to be the concluding clause (out of three) of vs. 51, then it must be interpreted as a summation of vss. 41ff., and vss. 53–58 may be understood as a response (employing eucharistic imagery) to the question of the Jews, 'How can this man give us his flesh to eat?' In the former case, the likelihood of 6:51c–58 being an interpolation is increased. If the latter were demonstrated, vs. 51 would constitute a tripartite conclusion to the second 'Bread of Life' discourse, which is primarily incarnational, *not* eucharistic. This would mean that vss. 53ff. are not suggestive of the function, let alone the indispensability, of the eucharist for salvation. Rather, an alternative interpretation must be found. Therefore, as well as evaluating the sacramental attitude of the evangelist and assessing the *religionsgeschichtliche* relationship between John 6:51c–58 and the letters of Ignatius, the 'contextual problem' of 6:51b/c must also be considered if the 'eucharistic section' of John 6 is to be understood properly. First, however, a brief account of some of the main discussion among recent scholars will be serviceable.

The incongruity of 6:51cff. with that which precedes and follows it has not only been argued by Bultmann, but by other scholars as well.[15] In 1956, G. Bornkamm

---

15 It is instructive to note that there is a high correlation between scholars who assent to all or to none of three propositions: a) that Ignatius' 'medicine of immortality' has to do primarily with a magical view of the sacraments, b) that the 'eucharistic interpolation' in John 6 had to have been added by a sacramentalist redactor, and c) that the break between the sections comes at vs. 51b/c, rather than between vss. 51/52, or elsewhere. Therefore, even a scholar such as Bornkamm, who argues (rightly) that Jn. 6:60–71 refers back to the incarnational section earlier in the chapter (*ZNW* 47, 1956, pp. 161–169) assumes that the section included

approached the same issue from a different angle, which carried fewer drawbacks. Bornkamm still believed 6:51cff. to be an interpolation, but he argued that the cause for the scandalization of vss. 60ff. was not the references to the eucharist implied by 6:51cff., but the descent of the Son of Man who not only gives the Bread of Life, but who also *is* that which is given. This would explain the parallelism between vss. 33, 38, 50f. and vs. 62. If the disciples are offended by Jesus' coming down from heaven as the Bread of Life, how much more will they be offended by the ascension of the Son of Man! This is further supported by the interpretation of *sarx* in vs. 63 as a reference to vss. 35–51b, *not* to vss. 51c–58. Thus, *sarx* (vs. 63) is not the 'flesh' of the eucharist but a contrast to the way of the Spirit, as developed in the Nicodemus story of ch. 3. All of this would suggest that vs. 51b was originally followed by vss. 59–71, and that vss. 51c–58 is a eucharistic interpolation added later by a redactor.

Such a view builds upon the best of Bultmann's theological insights and also reduces some of the liability of Bultmann's extensive disordering and reordering scheme, making Bornkamm's interpretation more believable than Bultmann's. As well as following Bultmann's error of ascribing the theology 6:51cff. to the magical notion of the eucharist as supposedly espoused by Ignatius, however, Bornkamm's approach rests upon a contextual interpretation of vs. 51 which is not necessarily correct.

In 1958, H. Schürmann[16] challenged Bornkamm on the grounds that vs. 51c is not an introduction to an exposition upon the eucharist, but that it is primarily a reference to the death of Jesus on Calvary. This is supported by the connection between vs. 51 and vs. 33, as the coming down from heaven of the Bread of God ultimately culminates in Jesus' sacrificial death on the cross. Therefore, John 6:26–58 may be considered to represent two sections: vss. 26–51 which refer to Jesus' death on the cross, and vss. 53–58 which represent subsequent Johannine teaching on the eucharist. Vs. 52 is not a grievance against the sacraments, but it is an objection to the suggestion of Christ's dying (cf. Mk. 8:27–33; Jn. 6:69). Schürmann continues his challenge to Bornkamm in his 1959 article, in which he argues that there are also eucharistic overtones in vss. 26–51b and 60–71. To differentiate vss. 53–58 from the rest of the chapter on the basis that it contains

---

vss. 27–51b, but *not* vs. 51c. Other scholars who assume all three of these propositions include H. Köster, 'Geschichte und Kultus im Johannesevangelium und bei Ignatius von Antiochen', *ZTK* 54, 1957, pp. 56–69; E. Lohse, 'Wort und Sakrament im Johannesevangelium', *NTS* 7, 1960, pp. 110–125.

16 Schürmann has actually made two significant contributions to this discussion: 'Jo 6:51c — ein Schlüssel zur grossen johanneischen Brotrede', *BZ* 2, 1958, pp. 244–262, in which he argues that vs. 51 is the culmination of the section beginning in vs. 41; and 'Die Eucharistie als Repräsentation und Applikation des Heilsgeschehens nach Jo 6:53–58', *TThZ* 68, 1959, pp. 30–45, 108–118, in which he argues that the eucharistic motif in vss. 53–58 is merely an accentuation of the same theme running throughout the entire chapter. See also, W. Wilkens, 'Das Abendmahlszeugnis im vierten Evangelium', *Evangelische Theologie* 18, 1958, pp. 354–370, (esp. 362ff.), in which he argues against interpreting vss. 51c–58 in terms of the *pharmakon athanasias* of Ignatius.

eucharistic themes can only be done as a matter of degree of explicitness, not as a matter of theological substance. Furthermore, the meaning of vs. 63 as suggested by Bornkamm is furthered by a sacrificial interpretation of vs. 51c. Therefore, it is doubtful that if there was an interpolation, it should have begun with vs. 51c. The significance of Schürmann's contribution to this discussion is that if vs. 51c marks not the beginning of a eucharistic interpolation, but the conclusion of an incarnational (sacrificial) discourse, then the meaning of vss. 53–58 must also be reconsidered. Thus, the eucharistic allusions of vss. 53ff. may not be understood as an interpolation, emphasizing the soteriological function of the eucharist, but as a Johannine development of the incarnation and its implications for discipleship by means of employing eucharistic allusions. Vss. 53–58 serve as a lens which collects the light of vss. 26–51 and reflects it back in a more concentrated form (pp. 108ff.).

Schürmann's first essay was followed quickly by a brief, yet affirming article by P. Borgen.[17] Borgen agreed with Schürmann that 6:51c 'binds the preceding and the following parts together ...' (p. 277), and that 'the discourse in John 6 ... is composed as a unity to interpret the quotation from the Old Testament found in John 6:31' (p. 278). In this terse essay may be observed some of the central components of Borgen's later monograph (*Bread*, 1965), in that he argued that 1. the entire section (6:31–58) is a *midrash*; 2. the theme, *arton ek tou ouranou edōken autois* (vs. 31) is paraphrased and interpreted in vss. 32, 33, 34, 35, 38, 41, 42, 48, 50, 51, 52, and 58; 3. *phagein* (vs. 31) occurs in vss. 49, 50, 51, 52, 53, and 58, and its synonym *trōgein* occurs in vss. 54, 56, 57, and 58 (pp. 277–278). Therefore, Borgen concludes that the entire section (vss. 31–58) is a literary and thematic unity, which reflects a midrashic development of the manna-giving and manna-eating themes of the Old Testament verse(s) referred to in 6:31.[18]

---

17 P. Borgen, 'The Unity of the Discourse in John 6', *ZNW* 50, 1959, pp. 277–278. With this article, and the following form-critical research of Borgen, the discussion was catapulted onto a new plane of investigation.

18 In Richter's criticism of Borgen's *Bread from Heaven* ('Zur Formgeschichte und literarischen Einheit von Joh 6:31–58', *ZNW* 60, 1969, pp. 21–55) is another example of the threefold cluster of issues to which scholars either gravitate or do not. Although he argues that Borgen's thesis actually does a 'boomerang' (demonstrating the formal unity of John 31–51b only, as the eucharistic theme of vss. 51c–58 is obviously out of character with the evangelist's central purpose as described in 20:31), Borgen's response to Richter ('*Bread from Heaven*; Aspects of Debates on Expository Method and Form', in his *Logos Was the True Light*, Leiden, 1981, pp. 32–46) actually demonstrates that *Richter's* objection does a boomerang, negating itself (pp. 43–45, n. 27). In other words, a) *Pisteuein* (20:31) is not only lacking in vss. 51cff., but also in vss. 41–51b. b) The occurrence of *zōēn (aiōnion) echein* in vss. 33, 35, 40, 48, 51b, 51c, 53, 54, 57 and 58, ' ... speaks against the view of Richter and in favour of the unity of the discourse as a whole'. c) Borgen contends that Richter performs 'arbitrary exegesis' by considering some references to Jesus and his mission as 'christological', and others not. The strength of Borgen's reply is confirmed by the accord of R. Schnackenburg ('Zur Rede vom Brot aus dem Himmel: Eine Beobachtung zu Joh 6:52', *BZ* 12, 1968, pp. 248–252) and J. Dunn ('John VI — A Eucharistic Discourse?', *NTS* 17, 1971, pp. 328–338).

In his 1971 article J. Dunn agrees with Schürmann that 'v. 51c belongs to the preceding context and that in consequence it should be understood metaphorically — its primary reference being to the redemptive death of Jesus' (p. 329f.). He also sides with Borgen's analysis of the unity of vss. 31–58 and believes Richter's attempt to refute Borgen's work has been unsuccessful. Believing Bultmann and Lohse (cf. n. 14) 'have overstated the contrast between what goes before 6:51c and what follows it' (p. 329), Dunn identifies several points of continuity between vss. 51c–58 and vss. 27ff.[19] Vss. 51c–58 are also connected to vss. 60ff. in that 'the repetition in v /. 57–8 of the precise thought of vv. 50–51b is clearly intended to find its answer in v. 62' (p. 329). Thus, Dunn believes Bornkamm is 'mistaken in his attempt to drive a wedge between the *sarx* of vv. 51c–56 and the *sarx* of v. 63' (p. 331). The main thrust of vs. 51c is a reference to the redemptive death of Jesus on the cross, and this motif is developed by means of the sacrificial connotations of the phrase, 'flesh and blood'. Says Dunn (*NTS* 17):

> And this is expressed more clearly in v. 51c: it is by his exaltation on the cross that he will give (note the future) his flesh for the life of the world. In other words, this is how John presents the offence of the cross, and we find ourselves at once within that complex event of Jesus' death, resurrection, ascension and gift of Spirit which John presents as a theological unity. The hard saying therefore is the talk of Jesus' incarnation *and his death*. (p. 331)

This being the case, the connection between vss. 31–51b and vss. 60ff. (cf. Bornkamm) would also apply to the relationship between vss. 51cff. and vss. 60ff. The presence of eucharistic terminology does not necessarily imply the advocacy of institutional sacramentalism. Therefore, Dunn's criticism of Lohse and company is justified.[20] The sacramentology of John 6:51ff. is as much a reference to the

---

19 Says Dunn (1971. p. 329):

> Moreover, vv. 51c–58 in most of their ... ideas are certainly uniform with their context, both preceding context and succeeding context. As to the former, note the following links: v. 51c explains v. 33; having eternal life (vv. 40, 47, 53–4) and resurrection at the last day (vv. 39, 40, 44, 54); eating and drinking (vv. 35, 53–6); the reappearance of *brōsis* (vv. 27, 55); reciprocal indwelling is very Johannine (v. 56; see also 19:20 [17:20?]; 15:4–5); *zōn* as an adjective (vv. 51, 57); Jesus as sent by the Father (vv. 29, 57); the identification of that which is eaten with Jesus himself (vv. 35, 48, 57); eating resulting in life (vv. 51, 57–8; bread from heaven (vv. 31–3, 41, 50–1, 58); contrast with manna (vv. 30–3, 49–51, 58). As to the latter: the reception in vv. 57–8 of the precise thought of vv. 50–51b is clearly intended to find its answer in v. 62.

> G. Burge agrees with Dunn (*The Annointed Community*, Grand Rapids, 1987, pp. 181–190) and includes a thoughtful section on John's 'corrective' views.

20 *Ibid.* In recent years several German scholars (U. Müller, 'Die Bedeutung des Kreuzestodes Jesu im Johannesevangelium. Erwägungen zur Kreuzestheologie im Neuen Testament', *KD* 21, 1975, pp. 49–71; U. Schnelle, *Antidoketische Christologie im Johannesevangelium*, Göttingen, 1987) have been emphasizing the 'theology of the cross' within John. By this is meant that the evangelist, like Paul, calls for solidarity with Jesus in his suffering and death as well as in his resurrection. Thus, Schnelle emphasizes that John 6:51c–58 is a eucharistic section which is used by the evangelist precisely because in participating in the eucharist, community members with docetising inclinations would be faced with the fleshly reality of

sacrificial death of Jesus on the cross as anything else, notwithstanding the many ways this passage has been misinterpreted as a new 'law',[21] emphasizing the soteriological necessity of the eucharist. Vs. 51c is not as much of an 'unbearable tension' as some scholars (Bultmann, Lohse, et.al.) would suggest. According to Dunn, John 6:51c is in complete continuity with that which precedes it and that which follows.

The most persuasive essay, however, regarding the place of John 6:51c is C.K. Barrett's 'The Flesh of the Son of Man' (in his *Essays on John*, Philadelphia, 1982, pp. 37–49; see also Barrett's essay, 'Sacraments', pp. 80–97). After reviewing some of the salient contributions on this topic, Barrett proposes his own solution to the problematic passage on the grounds of form and content. Regarding form:

> Most of the discussion of the question of redaction has proceeded on the assumption that the paragraph which may or may not be an original part of the Gospel is verses 51c (*kai ho artos de ...*) — 58 (... *zēsei eis ton aiōna*). ... But division at this point is not entirely satisfactory, for it means that after one short sentence Jesus breaks off, the Jews ask their complaining question (vs. 52: *Pōs dunatai houtos ...?*) and the discourse then resumes with a reiteration of the reference to *sarx*, expanded with further reference to the Son of man. It seems in fact to be John's method to break up his discourses by means of objections. (p. 40)

As evidence to support this observation, Barrett examines the occurrence of the objections and complaints of those in dialogue with Jesus, first in John 6, and then in other parts of the Gospel. It is most clear that vs. 60 marks the beginning of the next section (vss. 60–70), as vs. 59 punctuates the preceding section with a reference to the setting, and Jesus' dialogue with his disciples (vss. 61ff.) follows upon the objection, 'What a "hard saying" this is! Who can go along with that?' (vs. 60b). Similarly, Jesus' dialogue with the Jews (vss. 26ff.) was precipitated by the ironic

---

Jesus' suffering and death on the cross (pp. 216–228). Therefore, 'Zielpunkt und Zentrum des Kapitels ist der eucharistische Abschnitt in V. 51c–58, auf den die redaktionelle Arbeit des Evangelisten zuläuft und der in seiner antidoketischen Ausrichtung den Anlaß für die jetzt vorliegende Gestalt von Joh 6 bildete' (p. 228; cf. also, J. Becker, *Das Evangelium nach Johannes* Bd. 1, Gütersloh, 1979, pp. 195–206; and F.J. Moloney, 'John 6 and the Celebration of the Eucharist', *DownR* 93, 1975, p. 248). And, according to J. Forestell (*The Word of the Cross*, Rome, 1974, p. 193):

> Jn. 6:51 is probably a eucharistic formula, but in the context of the gospel it points to the universal life-giving purpose of Jesus' mission, especially of his death. ... There is nothing in the context of 10:15, 17 or 15:13 which points to the cultic character of Jesus' death. It is an act of self-devoting love on Jesus' part, undertaken in obedience to the will of the Father, to save from death those who believe in him.

21 In the otherwise excellent treatment of the Spanish authors, Mateos and Barretos (1983), they treat the eucharist as a 'new law', and miss the motivation for including vss. 53–58. On one hand, their interpretation seems quite promising as they speak of belief in Jesus as 'assimilating his life and death — his flesh and blood' (cf. p. 303): 'La Ley de la nueva comunidad es la asimilación a su vida y muerte (su cuerpo y su sangre), con el don total de sí mismo por amor a los demás (6:41–58).' However, to identify the eucharist as a 'new law of the community' (p. 343) misrepresents the way that the eucharistic imagery is used in John 6.

question of the crowd (vs. 25), and Jesus' other discourse sections in John 6 follow *in response to* the comments and questions of his discussants (cf. vss. 28, 30f., 34, 41f., *and* vs. 52). In response to each of these statements the Johannine Jesus embarks upon a christocentric development of a new theme. It thus seems entirely likely that this would also have been the case regarding vs. 52 as the most suitable starting point of the new paragraph rather than vs. 51c.[22] Each new section in John 6 is characteristically marked by the *interjection of Jesus' discussants*, *not* the preceding clause in Jesus' discourse.

A second confirmation of the unity of vs. 51ab with 51c has to do with the three-fold structure of the characteristic ending of each of Jesus' discourses in John 6. In vss. 27, 32f., 40, 51, 58, and 63f., the Johannine Jesus concludes each discourse, short or long, with a three-fold sentence which sums up the former discussion and leads into the next discourse.[23] Jesus' discussants, therefore, play a pivotal role in the progression of the narrative. By raising a question or making a comment, they prepare the hearer/reader for the subsequent teaching of the Johannine Jesus. In this sense, the question of the discussant becomes the question of members of the Johannine audience. Each of Jesus' responses either involves or concludes with a three-fold statement, which both reaches backwards to summarize the former discussion and extends forwards to prepare the way for the following discourse. Upon this point, most scholars using synchronic approaches to John 6 agree.[24] This means that John 6:51 should be considered a unitive conclusion to the discourse of vss. 43–51, which addresses the question of the Jews in vs. 41f. It also introduces a new theme, the suffering and death of the Son of Man,[25] which is developed using

---

22 Thus, the dialogue/discourse section of John 6 begins in vs. 25 and concludes with the reaction of the disciples in vs. 66. As a contrast to the typical Johannine narrative, in which Jesus (or some other agency of God) is the initiator, the typical Johannine dialogue/discourse begins with the initiative of Jesus' discussants, which leads into a dialogue with Jesus and often concludes with a discourse. This is especially evident in the three main discourses on the 'bread of life' in John 6 (vss. 35–40, 43–51, and 53–58). They all begin with Jesus' responding to a comment/question of the crowd/Jews (vss. 34, 41f., and 52). The same is true with the disciples and Jesus in vss. 60–66.

23 While it is less obvious in vss. 27, and 32f., the conclusions of each of Jesus' main discourses in John 6 (vss. 40, 51, and 58) all employ a tripartite summary of what has been discussed before and point ahead to what will be developed in the next few verses. Therefore, to divide vs. 51 between parts b and c is to go *against* the stylistic structure of the evangelist's typical tripartate constructions in Jn. 6.

24 See especially P. Ellis, *The Genius of John*, Collegeville, 1984, pp. 124–127; and G. Mlakuzhyil, *The Christocentric Literary Structure of the Fourth Gospel*, Rome, 1987.

25 The theme of the Son of Man, which Bultmann usually associates with the christology of the evangelist, provides a key unitive link between vss. 27, 53, and 62. What is alluded to in vs. 27 and described more clearly in vs. 51 is finally made manifest in vss. 53–56. The 'life-producing bread', which Jesus *gives* and *is*, is his *flesh*, given for the life of the world. Thus, the one who 'comes to' (vs. 35) him and who 'abides in him' (vs. 56) participates with him in his death, and *therefore* in his resurrection. According to Barrett ('The Flesh of the Son

eucharistic imagery in vss. 52–58. Thus, vs. 51c is *not* an opening sentence, but a *concluding clause*.

When John 6:51–58 is taken in this sense, the connection between John and Ignatius becomes far clearer. John's eucharistic allusions in 6:53ff. are to the emerging institutional sacramentalism of the mainstream church what Ignatius' references to the 'medicine of immortality' are to the theophagic practices of the Mystery Religions. In a rather odd reference to Paul's incorporation of 'the mysteries' (*Ro.* 7:1) as a basis for his eucharistic teaching in 1 Cor. 11, Ignatius stresses that the sacramental meal of the eucharist is far more efficacious than the rites of pagan religions. Not only is the 'power of Satan' overcome by the Christian eucharist, but the believer who shares in Christ's death will also share in his resurrection. It is important to note that Ignatius is in no way suggesting that he believes the rites of the Mysteries to be efficacious at all! He is simply 'borrowing' parasitically from the popular authority of their claims in order to stress the superiority of the Christian practice. It is the rhetorical employment of a motif from popular mythology, *not* an indication of pistic convincement as to its veracity. In some ways, Paul does the same.

Likewise, John nowhere mentions the institutionalization of the sacraments nor their being ordained by Jesus. The central 'sacramental' concern of the Fourth Evangelist is the *incarnation*, as God's Son is portrayed as being sent by — and yet returning to — the Father for the purpose of uniting humanity with God. Given also that John even seems to counteract any institutionalizing trends attributing baptism and the eucharist to 'ordinances' of Jesus (Jn. 4:2 and ch. 13), it seems highly unlikely that the evangelist's references to ingesting the flesh and blood of the Son of Man (vss. 53ff.) may be interpreted as pro-eucharistic statements in the ritualistic sense. Rather, just as Ignatius borrowed from the popular authority of Mystery Religions and Paul, so the evangelist has borrowed from the authority of emerging sacramentalism within first-century Christianity. The evangelist has done the same regarding the authority of the scriptures, John the Baptist, the law of Moses, etc. in order to emphasize the ultimate place of the Son — in whom the love of the Father is revealed *fully*. In using eucharistic terminology in 6:53ff., the evangelist is not emphasizing the importance of the eucharist but pointing to an abiding belief in the 'flesh and bloodness' of the incarnation, which is the true end

---

of Man', in his *Essays on John*, Philadelphia, 1982, pp. 37–49), 'The three references to the Son of Man cohere; what is more, the use of "Son of Man" in 6:53 introduces into verses 52–8 the theme of descent which is so characteristic of verses 35–50 and is implied by verse 62' (p. 48). Therefore, vs. 51a–c serves as a bridge between the sections preceding it *and* following it. The conclusion of D.M. Smith is therefore certainly justified (p. 146):

Thus it seems that 6:51c is not just an appendage, or a transition to the introduction of an alien sacramental idea, but rather a fitting culmination to what has preceded. In fact, if the allusion to Jesus' death were omitted, the preceding discourse would be deprived of a very important historical point of reference. In death, Jesus becomes the bread of life. ... In no other relationship can the heavenly bread be understood or received.

of all eucharistic rites and Christian discipleship. Thus, in this passage the incarnation is *not* used to emphasize participation in the eucharist. Rather, the emerging authority of eucharistic imagery in the late first century (vss. 53–58) has been co-opted in order to call for faithful solidarity with Jesus and the community of his followers, which is for the evangelist the *only* means of attaining abundant and eternal life. Says Lindars ('Word and Sacrament', p. 60):

> The object of these verses is thus, not to relate the discourse to the eucharist, but to exploit the eucharistic words for the needs of the discourse. Those who feed on Jesus as the Bread of Life must accept the fact that they feed on the one who was bound to die in order to accomplish the divine purpose. This is the "hard saying" (verse 60) which gives offence (*skandalizei*, verse 61; cf. 1 Cor. 1:18–24).

Findings

Given the high degree of confusion regarding sacramental terminology and scholarly discussions of John 6, it should be acknowledged that *nowhere* does John advocate a sacramental view of the eucharist cast in the form of an institutional rite, an ordinance of Jesus, or a magical view of the theophagic rites of Mystery Religions — even in John 6:51–58! Rather, the ultimate 'sacrament' for John is the *incarnation*, and to 'eat and drink' the 'flesh and blood' of Jesus is to assimilate the salvific reality of the incarnation by faith and communal faithfulness. In God's Word become flesh, the world is drawn to God by means of a believing relationship with Jesus.

1. Therefore, Bultmann is correct to identify an apparently critical stance toward sacramental themes on behalf of the evangelist, but he is wrong to assume that this is due to the evangelist's objection to 'the sacramentalism of ecclesiastical piety' or to an apparent objection to instrumentalistic views of sacraments as a magical way to receive eternal life. These problems were obviously wrestled with in the developing history of the church, but to transpose them onto the setting of first-century Johannine Christianity is anachronistic. The evangelist may have objected to the ways that sacraments developed institutionally, but he clearly felt they distracted from the religion of the historical Jesus as he understood it. He may even have felt that the rise of sacramental practices competed with authentic faith in Christ alone, as did thaumaturgic christologies, but this is not the same as concluding that he was an anti-sacramentalist, proper. Just as he has used Jesus' signs dialectically, he has also employed sacramental imagery dialectically to appeal for abiding solidarity with Jesus and his community.

2. An analysis of the letters of Ignatius of Antioch shows that his appraisal of the eucharist was *not* simply 'magical' or instrumentalistic. More accurately, Ignatius believed that the only way to be united with Christ in his resurrection was to express solidarity with him in his death. The context from which Ignatius was writing faced two acute pressures, the Judaizers from without, and docetising tendencies from within. While Ignatius countered the former by means of

expounding a high christology, he countered the latter and more acute problem by calling for solidarity with the *one* bishop and participation in the *one* worship service (and thus the breaking of *only one* loaf) of the community, thereby expressing one's solidarity with the *one* Lord, Jesus Christ, which is the faith leading to eternal life. In order to do this Ignatius co-opted the imagery of the Mystery Religions, but this is not the same as saying that he embodied their views or agreed with them. Clearly he did not. Rather, he built more centrally on 1 Corinthians 10–11, and perhaps even John 6:33. Thus, the parallelism between John 6:51–58 and the letters of Ignatius exists, but *not* in the way suggested by Bultmann. Just as Ignatius co-opted the imagery of the Mystery Religions to bolster his rhetorical appeal for unity, the evangelist (or *whoever* wrote the section) is co-opting emerging eucharistic imagery within the church to call for corporate solidarity and loyalty to Christ in the face of persecution under Domitian.

3. The contextual evidence for dividing the passage at 6:51b/c is weak indeed. It depends solely upon the mistaken theological judgment that the only meaning of '... and the bread which I shall give is my flesh, for the life of the world.' is a reference to the eucharist, which is then developed in the following verses (52–58). The contextual evidence suggests that just as in vss. 27, 32f., 40 and 58, the typical form of Jesus' last sentence before being addressed by his audience in John 6 involves a three-part summation of what has gone on before, preparing the way for the next question/reaction and following discourse. John 6:51 is no exception. Parts a and b summarize the preceding discussion, and part c of vs. 51 refers to Jesus' suffering and death, which is then developed using eucharistic imagery in vss. 53–58. It is *this* calling for *participation with Jesus in his suffering and death* which scandalizes the disciples (vs. 61) and even causes some of his followers to regard the cost of walking with him too high (vs. 66).

4. The result of this analysis is to conclude that just as there is insufficient stylistic and contextual evidence for identifying John 6:51c–58 as a redactor's interpolation, neither are there sufficient *ideological* grounds. Nevertheless, Bultmann's incisive observations still point the way forward as follows: a) His identification of the evangelist's critical stance toward the sacraments may reflect an ideological disagreement between the centripetal ways late first-century Christian leaders sought to counteract the centrifugal tendencies of the sub-apostolic era. An acute emphasis on cultic ritual involvement was one of these, and while it is anachronistic to assume the evangelist was an 'anti-sacramentalist', he may indeed have objected to institutionalizing attempts to centralize the church. He apparently disagreed with the rise of ordinance motifs and understood the unifying power of faith in Jesus Christ to be better expressed in relational and familial ways than in ritual ones. b) The comparison/contrast between John 6 and the letters of Ignatius is illuminating. Here we find two distinct, yet parallel, models for unifying the church under the leadership of Christ (christocracy). One calls for unity with the bishop—as to the Lord (cf. Matt. 16:17–19), while the other calls for an abiding immersion in the present leadership of the resurrected Lord (cf. Jn. 6:69; chs. 14–

16). It is highly unlikely that there were no tensions among middle to late first-century Christian leaders regarding the means by which parallel problems should be addressed. Exploring this possibility may suggest something of the dialectical situation out of which John 6 was written (cf. 3 Jn. 9–11). c) By examining the structure of vs. 51, something of the progressive/linear and yet circular/repetitive structure of the evangelist's forward-moving, didactic style is revealed. The evangelist works out his themes dialectically, introducing one theme, developing another, and bringing the light of each new understanding to bear on former ones. This suggests that not only is the evangelist a dialectical thinker himself, but as a conveyer of his insights, he seeks to bring his audience to the same kind of living and christocentric 'truth held in tension', which he has himself encountered. These findings — especially the parallels with the socio-religious situation of Ignatius and his audiences — will be developed further, in Chapter 9, below.

Chapter 7

The Dialectical Character of John 6

The previous three chapters have tested the validity of Bultmann's diachronic approach to the unity and disunity of John 6 and have produced the following conclusions:

1. There is no significant difference in style between the material attributed to the *sēmeia* source, the *Offenbarungsreden*, and redactional interpolations in John 6. Actually, the entirety of the chapter (and the Gospel) betrays a Semitizing style of Greek, and if not written by the same person (or editorial group), it certainly appears to have been. Thus, the stylistic unity of the chapter must be explained by Bultmann's 'imitation of style' hypothesis, which is itself a back-handed acknowledgment of the *stylistic unity* of John 6. On the other hand, the narratological contribution of the evangelist *is* distinguishable on the basis of stylistic evidence, but this does little more than belabour the obvious: John 6 was written by an author who combined two miracle stories with a discussion about the meaning of the first sign, leading into several typically Johannine christological discourses, which are followed by an adverse reaction of some disciples and the confirmation of the twelve. However, this says absolutely nothing about the existence of — let alone the literary character of — the sources thought to have been used by the evangelist. Stylistically and linguistically, John 6 is a basic unity.

2. In order to recreate the hypothetical sources used by the evangelist, and in order to reconstruct an acceptable order which may have existed before the adding of interpolations by the redactor, Bultmann must propose an extremely complex theory of disordering and rearrangement. However, this solution to other problems becomes a major problem, itself. The odds against the disordering happening as suggested by Bultmann are astronomically high, and the proposed reordering has *less* to do with solving problems intrinsic to the present order of the text, and *more* to do with alleviating further problems created by excising vss. 51c–58. The fact that a scholar as creative and brilliant as Bultmann had to work this hard to offer a coherent theory of composition suggests that the literary disunity of John 6 is less than obvious. In fact, Bultmann's new proposals are so problematic that accepting the text as it stands, and dealing with its tensions in ways other than by means of complex diachronic composition theories, is far more tenable.

3. Bultmann's approaches to contextual difficulties in John 6 are equally problematic. He has overlooked the evangelist's use of local irony in 6:25f. and 6:27ff. and has failed to see the extended irony throughout the entire chapter.

Rather, he has ascribed these authorial tensions to redaction-critical aporias, supposedly reflecting literary 'seams' between the signs and discourse sections of John 6. Regarding vss. 25f. and 27ff., Bultmann's method of operation is exposed. Whether contextual difficulties are suggested by rough transitions, or glossed over by smooth ones, Bultmann is entirely happy to propose a diachronic solution to *his* detection of a contextual difficulty.

4. Bultmann is wrong to say that the dialogue of 6:26–71 'has no real bearing on the situation produced in 6:1–25 ... ' (p. 218). This error is confirmed by the unifying theme of 'testing', which runs throughout John 6. Not only is Philip tested in vs. 6, but throughout the 'Bread of Life' dialogues and discourses the crowd, the Jews, and the disciples are tested, and each is called to choose the life-producing Bread, to be given by the Son of Man (vs. 27), as opposed to clinging to other kinds of 'bread' which are inferior and ultimately death-producing. The testing motif may be described as the divine-human dialogue by which persons are confronted by agents of, or witnesses to, God's saving love in the world. This leads to a response by the individual or group, which is characterized by one of the following reactions: *unbelief* (the refusal to believe in Jesus as the agency of God's salvation), *incomplete belief* (perceiving Jesus as a wonder-worker — or a prophet/king like Moses — but nothing more), or as *complete belief* (which is characterized as an abiding relationship with Jesus [vs. 56], even calling for solidarity with him in his death as well as in his resurrection [vss. 51–55]).[1]

A central problem with this human-divine dialogue is recognized by the evangelist and alluded to in various ways. A key flaw of human-made religion is that humans too easily confuse the 'bread' which God *gave* in the past with the 'Bread' which God *gives* in the present (vs. 32f.). Eschatologically, this is the flesh

---

1 R.E. Brown develops this concept most helpfully in Appendix III of his commentary ('Signs and Works', pp. 525–532), and he actually poses *four* reactions to the signs (p. 530f.): a) First there is 'the reaction of those who refuse to see the signs with any faith'. Unbelief (11:47) is understood as humanity's refusal to come out of darkness into the light (3:19f.), and people's sin is magnified by their having seen without believing (9:41; 15:22), with the only explanation being the foretelling of unbelief by Isaiah (12:37–41). b) Second, there is the 'reaction of those who see the signs as wonders and believe in Jesus as a wonder-worker sent by God', but fail to see in his words and works the 'revelation of who Jesus is, and his oneness with the Father' (2:23–25; 3:2f.; 4:45–48; 7:3–7). c) Third, there is 'the reaction of those who see the true significance of the signs, and thus come to believe in Jesus and to know who he is and his relation to the Father'. This reaction may be observed following several of Jesus' miracles (2:11; 4:53; 6:69; 9:38; 11:40), and in this sense Jesus' signs serve as a witness to who he is and whence he has come (5:36; 10:38; 11:41f.). d) Fourth, there is the 'reaction of those who believe in Jesus even without seeing signs' (20:29). 'Such disciples believe on the word of those who were with Jesus (17:20), and Jesus blesses them and prays that they may see his glory (17:24).' The first two kinds of belief are portrayed as negative by the evangelist (unbelief and incomplete belief), while the other two are portrayed as positive, and even salvific (complete belief and belief 'par excellence'). All four of these levels of belief may be observed in the narrative of John 6.

of the Son of Man, given for the life of the world (vss. 27, 51, 53, 62f.), and for the evangelist, the central focus of the 'sacramental principle' is the *incarnation*. Therefore, the central importance of Jesus' miracles, Old Testament typologies, and even eucharistic imagery is that which they *signify*: the spiritual reality of God's saving presence, revealed in Jesus, to which they point. The many ways that God has spoken in the past (cf. Heb. 1:1–4) are fulfilled and embodied in the final 'Word made flesh', to whom the evangelist calls his audience to respond in faith. He alone has the 'words of eternal life' (vs. 69).

5. The unity of sign and discourse in John 6 is also suggested by comparing the three traditions regarding the feeding and subsequent events in Mark 6 and 8 and John 6. In each of these traditions there is a common clustering of reported events: a feeding, a scene on or near the water, and a discussion about the meaning of 'bread'. As the feeding and a following discussion of its meaning were included in *both* Marcan traditions, it is highly likely that this was also the case for the Johannine tradition. In other words, the connection of sign and discourse was probably much earlier than Bultmann's composition theory suggests. Furthermore, the authenticity of the Johannine tradition is affirmed by the fact that Matthew's, and especially Luke's, redactions of Mark 6 and 8 tend to agree with the Johannine tradition. Therefore, the traditional origins of sign and discourse in John 6 are *not* as truncated as Bultmann suggests. While some parts of John 6 reflect later developments in Johannine Christianity, an interpretation of the loaves accompanied the Johannine narrative of the feeding, perhaps even from the early stages of the tradition.

6. The sacramentology of John 6:53–58 is neither presented as an institutional ordinance, nor does it represent a magical view of the eucharist, as scholars have believed (wrongly) regarding Ignatius' *pharmakon athanasias*. Rather, vss. 53ff. represent the borrowing from the popular authority of eucharistic motifs in order to emphasize the importance of believing solidarity with Christ — in his death as well as his resurrection. This was the *skandalon* which caused the departure of even some of his disciples, and as in Mark 8, the confession of Peter in John 6 is associated with the suffering of the Son of Man and its implications for discipleship. Thus, the spirit-flesh dualism of vs. 63 is not a reference to the insufficiency of outward rituals (Dunn), nor is it a reference only to the section preceding vs. 51c (Bornkamm). Rather, it concludes the 'exhortation of the "two ways" ' and calls for humanity to reject their inferior notions of death-producing 'bread' in exchange for the life-producing 'Bread' which Jesus gives and is (vs. 27).

7. Bultmann is correct to assume that vss. 60–71 refer to 'the way of the cross', but he is wrong to infer that vs. 51c is a reference primarily to the eucharist and *not* to the suffering and death of Jesus. When vss. 51–71 are interpreted (rightly) as a unitive section, it becomes clear that the adding of the new theme in vs. 51c — the cross — is centrally connected with the audience to which John 6 is addressed. Therefore, the latest targeted audience addressed by John 6 (and especially vss. 51–66) is the followers of Jesus within Johannine Christianity, who may be tempted to leave the community of faith in the face of suffering. As Ignatius appealed for

solidarity with the *one* bishop and the celebration of *only* one eucharist, and as the the author of Matthew added the 'succession of Jesus' narrative to Peter's confession (Matt. 16:16–19), so the confession of Peter in John 6 suggests something about the ecclesial means by which the Fourth Evangelist seeks to bolster faithful solidarity with Jesus and his followers within Johannine Christianity. The juxtaposition of Peter and the Beloved Disciple throughout the rest of the Gospel also suggest the character of the evangelist's ecclesiological views, in dialogue with parallel ideological views within developing Christianity. The issue here is not necessarily a power struggle between two individuals. The central issue is christocracy: the means by which the risen Christ continues to be the leader and shepherd of the community of faith.

8. Contrary to the reactions of many scholars who have sought to demonstrate the stylistic, contextual or theological unity of John, a proper evaluation of Bultmann's diachronic approach to John 6 inevitably produces two conclusions: a) While on the one hand Bultmann's cumulative evidence is insufficient to support the weight of his complex theory of composition; b) his insights and detection of subtle inconsistencies and perplexities are indeed worthy of providing the 'building material' for future constructs.[2] This latter point has too often been neglected by Bultmann's critics, to their peril. Therefore, the original query of the present study must again be raised. If the christological unity and disunity of John may *not* reasonably be attributed to tensions *external* to the thinking and writing of the evangelist, they must be regarded as *internal* to his thinking and writing; but some explanation must be posed as to how this may have been possible. This issue is clarified even further by R. Fortna's acknowledgment that the central motivation for the posing of a hypothetical Signs Gospel is *not* explaining stylistic evidence, but addressing John's theological tensions:[3]

> Finally, we consider the strongest evidence for a pre-Johannine Gospel combining signs and passion, namely the fundamental **theological unity** in the two halves and its sharp difference from the theology of the present Gospel.

---

2 This 'building material' may be summarized as follows: a) The interpretive comments of the evangelist (vss. 6, 14f., 23f., 26, 41f., 60f., 66, etc.) should be taken seriously, and as a group they suggest the way in which the unifying theme of 'testing' is understood by the evangelist and related to the central christological point of the narrative. b) The 'Bread of Life' dialogue/ discourse begins properly with the exhortation of the 'two ways' (death and life) in vs. 27, *not* at vs. 31 (contra Borgen, et. al.). c) A strikingly new theme *is* introduced in vs. 51c, but it is only secondarily a reference to the eucharist. Primarily, it is a reference to the suffering and death of the Son of Man (vss. 27, 53, 62), and the evangelist uses eucharistic imagery to call for believing solidarity with Jesus and the community of his followers. Therefore, vss. 60–71 *do indeed* refer to following Jesus no matter the cost, but the appeal which begins innocently enough in vs. 27 takes a radical turn at vs. 51, and it is developed for the benefit of the intended immediate audience in the remainder of the chapter.

3 In Fortna's first Excursus (A) at the end of his second monograph (1988), the dialogue with Ruckstuhl continues:

> It is patent that the central, indeed virtually the only, theological theme in the signs is a simple christology, the fact that Jesus is Messiah. While other issues are not absent, ... they are always secondary and implicit. (1988, p. 213)

Thus, Fortna's explicit identification of the *theological* motivation underlying his source-critical approach to John is highly significant.[4] He assumes the attributing of theological tensions in John to a *literary* dialogue between a redactor and his source(s) is to be preferred over a *reflective* dialogue within the mind of the evangelist (or the author of his 'non-reflective' source) and also over *rhetorical* dialogues with the evangelist's evolving audience. Upon this assumption hangs the marshalling of stylistic, contextual and ideological evidence within Fortna's and Bultmann's treatments of John 6, and the validity of this assumption must be evaluated. If there really is convincing evidence for hypothesizing sources underlying and redactions overlaying John 6, the critical scholar deserves to know this. However, the dearth of stylistic and contextual evidence supporting a

---

> I concede that my conclusions were in some ways hasty. Thus, Ruckstuhl diminishes the percentage of Johannine characteristics absent in the source by observing that many of them are used "exclusively in discourse material, most often in elevated speech" or "only exceptionally found in the narrative material" ("Language", p. 131–132). But ... the proportion of characteristics not found in the source remains significant, especially when we consider the likelihood that the Evangelist, perhaps unwittingly, will have imitated its pre-Johannine style. ... Thus, stylistic blurring is to be expected. (p. 210, n. 509)

With the final dearth of stylistic evidence for distinguishing variant sources and redactions in John, one wonders why source critics do not abandon this aspect of their arguments and simply concentrate on contextual and theological evidence. One can only take so much of the explanation that 'the redactor imitated the style of the evangelist' and the 'evangelist imitated the style of his sources — perhaps unwittingly', before one is forced to conclude that this amounts to an 'unwitting denial of the existence of stylistic evidence' by those who have argued the case most rigorously. In John 6 there are virtually *no* stylistic differences which cannot be attributed to the *story which is told*, and the *comments of the story-teller along the way*. Therefore, one must agree with D.M. Smith at this point:

> To attribute the phenomena which give the impression of the overall stylistic unity of the Fourth Gospel to the evangelist's sources ..., while it offers a way out of a difficult situation, becomes an increasingly suspect procedure the more it is utilized. (p. 83)

4 Fortna's admission confirms at least one aspect of Smith's first impression as he began his research on Bultmann's commentary. While Smith was entirely correct to acknowledge the multiple motivations and implications of Bultmann's work, he was nonetheless sensitive to the theological interests of Johannine source-critical explorations, and this 'hunch' is described coarsely in his introduction to his monograph (p. vii):

> The endeavor to show that Bultmann's literary and source criticism is simply a means of rationalizing and supporting his own theological views was abandoned at an early stage as both tendentious and unprofitable. His work is much more — and less — than that.

While Smith did well to lay aside such an impression, a particular aspect of it must be taken further. If Bultmann *has* sought to reconcile theological tensions within the Fourth Gospel by attributing them to dialogues between redactors and their sources (and it is inconceivable that Bultmann could have started with stylistic evidence alone), given the *lack of* contextual and stylistic evidence, an alternative approach to these theological tensions must be explored.

diachronic theory of the composition of John 6 causes one to return to Barrett's proposal that the evangelist *was* a 'dialectical thinker' (above, Chapter 3), and the rest of this chapter will be given to exploring the kinds of factors which contribute to dialectical and reflective thinking. In doing so, recent research-based studies in the field of cognitive development (especially regarding the factors contributing to one's ability to think dialectically) will be considered.[5] One study approaches faith in God along developmental lines (Fowler), and the other analyzes the characteristics of spiritually transforming encounters (Loder).

A. *Faith Development and Dialectical Thinking*

In his theory of faith development, J. Fowler has proposed that just as there are stages of psychological, cognitive, and moral development,[6] so there are stages of *faith* development which are generally common to all human beings. Over two decades of research, and after hundreds of interviews with individuals from various strata of life, Fowler has identified six stages of faith development which he believes are potentially common to all people. Says Fowler:

> These stages, which try to describe uniform and predictable *ways* of being in faith, are not primarily matters of the *contents* of faith. We are not suggesting that a person goes through a succession of world views and value systems, if we mean by those terms substantive beliefs, themes, images, and stories of faith. Rather, we are trying to identify and communicate differences in the *styles*, the *operations of knowing and valuing*, that constitute the action, the way of being that is faith. Our stages describe in formal terms the structural features of faith as a way of construing, interpreting and responding to the factors of contingency, finitude, and ultimacy in our lives. (*Becoming*, p. 52)

While it is the fifth stage of faith development (*Conjunctive Faith*) in which adults come to think dialectically, holding apparent contradictions in tension, there

---

5 J. Fowler, *Stages of Faith: The Psychology of Human Development and the Quest for Meaning*, San Francisco, 1981; and *Becoming Adult, Becoming Christian; Adult Development and Christian Faith*, San Francisco, 1984. See J. Loder, *The Transforming Moment; Understanding Convictional Experiences*, San Francisco, 1981. See also P.N. Anderson, 'The Cognitive Origins of John's Christological Unity and Disunity', in *Horizons in Biblical Theology* 17, 1995, pp. 1–24.

6 Fowler's work draws heavily on the findings of such well-known theorists as Erikson, Piaget, Kohlberg, Gilligan and Levinson (cf. especially E. Erikson, *Childhood and Society*, 2nd. ed. New York, 1963; J. Piaget, *Six Psychological Studies*, New York, 1967; L. Kohlberg, *The Philosophy of Moral Development*, San Francisco, 1981; C. Gilligan, *In a Different Voice; Psychological Theory and Women's Development*, Cambridge, Mass., 1982; and D. Levinson, *The Seasons of a Man's Life*, New York, 1978), but it goes beyond them in that it applies these findings to ways people think about matters of spiritual faith. See also relevant criticisms and developments of Fowler's work in *Faith Development and Fowler* (Eds., C. Dykstra and S. Parks, Biormingham, AL, 1986), and *Christian Perspectives on Faith Development* (Eds., J. Astley and S. Parks, Grand Rapids, 1992).

is value in at least an introduction to the other five stages. To summarize Fowler's theory of faith development, he believes that there are basically six stages of faith through which humans may develop, as they mature in their understandings of God and matters of 'ultimate concern'. Fowler believes all humans begin with an undifferentiated *primal faith*, and that just as an infant tests his or her environment,[7] so primal faith grows out of a sense of testing that which is trustworthy, providing the soil out of which further levels of faith may grow. The first of these is *Intuitive-Projective Faith* (Stage 1), and it is characterized by the pre-school child feeling like he or she is the centre of the world. Correspondingly, God is perceived as a projection of the child's felt needs. The second stage is *Mythic-Literal Faith*, and during this stage of faith development the 7–10 year-old child tends to distinguish between the 'real' world and make-believe stories, with a great emphasis placed on God's 'fairness'.

Stage 3 is called *Synthetic-Conventional Faith* by Fowler, and it is precipitated by the breakdown of literalistic constructs in the presence of implicit clashes between stories. Corresponding with early adolescence, this stage is *synthetic* not in the sense of being *artificial*, but in the sense that it involves 'pulling together and drawing disparate elements into a unity, a synthesis' (*Becoming*, p. 59). It is *conventional* in the sense that the individual has largely internalized the norms and values of his or her community and seeks to conform to those norms. Authority is located within traditional authoritative roles, especially when those roles are assumed by persons commanding personal respect, and matters of faith are deduced from such sources of authority. Stage 4 may be understood as *Individuative-Reflective* faith, and one's transition to it is usually facilitated by 'serious clashes or contradictions between valued authority sources', or 'the encounter with experiences or perspectives that lead to critical reflection on how one's beliefs and values have formed and changed, and on how "relative" they are to one's particular group or background' (*Stages*, p. 173). This sort of transition is characteristic of later adolescence and is commonly precipitated by such factors as leaving home or coming into contact with world-views conflicting with one's own. Whereas prior internalized values and beliefs may have been largely unexamined, the movement toward *Individuative-Reflective* faith involves the critical challenging of previously held notions. This stage involves 'de-mythologizing', and it is most aptly regarded as the autonomous understanding of truth held by a free-thinking adult, differentiating between one's authentic self and convictions and one's many societal roles and expectations.

---

7   The following discussion is taken from the sections in Fowler's two books in which his faith development theory is presented most clearly: in *Stages of Faith* (henceforth, *Stages*), pp. 119–213; see also the more condensed treatment in *Becoming Adult, Becoming Christian* (henceforth, *Becoming*), pp. 48–76.

While most adults attain an *Individuative-Reflective* level of faith,[8] not all move on to the fifth stage of faith development, which Fowler calls *Conjunctive* faith. The transition to Stage 5 involves a 'restlessness with the self-images and outlook maintained by Stage 4' (*Stages*, p. 183). Often occurring in middle-age, this transition is brought on not merely by a crisis of external sources of authority, but by *contradictions within oneself*, as the reflective adult must reconcile his or her own compromises of personal ideals, and admit 'that life is still more complex than Stage 4's logic of clear distinctions and abstract concepts can comprehend'. When this happens, 'stories, symbols, myths and paradoxes from one's own or other traditions may insist on breaking in upon the neatness of the previous faith'. Disillusionment with one's individuated faith presses one 'toward a more dialectical and multileveled approach to life truth' (*Stages*, p. 183).

Borrowing from Nicolas of Cusa (1401–1464) who 'developed the idea of God as the *coincidentia oppositorum* — "the coincidence of opposites" — the being wherein all contradictions meet and are reconciled' (p. 183), Fowler employs this motif to describe the fifth stage of faith, 'Conjunctive faith.' Thus:

> Carl Jung adapted this [Cusa's] idea in many of his psychological writings on religion, altering the term to the *coniunctio oppositorum* — the "conjunction of opposites." The stage of faith that emerges with mid-life or beyond involves the integration of elements in ourselves, in society, and in our experience of ultimate reality that have the character of being apparent contradictions, polarities, or at the least, paradoxical elements. (*Becoming*, p. 64)

Conjunctive faith moves beyond the dichotomizing logic of Stage 4's either-or approach to reality. It sees that issues have more than one side, and that even the hard fought and finally won battles for autonomy and integrity in Stage 4 must be set aside in the humbling aftermath, as it is learned that every new solution has its own set of new problems. One's parents seem to have been much wiser than previously thought, one comes to know that one has his or her own share of 'blind sides', one realizes that God is far beyond even the best descriptions of who God

---

8 Fowler's interview analysis (*Stages*, pp. 313–323) shows that of a total of 359 intensive interviews (conducted across a wide spectrum of ages, evenly divided between male and female, from Judeo-Christian traditions in North America), percentages (here rounded) of those who reached (at least) a Stage 4 level of faith are as follows: ages 0–6:0%; ages 7–10:0%; ages 13–20:5%; ages 21–30:43%; ages 31–40:54%; ages 41–50:90%; ages 51–60:59%; and age 61+:60%. In other words, by their 30's most of the population sampled had *at least begun* to operate on an Individuative-Reflective (Stage 4) level of faith. By their 40's the majority of those sampled in this age-range *were* operating at least on this level; and by their 50's nine tenths of those sampled in this age-range were operating on a Stage 4 level of faith development *or higher*.

On the other hand, those operating on (at least) Stages 5 were as follows: ages 0–6:0%; ages 7–10:0%; ages 13–20:0%; ages 21–30:0%; ages 31–40:15%; ages 41–50:13%; ages 51–60:24% age 61+:18%. Thus, of the total sample, only 15% were tested as being in transition to Stage 5, *Conjunctive Faith*, or operating on a higher level (Stages 5 or 6).

is, and one begins to see that no individual insight or religious expression has sole access to the truth of God. There are four hallmarks of the transition to Conjunctive faith (p. 65f.):

(1) An awareness of the need to face and hold together several unmistakable *polar tensions* in one's life: the polarities of being both *old* and *young*, ... *masculine* and *feminine*, ... *constructive* and *destructive* ... and the polarity of having both a *conscious* and a *shadow self.*

(2) Conjunctive faith brings a felt sense that truth is more multiform and complex than most of the clear, either-or categories of the Individuative stage can properly grasp. In its richness, ambiguity, and multidimensionality, truth must be approached from at least two or more angles of vision simultaneously. Like the discovery in physics that to explain the behavior of light requires two different and unreconcilable models — one based on the model of packets of energy and one based on the model of wave theory — Conjunctive faith comes to cherish paradox and the apparent contradictions of perspectives on truth as intrinsic to that truth.

(3) Conjunctive faith moves beyond the reductive strategy by which the Individuative stage interprets symbol, myth and liturgy into conceptual meanings. Beyond demythologization and the critical translation of the mythic and symbolic to propositional statements, Conjunctive faith gives rise to a "second naîveté", a postcritical receptivity and readiness for participation in symbol and myth.

This means (4) a genuine openness to the truths of traditions and communities other than one's own. This openness, however, is not to be equated with a relativistic agnosticism (literally, a "not knowing"). Rather, it is a disciplined openness to truths of those who are "other," based precisely on the experience of a deep and particular commitment to one's own tradition and the recognition that truth requires a dialectical interplay of such perspectives. Put another way, Conjunctive faith exhibits a combination of committed belief in and through the particularities of a tradition, while insisting upon the humility that knows the grasp on an ultimate truth that any of our traditions can offer needs continual correction and challenge.

For these reasons, persons of Conjunctive faith would be unlikely candidates for being 'true believers', in the undialectical and uncritical sense of single-minded devotion to a cause or ideology and would be unlikely 'protagonists in holy wars' (p. 67). They know that as well as the highest of ideals, each person also has a dark side of the self (Jung), and that even the most thoughtfully constructed organizational structures are still prone to new sets of problems. This stage of faith requires a dialogical approach to issues and realities by which knower and known are engaged in a multiplex structure of interaction. The strength of Conjunctive faith is that it gives rise to the 'ironic imagination — a capacity to see and be in one's or one's group's most powerful meanings, while simultaneously recognizing that they are relative, partial and inevitably distorting apprehensions of transcendent reality' (p. 198). The weakness is that this paradoxical understanding of truth may also become debilitating and paralyzing. Says Fowler:

Conjunctive faith involves the integration into self and outlook of much that was suppressed or unrecognized in the interest of Stage 4's self-certainty and conscious cognitive and affective adaptation to reality. This stage develops a "second naîveté" (Ricoeur) in which symbolic power is reunited with conceptual meanings. Here there must also be a new reclaiming and reworking of one's past. There must be an opening to the voices of one's "deeper self." ... Stage 5 can appreciate symbols, myths and rituals (its own and others') because it has been grasped, in some measure, by the depth of reality to which they refer. (p. 197f.)

The sixth stage of faith is *Universalizing* faith, and movement to it from Conjunctive faith involves the overcoming of paradoxes and divisions within oneself and within society at large, inherent to the dialectical awareness of Stage 5. Universalizing faith is a radical level of self-actualization in which the individual is willing to suffer — and even to relinquish his or her life — not for the sake of self-interest (Stages 1 and 2), nor for the sake of fitting into society as a well-adjusted yet autonomous adult (Stages 3 and 4), but for the sake of obeying the truth regardless of the consequences.[9]

> Persons best described by Stage 6 typically exhibit qualities that shake our usual criteria of normalcy. Their heedlessness to self-preservation and the vividness of their taste and feel for transcendent moral and religious actuality give their actions and words an extraordinary and often unpredictable quality. In their devotion to universalizing compassion they may offend our parochial perceptions of justice. In their penetration through the obsession with survival, security, and significance they threaten our measured standards of righteousness and goodness and prudence. Their enlarged visions of universal community disclose the partialness of our tribes and pseudo-species. And their leadership initiatives, often involving strategies of nonviolent suffering and ultimate respect for being, constitute affronts to our usual notions of relevance. It is little wonder that persons best described by Stage 6 so frequently become martyrs for the visions they incarnate. (*Stages*, p. 200)

According to Fowler, few reach a Stage 6 level of faith development, and those who do cannot operate on this level all the time. More common is the case where a free-thinking, autonomous adult (Stage 4) is forced to re-examine his or her individuated conceptions of faith in the light of contradictory experiences (which leads to a Conjunctive level of faith: Stage 5), but who is then confronted by transforming glimpses of truth, which call for the reckless abandonment of all else in order to facilitate the actualization of such images within the sphere of human activity (Stage 6). One may operate on more than one level at a time, especially regarding different issues and understandings, and persons often operate on stages lower than the highest ones they have achieved. But Fowler is basically correct to argue that persons generally will not 'skip' stages from lower to higher. In other words, one cannot distinguish one's autonomous beliefs (Stage 4) *until* one has

---

9 Examples of individuals who have operated on a Stage 6 level of faith development include such notables as Martin Luther King, Jr., Gandhi, Mother Teresa of Calcutta, etc. (which explains in part why *only one* out of the 359 persons interviewed scored in the *Universalizing Faith* category). Therefore, says Fowler:

> To say that a person embodies the qualities of Stage 6 is not to say that he or she is perfect. Nor is it to imply that he or she is a "self-actualized person" or a "fully functioning human being". ... Greatness of commitment and vision often coexists with great blind spots and limitations. (*Stages*, p. 201f.)

assimilated the views of one's social group (Stage 3), and one cannot move to a dialectical and conjunctive understanding of faith (Stage 5) *until* one has come to 'own' for oneself notions and experiences, which are later found to be contradictory. Thus, in many respects, faith development is entirely parallel to the natural process of human development. Regardless of religion, age or culture, humans by and large move from primal faith to more self-centred understandings of spiritual matters, to social and group-defined religious values, and (perhaps) to convictional beliefs which transcend self and society in obedience to 'the truth'. While Fowler's study has many problems with it, his theory is nonetheless based on extensive research and has been received positively across a wide spectrum of religious audiences.[10] However, its value for the present study is that Fowler offers an intelligible theory, based on empirical research, describing the process by which an individual comes to think dialectically about his or her faith. If the evangelist was indeed a dialectical thinker, as Barrett rightly assumes, it is reasonable to conclude that some of his transition from Stages 3 to 4 to 5, and perhaps even to Stage 6 faith, may be implicit in his distinctive portrayal of Jesus.

For instance, if the evangelist is confronting conventional understandings of what the Messiah should be like (Stage 3 faith), some of these notions may be inferred as they relate to the kind of Messiah to which the Johannine Jesus is contrasted. This is the typical level (Stage 4 faith) on which straightforward polemic is conducted: 'the truth is not X, but Y', and in this respect the analyses of Borgen, Brown, Martyn and others are structurally correct. The evangelist often 'corrects'

---

10 As Fowler himself is well aware of the limitations of his study, the extent of its application must be at least somewhat limited. Some of these limitations include: a) *Ethnocentrism*. Fowler's sample is admittedly limited to a North American (largely caucasian, and literate) population, and one wonders what sort of findings may have been derived from a rural Asian, African, or Latin American population. b) *Religiocentrism*. Again, Fowler has admittedly chosen a sample from the Jewish-Christian (late 20th century North America) population, but one wonders what would result from a sample of Iranian Shiite Muslims, or Voodoo adherents in Haiti. c) *Chronocentrism*. While it would have been impossible to conduct such a survey during another age (say, pre-Enlightenment Europe, or post-70 CE Palestine and Asia Minor), one is simply aware that the findings of Fowler's study are much more easily accommodated within the present ecumenical climate of America and Europe than they would have been during the 'Manifest Destiny' climate of the America of the 1890's or the European and American missionary movements around the same time. Fowler is aware of these and other limitations; therefore, he tailors the implications of his study accordingly.

Nonetheless, his work has been received in remarkably positive ways across various religious groups and even across various disciplines (cf. reviews in the *Anglican Theological Review* 65, 1983, pp. 124–127, by D. Browning; and the *Journal for the Scientific Study of Religion* 21, 1982, pp. 288f., by J.P. Keating, for representative samples). Regardless of the limitations of such a study, it does have significant implications for illuminating one's understanding of the factors contributing to a reflective and dialectical exploration of one's faith, whatever the age or culture. Fowler's model has incorporated recent feminist contributions (esp. Gilligan), and as his interviews included females, his model is far less vulnerable to feminist critiques than Kohlberg's.

the conventional notions of his audience. However, much of the christological disunity of the Fourth Gospel (unlike 1 and 2 John) is characterized not as the posing of the 'correct' christological view, but as the posing of 'conjunctive' motifs—held in tension, which betrays a dialectical (Stage 5) level of theological reflection. The difference between this level of believing and Stage 4 faith is that the reconciliation of contradicting elements stems not from deciding for oneself what one believes (as a contrast to other authoritative opinions), but from wrestling with the *internal* contradictions between one's perceptions and one's experiences.[11] This process is fundamental to the discipline of reflective theology, and if the evangelist were indeed a reflective theologian, even a first-century Jewish Christian within a Hellenistic setting, one is entirely justified in exploring the kinds of factors which may have contributed to such christological reflection.

B. *Dialectical Thinking and 'Transforming Encounters'*

A second cognitive model for understanding dialectical thinking as it relates to the process of theological reflection, is more of a 'crisis' model as opposed to a developmental one. Also in 1981, a significant study was published by J. Loder, in which he reflects upon the traumatic experience of nearly having been killed in a road-side accident, and the spiritual experiences which followed.[12] The combination of personal experience and extensive research makes this book extremely

---

11 In other words, the evangelist treats tensions with the Synagogue (reflected by the 'fear of the Jews' motif: 9:22; 12:42f.) as effecting a Stage 3 mentality, and he laments the refusal of some Pharisees to risk social alienation in order to follows Jesus ' ... because they loved the praise of men more than praise from God' (12:43). On the other hand, the evangelist commends autonomous faith for others (4:42; 9:38; 20:28; Stage 4), while his own approach to Jesus' flesh/glory (1:14) and signs (20:29) betrays the thinking of one who is operating on a Stage 5 level of Conjunctive faith. It is for this reason that many of John's christological tensions cannot simply be ascribed to the evangelist's socio-religious 'dialogues' with the Synagogue, Samaritans, or even other Christians. Jesus' discourses in chs. 5, 6, 8, 10, 13–17, etc. betray the dialectical thinking of one who refuses to reduce his christology to a definitive and monological statement. Thus, the 'dialogues' within the thinking of the evangelist must also be explored, as they relate to John's unitive and disunitive christology.

12 Citing such examples as the Damascus road event of the Apostle Paul, the scientific breakthroughs of Einstein and Schrödinger for science, Marx and Toynbee for history, and Freud and Jung for personality theory, Loder describes the experience of 'knowing' — generally and convictionally — as:

   ... first, foremost and fundamentally an event. At the center of an event is a nonrational intrusion of a convincing insight. It is constructed by the imagination and constitutes a leap that may be found in any seemingly closed sequential movement from proposition to proposition, and a similar sort of leap is found at the crux of every convicting event. This is the central common feature that makes every convictional event an act of knowing and every act of knowing an event. (p. 26f.)

valuable as a resource for understanding 'an anatomy of spiritual encounters',[13] and its findings are complementary to Fowler's. A particular value of Loder's contribution has to do with its challenging of current epistemological views,[14] but for the purpose of this study, Loder's identification of five steps basic to any experience of knowing 'as a transforming event' is most helpful.[15] These five steps include a) *conflict*, b) *an interlude for scanning*, c) *the constructive act of the imagination*, d) *release and openness*, and e) *interpretation*. Loder argues that these five steps accompany all transforming events of knowing, whether they be the 'Aha' experience of solving a nine-dot puzzle, or a 'Damascus road experience' like the one encountered by Paul.

The sense of *conflict* arises out of being confronted with an experience which is antithetical to one's situational context. It causes one to be alarmed, even shocked, and to take note of what is happening. This leads to an *interlude for scanning*, in which the individual searches within his or her frame of reference for solutions to the problems created by the conflict. If no suitable parallels are found, one's mind will eventually pose a tentative 'hypothesis' as a *constructive act of the imagination*. In other words, 'It is this third step, the construction of insight sensed with convincing force, that constitutes the turning point of the knowing event' (p. 33). The next step has two aspects to it: the sense of *release*, as the energy bound up in the conflict is liberated, and a sense of *opening*, in which the knower experiences an aspect of self-transcendence and the reality of moving beyond one's previously-held notions of truth. The fifth step is *interpretation*. In it the knower reflects backward upon the meaning of the event (and elements leading up to it), and looks forward, anticipating the implications this 'transforming moment' may have for the future. Therefore, the deep level of awareness which results from such transforming encounters may be called 'convictional' knowing. Loder rightly points out parallels between scientific, 'esthetic' and therapeutic ways of knowing, but he is also justified in developing a portrayal of the distinctive kind of convictional knowing which stems from transforming, spiritual encounters.[16] He also correctly

---

13 This is not his term, but mine.

14 Loder proposes 'a new theory of error' (pp. 20–27), in which he argues that solely 'objective' approaches to truth suffer from an 'eikonic eclipse' caused by their screening out 'subjective' content. Thus, 'the determination of truth is the end result of a rational process combining induction and deduction', and it must include the *image* as well as linear thought (p. 21). Loder also goes on to illustrate that, while the scientific method effectively 'tests' tentative hypotheses, it is nonetheless dependent on 'eikonic' experiences of knowing — the constructive images of the imagination — *before* an hypothesis may even be posed (cf. also P. Palmer, *To Know As We Are Known; A Spirituality of Education*, San Francisco, 1983).

15 In other words, if the dialectical christology of the evangelist consists of reflections upon christocentric encounters with God — whether they stem from knowing the man Jesus, or whether they have stemmed from mystical encounters with the risen Christ — Loder's analysis of transforming spiritual encounters is highly instructive for understanding the character and content of John's distinctive presentation of Jesus.

16 Loder analyzes the five-step account of the thinking process outlined by J. Dewey (*How We*

identifies the place of convictional knowing within human development theories, but also shows how it differs.[17]

The significance of Loder's contribution for the present study is that if the Fourth Gospel contains material which is a reflection upon the experience(s) of an individual (or group) who has 'beheld the *glory*' of Jesus as the Christ, insights into John's christological unity and disunity may be gained. What has been mistaken as an appeal to 'historical' authority in the Johannine tradition (esp. 1 John 1:1–3) is actually the valuing of a tradition assumedly built upon *transforming encounters with Jesus*, with which the post-resurrection life of the community is believed to be continuous. The supreme valuing is not of objective, factual-type content, but of the subjective, relational-type connectedness to the living Lord. This means that if John's christology has its origins in transforming encounters with Jesus (Jn. 6:20), which lead into future encounters with the eternal Christ (cf. Bultmann, p. 70f., esp. notes 2 and 3, re. Browning and Kierkegaard), the epistemological origin and structure of this content is personal and relational. Thus, any approach to John's christology which does not take its subjective aspect into consideration (albeit in a rational way) cannot but misapprehend the 'truth' of the Johannine witness. As a contrast to the gradual elevation of the significance of an event, characteristic of maturation within one's faith development, one's appraisal of a spiritual encounter is elevated *from the beginning*. This appears to have been the case for Paul, reflecting upon his Damascus road experience, and there are many parallel accounts of such 'encounters with Jesus' in John (1:41ff.; 6:20; 20:16; 21:7, etc.). Therefore, whether the evangelist may have had a mystical encounter with the risen Christ upon reading or hearing the gospel story from the 'eye-witness' generation, or whether the evangelist himself may have encountered the transforming presence of God's love in the man, Jesus, Loder's contribution applies. A transforming encounter involves the irruption of that which is beyond one's world and frame of reference in a way that shakes the foundations of one's preconceived notions of

---

Think, New York, 1933, pp. 106–118), and draws parallels between the five elements of scientific knowing and his own five steps of knowing (pp. 39–44). He also identifies parallels between his theory of knowing and 'esthetic knowing' (pp. 44–53) and 'therapeutic knowing' (pp. 53–60). As a contrast to these kinds of knowing Loder poses a four-fold model of the convictional knowing event involving 'the lived world', 'the self', 'the void', and 'the Holy' (pp. 68–91). This outline offers a wholistic consideration of the ways in which the knowing event affects the individual.

17 While Loder's study overlaps with Fowler's (both being published in 1981), he correctly locates his study within the mainstream of developmental studies (pp. 125–160). One of the interesting asides in this chapter is his connecting the developmental work of E. Erikson and J. Piaget with the 'transformation dialectics of the nineteenth-century philosopher Georg Friedrich Hegel' (p. 129). While the historical connection is unclear, there is certainly a great deal of continuity between the kinds of epistemological phenomena which Hegel sought to address and the work of recent developmental theorists. Thus, there may be more connections between developmental studies and theology (and even New Testament theology) than is currently acknowledged.

spiritual truth to the core, making all things new. Thus, the well-known patristic reference to John as the 'spiritual gospel' implies not its detachment from eye-witness encounters with Jesus, but *its radical proximity to them.*

C. *Rudolf Bultmann and Dialectical Theologizing*

While one may object that late twentieth-century studies ought not to be applied to a first-century piece of writing, one must also acknowledge that applying diachronic theories of composition to account for theological tensions is no improvement. The significant difference is that the studies of Fowler and Loder are based upon extensive research, accounting for ways in which people think dialectically about the contradictions of life. On the other hand, Bultmann's assumption that the same author *could not have thought* in ways which appear to be contradictory is untested and must be accepted on grounds of faith, not rational or empirical evidence. Therefore, while Bultmann's interpretive insights are incisive and valuable, and ought to be retained, his theoretical construct explaining John's composition is flawed because he adopts a Synoptic source-critical and redaction-critical model to account for John's christological unity and disunity. However, if another of Bultmann's models is chosen, such as his explanation of 'dialectical theology', a way forward emerges. In his 1927 address at Eisenach[18] Bultmann asked:

> What, then, is meant by *dialectic*? Undeniably it is a *specific way of speaking* which recognizes that there exists no ultimate knowledge which can be encompassed and preserved in a single statement. ... The dialectical method in philosophy depends on the conviction that every truth expressed is a partial truth and that whole truth which is its basis can best be found by first setting beside it the contrary statement. For the contrary statement ... must also contain a portion of the truth. By setting the two partial truths against each other and combining them, it may be possible to grasp the underlying principle. (p. 146)

In this statement Bultmann offers an *excellent* description of Conjunctive faith (Stage 5), and this appears to be precisely the level of faith development on which the Fourth Evangelist must have been operating. The anomaly between this essay and Bultmann's commentary on John is that while he assumes modern theologians and philosophers can (and do) think dialectically, he refuses to allow the evangelist to do the same. Instead, he adopts the model of a scribe, hovering over no fewer than three major texts and several minor ones, trying to compose a written gospel, which became subsequently disordered *before* anyone was able to remember the original order, and was later patched together (wrongly) by an editor who forged his dissonant content into the gospel and passed it off falsely as the account of an eye-witness. This is no less of a twentieth-century construct, and it simply is the

---

18 Later entitled 'The Significance of "Dialectical Theology" for the Scientific Study of the New Testament', in Bultmann's *Faith and Understanding* I, ed. R. Funk, E.t. L.P. Smith, London, pp. 145–164, citation, p. 146.

wrong approach for John.[19] This is why Barrett's essay on dialectical theology (above, Chapter 3) is so convincing. It demonstrates, based on a widely-known historical precedent (the definition of reflective thinking in Plato's *Theatetus*), a credible explanation for the evangelist's dialectical method of reflecting upon his understanding of the words and works of Jesus. Therefore, if Bultmann's keen theological insights should be combined with his understanding of how dialectical theologians regard the truth (which is corroborated by the studies of Barrett, Fowler, and Loder), new possibilities emerge for understanding John's christological unity and disunity, and the destination and purpose of the Fourth Gospel as well. Thus, making fullest use of Bultmann's contribution involves three corrections: a) While his theory of composition is radical (and also brilliant) his interpretive insights are most sound and hermeneutically helpful. b) Far from being demonstrable, his theory of composition is unsubstantiated, even by his own stylistic, contextual and theological evidence, and it may largely be disregarded. c) Yet, if another of his approaches is applied (that of the evangelist as a dialectical thinker), a way forward emerges with buoyancy. This way forward will now be applied to Bultmann's detection of the evangelist's ambivalence toward Jesus' signs and the tension between the flesh and glory of Jesus in John.

1. *The Evangelist's Ambivalence Toward Jesus' Signs*. The ministry of Jesus was by no means unambiguous and non-controversial. Therefore, to assume that

---

19 An easy fallacy of text-oriented scholars is to project their medium onto the works they study. Therefore, ideas and stories are reduced to the literary form of written sources or detached fragments of papyrus, rather than seeing the development of traditions as more dynamic than that. Parallel to modern philologists, Johannine diachronic scholars have often had to 'kill a living text' in order to dissect it, analyze its meaning and attribute its origin to one literary source or another. As the Russian form-critic, M. Bakhtin has said:

> Underlying the linguistic thinking that leads to the construction of language as a system of normatively identical forms is the practical and theoretical aim of studying dead foreign languages that have been preserved in written texts.
>
> It cannot be too strongly emphasized *that this philological aim has largely determined the character of all European linguistic thought*. It grew up and matured over the corpses of written languages. Nearly all the main categories, nearly all the basic approaches and skills were evolved while trying to breathe life into these dead corpses. (p. 42)

(Citation, V.N. Voloshinov, in *Bakhtin School Papers*, E.t., N. Owen, 1983). As Bakhtin argues elsewhere (*The Dialogic Imagination*), languages have both centrifugal *and* centripetal forces exerted upon them: the former arising out of human needs to stretch a language to accommodate ever-changing life experiences, and the latter usually being imposed upon a language by those who seek to maintain intelligibility and consistency. The parallel with Johannine studies is clear. The evangelist is obviously *not* a thinker who is satisfied with 'monologic utterances' (*Ibid*, p. 43). These reflect the needs of philologists, or dogmatists, but not the needs of a reflective, dialogical thinker, who is constantly pushing the limits of his christology to accommodate the polarities of christocentric experiences and socio-religious tensions he has encountered. John's is a 'living christology in written form', which must be analyzed as such, lest it be misunderstood and misjudged. Conversely, the christology of the Epistles is more ordered and linnear.

there *ever* may have been a 'single', unified tradition, posing only *one* interpretation of Jesus' words and works, is unfounded and wrong. Synoptic *and* Johannine traditions portray the disciples as being puzzled over the meaning of Jesus' teachings (cf. Mt. 13:10, 36; 15:15; Jn. 14:5, 8, 22; 16:17f.), and both traditions are also clear that Jesus' works were ambiguous as well (Mk. 1:27; 2:6, 12, 16; 3:6; 6:2–6, 54–56; 8:11, 14–21, etc.; Jn. 1:49; 2:22, 18; 4:53; 5:10–18; 6:14, 30, 66; 7:5, 12f., 25–27, 31, 40–44, 52; 9:16f., 25, 29, 38, 40; 10:19f., 24, 33, 42; 11:45–53; 12:37, 42, etc.). In fact, one thing common to Mark's *and* John's accounts of the reactions to Jesus' works is that they both betray mixed reactions to Jesus (far more than Matthew or Luke), oscillating back and forth between those who believe on account of the signs, and those who do not. The most significant difference between the Marcan and the Johannine traditions with respect to Jesus' miracles, however, is the divergent interpretations of the signs' meanings, rather than the mere inclusion of some rather than others. For Mark (and especially the pre-Marcan tradition) they are portrayed as *mighty acts of God's power* by which the Kingdom of God goes forward: binding the 'strong man' (Mk. 3:27), casting out demons (Mk. 1:23–27), healing the sick (Mk. 1:32–34) and proclaiming the gospel (Mk. 4:2; see also the formula-type summaries in Matt. 4:23–25 and Lk. 4:18f.). However, in John, Jesus' signs are regarded as *vehicles of revelation* which convey something of the character of God's Kingdom, which is one of 'truth' (18:36f.), and which can only be 'seen' by means of a transforming immersion in the Spirit, involving being born 'from above' (3:3–8). Therefore, not only do the Marcan and Johannine traditions differ significantly regarding Jesus' signs, but also regarding the character of God's Kingdom. Bultmann has described this difference well:

> The early tradition, as is shown by the miracle stories of the Synoptic Gospels, records the effect which the miracles had on the witnesses, but is not interested in their further consequences, and in this respect the Synoptic writers are virtually the same. In John, however, the miracles are closely related to the history of the Revealer. They are *sēmeia* in a special sense (see v. 26) and so compel men to take their stand for or against the Revealer. Vv. 14f. therefore have been added by the Evangelist. (p. 213)

Bultmann's error in logic is obvious here. While he assumes the attestations of Jesus' miracles are common to the 'early tradition', he also acknowledges that in the inclusion of these attestations, 'the Synoptic writers are virtually the same'. Thus, even though Matthew and Luke were probably completed in the 80's or 90's, and certainly a decade or two after Mark, they have retained the interpretive slant of the 'early tradition'. If John were written about the same time, though slightly later, the omission of attestations cannot be due simply to the passing of time. All the evidence suggests that John and Mark are the two 'bi-optic gospels', and that John's interpretation, as well as narration of events, was independent from Mark's perhaps since its earliest stages. The 45 similarities — and differences — between John 6 and Mark 6 and 8 cannot be explained any other way (see above, Tables 7 and 8). This being the case, the relationship between faith and signs in John and Mark is also significantly parallel — yet distinct.

For Mark faith *precedes* miracles, while for John the primary purpose of Jesus' signs is to evoke faith in the audience. Thus, faith *follows* the signs in John, and the origin of such a posture was the dialectical reflection of the evangelist. A probable explanation for many of the differences between Mark and John has to do with the human 'source' of the Marcan tradition having been less reflective than the human 'source' of the Johannine. Of course, we are not talking about an 'abstract cluster of ideas' as being the pre-gospel 'source' in each case, but actual *human beings*, who interpreted Jesus' ministry in divergent ways. Therefore, some of (indeed, many of) the differences between the bi-optic gospels must have existed from the early stages of the two traditions and may tentatively be attributed to differing cognitive experiences of at least two followers of Jesus, who perceived his ministry in fundamentally different ways. This is not to say that one was 'right' and the other 'wrong', or that a great deal of embellishment and paraphrase did not accrue over the years. They obviously did. It *is* to call for a correction in the ways 'traditions' are often researched and discussed. A docetic view of Jesus is one thing; a 'docetic' view of the *human* sources of gospel traditions is another.[20] For this reason the oft-discounted opinion of the compiler (Jn. 21:24f.), that the source of John was a follower of Jesus, deserves fresh investigation in the light of cognitive and sociological analyses. Rather than assuming his purpose was primarily 'historical' (however that word is understood), one must again explore the possibility that the Fourth Evangelist was a follower of Jesus who has reflected upon the existential meaning of Jesus' words and works over the years, doing so in a dialectical manner.[21] This is a primary difference between the pre-Marcan (which I shall call

---

20 Lindars refers to this docetising tendency as ' ... an abstraction from ... the pale ghost of John himself' (*Behind the Fourth Gospel*, London, 1971, p. 43). While the evangelist is not referred to in John by name, this is not the same as 'anonymity'. He makes no claims for himself, but is considered by the compiler to have been the 'beloved disciple', a follower of Jesus (21:24f.). The point I want to make is that *before* the Fourth Gospel was finalized, this was the literary opinion of someone very close to it, regarding its composition history. As a contrast to Luke's rendition of how his account was researched and written (Lk. 1:1–4), the opinion of John's compiler deserves at least to be explored, especially in the light of the highly unitive character of John 6. For the purpose of this study, it matters not *who* exactly this person may have been. The point is that 'eye-witnesses' do not *only* think in 'historical' terms; they also think in interpretive/reflective terms, and this possibility demands critical investigation as an epistemological factor in John's unitive and disunitive christology.

21 'Historical' is not necessarily a term denoting objectivity, but a tool of rhetorical argument, used most characteristically in Johannine debates to 'prove' one point or to 'disprove' another (cf. above, Introduction, n. 21). Its most common abuse in Johannine studies has to do with the over-stated question, 'Who *cannot* have written John?'. While this topic cannot be explored fully in this study, it must be stated that one has yet to find a single scientific treatment of the kind of 'history' an octogenarian eye-witness may have produced at the end of his life, as a reflection upon the ministry of Jesus. Thus, if the evangelist or his 'source' were an eye-witness, this would *not* insure the Gospel's historical integrity any more than the mere pointing out of discrepancies between Mark and John proves that Mark cannot have

'Petrine') and the Johannine traditions'[22] appraisals of Jesus' miracles. The former perceived Jesus as a thaumaturge, the latter did not — and perhaps never did. One further note. A fresh critical examination of Papias' view of Marcan and Johannine origins is demanded, not despite diachronic theories of composition (attractive

---

been based on apostolic preaching. Having researched the factor of age in legal testimony, A.D. Yarmey concludes about older eye-witnesses:

> Older persons may be more susceptible to such things as unconscious transference and negative stereotypes, which are more likely to influence their misidentification of peripheral figures, such as innocent bystanders. ... In addition, verbal descriptions given by the elderly are definitely poorer than those given by the young. ... Thus, the credibility of the elderly witness may be low. Finally, because of their tendency to make a relatively high number of omission errors, the elderly are likely to fail to identify a suspect when he or she truly is the wanted person.

(Citation from A.D. Yarmey, "Age as a Factor in Eyewitness Memory", in *Eyewitness Testimony; Psychological Perspectives*, ed. G.L. Wells, E.L. Loftus, Cambridge, 1984, p. 153f.). On the other hand, neither is P. Parker (*JBL* 81, 1962, pp. 35–43) justified in his absolutist response to advocates of John's author being the son of Zebedee:

> All this would be enough to make some NT professors, of a generation or two ago, feel that they had lived in vain. If there was one "assured result of biblical criticism" for such scholars of the 20's, 30's, and 40's it was that John the son of Zebedee, had nothing at all to do with the writing of this gospel. The very phrase "Gospel of John" ceded place to "Fourth Gospel" in recognition of its nonapostolic origin.
>
> Now it may be that our mentors in earlier decades undervalued this gospel's history. ... In the matter of authorship, however, I think their negative judgment was right. This gospel cannot possibly be the work of John the son of Zebedee, and cannot conceivably represent this point of view. (p. 35f.)

Despite the intensity of this appeal, a thorough investigation of all of Parker's evidence suggests that none of his points is absolutely convincing, and many of them (esp. contrasts between John and the Synoptics) may be explained on the basis that John's tradition simply differed from Mark's. This leads to a reiteration of the possibility that Mark and John represent 'bi-optic' perspectives on Jesus' ministry, perhaps going back to interpretive differences in perspective between ancient gospel traditions.

22 Without attempting to demonstrate the identity of the specific followers of Jesus who may have been the primary sources of the Marcan and Johannine traditions, they may simply be referred to as 'Petrine' and 'Johannine', in keeping with Papias' opinion that the preaching of Peter was a major source for Mark, and that John represents the apostle's recollections of Jesus' ministry, written at the end of his life. Obviously, a great deal of embellishment has accrued between the gospel presentations of the disciples as 'eye-witnesses' and the same apostles as 'prototypes' (cf. manuscript under preparation, 'From Personalities to Prototypes', Paul N. Anderson), but upon this fact many authorial assumptions have foundered. There are at least *seven* interpretive levels of comparison and contrast between the Petrine and Johannine traditions, of which 'eye-witness' and prototype are but the first and the last (including: a) the personalities of disciples, b) keen friendship/rivalry between them and contrasting presentations of one another, c) the portrayal of the differing ministries of Peter and John in Acts, d) the *kerygmatic* content of their spoken and written ministries, e) views of discipleship, f) differing *basileiologies* and g) [after their deaths] differing models of church government [christocracy] advocated by their followers), and scholars have failed to take these into consideration comprehensively before ruling out an authorial possibility.

as they are for a variety of reasons) but precisely because they fail the test of critical scrutiny.

Whatever view one adopts regarding John's composition, the signs of Jesus pose a major problem[23] of naturalism versus supernaturalism. This problem will remain unsolved in the present discussion, though not unexplored. It is worth noting that while the evangelist's dialectical attitudes toward the signs and sacraments are parallel, he denies the ordination of sacraments by Jesus. He does *not* deny his performing of miraculous signs. Significantly, however, Jesus' miracles were also a problem for all the gospel writers, and they all seek to give some account for why miracles did happen — and more importantly (for the present study) *why they did not*. Applying Fowler's faith development theory to the ways Jesus' miracles were interpreted, the Petrine tradition viewed them along the lines of an *Individuative-Reflective* (Stage 4) faith, while the Johannine tradition viewed them from the perspective of a *Conjunctive* (Stage 5) level of faith development. This meant that Mark's source was an individual (or group) who was clear about *who* Jesus was and *what* his miracles were about: the establishing of God's Kingdom by means of *works of power*. The only way such a perspective can be maintained without suffering a crisis of faith is for this individual or group to have experienced a sufficient degree of continuity between thaumaturgic interpretations of Jesus' ministry and future works of power. Therefore, if there were *any* connection between the memory of Peter's dynamic ministry as portrayed in Acts and Papias' view that the content of Peter's preaching was a central component of the pre-Marcan tradition, this may explain why Jesus is portrayed more in the role of a thaumaturge in Mark.[24] Mark's main traditional source (whomever it was) must have been an explosive personality who never seriously questioned the meaning

---

23 The Signs Gospel and *sēmeia* source hypotheses must face the same historical problems that apply to a unitive Gospel. If such a source contained independent, historical material, how does one account for its miraculous portrayal of Jesus' ministry? Was it a fabrication — even the historical-type detail? And, if it was, then what can be said about the evangelist's judgment for using such a propagandist document so extensively? It seems better to confess that Jesus' miracles remain a problem, but the unitive integrity of the Gospel is magnified *precisely because* they were a problem for the evangelist as well. He remains ambivalent toward Jesus' signs, yet he cannot find it within himself to deny their occurrence. This 'contradiction' argues in favour of his proximity to the 'eye-witness' tradition, not against it.

24 While C. Holladay (1973) has demonstrated that the *theios anēr* concept has only had a unified and coherent meaning in the twentieth century (cf. also H.C. Kee, *Miracle in the Early Christian World*, New Haven/London, 1983, pp. 297–299), there are, nonetheless, clear signs of tensions over the interpretation of Jesus' miracles in the New Testament. Thus, the tendency to regard Jesus' miracles as attesting works of power, designed to establish God's Kingdom with mighty signs and wonders may be referred to simply as 'thaumaturgic'. The Petrine tradition found such a concept meaningful, but the Johannine tradition objected to it. Thus, there was an *ideological conflict* between the two traditions, perhaps going back to their earlier stages, but certainly reflected in the later ones.

of Jesus' miracles, perhaps because he never faced fully the stark contradiction of the fact that miracles do not happen as often as one expects. Rather, just as the dynamic ministry of this individual must have been bolstered by his own self-confidence and faith, he apparently 'explains' the absence of wonders in his own ministry (and in the ministry of *Jesus*) as the result *not* of God's failure, but as *the consequence of a lack of human faith*.[25] While Peter or someone like Peter (as portrayed in Acts) was forced to think conjunctively (Stage 5 faith) about 'forbidden food' (it took a 'vision from God' to cause this crisis of stage-transition, Ac. 10:9–23) and about accepting Gentile Christians (it took the 'contradiction' of the Holy Spirit being poured out on the Gentiles, Ac. 10:44–48; 15:7–11 to move Peter to a conjunctive and inclusive posture), there is no story in Acts which portrays Peter actually facing the contradiction of wonders anticipated in strong faith, and yet denied. John, however, is portrayed as doing no miracles in Acts, and only witnesses to what he has '*seen and heard*' (Ac. 4:20). The theological interpretation of Jesus' miracles in the Petrine and Johannine traditions are remarkably congruent with the ministry gifts of Peter and John as portrayed in Acts. This fact deserves critical investigation.[26]

---

25 Whether or not this person was actually Peter or had anything to do with him, it may simply be recognized that in *all of* Peter's sermons as portrayed in Acts, some sort of wondrous act of God is central to his rhetorical appeal for repentance and belief in Jesus as the Christ (the outpouring of the Spirit: 2:14–18; Jesus was attested by *acts of power*, *wonders* and *signs*: 2:22; Peter's healing the lame man was the result of Jesus' power to heal: 3:16; 4:9–12; Peter seems to have 'divine knowledge' of Ananias' sin: 5:3; Peter's vision is the justification for his 'change of mind' regarding the acceptance of Gentile Christians: 11:5–14; and the filling of the Gentiles by the Holy Spirit — complete with speaking in other tongues — justifies Peter's according them 'full status' as believers: 11:15–18; 15:8).

26 As a contrast, the *only* words attributed to John (actually, Peter *and* John) in Acts may be found in the second half of the two-fold statement in Ac. 4:19f.:

"Judge for yourselves whether it is right before God for us to obey *you* rather than God!" And,

"For we cannot help but to speak about that which we have *seen* and *heard*."

The first part of this composite statement corresponds with Peter's (and the other apostles') statements in Ac. 5:29 and 11:17, but the second part is *remarkably Johannine* (cf. Jn. 1:14bc; 3:32 and esp. 1 Jn. 1:1–3). Therefore, as early as Luke's gathering of the material for his writing of Acts, John the disciple of Jesus and companion of Peter is associated with witnessing *only* to 'that which he has seen and heard'. Johannine scholars and experts on Acts have totally overlooked this correlation, as far as I know. It is also significant that John does no miracles in Acts, whereas Peter and Paul do. The points I want to make are not to argue that Peter's preaching had to have underlain Mark, nor that John the disciple must have been the author of the Fourth Gospel. Rather, even if there is nothing historical about the portrayals of Peter and John in Acts, and even if they had nothing to do with the traditions underlying the Gospels of Mark and John, respectively (arguments which seem to 'docetise' the leading figures of the apostolic age), they offer two distinct *typologies* which may broadly be considered 'Petrine' and 'Johannine'. Another point is significant as well: the spiritual gifts and ministries of apostolic preachers *must have influenced what they taught about Jesus' ministry*. This notion may open significant doors to understanding at least part of the reason

Throughout John, one may detect various ways of struggling with the problem of suffering, even in the light of God's sovereign love and goodness. Thus, the presence of *theodicy* within Johannine Christianity is reflected by the question regarding the cause of suffering: 'Rabbi, who sinned, this man or his parents, that he was born blind?' (9:2); and by the angered grieving underlying Martha's *and* Mary's exclamations, 'Lord, if you had been here, my brother would not have died!' (11:21 *and* 32). By the time the Gospel was finalized, its community had faced the death of the Beloved Disciple (21:22f.), Peter (21:18f.) and others (even Lazarus?). Therefore, even though this segment of early Christianity believed in the miraculous ministry of Jesus, and that they too would be entrusted with power to do wondrous deeds — perhaps even surpassing his (14:11–14) — they had to face the earthly realities that people still go hungry, Jesus' followers sometimes fight with each other, and even the disciples of the Lord die.[27] These human realities temper even the most visionary of aspirations, and the ideals of *Individuative-Reflective* faith become tempered by the frailty of human existence. It is because of suffering and unfulfilled expectations that the truth of Jesus' words and works is distilled into existentializing motifs. Thus, the miracle is not that the blind man can see, but that Jesus is *the Light of the world.* The final wonder is not that Lazarus is raised from the dead, but that Jesus is himself *the Resurrection and the Life.* Furthermore, Jesus assures them:

> He who believes in me will live, even though he dies; and whoever lives, and believes in me, will never die. (11:25f.)

It was also the experience of suffering within Johannine Christianity which called forth solidarity with the suffering Son of Man (15:18–25; 12:23–26; 6:51–58), and just as some disciples may have abandoned Jesus during his earthly ministry (6:66) due to unfulfilled messianic expectations, so future generations were faced with the same problem. When things do not turn out as expected, people are forced either to alter their expectations or to change their situations. To both of these options, the Johannine tradition advocates a christocentric reorientation: 'Lord, to whom shall we go? *You (alone)* have the words of eternal life!' (6:69)

---

for the discrepancy between the Johannine and Synoptic portrayals of Jesus' ministry. Interpretations of Jesus' ministry must have been influenced by the distinctive morphologies of the ministries of different apostolic preachers. This may also explain partially the origin of their differences regarding the relationship between signs and faith. (Cf. P.N. Anderson, 'The Cognitive Origins of John's Christological Unity and Disunity,' *Horizons in Biblical Theology* 17, 1995, pp. 1–24; and Appendix VIII, below.)

27 In his famous poem, 'A Death in the Desert', R. Browning had already surmised that weakness, suffering and even death must have played a formative role in Johannine Christianity. The poem opens not with Lazarus in a tomb, but with *the evangelist* having been in a grotto for sixty days. Three men and a boy come to the cave in order to 'see his face', or to hear him speak again as in days of old. In order to awaken him from his death-like sleep, Xanthus offers wine. Valens produces perfume, but *the Boy* (in whom the ethos of the Johannine tradition lives on) ' ... sprang up from his knees ... and spoke, as 'twere his mouth proclaiming first, "I am the Resurrection and the Life." ' At this, John opened his eyes.

A final insight into the evangelist's approach to Jesus' signs may be derived from the way John differs from the Synoptics regarding the relationship of faith to miracles, as affected by theodicy. In the Synoptic tradition, Jesus comes down off the Mount of Transfiguration, finds his disciples unable to cast the demon out of the convulsive child, and exclaims in disgust, 'You unbelieving generation, how long shall I stay with you ... and put up with you?' (Mt. 17:17; Mk. 9:19; Lk. 9:41). At Nazareth Jesus *could do* no miracles *because of the people's lack of faith* (Mk. 6:5f.; see Matthew's softening of Mark: Jesus '*would* do no miracles'; Mt. 13:58). To the woman with an issue of blood Jesus says, 'Daughter, your faith has made you whole.' (Mt. 9:22; Mk. 5:34; Lk. 8:48); and *faith* is the key ingredient for the raising of Jairus' daughter (Mk. 5:35; Lk. 8:50). The practical implication is conveyed in Mark's second ending: signs will accompany those with faith, and this will enable them to drive out demons in Jesus' name, speak in other tongues, pick up snakes and drink deadly poison with no ill effect, and they will be able to heal the sick by the laying-on of hands (Mk. 16:16–18). The pre-Marcan view continues long after Mark's original writing. Furthermore, Matthew adds a second interpretation of the mustard seed parable which connects miracle-working with facilitating faith:

> Truly I tell you, if you have faith as a grain of mustard you will say to this mountain, "Move from here to there!" And it will move; and nothing will be impossible for you. (Matt. 17:20b)

It is in 17:20a, however, that Matthew betrays the central question underlying the connection of miracles to faith. In response to the question of the disciples (17:19), 'Why couldn't we drive it out?' the Matthean Jesus responds with the Synoptic (Petrine) explanation of theodicy, 'It is because of *your lack of faith*.' (17:20a). Despite the differences of opinion between John and the Synoptics regarding the relation of miracles to faith, *both traditions address the same problem*: they explain why miracles do *not* happen according to expectation. In doing so, however, they pose differing explanations.

Therefore, the Fourth Evangelist's ambivalent attitude toward miraculous signs is the result of his own struggling with *theodicy*, and it marks the transition of having moved from an *Individuative-Reflective* (Stage 4) faith to a *Conjunctive* (Stage 5) level of faith. But the pre-Marcan (Petrine) tradition apparently had not faced the same crisis in the same way, and thus the failure of wondrous expectations is ascribed to human lack of faith, rather than leading to an ideological re-evaluation of the kind of Kingdom Jesus had come to establish. Rather, as in the case of the Synoptic tradition (although more acutely), the Johannine attitude toward Jesus' miracles and their relation to faith is not primarily the result of miracles having happened, but the result of their *not* having happened within developing Christianity. As M. Weber and P. Berger have pointed out,[28] the problem of theodicy is solved in many ways within world religions, and future eschatologies, messianic

---

28 See M. Webber's chapter on theodicy in his *The Sociology of Religion*, E.t., E. Fischoff, (1956 ed.), 1963, London, pp. 138–150; and P. Berger's *'The Sacred Canopy'; Elements of a Sociological Theory of Religion*, New York, 1967, pp. 53–80. Says Berger:

hopes, predestinarian views, providence theologies and dualistic anthropologies all have as their common root the attempt to explain or alleviate the problem of human suffering — given the assumption of a sovereign and loving god. They often do so by means of a theological construct, and the same is true for the Fourth Gospel's treatment of Jesus' miracles. The evangelist portrays them as revelatory signs precisely because he is convinced of their representative place in the actual ministry of Jesus; while at the same time, he believes their significance for a later generation transcends the outward results alone. In doing so, he corrects not a backwater signs source, but the prevalent interpreted value of Jesus' miracles in the entire Synoptic tradition. Jesus' signs were *not* intended to be thaumaturgical nature miracles. They 'signify' who God is in Jesus Christ and call for a believing response to God's saving/revealing initiative.

2. *Jesus' Flesh and Glory.* A related problem is the relationship between Jesus' flesh and glory. This problem centres on interpretations of John 1:14, and as is the case regarding many of the most salient New Testament debates within recent years, the parameters of the debate have been defined classically by Käsemann's response to Bultmann's opinion. Introducing his treatment of 1:14, Bultmann says:

> Just as the *et incarnatus est* marks the turning point in the Mass, so too here the character of the Prologue changes. ... Now the riddle is solved, the miracle is proclaimed: the Logos became flesh!
>
> It is the *language of mythology* that is here employed. ... In this mythology the concept of revelation receives a definite form; it affirms 1) that revelation is an event with an other-worldly origin; 2) but that this event, if it is to have any significance for men, must take place in the human sphere. (p. 60f.)

It is for this reason that Bultmann believes the incarnation is such a scandal. When humans are confronted with God's divine action toward them, coming in the form of a man and *only* a man (*Nichts als ein Mensch*), this shatters all human expectations of how God's redemptive power 'ought' to work. Therefore, salvation is not an other-worldly event which comes to humanity from the clouds of heaven. It lies in the paradoxical conviction that the eternal *Logos* became finite *sarx* (1:14a), and yet the very hiddenness of revelation becomes a stumbling block. The scandal of the incarnation is that 'the *doxa* is not to be seen *alongside* the *sarx*, nor *through* the *sarx* as through a window; it is to be seen in the *sarx* and nowhere else' (p. 63).

Based on this assessment that the fulcrum of the Prologue is 1:14a, and that the Prologue is the encapsulation of that which follows in the rest of the Gospel, Bultmann believes the core of the evangelist's christology is exclusively incarnational. This means that if the evangelist believes it is as Jesus' *sarx* that

---

Theodicy directly affects the individual in his concrete life in society. A plausible theodicy (which, of course, requires an appropriate plausibility structure) permits the individual to integrate the anomic experiences of his biography into the socially established nomos and its subjective correlate in his own consciousness. (p. 58)

God's salvation has come to humanity, other motifs such as Jesus' exaltation and supernatural knowing of people's thoughts and coming events *must* suggest different authorship. This is the terminal flaw with Bultmann's interpretation. The problem is *not* that he has overemphasized the flesh over the glory, as a failure of balance; but the problem is one of failing to retain the dynamic tensions in an otherwise 'living' christology, which alters the form and meaning of its content. In other words, the problem is not a matter of interpreting John's christology to be too elevated or too humiliated, but the failure to see these elements in dynamic tension. Bultmann has assumed too facilely that the evangelist *must* have been a Stage 4, *Individuative-Reflective* thinker, who is concerned only with one aspect of christology: its incarnational implications. Because the evangelist's level of reflection was obviously more *Conjunctive* (Stage 5) than this, his incarnational interests must be seen *in tension with* the exalted glory of the Lord.

In disagreement with his former mentor, E. Käsemann launched a serious challenge to Bultmann's opinion that 1:14a was the interpretive fulcrum of the Prologue. According to Käsemann, the fulcrum of the Prologue is not 'the Word became flesh,' but vs. 14:c, 'and we beheld his glory'.[29] Says Käsemann:

> We must maintain emphatically that, according to the Fourth Evangelist (and, for that matter, according to the Synoptists) he who has become flesh does not cease to exist as a heavenly being; that he undergoes no "transformation"; and that John ... did not feel the activity of the Word in his fleshly state to be a humiliation. ... It is not without reason that two millennia have loved the Fourth Gospel because it portrayed Jesus as the God who walked the earth.

While Käsemann appreciates Bultmann's insight that, 'the Johannine Christ brings with him no information about the nature of the heavenly and no specific teaching other than his proclamation of his own person,' he goes on to argue that the heart of the Gospel is not Jesus' humility, but his making manifest the glory of God. 'Incarnation for John is really epiphany.' (p. 160f.) However, in doing so, Käsemann *also* reduces the evangelist to a Stage 4 thinker and must dismiss all references to Jesus' humanity as being eclipsed by his divinity in John. Therefore, the discussion between Käsemann and Bultmann is one which argues not only the emphasis of 1:14, but whether the *Leitmotif* of the entire Gospel is the flesh *or* the glory of Christ. However, in removing the tension from the both-and-ness of John's conjunctive presentation of Jesus' humanity and divinity, the *most distinctive element* of John's christology is denied: namely, its unitive *and* disunitive tension (cf. above, Chapter 1).

Bultmann seeks to remove the tensions by assuming there was only one pole within the thinking and writing of the evangelist: Jesus' humanity. References to Jesus' divinity must have been inherent to *other* sources or interpolations. On the

---

29 E. Käsemann, 'The Structure and Purpose of the Prologue to John's Gospel', in his *New Testament Questions of Today*, London, pp. 138–167, 1969, citation on p. 160f. See also his *The Testament of Jesus*, Philadelphia, 1968, p. 9f.

other hand, Käsemann attempts to remove the tension by denying that one of the poles exists and by discounting as insignificant all references to Jesus' fleshly humanity. This is spelled out more clearly in his *Testament of Jesus*, and it is one of the key criticisms of his work by Bornkamm.[30] Along with nearly every other scholar who criticizes Käsemann's reference to John's 'naive docetism', Bornkamm points out that:

> If one follows Käsemann in interpreting John's version of the story of Jesus undialectically as a simple, straightforward story of God striding over the earth, a story infected with docetism and robbed of the reality of the crucifixion, then what one has encountered is not John, but the pre-Johannine tradition. (Ashton, p. 91)

Bornkamm's criticism is justified. John 1:14 is a representative encapsulation of the dialectical portrayal of Jesus which runs throughout the entire Gospel. Therefore, any attempt to remove one of the poles which create the tension does violence to the central fibre of John's christology overall. As in the case of the evangelist's attitude toward the signs, however, an explanation for this tension must be attempted. Bornkamm is partially right in his allusion to reflective developments within the tradition, but he is wrong to assume a clear break between Johannine and pre-Johannine traditions. John's dialectical presentation of Jesus' glory and flesh may even represent a continuous development between different phases of the same tradition, rather than two distinct traditions. Thus, the tension between John 1:14a and 1:14c may be explained by considering 1:14b, *kai eskēnōsen en hēmin*.

The word, *eskēnōsen*, not only bears with it associations with the 'tent of meeting' (Ex. 33:7–23) characteristic of *Shekinah* theologies,[31] but it also may illuminate the history of development regarding the themes underlying John 1:14. Within the *Shekinah* motif, the *sarx* and *doxa* of God's saving presence co-exist dialectically. That John contains very early, as well as later, christological content is fairly certain.[32] However, John's christology also goes beyond conventional

---

30 G. Bornkamm, 'Towards the Interpretation of John's Gospel' (Ashton, pp. 79–98; cf. also note e, p. 97).

31 See I. Chernus, *Mysticism in Rabbinic Judaism*, Berlin/New York, 1982; esp. 'Nourished by the Splendor of Shekinah', pp. 74–87. While one could develop an entire monograph on the connections between the Johannine 'tenting' motif and the Old Testament concept of God's *Shekinah* presence abiding with Israel (the condition of humanity is blindness to the glory of God: Ex. 33:20 → Jn. 1:18a; however, God enters the sphere of the *cosmos* in order to engage humanity in a saving/revealing 'dialogue': Ex. 33:7–11 → Jn. 1:1–5, 9–14a; this discourse with humanity is characterized as God's presence dwelling in Israel/God's children: Ex. 33:14 → Jn. 1:14b; and it is experienced as *glory* by those who encounter it: Ex. 33:18–23 → Jn. 1:14c–e), the significant aspect of the 'tenting' motif is that it implies an abiding and communing relationship with God. It reflects *a theology of encounter*.

32 The main peculiarity of John's christology is not that it portrays Jesus as Lord, the pre-existent Word, and the only-begotten Son. One would expect such exalted christological motifs to have existed in a late first-century document. What is peculiar about John is the paradoxical emphasis on the *flesh* of Jesus, his 'pathetic' (*pathos*-filled) portrayal, and the use of such

messianic prototypes. While Jesus is perceived to be a 'member of the set' of previous prophets and teachers, he is also experienced as one who is in a distinctive category all by himself. Thus, we have the superlative distinction between Jesus and earlier typologies (1:17f.; 5:19–46; 6:32f.; 7:46; 8:58). The emphasis upon Jesus's superiority to preceding agencies of God culminates in his portrayal in John as the eschatological agent of God's saving communication with humanity (Deut. 18:15–18). As God's eschatological 'Word', Jesus embodies the *Shekinah* presence of God in the world and calls for humanity to both encounter this reality and to respond to God's saving initiative. Therefore, considering the dialectical progression from perceptions, to modifying experiences, to new perceptions and modifying experiences, etc., John 1:14 should not be perceived simply as emphasizing either Jesus' humanity or his divinity. John 1:14a and c are held together by 1:14b 'and *dwelt* among us', which suggests that John's high and low presentation of Jesus is not founded primarily on a theoretical construct, but on *experiential* ones.[33] It is a living christology which has arisen out of encounter with God through Jesus, and which evokes the same for later generations. This revelatory tension runs throughout the entire gospel and finds its classic definition in the first ending of the gospel, ' ... but these are written that you might believe ...' (20:31).

Findings

Despite the valuable contributions made by Bultmann's commentary, his diachronic approach to John's composition is not supported by the literary and

---

quickly out dated titles as 'Rabbi' and 'prophet'. This suggests that John's christology contains material which is both very early *and* late. This is especially the case regarding the Prophet-like-Moses motif, based on Deut. 18:15–18, which had all but been omitted from middle-to-late first century christological statements (except Peter's reference in Ac. 3:22, and Stephen's *heilsgeschichtliche* recitation in Ac. 7:37; cf. J.A.T. Robinson's 'The Most Primitive Christology of All?', *JTS* 7, 1956, pp. 177–189). Thus, the tradition underlying John 6 must cover a chronological span of at least a generation or two. Within its scope, would-be followers of Jesus who perceive him in the role of the charismatic prophet are compared with docetising members of Johannine Christianity as though both are 'present realities' in the thinking of the evangelist. Thus, John's may indeed be the earliest — as well as the latest — christology among the four Gospels (cf. Robinson's *The Priority of John*, London, 1985), although it was the last to be 'published'.

33 The literary form of the Prologue, as a composition used in the *cultus* of Johannine Christianity, is also significant. As Loder describes the process by which an encounter is re-formed into an image, the function of the *cultus* is to further the transformation process by means of making such images come alive within the imagination and experience of the individual. Therefore, John's christology not only arises out of encounter, but it is presented in such a way so as to evoke the same kind of *eikonic* and transforming reality in the experience of the worshipper/reader. It is a 'living' christology which *presumes* a christocentric encounter with the living God — and *creates that which it presumes* (cf. K. Barth's introduction to his commentary on Romans 6th ed. Oxford, p. 28).

theological evidence. Nevertheless, his insights and astute observations are still of great benefit, as other solutions may be explored in addressing some of the central problems he detected. Therefore, the christological tensions in John 6 must be attributed largely to tensions within the thinking of the evangelist, and thus the dialectical style of his thinking and writing must be explored in order to gain a proper perspective on the origin and character of the Gospel's content. For this reason, the findings of recent developmental and cognitive studies have been employed in order to illuminate a better understanding of the dialectical character of John's christology and to explore how the evangelist may have come to think in such a way.

1. J. Fowler poses a developmental (psychodynamic) model for understanding the ways people mature in their faith and approaches to God. Pertinent to the present study is Fowler's theory that dialectical thinking about one's faith occurs only after an adult has arrived at his or her autonomous understanding of faith, and yet is challenged to reconcile the tensions between subsequent contradictory perceptions and experiences. Such an individual is not less convinced about the veracity of previously held convictions but becomes increasingly aware that while a particular aspect of truth may be represented by a belief, no particular notion contains the whole truth. Therefore, Stage 5 *Conjunctive* faith holds apparently conflicting aspects of truth in tension and affirms a both/and approach to faith, rather than an either/or stance. This is the sort of thinker the Fourth Evangelist must have been.

2. The contribution of J. Loder involves the exploration of the origin and character of transforming experiences and offers more of a 'crisis' (transformational) model than a developmental one. Central in Loder's analysis is the role of the 'image' as a construct within one's cognition, which becomes the threshhold of a new perceptual reality. The 'event of knowing', according to Loder, is a five-step encounter, involving the conflict caused by a new and contradictory experience and the subsequent dialectical process of reflective interpretation. Such an event is often formative in one's transition from one stage to the next (in developmental models); but differing from such models, a transforming spiritual encounter is more like a 'peak' experience than the scaling of a mountainside. The many 'Aha!' encounters with Jesus intrinsic to the Johannine witness suggest that a foundational origin of its epistemological content must have come from 'knowing events', which in their being reflected upon and proclaimed within the community of faith (and beyond), facilitate like transformations for future generations. This *theology of encounter* connects the Jesus of Galilee with the risen Christ of the Johannine community.

3. The lasting genius of Bultmann's contribution may not be his brilliant (though deficient) composition schema, but his incisive interpretive observations, combined with an uncanny sensitivity to nuances and perplexities in the text. Thus, given the failure of diachronic composition theories to convince, two of these major insights have been explored using a different composition model: that of the evangelist as a follower of Jesus, who is reflecting dialectically upon the significance of Jesus' ministry for future generations. a) The evangelist's ambivalence

toward Jesus' signs betrays the *Conjunctive* (Stage 5) thought of one who may have originally embraced more of a thaumaturgic view of Jesus' miracles (although not entirely similar to that of the pre-Marcan tradition), but in the light of the relative absence of such miracles, has modified his appraisal of their value. While the Synoptic tradition explained the relative dearth of the miraculous as the human failure to believe, the Johannine addressed this problem by existentializing the works of Jesus, calling them 'signs', and clarifying that the main value of Jesus' wondrous ministry *never was intended to be* limited to temporal blessings. Jesus' words and works are centrally vehicles of God's saving revelation, by which those who believe in him receive the ultimate gift of eternal life (20:31). b) The contradiction of Jesus' flesh and glory in John has its foundational origin in the contradictory experiences of the evangelist (or his tradition). In the man Jesus, the evangelist (or his tradition) has encountered the *Shekinah* presence of God, and he virtually spends the rest of his life reflecting upon and interpreting the implications of such transforming experiences. For this reason, he cannot be satisfied with delimiting christological categories. His is a living christology, having arisen out of encounter. Both the form and content of John's christology reflect a dynamic relation to its subject, and this clarifies a central aspect of why it has been so difficult — and yet so simple — to comprehend. Browning was not unaware of these twin aspects of the evangelist's dialectical reflection when he wrote:

> Such ever was love's way: to rise, it stoops.
> Since I, whom Christ's mouth taught, was bidden teach,
> I went, for many years, about the world,
> Saying "It was so; so I heard and saw,"
> Speaking as the case asked: and men believed.
> ... Left to repeat, "I saw, I heard, I knew,"
> And go all over the old ground again,
> With Antichrist already in the world,
> And many Antichrists, who answered prompt
> "Am I not Jasper as thyself art John?
> Nay, young, whereas through age thou mayest forget:
> Wherefore, explain, or how shall we believe?"
> I never thought to call down fire on such,
> Or, as in wonderful and early days,
> Pick up the scorpion, tread the serpent dumb;
> But patient stated much of the Lord's life
> Forgotten or misdelivered, and let it work:
> Since much that at the first, in deed and word,
> Lay simply and sufficiently exposed,
> Had grown (or else my soul was grown to match,
> Fed through such years, familiar with such light,
> Guarded and guided still to see and speak)
> Of new significance and fresh result;
> What first were guessed as points, I now knew stars,
> And named them in the Gospel I have writ.

Summary of Part II

Of fundamental interest to an analysis of the christological unity and disunity of John 6 is the question of its literary unity, and Bultmann's treatment must be taken into consideration before any final judgment can be made. The pivotal implication of Bultmann's contribution, and of those who follow his lead, is that if it can be demonstrated that various sources underlie, and various reactions overlie, John 6, a convincing case can be made for the attributing of John's christological disunity to tensions external to the thinking of the evangelist. On the other hand, if John 6 appears to be more unitive than Bultmann, Fortna and others argue, another explanation must be provided to explain the origin of these tensions. After considering thoroughly Bultmann's treatment of John 6, one must conclude that there is insufficient stylistic, contextual and ideological evidence to suggest more than one author. In fact, John 6 should be considered a basic authorial unity, although it was probably composed over several decades of oral and written development.

This being the case, Barrett's proposal that John 6 betrays all the characteristics of a dialectical thinker must be considered again. In the light of recent developmental and cognitive studies, John's dialectical approach to christology seems to have arisen out of at least two kinds of reflections: one, involving the existentializing of events from Jesus' ministry (especially his signs), and another involving the interpretation of christocentric encounters with God, which the evangelist must have experienced. These two kinds of experiences are suggested by the ways the evangelist portrays the two signs in John 6, and they will be explored further in Part III.

Part III

John 6: Three Levels of Dialogue

What first were guessed as points, I now knew stars,
And named them in the Gospel I have writ.
For men said, "It is getting long ago:
Where is the promise of His coming? " — asked
These young ones in their strength, as loth to wait,
Of me who, when their sires were born, was old.
I, for I loved them, answered, joyfully,
Since I was there, and helpful in my age;
And, in the main, I think such men believed.

Robert Browning
'A Death in the Desert'

The tensions inherent in the unity and disunity of John's christology cannot be ignored, as though the evangelist were speaking in dogmatic terms, nor can these tensions be ascribed to literary sources external to the thinking and writing of the evangelist. Therefore, the stylistic and literary unity of John 6 calls for a modified synchronic approach, but this must be done on more than one level alone.[1] There

---

1 Just as G. Theissen was compelled to pose alternative options to gospel criticism and Pauline studies (versus a synchronic *or* a diachronic approach to the gospels, Theissen adopts a 'functionalist' view in which he examines the social function of primitive Christian stories, cf. *The Shadow of the Galilean*, London, 1987, pp. 28–40; and, rather than focus on the external history of the Pauline corpus, Theissen finds he must explore the 'inner history of humanity' as it relates to Paul's dialectical reflection upon his experiences and situations, cf. *Psychological Aspects of Paul*, E.t., J.P. Galvin, Edinburgh, 1987), one must also adopt a comprehensive approach to interpreting John's distinctive presentation of Jesus as the Christ. While John 6 must be interpreted as a basic literary whole, to assume all of its tensions can be attributed to dialogues with other groups or the history of Johannine Christianity is too simplistic. And, to say simply that John is a 'synchronic' piece of literature, written only as a function of seeking to evoke a response from the reader, is to ignore its literary genre as 'interpretive history': a reflection upon the events in the ministry of Jesus.

The 'functionalist' approach adopted in Part III involves three levels of dialogue, which must all be considered in order to understand the content of John 6. They include the evangelist's reflective dialogue with his tradition, the literary means by which he seeks to engage the hearer/reader in a 'dialogue' with the narrative, and the dialectical situation in which Johannine Christianity found itself around the time of the writing of John 6. These

are at least three levels of dialogue represented by the Fourth Gospel, and each of these must be considered if an adequate appreciation of its content is to be acquired.

The first level of dialectic is the dialogue between the evangelist and his tradition. Reflecting back upon events and traditions produces new understandings of familiar stories, earlier perceptions and memories. As the ministry of Jesus is reinterpreted in the light of the needs of developing Johannine Christianity, the scope of otherwise 'historical' events becomes more universal — and at the same time more relevant — in its significance. Thus, the 'dialogue between the evangelist and his tradition' deserves consideration, and vss. 1–24 provide a suitable context for this endeavour.

The second level of dialectic involves the literary means by which the evangelist attempts to engage his audience in dialogue through the Gospel narrative. This is especially clear in the discussion following the feeding, which leads into a three-fold christological application of the manna motif (vss. 25–66). Whether or not the form-history of this dialogue/discourse section was as an oral homily or simply a written text, its exhortative purpose is clear. The hearer/reader is called to receive (ingest) Jesus as the 'true' bread of life, forsaking other kinds of 'bread' (vs. 27). Both of these literary forms are rhetorical in their function, and their goals are identical: to engage the hearer/reader in a conversational 'dialogue' which leads to a believing response to God's saving action in Jesus (20:31). Therefore, the rhetorical means by which the evangelist seeks to engage his audience in dialogue deserves to be considered, and vss. 25–66 provide an excellent context for this inquiry.

A third level of dialectic pertains to the socio-religious factors which may have influenced various aspects of John's christology. It is fairly certain that Johannine Christianity was involved in some rather intense debates with leaders of the local Synagogue, yet evidence also suggests that there were debates with followers of John the Baptist and with docetising Christians as well. These 'dialogues' would certainly account for some of the high/low tensions within John's christology, but these are not the only dialogues between groups represented in the Gospel. Less polemical, but dialectical nonetheless, is the dialogue with mainstream Christianity in the second half of the first century. These tensions may be cast into sharp relief by means of analyzing the contrast between Peter's confession in Matthew and John and considering the juxtaposition of the Beloved Disciple and Peter in the rest of the Gospel. The central concern reflected here is *christocracy*: the means by which the post-resurrection Christ continues to be the shepherd of the flock and the teacher of his disciples, and vss. 67–71 provide a springboard into this discussion.

These levels of dialectical tension must all be considered when accounting for John's christological unity and disunity, and Part III will sketch possible explana-

---

three kinds of dialogue lend themselves remarkably well to the literary structure of the chapter: vss. 1–24, 25–66 and 67–71.

tions as to how these may have existed within the thinking and writing of the evangelist. By means of reflecting upon the significance of Jesus' ministry, the evangelist has come to realize that what he first guessed were 'points' were later known as 'stars'. His Gospel witness is designed to convey the truth of insights received for the benefit of future generations — in order to be able to have said in the end: 'And, in the main, I think such men [and women] believed.'

Chapter 8

Not an Attesting Miracle ... But a 'Testing' Sign
(An Exegesis of John 6:1–24)

The Johannine version of the feeding and the sea crossing is radically distinctive, as contrasted to parallel accounts in Mark 6 and 8, and this distinctiveness extends both to matters of detail and interpretation. The distinctiveness of John 6:1–24 is especially striking, given its high degree of sequential and linguistic correlation with the Marcan tradition.[2]   Therefore, John's independent account will be analyzed as the evangelist's reflection upon (dialogue with) his tradition, whether his tradition is simply independent from Synoptic ones, or whether 'he is the tradition himself'.[3] Of special interest will be the distinctive characteristics of John's narrative and the evangelist's interpretive comments. Therefore, this chapter will include a translation of John 6:1–24, exegetical notes, and a concluding section drawing together inferences which may be made regarding the 'dialogue' between the evangelist and his tradition.

---

2 The many parallels, and yet differences, between John 6 and both Marcan accounts (cf. Tables 8 and 9 above, Chapter 5) suggest that a) The Fourth Evangelist *did not* borrow from Mark. If he did, he disagreed with Mark at every single point of linguistic similarity. b) If John did not borrow from Mark 6 or 8, John's tradition contains most of the material which each of those accounts omits. In other words, John is *complete* where they are *deficient*. c) John's narrative is much more unified, interpretively and ideologically. The theme of 'testing' runs throughout the narrative and culminates with Jesus' response to Peter's confession (vs. 70). These findings confirm the studies of E.D. Johnston ('The Johannine Version of the Feeding of the Five Thousand — An Independent Tradition?', *NTS* 8, pp. 151–154) and M. Smith ('Collected Fragments: On the Priority of John 6 to Mark 6–8', SBLASP 1, Missoula, 1979, pp. 105–108), which argue that John's tradition was not only independent from Mark's, but that it is also more reliable.

3 Whether the evangelist was 'the tradition himself', or whether he has reflected upon the stories of his teacher who was a follower of Jesus, the results of this approach will be identical. There is little advantage in assuming that Jesus was the teacher of the evangelist's teacher (Schnackenburg), rather than assuming that the evangelist was a follower of Jesus, as claimed by the compiler (21:24). Adopting a minimalist posture, John appears to contain at least some reflective memoirs of a follower of Jesus who was *other* than the primary source of the Marcan tradition. Especially in the light of M. Hengel's provocative monograph (*The Johannine Question*, London/Philadelphia, 1989) Papias' view of Marcan and Johannine authorship deserves renewed analysis and critical consideration.

John 6:1–24

Subsequently, Jesus departed across the Sea of Galilee upon Tiberias, but a large crowd followed him because they had seen the signs which he had done upon the infirm. So Jesus ascended the hillside, and there he sat down with his disciples.

Now the Passover feast of the Jews was near; and therefore Jesus, lifting up his eyes and beholding a large crowd coming toward him, says to Philip,

"Where shall we buy bread so that these people may eat?"

(Of course, this he said as a means of testing him; for he knew what he was about to do.) Philip answered him,

"Two hundred *denarii* of loaves would not even be enough for each one to have a bit."

One of his disciples (Andrew, the brother of Simon Peter) says to him,

"There is a laddy here who has five barley loaves and a couple of pickled fish; but what good are these among so many?"

Jesus said,

"Have the people sit down."

(Now there was a lot of grass in the area; therefore, the men sat down — about five thousand of them in number.) Then Jesus took the loaves and having given thanks distributed them to those who were seated. He also did the same with the fishes until all had eaten as much as they wished. Now when they were satisfied, he tells his disciples,

"Gather together the leftover fragments so that nothing is lost."

Therefore, they gathered and filled twelve baskets of fragments from the barley loaves which were left over by those who had eaten. However, seeing the sign[s] he had done, the people exclaimed,

"Truly this is the Prophet — the one coming into the world!"

But Jesus, knowing that they were about to come and carry him off in order to make him king, fled again into the hills by himself.

And when evening came, his disciples went down to the sea, and embarking in a boat, they set off across the sea to Capernaum. By now it had become dark, but Jesus had not yet come to them; and as a great wind was blowing, the sea became rough. So having rowed about twenty-five or thirty *stadia*, they behold Jesus walking upon the sea and drawing near the boat; and they were frightened. But he says to them,

"I AM! Fear not."

Then they wanted to take him into the boat, and [but?] immediately the boat was upon the land to which they were going.

On the next day, the crowd which was standing across the sea saw that there had been only one boat there, and that Jesus' disciples had departed in the boat alone, and that he did not come with them. Other boats came from Tiberias near the place where they ate the bread after the Lord had given thanks. Therefore, when the crowd saw that Jesus was not there, nor his disciples, they embarked in the boats and came to Capernaum, seeking Jesus.

Exegetical Notes

1. *Meta tauta,* literally 'after these things', need not imply the immediate following of events, more characteristic of *meta touto* (2:12; 11:7, 11; 19:28, etc. cf. Schnackenburg, II, p. 13; n.9 on p. 441). It simply denotes sequence, and as in 3:22; 5:1, 14, 22; 7:1; 13:7; 19:38 and 21:1, etc., the phrase may suggest 'later on' (Brown, p. 232), 'some time after this' (Cassirer), or simply 'subsequently'. Therefore, the sequence of Galilee (ch. 4) — Jerusalem (ch. 5) — Galilee (ch. 6) — Jerusalem (ch. 7) is not as problematic as Bultmann *et. al.* suggest, if *meta tauta* is taken

in the broader sense. Because John 6 is so clearly a self-contained unit (Schnackenburg II, p. 10), it may have been added as a unit by the evangelist or the compiler to an existing text (along with such passages as 1:1–18; chs. 11, 15–17, and 21; cf. Lindars, p. 50f.). This would mean that ch. 5 may have originally moved directly into ch. 7, and thus the debate about the Sabbath led into Jesus' proclamation in the Temple about the living water. On the other hand, ch. 6 does follow nicely from 5:46, ' ... and Moses wrote of me', and it also leads nicely into 7:3ff., where Jesus is requested to perform more signs to convince the brethren (Barrett, p. 310f.). One can appreciate how ch. 6 came to assume its present location, whether it was inserted there by the compiler, or even by the evangelist. Lindars' hypothesis is most convincing, as there is also a good deal of theological similarity between the sections added to an earlier edition of the Gospel, suggesting a common era within the developing history of Johannine Christianity. Fortna's assumption that *meta tauta* indicates a literary seam (' ... John's only attempt to ease the aporia his rearrangement has caused ...', *Gospel*, p. 56) is unconvincing. It simply involves a change of scene and implies nothing about a previous order of the text.

The triple use of the genitive article *tēs* is quite confusing, and this is reflected in the attempts of later copyists to clarify the passage. Although one is tempted to look for a connection between *peran tēs* ... and *Tiberiados* (cf. *peran* with the genitive in Jn. 1:28; 10:40; 18:1, where it means 'beyond' or even 'across from' the Jordan/brook of Cedron), most scholars translate it 'across the sea ... which is called Tiberias'. However, the fact that the following day people are reported to have set out from the *town* of Tiberias (6:23) causes one to suspect that vs. 1 is a reference, muddled though it be, to the town, Tiberias, upon which the sea is located, and near to which the feeding is to have taken place. Whatever one's translation, the triple genitive article is confusing, and any theory used to explain its inclusion as it stands cannot sustain much interpretive weight.

4. The mention of *eggus to pascha* is neither chronological nor theological in its purpose, but it is used to describe the religio-political situation in which the feeding *and* the misperception of Jesus' *messiahship* by the crowd (vs. 14f.) were to have taken place. To 'read into' the paschal reference the Pauline notion of a sacrificial lamb christology, or a cultic reference to the eucharist, is deflective. The primary function of the *eggus to pascha* theme in John is to increase the nationalistic intensity of the narrative in order to make an emphatic distinction between the kind of Messiah Jesus was anticipated as, and the kind of Messiah Jesus intended to be. Thus, when the three *eggus to pascha* passages in John are considered jointly (2:13; 6:4; 11:55) several matters become clear: a) his 'zeal' for his Father's 'house' is *not* the zealotry of the Zionist, who would rebuild the Temple in Zion in defiance of Roman occupation, but the power of Jesus' kingship (18:37), which is finally revealed in the resurrection (Jn. 2:13–22); b) the Jewish leaders are obviously afraid of the Roman backlash, which would follow a paschal messianic revolt (Jn. 11:45–55) and decide to offer Jesus up as a 'religio-political sacrifice' to the Romans; and c) in Jn. 6:4–69 Jesus is misperceived as an army-feeder like Elisha (vss. 9ff., an implicit connection with 2 Kings 4:42–44), the prophet-king, like Moses (vs. 14, explicit), and even the Holy One of God (vs. 69) who restores the Kingdom by means of spiritual acts of power (cf. Mk. 1:24). In each of these cases, a reference is made to the disciples' misunderstanding, which later reinterpreted Jesus' salvation as spiritual, *rather than political*, after his death and resurrection (2:21f.; 6:60–66; 12:16): an indication of a Stage 5, *Conjunctive* reinterpretation of Jesus' messiahship in the light of later events.

The historicity of such religio-political tensions associated with the feeding event is corroborated by the primary interpretive comment within the Marcan tradition (Mk. 6:34), where Jesus has compassion upon the multitude because they are like 'sheep without a shepherd'. The traditional associations of this phrase go back to the installation of Joshua as the successor of Moses (Nu. 27:15–17) and the vision of Micaiah ben Imlah upon the eve of the tragic battle of Ramoth Gilead (1 Ki. 22:17; cf. Jer. 8:22) — scenes which later contribute to a primary image of the Zion restoration as described in Zech. 10:2ff. This 'Zionist' motif was inherent only to the

Marcan tradition, as both Matthew and Luke omit such interpretive comments in the post-70 CE redactions of Mark. In the Johannine tradition, however, earlier *and* later interpretations co-exist together, and it may reasonably be assumed that vs. 4 was an integral part of the earlier oral tradition, as was Mk. 6:34 within the pre-Marcan tradition, rather than a later interpolation added to an extant text.

5f. Jesus' initiative in this section has nothing to do with his 'command over the situation', and thus assuming a hypothetical *theios anēr* role. Characteristic of the Johannine narrative (rather than the discourse sections), it is Jesus (or some other agency of God's discourse with humanity) who takes the initiative, suggesting that a response from humanity is to be expected within the immediate context. The evangelist interprets the story of Jesus (as well as the history of Israel and the world) as the saving and revealing divine-human dialogue, by which God initiates the 'conversation', and humans are called to respond faithfully to God's initiative. This may also be seen in the 'testing' of Philip, which is entirely reminiscent of Yahweh's 'testing' of Israel in the wilderness (Ex. 16:4; contra C.T. Ruddick, 'Feeding and Sacrifice; The Old Testament Background of the Fourth Gospel', *ExpT* 79, 1967/8, p. 340f., who sees the 'testing' motif as a reference to Gen. 22; cf. Guilding). What Mark 6 and 8 report as a discussion of the means of provision, the Johannine tradition interprets as a testing of the disciples' ability to respond in faith to God, the Source of all provision, at work in his apostolic envoy, Jesus. This is the unifying motif of *all of John 6*.

7. While Barrett is justified in looking for literary connections between the linguistic similarities inherent to the Johannine and Marcan narratives, Gardner-Smith is correct in assuming that 200 *denarii* is precisely the sort of illustrative detail that would have been lodged firmly within the oral transmission of traditional stories. This also explains why it is omitted from Luke's and Matthew's redactions of the written, Marcan tradition. It is also significant that only John includes the names of disciples in this discussion. Fortna's assumption that the addition of names is a result of the dramatizing work of the evangelist is not the best solution. The fact that the Johannine account is more graphic in its detail than the Synoptic ones may also be explained as a result of its proximity to the events themselves. After all, if Philip's home town were Bethsaida (1:44; 12:21), not far from the town of Tiberias, it would have been entirely understandable that he should have been asked about where to acquire bread. Again, Fortna's belief that the insertion of names is a redactional technique used by the evangelist goes *against* the style of the Synoptic redactions of Mark (cf. for instance Mt. 8:14–17; 9:18–26; 18:21; 24:3; 28:7; and Lk. 21:7; 22:39), and Fortna cites no other literary precedent, contemporary or otherwise, on which to base such a judgment. It seems odd, if the First and Third Evangelists were also trying to write 'believable and illustrative' Gospels, as the Fourth is supposed to have attempted, that rarely, if ever, do they add names (outside of a unit) to a Marcan narrative. Their redactional alterations are *nearly always* summarizing (changing lists of, or references to disciples' names to 'some of his disciples' or 'the disciples', etc.) rather than interpolative when it comes to *detail*. Assuming the Fourth Evangelist must have done the opposite is unwarranted.

9. The double diminutive *paidarion* need not be interpreted as a boy having lesser status or stature. It may also be taken as an endearing term, such as the Scottish, 'wee lad' or 'laddy'. It is again significant that John alone records the origin of the loaves and fishes, whereas Mark 6 and 8 simply mention generally that the disciples are able to produce the loaves and fishes. John also describes the loaves as *krithinous* (loaves made of barley which were a common staple for the poor) and the fish as *opsaria* (a preserved fish — either in dried, pickled, or relish form — normally eaten with bread, although, cf. Jn. 21:9, 10 and 13). If these two references have been added for 'illustrative' reasons alone (cf. the mention of *paidarion* in 2 Ki. 4:42, LXX) and had nothing to do with actual events, it must be said that the tradition underlying Mark 6 has done the same (the prophet commands, 'Give it to the people to eat!' 2 Ki. 4:43, cf. Mk. 6:37; and those

fed are in groups of one hundred, cf. 2 Ki. 4:43 and Mk. 6:40). Thus, whether or not these details represent the actual physical setting of the feeding, the connection with the Elisha story was a part of the early Marcan *and* Johannine traditions. This suggests an interpretation contemporary with the events themselves (Mk. 8:28), as Jesus' works were obviously associated with Elijah/Elisha typologies quite early (2 Ki. 2–8). What is conspicuous is that the pre-Marcan and Johannine traditions each present this connection with similar, yet different, details.

10. The descriptive detail of John's tradition is also evident in the description of the grass (*polus*, cf. *chlōrō*, Mk. 6:39). This means that it would have probably been springtime, as the grass would have been most plentiful in Palestine after the spring rains. This detail coincides with vs. 4 chronologically, and again, no symbolic meaning is attached to this detail, and there is nothing in 2 Ki. 4 reminiscent of green grass. It is simply a non-symbolic, illustrative detail carried over (like Mk. 6:39) from the oral tradition.

11. Cassirer translates *elaben* as 'seized', which accentuates the dramatic effect of the narrative and heightens the initiatory activity of God's agent, Jesus. The word, *eucharistēsas* simply means 'having given thanks'. It does not refer to highly developed eucharistic traditions. Rather, it is in keeping with the Jewish practice of giving thanks before meals, which would have been done by the head of a household, and it is in keeping with the motifs of 'blessing' the Lord out of gratitude for his blessings (Psalms 78 and 105; cf. Brown, p. 233f.).

12f. The phrase *hina mē ti apolētai* is pregnant with double-meanings. On one hand, it may simply be taken as 'in order that nothing be wasted', referring to scraps of bread. On the other hand, Judas is referred to in 17:12 as *ho huios tēs apōleias* (cf. also Jn. 6:64), and the connection with the 'losing' of some of Jesus' followers (vs. 66) is implied. There may also be a relationship between the gathering up only of the bread (as a contrast to fish in Mk. 6:43), and the christological development of Jesus as the 'bread of life' later in the chapter. Those who 'assimilate' the 'Bread of Life' do not perish, but live eternally.

14. Brown is correct in keeping the plural, *sēmeia*, along with Vaticanus, P[75] and other manuscripts. Says Brown: 'One can see how a plural might have been changed to a singular to make the reference to the multiplication clear; the opposite process is difficult to explain.' (p. 234) The significance of this textual reading is that it suggests that the crowd's reaction was based on cumulative experiences, rather than upon a singular one. However, vs. 26 suggests that in the 'seeing' of signs (possibly vss. 16–24 also, but probably not), the crowd had missed that which they were signifying. Therefore, although they had seen, they had not really understood, and the ironic play on words from Isaiah 6:9f. is implicit. Although they had listened, they had not understood; although they had seen, they had not perceived (cf. Jn. 12:40).

The 'Prophet coming into the world' motif is an explicit reference to the Moses typology, which is implied in John 5:19–47. Behind this motif is Deuteronomy 18:15–22, which is the foundational text for Messiah-Prophet expectations. Several themes in this passage bear a remarkably close resemblance to John's christology; and therefore, the connection between Deuteronomy 18 and John's christology is by no means insignificant. a) The Lord God will raise up a prophet like Moses from among their brothers, and the children of Israel are called to listen attentively to, or to 'hear' him (Deut. 18:15). Therefore, Jesus' reception among the brothers is a common Johannine theme (Jn. 1:11; 7:3, 5; 20:17), and those who believe in Jesus are portrayed as 'hearing' his words (3:29; 4:42; 5:24, 25, 28, 37; 6:45; 8:47; 9:27; 10:3, 8, 16, 27; 12:47; 18:37) as though responding to God, who sent him.

b) The sending of the Prophet is in accordance with Israel's request never to hear Yahweh's voice nor see his fire, lest they die (Ex. 20:19; Deut. 18:16). Correspondingly, the need for God's 'word' to be addressed to humanity is portrayed by the Johannine appraisal of the human situation: no one has ever seen God (Jn. 1:18; 6:46) except the one who has been at the Father's side (1:18) and who has been sent from the Father (6:46) to make him known.

c) Yahweh agrees to abide by the request and promises to send a prophet like Moses, into whose mouth he will put his words, and this messenger will speak everything (and *only* that which) Yahweh has commanded him (Ex. 4:15f.; 7:2; Deut. 18:17f.). Throughout John, these messianic motifs are absolutely characteristic of John's christology. The Samaritan woman's exclamations in 4:19, 25 are indicative of an expectation based upon this motif, as is Jesus' first encounter with his soon-to-be disciples (1:37–49). The revealing/saving mission of Jesus is portrayed in John as God 'speaking' through Jesus (1:1–18; 3:34; 6:63; 9:37; 14:7), thus fulfilling the typology of the Mosaic prophet of Deuteronomy 18:15–22. The Johannine Jesus is thus portrayed as God's agent, doing his *work*, who speaks *only* what he has *seen and heard* from the Father who *sent* him (3:11–13, 27, *31–34*; 4:32–34; 5:19–21, 30, 36–40; 6:27, 29, 33, 38, 47–51, 57f., 63; 7:17, 18, 28f.; 8:16b, 18, 23f., 26–29, 38, 40b, 42, 54; 10:15, 18, 25, 29f., 34–38; 11:27, 42; 12:13, 27f., 49f.; 14:10f., 20, 24b, 28–31; 15:10b; 16:5a, 27f.; 17:2–8, 21, 25f.; 18:36f.; 20:17, 21). This motif has at times been mistaken for subordinationism in John, but it is not. Primarily, it is a reflection of an 'agency christology' based on Deuteronomy 18:17f. The emphasis is not that the Son is limited to the Father's message because of lesser ability, but it is precisely the delimiting of his message solely to that which the Father has shown and spoken which comprises the faithful accomplishment of his emissary, and *thus* authoritative, mission. To speak (or do) more (or less) than this would be to negate the representative function of the prophet's work, and to diminish the authority of its divine commissioning.

The representative work of the agent carries with it two possibilities in terms of response: either one *accepts* the messenger and the message from the one being represented, or one *rejects* the agent, message and the sender. Either way, such a reaction is interpreted in John as response to the sender — in this case, *God* — as well as the one being sent. Therefore, the agency christology of John is inextricable from the Prophet-like-Moses motifs, which are based on Deuteronomy 18:17f. In the positive sense, those who receive the Son also receive the Father who sent him (1:10–13; 3:16–18a, 35–36a; 5:24; 6:40, 51–58; 8:19c; 12:44–46; 13:20b; 14:6f., 9; 17:7). Conversely, to reject Jesus is also to reject the Father (3:18b, 36b; 5:23; 8:19b). Furthermore, the agency motif carries over into Jesus' sending the *Paraklētos*, the Spirit of Truth (14:17; 15:26; 16:13), who convicts the world of sin and righteousness (16:8–11), and who speaks not of his own initiative, but only what he hears and is told to say (16:13–15). And, because it is Jesus who sends out his followers as apostles (6:57; 17:18; 20:21), those who accept them also accept Jesus and the one who sent him (13:20). Therefore, discipleship in John is understood in terms of *apostolicity*. To believe in Jesus as the Son of God — sent into the world with God's message — is also to be called into partnership with Jesus as an agent of God's truth, love and light in the world. The trademark of discipleship is to follow Jesus' ultimate example of love and to be willing to lay down one's life for one's friends (13:34f.; 15:12f.). And, to obey Jesus' commandments and to know his revelation is to be called his 'friends' (15:14f.). It would not be an exaggeration to say that much of John's theology, christology, pneumatology, and ecclesiology is based upon an understanding of Deuteronomy 18:18, which promises that God will continue his redemptive dialogue with humanity by means of the prophet(s) like Moses who speak all that God commands. This important connection has been overlooked by most Johannine scholars. John's subordinate *and* egalitarian christological themes are subsumed in the same schema: *John's agency christology*. They are two sides of the same coin.

d) The implication pertaining to God's word spoken through the prophet is that his audience will be held accountable for that which they have heard (Deut. 18:19). This motif is characterized throughout John by the relationship between truth and judgment. Jesus has not come to condemn the world as an eschatological judge, but the spiritual character of those who behold his witness is revealed by the exposing power of truth (3:17–21; 8:15, 31f.; 9:39–41; 12:46–48). Therefore, one's response to Jesus as God's messenger not only determines one's relationship to God in the future, but it is also indicative of the past and present character of that relationship. Exposure to the truth of God in Jesus brings about the true judgment of God, in that those who know the Father recognize the Son (6:44f., 65; 7:17; 8:47a; 10:3f., 14, 27; 11:25f., 40; 12:26, 36; 16:8, 10). Those who reject the Son do so because they have not known the Father (5:37–40; 6:64; 8:40, 42a, 43, 44, 47b; 10:26; 15:21; 16:3, 8–9). In this respect, the Son of Man does indeed come as an eschatological judge (5:22, 27–30; 8:15f.; 9:39), as his coming forces humanity to make a decision for or against the agent of God (the 'Son of Man' of Dn. 7:13f. is itself an apocalyptic adaptation of the Agent-of-Yahweh typology). Not only does Deuteronomy 18:15–18 describe the human-divine dialogue by which God promises to send his people a prophet like Moses, but Deuteronomy 18:19 also implies that people will be held accountable for their response to the prophet's message. Such is the *religionsgeschichtliche* origin of the evangelist's 'dualism of decision' ideology. On the other hand, the historical Jesus probably saw himself more as a prophet like Moses than the king like David of the Synoptic traditions. While the agency schema is central to John's christology, the evangelist did not invent it. It appears intrinsic to the self-understanding of the historical Jesus, even as based on Synoptic research.

e) As a proleptic answer to the question, 'How can we tell when a prophet *has not* (or *has*) been sent by Yahweh?', Deuteronomy 18:22 advises that if the predictive words of the prophet do not come true he is not to be listened to (cf. the accusation in Jn. 7:12, 'No; he deceives the people!'). The classic testing of this motif is found in 1 Kings 22, where the true prophet of Yahweh, Micaiah ben Imlah, is contrasted to the other 400 court prophets who are false prophets. They tell Ahab to go to battle, assuring him that Yahweh will grant him victory (22:6), but Micaiah warns him that to go to Ramoth Gilead is to meet his doom and for Israel to be scattered on the hillside, 'as sheep without a shepherd' (vs. 17; cf. Mk. 6:34). Influenced by a spirit of deception, Ahab goes to war, disguised as a charioteer, and is killed by a random arrow (vss. 22, 34). Micaiah's identity as a true prophet of Yahweh is attested by his claim that he speaks *only* that which Yahweh commands him (vs. 14), and that whatever Yahweh speaks through the prophet comes true — as a contrast to the predictions of false prophets (vs. 28). This motif is continued in Jeremiah 28:9 and Ezekiel 33:33, where the fulfillment of a prophet's prediction verifies that he has been *sent by God*.

In this sense, Deuteronomy 18:22 may explain at least part of the 'witness' motif in John. In several key instances the evangelist emphasizes that Jesus' words are fulfilled, thus confirming that he is sent from God (2:22; 4:29, 39, 53; 16:4; 21:18f.). Furthermore, it is stated explicitly in 13:19 that Jesus makes a prediction ahead of time *in order to provide the evidence* for his disciples to believe that he is who he says he is — the one sent from the Father —with the result being that those who accept the emissary also receive the sender (13:20, cf. 18:32).

From Deuteronomy 18:22 it is a short step to also considering divine signs and wonders as legitimizers of a prophet's divine commission. In fact, Deuteronomy closes with the lamentation that since the time of Moses there has not arisen in Israel a prophet like Moses, whom Yahweh knew face to face, and who did miraculous signs and wonders (34:10–12). The signs of Moses in the court of Pharaoh serve as confirmations that he is sent from Yahweh (Ex. 7:10–11:10), as are the miracles of Elijah (1 Ki. 18:16–46) and even more so, Elisha, whose superlative succession to Elijah (2 Ki. 2:9) would be confirmed by the doing of many signs (2 Ki. chs. 2–7) reminiscent of the signs of Elijah and even Moses. Ironically, on the basis of Deuteronomy 13:1–6 and 18:1–22 Jesus is accused of being a false prophet in John 7:14–52 (cf. W. Meeks, *Prophet*, pp. 32–61), as Jesus is accused of being demon-possessed (Jn. 7:20) and a deceiver of the people (Jn. 7:47). The confusion of the Prophet-like-Moses typology with the fulfillment of the King-like-David expectations in the minds of the Jewish leaders (7:26f., 31, 40–43, 52) results in their inability to comprehend that Jesus really is sent from God. Meeks has also pointed out that Jesus' rejection by those with Davidic (Zionist and 'kingly') expectations may be related to the 'geographical symbolism' of John (*Prophet*, pp. 313–316). It is the Samaritans and Galileans who receive Jesus, while the 'Jews' (*Judaiou=Judeans?*) of Jerusalem reject him (p. 316). This may suggest something about the geographical locale of at least part of the Gospel's tradition, but more importantly, it underscores the evangelist's perception of Jesus as God's agent, being sent unto his own, but ironically, being rejected by the same (1:11–13). Therefore, Jesus' signs, as well as his fulfilled words, serve the function of confirming the divine origin of his mission. They point to the divine sender, who speaks through him; but at the same time, they become stumbling blocks to those who do not recognize the voice of the Father.

Such a connection suggests at least a partial reason for the evangelist's ambivalence towards Jesus' signs. On one hand, he has matured to the place that he understands true faith to transcend dependence upon the miraculous; while on the other hand, the divine origin of Yahweh's messenger is attested by his fulfilled words and signifying works. Therefore, within the Johannine kerygma, the attestation of Jesus' words and works continues to be a significant christological motif — even to the extent that the evangelist believes he and other believers should be doing the same sort of works that Jesus had done (14:12) — while on the other hand, the evangelist is faced with the reality that miracles do not happen as often as expected. It may also be that requests for a sign were *actually* discouraged by Jesus during his ministry (4:48; 6:30ff.), and that the refusal to allow signs to be a prerequisite for faith is to the Johannine tradition what the adding of 'suffering' to popular Son of Man conceptions is to the Marcan tradition. A clarification of the kind of Messiah Jesus was — and was not.

15. In his 1967 monograph (*Prophet*), W. Meeks has argued convincingly that within the Jewish and Samaritan settings out of which Johannine Christianity emerged, Moses was regarded as a king as well as a prophet, and that 'the depiction of Jesus as prophet and king in the Fourth Gospel owes much to traditions which the church inherited from the Moses piety' (p. 318f.). What Meeks does not address satisfactorily, however, is the political background of 6:15, where Jesus flees the crowds and escapes into the mountains. According to Meeks (p. 99):

> The identification of Jesus as this prophet-king is by no means denied by Jesus' "flight" to the mountain; only the time and the manner in which the men seek to make him king are rejected.

The opposite seems to have been the case within the Johannine interpretation of the event, as it is precisely the popularistic understandings of leadership that Jesus is portrayed here as eschewing. While Jesus is quite clearly connected with the Prophet-like-Moses figure, sent from the Father, it does not seem so clear that the Johannine Jesus is all that ready to accept the conventional expectations that 'kingship' would entail. It is telling that of the 16 times that *basileus* occurs in John (1:49; 6:15; 12:13, 15; 18:33, 37-, 39; 19:3, 12, 14, 15-, 19, 21-), *not once* is it used by Jesus to refer to himself! In 18:37 he volleys the question back to Pilate, '*You* say I am a king,' but goes on to clarify the precise nature of his kingship: it is the *reign of truth*. In 18:36 Jesus contrasts the violent character of earthly kingdoms to the character of his kingdom, and in 6:15 Jesus *flees* (*pheugei*, Sinaiticus*, Diatesseron, etc.) the crowd *because* they want to make him their king. All of this makes one suspect that there is more to Jesus' fugitive withdrawal than the untimeliness and demeanour of such a coronation. This represents the evangelist's reflective dialogue with the events of his tradition, and his juxtaposition of the type of king Jesus is *not* (Bultmann, p. 213f.) serves as a foil to develop a clearer picture of the kind of 'king' the Son of Man has really come to be (6:27, 51, 53, 62f.). If he has a crown, it is inextricably bound to the cross.

Historically, Jesus must have been wary of being perceived in the same mould as contemporary prophetic and messianic figures, who sought to restore God's kingdom to Israel by dramatic and sometimes violent means. Most familiar in the region would have been Judas the Galilean, who in 6 CE sought to lead a rebellion against Roman suzerainty, believing that Jews owed allegiance to God alone, and that to pay taxes and homage to Quirinius was an act of disloyalty to God (Josephus, *War* ii:118; *Ant.* xviii:4–5; cf. D. Hill, 'Jesus and Josephus' "Messianic Prophets" ', in *Text and Interpretation*, ed. by E. Best and R. McL. Wilson, Cambridge, pp. 143–154). In fact, in the speech attributed to Gamaliel (Ac. 5:34–39), Jesus is compared to Theudas and to Judas the Galilean, as though if his activity were of human origin, his followers would soon be scattered. Just as it is likely that Jesus was killed by the Romans, in keeping with their standard way of dealing with aspiring Zionists, it is also true that Jesus is portrayed by all four gospels as wanting to distance himself from contemporary zealots and revolutionaries, who may have sought to re-enact the taking of Jericho, the deliverance of Cyrus, or the 'kingship' of the Maccabeans. This being the case, Jesus' reluctance to be carried away as a 'king' is perfectly understandable, and vs. 6:15 is to John what the 'messianic secret' is to Mark (8:34). Therefore, while Moses was indeed regarded in regal terms by Jesus' contemporaries, the Johannine Jesus appears reluctant to be considered a 'king' in the conventional sense. According to Hoskyns (*Fourth Gospel*, p. 290):

> The crowd, judging that one who is capable to feed them miraculously can also with miraculous power lead them against the Romans, decides to appoint as king the man whom God has manifestly appointed as His prophet. Movements of revolt were most frequent in Galilee, and they were led by men who were supposed to be prophets (Josephus, *Ant.* xvii.271, 272, xx.97, 98, 169; *B.J.* iii.42, 43).

A theological factor in this inclination also deserves consideration. A rather strong sentiment within the prophetic tradition regards Israel's request for a king as the abandonment of theocracy and the beginning of their demise (1 Sam. 8:11–18; 12:12–17; 13:13). Therefore, the requesting of a king is perceived not as the abandonment of Samuel's prophetic guild, but as the *abandonment of Yahweh* and his sovereign care for Israel (1 Sam. 8:7; 10:19). Yahweh is grieved over the appointment of Saul as king (1 Sam. 15:10, 23, 35), and even Yahweh's promise that David's throne would be established forever (2 Sam. 7:16) is tempered by the deconstructionist narratives of 2 Samuel 21–24, where credit for David's victories are distributed more evenly among his 30 fighting men (2 Sam. 23:24–39), among which Uriah the Hittite is listed as the *last.* Furthermore, Saul's and David's original qualifications to be king were measured in accordance with their *being filled with the prophetic spirit* (1 Sam. 10:6–12; 16:13). Mateos and Barretos rightly interpret the desire of the crowd to make Jesus king as identical to the idolatry of the Israelites in the wilderness (Ex. 32:4; p. 319). Indeed, the attempt to meet the needs that only God can fulfil by some other means than God's provision, is the epitome of idolatry in the Jewish scriptures.

The ideological tensions between the prophetic and royal forms of theocracy have also been at work in the interpretation of Jesus' ministry — even representing ideological differences between his followers. Therefore, the Johannine Prophet-like-Moses christology is set in contradistinction over and against the Marcan King-like-David messianism more prevalent in Jewish (esp. Jeruselocentric and Antiochene) Christianity. Certainly, one of the key objections to believing in Jesus as the one sent from God is that he does not fulfill messianic expectations which are Davidic. He comes neither from David's lineage nor from Bethlehem (7:42), 'the prophet' is not supposed to come from Galilee (7:52), and of course nothing good can come from Nazareth (1:46). Whether the origin of John's prophet christology emerged from the Samaritan (or Galilean) origin of the evangelist (cf. J. Bowman, *The Samaritan Problem*, Pittsburg, 1975; G.W. Buchanan, 'The Samaritan Origin of the Gospel of John', in *Religions in Antiquity*, ed. J. Neusner, Leiden, 1968, pp. 149–175; E.D. Freed, 'Samaritan Influence in the Gospel of John', *CBQ* 30, 1968, pp. 580–587; and J. Purvis, 'The Fourth Gospel and the Samaritans', *NovT* 17:3, 1975, pp. 161–198), whether affinities to Samaritan ideologies have come to the evangelist as a result of familiarity with the Septuagint (M. Pamment, 'Is There Convincing Evidence of Samaritan Influence on the Fourth Gospel?', *ZNW* 73, 1982, pp. 221–230), or whether they reflect the influx of Samaritan converts into Johannine Christianity (R.E. Brown, *Community*,

34–54), one thing is clear: John's messianism differs markedly from the Davidic ideology of the Marcan tradition, and this tension may be observed in its multiple forms throughout John's distinctive presentation of Jesus as the Christ. The Johannine Jesus did not come to restore David's throne in Jerusalem, but to bring truth, light and life to the entire world; and this may be observed in John's attitude toward a pneumatic form of christocracy, rather than an institutional (and Petrine) model. Once again, the Johannine rendition corrects the more prevalent Synoptic (esp. the Matthean) inclination.

The Johannine version of Jesus' fleeing into the hills to escape the crowds in John 6:15 may even be more accurate historically than the more pietistic Marcan version (Mk. 6:46), where he does so in order to pray. Politically, Jesus may have wanted to distance himself from the likes of Judas the Galilean, and other Mosaic or Davidic pretenders to kingship. As the 'One sent from Yahweh', in keeping with the Prophet-like-Moses tradition, the Johannine Jesus is portrayed as restoring the original theocracy of pre-monarchic Israel, where Yahweh interacted with his people by means of his spokesman, Moses, and his successor(s). Therefore, not only is the Prophet-like-Moses motif understandable as a central way in which Jesus' ministry would have been interpreted messianically by Galilean and Samaritan audiences, but it may also represent the early christological posture of the evangelist and is also at least partially responsible for the evangelist's ambivalence toward the signs and the lack of any Davidic allusions within John's christology. The true identity of the prophet is attested by his fulfilled words and confirming deeds, and the original understanding of theocracy within the Torah was that it was to be effected through God's dialogue with humanity by means of the prophet like Moses, in keeping with Deuteronomy 18:15–22. Thus, the 'bi-optic gospels' (Mark and John) differ not only in drawing upon independent traditions, but in their ideological perceptions of what Jesus came to do.

16f. As a contrast to Jesus' initiatory role in the feeding narrative, the disciples are *not* commanded to board the boat as they are in Mark 6:45. Their departure is simply reported by the evangelist. Their destination is Capernaum, and it is not clear whether they were returning after having been away for a day, or whether their absence had been longer. What Mark 6:47 reports as 'evening' (*opsias*), with the boat in the midst of the sea and Jesus on the land, John describes as 'darkness' (*skotia*), a familiar Johannine symbol for spiritual desolation (1:5; 19; 6:17; 8:12; 12:35; 20:1; cf. also *nuktos/nux*: 3:2; 9:4; 13:20), which is the natural condition of the world without Jesus (1:5; 8:12; 9:4; 12:35f.). Mateos and Barretos translate vs. 17 graphically, 'Los había cogido la tiniebla.' 'Darkness had *grabbed* them.' (p. 306).

19f. What Mark 6:47 reports in general terms as 'in the middle of the sea", John describes as 'about twenty-five or thirty furlongs' (*stadious*). The redactional tendency of both Matthew and Luke is to omit such non-symbolic illustrative details, and it simply deserves to be pointed out that John once more does the opposite. However, the most significant difference between the Marcan and the Johannine versions of the sea crossing is the different ways in which they report the appearance of Jesus and the disciples' reaction. The reports of each contain five components, each of which is portrayed in slightly different terms by Mark and John. These include:

a) The differing accounts of Jesus' appearance on the sea:

Mark 6:48	*John 6:19*
And seeing them being tormented as they rowed ... he comes to them walking on the sea, and intended to go by them.	... they beheld Jesus walking on the sea and coming near the boat.

Despite the similarity of phraseology (walking on the sea), the action of Jesus is different. In Mark, he seems to be *drifting past* the boat, but in John Jesus is *coming to* the boat. John's account *cannot here be explained* simply as an assimilation of, and alteration upon, the Marcan narrative. Its reporting of Jesus' action is radically distinctive, and not derivative from Mark. The immanence theme, particular to the Johannine version, is accentuated by the reaction of the disciples. John's and Mark's interpretive cleavage was *radical*, not subsequent.

b) The differing perceptions of Jesus' appearance by the disciples and their reactions:

Mark 6:49b–50a	*John 6:19c*
And seeing him walking on the sea, they thought it was a phantasm and cried out, for they all saw him and were troubled.	... and they were afraid.

These differences between John and Mark are the most significant in the sea-crossing accounts. The Marcan tradition regards Jesus' appearance as a phantasm, floating by the disciples' boat, causing them to cry out in fear (Matt. 14:26 lists 'out of fear' as the conjectured reason for their shouting). The Johannine tradition, on the other hand, interprets Jesus' appearance with distinctly theophanic overtones. Being filled with fear before the presence of God is characteristic of theophanic encounters in Exodus (Ex. 3:6; 20:18; etc.) and is certainly characteristic of the prophets' responses to being addressed by God at the beginnings of their callings (Is. 6:5; Jer. 1:6; Ezek. 1:28b; Rev. 1:17; cf. Bultmann, p. 215, n. 7). What Mark describes as being afraid of a phantasm, John interprets as *the fear of God* — reminiscent of OT theophanic encounters, and this difference is further confirmed by Jesus' words to the disciples.

c) The difference in Jesus' words to the disciples:

Mark 6:50c	*John 6:20b*
'Cheer up! It is I; don't be afraid.'	'I AM! Fear not.'

In both accounts the *egō eimi* is identical, but it is the Marcan qualification of the meaning of Jesus' words which is most telling. Jesus' statement in Mark is clearly a response to assuage their fears that he was a ghost, or something frightening. Thus, the Petrine account recalls Jesus giving words of assurance: 'Don't worry, it's only myself'. However, John 6:20 is starkly theophanic (Bultmann, p. 216, n. 1). While it is more subtly reminiscent of Ex. 3:14 than John 8:58, there are closer parallels between Jn. 6:20 and Ex. 3:14 than between Jn. 8:58 and Ex. 3:14. The Jn. 8:58 passage represents a christological claim within a debate with the Jews, while Jn. 6:20 represents a theophanic spiritual encounter as an *event*. As in the case of Moses before the burning bush, and the prophets before the transforming presence of the Lord, to encounter the Living God is at the same time to receive a calling to live out of the newness of that reality. Thus, Jn. 6:16–21 has subtle overtones representing the Johannine calling of the twelve (vss. 67–70). Out of spiritual encounters, spiritual callings emerge.

d) The differences in portraying Jesus' entry into the boat and the consequences:

Mark 6:51a–b	*John 6:21*
And Jesus went up to them and on into the boat, and the wind ceased.	Therefore, they wanted to receive him into the boat, and [but?] immediately the boat was upon the land to which they were going.

Whereas the Marcan account simply records that Jesus entered the boat and the wind ceased its blowing, the Johannine account records the disciples' response to Jesus' appearance and words: they were willing to/wanted to/were eager to take him into the boat. The emphasis of the Synoptic sea-crossing narrative(s) is that Jesus has command over the forces of nature (Mk. 6:51f.; Matt. 14:32f.; cf. also Mk. 4:39–41; Matt. 8:26f.; Lk. 8:24f.). On the other hand, the Johannine narrative portrays the event within the threefold structure of the divine-human dialectic, which involves God's addressing humans through his agent (the theophanic appearance and words of Jesus upon the sea), humans' response (they were willing to receive him — into the boat), and the result (and — or should *kai* be here rendered 'but'? — immediately the boat landed at the land to which they were headed). It is for this reason that Bultmann and others have considered vs. 21 to be 'the miracle of the landing', but the landing is still not portrayed as a nature miracle. It is made manifest not by the calming of the sea, but by *the calming of the disciples.* It is reported, thus, not as a nature wonder, but as an existential one.

e) The interpretive differences between the Marcan and the Johannine versions of the sea crossing are most profoundly revealed in the consequential interpretations of the feeding and the connecting of the two events to form a single motif. (Due to length, the following is a summary:)

Mark 6:51c–52, 56	*John 6:22–66*
The disciples were completely amazed (*lian ... existanto*), for they did not understand about the loaves, but their hearts were hardened. ... And they begged to touch the hem of his garment, and whoever touched it was saved.	On the next day the crowd came looking for Jesus, but he claimed that they sought him not because they saw the signs, but because they had eaten their fill of loaves. Later, even some of Jesus' disciples abandon him — the flesh profits nothing.

In both traditions the feeding and the sea-crossing narratives are brought together into a single interpretation, but the Marcan and Johannine renditions are remarkably different. For Mark, the significance of both events is that *Jesus is master over the forces of nature.* Therefore, the disciples should not worry, even if they have forgotten to bring their own bread. Interestingly enough, even though the second feeding in Mark (8:1–10) differs significantly in many of its details (to the extent that it may be considered to be a later variant of the same traditional account), its interpretation is virtually identical to that of Mark 6. As in the feeding of the 5,000, the feeding of the 4,000 is followed by Jesus' crossing the sea with his disciples (8:10–13); but the crisis is not a storm. Rather, it is that the disciples had forgotten to bring loaves along with them (8:14). In the ensuing discussion (8:15–21) Jesus rebukes his disciples for worrying about not having brought loaves (vs. 17) and calls them to remember the two (reports of the) feedings — as though that should stimulate their faith toward believing that Jesus *could* do it again if he wanted to. Typical of the Synoptic (and Petrine) approach to the miraculous, the Marcan Jesus implies that if one has enough faith in God's provision, one's needs will be met. John's approach to signs, however, is significantly different, and this is graphically illustrated in the Johannine interpretation of the feeding. The crowd has been satisfied by the loaves, but they have missed entirely the *significance* ('... you seek me *not* because you saw the *signs* ...' 6:26) of Jesus' works. The fact that the discussion of 'bread' in John 6 is developed exclusively in christological terms may suggest a reason for the departure of some of Jesus' disciples. If they had followed him with hopes that he would be a provider of bread (like Moses), which seems to have been encouraged in the Petrine tradition (and yet rebuked in the Johannine when the crowd does the same), the finality of Jesus' refusal to provide multiple feeding (offering only himself, vss. 48–58) must have been discouraging, to say the least. Whether for political or material reasons, they abandon Jesus because he is not the sort of king they anticipated.

In sum, the difference between the Marcan and the Johannine accounts of the feeding and the sea crossing may be described as the difference between the way 'salvation' is understood within the respective traditions. The Petrine tradition perceives Jesus' saving work in terms of seizing power over nature and spiritual forces of the age, while the Johannine tradition perceives it in terms of revelation, which involves the initiatory and saving action of God's dialogue with humanity. If a person's understanding of salvation tends to be determined by his or her perception of that from which he or she needs to be delivered, then this fundamental difference in ideology at the very least reflects significant departures between early Christian interpreters in their valuations of Jesus' 'saving' ministry. The probability that these two 'traditions' must have disagreed with each other ideologically is thus accentuated by Jesus' rebuke of the crowd in Jn. 6:26. The purpose of the feeding was *not* for people to 'eat ... and be satisfied' (*contra* Matt. 14:20; Mk. 6:42; Lk. 9:17; and Mk. 8:8; Matt. 15:37). This ideological tension is *not* between the Fourth Evangelist and a hypothetical source. It represents a fundamental ideological difference between the Petrine and Johannine traditions regarding the significance of Jesus' ministry overall. (See Anderson, *Sitz im Leben*, 1993, pp. 23–30.)

Disappointingly, not all scholarly studies have examined the difference between the Marcan and Johannine accounts closely enough. Heils is correct to observe that John's account involves both epiphany and rescue (common to all gospel sea-crossing narratives, p.17), but he fails to give proper credit to the 'theophanic' genre of epiphany which is distinctive to the Johannine tradition. Likewise, while W. Berg, after writing over 300 pages (possibly encompassing all the sea-crossing narratives in ancient literature, and then turning to the gospel sea-crossing narratives), treats all the gospel accounts as though they represented a single perspective on the event. Even in his identification of five ways in which the New Testament *Seewanderlerzählungen* have been interpreted by recent scholars, he fails to notice that the articles and books which interpret the sea crossing as a *göttliche Machttat* and a *soteriologische Epiphanie* (p. 333ff.; almost theophanic) are largely treatments of the Marcan and Johannine narratives, respectively. The differences between the Marcan and Johannine perspectives are foundational to the respective traditions, not later alterations of an identical traditional source. Such may never have existed.

22f. Verses 22f. are full of textual problems and perplexities, but this does not mean that vss. 22–24 may be facilely ascribed to a redactor. Indeed, as textual criticism illustrates, subsequent 'corrections' of earlier problems often make a passage *clearer*, rather than more muddled. As the many such examples in these verses illustrate, the textual problems of this passage demonstrate either that the Johannine compiler was a very poor editor, jumbling meanings here and there, or that he allowed various problems to stand — perhaps out of a concern to preserve the writing of the evangelist. The latter is, strictly from a redaction-critical perspective, more probably the case.

The first textual difficulty is not really problematic. In vs. 22, P^{75} and other early mss. read *ei mē hen*, and subsequent mss. have simply elaborated on the theme and described the boat as 'the one in which Jesus' disciples embarked' etc. The difficulties in vs. 23, however, are more serious. P^{75} reads *alla ēlthen ploia ek Tiberiados*, but the presence of the typically Johannine *de* in A, f¹, K; and *oun* in Sinaiticus; as well as the use of the double diminutive *ploiaria* in A, f¹, K, L; and *ploiariōn* in D; makes one wonder if there may have been a second-century text to which some of these changes may be attributed. On the other hand, the passage is somewhat awkward, and the discrepancies could be simply indications that future copyists have tried to make better sense out of the text. It would be fair to say, however, that none of the dozen or more variants makes a significant alteration of the meaning of the passage. All of them try to clarify the manner in which various boats left the town of Tiberias (which was near the place where Jesus had 'given thanks') in search of Jesus. The connection with vs. 1 may suggest that the Sea of Galilee was crossed, over to (or across from) the region of the town, Tiberias; and that Jn. 21:1 took its cue from a misunderstanding of 6:1. Then again, for an audience in Asia Minor, the Roman appellation would have simply been a more familiar reference to the lake.

The other textual variant in vs. 23 poses more of a theological problem than the others in this section. P^{75} and most other early mss. describe the location of the feeding on the previous day as the place where they ate the bread, *eucharistēsantos tou kuriou*; while D, 086, Diatesseron[l,v] and others do not include the phrase. This means that within the second century there was already a discrepancy between P^{75} and Tatian's Diatesseron. Because it is hard to imagine why such a phrase would have been omitted by such an orthodox document as the

Diatesseron, the phrase should be considered a cultic gloss which was added after the completion of the Gospel, probably expanding on Jn. 6:11. Therefore, it could not have been an interpolation added by the redactor of the Gospel. The value of identifying this interpolation is that it betrays quite clearly the eucharistic motif with which John 6:1–24 had come to be associated within second-century Christianity. This says nothing in itself of the way the narrative was originally used within Johannine Christianity, but it may suggest that a key context within which the retelling of the feeding/sea-crossing narratives occurred may have been times of table fellowship within the later Christian 'family'.

24. While vss. 22 and 23 are rather jumbled, the point of this transitional section in the narrative is made amply clear in vs. 24. When the crowd saw that Jesus and his disciples were no longer there, they embarked in boats themselves and went to Capernaum in search of Jesus. As typical of semeiological narratives, the scene closes with a response to the sign. However, the astute reader will have recognized by now that the enthusiasm of the crowds (which may have caused Jesus to get into a boat in the first place, 6:1), followed by their being carried away with Mosaic messianism (which caused Jesus to flee into the wilderness after the feeding, 6:14f.), may yet again receive a reticent welcome from the Johannine Jesus in the dialogue to follow.

Discussion

The dialogue between the evangelist and his tradition must be understood to have encompassed a broad measure of time. Whether or not the evangelist was himself the source of his tradition, the fact that John's account is parallel to — and yet different from — those in Mark 6 and 8 must argue for an independent tradition which had a different person or group as its origin. Thus, Mark and John are 'bi-optic' in the sense that they report two traditional 'perspectives' which must have arisen from different sectors of Jesus' band. As a story is told and retold, new insights arise, and new connections are made between familiar narratives and new meanings. Differences between the pre-Marcan and Johannine traditions not only encompass variations in the reporting of events, but more significantly, they betray two coherent clusters of ideological differences which extend from interpretations of Jesus' ministry to Kingdom theologies and to models of church government, whereby the risen Christ continues to shepherd his flock in the sub-apostolic generation. While most of the Johannine interpretation has been developed in the elaboration on the feeding (vss. 25–66), vss. 1–24 still offer a clear picture of some of the major distinctives of John's perspective regarding the feeding and sea-crossing events. Therefore, the following observations will be made regarding the evangelist's 'dialogue' with his tradition, as represented by John 6:1–24.

A. Given the corollaries between Mark 6 and 8 and John 6, it is obvious that a *cluster of events* (a large feeding, a sea crossing, subsequent discussions between Jesus and his disciples and Jesus and Jewish leaders, and the confession of Peter) must have occurred in Jesus' ministry, but that they have also been remembered differently by (at least) two sectors of Jesus' band. Both Mark 6 and John 6 recall the feeding as somewhat of a re-enactment of the Elisha story (2 Ki. 4), and they also reflect the historical probability that the original perception of the feeding by the multitude (and Jesus' followers) had to do with Zionist Messianism. This motif is diminished in the corollary accounts of Matthew and Luke. Given the dividing of people into companies of 50's and 100's, counting only the 'men', the similarities with later uprisings in the wilderness (Ac. 21:38; Josephus, *Ant.* xx 8,6), springtime (the Passover is near, vs. 4; cf. 2:13; 11:55) being the most common 'season' for Jewish uprisings, the Zionist theme of 'sheep without a shepherd', the impulse of the people to rush Jesus off for a hasty coronation (vs. 15), the recent loss of another 'messianic' prophet (John the Baptist, cf. Mk. 6:14–29), and the anticipation built upon Jesus' doing signs in the region, etc., all corroborate one thing. The early memory of the event was definitely clad in the messianic garb of Zionist or Galilean nationalism.[4] In fact, it seems to have taken Jesus' death and resurrection for even his disciples to abandon their nationalistic understandings of deliverance, and to see in Jesus another kind of salvation. In all four Gospels, the twelve did not understand fully what Jesus meant until *after* the resurrection.

Significantly, the Johannine and Petrine traditions show signs of having worked through these *Synthetic-Conventional* and *Individuative-Reflective* (Stages 3 and 4) nationalistic ideals and have interpreted the feeding as having another meaning. Also significant is the correlation between Jesus' epiphany on the sea and the disciples' transformed perceptions of the feeding as a result.[5] The Marcan source interprets the messianism of Jesus as that of a thaumaturge who has power over forces of nature (not necessarily military forces), and the point of the feeding and the epiphany is unitary: to give the disciples reason to believe they no longer need worry over earthly needs such as hunger and safety. Their *physical* needs were cared for in the past, and will be cared for in the future. While most of the 'revolt in the desert' themes of Mark 6 have eluded the accounts of Mark 8 and those of Matthew and Luke, the pre-Marcan thaumaturgic christology has not. Thus, in the Synoptic tradition the miracles of Jesus are remembered as 'attesting wonders', effected to arouse faith in Jesus as the Messiah and to facilitate continuity with his wondrous ministry in the life of the church.

---

4 The validity of the 1962 article by H. Montefiore ('Revolt in the Desert? (Mark 6:30ff.)', *NTS* 8, pp. 135–141) has been largely underestimated by Johannine scholars. However, Josephus cites at least five Prophet-Messiah leaders around this time, several of which seek to overthrow the Romans in acts of 'Holy War'. It is highly probable that this was the most prevalent messianic expectation against which Jesus had to struggle. It may have been such nationalistic hopes which drew a crowd that size to a rendezvous in the desert, the disappointment of which caused some to turn away (Jn. 6:66), and the threat of which brought a swift response from the Romans — crucifixion being the common sentence for such insurrectionists. However, the Johannine Jesus flees such designs on his future (6:15) and proclaims that his kingdom is a direct contrast to such struggles involving human force (18:36f.). See F. Hahn, 'The Eschatological Prophet', in his *The Titles of Jesus in Christology*, London, 1969, pp. 352–406; D. Hill, 'Jesus and Josephus' "messianic prophets" ', in *Text and Interpretation*, Cambridge, 1972, pp. 143–154; and P. W. Barnett, 'The Jewish Sign Prophets — A.D. 40–70; Their Intentions and Origin', *NTS* 27, 1981, pp. 679–697.

5 See discussion of vss. 16–21 above, pp. 179–182.

However, in the Johannine tradition by the time of its written form,[6] it is the disciples and others who are 'tested' by Jesus' works, and who are called to respond to that which God is doing through his apostolic envoy in the world. Therefore, the Prophet/King-like-Moses motif is reinterpreted by the Fourth Evangelist and existentialized into an agency christology based upon its foundational meaning described in Deuteronomy 18:15–22. There may have been other reflective developments along the way, but by the time John 4–7 was written, Jesus is perceived as the one through whom the Father speaks, the one to whom the scriptures point (5:39) and of whom Moses wrote (5:46). Jesus' mission is clearly portrayed in the role of the Deity's agency. This motif is also directly responsible for much of John's christological unity and disunity. The agent speaks nothing except what he is told by the sender, and he is therefore *like* the sender in all ways.[7]

As in the case of Mark 6, the Johannine interpretation of the feeding may have been influenced by the sea-crossing epiphany. Like Mark 6:45–52, the sea crossing in John 6:16–21 exhibits all the characteristics of what J. Loder refers to as a 'transforming' encounter (above, Chapter 7). Analyzed in terms of Loder's five-step anatomy of the experience of knowing, the disciple to whom the Johannine account is due must have undergone a mental 'dialogue' which went something like this: 1) He experienced a *conflict*. Being out in the middle of the sea and having last seen Jesus on the shore fleeing into the hills to escape the crowd, this disciple is stricken with awe at the sight of Jesus walking upon (*epi*) the sea.[8] 2) After a brief *interlude for scanning* and trying to judge what Jesus is doing, this person decides that he must be coming *to them* as he draws near the boat.[9] 3) With the utterance of Jesus' words,

---

6 There is no telling how Matthew and Luke would have interpreted the feeding narrative if they had been dealing with an oral tradition rather than a written one. Mark's interpretation must have been put into writing at the latest in the late 60's, and Matthew and Luke perpetuate the same interpretation. However, if John's tradition remained in an oral form until the 80's or even the 90's, this allows nearly twice as much time for reflective interpretation *before* the meaning of the narrative would have become fixed in writing. This would allow an early interpreter (even a follower of Jesus) more than ample time to reflect on these events and find new meanings and nuances in familiar stories, such as the motif of 'testing'. Such a motif would also be most meaningful during a time of 'testing' for Johannine Christians — say, during the reign of Domitian (81–96 CE).

7 This motif, as developed in Merkabah mysticism, is described by P. Borgen (*Bread,* p. 162): The basic principle of the Jewish institution of agency is that "an agent is like the one who sent him". In general this rule means that the agent is like his sender as far as the juridical effects are concerned. There were, however, rabbis who developed it into a "juridical mysticism" saying that the agent is a person identical with his principal. Thus not only his authority and function are derived from the sender, but also his qualities.

8 *Epi tēs thalassēs* may be translated walking *on* the sea, and it may also mean *along* the sea. By the time the tradition reaches Mark, Jesus is not only coming to them, but is about to go right past them; and by the time Mark's account is incorporated into Matthew, Peter is willing to try walking upon the water himself. John's tradition here appears to be the earliest — it is certainly the least developed.

9 One may also detect Loder's five steps in the knowing-event within the pre-Marcan (may

a *constructive act of the imagination* in the perception of this individual formulates a working hypothesis. Jesus' appearance is experienced and perceived as a theophany, and this cognition is the turning point of the knowing event. Therefore, Jesus' ambiguous words and actions are interpreted differently by the two disciples, who must have been the sources of the 'Petrine' and Johannine accounts of the sea crossing.[10] 4) What follows is a sense of *release* and *opening*, and the disciples desire to receive Jesus into the boat. 5) The final step in any knowing event is the *interpretation*, which reflects upon the significance of the event and the implications which it may have upon other events and understandings. Within the immediate context, the Johannine tradition offers *no* elaboration upon the meaning of the theophany on the sea. In this sense, John 6:16–21 is the least developed rendition of the gospel sea-crossing narratives and may be considered the most primitive (as also corroborated by ... *stadious eikosi pente hē triakonta*).

This suggests the sort of experience it must have been for one of Jesus' followers.[11] On the other hand, the theophanic experience of this individual has

---

we call it 'Petrine'?) tradition. a) The *conflict* in Mk. 6:48 is identical to the one in Jn. 6:19: the disciples were in the middle of the lake, and they saw Jesus coming to them, walking on the sea. b) However, in the *interlude for scanning,* the Petrine tradition differs from the Johannine. It seems that Jesus would pass right by them; they thought he was a 'phantom', and they began to shout out in fear (Mk. 6:48f.). c) This difference is accentuated further with the *constructive act of the imagination* which follows Jesus' words. Jesus' '*Egō eimi; mē phobeisthe!*' is interpreted as a comforting response to their distress. Thus, the working hypothesis is that Jesus' words are to comfort them and give them confidence. '*Don't worry,*' adds the Petrine tradition, 'it is I; don't be afraid.' d) The sense of *release* and *opening* comes after Jesus enters the boat and the wind and waves calm down. At this, the disciples wonder at Jesus' power over the elements, but the (Petrine) editorial comment suggests that ' ... they still did not understand about the loaves, as their hearts had been hardened' (Mk. 6:52). e) The *interpretation* continues to develop in vss. 53–56, as Jesus' divine power over nature and human illness is demonstrated before many.

The most extensive interpretation of Mk. 6:31–52, however, may be found in the tradition underlying Mk. 8:1–21. Here the interpretation which is implicit in Mk. 6:51f. has been made explicit (Mk. 8:17–21). Jesus *can* do the miraculous (provide more bread/have power over nature), and his disciples should believe in his ability to do so, rather than complain about being hungry.

10 Bretschneider's notion (1820) that the differences between John and the Synoptics proves John's a-historicity is unfounded. Jesus' words and works were indeed provocative and rarely free from ambiguity, and there was never a time in which *only one* interpretation of his ministry ever existed. Rather, there seem to have been variant interpretations of Jesus' ministry right from the beginning. This is not a matter of historicality, but of variant perceptions among his contemporaries. It is not inconceivable that the divergent experiences and interpretations (of two disciples in the boat?) may have evoked two sets of 'first impressions' which contributed to the development of two major ideological directions. Like Plato's and Xenophon's renditions of Socrates' *Symposium*, the recollections of a master's leading followers invariably *differ along ideological lines of interpretation*, let alone points of detail along the way.

11 Bultmann was right to declare, 'The *message of Jesus* is a presupposition for the theology

influenced his understanding of the meaning of the feeding, and this reflection may be observed further in the Johannine development of the 'Bread of Life' dialogues and discourses. What 'actually' may have happened on the sea that night, or whatever Jesus may have 'really' intended to do, must finally be left open for speculation. What *is* significant about the similarities and contrasts between the Petrine and Johannine traditions is that we seem to have two fundamentally distinctive experiences and interpretations of the same set of ambiguous events, and upon these *eikonic* constructs were based two 'bi-optic' accounts of what Jesus said and did, and what that should mean to his followers. In short, at least some of the differences between the Synoptic and John may have been due to consequences following the diverging 'first impressions' of two men in the same boat. At the startling appearance and words of Jesus, while one may have exclaimed something like, 'My God! It's a *ghost*!' (cf. Matt. 14:26 and 26:74!); the other may have confessed under his breath, 'My Lord, and my God!' (cf. Jn. 20:28).

B. The *independence of the Johannine narrative* is also corroborated by a redaction-critical analysis of Matthew's and Luke's assimilation of the Marcan narrative. When contrasted with the two closest parallels to John 6:1–24 (other than the Marcan ones), the accounts of Matthew and Luke, it soon becomes obvious that *if* John were written like them, as a compilation of a written narrative source (Mark) and a sayings source (Q), then John's redactional style is *diametrically opposite* their styles of redaction. Like Mark, John reflects greater proximity to the oral tradition, unlike Matthew and Luke, as is evidenced by a plenitude of non-symbolic, graphic, illustrative detail. While Barrett (p. 44) correctly points out six such connections between John 6 and Mark 6 or 8, most of this material is *uniquely found in John*.

Table 10:
'Non-Symbolic, Graphic Detail Distinctive to the Johannine Tradition (Jn. 6:1–25)'

— the locale to which they were headed (Tiberias, vs. 1)
— Jesus' ascending the hillside and sitting down with his disciples (vs. 3)
— (Lifting up his eyes) Jesus beheld the crowd coming to him (vs. 5)
— the vivid dialogue between Jesus and Philip and Andrew (vss. 6–9)

---

of the New Testament rather than a part of that theology itself' (*Theology of the New Testament* Vol. 2, p. 3). His mistake (and a mistake of recent scholarship, although it is rarely stated so bluntly) is to assume that the Synoptic/Johannine problem is 'three witnesses against one', thus proving the Synoptic witness to be more 'historical' than John. The gospels are *bi-optic*, and this is foundationally the result of differences between the apostolic sources of Mark and John. There may even be a direct link between the Fourth Evangelist's experience of Jesus as the 'I AM' of Ex. 3:14 and his paraphrasis of the ways Jesus may have spoken of himself with 'I am' metaphors and even the theophanic claim of Jn. 8:58. On the other hand, Peter's personal affinity to matters concerned with power may have influenced the jealousy over the 'sons of Zebedee accounts', his portrayal of Jesus' 'dynamic' ministry, and even his inclination to include Jesus' teaching on the *Kingdom* of God in his sermons.

— Andrew's relation to Peter (vs. 8)
— the fishes being a particular sort of preserved relish (*opsarion*, vs. 9)
— the loaves made of barley and contributed by a young lad (*krithinos, paidarion*, vs. 9)
— the quantity of grass (*chortos polus*) in the area — making sitting down easier (vs. 10)
— the barley loaves being mentioned as what has been gathered up (vs. 13)
— the crowd perceiving Jesus as the Prophet who is come into the world (vs. 14)
— causing Jesus to withdraw into the hills (again) because the crowd wanted to carry him off as their king (vs. 15)
— the disciples having rowed 25–30 furlongs (*stadious*, about 3–4 miles, vs. 19)
— the crowd's seeking them the following day (vs. 22)
— and then coming in boats from Tiberias to Capernaum in search of Jesus (vs. 23f.)

All of these details are unique to the Johannine tradition and are more suggestive of the oral account of a first-hand story teller than fabrications of an historicizing novelist. Except for vss. 4–6 and 14f. there is nothing explicitly interpretive about any of these details, nor are any of them used symbolically elsewhere in the narrative. For instance, no elaboration is performed upon what good fortunes will befall young lads who share their lunches with those in need; nor is any mention made of barley loaves being the least of breads — and yet the best of foods — having been blessed by Jesus; nor is there any further mention of the distance the disciples had rowed being suggestive of the inadequacy of human rigour when it comes to faith. Whether the evangelist is just a convincing dramatist, or whether he is simply describing a scene with which he has been familiar, his ability to make the reader feel the realism of the scene is striking.[12] The literary form of the narrative in John 6 is not that of an allegory, devised to convey a set of abstract ideas illustratively. It is a narrative which makes the reader feel at home in the setting, and which interprets the events of Jesus' ministry in such a way as to lead the reader into the transforming event of 'knowing' the christocentric truth of the narrative. But realism does *not* imply novelizing categorically. The non-symbolic, illustrative detail of John 6 serves no semeiotic or explicit rhetorical function. It appears simply because it, like Mark 6, never strayed too far from its oral renditions.

The weakness of the theory that John 6:1–24 is a redaction of Mark 6:31–52, or some other written source, is illuminated by a redaction-critical analysis of Mark's narrative contrasted to the ways it was edited by Matthew and Luke. Even a cursory overview manifests two conclusions: a) the kind of material they *omit* is the *graphic, illustrative, non-symbolic detail,* which is precisely the kind of material so characteristic of John's account; and b) the kind of material they *add* is *summarizing conjecture* (often pietistic) about motives and the transpiring of events, which is less characteristic of the Fourth Evangelist's narratological style.

---

12 Haenchen's conclusion that John's portrayal of events in Jn. 6:1–15, when considered with the Synoptic accounts, 'is to be understood as cold and colorless' (p. 276), is ludicrous. The human element does not 'recede' in John's account, but rather is infused with prolific illustrative detail and conversations between 'actual' people, and it is interpreted in the light of God's saving dialogue with humanity — itself an overture of love.

For instance, Matthew and Luke have *omitted* the following detail from the Marcan narrative.

Table 11:
'Marcan Detail (Mk. 6:31–52) Omitted by Matthew *and* Luke'

— Jesus' invitation to the 'apostles' to come away into the wilderness and rest after the ministry tour — they themselves had had nothing to eat (Mk. 6:31)
— the crowd saw them, ran together, and arrived before them (Mk. 6:33)
— 200 *denarii* worth of loaves (*dēnariōn diakosiōn*, Mk. 6:37)
— Jesus' question about how many loaves they had (Mk. 6:37f.)
— the *green* grass (*chlōrō chortō*, Mk. 6:39)
— some of the groups were composed of a hundred people (Mk. 6:40)
— Jesus also divided the fishes to all (Mk. 6:41)
— fishes are also gathered (Mk. 6:43)
— Bethsaida is the destination of the boat (Mk. 6:45)
— Jesus was alone *on the land* (*epi tēs gēs*, Mk. 6:47)
— he intended to bypass them on the sea (Mk. 6:48)
— they all saw him and were troubled (Mk. 6:50)
— they were amazed beyond measure and stricken with awe (Mk. 6:51)
— and they did not yet understand about the loaves (Mk. 6:52)

These are merely the elements of details that *both* Matthew and Luke omit from Mark's account, but the same type of omissions have been made individually by either Matthew or Luke. For instance, Matthew and Luke alone exclude at least three Marcan details or sections apiece.

Table 12:
'Marcan Detail (Mk. 6:31–52) Omitted by Matthew Alone'

— 'he began to teach them many things' (Matt. 14:14; cf. Mk. 6:34)
— 'and farms' (Matt. 14:15; cf. Mk. 6:36)
— 'groups of fifty each' (Matt. 14:19; cf. Mk. 6:40)

Table 13:
'Marcan Detail (Mk. 6:31–52) Omitted by Luke Alone'

— the entire sea-walking narrative (as quite possibly he believes that it is a doublet of Mk. 4:35–41?)
— 'on foot from the towns' (Lk. 9:11; cf. Mk. 6:33)
— 'And coming out he saw a great crowd' (Lk. 9:11; cf. Mk. 6:33)

By now it should be clear that it is precisely the non-symbolic, illustrative detail — so distinctive in John's account — that has been omitted by the two *known* redactions of Mark's feeding and sea-crossing narratives: those found in Matthew and Luke. Regarding the sort of material which the evangelists-as-redactors have *added* to their renditions of these narratives, it is also clear that their additions are very different from the type of interpolations which have been ascribed to the Fourth Evangelist by diachronic scholars. Interpolations added by Matthew and Luke include the following examples of common-sense conjecture.

Table 14:
'Interpolations Added by Matthew (Matt. 14:13–33)'

— and he healed their sick (14:14; cf. Mk. 6:34)
— 'They need not depart' (Matt. 14:16; cf. Mk. 6:37)
— 'apart from women and children' (Matt. 14:21; cf. Mk. 6:44)
— 'by himself' (Matt. 14:23; cf. Mk. 6:46)
— 'many furlongs from land' (Matt. 14:24; in place of 'in the midst of the sea', Mk. 6:47)
— 'from fear' (Matt. 14:26; cf. Mk. 6:49)
— the narrative of Peter walking to Jesus on the water (Matt. 14:28–33)

Table 15:
'Interpolations Added by Luke (Lk. 9:10–17)'

— 'and welcoming them he began to speak to them about the Kingdom of God and cured
    those in need of healing' (Lk. 9:11; cf. Mk. 6:34)
— 'lodge and' (Lk. 9:12; cf. Mk. 6:36)
— the rhetorical comment of the disciples, "unless we are to go and buy food for all these
    people" (Lk. 9:13; cf. Mk. 6:37)

Virtually all of these interpolations are either summaries and condensations of the Marcan text, or they are speculations about what one would expect to have happened. Therefore, the theological aside, 'and he was moved with compassion for them, for they were as sheep without a shepherd' (Mk. 6:34) is summarized by Luke as 'and welcoming them' (Lk. 9:11); and the discussion between Jesus and his disciples (Mk. 6:37b–38) is summarized by Matthew as, 'We have nothing here but five loaves and two fishes' (Matt. 14:17). And, elaborating on Mark's indication that Jesus began to teach the crowd, Luke adds that he began to speak to them about the Kingdom of God and heal the sick (Lk. 9:11; cf. also Matt. 14:14) — which is, of course, the sort of thing the Lucan Jesus obviously would have done. No special familiarity with the primitive tradition is required in order to make such conjectural statements. In contrast, the type of detail supposedly 'added' into John's text (6:4, 6, 14f., 23f., 26, etc.) is very *unlike* the genre of interpolations added by Matthew and Luke. They are clarifications of time and place, commentaries upon the intentions of the crowd and Jesus, and they report the response of the crowd to Jesus' works and his subsequent response to the inadequacy of *their* responses. These *are* interpretive comments, but they are intrinsic to the tradition and its basic perspective, rather than superimposed additions to an existing, written source.

Therefore, *if* Matthew's and Luke's redactions of Mark tell us anything about how John may have been written, John *could not have been* a redaction of another written source, Marcan or otherwise. Furthermore, John's narrative, while matching many of Mark's illustrative details and phraseology (Barrett), contains so much additional detail which is distinctively Johannine, that the view of P. Gardner-Smith is confirmed. The Johannine is a tradition pervasively independent from the Synoptics, with its own claim to authenticity, every bit as authoritative as the Marcan account. In fact, the use of non-symbolic detail and insightful commentary is *even more pervasive* in John than in Mark. This corroborates the opinion of

Papias from a redaction-critical perspective. Thus, John represents an alternative interpretation of basically the same events narrated by Mark, but from the perspective of a sector *other* than the source of the Marcan tradition. The only way Fortna is able to conclude that John 6:1–25 is a redaction of an earlier Signs Gospel which is 'similar to if not identical to Mark's account' (*Gospel*, p. 62), is to 'de-Johannify' the text and then to 're-Marcanize' it.[13] This methodology demonstrates *less* about the way John was written, and *more* about the fact that if John's tradition *and* interpretation are altered sufficiently, one can indeed come up with something which looks more Marcan than Johannine. The question is whether or not this is at all significant! Whether this says anything about the history of the text, and whether it does so in a way that is qualitatively superior to assuming that the evangelist was or was connected to a follower of Jesus who reflected dialectically upon the meaning of Jesus' words and works, is another matter.[14] John 6:12

---

13 In other words, Fortna 'de-Johannifys' John 6:1–14, 15b–25 by identifying (correctly) the characteristics of the evangelist's style. Then, he attributes to the 'redactional' style of the evangelist such features as: the *meta tauta* as a Johannine connective (vs. 1); the *hoti* clause of vs. 2b as explanatory; *oun historicum* (vss. 5, 11, 14, 15); the inclusion of disciples' names (vss. 5–8) as being narratological; vs. 6 as being Johannine on *ideological, stylistic* and *contextual* grounds; the phrase 'in order that nothing be lost' (vs. 12) as an interpretive comment; and 'seeing what he did was a sign', *hoti*, and ' ... coming into the world' (vs. 14) as ideologically and stylistically Johannine. Regarding the sea-crossing narrative, the Johannine 'interpolations' (my term, not Fortna's) include the explanatory clause of vs. 17b and the references to time, number and additional detail (vs. 22). On all of these accounts, Fortna is correct. These *are all marks* of Johannine style and interpretive ideology, which Fortna excises from the 'source'.

Where he is wrong is to assume that this must imply a 'dialogue' between the evangelist and a written document. Thus, in order to 'reconstruct' the sort of tract this must have been, Fortna 're-Marcanizes' the narrative. Using Mark 6:31–52 as the standard, he adds such phrases as *tois mathētais autou* (Mk. 6:41 added to Jn. 6:5), *kai ephagon (pantes) kai echortasthēsan* (Mk. 6:42 added to Jn. 6.12), and *kai apotazamenos autois apēlthen* (Mk. 6:46 added to Jn. 6:15b). Little wonder that Fortna's Signs Gospel must have looked so much like Mark! What is intriguing is that he still maintains that it represents a tradition which is *independent* from Mark.

14 There is no theoretical or practical advantage in assuming the evangelist's reflection is upon a written Signs Gospel rather than upon his own version, or prevalent versions, of the gospel story. Despite the fine piece of scholarship and sensitive interpretation represented by Fortna's 1988 monograph (*From Narrative Source to Present Gospel; The Fourth Gospel and its Predecessor*, Philadelphia, 1988; — this book deserves to be read and taken seriously by those who agree with Fortna's Signs Gospel hypothesis as well as by those who do not), his diachronic theory of composition is not required in order to arrive at similar interpretive conclusions. In fact, of the six essays at the end of Fortna's second monograph (pp. 225–314), most of these 'reflective dialogues' may also be applied to a model which sees the evangelist as reflecting upon *his own tradition*. Given the literarily unitive character of the Fourth Gospel, the evangelist as a reflective theologian, reflecting upon his own version of traditional stories and in dialogue with other traditions and issues faced by his evolving audience, seems more adequate.

confirms not only the independence of the Johannine witness, but its traditional authenticity as well.

Findings

The evangelist's dialogue with his tradition in John 6:1–24 brings one to the following conclusions: 1. The underlying christology of John 6 (and most of the Gospel) is the Prophet-like-Moses typology base on Deuteronomy 18:15–22, and this typology accounts for much of John's christological unity and disunity, *in and of itself.* a) Much of what has been mistaken for either subordinationist or 'equal-to-God' motifs in John have actually been central components of the *agency typology*, whereby the agent speaks as God's ambassador and is therefore able to do *only* what the sending Father tells him. This is the representative basis upon which the voice of the agent is to be equated with the 'Word' of God. b) The confirmation of the agent's authenticity is that all of his predictive words are fulfilled, and there is no deception in his teaching. Thus, the agent's words (and works, as well) become authenticating signs that he has been sent from God, and this at least partially explains the evangelist's ambivalence toward the signs — valuing them, and yet deeming their main import to be their function as a means to the greater end of revelation. It also explains the content of the Johannine 'sending' motif (Jn. 11:27; 17:3, 8, 18, 21). c) A third tension addressed by the agent typology has to do with the difficulty of interpreting the significance of Jesus' ministry. Within John 6 one may identify strands of the earliest christology (Moses/Elijah/Elisha typologies) which appear to be undergoing the evolutionary process of interpretation: i.e. '*What kind of prophet* is this one of whom Moses wrote?'.

2. John's account is not a redaction of earlier written sources, as were Matthew's and Luke's. The non-symbolic, illustrative details and christologically interpretive remarks, so characteristic of John's account, are precisely the types of words and phrases that Matthew and Luke leave out. It is assumed they too wished to write believable and graphic prose, so it cannot be accepted facilely that such a motive is an adequate explanation for the distinctive character of the Johannine narrative. Rather, John 6:1–24 is more like Mark, in the sense of betraying the literary characteristics of an oral tradition reproduced in written form, complete with interpretive asides and large amounts of non-symbolic, graphic detail. However, John is also unlike Mark (chs. 6 and 8), in that John 6 contains more of this detail and represents a far more unified account and interpretation of parallel traditional themes and events.

3. The evangelist's dialogue with his tradition may best be understood as his reflection upon either his own experiences or traditional stories about Jesus' ministry. Indeed, verbal similarities between John and Mark suggest contact during the *oral* stages of their traditions, given the character of the material. Within his interpretive dialogue, it is clear that he understands the motivation behind Jesus'

action to be one of 'testing' Philip (and others), and this unified motif runs centrally throughout the rest of the chapter. It represents the *Conjunctive* process by which new meanings are found in familiar stories, brought about by the crises of subsequent contradictory experiences, and the evangelist's reflections may be observed in his christocentric development of the 'living bread' motif in the rest of the chapter. On the other hand, Jesus' appearance on the sea is interpreted as a *theophany*, a transforming encounter through which the glory of God is revealed and experienced. The evangelist does not expand or develop the implications of this event at all. Its significance was ultimate from the beginning, and contrary to the 'epiphanies' of the Synoptics, John 6:16–21 represents not a wondrous stilling of the elements, but an awesome calming of the disciples.

Thus, John's narrative serves as a vehicle for reporting God's redemptive dialogue with humanity, whereby God (through his agent, Jesus) addresses the world, the world responds (having been 'tested'), resulting in the receiving or forfeiture of God's saving love. This is the unifying theme which runs as a connective thread throughout the entire chapter — and the Gospel as well. Thus, to the Fourth Evangelist, Jesus' words and works are *not* 'attesting miracles' — but *'testing' signs.*

Chapter 9

The Exhortation of the 'Two Ways'
(An Exegesis of John 6:25–66)

While the evangelist's dialogue with his tradition may be examined by considering the narrative common to John 6 and the Synoptics, the evangelist's dialogue with his audience may best be explored by analyzing the dialogues and discourses which interpret the previous events. The fact that vss. 25ff. mark the beginning of a new literary form is evident by the initiative passing from the agent of God to his audience. Whereas in 6:1–24 and 6:67–71 the divine/human 'dialogue' is portrayed in terms of God, or the agent of God, addressing humanity (with the consequence that humans must respond to the divine initiative) in vss. 25–66 the initiative shifts to the *audience* of the agent. They come to him, ask questions, make bold over-statements, and at nearly every turn Jesus' response provides a corrective to their short-sightedness.

As in most of the other dialogues with Jesus in John, the rhetorical role of the Johannine dialogue has two major components: a) The discussants betray a superficial understanding of some spiritual matter in their preliminary approaches, each of which allows the Johannine Jesus to add corrective insight upon insight. These often culminate in one or more christocentric discourse which conveys the 'true' perspective on the matter in remarkably clear fashion. b) Parallel to the function of a Socratic dialogue, the reader is drawn into the dialogue/discourse by being subsumed into the identity and inquiry of the discussants[1] and is then

---

1 The words 'discussant' and 'actant' are borrowed from J.D. Crossan, 'It Is Written: A Structuralist Analysis of John 6', SBLASP 1, Missoula, 1979, pp. 197–214.

It is significant that not only Barrett has made use of Plato's definition of 'thinking' as 'the conversation which the soul holds with herself' ('Dialectical', p. 50; cf. *Theatetus* 189f.) as a means of understanding the evangelist's dialectical thought; form-critic, M. Bakhtin also founded his theory of the *dialogical* structure of language and literature largely upon the same passage from *Theatetus*. Of particular interest to the present discussion is the relationship between one's ability to think dialectically and his or her use of dramatic *dialogue* to facilitate others' doing the same. Bakhtin explains his dependence upon and departure from this inward dialectical model to an outward one in his *The Dialogic Imagination*, ed., M. Holquist, Austin/London, 1981, pp. 84–258, esp. p. 134.

As in the case of Barrett's introducing the dialectical model of theological reflection to Johannine studies, Bakhtin's adoption of a dialogical model had ideological and epistempological implications, as well as literary ones. As Clark and Holquist have

corrected/taught by the master. Therefore, it is not just Nicodemus who comes to Jesus by night, but all would-be believers in the Johannine audience who may wish to come to Jesus (though perhaps secretly) or, more universally and existentially, any religious seeker of truth who is thoroughly acquainted with the way religion 'ought' to work, but who is nonetheless mystified by the life of the spirit (*anōthen*) — which like water and wind, cannot be contained in or confined to human-made structures. As a representative of religious certainty, Nicodemus is exposed as being 'in the dark' regarding things spiritual, to which John's christocentric corrective is posed. Thus, the narrative in John 3 is constructed in such a way as to draw the reader into its content, thereby engaging him or her in an imaginary dialogue with the Johannine Jesus.

Likewise, in John 4, it is not merely a woman by a well in Samaria who is drawn into dialogue with Jesus, but all children of Abraham (and Jacob) in the Johannine audience and beyond. This dialogue especially co-opts any who for some reason feel alienated by ethnocentrism (of Judeans, 'the Jews' or others), and yet who would still like to worship God meaningfully and be treated with respect (by their southern cousins or others). More universally and existentially, anyone who lives in fear of social ostracism or divine judgment, would feel himself or herself 'engaged in dialogue' with the redemptive Johannine Jesus. The sense of being fully known, and yet fully accepted, bears messianic overtones, and the one who has found the source of living water becomes the apostolic source of refreshment for others.

Therefore, in John 6 it is not merely members of the crowd who come to Jesus asking for more bread, but all who experience the agony of daily hunger and look for some means of deliverance. Perhaps they seek a second Moses who will come as an eschatological redeemer to reverse the social order, overthrow the Romans, and provide every household with its own vine and fig tree — or perhaps they expect a second Elijah/Elisha, who will reverse the natural order causing water to well up from the ground and manna to descend from the heavens. More universally and existentially, the dialogue/discourse draws in all who have hungered for bread and borrows from the realism of human hunger to make a christocentric application: all desire is ultimately a desire for God. It was not Moses who gave them bread, but the Father who *gives you* eternal sustenance, available now through the 'ingesting' of the truly heavenly bread, Jesus, given for the life of the world. Therefore, the hearer/reader in the Johannine audience is drawn into the dialogue/ discourse by being assumed into the role of the discussants who come to Jesus with

---

concluded about his theories (K. Clark and M. Holquist, *Mikhail Bakhtin*, Cambridge, Mass./ London, 1984, p. 348, emphasis mine):

Dialogism is Bakhtin's attempt to think his way out of ... all-pervasive monologism. Dialogism is not intended to be merely another theory of literature or even another philosophy of language, but it is an account of relations between people and between persons and things that cuts across religious, political and aesthetic boundaries. ... *Dialogism liberates precisely because it insists that we are involved in the making of meaning.*

otherwise 'innocent' questions but find themselves drawn beyond the surface dialogue into an intimate and transforming spiritual encounter. Such is the rhetorical function of the Johannine dialogue/discourse. The works and words of the Johannine Jesus are not simply narrated as decisive words and delivering deeds, wondrous in and of themselves. They function so as to draw the reader into an inward, human/divine 'dialogue' designed to lead to a transforming encounter with God through believing in the Johannine Jesus.[2]

The ironic questions of the crowd, the refusal to understand by the Jews, and the grumbling abandonment of some of the disciples in John 6 all serve the literary function of involving the reader in a dialogue with the christological content of the narrative. Within each inappropriate approach and response to the Johannine Jesus lie the rhetorical seeds of exposing fallacious understandings of God's workings and convincing the reader to respond to the divine initiative more faithfully. Epistemologically, the 'reflective dialogue' in the mind of the evangelist has influenced his use of something like a Socratic dialogue (replete with the rhetorical use of irony and misunderstandings) in order to evoke a 'dialogical' and reflective response within the mind of the hearer/reader. As the Russian form critic, M. Bakhtin has observed:[3]

> The device of "Not understanding" — deliberate on the part of the author, simpleminded and naive on the part of the protagonists — always takes on great organizing potential when an exposure of vulgar conventionally is involved. Conventions thus exposed — in everyday life, mores, politics, art and so on — are usually portrayed from the point of view of a man who neither participates in nor understands them.

However, the device of 'misunderstanding' does not simply make an abstract point for the sake of argumentation. It always levies its rhetorical point toward a particular sector of the author's audience, and the targeted notions of this person or group are depicted symbolically by the simpleminded discussants in the dialogue. Parallel to what Bakhtin observes elsewhere:[4]

---

2 W. Meeks describes this dialectical method of composition in his provocative essay, 'The Man From Heaven and Johannine Sectarianism' (Ashton, 1986, pp. 141–173):

> The reader cannot understand any part of the Fourth Gospel until he understands the whole. Thus the reader has an experience like that of the dialogue partners of Jesus: either he will find the whole business so convoluted, obscure and maddeningly arrogant that he will reject it in anger, or he will find it so fascinating that he will stick with it until the progressive reiteration of themes brings, on some level of consciousness at least, a degree of clarity. While an appeal to the reader's subjective experience may appear highly unscientific, I have tried to show that such an experience is grounded in the stylistic structure of the whole document. ... *The book functions for its readers in precisely the same way that the epiphany of its hero functions within its narratives and dialogues.* (p. 161f.)

3 Bakhtin develops the role of 'the fool' in literature, in his 'Forms of Time and Chronotope in the Novel', *The Dialogic Imagination*, pp. 84–258; citation, p. 164.

4 M. Bakhtin, 'Discourse in the Novel', in his *The Dialogic Imagination*, p. 403. While Bakhtin here alludes to the mimicking function of the protagonist's feigned incomprehension in the modern novel, the rhetorical function of his/her misunderstanding discussants is also found

Stupidity (incomprehension) in the novel is always polemical: it interacts dialogically with an intelligence (a lofty pseudo intelligence) with which it polemicizes and whose mask it tears away.

The rhetorical form of 6:25–66 has been correctly identified as 'homiletical' (by Borgen, Brown, Lindars), in the sense that it calls forth a response to the exhortation of vs. 27: 'Seek not the food which is death-producing, but the food that endures into eternal life, which the Son of Man will give you.' However, the 'main text' of the exhortation is *not* an Old Testament quotation (vs. 31), but the *narration of Jesus' ministry* (vss. 1–24, probably still in oral form), which by the time of the writing of John 6 seems to have acquired something near the degree of authority possessed by the Jewish scriptures.[5] Thus, contrary to Matthew and Luke, which have incorporated and expanded upon the earlier Petrine interpretation of the meaning of the loaves (fixed in written form in Mark), John's reflective development of the 'bread' motif seems to have undergone at least three or four interpretive evolutions. Each of these interpretations involves an exhortation to choose the 'Food' which Jesus gives and is over inferior kinds of food. Therefore, the focus of this chapter will be to consider the means by which the evangelist seeks to engage his readers in dialogue with the text, thereby facilitating a believing response to God's eschatological gift of 'Living Bread': *Jesus.*

John 6:25–66

And finding him on the other side of the sea they asked him,
  "Rabbi, when did you get here?"
Jesus answered and said to them,
  "Truly, truly I say to you, you seek me not because you saw the signs, but because you ate of the loaves and were satisfied. Work not for the food that is perishable, but for nourishment that endures into life eternal, which the Son of Man will give you; for it is on him that God the Father has stamped his seal of verification."
Therefore, they said to him,

---

widely within the classical, Greek biography. See also Plato's presentation of Socrates' posing of questions as epistemological 'midwifery' (esp. *Theatetus*, 149–152). Socrates' dialogues serve precisely the same function, and parallels between Plato and the Fourth Evangelist are more than a few on this account. In John, the rejection and death of Jesus are portrayed in the ironic dualism of Plato's Allegory of the Cave.

5 According to E.D. Freed, *Old Testament Quotations in the Gospel of John,* Leiden, 1965:

In view of the evidence presented in Chapter 6 with regard to the use of *hē graphē* and other formulas to introduce quotations from N.T. writings we have to conclude that some of the sayings of and about Jesus were very early put into writing and used with the same authority in the early church as O.T. scripture. (p. 119)

See also W. Sproston, ' "The Scripture" in John 17:12', in *Scripture: Meaning and Method; Essays Presented to A.T. Hanson,* ed. B.P. Thompson, Hull, 1987, pp. 24–36.

"What must we do in order to be able to do (effect?) the works of God?"

Jesus answered and said to them,

"The work of God is this: that you believe in the one God sent."

So they asked him,

"Then what is the sign you demonstrate, in order for us to see and believe you? What work do you do? Our fathers ate manna in the wilderness; as it is written, 'He gave them bread from heaven to eat'. "

Therefore, Jesus said to them,

"Truly, truly I tell you, it was not Moses who *gave* you bread from heaven, but my Father who *is giving you* the authentic, heavenly bread; for the bread of God is the one who by coming down from heaven is life-producing for the world."

Then they begged him,

"Sir, give us this bread all the time."

Jesus declared to them,

"I myself am the life-producing bread; the one coming to me by no means hungers, and the one believing in me will never thirst again.

But as I've told you, despite having seen [me] you still do not believe. All whom the Father entrusts to me will come to me, and I shall not by any means exclude anyone coming to me, since I have come down from heaven not to do my will but the will of the one who sent me.

And this is the will of the one who sent me, that I should lose none of those entrusted to me, but that I should raise them up on the last day. For this is the will of my Father, that everyone who beholds the Son and believes in him should possess eternal life, and that I should raise him up on the last day."

Therefore, the Jews grumbled about him because he said, "I am the bread which has come down from heaven". And they complained,

"Isn't this Jesus, the son of Joseph, whose father and mother we know? How in the world can he now claim, 'I've descended from the sky'?"

Jesus answered and said to them,

"Do not grumble amongst yourselves. No one can come to me except the Father who sent me should draw him, and I shall raise him up on the last day.

As it is written in the prophets, 'And they shall all be taught by God.' Those who come to me include everyone who listens to and learns from the Father; not that anyone has seen the Father, except the one being from God. He alone has seen the Father.

Truly, truly I tell you, the believer possesses life eternal. I am the life-producing bread. Your fathers ate plenty of manna in the wilderness, but they died. This is the kind of bread that comes down from heaven so that anybody may partake of it and not die. I am the bread which possesses life within it; if anyone eats of this bread, he (or she) will live eternally; and indeed, the bread which I shall offer is my own flesh for the life of the world."

Therefore, the Jews began to fight amongst themselves saying,

"How can this man give us [his] flesh to eat?"

So Jesus said to them,

"Truly, truly I say to you, unless you eat the flesh of the Son of Man and drink his blood, you possess no life within yourselves. The one who feeds on me — of my flesh, and drinks me — of my blood, will possess eternal life, and I shall raise him up on the last day. For my flesh is the ultimate nourishment, and my blood is the ultimate refreshment. The one who feeds on me — on my flesh, and drinks me — of my blood, abides in me and I in him (or her). Just as the living Father sent me, and I live because of the Father, even so the one feeding on me — that one will possess life through me.

This is the bread that has descended from heaven; an exact opposite from that which
the fathers ate, and died; the one who feeds on this bread will live into eternity."
He said these things in the Synagogue while teaching in Capernaum. Therefore, many of
his disciples who were listening in said,
"That's a harsh word; who can go along with it?"
But Jesus, inwardly aware that his disciples were grumbling about this, asked them,
"Is this all that scandalous to you? Just wait till you behold the Son of Man ascending
to his place of origin!
That which is life-producing is Spirit; the flesh is bankrupt. The words I speak to you
are Spirit and they are Life.
But among you there are still some who just don't believe." (For Jesus knew from the
beginning those who would not believe and he who would betray him.) And he said, "This
is why I told you that no one can come to me except he (or she) be enabled by the Father."
From that time on many of his disciples slipped away into the background and never walked
in his company again.

Exegetical Notes

25. The ironic question of the crowd initiates the dialogue with Jesus by means of the
euphemistic '*Rabbi, pote hōde gegonas*?' The *local irony* is evident by the fact that while the
crowd is willing to call Jesus 'Rabbi', they comprehend so little of his teaching (vs. 26f.). Thus
the implicit query underlying their question, 'How long have you been here?' is actually, 'How
did you actually get here so fast without a boat ... and (more pointedly) *how long* will it be until
we get *another feeding*?'

26. The Johannine Jesus reads the implicit and naive question perfectly and exposes their
real motive for seeking him (vss. 22–24). Even though they have been filled by the bread (vs.
11) they have not experienced the fullness of the feeding because they have not perceived its
revelational significance. The fact that the supposedly positive result of *all five* Synoptic feeding
accounts (*ephagon ... kai echortasthēsan*, Mk. 6:42; Matt. 14:20; Lk. 9:17; *also* in the feeding
of the 4,000 narratives: Mk. 8:8; Matt. 14:20) is practically quoted as a direct contrast to the
authentic meaning of the feeding (*ouch hoti eidete sēmeia all' hoti ephagete ... kai echortasthēte*)
is *not* coincidental. As in vs. 14f., the Johannine interpretation of the feeding is concerned to
correct the prevalent interpretation. The evangelist's awareness need not have come from his
knowledges of any of the written Synoptic Gospels (although he may have known Mark). More
probably, the evangelist's acquaintance with the Petrine interpretation of the feeding and sea
crossing had its origins in the oral stages of the pre-Marcan tradition, as well as its later renderings,
and John's 'corrective' interpretation represents *setting the record straight*: not with regard to
chronology or such trivialities as 'what actually happened', but with the central issue of what
Jesus' words and works *were intended to mean*. The significance of the feeding and the sea
crossing is *not* that Jesus has divine power over the natural world. Rather, it is that in the works
of Jesus something of God is revealed, and it is the beholding of them as *sēmeia* (the means by
which the divine-human dialogue is effected) that they derive their true significance.

27. Having exposed the misunderstanding of the crowd through their euphemistic question
in vs. 25, and having challenged the short-sightedness of their perspective regarding the feeding
(vs. 26), the evangelist now articulates the central exhortation of John 6.

"Work not for the food that is perishable, but for nourishment that endures into eternal life,
which the Son of Man will give you; for it is on him that God the Father has stamped his
seal of verification."

Here, we have in kernel form the 'two ways' of the Johannine Gospel. While parallel in function, the thematic contrast to the 'two ways' of the *Didache* (1–10) is obvious. The thrust of the *way of life* in the *Didache* (1:2–4:14) is described basically in terms of following the two commandments of Matthew 22:37–39, the ethical teaching of the Torah and the teachings of Jesus (especially the Sermon on the Mount). Similarly, the *way of death* in the *Didache* (5:1–6:3) is described by an itemization of wicked deeds (cf. Ro. 1:29–31; Gal. 5:19–21; etc.). The two ways in John, however, are described in *revelational* and *epistemological* terms. The *way of life* involves seeking truth, walking in the light, knowing the Father, believing in the Son, beholding his glory, etc. Similarly, *the way of death* in John involves disobeying the truth, remaining in darkness, not knowing the Father, and thus neither recognizing the Son nor beholding his glory. Vs. 27 therefore serves as the *pivotal fulcrum* of John 6. It builds on the narrative events and the inappropriate response of the crowd, characterized as the desire for bread, rather than Bread; and it sets the stage for the following interpretation, which from dialogues to discourses develops homiletically the Johannine version of the 'two ways'.

Ergazesthe mē ... has less to do with the Pauline notion of grace versus works-righteousness (although associations with Torah as *brōsin* are clearly implied, cf. Deut. 8:3), and more to do with responding to the living Word of God, which sweeps over the land accomplishing God's purposes and transforming all in its wake (Is. 55:9–11). Therefore, the meaning of the working/seeking motif seems to be more in keeping with Isaiah 55:1–3a (JB) (Lindars, p. 254). It is an invitation to be responsive to God's saving/revealing initiative (cf. Jn. 4:14; 7:39).

> Oh, come to the water all you who are thirsty,
> though you have no money, come!
> Buy and eat; come, buy wine and milk
> without money, free!
> Why spend money for that which cannot nourish
> and your wages on what fails to satisfy?
> Listen carefully to me, and you will have good things
> to eat and rich food to enjoy.
> Pay attention, come to me;
> Listen, and you will live.

Ho patēr esphragisen ho Theos is a rather difficult phrase to interpret. On one hand, it means literally 'the Father God has sealed'. However, the meaning is ambiguous (a reference to baptism, the works, the transfiguration, etc.?). Judging from the use of the same word in 3:33 though, the phrase in this context seems to be more of an attestation of the veracity of the Johannine *marturia*. He who receives the witness of the Son 'attests' that God is true (3:33). Likewise, the Father has (divinely) 'attested' that the bread offered by the Son of Man is truly efficacious in its life-producing function. Thus, interpreted within the context of John 6, the 'sealing' work of God the Father seems to refer to the semeiological function of the *feeding*. The purpose of the feeding is to be a seal of attestation, a *sign* that the Son is sent from the Father and that the Bread he has to offer is therefore *eternally* nourishing. Then again, it could refer to the Father's witness to the Son (5:37; 8:18) or even to Jesus' paradoxical glorification on the cross.

28. The misunderstanding of the crowd is still implied by the possible double meaning of the question. 'What must we do in order to effect the works of God?' asks the crowd; a perfectly respectable question for those whose this-worldly intention is ambiguous. It could be taken to mean 'What must we do in order to do (or acquire) such wonders ourselves?' (Ac. 8:19). Lindars may also be correct in interpreting vs. 28 as a genuine asking of 'the right question, so as to bring the dialogue quickly to the desired point for the discourse' (p. 255). But it is not a reference to the Pauline doctrine of justification. In this context, *ergazōmetha* alludes to *effecting* the works of God, implying the acquiring of another feeding, couched in a subtle play-on-words.

29. The *double entendre* of vs. 28 is obviated by Jesus' response in vs. 29. Here the parallel to the Pauline idea of justification by faith is clear. However, the development of the idea is distinctively Johannine. Faith does not replace 'works' as the means to righteousness (Ro. 1:17), but the exercising of faith is the essential means by which the 'work' of God is done. The point is that believing involves a positive response to the divine initiative of God, operant through the one sent into the world. Thus, the *work* of God is to respond to God's initiative, revealed incarnationally, and this is the end of Jesus' *works*.

30. The irony of the question in vs. 30 would by now be obvious to the Johannine audience. a) Jesus' question to Philip (vs. 5f.) *tests* him, and his and the other disciples' responsiveness to Jesus' instructions (vss. 10–13) is ultimately represented by their willingness to take Jesus into the boat (vs. 21). This implies a successful passing of the test. b) The crowd, however, *misunderstands* Jesus totally, and this is made obvious by their wanting to make him a prophet-king after the feeding. c) Their misunderstanding *continues* on the following day, when they come seeking Jesus in hopes of receiving more bread (vss. 22–26). d) They *appear* to be 'getting it right', as they are willing to do what it takes to do God's works and receive the non-perishable Bread of the Son of Man — attested to and sealed by God (vs. 27f.). e) Their question in vs. 30, however, *betrays* the fact that they *have been missing the point all along*. They still don't consider the feeding an attestation by God and now ask for a sign before believing. Therefore, the question in vs. 30 is not an insurmountable aporia which proves that it had to have followed vss. 34f. (Bultmann, p. 221). It emphasizes not only the misunderstanding of the crowd, but their *provocation* of Jesus as well (cf. Ps. 78:40–43, 52–53).

R. Brown is quite right to draw a connection between John 6:26–34 and Matthew 4:1–11; Mark 1:12f.; and Luke 4:1–13 (*NTE*, pp. 261–264). As Jesus was tempted by Satan in the wilderness to change stones into bread within the Q tradition, in the Johannine narrative the role of 'tempter' is assumed by the *crowd*. Despite having witnessed a sign, they do not perceive it as such, and this is implied by their attempt to solicit another feeding, challenging Jesus to do another sign. The similarities between John 6 and Matthew 4:1–11 and Luke 4:1–13 are several: a) The interpretive theme of testing (temptation) is prevalent in the narrative (*peirazōn*, Jn. 6:6; *peirasthēnai*, Matt. 4:1; *peirazomenos*, Lk. 4:2). b) The 'temptation' is to be/do what Jesus has just been attested to have been /done ('This is my Son ... ', Mt. 3:17; Lk. 3:22 — 'If you *are* the Son of God ...', Mt. 4:3; Lk. 4:3; and '... not because you saw the signs ...', Jn. 6:26 — 'What sign will you do, then, that we might see and believe?', vs. 30). c) The temptation is to produce bread supernaturally (stones into bread, Matt. 4:3; Lk. 4:3; another sign like the one the day before, Jn. 6:30). d) In both cases a citation from the Old Testament is used as a means of bolstering the appeal of the tempter(s) (Matt. 4:6; Lk. 4:10f. → cf. Ps. 91:11f.; Jn. 6:31 → cf. Ps. 78:24f.; Ex. 16:4; Neh. 9:15). e) Jesus counters the tempter(s) by appealing to God's authentic way of working and by citing another scriptural reference (Matt. 4:4, 7, 10; Lk. 4:4, 12, 8 → cf. Deut. 8:3; 6:16, 13; and Jn. 6:45 → cf. Nu. 11:29; Is. 54:13; Jer. 31:31ff.).

Despite these similarities between the Q tradition underlying Matthew 4:1–11, Luke 4:1–13 and John 6:26ff., however, the temptation motif serves functions within the progression of the Synoptic and Johannine narratives which are radically different. The function of the temptation story in Mark 1:12f., and in its expanded renditions in Matthew and Luke, is to emphasize Jesus' preparation for ministry. Having been identified as being God's Son at the baptism by the descending dove and the declarative voice from heaven (Mk. 1:10f.; Matt. 3:16f.; Lk. 3:22), the Synoptic Jesus is tested and tempted as a means of preparation for his ministry. In John, however, the tempting of Jesus by the crowd is a testing of Jesus' *audience* (6:6). It portrays not the preparation of Jesus for ministry, but the crisis of whether those being tested will see, believe and follow him. The exceptions are the twelve, and yet even one of them is a devil (*diabolos*, Jn. 6:70; cf. Matt. 4:1, 5, 8, 11; Lk. 4:2, 5, 9, 13). The significance of the correlation between the Synoptic and the Johannine 'temptation' narratives regards the ways the tempters are portrayed, and it provides an insight into the style of personification within the gospel traditions. In John they are portrayed as the crowd, 'the Jews', some of the disciples and Peter; whereas in the Synoptics the role of tempter is reserved for the devil, Satan. Therefore, even if some kind of disputation occurred following a feeding in the ministry of Jesus, it is significant that the Fourth Evangelist portrays those who misunderstand Jesus' signs as those who assume the role of tempter. They represent a key misconception (and a Petrine one, at that) which the Johannine Jesus soon corrects.

31. The rhetorical device used by the crowd quotes Psalm 78:24, which is itself a midrashic conflation of Exodus 16:4, 15 and Numbers 11:7–9. The Greek rendition in the LXX is nearly identical to the citation in John 6:31: *Arton ek tou ouranou edōken autois phagein* (Ps. 78:24), and Borgen even concedes that in some respects the Johannine rendition is closer to Psalm 78:24f. than to Exodus 16:4, 15 (*Bread*, p. 40). Lindars is absolutely correct to assume (albeit tentatively) that the reference in Jn. 6:31 is to Ps. 78:24 rather than to Ex. 16:4 (p. 257). Thus, given the linguistic similarities, Borgen errs in not considering more closely the *rhetorically formal similarities* between Psalm 78 and John 6. Strikingly, the rhetorical use of manna in Ps. 78 and Jn. 6 even transcends the formal differences between a psalm and a gospel narrative. While both of these passages are midrashic developments of Exodus 16 (and Numbers 11), John 6 also adapts some of the interpretive content of Psalm 78 to fit the situation of the Johannine audience. The literary connection between John 6:31 and Psalm 78:24 is significant in two respects: a) In both passages the manna motifs of Exodus 16 and Numbers 11 are developed rhetorically in order to persuade an audience towards exercising a particular understanding of faithfulness to God. b) In both cases the manna motif is not the key theme being developed, but rather, it is a *secondary text* which has been incorporated in order to bolster the central argument as a rhetorical trump. (See Anderson, 1993, pp. 11–16.)

The audience to which Psalm 78 was addressed is difficult to identify precisely, but the purpose of the psalm was clearly to call for Judah to remember the saving acts of God in the past, and (unlike Israel, implying a date between 721 and 587 BCE) to trust in God fully and to obey his commands, being grateful for his means of provision for them through David's shepherding care in Zion. In other words, the exhortative thrust of the psalm is to draw a connection between God's acts of salvation and provision in the past with the same (to be recognized as the Judean monarchy) in the present. Likewise, in John 6 the 'testing' of the actants in the narrative is designed to test the Johannine audience regarding whether or not they will be responsive to God's saving and providing activity in Jesus. The provision of loaves and fishes in the desert and the sea-crossing narrative are clearly reminiscent of God's mighty acts of deliverance of Israel in the wilderness. But the true test comes with whether the audience will respond to God's eschatological activity of provision and deliverance in the present, which is to be found in the spiritual and existential Bread which Jesus gives and is.

The second parallel between John 6 and Psalm 78 regards the way in which the manna motif is used and developed. Contrary to Borgen's otherwise excellent treatment of the manna motif in John 6 and contemporary Jewish literature (*Bread*, pp. 28–98), the citation of Exodus 16:4, 15 is *not* the starting point of the 'homily'. It is a secondary text, employed as a rhetorical trump within the development of another theme. For instance, in Psalm 78 the manna motif is introduced at vs. 24f., but it is listed centrally among the other acts of God's provision within a larger appeal for the audience to exercise faithful obedience. The converse of such a believing response is epitomized by Israel's request for *flesh* (vs. 20), and in vss. 26–33 the psalmist combines the Numbers 11 narrative with that of Exodus 16. The conflation of the texts from Exodus and Numbers heightens the irony of Israel's unfaithfulness. Rather then being satisfied with Yahweh's provision of manna, Israel remembered the flesh pots of Egypt (Ex. 16:3) and craved meat to eat (Nu. 11:4f., 18). To the feeding narrative, the Numbers account adds the consequence of eating the flesh which they craved: they *will* eat it for a whole month, until it comes out of their nostrils (11:20)! And even while the meat was between their teeth they were stricken with a severe plague and many died (11:33f.). Their punishment was to receive the object of their cravings — and its consequences.

Therefore, the use of the manna-versus-flesh motifs of Exodus 16 and Numbers 11 is developed midrashically in Psalm 78 as follows: a) Manna is equated with the perfect provision of God, given to meet the needs of Israel in the wilderness. b) Flesh (*sarx*, LXX) is equated with that which Israel craved, despite the perilous consequences of Egyptian bondage and sickness and death in the wilderness. It is given as a result of Israel's 'grumbling' in the desert, the consequence of a lack of covenant faithfulness and ingratitude for Yahweh's true provision — the manna. c) The manna/flesh dichotomy is then applied to the situation of the psalmist's audience. To be grateful for God's provision in Mount Zion, through his servant David, is to receive the manna from heaven — the bread of angels ('the strong', vs. 25) — God's true source of provision for their contemporary situation. On the other hand, not to be content and to *grumble* is like craving the flesh pots of Egypt, which results in sickness and death. Therefore, the message is clear: trust in God, and receive gratefully his present source of provision through Zion. As B. Malina (*The Palestinian Manna Tradition*, Leiden, 1968, p. 35) concludes about the rhetorical use of manna in Psalm 78:

> The manna (and the quail, simply called "winged creatures") seems to have come but once. Obviously, the psalmist is not interested in the manna itself. Rather he seizes upon the traditional data of the desert wanderings to point up God's mercy and Israel's continual rebellion. Thus the manna (and quail) is here presented as an item of haggadic midrash; the data is appropriately expanded to help the psalmist prove his point.

The Johannine treatment of the same motifs is parallel, although somewhat different. In John 6 the central exhortation is, 'Work not for the food which perishes, but for nourishment that abides eternally, which the Son of Man will give you' (vs. 27). The 'testing' motif of Deuteronomy 8:2f. is prevalent throughout the entire chapter, but ironically, while the failure of Israel in the Old Testament narratives was that they refused to be grateful for the manna, provided by Yahweh in the wilderness, the failure of Jesus' discussants in the Johannine narrative lay in their inability to see beyond the manna as bread to seeing it as *God's provision*, which is now eschatologically present in Jesus as the ultimate life-producing Bread. Therefore, for the Johannine audience, the tables are turned: a) For those who would question Jesus' authority, clinging to Moses' precedents and even challenging Jesus to surpass them, the Johannine Jesus corrects the crowd's assertion that Moses was the giver of the manna in the wilderness. Jesus corrects their interpretation of the manna motif and clarifies the true origin of the manna according to Exodus 16:4 and Psalm 78:24. The source of the giving was not Moses, but it is *the Father* who gave — *and who gives* — the life-producing Bread for all the world (Jn. 6:32f.). Thus, the interpretation of the manna motif by the Johannine Jesus shifts the locus of import from that which is given to *the one who gives*. The significance of the manna in the wilderness was not that it was a wondrous 'bread of angels', but that its *origin* was heavenly. Likewise, the significance of Jesus' ministry is not that he provides barley loaves for the crowd, but that he is *sent from above*, and the nourishment he provides has been attested by the Father (vs. 27).

b) The death-producing cravings for flesh in the Numbers 11 and Psalm 78 midrashim are in the Johannine narrative equated with the crowd's craving for more loaves (manna). This interpretive move is unique within the Jewish midrashic developments of the manna motif. In the Old Testament (Nu. 11:6–9; Ps. 78:23–25; 105:40; Neh. 9:15, 20), Philonic (*Leg. All.* III 162, 173; *Fug.* 137; *Mut.* 259), Midrash Rabbah (Gen. 48:10; 51:2; 66:3; Ex. 5:9; 24:3; 25:1–8; 33:8; 38:4; 41:1; Deut. 10:4), and even the Pauline (1 Cor. 10:3) interpretations of the manna motif, manna is portrayed as a prototype of God's miraculous provision in the wilderness — a spiritual food, which also became associated with divine knowledge, based upon the Torah.

As a striking contrast in John 6, possibly for the *first time* in the history of Jewish-Christian interpretation of the manna motif, manna is regarded as *death-producing* and *inferior* to another kind of 'Bread'. Therefore, as in Psalm 78:27–33, *sarx* is of no avail (Jn. 6:63), but that which here is death-producing is not the flesh of quails — effecting illness and death even as it was between their teeth. It is the *manna* which is now considered death-producing, for the forefathers ate manna and died, but whoever eats of the 'Bread' which Jesus gives and is will live eternally (vs. 58).

c) As in Psalm 78, the rhetorical use of the manna tradition is intended to evoke a believing response to God's saving action in the present. Whereas the crowd marshalls the manna motif as a challenge to Jesus: first, tempting him to provide more loaves, and second, claiming Moses' (of whom they were 'disciples') superiority over Jesus, the Johannine narrative invokes the existentializing interpretation of the manna narrative found in Deuteronomy 8:2f., 16 and its corollary in Neh. 9:20. Here we have an identical parallel between the Johannine and the Deuteronomic traditions, in which existentializing is employed as a means of dealing with the problem of suffering. The crisis in the wilderness was not only a time of God's provision for Israel, but it was also their 'testing', designed to teach them humility and covenant faithfulness. Thus, Yahweh is not understood only as the source of provision, but also as the source of their hunger (Deut. 8:3), seeking to teach them that 'man does not live by bread alone but by every word that proceeds from the mouth of Yahweh'. Likewise, the Johannine narrative portrays not only the testing of Philip, but the testing of the *crowd*, the *Jews*, and the *disciples*. Unlike Psalm 78, John 6 is more than a midrashic development of Old Testament texts for the purpose of arguing a point. It is also a narration of events, dialogues and reactions to discourses, which portrays the audiences of the Johannine Jesus as failing the test. The crowd fails to understand, the Jews grumble, and *even* some of the disciples abandon him. Thus, the three-fold exhortation of the 'two ways' exposes three kinds of inferior 'bread', each of which may represent an acute 'test' within various epochs of Johannine Christianity.

Therefore, the rhetorical use of the manna motif by the Fourth Evangelist serves as a proleptic attack upon those in the Johannine audience who would either be overly concerned with a) receiving physical bread (along with associated expectations for a thaumaturgic Messiah); b) challenging the Johannine Jesus with the primacy of Moses and the Torah; or c) pondering the abandonment of Johannine community. By expressing the notion to be refuted through the questions and statements of Jesus' discussants, the evangelist 'hooks' the hearer/reader into the narrative and exposes the inadequacy of such notions by sketching the *failure* of the test by Jesus' discussants.

32f. In contradistinction to the bread which *the Father* gave (*dedōken*) to the children of Israel in the wilderness, the bread which he now gives (*didōsin*) is for the life of the world. This is the Johannine equivalent of accusing the adherents of Mosaic piety of *idolatry*! To dwell on the ways God has spoken in the past diminishes one's ability to hear the Word of the Living God in the present. This is no mere exegetical triumph. It is the scandalous declaration that biblical exegesis itself has been supplanted by the eschatological Word of God, coming down from heaven and giving life for the world (cf. Martyn, p. 128).

34. Contrary to Bultmann (p. 225), the crowd still does not understand that Jesus is referring to himself, but would like to receive this heavenly bread all the time. This ironic failure to understand is exposed for what it is in vs. 36.

35–40. Thus begins the first of the extended discourses within the Johannine debate over the meaning of the feeding. The Johannine Jesus co-opts the hunger/satisfaction motif and gives it a radically christocentric meaning. It is Jesus himself who is the life-producing Bread. All who (figuratively) come to him will never hunger, and all who believe in him will never thirst. Bultmann correctly interprets vs. 35: 'The whole paradox of the revelation is contained in this reply. Whoever wants something from him must know that he has to receive Jesus *himself.* ... Jesus *gives* the bread of life in that he *is* the bread of life' (p. 227). Where Bultmann is wrong is in his assessment that the rest of John 6 is concerned with *anything other* than this central motif. Just as vs. 31 is an echo of vs. 27a, ' ... the food which perishes', vs. 35 is a clarification of vs. 27bc, ' ... but for the nourishment which abides into eternal life, which the Son of Man will give you'. Thus, the 'key text' being developed 'midrashically' in John 6 is *not* Exodus 16:4, 15, (or even Ps. 78:24) but the *words of Jesus* in vs. 27, as informed by his *works* in vss. 1–21. In contrast to the life-producing Bread which he gives and is, the manna motif is introduced in vs. 31 to magnify the eternal effect of 'eating' the true Bread which has come down from heaven for the life of the world.

36. The misunderstanding and lack of belief implicit in the crowd's reactions to Jesus' works and words (vss. 2, 14, 22–25, 28, 30f., 34) is exposed explicitly in vs. 36: ' ... you have seen [me], and still you do not believe'. (The inclusion of *me* in P⁶⁶ and P⁷⁵ suggests an early, and perhaps the original rendition; Brown, p. 270, contra Lindars, p. 260.) The emphasis here is christocentric, not semeiotic.

37–40. These verses explain the scope of Jesus' saving and revealing work. It is to embrace all who come to (believe in) Jesus, and to raise them up on the last day. While Bultmann believes that vss. 39c, 40c, and 44c are all redactional insertions, such a move is not confirmed by contemporary examples. Indeed, the manna motif in 2 Baruch, also a first-century text, suggests that the second provision of manna and the resurrection of the faithful were considered twin effects, associated with the eschatological coming of the Anointed One. (E.t. by A.F.J. Klijn):

> And it will happen that when all that which should come to pass in these parts has been accomplished, the *Anointed One will begin to be revealed.* ... And it will happen at that time that *the treasury of manna will come down again from on high,* and they will *eat of it* in those years because these are they who have arrived at the consummation of time.
> And it will happen after these things when the time of the *appearance* of the Anointed One has been fulfilled and he *returns with glory,* that then *all who sleep in hope of him will rise.* And it will happen at that time that those treasuries will be opened in which the number of the souls of the righteous were kept, and *they will go out and the multitudes of the souls will appear together, in one assemblage,* of one mind. And the first ones will enjoy themselves and the last ones will not be sad. For they know that the time has come of which it is said that it is *the end of times.* (2 Baruch 29:3, 8–30:3; emphases mine)

Whether the Johannine discourse is close to something Jesus may actually have taught, or whether it is entirely the work of the evangelist, Jesus' feeding of the multitude is portrayed as an eschatological sign of the last days in which the Anointed One will come. On that day manna will come down from the heavenly treasuries, and the righteous will be raised from their 'sleep', forming a part of the eschatological assembly. The condition of the Johannine eschatology, however, is that the righteousness of the world is accorded with individuals' ability to perceive the divine origin and mission of the Anointed One, and to receive him in faith (6:40). Therefore, all who receive the one who comes from above unto his own are given the authority to become the children of God (Jn. 1:11–13).

The significance of the 2 Baruch parallel for analyzing the christological unity and disunity of John is that a contemporary Palestinian manna tradition (first century?) combines a messianic anticipation of the Anointed One with the eschatological outpouring of 'the treasury of manna' from on high and the assembling of the treasuries of the 'souls of the righteous'. This is a clear association of the outpouring of manna with a future eschatology, suggesting that vss. 39c, 40c, 44c and 54c, *need not* be considered interpolations. The eschatology of John 6 holds the future hope of the resurrection in tension with God's present activity in giving his Son for the life of the world (vs. 32). This is an example of 'dialectical tension' within a prevalent cluster of beliefs, which the evangelist has employed in his narrative. Thus, the tensions between present and future eschatologies in John are not as problematic as otherwise assumed, and certainly do not require a diachronic theory of composition to explain their presence in John 6. G.R. Beasley-Murray also makes this clear in his book, *Gospel of Life*; *Theology in the Fourth Gospel*, Peabody, 1991.

41f. While the failure of the crowd to respond to God's eschatological source of life-producing nourishment for the world is characterized as their failure to distinguish between the loaves which satisfy only for a day and the Bread which comes down from above, which abides into eternity (vs. 27), the Jews' failure of the test is marked by their 'grumbling' (*egogguzon*). The grumbling of the children of Israel in the wilderness is recalled as the prototype of unbelieving rebellion. Whether in need of water (Ex. 15:24; 17:3) and food (Ex. 16:2f.), or whether it had to do with fear of the Canaanites (Nu. 14:2), the grumblings in the desert are remembered by future interpreters as the sins of rebellion (Ps. 78:8, 17, 40, 56; 106:32f.; Neh. 9:17, 26): unbelief (Ps. 78:22, 32, 57; 106:24f.), lack of covenant faithfulness to Yahweh (Ps. 78:8, 10, 37, 57), arrogance (Deut. 8:16; Neh. 9:16) and disobedience (Neh. 9:16, 26). The Jews' problem is quite different from that of the crowd. The crowd does not really grasp the meaning of Jesus' ambiguous works and words, but the Jews appear to have, and it is precisely this understanding that was intolerable.

Typical of the normal Petrine/Johannine christological disagreement over the reporting of events in Jesus' ministry, the hometown audience of Mark 6:1–5 refuses to believe that Jesus (the carpenter, Mary's son and brother of James, Joseph, Judas and Simon; vs. 3) can perform wonders. Conversely, the Johannine audience (the Jews) exclaims, 'Isn't this Jesus, whose father and mother we know? How in the world can he now claim, "*I have come down from heaven*"?' The Jews recognize this as a messianic claim, and this is the source of their consternation.

43f. Jesus responds to their question with a reassuring, *Mē gogguzete met' allēlōn*; and then he explains how his mission speaks to the human condition. 'No one can come to me except the Father who sent me should draw him, and I shall raise him up on the last day.' (vs. 44) This is not a statement about predestination nor about divine election. The verb is not '*may* come' but '*can* come'. It is simply an assertion by the Johannine Jesus that even belief in Jesus as the Anointed One, sent from the Father, requires divine assistance in order to be effected. Ironically, those who search the scriptures most exhaustively (5:39) and who are the teachers of Israel (3:10) are the very ones who are most in need of being taught by God about the things of the Spirit. Perhaps their lack of enlightenment is due to a preference for darkness (3:18–21), or perhaps their sin (obstacle) is that they claim to know (9:41). Either way, the Johannine portrayal of the life of faith is that it begins and continues solely by means of divine enablement and human responsiveness to it. As in John 14:6f., the issue is not a matter of divine exclusivity and allowance, but a correct diagnosis of the human situation — absolutely dependent upon divine enablement to see the way forward and to walk in it. It is a matter of God's revelation and human response.

45. In this verse Jesus declares the effect of the coming of the Word of the Lord, which transforms all within its wake (Is. 55:6–11). No longer will Israel be instructed with nonsensical utterances (Is. 28:10, 13), but Yahweh will himself speak with his people (vs. 11). All of Israel's children will be *taught by Yahweh*, and great will be their *peace* (Is. 54:13; cf. Nu. 11:29).

Contrary to Borgen (*Bread*, p. 38), the citation of Isaiah 54:13 in vs. 45 is not a 'subordinate quotation' used to complement a primary Old Testament text in John 6. The manna motif in vs. 31 is actually introduced as the antithesis of the life-producing nourishment given by the Son of Man. Just as manna is revealed to be death-producing as a means of sustenance, the monopoly upon the truth derived from the interpretation of the scriptures by the Jewish leaders is revealed to be bankrupt by their faithless grumbling in vs. 41f. The reconstructive synthesis is articulated in vs. 45, where the grumbling of the Israelites is transformed by the spiritual anointing (Nu. 11:25) of the elders. As in the case of Psalm 78:24f., Isaiah 54:13 is a midrashic reformulation of Numbers 11:29, where Moses cries out, 'Oh, that *all* were prophets, and that Yahweh would pour out his Spirit upon them!' This same motif is echoed in Jeremiah 31:33f., where the New Covenant is described as an internalization of Yahweh's law, now residing in his people's minds and written upon their hearts, with *all* knowing Yahweh and *having no need of human teachers*. Therefore, that which is yearned for by Moses in Numbers 11:29, and anticipated in Isaiah 54:13 and Jeremiah 31:33f., is declared to be imminent in John 6:45. Likewise, the spiritual gift of leadership in Nu. 11:29 is extended in Joel 2:28–32 to include women as well as men, and the young as well as the mature. Thus, one may detect the ethos of Moses' yearning and its OT developments within Johannine ecclesiology: the internalization of covenant, the inclusivity of ministry and the inspired character of divine pedagogy.

In responding to God's saving initiative in Jesus the promise that all shall be taught by God becomes actual. The implications for the Johannine understanding of apostolicity are centrally connected to these notions. Just as the Father has sent Jesus, so Jesus sends (all of) his disciples to be apostles. Thus, he sends them out, breathes his commissioning Spirit upon them, and gives them the authority (responsibility) to forgive sins (Jn. 20:21–23). As a contrast to the institutional view of later Petrine christocracy (cf. Matt. 16:17–19), the Johannine ideology assumes that all who 'come to' Jesus will be 'taught by God'. This notion is developed more fully in the *Parakletos* passages of Jn. 14–16. True disciples of Jesus continue to be instructed by the present Spirit of the resurrected Lord (Jn. 16:7–15), and this conviction is cited in Jn. 6:45 as being prohesied by Isaiah.

46. This verse clarifies the anthropological need of humanity to be taught by God. No one has seen God at any time except the one who has been with him from the beginning (1:1, 18) and who has been sent from him (7:29).

47–51. This passage is a christological development of the manna motif as it relates to vs. 47: 'Truly, truly, I tell you, the believer possesses life eternal.' The development of the motif is as follows: a) Jesus identifies himself as the life-producing Bread (vs. 48). b) This kind of bread is set in contradistinction to the death-producing manna, provided in the wilderness (vs. 49). c) As believing is to Jesus, eating is to this life-producing Bread which comes down from heaven (vs. 50). d) Jesus again asserts that he is the life-producing Bread, which if eaten effects eternal life (vs. 51ab). e) The connection is finally made between the Bread which Jesus is and his *flesh, given for the life of the world* (vs.51c). Therefore, this paragraph is an excellent example of the Johannine interweaving of various themes — the mixing of metaphors and the somewhat redundant emphasizing of central motifs. Despite the mention of 'eating', and Jesus' 'flesh', given for the life of the world, the reference is clearly to *Jesus' death on the cross*, not primarily the eucharist.

The radical shift of emphasis between vs. 51b, and c does not expose an interpolation into the text, but rather suggests that a new problem is being addressed. It is now the followers of Jesus who are put to the test to see if they are able to 'drink the cup' of suffering and 'eat the bread' (of affliction) offered by the Son of Man. The 'bread' which the Son of Man offers is his flesh, given for the life of the world, but the receptacle on which it is offered is a 'platter' hewn into the shape of a cross.

52. The grumbling of the Jews has by now escalated into a fight (*Emachonto*), and the issue under debate is the means by which Jesus gives [his] flesh to eat. The textual difficulty is more problematic than the one of vs. 36, as P[66] includes *autou*, yet P[75] and several other early manuscripts omit it. Whatever the original reading, the question is ambiguous. It could be a reference to the Christian observance of the eucharist, or it could simply reflect the confusion

of the Jews over what Jesus was predicting about his mission. Within the later stages of the tradition the former is more likely to have been the case, but the evangelist is clearly using the question of the Jews as a foil, against which to appeal for corporate solidarity with Jesus within the Johannine community.

53–55. As in vs. 25 Jesus infers and answers the real question being posed. The concern of the Jews is not to find out 'how' Jesus gives [his] flesh, but to ask, 'Do we *really* have to go along with this new "bread from heaven" teaching? Do not the prototypical manna in the wilderness and the sapiential nourishment of the Torah suffice?' To this implicit set of questions Jesus responds, 'Unless you eat my flesh and drink my blood, you have no life in yourselves' (vs. 53). The answer is clear. Without coming to Jesus, believing in him, and ingesting his flesh and blood one does not possess eternal life.

The move from *phagein* to *trōgein* in vs. 54 is not necessarily a clear reference to the coarse munching sound made by animals as they feed (munching, gnawing, etc.), inserted to highlight the physicality of the eucharistic meal. Rather, *trōgein* is equally well associated with 'feeding upon' — as it relates to the internalization of the Bread which Jesus is. The phrase used by Mateos and Barretos is 'asimilar su realidad humana' (to assimilate his human reality, p. 343), and the word simply means 'to feed upon', or 'to draw nourishment from'. The overtones are eucharistic, but there is no indication that the eucharist within Johannine Christianity was ever anything as formalized as an institutional rite, bolstered by ordinance sayings. Quite likely, the Johannine 'eucharist' (if it can indeed be called that) was more of a fellowship-meal setting in which gratitude for alimental sustenance and spiritual provision in the death and resurrection of Christ were regularly expressed. Like the corporate breaking of bread in Acts 2–4. The Johannine 'common meal' was probably more like the weekly Passover celebration of the '*Therapeutae*' sect mentioned by Philo, or even the fellowship meals used within the Corinthian church *before* they were abused and had to be replaced by a ritualized meal (cf. 1 Cor. 10:3, where the manna tradition is also associated with giving thanks for God's acts of deliverance). Anything more formalized than that would have been anachronistic to the first-century Johannine situation. The Johannine corporate meal was not patterned like the more organized eucharistic rite emerging within the Jewish/Christian traditions, which sought to provide a Christian sequel to the Jewish Seder service. This accounts for some of the differences between the Synoptic and Johannine portrayals of the last supper. The question is *not* 'Why did John *omit* references to the meal being a Passover celebration?'. Rather, and more importantly, 'Why did the Petrine tradition *seek to insure* that the Seder-meal setting was firmly lodged at the centre of its narration of reported events?' Its motivation was not only theological, but socio-religious. It provided the organizational means of offering an alternative to cultic Judaism, and later, the centralizing means of appealing for corporate solidarity in the face of Roman persecution. Conversely, the Johannine tradition offered an alternative approach to enhancing corporate solidarity: the appeal to stay with Jesus and his followers in the 'family' of faith.

56f. In these verses the theme of mutual abiding (cf. 15:1–5) comes to the fore as the clarification of what true 'communion' is all about. It is an abiding immersion in — a spiritual coming into union with — Jesus Christ. It involves solidarity with him in his suffering and death, with the consequence that one will also share in his resurrection (Ro. 6:3–7). This solidarity with Christ — corporately and individually — was the central concern of Bishop Ignatius' appeals to the Ephesian and Roman Christians. The *pharmakon athanasias* was not the breaking of *a loaf*, but the breaking of *one* loaf as opposed to splitting off into factions and schismatic groups. Thus, the worry for Ignatius was *not* that Christians should fail to partake of the eucharist, lest they be damned. His concern was that if they were unwilling to face temporal hardship and martyrdom (especially acute, given the impending threat of his own martyrdom), they would also forfeit the eternal benefit of solidarity with Christ in his resurrection. A similar situation was faced by

Johannine Christianity, as vss. 53–58 form the central appeal for corporate solidarity with Christ, hemmed by the reference to his death on the cross (vs. 51) and his abandonment by even some of the disciples (vs. 66).

58f. Borgen is correct in arguing that vs. 58 is the summarizing conclusion to not only vss. 51c–57, but to the preceding section as well. What he misses, however, is that in echoing vs. 31, vs. 58 is actually reaffirming the latter of the 'two ways' (death and life) mentioned in vs. 27. The central exhortation is, 'Work not for the bread which is perishable, but for nourishment that endures into eternal life, which the Son of Man shall give you'. To this central thrust, the manna motif is a well-developed illustration of the need for this eschatological Bread, based upon Israel's history. However, the exhortation does not end here. A reference is made to the setting in which the discussion is to have taken place (in or near the Capernaum Synagogue), but then the dialogue with the crowd and the Jews subsides, and the reaction of some of Jesus' disciples is taken up.

60. Despite the reference to locale (vs. 59) and the change of discussants, the setting is still the same, and the exhortation/dialogue continues into vs. 66. The classic interpretive problem here is identifying the source of the disciples' scandalization. As Martyn has proposed a two-tiered approach to John 9, this should also be done for John 6, and especially for vss. 60ff. On the first level, the narration of events (*einmalig*), the dispute of the disciples was probably similar to the reported disputes over the meaning of the feeding, as portrayed in *Mark 6 and 8*. In both of these accounts the disciples do not understand the meaning of the loaves (Mk. 6:52; 8:21), which is, according to both Marcan accounts, that Jesus can supply bread wondrously. Therefore, the disciples should neither fear the forces of nature (6:51) nor worry about not having enough bread to eat (8:14, 17–20). In this sense, the pre-Marcan interpretation of the feeding is indeed parallel to the popularistic. It is quite likely that among those who came to Jesus, looking for a sign (Jn. 6:2), at least some of them were followers (or would-be followers) of Jesus. They may also have been among those who wanted to make Jesus a king (vs. 14) and who followed him the next day, in search of another handout. Therefore, when it became obvious that Jesus was *not* leading up to another feeding (nor a Passover revolt against the Romans), these followers of Jesus abandoned the cause. On this level, vss. 60–66 represent an actual defection.

The use of the word, *mathētōn*, rather than *ochlos*, is significant as it relates to the evangelist's dialogue with his audience. This is especially the case in the light of the impending crucifixion overtones following vs. 51 and the subsequent call for corporate solidarity with Jesus in his death as well as his resurrection. On the second level of interpretation, reflecting the situation fairly contemporary with the writing of the narrative, the abandonment of *even* some of the disciples serves as a rhetorical hook. It is used to draw any would-be deserters of the Johannine community into the narrative, thereby convincing them to be faithful. This rhetorical move may be observed within the writings of a third-fourth century gnostic group, the Borborites, who *used John 6:53–66* to justify their grotesque cultic rites (involving abortion and ingesting the fetus and other body parts/fluids, a form of ritual cannibalism), and to call for allegiance to their cause. *They* took *trōgein* literally. If someone did not go along with their practices, he or she was identified with the disciples of Jesus who abandoned him, not having been 'established in fullness' (cf. B. Layton, *The Gnostic Scriptures: a New Translation with Annotations and Introductions,* London, 1987, pp. 199–214). Likewise, vss. 53–66 were crafted so as to address effectively Johannine Christians during a time of community crisis.

61f. Now it is the *disciples who grumble* and thereby demonstrate their unbelieving rebellion. Jesus counters their unbelief with the *anabainein* theme in an attempt to bolster the exhortation that the bread given by the Son of Man is indeed life producing. Even though they may not have perceived the eschatological, saving work of God in the one who is come down from heaven (*katabainein*), they will certainly be confronted with the truth of Jesus' words, should they see him exalted. Whether the audience is tempted to depart from the Johannine community to rejoin the Synagogue or to escape Roman persecution the message is the same. To deny Jesus before humanity is to be denied by the ascended Son of Man before the Father (cf. Mk. 8:37f.). *This* scandal will be *eschatological indeed*.

63–65. Verse 63 is neither an abhorrence of the cannibalistic overtones of eucharistic rites, nor is it a quasi-docetic rejection of the flesh of Jesus. It is a reference to the two ways of seeking (vs. 27), the two kinds of bread (vss. 30–33), and the choice of either adhering to or rejecting the cross of Jesus — as marked by one's willingness to remain loyal to him and signified by corporate solidarity, risking suffering and even death (vss. 51–58). This interpretation is confirmed by the following of vss. 63f. by vs. 65. The point is that the way of the flesh is bankrupt, but the way of the Spirit is life producing. Even some of Jesus' followers still do not believe, and as in the case of the Jews (vs. 44), it is impossible to work for (seek effectively) the life-producing Bread, to come to Jesus, to ingest his fleshly suffering, and to believe in him without the Father's enablement. The anthropological reality is that just as no one has seen God at any time, even recognizing God's activity in the world requires divine assistance. The saving function of the christocentric revelation of the Father through the Son in John is not a matter of bringing 'new' knowledge to humanity. It involves the process of opening the eyes of the world to the reality of God's saving presence at all times and the invitation to see with new eyes.

The exhortative theme of the Johannine interpretation of the feeding, as articulated in vs. 27, is restated in vs. 63. The theme of testing runs throughout the entire chapter, and as in Deuteronomy 8:2, the feeding in the desert is reflected upon as a time of Israel's testing. This is precisely what has transpired in the Johannine reflection upon the feeding of the multitude, and the resultant conclusion is also identical. The meaning behind the provision of manna was to teach Israel that true sustenance comes not from bread alone, but from every Word that proceeds from the mouth of Yahweh (Deut. 8:3). And, the significance of Jesus' feeding the crowd points to the life-producing effect of Jesus' words, which are themselves Spirit and Life (vs. 63c).

66. However, not all pass the test. The slipping away of some of the disciples serves as an object lesson to any in the contemporary Johannine intramural audience tempted to make similar defections. It is no accident that the disciples' response is saved for the conclusion of the dialogue/discourse. As in the case of Amos 1:3–2:5, the prophet's audience can almost be heard to be cheering in the background as Amos pronounces judgment on all of Israel's neighbours. It is only when the final group is addressed that members of Israel come to terms with the real focus of the prophet's confrontation (Am. 2:6–16). It is *they*, Israel, for whom the prophetic admonition is most incisively aimed. Therefore, all the exposing of the faults of others simply serves as a prelude, preparing the way for the acute concern of the prophet: to address the situation of this particular audience. The same may be said for John 6. The existentializing of 'bread' is undoubtedly familiar to the evangelist's audience by now, debates with Jewish leaders have probably become less intense, but for those contemplating the cost of discipleship, the evangelist's message brings with it the power of convicting truth.

Discussion

John 6:25–66 is the Johannine 'exhortation of the "two ways" '. The 'primary text' of the exhortation is the narration of Jesus' words and deeds which precedes it, and the exhortation proceeds by means of a series of dialogues which lead into three main discourses of Jesus, each of which develops a christocentric understanding of the 'life-producing Bread' which Jesus gives and is. The pivotal text of the exhortation is vs. 27, and Bultmann was entirely correct to assume that this verse must have been the beginning of the 'Bread of Life' discourse.[6] Contrary to Bultmann's diachronic theory of composition, however, the evangelist has crafted the following dialogues and discourses to follow a consistent pattern whereby Jesus' discussants ask ironic questions, make bold overstatements, and generally provide a foil for the Johannine Jesus to pose the existential question to the present Johannine audience in the face of persecution and 'testing': 'Which will *you* choose? The 'bread' which leads to death, or the Bread which leads to Life Eternal?' In order to convey this message, the evangelist has employed a variety of literary techniques designed to engage the reader in an imaginary dialogue with the christocentric content of the chapter. Thus, 'what' the evangelist is saying will be considered after examining 'how' he goes about doing so.

A) The *literary means* by which the evangelist seeks to engage his audience in dialogue are multivalent and mutually re-enforcing. 1. His *use of irony* becomes clear with the first interaction between Jesus and the crowd. The humour in their question would have been obvious to the Johannine audience. They come asking, 'how long' Jesus had been there, but their hidden agenda is clearly to inquire, ' ... and *how long will it be* until lunchtime?' The Johannine Jesus exposes their hidden question immediately with his knowing response: 'You seek me not because you saw the signs, but because you ate the loaves and were satisfied.' The irony continues, however, with the obvious misunderstanding of the crowd. They mistake 'works of God' for outward deeds as opposed to the ongoing spiritual activity of coming to and seeking the living God (Is. 55:1–3; cf. Ps. 42:1–2; Jer. 2:13). They betray the fact that they have not 'seen the sign' the day before (vs. 36) in requesting another sign and further exhibit their preoccupation with material bread by requesting, 'Give us this bread *all the time*' (vs. 34).

The evangelist's use of irony continues with a second type of 'bread', the Jewish Torah. Alluded to in vss. 30–33 in the discussion with the crowd, the issue becomes explicit with Jesus' citation of Is. 54:13 in vs. 45. The dialogue has thus shifted from the crowd's use of 'manna rhetoric' to try to obtain more loaves (vs. 30f.) to Jesus' christocentric identification of the truly life-producing 'Bread', which involves a dualistic contradistinction between that which Moses *gave* and that which *God gives* (vs. 32f.). This affront to Mosaic piety and implicit depreciation of the Torah bring a sharp objection from 'the Jews' (vs. 41f.). 'How does he now say that he has come down from heaven?', they grumble. The irony of their objection is striking. First of all, they have forgotten the true source of the Torah's authority (*and* Moses') as being the 'givingness' of God (vs. 32; cf. Jn. 19:11). Their high

---

6 Bultmann, p. 222. This is a clear example in which Bultmann has identified correctly the formal elements of a passage (vs. 27 being the pivotal fulcrum of the chapter) but has posed the wrong composition-hypothesis to account for it.

regard for Moses and the Torah (5:37–47) borders on idolatry, which is fundamentally the placing of anything before one's allegiance and service to the living God (Ex. 20:4–6). Second, they miss the point entirely when Jesus speaks of his divine origin, assuming that he was referring to the physical act of coming down from the clouds, like manna from heaven. The reference is obviously to Jesus' divine commission as God's agent (Deut. 18:15–18), sent to speak *only* that which he is commanded, and thus to represent God fully on earth (cf. Jn. 5:19–47). The irony of their miscomprehension must have struck members of the Johannine audience with utter hilarity. The scriptures point to Jesus, and it was of *him* that Moses had written (5:37–47), but here the Jews come back again, seemingly oblivious to their impending midrashic defeat! The rhetorical method of the Johannine Jesus is to grant them their penultimate authorities, but to point to the ultimate source of all authority, life, and being-itself — God — whom Jesus reveals and represents with eschatological finality. Just as the crowd's statements served as a foil for the next audience addressed by Jesus (the Jews of the Synagogue — cf. Jn. 9:22; 16:2f.), so the question of the Jews (vs. 52) provides a foil for the primary audience of the evangelist at the time of writing, some of whom must have been undergoing the 'testing' of persecution. This is where the evangelist's use of irony takes on the subtle face of paradox.

At vs. 51 the dialogue/discourse section takes a radical turn. Until now, Jesus has been inviting the crowd and the Jews to 'come to him and eat', and in doing so to believe in him and to receive him as God's eschatological provision of eternal 'nourishment', which leads to being 'taught by God' (vs. 45). Now it becomes clear that Jesus' being the life-producing Bread actually involves *death*. The giving of his *flesh* for the life of the world is a graphic reference to his suffering and death on the cross. At this point the evangelist's use of irony becomes more subtle, in the light of the grave situation faced by Johannine Christians around the time of the writing of John 6.[7] In calling believers to affirm their solidarity with Jesus and his community of followers in the fact of persecution, the evangelist conflates two separate debates from different eras of the early Christian movement and calls for the followers of Jesus to make a paradoxical decision: he or she must choose the way of the cross (which may lead to death) in order to receive the *life* which Jesus came to offer.

If the evangelist's audience would have been familiar with the accusation that Jesus' followers practised 'cannibalism' in their eucharistic rites (although there was probably not an institutionalized form of eucharistic liturgy within Johannine Christianity at this time, cf. above, Chapter 6), they may have also been familiar with the standard Christian response, appealing to Jesus' words of the institution. Thus, the hearer might have been preparing for a splendid Synoptic-type or Pauline

---

7 It is not entirely adequate to assume the evangelist was using the 'cannibalistic eucharist' debates ironically, but it would have matched his style in the preceding dialogues and discourses, and it certainly would have been effective as a rhetorical tool.

repartee, emphasizing the eucharist as the fulfilment of the Passover meal (cf. Mk. 14:12–26; Matt. 26:17–30; Lk. 22:7–23) or the eschatological messianic banquet (Lk. 22:25–30; 1 Cor. 11:23–26). However, Jesus does not do this. Instead, he emphasizes the implication of 'eating the flesh' and 'drinking the blood' of the Son of Man. It involves *remaining* in Jesus (vs. 56), and assuming the same sort of relationship to Jesus as he has with the Father who sent him (vs. 57). The problematic implication is that Jesus was sent to give his 'flesh for the life of the world' (vs. 51), and *solidarity with him implies the same for his followers*. The irony continues in the obvious anachronicity of the disciples' 'grumbling' (vs. 60f.). Historically, followers of Jesus probably did abandon him when they realized he was not the sort of militaristic (or materialistic) Messiah they had expected him to be (vs. 66). However, the evangelist makes it appear that these disciples are offended over Jesus' 'cannibalistic' references to the eucharist. The exhortation of the 'two ways' comes full circle in Jesus' reference to the ascending Son of Man (vs. 62) and the profitlessness of the flesh (vs. 63). The only means of attaining eternal life is through adherence to Jesus' words, and the context within which these are to be heard can be nowhere other than the community of faith. Therefore, the evangelist has 'borrowed from the emerging popular authority' of eucharistic imagery in order to call for solidarity with Jesus and the community of his followers in the face of suffering. The unwitting disciple may smugly have anticipated the rhetorical defeat of those who accused Christians of cannibalism, but would eventually have had to face the centrality of the Johannine Jesus' message: the Food which abides into eternity is that which the Son of Man offers, and 'eating' this 'bread' involves solidarity with Jesus in his *death* as well as in his *resurrection*.[8]

2. A second literary device used by the evangelist is to *co-opt the traditional use of manna as a 'rhetorical trump'*, and to turn it on its head, thereby creating a conceptual change in the mind of the hearer/reader.[9] As was demonstrated above (Chapter 3), Borgen's analysis of the homiletic pattern of Jn. 6:31–58 is only partially right. He demonstrates convincingly that the order of this passage *does*

---

8 In this sense the perspective of the Fourth Evangelist is entirely parallel to Ignatius (*Eph.* 20) and Paul (Ro. 6:5; 8:1f., 11–17), who understand solidarity with Jesus in his death as being a necessary correlative to participating with him in his resurrection.

9 As Loder has demonstrated, any experience of knowing must, by definition, begin with some sort of epistemological crisis which dislocates the understanding of the knower in order for it to undergo a reflective process and arrive at a new perspective (above, Chapter 7, notes 12–17).

This is precisely what J. Riches and A. Millar argue that Jesus must have done in posing a new understanding of the Jewish conception of the Kingdom of God ('Conceptual Change in the Synoptic Tradition', in *Alternative Approaches to New Testament Study*, ed., A.E. Harvey, London, 1985, pp. 37–60). In a socio-religious context where manna had commonly been associated with the superior gift of God, to turn the use of manna as a 'rhetorical trump' (a category or suit that wins over all others by virtue of its superior value) on its head, and to associate it with food which leads to *death* must have provided more than a little shock for a Jewish-Christian audience. It made the point stick.

make sense as it stands, and even that one may detect a progressive unfolding of the meaning of Jesus as the 'Bread' which God gives *now*, as contrasted to that which was given in the wilderness. However, Borgen has adopted the wrong midrashic pattern for John 6, and the 'homily' (exhortation) does *not* begin at vs. 31. Rather, it 'begins' at 6:1 with the narration of Jesus' words and works, and the pivotal fulcrum of the exhortation is stated in vs. 27 and developed throughout the rest of the chapter.[10] In reality, neither Jesus nor his discussants is interested in 'exegeting' the authentic meaning of 'manna' midrashically. Verse 31 *does not* launch the development of various meanings of 'manna', as though it were the primary text (cf. Exodus Rabbah 25:1–8) to be exposited. Rather, in reflecting upon Jesus' signs, various ways of responding to him are 'exegeted' by means of developing various meanings of 'death-producing food' (in contrast to the Food which Jesus gives and is), of which the craving for outward manna (bread) is one. Therefore, in John 6 manna is not exegeted as a primary text, but is used (unsuccessfully by Jesus' discussants) as a secondary text — a rhetorical trump — which is corroborated by its linguistic and rhetorical similarity to Ps. 78 rather than Ex. 16.[11] The employment of manna as a *secondary proof text* assumes a different rhetorical form than the one suggested by Borgen and may be observed in the way the Psalmist *and* the Fourth Evangelist follow the standard form of manna rhetoric:

Table 16:
'The Rhetorical Use of Manna Pattern in Psalm 78'

A. *Main point of exhortation*: Put your trust in God, Oh my people, and do not be like your forefathers — a stubborn and rebellious generation (vss. 1, 7f.).

B. *Development of point using either/or categories*: God did many miracles inviting their trust (vss. 11–16), but the sons of Ephraim continued to sin, putting God to the test, demanding the food they craved (vss. 9f., 17–20). Therefore, God's wrath broke out and he sent fire, but they still did not trust (vs. 21f.).

C. *Introduction of manna as a rhetorical trump*: God even opened the doors of heaven and rained down *manna for people to eat*, and he gave them the 'grain of heaven'. Mortals ate the 'bread of the angels' — as much as they desired. He also rained down flesh (flying birds as thick as sand on the shore), satisfying all their cravings, but despite all this, they went on sinning. Even as the flesh was between their teeth God's anger rose up against them, putting to death even the strongest of them, and yet they still put God to the test (vss. 23–41).

---

10 The two uses of *meta tauta* at Jn. 6:1 and 7:1 suggest that the entire chapter is meant to be taken as a literary unit (cf. J.D. Crossan, 'It Is Written: A Structuralist Analysis of John 6', *Sēmeia* 26, 1983, pp. 3–21). Just as the signs are primarily about Jesus, so the 'bread of life' discourses are not about bread — or even manna — but about *Jesus*, as the Bread of Life.

11 Borgen's dismissal of Ps. 78:24f. as the closest parallel to Jn. 6:31 is unconvincing (*Bread*, pp. 40f., 63; cf. Barrett, p. 288f.; and Lindars, p. 256f.). Both linguistically and rhetorically, Jn. 6:31 is most closely parallel to Ps. 78:24f., and this may be seen by the way manna is developed rhetorically in both texts (but less so in Ex. 16). On the other hand, John 6 is *not* a psalm, as is Ps. 78, but the formal differences do not outweigh the rhetorical similarities, especially with regard to the way the manna motif is employed.

D. Continued development and implications: God did miraculous signs in Egypt (vss. 42–51), he delivered them from the oppressor (vss. 52–55), but they still put God to the test (vs. 56). Therefore, God was angered. He consumed their young men with fire, put their priests to death by the sword, and rejected the tribe of Ephraim, choosing *Judah* instead.

E. Reiteration of main point: Therefore, God chose David his servant to be a shepherd to his people, and to lead them with skilful hands (implied exhortation: be thankful for God's provision through David's kingdom, and not ungrateful as the fathers in the wilderness, who craved something more.) You saw what happened to the Northern Kingdom ... will *you* be next? (vss. 68–72).

Roughly the same rhetorical structure may be observed for most of the midrashic developments of the manna motif (cf. above, Chapter 3, notes 9–12; Tables 1 and 2; and below, Appendix VII) in ancient Jewish literature, and this appears to be precisely the sort of means by which the crowd sought to convince Jesus to provide more barley loaves. The use of manna as a 'rhetorical trump' by the crowd in John 6 is as follows:

Table 17:
'The Use of Manna as a "Rhetorical Trump" by the Crowd in John 6'

A. *Main point of the crowd's request*: 'How long have you been here?' (implying 'And just *how long will it be* until we receive another feeding?' vs. 25f.).

B. *Development of point using either/or categories*: In response to Jesus' exhortation to seek not the food which produces death, but that which is life-producing, the crowd asks, 'What must we do in order to do (get?) the works of God' (and thus receive the life-producing food, vs. 27f.)?

C. *Introduction of manna as a rhetorical trump*: 'Then what sign will *you* do for us? Our fathers ate *manna* in the desert.' (vs. 30f.) The challenge is clear; the gauntlet is thrown down.

D. *Continued development and implications*: 'As it is written, "He gave them bread from heaven to eat." ' In other words, 'If you really claim to be a Prophet like Moses (Elisha), show us another sign — after all, *he* gave us bread from heaven (the food of angels) to eat' (vs. 31f.). 'Are you what you claim to be, or not?'

E. *Reiteration of main point*: Therefore, they said to him (regarding the bread which comes down from heaven), 'Lord, give us this bread *all the time*.' (vs. 34).

Whether or not an actual dialogue like this ever took place,[12] the evangelist certainly constructs the scenario in such a way as to show Jesus refuting the manna-

---

12 Scholars are fond of explaining the differences between the two 'bi-optic' Gospels by asserting that Mark was 'historical' but John was not. Therefore, the dramatic style of this dialogue, and those in John 9 and 11, etc., have led many to assume that a dialogue like this never happened, but existed only in the creative mind of the evangelist. This may have been the case, but if so (rather than the evangelist's reflection upon an actual cluster of debates), it must be acknowledged that the evangelist represents the crowd's use of the manna rhetoric in perfect keeping with the way people would have been likely to approach Jesus within that socio-religious context. The account is also much clearer in John than in Mark 8, and one gets the impression that the Fourth Evangelist has original insight into the meanings and nuances of the dialogues that none of the Synoptists ever did.

rhetoric at every turn, and finally *over-trumping* the 'highest card' of his discussants. At their deflective request for more loaves (A), Jesus exposes their true agenda and makes an either/or distinction between eating one's fill of the loaves and seeing the *significance* of the feeding (cf. Is. 55:1–3). At the further development of their main point (B), Jesus points them to the kernel of doing God's works, which implies a relationship of trust. At their introduction of the manna theme and its implications (C and D) Jesus corrects their exegesis of Ps. 78:24. 'It is *not* Moses who *gave* you the bread from heaven, but *my Father who gives* you the true Bread out of heaven.' However, in doing so, he does not simply replace their exegesis with his—but with the eschatological implication of the text (Martyn, p. 128). The distinction is two-fold. First, it makes it clear that Moses never was the source of bread (the Law, or any other spiritual gift), but God. Therefore, the use of manna (or the Torah) as a rhetorical trump is founded on a fallacious assumption: that Moses was the giver instead of God.

The second distinction has to do with the kind of bread which manna is, versus the *true* Bread which Jesus is. For the first time in the history of the Jewish-Christian exposition of the manna theme is manna regarded as anything less than the wondrous food provided miraculously in the wilderness. In fact, the Johannine Jesus actually refers to it as death producing, in contrast to the Life which comes through him (vss. 49f., 58). Finally, in response to the crowd's reiteration of their original point: 'Give us this bread all the time.' (E), Jesus begins the first of his three Bread of Life discourses. In effect, what the Johannine Jesus has done is to perform a rhetorical *coup d'état* on his discussants, who used manna as a rhetorical device to obtain more bread. He has turned the entire enterprise on its head, developing three christocentric elaborations on the life-producing 'Nourishment' which Jesus gives and is, contrasted to various kinds of death-producing 'food'.[13]

---

13 This is precisely parallel to what Philo has done to the Greeks of Alexandria and their appeal to the *gnosis* and *sophia* of the Encyclical educational system (*Congr.* 154–180). The way Philo demonstrates the superiority of 'self-taught' knowledge is to point out the fact that the Encyclical schools employ the finite (physical) faculties of the student (155f.). Their learnings can only come through toil and suffering, as contrasted to the spiritual knowledge which comes from the God of Israel (158–172). Therefore, divine (spiritual) manna is introduced as a *rhetorical trump* (Ex. 16:4) to show that the highest values of the Greek ethos (divine knowledge and wisdom) may be found in the Jewish educational system instead. Thus, says Philo (*Congr.* 174):

> But the multitude, the common herd, who have never tasted of wisdom, the one true food of us all, think that those who feed on the divine words live in misery and suffering, and little know that their days are spent in continued well-being and gladness.

Therefore, Philo has overturned the Greeks' appeal to *sophia* by claiming to receive manna, the food of God's wisdom; and in John 6, Jesus overturns the conventional use of the manna-rhetoric and 'wins' the argument dramatically. Borgen is correct to assume a parallel between Philo's *Congr.* 174 (and context) with John 6:31 (and context), but the parallelism is *inverse*. The Fourth Evangelist has placed the Jewish study of the Torah and the manna-rhetoric in the same position that Philo places the Greek Encyclia and their appeal to *sophia*. Thus, Jesus

B) Regarding the *christological content* of John 6:25–66, 'what' is said is illuminated by having considered 'how' it is presented. One may observe in the method of the evangelist a linear/progressive and cyclical/repetitive style of narrative construction, designed to engage the reader in a 'dialogue' which results in an encounter with the christocentric content of the exhortation.[14] Obvious in the three-fold application of the Bread of Life motif is the fact that John's christology does *not* represent a formalized, credal understanding of Jesus, but a fluid, living appreciation of who he was — and continues to be — for his followers in the world. Whereas the Synoptic interpretation of the feeding and sea crossing must have been confined to written form in the 50's or 60's (as Matthew and Luke later assimilate the interpretation of Mark 6 and 8), the Johannine tradition shows signs of ongoing interpretation, perhaps into the 80's or 90's. Therefore, one may infer at least three (and perhaps four) acute issues within Johannine Christianity, which have been addressed christologically (using the typologies of two kinds of 'bread', vs. 27) by the evangelist.

1. The first issue has to do with the obsolescence of the earlier Petrine interpretation of the feeding as a *thauma*: 'Jesus has power over nature (sea danger, illness, hunger, etc.); if you will simply believe strongly enough and not doubt (Mk. 6:51–56; 8:16–21) your physical needs will be met'. This notion probably was never as strong in the Johannine tradition as it was in the Petrine, but what is significant about John 6:26 is that the sign-seeking crowd is used to embody the Synoptic (prevalent Christian) interpretation of the result (and thus, the meaning) of the feeding: 'they all ate and were satisfied', and the Johannine Jesus *rebukes* them for it. This represents the Fourth Evangelist's facing the facts that despite one's maximum employment of faith, hunger still continues, and illness and death continue to take their tolls. The impact of such reflection catalyzes a Stage 4 level of faith into a Stage 5, *Conjunctive* one.[15] In doing so, the evangelist takes on not

---

is 'tempted' by means of Jewish manna rhetoric, and he 'over-trumps' the highest card of his discussants.

14 G. Mlakuzhyil (*The Christocentric Literary Structure of the Fourth Gospel*, Rome, 1987, pp. 134–137) outlines the 'spiral structure of the Prologue', but Meeks' description is better ('The Man from Heaven in Johannine Sectarianism', in J. Ashton, p. 150):

The result is not only a dramatic effect produced by the connections between discourse and narrative, but also a certain distance for the reader from the ambiguous and paradoxical statements, so that the internal tensions of the material begin to work in a progressive, didactic spiral.

15 While the evangelist may have been familiar with Mark, the ' ... ate and were satisfied ...' result of the feeding must have been well known, even by those who had not read any of the Synoptics. What vs. 26 represents, from an ideological point of view, is the Johannine attempt to 'set the record straight' — against the mainstream of oral and written tradition — that Jesus' words and works were *not* nature wonders (alone), but *vehicles of revelation* (signs). Thus, the evangelist was not merely arguing against a hypothetical miracle tract. He was taking on the entire, mainstream Christian tradition, which had assumed, in his view, an unreflective and experientially inadequate interpretation of the meaning of Jesus' works.

a backwater *sēmeia* tract, but the prevalent valuation of Jesus' miracles in the Synoptic tradition, and the Johannine critique may have spanned decades.

2. The second crisis alluded to is the conflict between the Christians and the Jews of the Synagogue. J.L. Martyn is correct to argue that this debate must have been especially intense within Johannine Christianity, but he is wrong to assume this is the most acute debate at the time of the writing of John 6.[16] In fact, the Christian answers to 'the Jews' seem to have been well formulated and predictable by the time John 6 was written, and the separation with the Synagogue seems to have been over its most intense stages. Nonetheless, the dialectical relationship with the Synagogue suggested by John 9 and 1 John 2:18–25 is still alluded to residually in Jesus' debates with the crowd and the Jews in John 6.

3. The most acute struggle faced by Johannine Christianity at the time of the writing of John 6 had to do with the impact of docetising tendencies within the late first century upon the Christian movement. Thus, it is probably a group with docetising inclinations at which the exhortation of the 'two ways' is aimed most intentionally, and Brown may even be correct in his scenario of how it may have happened.[17] It must be recognized, however, that the primary motivation for the evangelist's corrective was probably less a function of his desire for them to 'get their theology straight', and more a concern about the *ethical implications* of a christology which de-emphasized the fleshly humanity of Jesus.[18] In this respect,

---

16 See S.T. Katz, 'Issues in the Separation of Judaism and Christianity After 70 C.E.: A Reconsideration', *JBL* 103, 1984, pp. 43–76; and R. Kimelman, '*Birkat Ha-Minim* and the Lack of Evidence for an Anti-Christian Jewish Prayer in Late Antiquity', in *Jewish and Christian Self-Definition* Vol. 2, ed., E.P. Sanders et. al., London, 1981, pp. 226–244.

17 R.E Brown's reconstruction of the various issues which may have contributed to John's distinctive portrayal of Jesus' ministry (*Community*) offers one of the clearest and most convincing hypothetical reconstructions of what may have been the history of Johannine Christianity. While Brown makes no claim to have solved the problem of John's christological unity and disunity, some of the tensions may be understood more clearly by means of his reconstruction (i.e. the explanation that debates with the Jews may have pushed John's christology higher, and, this emphasis may have influenced the development of docetism within the Johannine community, etc.). What is interesting, however, is that even in the debates with the Jews, and in emphasizing the flesh of the Son of Man, *dialectical* (*Conjunctive*) responses are used by the Johannine Jesus, rather than dogmatic (Stage 3 or 4) ones.

   Thus, in response to the accusations of the Jews that Jesus had made himself 'equal to God' (Jn. 5:18; 10:30, 33), the evangelist does not simply give the other side of the argument to 'prove' them wrong. Rather, the Johannine Jesus emphasizes that he never claimed to be equal to God, but that his word should be *equated with* God's, because he has been sent by the Father, and he speaks *only* what the Father tells him to say (5:19–47; 10:36–38). Likewise, when the evangelist confronts docetising Christians, he does not do so polemically (Stage 3 or 4 faith) but argues *Conjunctively* (Stage 5 faith) and emphasizes the both-and-ness of solidarity with Jesus' resurrection and death (6:51–63).

18 While R. Wallis outlines the non-theological factors which contribute to the formation of a cult, and sect-identity ('The Cult and Its Transformation', in his *Sectarianism*, London, 1975,

the exhortation of the 'two ways' is entirely parallel to the situation addressed by the writer of the *Didache*. As J. Draper has demonstrated in his 1983 Cambridge thesis,[19] the posing of 'two ways' before members of a community of faith in ancient Judaism always served the function of bolstering corporate solidarity against internal and external sources of threat. John 6 is no different. Paradoxically, seeking to save oneself from persecution is actually the 'way of death', whereas the 'way of life' involves ingesting the flesh-and-bloodness of Jesus and *embracing the cross*. A fourth crisis is alluded to in vss. 67–71.

Findings

John 6:25–66 may be considered the 'exhortation of the "two ways" ', as responses to Jesus' words and works are sketched in terms of food which perishes and food which endures into life eternal (vs. 27). By means of dialogues and discourses, the evangelist seeks to draw the reader into an engaging 'dialogue with the text', leading to a transforming encounter with Jesus by faith.

1. As a contrast to the standard Johannine portrayal of Jesus' ministry as a 'scenario' of God's saving/revealing discourse with humanity, the Johannine misunderstanding dialogues with Jesus *shift the initiative* from God, or God's agent, to Jesus' *discussants*. By means of naive questions and bold overstatements, these individuals and groups approach Jesus, only for their ignorance to be exposed by his replies and teaching. A further function of these dialogues is to provide a specific corrective to particular needs of those in the audience. This is done by assimilating the misconceptions of the targeted audience into the questions and statements of the discussants, to which Jesus provides the correct perspective.

---

pp. 35–49), the point I want to make is that high christologies by themselves would not have been a terribly difficult problem within Johannine Christianity. Certainly, the evangelist's own christology had very high elements in it. Neither would a de-emphasis upon Jesus' flesh have been overly problematic, in and of itself. Theological problems become most acute when the *implications of those beliefs* come into full view. Therefore, the most threatening aspect of docetism would have been the implication that if Jesus did not suffer, *neither do his followers have to suffer in the face of persecution*. This is not to say the evangelist was not concerned that christological truth be held in proper tension. It is to say that even in his emphasis on the 'flesh and bloodness' of Jesus, his main concern was to affect the lives and actions of individuals, not just their ideas. Schnelle's work (1987) would support this thesis.

19 In his 1983 Cambridge Ph.D. thesis ('A Commentary on the Didache in Light of the Dead Sea Scrolls and Reflected Documents'), Draper points out that the 'Two Ways teaching' is a Christian adaptation of the Jewish 'Covenant imagery of Deuteronomy, but [which] was modified under the influence of Iranian dualism' (p. 329f.). The primary function of exhortations of the 'Two Ways' is to inculcate the values of the religious community within the belief systems of its members, and to call for corporate solidarity with, and appropriate action within, the community of faith. The same may be said about the function of John 6:27 and the following exhortation.

2. The evangelist has also employed a variety of literary techniques to make this engaging function of the text more effective. Two of these include the use of *irony* and the *reversal of conventional Jewish manna rhetoric*. The questions and statements of the crowd, the Jews and the disciples — combined with Jesus' responses — all involve the effective use of irony by the evangelist. The function of irony is to shock and create a disturbance within the mind of the reader in order to prepare him or her for receiving the intended message of the narrator, and this is done throughout John 6. Parallel to Psalm 78, the manna motif is used by the crowd in John 6 as a secondary text, a rhetorical trump, in order to convince Jesus to provide more barley loaves. However, at each of the five steps characteristic of the Jewish rhetorical use of manna, the Johannine Jesus exposes the shallowness of their cravings, and the fallacies of their exegesis — bordering on idolatry. In effect what the Johannine Jesus does is to 'over-trump' the highest card of his discussants, and for the *first time* in the history of Jewish/Christian *midrashic* use of the manna motif, is it described as *inferior* and *death producing* in contrast to the life-producing Bread, which Jesus gives and is.

3. Within the three discourses which follow the manna debate and behind the misunderstanding views of Jesus' discussants, one may infer a three-fold corrective interpretation of Jesus as the life-producing Bread, each of which represents an acute crisis within Johannine Christianity. The first represents the obsolescence of the Synoptic (Petrine) interpretation of the feeding and sea-crossing narratives; the second represents struggles between the Johannine community and the Synagogue; and the third represents the centrifugal consequences of docetising tendencies within Johannine Christianity. This third issue was the most pressing at the time John 6 was written, and the exhortation of the 'two ways' must finally in its written form be interpreted as an appeal for solidarity with Jesus and his followers in the face of persecution. To do this, the evangelist 'borrows from the authority' of current sacramental debates in order to represent graphically the cost of discipleship and the way of the cross. To participate in the resurrection one must also share in Jesus' suffering and death, and figuratively 'eat and drink the flesh and blood of the suffering Son of Man'.

Chapter 10

Returning the 'Keys of the Kingdom' to *Jesus* (An Exegesis of John 6:67–71)

The third section in John 6 returns to the same narratological sequence of initiative and response as was characteristic of vss. 1–24. In John 6:67–71 *Jesus* again assumes the initiative, and as in vss. 5–12 and 19f., this evokes a response from the disciples. As a contrast to the sequence in which discussants come to Jesus and receive a 'lesson in the truth' from Jesus (as a corrective to specific problems within the Johannine audience), the most common sequence of the Johannine narrative is not corrective, but revelational. It portrays a scenario of God's saving/revealing dialogue with humanity in a way which calls for a response to God's initiative.[1] Between these two *modes of dialogical sequence* the narrative of the Fourth Gospel progresses, with each approach having its own kind of rhetorical effect.

The difference between these two modes of narrative progression is this: a) Where the *agent of God* is the initiator, the rhetorical thrust of the narrative is to convince the reader that in Jesus (as well as through Moses, the scriptures, John the Baptist, etc.) God has spoken in the fullness of time (cf. 2 Cor. 5:19; Heb. 1:1f.). This calls for a believing response to the saving initiative of the Father through the Son, which brings with it such life-producing results as the knowing of truth, being in 'the light', being transformed by the love of the Father, and ultimately experiencing the zōē and *doxa* of God eternally (Jn. 20:31). Conversely, the refusal to respond believingly to God's saving initiative in Jesus is portrayed in John as the basic sin, and a negative response to Jesus brings with it such death-producing effects as remaining in darkness, being alienated from the Father, and living in self-deception (Jn. 3:18–20). Therefore, the rhetorical structure of the Johannine narration of Jesus' ministry portrays the threefold pattern of God's discourse with humanity involving God's initiative, a human response to God's initiative, and the consequence of such a response — described in soteriological terms. This is the structural pattern with which the Fourth Evangelist interprets the history of Israel, the eschatological advent of Jesus, and the purpose of the Gospel as described in

---

1 For a fuller treatment of revelation as a human-divine dialogue, see W.J. Abraham, *Divine Revelation and the Limits of Historical Criticism*, Oxford, 1982. For a perceptive treatment of the function of the 'scenario' within literature, see M. Bakhtin, (V.N. Voloshinov), 'Discourse in Life and Discourse in Poetry', E.t. by J. Richmond, in *Bakhtin School Papers*, 1983, pp. 5–30, esp. p. 18.

20:31. The appeal is universal in its scope, and it may be said to embrace audiences internal and external to Johannine Christianity.

Table 18:
'Divine Initiative and the Revelational Scenario/Discourse in John'

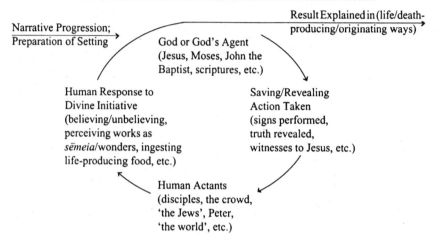

b) Where *Jesus' discussants* take the initiative, leading into a dialogue with Jesus and followed by one or more of his discourses, the rhetorical target is more specific. It may largely be assumed that the dialogues of John begin with a specific person or group representing a particular approach to God, the truth, Jesus, etc., which is revealed to be inadequate by the Johannine Jesus. Like the signs and the other events of Jesus' ministry, these dialogues have been included in the Johannine text because of their applicational value as perceived by the evangelist. However, this does not mean that all targeted audiences would need to have shared the same external situation as the discussants in the narrative. For instance, one need not to have lost a brother by death to relate to the grieving anger conveyed in the exclamation of Martha *and* Mary in 11:21 and 32, 'Lord, if you had *only* been here my brother would not have died!' Nor does one have to have been a Samaritan woman or a Galilean follower of the John the Baptist to find oneself drawn into the feeling of being 'known' by the Johannine Jesus (4:29; 1:48). Therefore, the rhetorical function of the Johannine dialogues is to draw members of the audience into a believing relationship with Christ by means of correcting a particular aspect of inadequate faith. This is the primary rhetorical function of the Johannine misunderstanding dialogue.

These correctives are then reinforced by Johannine discourses in order to reconstruct a picture of what a believing response to God ought to look like. In order to do this, Old Testament typologies are drawn into the discussion as illustrations of what an adequate response to God's saving/revealing initiative entails. Thus, the lifting up of the serpent in the wilderness is employed (3:14f.) as a parallel to the saving/healing work of God through Jesus as the Son of Man, available to all who look to him and believe; and, the exegesis of the crowd is corrected in 6:32ff., where the emphasis is laid upon the true source of the manna (God) as the one who has provided genuinely life-producing nourishment in Jesus as the Bread of Life. Even in the correcting of scriptural interpretations, the overall concern of the evangelist may be detected. His interpretations of Israel's salvation history, the ministry of Jesus, christology, and pneumatology all share a common function. They all represent the effectual means by which God has spoken to humanity, calling for a believing response on the part of those who encounter — and indeed are encountered by — the revelational Word of God. S.M. Schneiders has described it succinctly:[2]

> The central concern of the Fourth Gospel is the saving revelation which takes place in Jesus. This revelation, however, must be understood as a dialogical process of Jesus' self-manifestation as the one being continuously sent by the Father (7:16–18) who is thereby encountered in Jesus (10:30; 14:9–11) and the response of belief on the part of the disciple (17:8).

Table 19:
'Human Initiative and the Rhetorical Misunderstanding Dialogue in John'

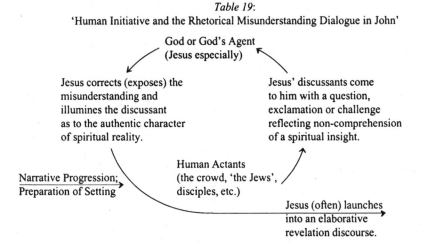

This is where distinguishing between parts of John 6 which are 'sapiential', as opposed to 'sacramental', as opposed to 'christological' is insufficient. All of John is christological, but christology for the Fourth Evangelist is a subset (central though it be) of the larger set to which also belong Jewish and gnostic *sophia* and *logos* mythologies, Old Testament typologies (the examples of Abraham, Moses and Elijah, as well as the images of manna, the vine, the shepherd/flock, etc.), and contemporary sacramentologies. From time to time the evangelist borrows one or

---

2 S.M. Schneiders, 'Women in the Fourth Gospel and the Role of Women in the Contemporary Church', in *BTB* 12, 1982, p. 39.

more of these other motifs in order to make a christological point, but this does *not* mean that the point being made *ceases* to be christological. Rather, even in the co-opting of other motifs the evangelist furthers his christocentric purpose: to evoke a believing response to God's initiating and sustaining love through his reflective portrayal of the 'significance' of Jesus' ministry (20:31). This divine/human, saving/revealing dialogue is the heart of the Fourth Evangelist's theology.

This brings us to vss. 67–71 of John 6. With vss. 1–24 reflecting the evangelist's dialogue with his tradition, and with vss. 25–66 portraying the evangelist's dialogue with the audience(s) addressed in John 6, the remaining five verses are suggestive of some of the tensions internal and external to Johannine Christianity at the time of the final writing of the chapter. Before translating and exegeting the text, however, the one critical issue not treated in Part II should be addressed briefly: namely, *the order of John 5 and 6*. Bultmann's grounds for reversing the order of chs. 5 and 6 are as follows:

> The present order of chs. 5 and 6 cannot be the original one. Since in 6:1 Jesus goes "to the other side" (*peran*) of the lake, he must have been at the lake-side beforehand; but in ch. 5 he is in Jerusalem. Thus ch. 6 has no connection with ch. 5. On the other hand it would follow on ch. 4 very well. Correspondingly 7:1 assumes that Jesus had been staying in Judaea (Jerusalem) up till then, and ch. 7 would thus link up with ch. 5. So the original order must have been chs. 4, 6, 5, 7. (p. 209)

The order of John 5 and 6 is the primary source of evidence for those who would postulate some sort of disordering/reordering theory, and without citing these chapters, most of these theories would have very little else upon which to construct their arguments (although, cf. Jn. 3:31–36; 14:31ff., etc.). While the connection between the life-producing water and the life-producing bread in chs. 4 and 6 is interesting, and while the beginning of ch. 6 and the Passover motif of 6:4 seem abrupt and non-sequitur, respectively, the strongest justification for reordering John 5 and 6 must be the apparent continuation of the debate with the Jerusalem Jews over the healing on the Sabbath in 5:16–47 and 7:15–24. A fundamental weakness with Bultmann's theory is that it assumes most of John 4–7 existed side-by-side *before* the evangelist incorporated it into his version of the Gospel, and furthermore, that it must have existed in *another* order. This was not necessarily the case. What seems more likely is that there were at least two, and possibly more, editions of John, as argued by Brown, Lindars, Schnackenburg and others. This being the case, John 6 was probably *inserted between chs. 5 and 7 as a unit* during a later edition of the Gospel, and the reason it was inserted at this place (among other reasons) was to expand upon John 5:46, ' ... for he (Moses) wrote about me (Jesus)' (cf. Lindars, pp. 206–209).[3]

---

3 M. Shorter ('The Position of Chapter VI in the Fourth Gospel', *ET* 84, 1973, pp. 181–183) offers a similar solution to Lindars' and keeps chs. 5 and 7 together, placing Jn. 6 after Jn. 10:21. She makes the same mistake as Bultmann and others, however, in assuming that all

Among the composition theories put forward, Lindars' is the most attractive, as it handles the major literary aporias with a minimum amount of speculation. According to Lindars (p. 50f.), the major literary problems in John, such as the hymnic character of the Prologue (esp. 1:1–5, 9–14, 16–18), the unity of John 6, the Lazarus material (11:1–46; 12:9–12), the following of the odd break in 14:31 by chs. 15–16 and ch. 17, and the addition of ch. 21 (also 19:35 and 'beloved disciple' passages) by a later editor, may all be explained by the theory that the evangelist himself introduced this 'supplementary material' when he expanded his work. Likewise, such sections as 7:15–24; 10:26–29; and 3:31–36 may be explained as the evangelist's technique to 'hold over part of the material from one section to form the nucleus of the next section' (p. 50).

Such a theory of composition has the following advantages: a) It poses a minimum number of diachronic literary solutions to address other kinds of problems and deals primarily with aporias involving apparent interruptions of sequence or abrupt changes in literary form. b) It leaves theological problems to be dealt with theologically, rather than excising passages which are 'difficult' or which appear to be 'unmotivated' by the context. c) Such a theory reveals how the ministry of Jesus would have been hemmed by the witness of John the Baptist (1:6–8, 15, 19–34 and 10:40–42) during the first edition of the Gospel, when his ministry would have been most pronounced in the memories of early Christians and others; while during the second and third Christian generations, other themes would have been more prevalent (Logos christology, the Lazarus story, etc.). d) Such a theory allows 14:31 to have moved directly into ch. 18, as chs. 15–17 appear to be later Johannine compositions. e) The one transposition Lindars believes the evangelist has made is to have moved the Temple-cleansing narrative to the beginning of Jesus' ministry (2:13–22) in order to make room for the Lazarus narrative as the motivation for the Jews' desire to kill Jesus.[4] This reconciles the Johannine account with those of the Synoptics, and it draws together such passages as 2:22 and 12:16. These are but a few of the problems that are solved by means of Lindars' two-edition theory, and unlike the theories of Bultmann, Teeple and others, there are very few new problems created in its wake.

The specific value of Lindars' theory for the present study, however, is twofold: a) It manages both the unity of John 6 and the connection between chs. 5 and 7 effectively with minimal complication. b) More importantly, if John 6 were added to the main part of the Gospel during a subsequent edition along with other

---

the content of John must have existed side-by-side at the same time before the majority of the Gospel was completed.

4 One key objection to Lindars' moving of the Temple-cleansing from John 12 to John 2 has to do with evidence put forward by L. Morris (*The Gospel According to St. John*, Grand Rapids, 1971, ad. loc.) and others. If Morris is correct, that the construction of the Temple in Jerusalem began in 20 BCE, the comment by the Jews, 'It has taken forty-six years to build this temple ... ' (Jn. 2:20) would make the event of the Temple-cleansing around 26 CE, towards the *beginning* of Jesus' ministry.

identifiable material, a comparison between the issues addressed in this later material may illumine one's understanding of the situation underlying John 6. Therefore, as the present chapter will attempt to assess the socio-religious context out of which John 6 may have emerged, some of the content from the other 'second edition' material (according to Lindars' proposals) will be drawn into the discussion.

John 6:67–71

Therefore, Jesus said to the twelve,
  "Can it be that you also wish to depart?"
Simon Peter answered him,
  "Lord, to whom shall we be released? You have the words which produce eternal life."
  "And we have believed and have come to know that you are the Holy One of God!"
Jesus answered them,
  "Is it not I who have chosen you, the twelve? And yet, one of you is a devil!"
(Now he actually meant *Judas*, son of Simon [Iscariot], for this one was about to betray him, being one of the twelve.)

Exegetical Notes

67. Here the first mention of 'the twelve' is made in John, although the 'twelve baskets' of 6:13 also clearly alludes to Jesus' disciples. The question, *Mē kai humeis thelete hupagein?*, must have been received with shock by the Johannine audience. The dramatic tension of the narrative has steadily been building throughout John 6. The crowd misunderstands, the Jews grumble, even some of Jesus' followers abandon him — to walk with him no more. But what about 'the twelve'? Surely, *they* will respond faithfully! ... Or *will* they?

68. Simon Peter comes to the rescue and as in the Synoptic tradition serves as the spokesman for the twelve. In his response he echoes Jesus' claim in 6:63 that indeed, his words (*rēmata*) are spirit and life, but between vss. 63 and 67 the subject of the clause shifts from the words themselves to the *source* of the words. The implication is that Peter's confession in John 6 is designed to reaffirm the source of life-giving words: *Jesus*. When contrasted with the Matthean addition to the Marcan confession account (cf. Matt. 16:17–19) in which Jesus is portrayed as endowing Peter with his authority, it becomes clear that in John 6:68f. it is *Peter* who reaffirms Jesus' sole authority. In other words, Peter is portrayed as figuratively *returning the 'keys of the kingdom' to the Johannine Jesus*.

It is seldom realized just how *shocking* Peter's confession in John would have seemed to a Christian audience in the last third of the century, during the pinnacle of Peter's popularity! It is doubtful that the evangelist knew the Matthean rendition of Peter's confession in its written form by the time John 6 was written, and he may not even have been familiar with the written form of Mark. However, one may assume with reasonable certainty that in the years following Peter's death, the popularity of Peter would have increased sufficiently for the evangelist to be familiar with at least the sentiment underlying the 'entrusting of the keys' narrative in Matthew, let alone its conventional function among the churches. When Matthew's and John's renditions of the confession narrative are considered side-by-side, it is clear that in John it is not Jesus who gives authority to Peter (and those who follow in his wake), but *it is Peter who affirms the sole authority of Jesus.* What may appear to be a slight variation in detail is actually an indication of a fundamental difference in ideology. Peter's confession in John is meant to disturb.

Therefore, vs. 68 is both constructive *and* deconstructive. It corrects the view that the means by which christocracy occurs is to be understood as mediated through an institutional model, and it affirms the life-giving function of the voice of Jesus, which in turn alludes to the pneumatically-mediated, christocratic model developed more fully in the *Paraklētos* sections of chs. 14–16. The deconstructionist/reconstructionist words of Peter, the negative reaction by Jesus, and the attempt of the final compiler to even out the difficulty caused by Jesus' sharp response to Peter in vs. 70 suggest a shift in initiative between Peter's two statements. Having affirmed the true source of life-producing words, Peter's second statement draws a rebuke from Jesus. This suggests a misunderstanding on Peter's part, which undoubtedly affects one's understanding of his confession.

69. The words, *hēmeis pepisteukamen kai egnōkamen* ... certainly have the ring of Johannine orthodoxy, but the content of such knowledge and belief, ... *hoti su ei ho hagios tou theou*, poses a striking contrast to Synoptic versions of Peter's confession as well as standard Johannine terminology. Obviously, the textual problems related to this phrase are attempts to harmonize the Johannine rendition of Peter's confession with those in the Synoptics. But more interesting is the connection with the way the title, 'the Holy One of God', is used in the Synoptic tradition. Found only in Mark 1:24 and Luke 4:34 in the rest of the New Testament, the phrase, *ho hagios tou theou*, occurs in these two instances on the mouth of the demoniac in the Capernaum Synagogue. Despite such similarities as the setting and references to an evil spirit(s) (Mk. 1:23, 26f., Lk. 4:33, 36), a demon (Lk. 4:33, 35), and a devil (Jn. 6:70), the Johannine rendition is probably not suggesting that Peter is to be equated with the demoniac of the Marcan tradition (which Luke incorporates).

Several inferences may be drawn regarding the associated parallels between the two narratives: a) 'Holy One of God' may indeed be closer to Peter's actual confession than the more confessional Marcan account (8:29, 'You are the Christ.'), as Mark 8 was obviously a synthesized rendition of the feeding, sea crossing, interpretation of the loaves and confession accounts. At least one explanation for the changing of the number of the baskets from 12 to 7 is the possibility that if the number of baskets were associated with the number of disciples who gathered the fragments, the 12 baskets in the Petrine account would have been associated with the twelve disciples responsible for Jewish Christianity (Ac. 1:12–26), while the 7 baskets in the Mk. 8 tradition would match the number of the seven leaders chosen to care for the Gentile Christians in Acts 6:1–7. Mk. 8 thus resembles the way the Petrine feeding narrative would have been communicated among the Gentile churches. If this were the case, *ho Christos* certainly would have been the Hellenistic equivalent of the more Semitic *ho hagois tou theou*. The fact that the rendition of the story for a Gentile audience had obviously come into contact with those who were already familiar with the Mk. 6 account may be seen in the 'dovetail section' (Mk. 8:17–21), where the Marcan Jesus explains the meaning of the feeding of the five thousand *and* the four thousand. Both sets of numbers are reiterated (12 and 5,000; 7 and 4,000), and both renditions are given the same interpretation: Jesus has power over the forces of nature to multiply loaves *if* he chooses. Thus, 'Fret not. You will not go hungry.' promises the pre-Marcan Jesus.

The fact that *ho hagios tou theou* is a Petrine christological reference may also be inferred from Acts 3:14, where Peter calls Jesus *ton hagion kai dikaion*, and Mark 1:24, where the source of Mark's account is quite possibly the preaching and teaching of Peter. In other words, the fact that the only four places in which this phrase (or something like it) occurs in the New Testament all happen to be either of likely Petrine origin or attributed explicitly to Peter seems to be more than a coincidence. John 6:69 may therefore be considered more authentic as a Petrine confession than is normally assumed, and possibly more authentic than the Marcan, 'the Christ'. As in the case of including only one feeding (the 5,000), only one sea crossing, and moving Peter's confession to follow the feeding of the *five thousand,* Luke also *agrees* with the Johannine tradition in adding *tou theou* to the christological title used in Mark's rendition of Peter's confession (Lk. 9:29). Add the 'criterion of dissimilarity', and Peter's confession in John cannot but grow in one's appraisal of its authenticity.

b) The significance of the demoniac referring to Jesus as *ho hagios tou theou* within the tradition underlying the Marcan narrative is that the phrase bespeaks a Petrine understanding of the means by which the Kingdom of God goes forward, and it is precisely this notion that is being countered in John 6:69f. In Mark, the Kingdom of God goes forward by overpowering the Kingdom of Satan (3:23–27). Just as one must first bind the strong man before plundering his house, so the Kingdom of God goes forward by loosening Satan's grip on the world, and this is done by *dunameis* — works of power such as the casting out of demons, the healing of the sick and the preaching of the Gospel (Mk. 1:15, 34, 39, etc.). In John, however, the Devil is one who murders and lies because *the truth* is not in him (8:45), but the 'prince of this world' is judged and driven out by the lifting up of the Son of Man (12:31). Just as darkness is 'extinguished' by the very shining of light (1:5), so the establishing of Jesus' Kingdom comes not by human might or works of power (18:36) but by the power of truth (18:37). This ideological difference between the Petrine tradition and the Johannine betrays a fundamental disagreement within early Christianity regarding not only interpretations of Jesus' ministry, but more significantly, regarding the ministry of the church as well. This difference is especially illuminated by John's treatment of Peter's confessing Jesus to be 'the Holy One of God'.

Borrowing heavily from the Davidic tradition in which Israel is redeemed, purged of her idolatry, and established as an everlasting city of God upon Mount Zion by Yahweh, the 'Holy One of Israel' (Isaiah, chs. 10, 29, 30, 31, 37, 40, 54 and esp. 60:14; Ps. 78 and 89; and Zech. 9 and 12), the Synoptic interpretation of Jesus' restoration of theocracy to Israel is entirely monarchic in its basileiology. This is not to say that the 'Holy One of God' and the 'Holy One of Israel' are by any means equivalent, or even connected. At the very least, though, they share a common origin — the legacy of Davidic power. The Marcan Jesus compares himself to David when his lordship over the Sabbath is questioned by the Jewish leaders (Mk. 2:25–27), he is called the 'Son of David' by blind Bartimaeus (twice, Mk. 10:47, 48), the crowd shouts ' Blessed is the coming of our father David!' (Mk. 11:10), and climactically in Mark 12:35–37 the Marcan Jesus asks:

> How is it that the teachers [of the law] say that the Christ is the son of David? David himself said, speaking by means of the Holy Spirit,
>   "The Lord said to my Lord,
>   'Sit at my right hand until I subdue your enemies under your feet.' "

The Zionist enthronement Psalm from which the above citation is taken (Ps. 110:1) also serves as the climactic Old Testament citation in Peter's great sermon in Acts 2 (vss. 34f.), and it provides the basis for Peter's urgent (and effective) call to repentance (Ac. 2:38–41). Elsewhere in the Petrine tradition, believers are called to be 'a royal priesthood, a holy nation, a people belonging to God' (1 Pet. 2:9), founded upon the cornerstone of Zion (1 Pet. 2:6–8; cf. Is. 28:16; 8:14; Ps. 118:22). This new 'kingdom' is to be based upon submission to 'every authority instituted by men' (1 Pet. 2:13), but 'shepherds of God's flock' ought not to be negligent or self-serving (1 Pet. 5:2–4), and self-control and alertness must be used to resist the devil who 'prowls around like a roaring lion seeking whom he may consume' (1 Pet. 5:8f.).

The point of the above discussion is to illuminate the Marcan understanding of how the advent of God's Kingdom in Jesus plunders the 'house of the strong man', and how it becomes established as a result. This has everything to do with the evil spirit's recognition of Jesus as 'the Holy One of God' in Mark 1:24. Just as blind Bartimaeus called out to the 'Son of David' for miracle-producing mercy (Mk. 10:47f.), the reference to Jesus as 'the Holy One of God' is a statement acknowledging Jesus' divine power to re-establish God's Davidic kingdom on earth. It is precisely this understanding that underlies Peter's confession in John 6:69 — *and* the rebuke of the Johannine Jesus in vs. 70. In that sense, the Johannine corrective of the prevalent Synoptic valuation of miracles (vs. 26) continues in vss. 67–70. Now, however, the issue at stake is the character of God's continuing rule.

c) It is entirely conspicuous that John is nearly devoid of Davidic messianic motifs. The reference to the Kingdom/Son of David at the triumphal entry is missing (Jn. 12:13–15; also, Luke has omitted it, cf. Lk. 19:38; but Matthew has added a variation of Mk. 11:9f., ' "Hosanna to the Son of David!" ', Mt. 21:9). In John, however, Moses is the one through whom the God of the Old Testament has (primarily) spoken (Jn. 1:45; 5:46; 9:26; as contrasted to Mk. 12:36; Ac. 1:16; 2:25; 4:25, where God speaks through his servant, David). But most importantly, the Johannine tradition portrays one of the primary reasons for the Jews' ('*Judeans*'?) rejection of Jesus as being their inability to perceive him as fulfilling *their* conception of a *Davidic* Messiah. In John 7:40–44, 52 people respond to Jesus' words dividedly. Some perceive him as 'the Prophet', and some as 'the Christ', but others *err* by objecting:

> How can the Christ come out of Galilee? Has not the scripture said that the Christ will descend *from the seed of David* and will come from *Bethlehem, the village where David was*? ... Search and see for yourself that out of Galilee *no prophet* is to be raised!

The Johannine use of irony is powerfully subtle, yet clear, as to why at least some of the Jews failed to recognize Jesus as the one sent from the Father (cf. Deut. 18:18). To desire a 'king' (like David) represents the abandonment of theocracy (cf. 1 Sam. 8:7ff.), instead of being thankful for the pneumatic/charismatic model of theocracy, following God's promise to raise up prophets like Moses (Deut. 18:15–18). Close parallels apply to the ideological differences between the Petrine and the Johannine understandings of *christocracy*. Thus, among the crowds there was widespread *grumbling* (Jn. 7:12). Some were saying that Jesus was a good man, while others accused him of misleading the people (Jn. 7:12, which was *precisely* the accusation to be made of a false prophet according to Deuteronomy 18:9–12, 20–22). Ironically, in the 'fulfilled words' (Jn. 2:19–22; 12:30–33; 13:19; 18:9, 32), and in the signifying works of Jesus, his divine agency as the prophet like Moses has been confirmed (Deut. 18:22). But, in the expectation of a Mosaic thaumaturge (6:14), the Holy One of God (6:69 — there may also be overtones of a Joshua typology, leading Israel into 'Holy War' against the 'enemies of God'), or a king like David (7:40–44, 52), the crowd, the Jews, some of Jesus' followers, and even his own brothers (7:3–5) fail to recognize Jesus as having been sent by God. According to the paradoxical theology of the evangelist, however, his glory is seen solely in his fleshly humanity (Bultmann, p. 60ff.).

Therefore, the christological aspect of Peter's confession in John 6:69 serves the same function as his refusal to allow the Son of Man to suffer and die in Mark 8:32. In both accounts, Peter not only affirms the miraculous triumph of the Messiah, but implicit is the hope that *the followers of the Messiah would also escape tribulation and be exalted in the end*. The extended discourse in Mark 8:34–38 confirms that the Marcan Jesus understood Peter's implicit concern and confronted it with a call to discipleship which involves the risk of suffering and death:

> If anyone wishes to come after me, let him deny himself, take up his cross, and follow me.
> For whoever wishes to save his life will lose it; but whoever releases his life for my sake and the gospel, will save it. For what does one profit by gaining the entire world in exchange for his soul?
> For whoever is ashamed of me and my words in this sinful and adulterous generation, likewise will the Son of Man be ashamed of him, when he comes with the glory of his Father and with the holy angels.

Besides the obvious parallels to the eschatological ascending (and descending) of the Son of Man

(Jn. 6:62f.), the profitlessness of the flesh (vs. 63) and the paradoxical receiving of life through releasing it (vss. 51–58), the Johannine equivalent to the Marcan Jesus' declaring the cost of discipleship (for the sake of those contemplating abandoning Jesus) is obviated by the context. 1) Even some of Jesus' disciples abandon him and walk with him no more (6:66). 2) Jesus asks if the twelve will abandon him as well (6:67). 3) Peter speaks out for the twelve and affirms that they will stay with him because he is the Davidic, 'Holy One of God', whose everlasting kingdom will be established with miraculous power in Zion (implied, 6:68f.). 4) It is precisely this notion to which the Johannine Jesus objects, and this can be seen in Jesus' response to Peter's confession. Just as the Johannine Jesus rebukes the crowd for experiencing the feeding in keeping with the Synoptic (Petrine) rendition (Jn. 6:26), in vs. 70 Jesus rebukes Peter for implying that as a Davidic thaumaturge he is to set up a kingdom of power on Zion — implying that his followers will be victorious and not suffer. Thus, the christological 'title' used by Peter in Jn. 6:69 is *not* a reference to Jesus' 'holiness'; it is a reference to the 'Holy War' aspirations of the power-based messianism which Jesus rejected in 6:15 and elsewhere in John (18:36).

70. Jesus' response to Peter has often been translated in the interrogative, 'Have I not chosen you, the twelve, and yet ... ?', but a perfectly acceptable rendering of the phrase could also be the declarative, 'I have not chosen (*elected*) you, the twelve, and yet ... '. Put otherwise, 'I have *not* elected you, the twelve, to be spared tribulation unscathed; and that suggestion by one of you betrays the Devil's deception.' Thus, the absence of a Johannine calling narrative. Conversely, as Barrett has pointed out, the emphasis is not on election, but upon *who does the electing* (p. 307). As in Mk. 10:28, Peter's initiative and ready commitment must cede place to the initiative of Jesus (God's agent), who chooses whom he will, and who calls his followers to abandon earthly security in order to be securely bound to Jesus in their faithful responsiveness to his will. Thus, Jesus emphasizes that it is *not they* who have chosen him, but *he* who has chosen them.

This emphasis upon the divine initiative, combined with Jesus' rebuking the second part of Peter's confession (vs. 69) confirms that in vss. 67–71 we have both a revelation scenario and a brief rhetorical (misunderstanding) dialogue. Peter's response to Jesus' initiative is ambivalent. The first part is fully adequate (vs. 68), but the second (vs. 69) comes across as a shift to human initiative, orthodox though it seems. But like the crowd, the Jews, and some disciples, it is now *Peter* who fails the test.

Therefore, the choice between the 'two ways' (vs. 27) entails different variants of the same choice for Jesus' discussants in John 6. The temptation is to seek the 'food' which satisfies for a day, and to forfeit the 'Food' which abides into life eternal. While in each case the 'Bread' is Jesus, the evangelist addresses the greatest weakness of each group with a dramatization of the overarching truism, 'The one who loves his life will lose it, but the one who disregards (releases) his life in this world will retain it into life eternal' (12:25; cf. also *Mk. 8:35*). Therefore, the *crowd* must be willing to look beyond their desire for barley loaves to the Bread which nourishes into eternity; the *Jews* must be willing to de-idolize their rich religious heritage, complete with its manna traditions and the receiving of the Torah as 'bread from heaven', and look to that eternally life-producing Bread which Jesus is, and which God has now given as an eschatological gift of salvation for the world; and, the *disciples* — even those who had believed and received Jesus as the Bread of God — must now ingest the cost of discipleship as the 'bread of suffering' (6:51) and the 'cup of affliction' (18:11), affirming solidarity with Jesus in his death if they hope to be raised with him in the *eschaton*.

While all three of these exhortative motifs would have been intended to strike home within the Johannine audience, and there may even be some indication that three chapters of Johannine Christianity are portrayed by the discussants' concerns, one also gets the impression that the Johannine exhortation rises to a climax in its intensity. To call another to suffer social and religious alienation is one thing; but, to call a disciple to be willing to die for a cause is the ultimate challenge, and this is what underlies Jesus' response to Peter in Mark 8 *and* John 6.

Thus, the motifs of John 6:25–70 and the Matthean interpretation of the Q temptation narrative are entirely parallel. The first temptation is to produce bread out of stones miraculously (Matt. 4:3; cf. Jn. 6:25–31); the second is to do a miraculous sign at the temple in Jerusalem, and thereby command the respect of the (Jewish) world by the assistance of the angels (Matt. 4:5f.; cf. Jn. 6:30–58); and the third temptation is to gain the 'kingdoms of this world' by worshipping the devil, thus forfeiting theocracy (Matt. 4:8f.; cf. Jn. 6:51–70). With these parallels in mind, it is not hard to understand why the tempter in both Matthew 4:5, 8, 11 and in John 6:70 is called *diabolos*. The major difference is that while in the Q narrative Jesus is tempted, in John 6 (cf. esp. *vs. 6*) it is Jesus' discussants who are explicitly tested (as in Mk. 8:11–21, 27–37). The Johannine use of irony is again evident: those who come to Jesus, testing him, find themselves tested ... and they largely fail the test.

71. As in the case of the Matthean confession, an interpolation has been added in order to enhance the portrayal of Peter. The difference, however, is that Matthew 16:17–19 has been added by the First Evangelist, and it contains a prescriptive interpretation of the means by which christocracy ought to occur. On the other hand, the Johannine interpolation is much less theological in its content and seeks only to alleviate the problem of Jesus' calling Peter a devil. Thus, the clarifying gloss in amplified form is: 'Jesus was not referring to the Simon called "Peter" (vs. 67), but actually to *Judas the son of Simon*, Iscariot (cf. 12:4; 13:2, 26), who was *also* one of the twelve, and yet we all know that *this* was the one who was about to betray him (cf. 6:64b).' It may also be the case, although less likely, that the compiler has added the Judas/ betrayal theme (from 12:4) to 6:64b in order to alleviate the harshness of 6:64a. On the other hand, vs. 64b offers understandable justification for a later editor to rectify the tarnished memory of Peter as he has in 21:15–17. This would also be all the more likely if it were the compiler who inserted ch. 6 between chs. 5 and 7. Just as he added 18:1a as a bridge for chs. 15–17 to be inserted more gracefully, he has added 6:71 to 'explain' the harsh words of Jesus to Peter.

Whatever the case, it is probably true that the genre of the final editor's additions was less a series of theological additions and more a cluster of minor clarifications of detail (2:6c; 3:34; 4:9c; 6:64b, 70; 14:22b; 19:35; 21:20b, 23, 24f.) and the translating of Aramaisms into Greek (1:38d, 41c, 42d; 4:25c; 9:7c; 19:13c, 17c; 20:16c). The relatively minor editorial work of the compiler is further demonstrated by the fact that he has allowed several problems regarding sequence and transition (1:1–5/6-8/9–14/15/16–18/19ff.; chs. 5, 6, 7; 14:31/15:1ff., etc.) to stand. These jagged edges within an otherwise fluid text suggest that the compiler (and he was more of a *compiler* than a thorough-goingly reconstructive redactor) sought to preserve — and to clarify at times — the witness of the evangelist. Just as the compiler has clarified that the Judas of 14:22b was *not* Judas Iscariot, in 6:70 he has sought to clarify that the 'Simon' which Jesus rebuked was *not* Simon Peter.

Therefore, the problem rectified by the compiler's interpolation in John 6 was *not* the difficulty of an otherwise unacceptable text which needed a eucharistic section in order to bolster the church's defence of its cultic sacramentology (Bultmann, p. 219f.). He could have done this with *greater clarity and effect* by adding an institution of the eucharist narrative to *ch. 13*, especially if his work also involved the adding of Synoptic-type detail and wording. The primary issue underlying John 6 *never was sacramentology*, but sacramental themes *were* used to highlight the main emphasis of John 6 and the rest of the Gospel: that in Jesus, God has spoken to the world in a way that is life-producing, but one's ability to receive the gift of Life hinges upon one's believing response to the eschatologically present Word of God. Similar moves may be observed in 6:45 and 10:35b, where the sapiential motif and the authority of scripture are co-opted in order to make christological points. The employment of such motifs does not mean that the evangelist was a sapiential enthusiast, a biblical literalist, *or* a rigid sacramentalist. Such conjectures are anachronistic and wrong. Therefore, it was not the lack of eucharistic content which scandalized the compiler, but the apparent defamation of Peter, which was misunderstood.

Obviously, for an audience in the 80's and 90's, in Jesus' sharp response to Peter in vs. 70, it was not simply Peter as a person who was being rebuked, but the perspective he represented which was being corrected. Thus, the acute christological issue within Johannine Christianity at the time of the Gospel's writing was less a matter of getting one's *sachliche* notions about the 'how' and 'what' of Jesus right, and more a manner of clarifying 'who' Jesus is meant to be for the church and the world, and 'by what manner' those who would follow him are to live under his lordship. The primary concern for the evangelist in the writing of the Gospel is not to set forth an orthodox dogma, nor is it to record in literary form the 'historical' account of what Jesus said and did. Rather, it is an ecclesial manifesto which describes the effectual means by which the risen Lord continues to be the shepherd of his flock and the leader of his people, across the boundaries of time and space. It is a matter of *christocracy,* and this is what the compiler failed to see here (although he embraces it elsewhere), as evidenced by his 'clarification' of vs. 70 in vs. 71.

Discussion

Overall, John 6:67–71 has received lighter treatment than the rest of the chapter. This is partially due to the popularity (controversiality) of other sections, and partially due to the somewhat confusing nature of Peter's confession, Jesus' harsh response, and the abrupt introduction of the Judas theme. However, few scholars if any have considered the socio-religious function of vss. 67–71 as the section applies to the immediate audience of 'the disciples' within Johannine Christianity, and it is this topic that most of the following discussion will develop.

By the time of the writing of John 6 (probably in the late 80's-early 90's CE) the issue of physical bread versus spiritual nourishment as a main aspect of Jesus' messianic 'deliverance' had become *tertiary*. Messianic hopes which saw Jesus as a thaumaturgic wonder worker and a political deliverer were either transferred to other such figures after his death, or they were reinterpreted by his followers and modified to form the kerygma of the apostles. The issue of the church-Synagogue separation had become *secondary* by the time second-edition material was added to the Gospel. If Lindars' assessments are correct, that John 9 was a part of the *first* compilation of the Gospel by the evangelist, it would have thus represented an earlier stage in the composition of the Gospel (and Johannine Christianity) than the final form of John 6. And, despite the extensive arguments of J.L. Martyn and others,[5] Jewish persecution of the Christians *did not begin at Jamnia.* Jesus was

---

5 See above, Chapter 9, note 16. This is especially corroborated if Lindars' two-edition hypothesis is correct. If John 6 was added during a second edition, this would mean the situation underlying John 9 would have represented a time *earlier* in the history of Johannine Christianity than the situation underlying John 6. This is also corroborated by the apparent progression from debates with the Synagogue to debates with Docetists in the Johannine epistles, the letters of Ignatius, and the situation represented by John 6. For a fuller argumentation of this possibility, see P.N. Anderson, 'The *Sitz im Leben* of the Johannine Bread of Life Discourse and its Evolving Context', presented in the 1993 SNTS Johannine Literature Seminar, to be published in 1996 in a collection of essays on John 6 by E.J. Brill.

executed as a blasphemer by the Jewish leadership (with the help of the Romans) in the early 30's, and after the death of Stephen in the mid-late 30's a 'second wave of persecution' broke out (Ac. 8:1ff.). The *Birkat ha-Minim* in the later part of the century was merely a formalization of what some rigourist Jews had held for two generations or more, that Christians were heretics and ought to be rooted out if Israel were to receive the full blessing of God. Therefore, the debate with the Jews in John 6 (contra Martyn's critique of Borgen's monograph, cf. above Chapter 3, note 5) reflects not a 'heated' and current debate within Johannine Christianity, but a 'cooled' debate with the Synagogue, which by the time of its completed writing was probably less controversial and safe to handle. The *primary and acute* internal issue underlying the Johannine situation at the time of the writing of John 6, however, was that its familial model of church organization had been overstressed by internal centrifugal pressures, and now even some of the faithful were tempted to abandon the community of faith. As a reflection of the need to address this problem, the call to abiding perseverance and faithfulness may be heard throughout the later strata of the Johannine writings. John 6 is no exception.

The means by which the evangelist attempts to confront these centrifugal pressures is the same method which had been effective for an entire generation or more: to appeal to believers' love for Christ and one another, and to call for *unity* within the 'family' of faith. However, these centripetal measures are only as effective as the personal appeal of the evangelist. But with his increasing age, the passing away of the 'eye-witness' generation, more appealing expressions of Christianity elsewhere, competing heterodox groups, increasing persecution from Roman authorities during the reign of Domitian, lingering antipathy from Jewish groups, and pressures felt from mainstream (Jerusalocentric, Antiochine or Roman) Christians seeking to 'centralize' the Christian movement, the evangelist has sought not only to tell his own story of Jesus in order to say: 'This is what happened.' Rather, as a reflective and dialectical thinker, the evangelist has sought to articulate in written form his understanding of the kind of theocracy Jesus came to bring originally, and to provide an outline for the way the risen Christ should continue to lead his people. Ideologically, it is a matter of christocracy — the effectual means by which the risen Christ continues to nourish and shepherd his flock. This is outlined more fully in John 15–17.

Therefore, some of the aspects underlying the evangelist's interests at the time of his writing John 6 may be identified in the following ways: a) John 6:67–70 (combined with 19:26f. and 20:21–23) is to Johannine Christianity what Matthew 16:17–19 is to Matthean Christianity: an advocating of a particular model of christocracy. b) The juxtaposition of Peter and the Beloved Disciple in John is not simply a matter of competing personalities, or even traditions (primarily). Rather, it reflects a fundamental difference in ideology between later Johannine and later Petrine understandings of what christocracy ought to look like and how it ought to operate. c) The most acute problem with docetic inclinations in the late first century was not primarily that people believed the 'wrong' things about Jesus, but that they assumed if he really did not suffer and die, they might not have to either. Wrong belief was, of course, the way the root of the problem was identified. But these notions themselves probably did not call for corrective action until people began to *act upon their beliefs*: abandoning the community of faith (and their loyalty to Christ) and encouraging others to do the same (thus, the 'deceivers' of 1 Jn. 4:1–3). d) The christological unity and disunity of John is not due to redactors disagreeing with and editing earlier sources. It betrays the reflection of an early Christian thinker who, in facing each new situation, must reconcile the tensions between his perceived and experienced realities in ways coherent with his christocentric understanding of truth. While all of these topics cannot be explored fully in this chapter,[6] the first and the fourth will be developed concisely.

1. The Fourth Evangelist's acute ecclesial interests must be understood *in the context of intramural tensions between Johannine Christianity and the mainstream church*. R.E. Brown has identified five correlations between Matthew 16:17–19 and the rest of John (p. 302), but he does not develop the implications of these (and other) connections. As these connections with the Matthean institution of Peter are examined, it becomes clear that one of the acute tensions within Johannine Christianity around the time of the writing of John 6 is with Petrine ecclesiology, and in particular, the model of christocracy found in its latest stages represented by Matthew 16:17–19. These tensions cannot really be considered 'polemical', as they are more subtle than John's clear 'us/them' treatment of the followers of John the Baptist (Jn. 3:26, 30; or versus *Apollos*? cf. Ac. 19:1–6→Jn. 3:5–8) and 'the Jews' (Jn. 10:34b, etc.). Two explanations of this subtlety are that, a) Antiochine Christians would not have been considered 'them' quite so easily, but would still have been regarded as the larger family of faith; and b) as the tensions would have been current, the conflict-avoidance inclinations of the evangelist may have influenced his intramural and subtle approach to his perceived threat — a misrepresentation of the authentic means by which the post-resurrection Christ was to lead his people. Therefore, these tensions are more dialectical than polemical, and this is the historical situation inferred by E. Käsemann (*Testament*, p. 39f.):

---

6 See P.N. Anderson, 'Was the Fourth Evangelist a Quaker?' (*QRT* #76, Vol. 25, No. 2, 1991, pp. 27–43), which develops more fully the later ideological stages of the Johannine tradition, as contrasted dialectically to the later stages of the 'Petrine' tradition. The Fourth Evangelist was not solely concerned to correct the institutional model of christocracy which was evolving into a model parallel to Judaism in the late first century, but he was also concerned to develop his own understanding of the way the risen Christ ought to continue to be the Shepherd of the flock and spiritual leader of the community of faith. This pneumatic view of christocracy involves a) *worship* (which is in Spirit and in Truth, not confined to region or custom), b) *agapeic ministry* (*kenotic* love is the trademark of all discipleship), c) *sacramental fellowship* (which is present within the gathered community of faith — there it is that the work of the *Paraklētos* is encountered most fully), d) *universal apostolicity of believers* (to encounter the risen Christ through faith is to be called as a witness to this

We have seen how our assumption of John's historical position throws light upon his christology. The difficulties of his ecclesiology and the peculiar dialectical relation to tradition can also be more thoroughly understood on the basis of our assumption. The man who lives on the fringe of the prevailing development of the Church can oppose its trends and simultaneously be subjected to them, as his very reaction shows. ... By contradicting the present in his faithfulness to the past, he is already contributing to the scaffolding of the future.

Representatives of both Petrine and Johannine ecclesiologies were most likely involved in a series of ongoing dialogues about the best way to run the church (cf. above, Chapter 7, note 22, esp. f and g). These dialectical tensions may be seen in clear relief against the backdrop of the Matthean addition to Peter's confession, as its tenets are contrasted with their parallel equivalents in John.

From Matthew's reformulation of Mark 8:27–38, the most modest inferences to be drawn are that by the time of Matthew's redaction of Mark: a) The use of formulary references to Christ had proliferated, suggesting Matthew's christology had become more elevated than Mark's (cf. Jn. 1:49; 11:27; 20:31). b) The audience of Matthew's rendition would have been more internal (to the 'disciples') than Mark's (cf. Jn. 6:60–70). c) And (Simon) Peter's role is magnified, both in its favourable and unfavourable aspects (cf. Jn. 6:67–70; 13:6–10; 21:15–17). Parallel developments can be inferred in the Johannine tradition, and these themes are even more accentuated in the Matthean interpolation of 16:17–19.

The primary concern of the Matthean addition to the confession narrative is to establish the christocratic foundation of the church. In other words, Matthew 16:17–19 is not solely concerned with the succession of Peter, *but the succession of Jesus*. The parallels between these verses and Nathan's blessing upon David and his everlasting throne are not incidental (cf. 2 Sam. 7:4–16). In both cases the prophetic/institutional means is established through which God will shepherd his people. The blessing of (*makarios*, Matt. 16:17) Peter serves the sociological function of imbuing the institutional leadership of the church with the 'authority' of the charismatic leadership of Jesus. The Matthean institution narrative was added to a written gospel within a few years after Peter's martyrdom, and given Peter's indelible influence upon the nascent Christian movement, it is understandable how Matthean Christianity would have wanted to preserve his leadership and ministry in institutional form. Thus, as the proclamation of Jesus' 'gospel' was to the post-resurrection church, so was the preservation of the ministries of the apostles to the sub-apostolic generation. However, despite this sociological function, the christocratic thrust is clear: the means by which Christ will continue to lead the church is through Peter (and his successors), and against it (them) the gates of Hades shall not prevail.

---

transforming reality), and e) *the authority of truth* (the greatest authority is not human might but the convincing power of truth, and Jesus' kingdom is one of truth).

While Brown is correct in his identification of parallels between the Matthean institution narrative and themes in John, he has failed to note that the same issue, christocracy, is also the primary concern of these passages — and of much of John's christology. However, John's christocratic model differs radically from the Matthean, and this will be illustrated by a comparison/contrast between the main themes in Matthew 16:17–19 and their parallel equivalents in John.

a) Peter is 'blessed' in Matthew 16:17 because he has made the 'correct' (inspired?) christological confession: whereas in John the two macarisms occur in conjunction with believing *without* having seen (20:29), and with *doing* service for others after the example of Jesus (13:17). The John 13 macarism is especially relevant to Matthew 16:17–19. In the Matthean passage Jesus' blessing is unconditional, but not in the Johannine. In John 13:17 one is only blessed if one *does* the things Jesus has modelled, and this follows directly upon Peter's exaggerated response to Jesus' washing of his feet. The instructive point being made, using Johannine irony effectively, is that leadership after the example of Jesus involves *serving* one another. That this theme is levelled at the kind of leadership Peter represents is suggested clearly by vs. 16, 'Truly, truly I say to you, the servant is not greater than his master (*kuriou*), neither is the *apostle* (*apostolos*) greater than the one who sent him'. Just as the Matthean blessing of Peter as the successor of Jesus served to install an institutional means of apostolic succession for one segment of sub-apostolic Christianity, the Johannine blessing of the *doer* of ministry after the kenotic example of Jesus provides a corrective to any 'apostles' who might consider themselves *above their Lord* — let alone other disciples.[7]

b) Whereas in the Matthean tradition the model confession is made by Peter, in John it is made by Martha (a *woman*, 11:27). In general, the treatment of women in John is more elevated than in Matthew. This is illustrated by the fact that the Samaritan woman becomes a follower of Jesus and even an 'apostle to the Samaritans' (Jn. 4:7–42); Martha's sister Mary has the 'honour' of serving Jesus as she anoints his feet (cf. 12:1–8— 13:14); Mary is more than simply the mother of baby Jesus (she inaugurates his first miracle and is present at the cross); and Mary Magdalene is the *first* one to whom the resurrected Jesus appears (20:14–16), whereby she becomes the 'apostle to the apostles'.[8]

---

7 According to G.F. Snyder ('John 13:16 and the Anti-Petrinism of the Johannine Tradition', *BR* 16, 1971, pp. 5–15), John 13:2–17 must be taken as a literary unity, and its 'anti-Petrinism' is not *ad hominem*, but it ' ... is a direct attack on both Gnostic and Orthodox understanding[s] of ... apostleship' (p. 15). In John, Petrine apostolicity threatens christocentricity.

8 While the only 'ordinance' of John (13:14, the footwashing) is meant to be taken in the exemplary sense, not in the ritualistic sense, nonetheless, S.M. Schneiders (*op. cit.*) has suggested that Mary was portrayed as administering the 'sacrament of footwashing' to Jesus in Jn. 12:1–8 (pp. 43–45). See also R.E. Brown, *Community*, p. 190, n. 336; and J.A. Grassi, 'The Role of Jesus' Mother in John's Gospel: A Reappraisal', *CBQ* 48, 1986, pp. 67–80. John's portrayal of women even bolsters the historicity of its tradition.

c) While Peter is called *Simōn Bariōna ... Petros* in Matthew 16:17f., and *Simōn ho huois Iōannou ... Kēphas Petros* in John 1:42, the confession of faith in John 1:49 is reserved for Nathanael, *not* one of the twelve, and Peter is only present in the narrative as the brother that *Andrew* brings to Jesus (Jn. 1:40f.). In fact, Peter never appears in the Johannine narrative as an actor until his ambiguous confession in 6:68f. and not again until his overstated humility in ch. 13. Neither Peter nor any other of the disciples is explicitly called by Jesus in John, but one gets the impression that the twelve are simply the remnant of those who do not defect (6:66f.). See also John 21:15–17 for Jesus' threefold pastoral correcting of 'Simon, son of Jonas'. True discipleship and pastoral service in John is based on a transforming encounter with Jesus, rather than position or privilege. Thus, the juxtaposition of Peter and the Beloved Disciple in John has more to do with conflicting ideologies than personalities.

d) Indeed, flesh and blood (*sarx kai haima*) have not revealed the content of such a confession to Peter, but 'my Father who is in the heavens', according to Matthew (16:16f.); yet according to John 1:9, Jesus is the True Light which enlightens *everyone coming into the world*, and the Gospel witnesses to all members of its audience that 'Jesus is the Christ, the Son of God, in order that believing, you might have life in his name' (20:31). *All who believe* are given the authority (*exousian*) to become the children of God, and it is this spiritual birth (cf. 3:3), not the ability to make a formulary confession, which is considered of divine origin rather than the will of flesh and blood (*ouk ex haimatōn oude ek thelēmatos sarkos*, Jn. 1:12f.). Furthermore, *adhering* to the life-giving words of the Johannine Jesus and *solidarity* with him in the Johannine 'family', comprise the antithesis of the profitless 'flesh' in John 6:63. It is coming to, abiding in, and staying with Jesus which requires divine enablement,[9] and in John 6 *this* is considered the 'way of life' (vs. 27).

e) In Matthew 16:18 Peter (his confession?) serves as the foundational rock (*tē petra*) upon which the church is to be built, and against which the gates of Hades shall not prevail. This is not a reference to the spiritual victory of the church over demonic forces, but is rather a post-mortem eulogizing of one (Peter) whose memory will extend beyond the grave (as in Jb. 38:17 and Is. 38:10) by means of the institution founded upon his name. The Johannine equivalent is 21:15–19, and here Peter's memory is also preserved-and-rectified by means of a threefold confession following Peter's threefold denial (18:15–18, 25–27; around a 'char-

---

9 The statements in John 6 which refer to the necessity of the Father's 'drawing' in order for people to 'come to' Jesus (vss. 44, 65) are not references to predeterminism. They are references to the anthropological condition (Jn. 1:18) of needing divine enablement for perceiving the initiating 'word' of God, as well as responding to it. There is a dialectical tension between the initiative (sovereignty) of God and human responsiveness (responsibility), which are intrinsic components of the human-divine dialogue. On one hand, no one can come without the Father's drawing; on the other, *all* who receive the Son are given the authority to become the children of God, as many as believe on his name (Jn. 1:12).

coal fire', *anthrakian*, 18:18; 21:9). As in the case of the Matthean interpolation, John 21 represents a later stratum of the evangelist's tradition which preserves the memory of Peter as a disciple of central importance. However, it is not so much the reinstatement of Peter as 'head' of the church, as the chiding of Peter and the correcting of his (other pastoral leaders'?) failure(s) to live up to leadership (shepherding) responsibilities. It is no accident that in the Johannine gospel narrative, between Jesus' 'parable' of the unfaithful hireling shepherd (Jn. 10: 12f.) and his threefold injunction to feed-shepherd-feed (*boske-poimaine-boske*) Jesus' lambs-sheep-sheep, is the death of the Good Shepherd on the cross (cf. 10:11) in ch. 19, at which Peter is *nowhere to be found*. Therefore, John 21:15–17 only partially rectifies Peter's portrayal as the disciple of primacy. Far from simply being a reinstatement of his authoritative position, this is Peter's proverbial 'hour in the woodshed' in which he (and all who would follow in his wake) is chided for a lack of exercising sacrificial love for Jesus and his flock. This was demonstrated by his unfaithful example in chs. 18 and 19 and by his lingering lack of comprehending *agapē* love in 21:15–17. The Johannine interest, however, is not to demean Peter as a person, but to point to *Jesus* as the True and Good Shepherd, whose voice is known by all members of the flock. It even extends to sheep 'not of this fold'. Regarding christocracy, John makes it bluntly clear that while some (including such leaders as Diotrephes? cf. 3 Jn. 9f., etc.) may have been entrusted with shepherding responsibilities, there is but *one* Shepherd of the flock, *Jesus*, and that he will continue to lead, guide, instruct, and care for his fold through the pneumatically-mediated work of the *Paraklētos*. Even the images of 'rock' (Matt. 16:17) versus 'flock' (10:16) and 'vine' (15:1–5) are suggestive of static/dynamic differences in Matthean and Johannine understandings of the structural means by which this christocratic activity is to take place.

The same kinds of tensions between the Jewish-Christian 'episcopal', and the Gentile-Christian 'presbyterian' models of church government, as confronted by Paul, are evident in the prototype of the Beloved Disciple juxtaposed to Peter in John. It represents the last stages of the ideological differences between the Petrine and Johannine traditions, before they were written down in what later become canonical writings, which contributes to the obfuscation of otherwise incisive distinctions.

f) In Matthew 16:19a Jesus gives Peter the *keys of the Kingdom of the Heavens*, but in John 19:26f. the Beloved Disciple is entrusted with the care of *the mother of Jesus*. These two 'entrustments' serve identical functions within their respective segments of developing Christianity. Jesus is portrayed as handing over what is most dear to the sacred entrustment of his leading disciple, with the implication that Jesus' redemptive activity in the world will continue to go forward by means of the ministries of those who succeed him. Again, the difference in that which is entrusted to Jesus' successors is striking. The keys of the Kingdom of the Heavens is an *instrumental* image associated with *power*. The mother of Jesus is a *familial* image associated with *relationships*. In the contrast between these two images the differences between Petrine and Johannine christocracy models are projected in sharp relief. The entrustment of the keys of the Kingdom of the Heavens to Peter is the archetype of an *institutional* model of church government, while the entrustment of the mother of Jesus to the Beloved Disciple is the archetype of a *familial* model. In other words, the 'basileic currency' of the institutional model is *power* within a hierarchy, while within the familial model it is *love* within an egalitarian community.

The parallels between these tensions and those between Samuel's school of the prophets and the establishment of Israel's monarchy are plentiful. As a comfort to the grieving Samuel, Yahweh says, 'It is not you they have rejected, but they have rejected *me as their king*' (1 Sam. 8:7). Therefore, just as Yahweh gave his children the 'flesh they crave', when manna would have been enough (causing them illness and death, cf. Nu. 11:4–20), so he gave them the monarchy they craved, even though it was not his first choice for them, nor was it necessarily in their interest (Deut. 18:15–18; Nu. 11:29; 1 Sam. 8:8–22). These tensions quite possibly had their roots in earlier stages of the Petrine and Johannine traditions, and this may account for the Johannine emphasis on prophet/teacher christological motifs, combined with the dearth of (antipathy to?) Davidic imagery in John. However, it is not until the approaching death of the Beloved Disciple and the prospect of the absence of his centripetal influence on the community's viability that the threat of institutionalizing trends, seeking to make Christianity a viable alternative to the more established Judaism, becomes *acute*.

g) In Matthew 16:19b it becomes clear what kind of authority the keeper of the keys has been granted: it is the authority to bind (*dēsēs*) and to loose (*lusēs*) on earth, with the understanding that the same will be granted in heaven. The meaning of this passage may be taken in a twofold sense, involving matters of faith (institutional doctrine or policy?) and the forgiveness of sins. The fact that the echo of this phrase may also be found in Matthew 18:18, sandwiched between the passages on accountability (vss. 10–17) and the need for (*Peter's*) forgivingness (vss. 21–35) suggests that some corrective to the potential abuses of divine-right binding and loosing in the name of Peter may already have been posed as a balance to 16:19b within Matthean Christianity. These may even represent Matthean adjustments to Johannine (oral) critique, though this cannot be demonstrated. John, however, deals with the matter more directly. The authority to forgive sins is not withheld for one disciple alone and those who follow after him, but it is granted to *all the disciples* by the Johannine Jesus: 'If you (plural) forgive the sins of any, they are forgiven; if you retain any, they are retained' (20:23). However, in terms of the binding and releasing, regarding matters of faith or the making of decisions (cf. Matt. 18:19), the Johannine corrective is all the more striking. Not only is the Johannine Jesus hailed as the only one who has the words of eternal life, but (in juxtaposition to Matt. 16:17–19) the '*reinstatement of Jesus*' is heralded by none other than *Peter*. Therefore, the *Leitmotif* of John 6:68 is the 'returning of the keys of the kingdom to Jesus' by means of Peter's implicitly deconstructive and explicitly reconstructive confession: 'Lord, to whom shall we go? *You* (alone) *have the words of eternal life'.*[10]

Table 20:

'Matthew 16:17–19 and its "Christocratic Correctives" in John'

Matthew 16:17–19	John
a) Peter, the 'chief of the apostles', is 'blessed' (vs.17) for making the correct (inspired?) confession.	Jesus commissions *all* of his followers — just as the Father has sent him (21:21f.); and 'blessedness' results from *serving* one another (13:17) and from *believing* without having seen Jesus' signs (20:29).
b) The model confession is made by a man — Peter (vs.17) — one of the twelve.	The model confession is made by Martha — *a woman* (11:27) — and is reiterated by the evangelist climactically (20:31). The first confession is made by Nathanael — *not* one of the twelve (1:49 — of Mt.).
c) *Simōn Bariōna ... Petros* (vs.17f.) is 'named' by Jesus as chief of the apostles, apparently having been called first (Matt. 4:18ff.).	*Simōn ho huios Iōannou ... Kēphas ... Petros* (1:42) is 'named' by Jesus, having been brought to Jesus by Andrew (1:40f.); and *Simōn Iōannou* is exhorted thrice by Jesus regarding *the character of agapeic shepherding* (21:15–17).
d) 'Flesh and blood' have not revealed the content of Peter's confession, but the heavenly Father (vs.17).	That which is of divine origin — not of flesh and blood, nor of human intentionality — is the authority to become the 'children of God', available to *all who believe* in the Son (1:12f.).
e) Peter (his confession?) becomes the foundation rock (*tē petra*) upon which the church will be established (vs.18). Oblivion (the 'Gates of Hades') will not prevail against the absence of Peter's ministry. His legacy and memory will continue.	John's models for the church are more fluid ('flock', 10:16; 'vine', 15:1ff.), and the permanence of church vitality is insured by the sending of the *Paraklētos* (chs.14–16). The *Holy Spirit* will bring to remembrance all that Jesus has taught in his (*and* the Beloved Disciple's, 21:23) absence (16:14f.).
f) Jesus imparts to Peter instrumental 'keys of the Kingdom of the Heavens' (vs.19a), suggesting an institutional model of church government.	Jesus entrusts the Beloved Disciple with his mother (19:26f.) — *a relational image*, suggesting a familial model for the church, and portrays Peter as 'returning' authority to Jesus (where it implicitly belonged all along, 6:68f.).
g) Jesus imbues Peter (and those who succeed him) with the spiritual authority to 'bind' and 'loose', affirming that the same will be 'bound' and 'loosed' in heaven (vs.19b).	Jesus fills (all) his followers with the Holy Spirit and promises that any sins they forgive or retain will be forgiven or retained accordingly (20:22f.). Apostolic inclusivity entails priestly responsibility.

---

10 Just as the confession of Peter in Matthew serves as more than a concise statement of faith

2. As well as being engaged in dialogue with other groups internal and external to Christianity, *the Fourth Evangelist also has his own agenda to advance*. It is for this reason that his internal method of dialectical thought — as it relates to the evangelist's external method of rhetorical engagement — must be considered. It relates centrally to John's christological unity and disunity. While some of John's christological unity and disunity *may* be attributed to the evangelist's addressing of particular concerns relevant to Johannine Christianity, not all of them can be. This may be illustrated by comparing and contrasting the method of dealing with socio-religious threats within John 6 and within the Johannine Epistles. While entire continuity cannot be assumed between the situations of the evangelist and the Epistle-writer, one can at least assume the situations underlying the Johannine Gospel and Epistles are similar. Therefore, regarding three particular crises faced by Johannine Christianity, a comparison between John 6 and 1, 2 and 3 John will throw the dialectical christology of the evangelist into sharp relief.

a) The first threat common to John 6 and 1 John is the set of problems associated with Christian Jews becoming Jewish Christians.[11] They are called 'di-theists' by members of the Synagogue, and the crisis faced by these Christians is that they were excommunicated from the very Judaism of which they understood Jesus to be the fulfilling Messiah. Apparently, some of these Jewish converts to Christianity had been persuaded by Jewish leaders that Jesus was not the Christ, or if he was, that he was subordinate to the Father. According to 1 John 2:19, a group of them had already lapsed back into Judaism, and the Epistle-writer deals with this loss on a Stage 3 (*Synthetic-Conventional*) level of faith development. He 'explains' their departure as a function of their never having *really* 'belonged to us' (vs.19b). The 'party platform' is hardened as the Epistle-writer poses the 'litmus test' of faith: 'Who is a liar? It is the one who denies that Jesus is the Christ. Such a person is the antichrist (because) he denies the Father and the Son' (vs. 22). On the positive side, 'to remain in the Son is also to remain in the Father, and the result of this is eternal life (vss. 23–25). This was obviously a Jewish/Christian schism, and the Epistle-writer has confronted it with an either-or approach to orthodox faith.

As a contrast, the evangelist co-opts Jewish Christian members of his audience by means of 'engaging them in dialogue' with the Johannine Jesus. In John 6:30–

(it allows the Mattean Jesus to imbue Peter — and those who follow in his wake — with vicarious authority), the same is true for John. In both cases, Peter's confession serves the function of establishing the means by which the departed Jesus will continue to be present with his followers. The model of christocracy according to Matthew is based on an institutional model, while the Johannine is based on a familial model. Both claim to have been in keeping with the will of Jesus, and there must have been a series of ideological tensions between advocates of both models, especially in the late first century (see Tables 20 and 21).

11 Although he is reluctant to interpret the Johannine Gospel alongside the Epistles, J.L. Martyn's analysis of this process is most enlightening (along with Brown's). See also D. Rensberger's extension of Martyn's thesis in his *Johannine Faith and Liberating Community*, Philadelphia, 1988.

50 the Johannine Jesus confronts the Jews' adherence to Moses and the Torah by exposing their idolatry, 'exegeting' the human situation, and upholding the original vision of Judaism. Therefore, Jesus overturns their exegesis (vs. 32) and points out that those who called Christians '*di*-theists' are actually '*a*-theists'. They had placed their own traditions before the place of the Living God of Israel, and that is idolatry. 'It is *not* Moses who gave, but my Father who *gives* you the true bread from heaven.'

Next he upholds as the original vision of Judaism the notion that *all* should be 'taught by God' (vs. 45, cf. Is. 54:13 and Nu. 11:29). This challenges centrally a Stage 3 (*Synthetic-Conventional*) understanding of the Jewish faith, which uses the fear of excommunication as a source of negative motivation, and which confines the more universal truths of the Torah to a set of 'purity laws'.[12] As a corrective, Jesus raises an interpretation of the original yearning of Moses (Nu. 11:29), 'If only *all Yahweh's people* were prophets, and that Yahweh would put his Spirit upon them!'[13] As a contrast to conventional Jewish religion of the time, the religion of Jesus excludes no one who comes to him (Jn. 6:37), and those who are learning from the Father already, recognize the Father's Truth in his teaching (vs. 45b). Finally, Jesus explains the reason for the need to be drawn to God (vs. 46). It is not because of God's aloofness that the Father must send the Son (and in this respect the Johannine agency christology differs radically from the Gnostic Redeemer-myth), but because of the basic conundrum of the anthropological situation: '*No one has seen God at any time!*' (Jn. 1:18). However, the one who is 'from God' has seen the Father (Jn. 6:46), and while the Jews search the scriptures (Jn. 5:39), *he* 'exegetes the Father' to the world (Jn. 1:18). This represents a Stage 5 (*Conjunctive*) level of faith which at times may reach a Stage 6 (*Universalizing*) level. It understands that God's Truth is beyond any finite comprehension of it, and yet, this is the very Truth which demands utter loyalty, even unto death.

b) The second crisis alluded to in the Epistles *and* in John 6 is the threat of docetising Christians who, out of refusing to believe that Jesus suffered and died, refuse also the calling to suffer for their Lord is the face of persecution. The crisis

---

12 See J.K. Riches, *Jesus and the Transformation of Judaism*, Edinburgh, 1980, esp. pp. 112–144. In the respect that Jesus is here teaching that all people, in coming to him, may be taught of God, and that one's relationship with God is to be based on love rather than fear, these are the sort of things the historical Jesus may indeed have said. In fact, regarding various other aspects of John's portrayal of Jesus (such as the prophet of Deut. 18 and the messenger of Malachi 3, and as one who emphasizes the love of the Father as central to his coming, etc.) seems very close to the sort of portrait of Jesus emerging from the 'third quest for the historical Jesus' and the Jesus Seminar. Allow for Johannine paraphrase, an independent tradition and several decades of oral rendering within an Asia Minor setting, and the bulk of John's content appears remarkably authentic.

13 John not only has a prophet/agent christology, but also a prophet/agent pneumatology and 'mathēteology'. The original yearning and vision of Moses is for there to be not just one, nor just a handful of prophets, but that *all* should be taught by the Lord (Nu. 11:29). The Johannine Jesus shares this concern (Jn. 6:45).

alluded to in 1 John 4:1–3 is *not* the same one described in 1 John 2:18–25. Just as the epistles of Ignatius betray two distinct threats (Judaizers and docetising Christians, cf. above, Chapter 6, note 11), the same two threats (and a chronological distinction between them) may be inferred from 1 and 2 John and John 6. Whereas those who refuse to believe that Jesus is the Jewish Messiah have already 'gone out from us' in 1 John 2:18ff., the second threat is still on the rise. Thus the Elder sounds the alarm and describes how to recognize it: those who refuse to acknowledge that Jesus Christ has 'come in the flesh' (1 Jn. 4:2f.). They represent the spirit of the antichrist (of which there are *many*, cf. 1 Jn. 2:18), ' ... which you have heard is coming and *even now* is in the world' (1 Jn. 4:3). However, by the time 2 John is written, converts of this second antichristic threat have also departed, and the Epistle-writer seems to be lamenting their departure: 'Many deceivers, who do not acknowledge Jesus as coming in the flesh, have departed (*exēlthon*) into the world. A person like these is a deceiver and the antichrist.' (2 Jn. 7) Again, the way the Epistle-writer addresses this second group is completely different from the way the evangelist does. The Epistle-writer operates on a Stage 3 level of faith: 'We are right; they are wrong!' This attitude represents the mentality of a sect, seeking to maintain itself, rather than the confidence of a dialectical thinker, exploring the truth he has encountered in Christ.

In John 6, however, the evangelist employs a *Conjunctive* (Stage 5) approach to the docetic problem. Rather than labelling potential lapsees or their leaders as 'deceivers' or as 'antichrists' (*the Jews* had called Jesus 'a deceiver' and 'demon-possessed', cf. Jn. 7:12, 20; 8:48, 52), the evangelist exposes the true cost of discipleship. To be a follower of Jesus is to adhere to him in his death (to ingest his 'flesh-and-blood-ness') if one expects to be raised with him in the *eschaton*. Schnelle's observation about the evangelist's choice of eucharistic imagery in order to drive this point home is significant.[14] Just as the evangelist has hit the Judaizers at their places of greatest vulnerability (rightly exegeting and following the Torah, Moses and the Father), the evangelist has targeted one of the most vulnerable aspects of docetising tendencies: their abhorrence of the eucharist. This is not, however, to say that his final goal, or even his preliminary concern, was to motivate people to take the eucharist as though this would have been the only way to receive eternal life. It is also anachronistic to assume that Johannine cultic practice accommodated a *symbolic* meal of commemoration at this time, rather than *actual* fellowship meals. Rather, the use of eucharistic imagery by the evangelist jolts

---

14 U. Schnelle, 'Excurs: Was ist Doketismus', in his *Antidoketische Christologie im Johannesevangelium*, Göttingen, 1987, pp. 76–83. Schnelle points out that one aspect of docetism was the fact that its adherents refused to believe that the eucharist was really the flesh and blood of Jesus (cf. Ignatius). Therefore, it stands to reason that the Fourth Evangelist would have used the eucharist as a provocative test of their faith. There is a difference, however, between using eucharistic imagery as provocation and raising it as a soteriological requirement. It seems the evangelist is employing eucharistic imagery more semeiotically than legalistically or instrumentally. Sacramentality for John is *incarnational.*

docetising members of his audience into facing the harsh reality that the *only* road to life eternal involves 'the way of the cross'.

c) The third threat alluded to in both the Johannine Epistles and John 6 is less explicit, but every bit as real. It assumes that 3 John 9f. represents at least something of a problem faced by later Johannine Christianity, and that there may be a connection between the Johannine version of Peter's confession and an understanding of christocracy — the acute source of dialectical tension with other Christian groups. In 3 John 9f. 'the Elder' accuses Diotrephes *not* of being a schismatic or a secessionist, but of *wielding his authority* in a heavy-handed manner. He 'loves to be *first*' (loves primacy?), 'refuses to welcome the brethren', and he 'casts out of the "church" ' any who are willing to take them in. This scenario implies that Johannine Christians may have (at least sometimes) found themselves on the *outside* of centralizing measures employed by the institutionalizing church! The fact that the word, *ekklēsia* occurs *only* in the gospels at the references to Peter and his authority in Matthew 16:18 and 18:17, and only in the Johannine Gospel and Epistles in 3 John (6, 9 and 10) is highly significant. By this time the formative community had become 'the church', and not long after his death the authority of Peter had soon become well established as the 'keeper of the keys' and the 'protector of the kingdom' against heretical threats. The writer of 3 John does not polemicize against Diotrephes and his kin (probably because he identifies him and others like him as allies, rather than adversaries), but he simply seeks to encourage those who had been discouraged by such 'cool' welcomes.

The evangelist, by contrast, offers a corrective which is more than pastoral. It is a radical assault on the ideological basis for such problems, resulting from the abuse of Peter's authority and a fundamental misunderstanding of the kind of theocracy Jesus came to restore to Israel. It is not the theocracy of earthly kingdoms, founded on Zion and enforced with a new set of codes and purity laws. This would be the kind of Stage 3 approach to religion from which Jesus came to deliver the true Israelites (the people of vision, cf. Philo, *Mut.* 258; Jn. 1:47). Rather, the theocracy which Jesus came to bring historically was probably more akin to the apostolic ministry of the Mosaic prophet, who speaks only what God has commanded (Deut. 18:15–18), thereby calling Israel to be taught by God (Is. 54:13) and to be stewards of the prophetic word themselves (Nu. 11:29). Therefore, by portraying Peter as returning authority to Jesus, the apostolic commission becomes available to *all* followers of Jesus, and *not* just Peter, or even the Beloved Disciple. As the Father sends him, so Jesus sends his *followers*, endows *them* (plural!) with the Holy Spirit and gives *them* (plural!) the authority to forgive ('release') people's sins (Jn. 20:21–23). The dialectical tension represented here is not merely the Corinthian *charisma* versus *exousia* debate; it represents the Johannine equivalent to Paul's appeal (against Cephas and 'Super Apostles' cf. 2 Cor.) to *transforming encounter with the risen Christ* as the *only* basis for apostolicity. Therefore, the true succession of Jesus *is* represented by Peter's confession in John. In contradistinction to institutionalizing tendencies in the main body of the church, however, apostolic succession comes not through an office, nor a hierarchical position. It results from a christocentric encounter with the living God, and it is epitomized by the confession, 'To whom shall we go, Lord? *You* (alone) have the words of eternal life!'[15]

Table 21:
'Three Acute Intramural Crises Faced by Johannine Christianity'

Extramural events affecting Johannine Christianity	Intramural crises faced by Johannine Christianity	Evidence in Johannine literature and elsewhere
Crisis # 1: Tensions with the Local Synagogue: 55–85 CE		
46–70 The Gospel comes to Asia Minor — Paul 'lectures' to 'the Jews', travels with Priscilla, Aquilla, Gaius and Aristarchus, etc. Apollos and co. also join the mission to the Jews.	Many Jews are convinced and become followers of 'the Way', but others were offended and maligned 'the Way'. As the evangelist joins the work, he brings along an independent Jesus tradition of Palestinian origin.	Ac. 18:18–19:20. Pauline traces in 1 Jn. 2:2 (*hilasmos*); 2 Jn. 1 (women in leadership); 3 Jn. 1. Many similarities exist between Johannine and Pauline theology.
70–80 Post Temple Judaism undergoes something like a fundamentalist shift—power shifts from Temple Sadducees to the Torah and the Pharisees. Jesus does not fit into their 'scriptural' view of salvation.	Already strained relations with the Synagogue become more acute, and pressure is brought to bear on Christian Jews. This causes some to leave the Synagogue, while some become cryptic.	See Nicodemus (Jn. 3), debates with 'the Jews' (Jn. 5,7,8 and 9), John the Baptist and signs-rhetoric, and various *marturia* motifs (esp. Jn. 5:36–40; see also Re.2:9f.). John's first edition betrays this tension.
80–90 The *Birkat ha-Minim*, in the mid 80's or 90's, added formal weight to the ostracism of Christian Jews — forcing them to recant, leave or go cryptic. However, the Jewish 'mission to the "ditheists" ' begins, causing a *Johannine intramural crisis.*	Friends of those who departed from the Synagogue come and appeal to their loyalties to Moses, Abraham and the Jewish 'way'. *Crisis #1: This causes some Jewish Christians to leave the Johannine community and to lapse back into 'the world': i.e. the Jewish Synagogue.*	The first acute crisis is evident in the last stages of the first edition of John (*aposunagōgos*, 9:22; 12:42; 16:2, etc.) and in 1 John (the first 'antichristic' group has already departed —2:18–25). Explanation: They never really did 'belong to us'/know the Father (*Jn.6:30–51* typifies this crisis). Ignatius mentions Jewish pressures as an early threat.

---

15 Apostolicity for the evangelist involved an encounter with Jesus and a commission by him. The distinctively Johannine interpretation, however, is that this encounter occurs within the worship setting of the community of faith, and living out of that experience becomes a

Crisis #2: The Departure of Gentile Christians in the Face of Roman Persecution:
81–96 CE

46–81	The gospel appeal is extended to the Gentiles as well as to the Jews of Asia Minor, and some become Christians. Growing estrangement with the Synagogue intensifies the Gentile mission.	Just as Paul was impressed that (perhaps God-fearing) Gentiles respond readily to the gospel, so the Fourth Evangelist identifies the 'light that enlightens everyone coming into the world' as Jesus (Jn.1:9).	Clearly the church grew rapidly among Gentiles in Asia Minor (Ac.17–20), and tensions continue to be felt between Gentile Christians and Jewish Christians (post Gal.2).
81–90	During the persecution under Domitian (81–96), both Jews and Christians are persecuted for refusing to participate in emperor laud. Some are tortured and even killed (Jn.10:12f.), although Roman persecution of Christians was probably more local and occasional than widespread and systematic.	While Jews were accustomed to religious persecution, Gentile Christians were not. For them, faith in Christ bore unprecedented costs, and some denied Christ and the community of faith. This led to the second antichristic schism, which was a docetising one. 'Antichrist', the ultimate perjorative Johannine label, finds a *second* target.	Roman persecution is clearly in the background of all of Revelation (esp. 2:13), and at the time of writing 1 Jn.4:1–3 this threat is still on the way. Pliny's and Trajan's correspondence (#s 96–97) obviates the harshness of Roman penalties against Christians in particular, which appears to have been an *established* practice, going back to at least Domitian.
90–96	The Gentile Christian faced three options in the face of emperor laud: a) to refuse outright and to either suffer or die, b) to deny being a Christian and leave (be forced out of) the church, and c) to try to remain in the community of faith, having exercised emperor laud, defending one's action on the basis of docetising appraisals of Christ: If Jesus did not suffer ... *how can one expect his followers to suffer?* Inadequate belief leads to inadequate praxis.	Intramural *Crisis #2: Gentile Christians encourage others to deny the humanity of Jesus and to break away from the community of faith.* Having escaped Roman persecution by adjusting their appraisals of Christ's example, they are met with condemnation by 'the Elder' and excluded from Christian fellowship. They appeal to other Gentile Christians to join them, and by the writing of 2 Jn. 7 a *second* group has also 'departed' (*exēlthon*; see 1 Jn.2:19) into the world. These Gentile schismatics evolve into the second-century gnostics who still used the Johannine Gospel.	By the writing of 1 John 4:1–3, the docetic threat is clearly on the horizon, but it apparently has not yet peaked. 'The Elder' warns his audience as to how to identify the threat: "by this you can recognize...". On the other hand, by 2 John 7, this threat seems to have come and largely gone. The fleshly christology of the second edition material in John corrects these docetising trends (*Jn.6:52–58* typifies this crisis). Ignatius mentions Docetists as a *later* threat, and the same sequence is found in the Johannine corpus.

spiritual calling. In this sense, apostolicity is perceived in more Pauline than Petrine terms. Or, should it be stated that *Paul's view* is more Johannine than Petrine?

Crisis #3: Tensions with the Mainstream Church

46–81	In the mission to the Jews and Gentiles of Asia Minor, both Petrine and Johannine renditions of Jesus' ministry were a part of the kerygmatic life of the church. Followers of Paul and even Apollos also were in the picture as the faith identity of Johannine Christianity developed.	The evangelist corrects the thaumaturgic slant of the Petrine tradition (*not* a *sēmeia* source) at several points, but esp. Jn.6:26, where the Johannine Jesus equates the perceived result of the feeding in *all five* Synoptic feeding accounts with the failure to 'see' the sign. This corrective extends over decades.	The dialogue with the crowd (Jn.6:25–40) typifies this corrective. Correctives to Apollos' party include the emphasis on the Spirit (Jn.3:5) re. baptism and John the Baptist's pointing to the priority of Jesus (Jn. 1:26–34; 3:30; 10:41). The Jerusalem council settles early tensions (Ac. 15).
81-90	As persecution under Domitian rises, the church develops several approaches to insuring corporate unity and faithfulness. The mainstream church develops more of an institutional model, patterned after the Sanhedrin model and bolstered by the memory of Peter receiving the 'keys of the kingdom' from Jesus.	The Fourth Evangelist's approach to instilling *corporate unity and solidarity* is to appeal for *sacrificial love* one for another and ingesting the 'flesh-and-bloodness' of Jesus (i.e. embracing the cross if one wishes to share in the resurrection). The Elder appeals to the identity of the individual: 'If you love God, love your brother.'	Jesus' appeals for unity in the community of faith bolster this appeal (Jn.14–17). The *Paraklētos* is the unifying element in the church, and Jesus is portrayed as entrusting *his mother* to the Beloved Disciple — a symbol of relational ecclesiology (*Jn. 6:60–69* typifies this issue).
90–100	Eventually the Beloved Disciple dies, and his followers feel some responsibility to preserve his witness for the church and beyond. In particular, the juxtaposition of the Beloved Disciple and Peter become 'foils' for Johannine restorationist energies. They argue that Jesus never intended to erect a new institution parallel to Judaism. He came to gather into his fold all who abide in the Truth and who respond believingly to God's saving initiative through Jesus. Matt. 18:20 may reflect Matthean	However, in the face of rising institutionalism within the mainline church, such a message becomes a threat. For instance, 'Diotrephes, who loves to be first' (*philoprōteuōn*) excludes the brethren and even excommunicates those who would take them in (3 Jn.9f.). In response, the Elder writes to the *ecclēsia* about him and probably is the one who finally compiles the Fourth Gospel and sends it off as the witness of the Beloved Disciple (Jn.21:24f.). Thus, John was 'published' to declare Jesus' 'original intentionality for his church' in the light of the third Johannine intramural crisis.	Ignatius heightens the value of the institutional church and its hierarchical leadership to stave off defections. The 'office' of Peter takes on soteriological implications in Antioch and is advocated in Asia Minor. Peter is central to *two* misunderstanding dialogues in John (13:6–17; 21:15–17), and both are corrective of inadequate church leadership. Peter is also portrayed as 'returning the keys of the kingdom' to Jesus (6:68f.), which sets the stage for the Johannine teaching on the *Paraklētos*. By the 'publishing' of the Gospel, the evangelist

accomodation to the	*Crisis #3: The threat of*	appeared to have died
Johannine critique, and	*rising institutionalism in the*	(21:18–23), and by the early
'... his witness is true.'	*late first-century church and*	second century, Johannine
(Jn. 21:24c) carries	*the local marginalization of*	Christianity becomes
clear ideological	*Johannine Christians.*	subsumed into the
overtones.		mainstream church —
		continuing as a catalyst
		for christocratic reform
		and a challenge toward
		christocentric belief.

The dialectical tension within nearly every aspect of the evangelist's thinking is the most distinctive characteristic of John's christology, and this is the primary source of John's christological unity and disunity. By the time the Johannine Epistles are written, the dynamic tension of Johannine christology has been lost, and factious groups adhere to one aspect or another of the Johannine understanding of truth, thereby negating the dynamic veracity of such concepts. In fact, the most convincing evidence to suggest that 1 John was *not* written by the Fourth Evangelist is put forward by J. Lieu, who has observed that 'there is a significant shift of focus between the Gospel and Epistles ...'.[16] Such a shift is reflected in the movement away from Jesus as the way, the truth, and the life toward the community's *definitive understanding of Jesus* being equated with 'the truth', adherence to which becomes 'the way of life'. While such a shift does not prove that 1 John was the chronological successor to the Gospel, according to Lieu:[17]

> The Gospel balances realised eschatology with more traditional statements of future hope, a strong sense of election with an emphasis on the individual's responsibility to respond, predeterminism with the universal scope of God's salvation, the world as opposition with the world as the sphere and goal of the mission of the Son, tradition with the creativity of the Spirit, God as the one whom Jesus makes known with Jesus as the only way by which

---

16 J. Lieu, *The Second and Third Epistles of John,* Edinburgh, 1986, p. 205.

17 *Ibid.* Schnelle also believes that at least 1 John was published before the Gospel, and so does K. Grayston, *The Johannine Epistles*, Grand Rapids/London, 1984, pp. 9–14. A possible scenario is that the Epistle-writer and the compiler of the Gospel may have been the same individual. He was probably a leader, along with the evangelist and others, but felt the weight of community responsibilities quite heavily. In response to specific problems he wrote 1 John first and was one of those who convinced the evangelist to put his memoirs into writing, perhaps offering scribal assistance. However, the evangelist may have died before the Gospel was finished (Jn. 21:23), and certainly before it was 'published'. After its 'publication' the compiler used it (along with other forms of influence) to try to restore unity and harmony within Johannine Christianity and beyond. Intramurally, the motivation for 'publishing' the Fourth Gospel may be reflected in the christocratic tensions underlying 3 John.

Ironically, the same source of several heretical excesses (the dialectical christology of the Fourth Evangelist) would then have been employed — in written form — in order to combat some of the very problems it had caused. Without the dynamic tension, Johannine christology becomes other than itself.

God can be known. In each case it might seem that I John holds on to the first member of those partnerships far more firmly than he does the second, that a creative dialectic has been surrendered in the interests of the security of dogmatism and exclusivism. (p. 205f.)

Findings

John 6:67–71 may be considered a vignette of the Johannine understanding of christocracy: the effectual means by which the risen Christ continues to lead the church. When compared and contrasted with Matthew's addition (Matt. 16:17–19) to Mark's account of Peter's confession, it becomes clear that the differences in the accounts of Peter's confession in John and Matthew represent two distinct — and perhaps competitive — understandings of the institutional means by which christocracy is to take place. These differences represent the latest stages of the pre-literary dialectical relationship between the Petrine and Johannine traditions, in which Peter and the Beloved Disciple serve prototypical functions as models of church leadership.

1. For the type of Christianity represented by Matthew, Peter assumes the role of 'successor to Jesus', with the implication that those who follow in his wake also receive the mantles of institutional authority and pastoral responsibility. By the time of Ignatius' writings, the Petrine system of the monepiscopate gained considerable acceptance, and Ignatius appealed for solidarity with the 'one bishop' as equivalent to solidarity with the one Lord. In John, however, Peter is portrayed as 'returning the "keys of the kingdom" to Jesus', and what is at stake is the Johannine understanding of the means by which christocracy is meant to occur. The Johannine model is not hierarchical like the Petrine, but *familial*. It involves relationships to Christ and one another which are not based on power, but on love, and one may infer that church leaders must have debated the primacy and preferability of these two models. In fact, such church-governance issues were most probably the source of the ecclesiological tensions underlying 3 John, rather than theological (christological) ones. Diotrephes was probably less threatened by Johannine docetising heresy than by *the questioning of his ecclesial authority* and the advocating of a pneumatic and egalitarian mode of christocracy as Jesus' original intention.

2. Within the dialectical situation of the early church, one of the most acute issues was the threat of docetism as a christological *and* an ecclesiological problem. While the refusal to believe in the fleshly humanity of Jesus posed obvious consternation to the author of John (and even more evidently in the author of 1 and 2 John), the *implications* of this doctrine were probably the greater source of socio-religious aggravation. If people did not believe that Jesus suffered and died, but only appeared to, they need not have suffered or died as his followers. Thus, in the face of persecution, even some of Jesus' followers must have been tempted to abandon him (Jn. 6:66). It was in response to the common threat of docetising, centrifugal

tendencies, that Petrine *and* Johannine centripetal models of christocracy emerged and thus must have clashed with each other most severely. This may be inferred in 3 John *and* John 6:60–71.

3. As a contrast to the Johannine Epistles, however, the christology of the Fourth Evangelist is less dogmatic and far more tolerant of ambiguity. This is the strongest argument for a difference in authorship between the Epistles and the Johannine Gospel. Rather than confronting potential threats by calling ideological adversaries 'antichrists' and exposing their errors (*Synthetic-Conventionally*), the author of John adopts a far more *Conjunctive* approach to christological truth. John's christology represents the confidence of one who is not easily threatened by diversity, but who reserves the right to push one's understandings in opposing directions at the same time. John's is a 'living christology', and to reduce it to a cluster of notions, or an outline of beliefs, is to alter the structure of its epistemological origin and character. Such an act is to eliminate the dynamic status of its tension, and thereby to negate the veracity of its content. The christology of the Fourth Gospel is both unitive *and* disunitive because it represents a living epistemology born out of encounter; and this is both its genius and its scandal.

Summary of Part III

There are at least three levels of dialogue underlying John 6 and the rest of the Gospel, and each of these must be considered if one is to grasp the full meaning of its content. The evangelist's 'dialogue with his tradition' is especially clear in John 6:1–24, where the accounts of the feeding and the sea crossing are narrated. As a contrast to parallel accounts in Mark 6 and 8, the Johannine reflection upon the meaning of these events values them not as thaumaturgic demonstrations of Jesus' power over nature, but sees them as scenarios of God's saving/revealing discourse with humanity. Therefore, Jesus' words and works are not 'attesting wonders' but are 'testing signs' which call for a response to God, who is at work in and through such events.

In the dialogue/discourse section (vss. 25–66) the function of the narrative takes on a literarily dialogical role, in that it is written to engage the reader in a rhetorical dialogue with the content and subject of the narrative. This section may be understood as 'the exhortation of the "two ways" ', as two kinds of 'food' (death-producing and life-producing, cf. vs. 27) are juxtaposed in a three-fold development throughout this section. By means of extended irony and overturning the use of manna as a 'rhetorical trump' by the crowd, the evangelist has actually provided an exhortation which addresses at least three sets of particular needs in the Johannine audience. The significance of Jesus' ministry is other than thaumaturgic; God's agent, Jesus, is the fulfilment of Judaism and the one to whom Moses and the Torah point; but to follow him is to ingest the paradoxical 'bread of life', which is figuratively served on a platter hewn into the shape of a cross.

As contrasted to the function of Peter's confession in Matthew 16:16–19, the Johannine rendition portrays Peter as returning authority (the 'keys of the Kingdom') to Jesus. This represents not primarily a battle between two personalities in the early church, but a conflict in ideology between apostolic and sub-apostolic leaders seeking to be faithful to their understandings of the sort of religion Jesus came to bring. Peter's confession in vs. 68f. is symbolic of the Johannine understanding of christocracy, which is developed more fully in the *Paraklētos* discourses of John 14–16. John's is a dialectical christology. It is born out of transforming encounters with God through Jesus. These are reflected upon dialectically by the evangelist and attributed new meanings in the light of new situations faced by the church. Finally, the evangelist has sought to engage the reader in a transforming dialogue by means of writing his Gospel, and after his apparent death (21:23–25) the compiler has completed and passed it on, not as merely the witness of the Beloved Disciple, but as the original intention of Jesus. In this sense, 'His witness is *true*.' is more ideological than factual in its intent. Thus, the latest stages of John's composition should be read in the light of 3 John. The Fourth Gospel was written to preserve and extend the Johannine evangel; and it was 'published' to be *a manifesto of radical christocracy*. As the Russian form critic, M. Bakhtin has said:[18]

> There is neither a first word nor a last word. The contexts of dialogue are without limit. They extend into the deepest past and the most distant future. Even meanings born in dialogues of the remotest past will never be finally grasped once and for all, for they will always be renewed in later dialogue. At any present moment of the dialogue there are great masses of forgotten meanings, but these will be recalled again at a given moment in the dialogue's later course when it will be given new life. For nothing is absolutely dead: every meaning will someday have its homecoming festival.

---

18 With these words M. Bakhtin closed the last article he ever wrote: 'K. methodologii gumanitarnyx nauk', *Estetika slovesnogo tvorcestva* (Moscow, 1979) p. 373; E.t., K. Clark and M. Holquist, *Mikhail Bakhtin*, Cambridge/London, 1984, p. 350.

Conclusion

On 'Seamless Robes' ... and 'Left-Over Fragments'

In 1858, even a scholar as independent and free-thinking as D.F. Strauss proposed that John was like a 'seamless robe' (Jn. 19:23), woven together from top to bottom, forming a literary unity which may be gambled over, but not divided.[1] Over the intervening years, such scholars as Wellhausen, Bultmann and Fortna have set the Johannine aporias in sharp relief, arguing that not only is John composed of disparate sources, but that these may be identified by means of critical methodologies, thus clarifying the content of the Gospel. Ironically, however, just as John's *disunitive* features have evoked the strongest objections to Strauss' metaphorical allusion over a century ago, it is now John's *unitive* features which frustrate even the best of diachronic studies. As well as 19:23, John 6:12 should be kept in mind: 'And when they had eaten their fill, he tells his disciples, "Gather up the left-over fragments, that nothing may be lost." '

If one may misuse a text equally, just as John (with its two editions) may not be considered a 'seamless robe', woven from top to bottom as a single piece of literary construction, *neither* is John an aggregate of 'left-over fragments', to be broken, blessed, distributed — and then gathered up again into their respective literary 'baskets' (Jn. 6:10–13). John's unity is every bit as extensive as its disunity, and therein lies the challenge for diachronic and synchronic approaches alike.

The purpose of this thesis has been to examine the tensions associated with the unitive and disunitive aspects of John's christology in order to understand more clearly their origins and meanings. The high/low aspects of John's distinctive

---

1 The citation used here is found in W.F. Howard's *The Fourth Gospel in Recent Criticism and Interpretation*, London, 1931, p. 258. Oddly enough, H. Teeple (*The Literary Origin of the Gospel of John*, Evanston, 1974, p. 263, n. 1) takes Howard to task for a relatively minor inclusion of *Vorrede zu den* ... with the actual title (*Gesprächen von Ulrich v. Hutten* vii, p. 556), and then he apparently misses the point of what Strauss is saying. According to Teeple:

   Strauss in 1858 opposed the view that the gospel is a "seamless robe" by declaring that it has been "patched together out of miscellaneous shreds of diverse materials." (p. 18)

Granted, the passage is dense and interwoven with subordinate clauses, so that the meaning is easy to miss, but the fact is that Strauss appealed *against* those who were dividing the Fourth Gospel, because it is so unitive as a literary piece of solid construction. It is the *opinions of (diachronic) scholars* that are stitched together out of such diverse kinds of fabric, and that in the long run, it is *their arguments* that cannot possibly hold together. (See also M. Hengel's note #1 on p. 136 of *The Johannine Question*, London/Philadelphia, 1989.)

christology, the evangelist's ambivalence to Jesus' signs, and the question of the Son's relationship to the Father all pose major problems which demand to be addressed. Thus, the question explored in this thesis has been, 'To what extent is the christological unity and disunity in John attributable to tensions external to, or internal to, the thinking of the evangelist?' Findings are as follows:

1. While recent approaches to John's christology have largely been interested in (and motivated by) its unitive and disunitive elements, the topic has rarely been explored directly, seeking to make use of cognitive and other related studies pertaining to the origin and character of dialectical thinking. Of the two main literary approaches to John — diachronic and synchronic ones — the primary motivation of the former has been to identify John's christological tensions as being external to the thinking of the evangelist, while synchronic studies have tended to minimize their significance. A third approach combines synchronicity of authorship with diachronicity of audience. This moves the poles of the tensions to the 'dialogue' between the evangelist and the rhetorical targets of his evolving context. A high correlation exists between recent commentators' understandings of John's christological unity and disunity and the theory of composition adopted by each scholar. This fact suggests that as progress is made in understanding more about John's christolgoical unity and disunity, one's insight into composition issues will be enhanced, and vice versa. It may also be assumed that John 6 serves as a fitting testing ground, with conclusions arising from the analysis of this chapter being applicable to other parts of the Gospel.

2. The studies of R. Kysar, P. Borgen and C.K. Barrett represent three approaches to John 6, but more significantly, they clarify the kinds of issues which advance an adequate analysis of it. a) While there is *not* an 'emerging consensus' among scholars posing diachronic analyses of John 6, one thing is certain: meaningful analyses of the unitive and disunitive features of John 6 must take into consideration Bultmann's unique contribution. Posing new solutions to many of Bultmann's insightful questions remains a fruitful enterprise. b) While Borgen has demonstrated convincingly that John 6:31–58 is a formal and thematic unity, he has adopted the wrong midrashic pattern. The development of the manna motif does not represent an exegetical paraphrase of Exodus 16:4, where the manna reference serves as the primary text. Rather, it bears a closer formal and thematic similarity to the rhetorical use of manna as a secondary text, whereby another point is 'proven' using manna as a 'rhetorical trump'. This is corroborated by earlier and contemporary midrashic literature, and the crowd's use of the manna proof-text is overturned by the Johannine Jesus and co-opted into the 'exhortation of the "two ways" '. The 'text' being developed midrashically in John 6 is not an Old Testament passage, but the works and words of Jesus. c) A key explanation for unitive and disunitive thought may be explored in relation to reflective thinking as the 'dialogue which the soul holds within herself' in considering anything. Barrett is entirely justified in employing this well-known precedent from Plato's *Theatetus*, and the

christological unity and disunity of John 6 deserves to be explored further using such a dialectical-reflective model. d) A further level of dialogue — a rhetorical one — may be explored by applying M. Bakhtin's form-critical analysis of the misunderstanding dialogue. Misunderstanding, or stupidity, in the novel is always rhetorical, and the targeted audience is suggested by the identity and/or beliefs of the misunderstanding discussants. Thus, the crowd, the Jews, the disciples and Peter provide a cursory guide to at least three or four impending crises within the history of the Johannine community. These struggles are mirrored in, and corroborated by John, the Johannine Epistles and the writings of Ignatius.

3. An analysis of Bultmann's treatment of John 6 suggests the following conclusions: a) There is not sufficient stylistic or linguistic disunity in John 6 to infer more than one literary source (*all* of John may be considered 'Semitising Greek'), and the fact that narratological and interpretive comments are present says nothing about whether they must have been added by a later hand. They were more likely intrinsic to the developing Johannine tradition, itself. b) The contextual difficulties identified by Bultmann are not as problematic as he argues. They do, however, play a central role in his disordering and reordering the discourse material in John 6, so as to bolster the credibility of his theory of composition. More realistically, they betray the evangelist's use of irony, serving to dislocate — and then to relocate — the reader's thinking along the lines of the ethos of the Johannine Jesus. c) The theological difficulties in John 6 would be very problematic if indeed John 6:51c–58 were meant to be taken as an explicit appeal for the salvific necessity of participating in the eucharist. Such a view would indeed be incompatible with the evangelist's christocentric soteriology. This, however, is anachronistic, and connections between this passage and Ignatius' 'medicine of immortality' as a bald reference to a magical view of the eucharist interpret both Ignatius and John wrongly. The appeal in both cases is for corporate solidarity with Christ and the community of faith in the face of persecution. Where Paul uses familiar Mystery Religions' theophagic motifs to emphasize the unity of the body of Christ, and where Ignatius refers to the familiar Pauline motif (the breaking of *one* loaf as the corporate expression of unity), John uses familiar eucharistic imagery to emphasize the importance of being nourished by Jesus' giving of his flesh for the life of the world (6:51c). Thus, John 6 represents a literary, stylistic and theological unity, which must be addressed by means *other* than literarily diachronic ones if one is to take seriously the Fourth Gospel as a piece of literature in its own right.

Despite the fact, however, that Bultmann's solutions to these problems cannot bear the weight of his hypothetical constructs, he has nonetheless identified unevennesses in the text and theological tensions with such uncanny sensitivity that these interpretive insights provide foundational material for alternative constructs. a) The insight that vss. 4, 5, 14f., 23, 26, 66, etc. represent the interpretive comments of the evangelist suggests that the evangelist regarded the entire episode as a time of *testing*. It stands to reason that he should have employed this narrative to address the needs of a community undergoing various times of testing, itself. b) The insight that vs. 27 is the beginning of the 'Bread of Life' discourse is also accurate. Verse 27 serves as the pivotal fulcrum of the entire chapter (not vs. 31), and it poses two choices for the Johannine audience: the *way of death* and the *way of life*. c) The theme of vss. 60–71 is indeed 'the way of the cross', and a radically new theme begins at vs. 51c. However, these verses have one and the same motif: the cross, which is developed by means of eucharist imagery in vss. 53–58. It is *the way of the cross* which scandalizes the would-be followers of Jesus, not a pro- or an anti-sacramentalist motif. This would have been abundantly clear to the original audience.

4. Because John 6 must be considered a basic literary unity, alternative means of addressing its theological and contextual tensions must be considered. Therefore, recent advances in cognitive studies should be explored to see how far they illuminate the origin and character of the dialectical thinking of the Fourth Evangelist. Two such studies include a developmental model, represented by J. Fowler, and a transformational model, devised by J. Loder. The value of Fowler's theory of Stages of Faith Development is that it illustrates the way in which people's understandings about God grow in accordance with cognitive development. His analysis also illumines an understanding of how dialectical thinking takes place as well as the sorts of factors which may have contributed to the evangelist's existentializing of Jesus' signs. The strength of Loder's model is that it provides an anatomy of transforming encounters. His five steps of the 'event of knowing' facilitate a better understanding of the character and origin of the evangelist's christological content, and in particular, what it may have been like for a first-century follower of Jesus to encounter in him theophanically the transforming presence of the love of God.

When applied to John 6, the findings of these two studies illuminate the narrative of John 6 as follows: a) In the evangelist's interpretation of the 'significance' of the feeding one can infer a progression of reflective maturation in the evangelist's understanding of the meaning of the feeding on various levels. This development is alluded to in the evangelist's interpretation of the sign as Jesus being the Bread of Life in several ways. b) By contrast, the Johannine sea crossing is an early (undeveloped) account, which interprets the appearance of Jesus as a *theophany*. While the Johannine tradition may have gradually come to interpret the meaning of the feeding differently from the interpretations in Mark 6 and 8, the Johannine rendition of the sea crossing represents a fundamentally different set of 'first impressions' from the pre-Marcan (Petrine) tradition. This difference may be attributed to two dissonant perceptions of the same external set of events between at least two followers of Jesus or sectors of his band. These and a matrix of other perceptual differences may account for much of the interpretive divergence between the 'bi-optic Gospels', Mark and John. In other words, at least two of Jesus' followers understood his mission and ministry in significantly different ways, and some of these differences extended well into the sub-apostolic era.

5. The evangelist's dialogue with his tradition may be examined most effectively in John 6:1–24, where the contrasts and comparisons with parallel accounts in the Synoptic tradition magnify John's distinctives most clearly. While John's sequence of events differs very little from the Marcan accounts, John's interpretive detail is radically different, and this is highly significant. It represents a fundamental difference in ideology between the Johannine and pre-Marcan traditions. John interprets the feeding *not* as the testing of Jesus (which is the primary point of the feeding narrative according to Mark 6 and 8) but as *the testing of humanity*: first Philip and later the crowd, the Jews and other disciples. Likewise, the sea crossing is not interpreted as a sign of Jesus' power over the forces of nature, as it is in all the Synoptic accounts, but it is cast in the form of a theophany. It betrays little interpretive development beyond what may have been the first impression of someone's 'spiritual encounter' experience. An implication of these differences is that John's independence from — and yet similarity to — the Synoptic accounts is that there may *never* have been just one, singular tradition, interpreting Jesus' words and works in a uniform way, whence a later tradition departed in its own Johannine direction. Rather, it is highly likely that from the beginning, Jesus' ministry was interpreted differently, even by some of his followers, and that Mark and John reflect some of those differences.

These interpretive differences are also suggested by the Old Testament references alluded to in Mark 6:34 and John 6:14: evidence of divergent trajectories within the Marcan and Johannine kerygmata. The Marcan reference to Zechariah 10:2 portrays Jesus as the Messiah sent by God to restore Israel by re-establishing his kingdom in Jerusalem, on Mount Zion. This was clearly a Judean motif which is even more fully developed in the Matthean tradition. On the other hand, John 6:14 refers to Jesus as the prophet like Moses of Deuteronomy 18:15–22, who will be sent by God to speak *only* what he has heard from God, and the veracity of his agency-identity will be confirmed by his fulfilled words and attesting signs. These differences of interpretation are far from minor discrepancies regarding 'historical' detail. They represent major ideological differences between the 'Petrine' tradition's (as represented by much of Mark, Matthew and 1 Peter) and the Johannine tradition's (as represented by John and 1 and 2 John) understandings of Jesus' ministry, the nature of the Kingdom of God, the scope of apostolic ministry, and the means by which the risen Christ should continue to lead his flock. The Matthean tradition poses an institutional model of church organization, while the Johannine tradition poses a familial and egalitarian model of the same.

Based upon a redaction-critical analysis of the Matthean and Lucan redactions of Mark 6 and 8, it is highly doubtful that John is a redaction of a written source (a *sēmeia* source or Mark) as the First and Third Gospels are. The kind of material most characteristic of John (a large quantity of non-symbolic, illustrative detail) is *precisely* the kind of material omitted by Matthew and Luke. On the other hand, the kind of material added by Matthew and Luke (summaries and common-sense conjecture about what might have happened) is radically different from the interpretive detail so intrinsic to the Johannine narrative. Therefore, John 6:1–24 betrays a dialogue between an evangelist and his tradition which involves a good deal of reflection (cf. Fowler's model) upon the meaning of the feeding of the multitude. On the other hand, the evangelist's interpretation of the sea crossing has little to do with the calming of the sea or Jesus' power over nature. Rather, it is cast in the form of a theophany (cf. Loder's model) and represents the 'calming of the disciples'. The assumption that stories about Jesus' works uniformly ended in an attestation of the miracle by witnesses, and that the Fourth Evangelist has omitted these endings, is fallacious. There is no stylistic, contextual or theological evidence favouring such a move in John 6, and the 'de-Johannification' of the feeding, followed by a re-Marcanization of the text does not an actual *sēmeia* source imply. John's corrective target was the prevalent Christian interpretation of Jesus' miracles common to *all five* Synoptic feeding accounts. These thaumaturgic attestations are characteristic of the Petrine (pre-Marcan material *and* Peter's sermons in Acts) kerygma, and the Johannine account demonstrates that there was at least one tradition which interpreted Jesus' works *not* as 'attesting miracles', but as 'testing' signs.

6. The evangelist's dialogue with his reader may be observed most clearly in John 6:25–66, where the initiative shifts from Jesus as God's agent to Jesus' discussants. The section reflects a homily, perhaps given as a Christianized form of midrash. However, it did not start with the scripture citation of vs. 31. Rather, the *whole* chapter comprises the Johannine 'exhortation', and the 'text' with which it begins is not an Old Testament passage, but the narration of *events in the ministry of Jesus*. Following the narration of the signs and the beginning of the dialogue with the crowd, the evangelist's dialogue with his audience begins with the exhortation of the 'two ways'. As the *Didache* posed the way of life versus the way of death, the Johannine Jesus identifies two kinds of food: one which is death producing, and the other which is life producing (vs. 27). Thus, the invitation to choose the life-producing Bread over other kinds of 'bread' is the exhortative fulcrum of John 6.

The motif of testing continues throughout the dialogue and discourse section, as the crowd, the Jews and Jesus' disciples are tested regarding their choosing or rejecting the life-producing Bread which Jesus gives and is. In the first testing, the crowd must choose whether they will be satisfied by the truly nourishing words and works of Jesus, or whether they will continue to seek only more bread for their stomachs. The fact that Jesus' sharp reply to the crowd (vs. 26) accuses them of seeking him because they had 'eaten the loaves and were satisfied', rather than because they had seen the signs, is highly significant. Here we have the Johannine Jesus refuting the Petrine interpretation of the feeding, a close form of the identical phrase ('they ate ... and were satisfied') being found *in all five Synoptic feeding accounts*. Thus, the Fourth Evangelist's correction of the Synoptic tradition (though he need not have been familiar with it in written form to disagree with the prevalent interpretation) is not concerned with corrections of detail or chronology, but with *ideological* differences regarding the character of Jesus' ministry.

The means by which the Johannine Jesus corrects the Petrine and thaumaturgic interpretation of the result of the feeding is to turn the manna-rhetoric of the *crowd* on its head and to 'over-trump their highest card'. Contrary to Borgen and others, the reference to manna in vs. 31 is *not* made in order to perform an exegesis on the meaning of the text. It uses the manna motif as a rhetorical trump, as a secondary text furthering another goal, which in this case is to acquire more bread from Jesus. By employing extended irony, the crowd which comes to test Jesus is portrayed as being tested unwittingly, and the exhortation of the 'two ways' confronts them at their place of greatest vulnerability: to forsake their craving for temporal bread in order to assimilate the Bread which is eternally life-producing.

The second group addressed in John 6 (symbolically or otherwise) is the *Jews*, who refuse to believe that Jesus came down from heaven. Their unbelief is parallel to the acute socio-religious conflict alluded to in the first edition of the Gospel (cf. John 5:16–47; 7:14–52; 8:12–10:39; esp. 9:22), where Johannine Christianity is faced with accusations of ditheism in its individuation from the Synagogue (cf. also 1 John 2:18–25). For the first time in the history of Jewish-Christian midrashic use of the manna tradition is the bread of Moses actually considered inferior and death-producing. Thus, the 'way of life' for Christian Jews becoming Jewish Christians is to accept Jesus as having been sent from the Father, and to transfer their faith in the 'bread' of the Torah to that Bread which Moses, the manna, and the Torah prefigure: Jesus, the Bread coming down out of heaven for the life of the world. The Old Testament citation in vs. 31 is not from Ex. 16:4, 15, but it is closest in wording and usage to Psalm 78:24f. As in the midrash of Psalm 78, John 6 uses the manna motif rhetorically (along with the quail and grumbling motifs of Nu. 11) to equate the Jews' desire for the manna and Torah of Moses with the death-producing craving for quail (flesh, vs. 63) in the wilderness. Thus, the exhortation is to not 'grumble' as did the unbelieving Israelites in the wilderness (Nu. 11), but to be thankful for God's present saving activity, the Bread of God, present in Jesus.

The third group addressed in John 6, the *disciples*, represents the primary group addressed by the evangelist near the time that John 6 was written. The acute dilemma facing Johannine Christianity during this time is the threat that Gentile Christians will also abandon their faith in the face of persecution. This threat is suggested by the following evidence: a) The impending schism which is alluded to in 1 John 4:1–3 (those who refuse to believe that Jesus has come in the flesh) has become actual by the time 2 John 7 is written. b) Material in the second edition added to the Gospel contains several references to the significance of Jesus' *humanity* (1:14; 6:51, 53–56; 11:35; 15:13, 20), suggesting that incipient docetism was becoming a problem. c) The abandonment of the 'scandalized' disciples (6:60–66) is used rhetorically to convince those most contemporary with the writing of John 6 not to leave the community of faith. Therefore, the acute problem with docetism, in the thinking of the evangelist, appears to be less a matter of 'correct' christological beliefs for the sake of preserving an orthodox standard, and more the *implication* of such beliefs: namely, that if Jesus did not suffer, then neither do his followers need to do the same. The evangelist refers to such an overly spiritualized view of Jesus as 'profitless flesh' (6:63) and employs eucharistic imagery to highlight the indispensability of solidarity with Jesus in his suffering and death if one expects to be raised with him on the last day as well. Thus, the choosing of the 'way of life' for the latest targeted audience of John 6 implies solidarity with Jesus in his suffering, and *therefore* in his resurrection. For this group undergoing the persecution of Domitian, as well as for Jewish Christians who had earlier been persecuted by leaders of the Synagogue, the life-producing Bread is the nourishment of the flesh and blood of the suffering of the Son of Man — given for the life of the world (6:51c). To follow Jesus is not to escape persecution, or even premature death. Just as the 'exaltation' of the cross was Jesus' paradoxical glorification, so will abiding in this knowledge be existential 'nourishment' for disciples undergoing hardship for the sake of their faith.

7. The fourth 'dialogue' to consider in one's analysis of John 6 involves the intramural dialectical situation of Johannine Christianity around the time it was written. The contrast between *Peter's confession* in John 6 and its parallels in the Synoptics reflects a fundamental disagreement between the later Johannine and Petrine traditions. This is especially true of the Matthean rendition of Peter's confession and the subsequent interpolation by the First Evangelist, which inaugurates an institutional model to provide for the earthly succession of Jesus (Matt. 16:16–19). John 6:67–71 offers a double corrective to the later Petrine tradition regarding the means by which christocracy occurs, as well as the character of the Kingdom of God on earth. The Johannine rendition of Peter's confession portrays Peter as *returning* the 'keys of the Kingdom' to Jesus: 'Lord, to whom shall we go? You (*alone*) have the words of eternal life.' Thus, the means of christocracy is not the succession of Jesus by a human institution or hierarchy, but by the ongoing leadership of the Paraclete, who will lead the community of faith — individually and corporately — in the way of Truth. Jesus' negative response to being called 'the Holy One of God' is the Johannine equivalent to the Synoptic Jesus' rebuke of Peter's unwillingness to allow the Son of Man to suffer and die. The ideological significance of the confession in John 6:69, however, is that it is cast in Synoptic (Petrine) language (Mk. 1:24; Lk. 4:34), where the Kingdom of God requires thaumaturgic works of power to destroy the kingdom of Satan and the demons. John's omission of exorcisms and his existentializing view of Jesus' signs suggest that implicit in Jesus' correcting of Peter in John 6:70 is an ideological disagreement between the Johannine and Petrine traditions regarding the character of God's reign on earth. Rather than going forth by means of works of power and force (18:36), the Johannine understanding of the Kingdom is that it is established by means of the exposing, convicting and enlightening power of Truth (18:37). The Fourth Evangelist may have come to such insights after reflecting upon the contradiction between his belief that he and other Christians would continue to do 'even greater works' than Jesus had done (14:12, in the first edition of Gospel material) and the

contradictory experience(s) of (prayer) requests not being met, as well as the possible dearth of miracles within his later experience. Thus, the evangelist's view of the relationship between signs and faith, and his understanding of the nature of the Kingdom were likely to have been influenced by the problem of theodicy, leading to his distillation of the eternal truth conveyed by Jesus' works and words. Likewise, if John or significant portions of John were written by a follower of Jesus, as the compiler believes (21:24f., and as diachronic analyses have yet to demonstrate otherwise), the evangelist's understanding of Jesus as the Christ seems to be an integration of one's experiencing the presence of God in the man, Jesus (6:20f.) and this person's connecting of Jesus with the prophet like Moses (Deut. 18:15–22), who would speak only what he had heard from the Father, and whose words and works served to testify that he was indeed sent from God. Then again, the historical Jesus probably saw himself more as a prophet like Moses than the Synoptic king like David.

8. Therefore, the christological unity and disunity in John is attributable to the following factors: a) Some aspects of John's christological unity and disunity may not be as problematic as they seem, but reflect the dialectical process of theological reflection in keeping with contemporary examples. Two of these include the tension between a present and future eschatology, and the apparent tension between determinism and free will in John. Aspects of Paul's eschatology included a tension between the already and the not yet (1 Cor. 15), and 2 Baruch associates the eschatological pouring out of manna from heaven with the raising of souls in the *eschaton*. Thus, John 6:39c, 40c and 54c are not exceptional, but *representative of contemporary eschatologies*. In that sense, it is not unlikely that they may have existed side by side within John's tradition as well. And, while John 6:44, 65 speak of the impossibility of coming to Jesus without divine enablement, the Son has come to all the world (1:12; 3:16) in order for all humanity to respond to the divine initiative in Jesus. This is not predeterminism, but the *dialogical character of revelation*. God's decisive initiative within his saving/revealing discourse with humans calls for their voluntary response. On one hand, *no one can come* to God without divine facilitation; on the other, *all who come and believe* are enabled to become children of God.[2]

b) What has appeared to be subordinationism versus egalitarianism between the Father and the Son in John is actually a reflection of the *evangelist's agency christology*. The Son is to be equated with the Father precisely because he represents the Father identically. As the prophet like Moses, who according to

---

2 See the excellent treatments of these two issues in G. R. Beasley-Murray, *Gospel of Life: Theology in the Fourth Gospel*, Peabody, Mass. 1991, pp. 1–14; and D.A. Carson, *Divine Sovereignty* and *Human Responsibility; Biblical Perspectives in Tension*, 1981, respectively. See also R. Kysar's excellent treatment of experiential factors in Johannine Christianity which must have produced such tensions within Johannine dualism (pp. 58–77) and eschatology (pp. 97–127) in his *John the Maverick Gospel* (revised), Louisville, 1993.

Deuteronomy 18:15–22 would be sent by God as the eschatological agency of God's dialogue with humanity, Jesus' authority is based on his speaking *only* that which he had received from the Father. His authenticity is attested by his fulfilled words and his signifying deeds (Deut. 18:21–22), and it is because of this representation that he is to be equated with God and his words heeded as God's. In John, subordinationist and egalitarian christological motifs are both central component parts to John's pervasive *agency christology*. They are two sides of the same coin.

c) The evangelist's ambivalence toward Jesus' signs is an indication of his *reflective dialogue with his tradition*, in which he continues to find new meanings in the significance of Jesus' words and works. In the case of John 6, it appears that the evangelist's understanding of the significance of the feeding of the multitude has matured over the years. While he once may have been more sympathetic to Petrine thaumaturgic interpretations of Jesus' ministry, he eventually found them inadequate, probably for reasons of experience. Then again, Johannine semeiology may have differed from the Marcan from its earliest stages. Symbolization results, however, from *theodicy*. Thus, while he values the wondrous aspects of Jesus' ministry, in the relative dearth of miracles over the intervening years he has come to see other value in Jesus' words and works, still in keeping with his agency christology. In the works of Jesus, as well as his words, the saving initiative of God may be perceived, and the audience is called to respond to the 'Word' of God, working in and through Jesus' signs. This happens over at least three or four crises in the community's history, and these may be inferred in the Bread of Life dialogues and discourses.

d) The tension between the flesh and glory in the evangelist's christology is the result of an *encounter theology*, and the theophany on the lake is a prototypical example of such an encounter. It may even have been formative. Analogous to Paul's experience on the road to Damascus, the memory of this event remained transcendent from the earliest stages of the tradition to its later written rendition, and its slant is fundamentally different from the pre-Marcan account. For the one who has encountered something of God's saving presence in the man, Jesus, the event of knowing never ceases to remain at least partially inexplicable and genuinely inexhaustible. Whether the evangelist was himself an eye-witness, or whether he simply stands centrally in that tradition, his is a christology which has arisen out of such transforming encounters, and his Gospel is written to facilitate the same for the reader.

e) A final explanation for some of John's unity and disunity involves *the dialogical means by which the evangelist seeks to engage the reader in an imaginary conversation with Jesus*. By means of local and extended irony, misunderstanding dialogues, discourses which employ rich metaphors christocentrically, and by portraying the stories of other people who encounter Jesus in the narrative, the evangelist woos, cajoles, humours and shocks the reader. In doing so, he seeks to create a *crisis* — a temporary sense of disturbance and

Table 22:
'Epistemological Origins of John's Dialectical Christology'
(unitive and disunitive issues included in parentheses)

The evangelist's theology of the *divine-human
dialectic* cast in the form of the Prophet-like-
Moses *agency Christology* (egalitarian/
subortionationist relation of the Son to the
Father; free will/determinism; an incarnational
sacramentology; the Johannine sending and
witness motifs; signs and fulfilled words as
authenticators of Jesus' "sent-ness"; the ironic
rejection of Jesus by the Jews) based on
Deut. 18:15–22.

| *Literary and composition factors* in the dialectical appearance of the Fourth Gospel (the *addition of supplementary material*: Jn. 1:1–18; chs. 6, 15–17, 21, etc. reflecting anti-docetic correctives and christocratic interests; the *linnear-progressive* and *circular-repetitive style* of the evangelist's narration; *the evangelist's use of irony*, serving first to dislocate — and then to relocate — the reader's thought in desired directions; *the evangelist's desire to evoke a believing response from his audience*, having distinctive implications during different phases of the community's history). | The *dialectical* ← (Conjunctive) *thought* → *of the evangelist* | *Groups and individuals* in the audiences engaged by the evangelist (*John the Baptist adherents*, possibly later followers of Apollos: spirit-versus-water baptism debates, the Christodoxic testimony of John, etc.; *Jewish Christians* experiencing pressure from the Synagogue: high christological motifs, 'I am' sayings, Elijah- and Moses-type signs, etc.; *Gentile Christians* under persecution by Romans: anti-docetic and incarnational motifs, the cost of discipleship, etc.; *representatives of the main church*: the juxtaposition of Peter and the Beloved Disciple, the promise of the Paraclete, John's familial and pneumatic ecclesiology). |

The evangelist's theological reflection as a
*cognitive dialogue between earlier perceptions
and later experiences* (appreciation for miracles/
their relative dearth in real life; theophanic
encounter with God in Jesus/tendencies to
formalize such experiences; the Jews being the
source of salvation/the Jews' rejection
of the Saviour; the Gentiles' responsiveness to
the Gospel/Jesus' being the only way to the Father;
the delay of the parousia/what Jesus really said;
salvation as present reality/as a future hope).

dislocation—as this is the *first and prerequisite* step in any experience of knowing. The evangelist adapts to the specific needs of his sector of early Christianity, but never does he stray far from his christocentric understanding of God's love, which is always and continually initiating a saving/revealing dialogue between God and humanity.

Therefore, it is because John's christology has arisen out of believing responsiveness to the 'divine-human dialogue' revealed in Jesus and the inward 'dialogues' between one's perceptions and contradictory experiences that the evangelist cannot be satisfied with monological statements about Jesus, left on their own. The veracity of John's christology exists not in spite of its dialectical tensions, but *because* of them. John's is a living (*Conjunctive*) christology, and while its skeletal form may be reconstructed by means of amassing a catalogue of Johannine propositions about Jesus, to do so is self-negating because the living tension of the Johannine dialectic is lost. The unitive and disunitive features of this distinctive portrayal of Jesus comprise the genius of John's christology—but also its scandal. It is a christology which is based upon encounter, and it must also lead to encounter, lest it be rejected or miscomprehended. Therefore, John 20:31 represents not only the *end* of the Gospel's purpose, but the *beginning* of its comprehension as well:

> "These (signs) are written that you may believe that Jesus is the Christ, the Son of God, and that believing, you might have life in his name."

Implications

A few implications for the various approaches to John's christology (Chapter 1) may be drawn, as they relate to historical, theological, literary and text-centred studies:

> 1. If John does indeed represent the reflective work of a dialectical thinker, a third alternative may be posed in favour of the false dichotomy which has tended to consider John *either* the 'historical' report of an eye-witness, *or* the 'historicized drama' of a novelist. John is neither. John represents a later development of a tradition which was independent from the Synoptic and pre-Synoptic (Petrine) tradition(s) from its earliest stages. While much of the Johannine tradition appears to be grounded in actual events of Jesus' ministry, this is not its most significant 'historical' value. To be concerned primarily with the 'objective' facts of history is to trivialize its meaning. In other words, dates and places and names derive their significance from their relationship to events which are perceived to be important to contemporary and future generations, not vice versa. Thus, the most significant 'historical' content in John is less a tabulation of what 'really' happened, and more the *subjective* (ideological) connecting of how the memory of 'what happened' relates to the present and the future. In this sense, there may be more 'historicity' in the Johannine paraphrases of Jesus' teachings than is commonly assumed.
>
> 2. This means that interpreting the significance of Jesus' ministry never ceases but is an ongoing activity. Thus, the evangelist's christology *never was* a totally-fixed and well-defined set of non-contradictory propositions about who Jesus was and what he came to do.

He continued to make new connections between Jesus' words and works and the later needs of developing Christianity. Therefore, analyses which apprehend his christology adequately must approach it as a dynamic phenomenon — a dialectical exploration of the set of contradictions and continuities which 'argue back and forth' between one's perceptions and subsequent experiences.

3. The epistemological structure of what one believes determines the means by which one attempts to convince others of such knowings. Thus, literary analyses may anticipate high dividends in developing more fully the relationship between the evangelist's transforming encounters with the truth of God in Jesus and the dialogical means by which he seeks to lead the reader into similar experiences of convictional knowing. In other words, if the destination and purpose of John (20:31) is to facilitate a believing encounter with Jesus, leading to experiencing 'life in his name', the literary interest is to analyze the means by which (' ... but these are written') the evangelist has attempted to evoke such a response from the reader.

4. While the evangelist's use of Old Testament typologies, agency schemas, and Hellenistic concepts is obvious, the more telling questions are not 'What ideas does he use?', and 'Whence did they come?', but '*Why* does he use them?', and '*What sort of an experience* are they intended to effect?'. The evangelist's use of the scriptures, the witness of John the Baptist, sapiential themes, and even his christology serve the over-arching purpose of confronting his audience with the saving and revealing dialogue between God and humanity. This suggests yet another tension. The entirety of the Fourth Gospel is christocentric, but christocentrism serves another end: the leading of all humanity to the Ground and Source of all Being, who effects the healing of the world.

Postscript

One of the central implications of John's christology has to do with its relationship to one's understanding of truth. In the scientific age, epistemological interests revolve around such questions as, 'How ... ?', 'Of what kind ... ?', 'When ...?', etc., and the implied assumption underlying these questions is that 'objective' content is to be equated with truth. While this may be the prevalent mythology of the present age, the problem is that truth encompasses both objective and subjective content. The christology of the Fourth Gospel illustrates the reality described by Bonhöffer:[3] 'The question may not run, "How is the incarnate one thinkable?", but "Who is he?" ' Thus, truth, in the christological sense, must be understood in subjective, personal terms, as well as objective ones.

Scholars have been wrong in their assumption that John's high (and low) christology (as well as other christological tensions) suggests that the evangelist's point of reference must have been far removed in time and space from its subject. The high degree of dialectical tension in John's christology, far from 'proving' that the evangelist *could not have been an eye-witness*, may actually suggest the opposite. The analogy to love, or any other subjective aspect of truth, here applies. Those who are able to give a reasoned definition of love and its categories are not

---

3 D. Bonhöffer, *Christ the Center*, E.t. by E.H. Robertson, San Francisco, 1978, p. 102.

those immersed in a profound love relationship, or even those who have been catapulted into the throes of impassioned infatuation. The one who has come to love most profoundly would be the least easily satisfied with single, monofaceted definitions of love. At least this person would have to say, 'Yes, that's true, but also so is this ... and this as well; but on the other hand ...!', until the spectra of merismus and hyperbole are exhausted. Therefore, the evangelist's 'living' christology appears to be continuously groping for new ways to articulate the truth which has been glimpsed through his spiritual encounters with Jesus. His refusal to delimit his knowledge of Jesus as the way, the truth, and the life, within monological christological statements which are simply 'true', reflects not the evangelist's low esteem of truth, but the *highest respect that is possible*. On this topic, the evangelist would no doubt resonate with the instructive words of Lessing:[4]

> If God had in his Right hand all truth, and in his Left only the drive toward truth, although with the inevitable result that I would err: should he keep his silence and say to me, "Choose!", I would humbly choose his Left, and would say, "Father, give me this! The pure truth is for Thee alone."

---

4 Translated from G.E. Lessing, *Werke* Bd. 6, Zürich, 1965, p. 269f.

Appendices

I. John's Exalted Christology

The Gospel of John has long been noted for its 'high' or exalted christology. While there is a great degree of interconnectedness between individual passages, one may nevertheless detect several groupings. a) There are those passages which emphasize some aspect of *the Son's equality or oneness with the Deity*. Verses 1:1, 18; 5:18; 8:16–23, 58; 10:29–30, 33, 38; 12:41; 14:10; 20:28 reflect a christology which regards the status of the Son as equal to or one with God, the Lord, or the Father. The Johannine Jesus is *monogenēs*: the only begotten one. The *Logos* was with God, and was God. "Before Abraham was, *Egō Eimi*!" declares the Son.

b) A second theme of Johannine high christology is *the glorification of the Son of Man* (the glorification of God's Son, 11:4; and, the glorification of the Son, 17:1a, 5, 10, 22–24.). Such passages as 1:51; 3:14; 6:62; 8:28; 12:23–36; 13:1, 13a all refer to some aspect of the Son of Man (or Jesus) ascending, being lifted up or being glorified. This is in keeping with the descent/ascent schemas of the christological hymns (Phil. 2:5–11; Col. 1:15–20; Heb. 1:1–4), but in John, glorification is paradoxically connected with *the cross*.

c) A third aspect of high christology in John is the emphasis put upon *the agency and work of the Son*. This aspect of John's christology is comprised by at least five sub-themes. First, the Father commissions and sends the Son (3:16b–17, 34–35; 5:22, 26; 7:16, 28–9; 10:36a; 11:27c, 42; 13:3; 16:27–28; 20:21).

Second, the Son does his 'work' and fulfills his mission (1:3, 5a, 10, 29, 33; 2:11; 3:32; 4:34; 5:21, 30, 36; 6:38, 63; 7:7; 9:4; 10:25, 32, 38; 12:27; 13:1, 14; 17:4).

Third, the mission of the Son becomes the mission of the believer/disciple (13:14–16, 20, 34, 35; 14:12–14, 15, 20–21, 23–24; 15:9–17, 27; 16:1, 4, 23–24, 33; 17:6–26; 18:36; 20:21–23).

Fourth, the *Paraklētos* will be sent to empower disciples to accomplish their common mission (14:16–18, 25–27; 15:26; 16:7–11, 12–16).

Fifth, the work of the Son, Spirit and disciple will be completed through their witness in the world, leading the world into the Father's saving love through the Son (1:10–13; 12:32, 44–46; 14:6; 17:20–23).

These five themes become an *ongoing cycle of apostolic witness*, as the Father sends the Son, the *Paraklētos* is sent by the Father and the Son, the believers are sent by the Son into the world — in order to witness about Christ in order to bring people through him to the Father, who sent the Son and the Spirit — and so forth. The agency of the Son is somewhat encapsulated by such passages as 3:31–36; 13:3; and 17:2–5.

d) Finally, Jesus is portrayed as *having supernatural knowledge*. He knows Nathanael from afar (1:48f.); he knows what is in the hearts of humans (2:24f.); the Samaritan woman experiences herself as being known by Jesus (4:39); and Jesus knows what will transpire beforehand (4:1; 6:64; 13:1, 3, 13). Nowhere in the canonical scriptures is Jesus' *divinity* portrayed more graphically than in John.

II. John's Subordinated Christology

The Son's subordination to the Father has often been equated with a 'low' christology in John, although this may not reflect a satisfactory understanding of either issue. For the sake of simplification, the aspects of John's 'low' christology may be divided into four groups. a) *The Son's dependence on the Father* is the theme which makes it very clear that the Son works not of his own accord, but in keeping with the Father's will. Verses 5:19, 30, (cf. also above, App. I, the second section of part c); 7:16; 8:16, 28; 12:49; 14:10 suggest that Jesus is *totally* dependent upon the Father for all he does and says. Another verse is even stronger (14:28): 'The Father is *greater than* (*meizōn*) the Son.' Here the Son is clearly portrayed as subordinate to the Father. Put positively, the Son's mission is to *glorify the Father* (12:28; 13:31b; 14:13; 17:1b, 4).

b) A second group of verses refers to *the fleshly existence of the Son.* Depending on their interpretation, such verses as 1:14a; 6:51, 52, 53, 54, 55, 56, 63 refer to the *sarx* of Jesus, and therefore his fleshly humanity. In the rest of the New Testament, other than in the Johannine Epistles, the word *sarx* is *not used at all* with reference to Jesus' human existence (as 1 John 4:2–3 and 2 John 7 articulate an emphasis on believing that Jesus Christ has come *in the flesh*). Also, out of his side flow blood and water (19:34), and Thomas touches the flesh-wounds in his hands and side (20:27).

c) A less emphasized aspect of Jesus' humanity in John is its *'pathetic'* (*pathos*-filled) *portrayal of Jesus.* While the suffering of the Son of Man is less clear in John than in the Synoptics, the portrayal of Jesus' *pathos* is illustrated by his reactions to events and his interactions with other people. Especially significant are the Johannine dialogues (1:38–51; 2:16–20; 3:1–12; 4:7–26; 5:6–8, 14, 17ff.; 6:25–58, 60–70; 8:12–58; 9:2–5, 35–41; 10:24–38; 11:3–16, 21–34, 39–44; 13:6–10, 31–38; 14:5–7, 8–14, 22–24; 18:4–9, 19–24, 29–38; 19:8–11; 20:15–17, 26–29; 21:15–22), in which Jesus interacts with another individual or group.

d) Finally, the *emotions* of Jesus are presented in such a way that the reader is confronted with a very 'human' portrayal of Jesus. He weeps (11:35), his heart is deeply troubled (11:33, 12:27; 13:21), he groans (11:33, 38), on the cross he thirsts (19:28), and he loves his own (11:3, 5, 36; 13:1, 23, 34; 14:21; 15:9, 10, 12; 19:26; 20:2; 21:7, 20). While Jesus also knows what will befall him (4:1; 6:64; 13:1, 3, 11) and knows what is in humanity (1:48; 2:24–25; 5:42), it may *not* be said that the Johannine Jesus is portrayed as an emotionally detached, non-human phantasm. He is portrayed as a feeling, thinking human being. Nowhere in the canonical scriptures is Jesus' *humanity* portrayed more extensively than in John.

III. Johannine Signs as Facilitators of Belief

It seems quite clear that the Johannine signs are included in order to evoke a believing response from the audience. This is expressed in at least eight ways. a) Statements are included which reflect the notion that *miraculous signs authenticate one's divine origin and authority*. A sinner cannot do miraculous works (9:16), but they are expected of the Messiah (2:18; 3:2; 6:30; 7:31; 10:41–42). The point is also made, with irony, in that in spite of miraculous signs people still do not believe (10:25; 12:37).

b) After seeing a sign and witnessing Jesus' glory in some way, the Johannine narrative records the effect on others, as *people believe as a result of seeing a sign* (1:50; 2:11; 4:53; 6:2, 14; 11:15, 45, 48; 12:11, 18–19; 20:8, 27–28).

c) Sometimes *people believe simply on the basis of Jesus' words* (4:42; 5:24; 7:40–41; 8:30; 14:11a).

d) Sometimes *a prediction is made by Jesus for the expressed purpose of evoking faith upon its fulfillment* (12:32–33; 13:19; 14:29; 16:4; 18:32; 21:19).

e) The *fulfillment of scriptures as a basis for belief* is also recognized by the disciples, especially after the resurrection (2:22; 12:13–16, 38–41; 13:18; 17:12; 19:24, 28, 36–37).

f) Another characteristically Johannine motif is that *witnesses have come to testify that Jesus has been sent from God*. John the Baptist (1:7, 8, 15, 19, 32, 34; 5:32–35), the Samaritan woman (4:39), the Father (5:37; 8:18), Jesus himself (3:11, 32; 4:44; 5:36; 8:14, 18), Jesus' works (5:36; 10:25), and the *Paraklētos* (15:26) all bear witness to Jesus' origin and his mission. This testimony is thus intended to convince the reader that Jesus is sent from the Father.

g) In two cases, *a divine voice is sounded for the pistic benefit of those who are present* (11:41–42; 12:28–29).

h) Finally, *the Gospel itself is written in order to evoke a believing response from the reader* (20:31). The Johannine Gospel is a signifying witness in written form, designed to facilitate saving and abiding belief.

IV. Johannine Signs and the Existentializing Work of the Evangelist

In contrast to using signs to evoke faith, the Fourth Gospel also betrays antipathy toward the kind of faith that is dependent upon miracles for its sustenance. a) Belief on the basis of the miracles themselves is encouraged, but it is also regarded as ultimately being *incomplete belief* (10:37–38; 14:11b). If people cannot believe in Jesus fully, they are encouraged at least to begin by believing in the signs as a step in the right direction, penultimate though it be.

b) The evangelist also portrays Jesus' apparent *frustration with those who require 'signs and wonders' before they will believe* (4:48). This point is made dramatically by Thomas' skeptical attitude and demand for physical proof before believing (20:25). Blessed (and more mature?) belief is independent from the need to see as a prerequisite for faith (20:29).

c) The evangelist also seeks to *answer the question as to why people do not believe despite the presence of ample signs.* Several possibilities emerge: people lack understanding (3:10–12); refuse to leave their darkness and come to the light, lest their deeds be exposed (3:18–21); are not indwelt by the word of the Father (5:38); did not believe Moses' writings (5:47); do not understand the source of Moses' signs being God (6:31–36); are offended by the incarnation and its implications (6:64); are 'from below' instead of 'from above' (8:23); are not seekers of truth (8:45–46); or are not members of Jesus' flock (10:25–26). Ultimately, the evangelist can only explain this problem by viewing it as a fulfillment of the scriptures (12:37, 39). In the rejection of Jesus, the prophecies of Isaiah 6:10 and 53:1 are fulfilled. For the Fourth Gospel, sin is equated with *the refusal to believe*, and this extends to both action and being (16:9f.).

d) There are sections which *place the emphasis more on the existential significance* and less on the miraculous import of the signs. Even though the crowd perceived him to be a prophet like Moses, Jesus did not want to be made a king (6:14f.). The fact that some had not focused on the existential meaning of the feeding miracle (but only the alleviation of hunger) meant they hadn't really 'seen' the sign (6:26), as Jesus is the *true* bread which comes down from heaven (6:51). True sight is to believe in him as the Son of Man (9:35–38), while ironically, to claim to 'see' without believing is to remain utterly blind (9:39–41). Finally, the purpose behind Lazarus' illness (as well as for the blind man's, 9:3) is that through it the glory of God might be manifested (11:4). Notice also the undercurrent of *theodicy* in ch.11. *If only* Jesus had been there, Lazarus wouldn't have died (11:21, 32); ... and, he who opened the eyes of the blind man *should have been able* to have kept this one from dying (11:37)! The reflective interpretation of the Johannine signs suggests that their key significance is other than the mere awesomeness of the miraculous. They are also christological, and they are designed to convey the existential significance of Jesus' works for later audiences.

e) The *spiritual is often prioritized over the physical* in John. Regarding signs, Jesus is wary to 'entrust' himself to those in search of signs (2:23–25); and true, righteous judgment is not limited to outward appearances alone (7:24; 8:15), but it involves judgment according to truth and light (7:18; 3:17–21). Facilitative though it be, signs faith in John is largely preliminary. 'Blessed' belief is that which transcends the need to see outwardly before trusting inwardly.

V. Realized Eschatology in John

The realized eschatology of John may be perceived in several ways. a) On one hand, it has to do with *the fullness of time being reached in the ministry of Jesus*. The 'hour' is coming for the Son of Man to be glorified (12:23, 27; 13:1; 17:1), and this has to do primarily with the Passion events.

b) A second aspect of John's realized eschatology is *the presence of the future*. 'The hour is coming *and now is*' when true worshippers will worship the Father in spirit and truth (4:23); when the dead will hear the voice of the Son of God and ... live (5:25); and when believers will be scattered, each to his own home (16:32).

c) A third aspect is the way in which *saving events are actualized in the here and now. Now* is the time for the world to be judged and for the Prince of the World to be driven out (12:31). Jesus' followers are *already* clean through the word he has spoken (15:3). He who believes in Jesus is not condemned (3:18a); and Jesus is come in order that people might experience abundant life (10:10). Thus, John's eschatology seems to emphasize its realization in the here and now. It is *salvation in the present tense*.

VI. Futuristic Eschatology in John

There is, however, an inclination towards a futuristic eschatology in John, and its aspects are roughly parallel to the three aspects above in Appendix V. a) There are many instances in which an event does *not* transpire because *the timing in Jesus' ministry is not yet fulfilled* (2:4; 7:6, 8, 30; 8:20). Thus, his 'hour' had not yet come, and the eschatological explanation is that Jesus' 'hour' was still in the future.

b) John's futuristic eschatology *alludes to several events in the future which are impending but not yet actualized.* The hour 'is coming' when people will worship neither on the Samaritan mountain nor in Jerusalem (4:21, although cf. v.23); those in tombs who hear the voice of the Son of Man will come forth (5:28–9); those who put believers to death will think they are serving God (16:2); and when Jesus will speak plainly without figurative language (16:25, although cf. vs.29). Jesus also promises to come again and receive his disciples unto himself (14:3), and he promises to send the *Paraklētos* to continue his ministry among his followers (14:16–29; 15:26; 16:7–15).

c) A third aspect of John's futuristic eschatology is the emphasis on *those events which will happen 'on the last day'.* Those who believe in the Son will be raised up on the last day (6:39, 40, 44, 54). Martha articulates a view (which seems to represent the conventional understanding) that people will rise again in the resurrection at the last day (11:24); and the words of Jesus will judge unbelievers on the last day (12:48). Thus, John's eschatology seems to emphasize also the anticipation of its future actualization. In this sense, it is *salvation as a future hope.*

VII. Philo's Use of Manna as a Secondary Text

Even though there is not the space for a full demonstration of the argument here, a few examples of the rhetorical form of the manna motif used as a secondary text may be helpful. This pattern may be clearly identified in the two Philonic passages discussed in greatest detail by Borgen, *Mut.* 253–263 (pp. 99–121) and *Leg.all.* III 162–168 (pp. 122–146). In both cases, it is instructive to note that the discussion does *not* begin with an exegesis of Ex. 16:4, or some elaboration upon heavenly bread (although, beginnings and endings are notoriously difficult to identify within Philo's circular and rambling style). Rather, in each case, *another theme* is set forth as the exhortative thrust of the writer, and after some discussion the manna motif is brought in as a secondary and verifying text, supporting the original idea. The outlines are as follows:

Mut. 252–263

(A) *Main point of argument*: It is understandable that even the man of virtue may settle for instruction from below (praying that Ishmael, seed of Hagar, be kept alive, 253–255), even though God's promise is to provide self-taught instruction from above (the virtue of Isaac, son of Sarah, 253–255). But, even though man in his weakness asks for one thing (Ishmael), God in his kindness, may give two (Sarah's son as well, 253).

(B) *The discussion of the main point in dualistic terms*: The folly of the way of the flesh is heightened by means of rhetorical questions. 'Have the eyes been taught to see, do the nostrils learn to smell, do the hands touch or the feet advance in obedience to the orders or exhortations of instructors?' (256). Thus, 'Does our mind attend the school of the professor of wisdom and there learn to think and to apprehend?' (257). The 'nation of vision' alone receives its 'food' from heaven, while men receive theirs from the earth (258).

(C) *God's giving of manna as rhetorical trump*: 'The earthly food is produced with the co-operation of husbandmen, but the heavenly is sent like the snow by God the solely self-acting, with none to share his work. And indeed it says "Behold I rain upon you bread from heaven" (Ex. 16:4).' (259).

(D) *Continued discussion and implications*: 'Of what food can he rightly say that it is rained from heaven, save of heavenly wisdom which is sent from above on souls which yearn for virtue by Him who sheds the gift of prudence in rich abundance ...?' (259–260).

(E) *Reiteration of the original theme in the light of the present discussion*: Even though God may allow 'both forms of virtue' (the virtue of Ishmael, fleshly seed of Hagar = others-taught knowledge, versus the virtue of Isaac, spiritual seed of Sarah = self-taught knowledge), ' ... where man is weak he will claim the former, where he is strong the latter comes ready to his hands.' (263). The main point (A) is proven with the help of manna rhetoric (C) as a proof text — a rhetorical trump.

Leg. All. III 161–178

(A) *Main text being exegeted*: Gen. 3:14 [*not* Ex. 16:4] (God, saying to the serpent) 'Earth shalt thou eat all the days of thy life.' and thus, the implied exhortation: But you, being human, have a living soul (Gen. 2:7), which requires another kind of nourishment that is spiritual (161).

(B) *Discussion of the main point in dualistic terms*: There are two aspects of humanity, body and soul. Thus, the ' ... the body [being] fashioned out of earth has food akin to it which earth yields, while the soul being a portion of an ethereal nature has on the contrary ethereal and divine food ...' (161).

(C) *The use of 'heavenly food' as scriptural 'proof' of main point*: (i.e. manna used as a rhetorical trump): 'That the food of the soul is not earthly but heavenly, we shall find abundant evidence in the Sacred Word.' (162). What follows over the next 15 sentences, then (162–176), is a five-fold development of the manna theme (162–166, 167–168, 169–171, 172–173, and 174–176), at each turn, making a slightly different application of some aspect of the manna-giving story.

(D) *Continued discussion and implications*: 'Now those of whom we have been speaking pray to be fed with the word of God. But Jacob, looking even higher than the word, says that he is fed by God himself.' (177, cf. Gen. 48:15f.). The life-producing word of God also has implications regarding physical healing in the simplest sense ... both through medical science and through the physician's skill ... though it is He Himself that heals alike by these means and without them.' (178). Salutary implications of (A) are clarified.

(E) *Reiteration of main theme in the light of the present discussion*: 'Now His mode of dealing is the same in the case of the soul. The good things, the food, He Himself bestows with His own hand, but by the agency of Angels and Words such as involve riddance of ills.' (178). Again, the midrashic interpretation of the main text (A) and its implications (D) are demonstrated by the profuse employment of manna (C) as a *rhetorical trump*.

One also could find parallel structures in the other manna references in Philo, and such a rhetorical pattern is even more clearly identifiable within *Exodus Rabbah* and *Exodus Mekilta*, where Ex. 16:4 is used as a secondary text, bolstering another point, or confirming the midrashic interpretation of *another text*. The implications of this pattern are developed further, above in Chapters 3 and 9. In virtually *all* of the ancient Jewish literature on the manna motif, except *Exodus Rabbah* 25:1–8 and a few other passages, it is not primarily the meaning of manna that is exegeted. Rather, some other text or motif is explored with the assistance of manna rhetoric, and John 6 is no exception.

VIII. The Papias Tradition, John's Authorship and Luke/Acts

The prevalent view of Johannine scholars is that Papias' connecting of John the apostle with the authorship of the Fourth Gospel (ca. 150 CE — cited by Irenaeus ca. 180 CE, who is then cited by Eusebius ca. 325 CE) is untrustworthy historically. Supposedly, Irenaeus was motivated by religious interests to levy a "fourfold gospel" against Marcion and the heretics and thus connected the four gospels fictitiously with either first-hand or second-hand apostolic authorship. Given John's divergence from the Synoptics and internal ambiguity about its own authorship, scholars have largely concluded that the Fourth Gospel could not have been written by an apostle such as John. If this is true, the origin of John's tradition becomes a problem, and source theories have been posed to address this issue, as well as to explain the character of John's theological tensions. The purpose of the essay is not to cover old ground within this debate, but to contribute new findings, and questions, which may further the discussion. In particular, Papias' identifying John (or someone like him) as the primary source of the Johannine Gospel will be explored using Luke/Acts as first-century sources of external reference.

Given the impressive degree of authenticity restored to the Papias tradition by M. Hengel's recent monograph (*The Johannine Question*, London/Philadelphia, 1989), the unbroken traditional connection from John to Polycarp (and perhaps Ignatius) to Papias to Irenaeus is one deserving of renewed critical consideration. What one finds, however, when considering the relationship of John to the Johannine tradition, is that Papias is *not* the earliest historical source. Luke/Acts is. As far as I know, this connection has been completely overlooked by all sides of the debate. Nonetheless, the evidence is as follows:

In Acts 4:20, John the apostle is portrayed as making a statement which has an unmistakably Johannine ring. Actually, Peter *and* John are quoted in vss. 19–20 as speaking, but the statement contains two sentences. The first, 'Whether it is right before God to listen to you, rather than to God, you decide.' is reiterated by Peter (and the apostles) in 5:29, "We must obey God rather than humans!" See also 11:17 for a characteristically Petrine aphorism.

This is precisely the sort of Socratic rhetoric that Luke understands Peter to have used in challenging the authority of the Sanhedrin in Acts 4, 5 and elsewhere in Acts 11. Interestingly, this human/divine dichotomy of authority is also remarkably close to the kind of thing Peter might have actually said, if the Matthean memory of him (let alone 1 Peter) is at all representative of his interests. The Petrine view of authority characteristically hinges upon divine commissioning. Based on the kind of authority-imbued (and wielding) institution erected in his memory, Luke was not far off in such a portrayal.

Likewise, his portrayal of John seems equally characteristic. Using typically Johannine syntax and construction, Luke renders the second part of the statement: 'For we cannot help speaking about that which we have *seen* and *heard*!' One *could not have uttered* a more characteristically Johannine statement! The *ou ... gar* syntax, followed by verb-last construction, and the centrality of *eidamen* and *ekousamen* make this *an unmistakable reference to characteristically Johannine* rhetoric. Most similar to 1 John 1:1–3, the passage is also reminiscent of John 1:1–18, and especially *the testimony of the Johannine Jesus* in John 3:32 (see also Rev. 1:9–19; 22:8 — not that these were written by the same author, of course). Indeed, *seeing and hearing* are central components of the Johannine 'witness motif' — the witness attests to what he/she has seen and heard (note the identical sequence of the verbs), and the audience must respond to the revelatory message of the messenger (see Jn. 3:32; 5:37; 8:38, etc.). Even the author of 1 John employs the Johannine witness motif as the basis for his authority, and the statement is remarkably similar to Acts 4:20: 'We announce to you what we have *seen* and *heard* in order that you might have fellowship with us.' (1 Jn. 1:3)

Obviously, just as the first part of the composite statement attributed to Peter and John (note also the matching *sequence* of names and statements) employs a rhetorical statement with a

Petrine ring to it, the second part employs a statement entirely characteristic of recognizably Johannine rhetoric. The close conjunction of seeing *and* hearing verbs is nearly absent from Luke and rare in the rest of Acts. Of some 237 occurrences of 'seeing' verbs in Luke/Acts, and some 162 occurrences of *akouō*, only 8 of these occur together (Lk. 2:20; 7:22; Ac. 2:33; 4:20; 8:6; 9:7; 19:26; 22:15). Of these, *only one* pair appears in the first person and in the same sequence (as in Jn. 3:32 *and* 1 Jn. 1:3): Acts 4:20. This implies Acts 4:20 is largely uncharacteristic of Luke's style and represents an intentional identification. The implications are as follows:

A) The earliest historical connecting of the apostle John and the Johannine tradition is *not* Irenaeus, or even Papias, but *Luke* a century or so earlier. Even if he was wrong, or misguided, the least one must admit is that as early as the 70's or 80's (and possibly earlier, if one considers this as a part of Luke's tradition), Luke has articulated an unmistakable connection between the apostle John and a Johannine-sounding saying. This fact has been hitherto completely overlooked by all sides of the debate and deserves critical consideration.

B) Furthermore, this connection must have antedated the writing of the Johannine Gospel and Epistles. Thus, Luke must have drawn the connection from the *oral* — not the written — stages of the Johannine tradition. Put otherwise, Luke either had met John or had heard stories about him from others who apparently had. Was John one of those (who were 'from the beginning' — *ap archēs* — cf. Lk. 1:2 and 1 Jn. 1:1) 'eye-witnesses and servants of the Word (*logos*, cf. Jn. 1:1)' mentioned in Luke 1:2? If John was indeed considered a 'pillar' in the church (along with Peter and James, Gal. 2:9) by Paul and others, it is highly improbable that Luke's 'orderly' investigation would not have achieved familiarity with his influence and tradition.

C) This is the only explanation for the little-considered fact that where Luke diverges from Mark and Matthew, he often converges with *John*. Many gospel critics attribute the similarities between Luke and John to Johannine dependence on Luke or their use of a common source. However, this is unlikely for three reasons: First, these similarities are most commonly identifiable in sections *other than the L tradition* units. They accompany Luke's treatment of the Marcan tradition as much as anything. This suggests Luke's intentional preference for tradition which is Johannine and not Marcan (nor from Q), as far as we know. It is also a fact that Johannine/ Lucan contacts do not show any evidence of John's incorporation of other Lucan material.

Second, if Matthean and Lucan redactions of Mark are at all suggestive of typical gospel redactional work, the two main characteristics — i.e. the replacement of non-symbolic illustrative detail with generalizing terms, and the replacement of theologically interpretive asides with common-sense conjecture about what Jesus and the disciples must have been up to — are totally missing in John. If John is not derivative from Mark (as the above study demonstrates), John is even less likely to have been based on Luke, based on redaction analysis.

Third, even more convincing is the fact that John/Luke agreements often couple Luke with John — *against* Matthew (Q) and Mark. This *cannot* be explained on the basis of Johannnie dependence on Luke. The relationship can only have been the reverse. Following are but a few examples which lend themselves to three categories: sequence and inclusion, wording and detail, and thematic agreements between Luke and John, where Luke *also* disagrees with Mark and Matthew.

1. *Sequence and inclusion commonalities unique to Luke and John*:
— Rather than two sea crossings, as in Mark and Matthew, Luke includes *one* — as in John.
— Rather than two feedings, as in Mark and Matthew, Luke includes *one* — as in John.
— Rather than placing Peter's confession after the feeding of the 4,000, as in Matthew and Mark, Luke places it *after the feeding of the 5,000* — as in John.
— Only John and Luke contain references to Mary and Martha being sisters who were very close to Jesus, as well as references to a man named Lazarus.
— Only Luke and John include the miracle of the great catch of fish, with similar details, although Luke employs the narrative as part of the calling of the Twelve, and John (the compiler)

employs it as an appearance narrative. Obviously, the disparate location of the events in John 21 and Luke 5 dispels any notion of borrowing from either of the gospels in written form. However, it is entirely conspicuous that Luke replaces the Marcan calling narrative with an adaptation of this Johannine pericope. Luke must have drawn it from the Johannine oral tradition, but rather than emphasizing the ecclesial role of Peter (shepherding/tending the flock), he employs it to emphasize the evangelistic calling of Peter and the rest (fishing for men).

2. *Similarities of wording and detail between Luke and John exclusively*:
— It is the *right* ear of the servant that is severed.
— Luke adds *tou theou* to Peter's confession (Lk. 9:20) in accord with the Johannine *ho hagios tou theou* (Jn. 6:69 — probably closer to the actual confession than the later, Hellenized rendition).
— Only Luke and John mention that Peter arrived at the tomb, as well as the linen cloths lying by themselves (Lk. 24:2 — missing from some ancient mss. but present in P[75]; see Jn. 20: 3–9).
— Luke and the Fourth Evangelist are the only New Testament writers to refer to the Holy Spirit as 'wind' (Ac. 2:2; Jn. 3:8).
— Only Luke and John record Jesus' anointing by the woman as the anointing of his *feet* with costly perfume (a *less likely* rendition than the more 'kingly' anointing of his head in Matthew and Mark — Jn. 12:1–11; Lk. 7:36–50) and her wiping his feet with her hair.
— Satan enters Judas as part of the betrayal (Jn. 13:27; Lk. 22:3).
— Jesus extols the greatness of servanthood, portraying himself as the exemplary servant (Jn. 13:4–5, 12–14; Lk. 22:27).
— Only John and Luke record the disciples' questioning over who would betray Jesus (Jn. 13:22–26; Lk. 22:23).
— Both John and Luke report Pilate as declaring 'I find no crime' in this man (Jn. 19:6; Lk. 23:4).
— Only John and Luke identify a *second Judas* — not Judas Iscariot (Lk. 6:16; Jn. 14:22).
— The road to Emmaus and the Lucan appearance narratives are filled with Johannine nuance and detail (Jn. 20–21; Lk. 24:13–49): Jesus' sudden standing with them in their midst, the emphasis on Jesus' flesh-wounds, Jesus' eating fish and bread with them, the appearance of the Lord to Simon and the emphasis on forgiveness of sins.

3. *Thematic similarities distinctively common to Luke and John*:
While these connections are the least obvious, they still raise the question of whether Luke's departure from Matthew and Mark reflects some degree of Johannine influence theologically.
— Jesus embraces Samaritans.
— Jesus shows special concern for women.
— Jesus emphasizes the priority of the Spirit as it relates to the power of the Kingdom.

In some ways, one feels hesitant to align oneself with a position often associated with non-critical traditionalism. But the fact is that the last century of Johannine scholarship has failed to produce a convincing alternative that withstands the test of critical scrutiny. Diachronic theories regarding the composition of the Johannine Gospel's text are appealing for a variety of reasons, but in assenting to them the critical scholar must acknowledge the following: a) The stylistic and contextual evidence suggesting the evangelist's use of earlier sources is genuinely lacking. Source theories have been marshalled to compensate for the fact that John's tradition is both independent and fairly reliable, and to account for much of John's theological tension. b) While there *is* theological tension in John, given the fact that John represents a completely independent tradition (perhaps even from its earliest stages) the view that the evangelist's dialogue must have been with an alien document (as opposed to a dialogue with the prevalent Synoptic interpretation of Jesus' intentionality) is an inadequate hypothetical construct. It has no textual evidence or precedent to support its veracity. Clearly, the evangelist was a dialectical thinker, and he even engaged his own tradition dialectically. The view that theological tension must imply more than one source overlooks 'partners' in dialogue, such as one's audience, one's evolving understanding of the meaning of events, and the incessant cognitive dialogue between one's perceptions of the way things are meant to be and the way things turn out experientially. c) Papias is not the earliest known writer to connect John with the Fourth Gospel. Luke is, and this fact has been hitherto overlooked by Johannine and Lucan scholars alike. The explicit connections of Acts 4:20 are also made implicitly in Luke 1:2, and those who discard the opinion of the Johannine compiler (Jn. 21:24f.), that John's tradition stems from an eye-witness source, must acknowledge that they do so *against two first-century historical opinions*: the compiler's and Luke's. d) The fact of Luke's agreement with the Johannine witness, against Mark and Matthew (and thus Q), can *only* be explained on the basis of Lucan dependence on the Johannine tradition — probably within its oral stages. These facts cannot be explained as adequately on the basis of Johannine dependence on Luke. This view is the result of allowing the prevalent opinion regarding John's non-authorship to dictate outcomes, rather than the redactional facts. e) Given the three facts: that critical scholars have largely left unexplored the findings of C.H. Dodd and F. Mussner regarding the epistemological morphology and origin of the Johannine tradition; that the portrayal of Jesus' ministry in John is entirely parallel to the religious-anthropological findings of the 'Third Quest for the Historical Jesus' (even though it is rendered in its own distinctive 'Johannine paraphrase'); and that the Marcan tradition was itself a largely 'theological' (not simply 'historical') work, one wonders whether critics of the post-modern era will overturn many of the prevalent opinions about John by further critical investigation. Unless more convincing evidence is produced, this may indeed eventuate.

The purpose of this essay is not to argue a definitive view of Johannine authorship. That is far beyond the scope and interest of this brief appendix. It is, however, to contribute new findings and questions to the larger debate, wondering how they will affect interpretive approaches to John. At least it is to demonstrate that *exploring the cognitive origins of John's independent witness*, perhaps even stemming from the earliest traditional stages, is a *warranted venture*. Finally, however, one cannot base one's interpretation entirely on a single view of authorship. One must always interpret the text with a considerable amount of presuppositional modesty, allowing for diverging opinions. However, given the facts of Luke's connecting the Johannine tradition with John the apostle as early as the 70's, and the compiler's connecting of the Fourth Evangelist with an eye-witness source in the 90's, and given the fact that diachronic theorists have failed to produce convincing alternatives, perhaps Papias (at least in regards to John's origin) was *right*.

Bibliographies

I. The Christology of John

Agourides, S., 'The "High Priestly Prayer" of Jesus', SE IV, Berlin, ed. F.L. Cross, Berlin, 1968, pp. 137–145.

Anderson, P.N., 'Acts 4:20: A First Century Historical Clue to Johannine Authorship?' (unpublished paper presented at the Pacific Northwest Region AAR/SBL Meeting, May 1992).

——, 'The Cognitive Origins of John's Unitive and Disunitive Christology', *Horizons in Biblical Theology* 17, 1995, pp. 1–24.

——, 'Revelation and Rhetoric: Two Dialogical Modes of Narrative Progression in the Fourth Gospel' (unpublished paper presented at the Pacific Northwest Region AAR/SBL Meeting, May 1990).

Appold, M., 'Christ Alive! Church Alive! Reflections on the Prayer of Jesus in John 17', *CTM* 5, 1978, pp. 365–373.

Ashton, J., *The Interpretation of John* IRT 9, Philadelphia/London, 1986.

——, *Understanding the Fourth Gospel*, Oxford, 1991.

Barrett, C.K., 'Christocentric or Theocentric? Observations on the Theological Method of the Fourth Gospel', in his *Essays on John*, London, 1982, pp. 1–18.

——, ' "The Father is Greater Than I" (John 14:28): Subordinationist Christology in the New Testament', in his *Essays on John*, London, 1982, pp. 19–36.

——, 'The Prologue of St. John's Gospel', *New Testament Essays,* London, 1972, pp. 27–48.

Bauckham, R., 'The Sonship of the Historical Jesus in Christology', *SJT* 31, pp. 245–260 (esp. pp. 253ff.).

Beasley-Murray, G.R., *Gospel of Life; Theology in the Fourth Gospel*, Peabody, Mass., 1991.

——, *John* WBC, vol. 36, Waco, 1987.

Becker, H., *Die Reden des Johannesevangeliums und der Stil der gnostischen Offenbarungsreden*, Göttingen, 1956.

Becker, J., 'Wunder und Christologie. Zum literarkritischen und christologischen Problem der Wunder im Johannesevangelium', *NTS* 16, 1969/70, pp. 130–148.

——, 'Ich bin die Auferstehung und das Leben: Eine Skizze der Johanneischen Christologie', *ThZ* 39, 1983, pp. 138–151.

Berger, K., 'Zu "Das Wort ward Fleisch", Joh. 1:14a', *NovT* 16, 1974, pp. 161–166.

Betz, O., 'The Concept of the So-Called "Divine Man" in Mark's Christology', in *Studies in New Testament and Early Christian Literature*; essays in honor of Allen P. Wikgren, ed. D.E. Aune, Leiden, 1972, pp. 229–240.

——, 'Das Problem des Wunders bei Flavius Josephus im Vergleich zum Wunderproblem bei den Rabbinen und im Johannesevangelium', in *Josephus Studien; Untersuchungen zu Josephus, dem antiken Judentum und das Neuen Testament* (Otto Michel, 70. Geburtstag), ed. O. Betz, K. Ellinger and M. Hengel, Göttingen, 1974, pp. 23–44.

——, *Der Paraklet; Fürsprecher im häretischen Spätjudentum, im Johannes-Evangelium und in den neu gefundenen gnostischen Schriften*, AGSU 2, Leiden, 1963.

Beutler, J., 'Psalm 42/43 im Johannesevangelium', *NTS* 25, 1978, pp. 33–57.

Bittner, W.T., *Jesu Zeichen im Johannes evangelium*, Tübingen, 1987.

Blank, J., *Krisis; Untersuchungen zur johanneischen Christologie und Eschatologie*, Freiburg, 1964.

Boice, J.M., *Witness and Revelation in the Gospel of John*, Grand Rapids/Exeter, 1970.

Boismard, M.-L., 'Jesus the Savior According to St. John', in *Word and Mystery; Biblical Essays on the Person and Mission of Christ*, ed. L.J. O'Donavan, Glen Rock, N.J./London, 1968, pp. 69–85.

——, *Moses or Jesus; An Essay in Johannine Christology*, E.t., B.T. Viviano, Minneapolis/ Leuven, 1993.

——, 'La royauté du Christ dans le quatriéme évangile', *LV* 11, 1962, pp. 43–63.

Boobyer, G.H., 'Jesus as "Theos" in the New Testament', *BJRL* 50, 1967–8, pp. 247–261.

Booth, K.N., 'The Self-Proclamation of Jesus in St. John's Gospel', *Colloquium* 7, 1975, pp. 36–47.

Borgen, P., 'God's Agent in the Fourth Gospel', in *Religions in Antiquity; Essays in Memory of E.R. Goodenough*, Leiden, 1968, pp. 137–148; also reprinted in J. Ashton, *The Interpretation of John*, IRT 9, 1986, pp. 67–78; and in *Logos Was the True Light*, pp. 121–132.

——, 'Logos Was the True Light', in his *Logos Was the True Light*, pp. 95–110; also in *NovT* 14, 1972, pp. 115–130.

——, 'Some Jewish Exegetical Traditions as Background for Son of Man Sayings in John's Gospel (John 13:13–14 and context)', in de Jonge, *L'Evangile de Jean*, Leuven, 1977, pp. 243–258.

Boring, M.E., 'The Influence of Christian Prophecy on the Johannine Portrayal of the Paraclete and Jesus', *NTS* 25, 1978, pp. 113–123.

Bousset, W., *Kyrios Christos; A History of the Belief in Christ from the Beginnings of Christianity to Irenaeus*, E.t., J.E. Steely, Nashville, (5th ed., 1965) 1970.

——, 'Ist das vierte Evangelium eine literarische Einheit?', *ThR* 12, 1909, pp. 1–12, 39–64.

Bowker, J.W., 'The Origin and Purpose of St. John's Gospel', *NTS* 11, 1965, pp. 398–408.

Braun, F.-M., *Jean le Théologien I*: Jean le Théologien et son evangile dans l'église ancienne, 1959; *II*: Les grandes traditions d'Israël, 1964; *III*: Sa Théologie: Le mystèrie de Jésus-Christ, 1966, Paris.

Breck, J., *Spirit of Truth; The Holy Spirit in the Johannine Tradition* Vol. 1, Crestwood, N.Y., 1991.

Brodie, T.L., 'Jesus as the New Elijah: Cracking the Code', *ET* 93, Nov. 1981, pp. 39–42.

Brown, R.E., 'The Theology of the Incarnation in John', in his *New Testament Essays*, New York, 1965, pp. 132–137.

——, 'Appendix II: The "Word" ', *Gospel*, pp. 519–524.

——, 'Appendix III: Signs and Works', *Gospel*, pp. 525–532.

——, 'Appendix IV: EgoEimi — "I Am" ', *Gospel*, pp. 533–538.

——, 'The Kerygma of the Gospel of John; The Johannine View of Jesus in Modern Studies', *Int* 21, 1967, pp. 387–400.

——, 'The "Paraclete" in the Fourth Gospel', *NTS* 13, 1966, pp. 113–132.

Bühner, J.-A., *Der Gesandte und sein Weg im vierten Evangelium. Die kultur- und religionsgeschichtlichen Grundlagen der johanneischen Sendungschristologie sowie ihre traditionsgeschichtliche Entwicklung*, WUNT 2:2, Tübingen, 1977.

Bultmann, R., *Theology of The New Testament* Vol. II, E.t., K. Grobel, New York, 1955, pp. 3–92.

——, 'The Eschatology of the Gospel of John', in his *Faith and Understanding*, E.t., L. Pettibone Smith (1928), London 1969, pp. 165–183.

——, 'The History of Religions Background of the Prologue to the Gospel of John', in J. Ashton, *Interpretation*, pp. 18–35 (Ashton's E.t. of 1923 Gunkel festschrift).

Cadman, W.H., *The Open Heaven; The Revelation of God in the Johannine Sayings of Jesus*, ed. G.B. Caird, New York, 1969.

Cahill, P.J., 'The Johannine *Logos* as Center', *CBQ* 38, 1976, pp. 54–72.

Carey, G.L., 'The Lamb of God and Atonement Theories', *TynB* 32, 1980, pp. 97–122.

Carson, D.A., *The Gospel According to John*, Grand Rapids, 1991.

——, *Divine Sovereignty and Human Responsibility*, London, 1981.

——, 'The Purpose of the Fourth Gospel: John, 20:30–31 Reconsidered', *JBL* 108, 1987, pp. 639–651.

Casey, M., *From Jewish Prophet to Gentile God; The Origins and Development of New Testament Christology*, Louisville, 1991.

Charlesworth, R.H. (ed.), *John and Qumran*, London, 1972.

——, *The Beloved Disciple. Whose Witness Validates the Gospel of John?* Valley Forge, 1995.

——, and R.A. Culpepper, 'The Odes of Solomon and the Gospel of John', *CBQ* 35, 1973, pp. 298–322.

Coetzee, J.C., 'Christ and the Prince of this World in the Gospel and the Epistles of St. John', *Neot* 2, 1968, pp. 104–121.

Collins, R.E., 'The Search for Jesus. Reflections on the Fourth Gospel', *Laval Théologique et Philosophique* 34, 1978, pp. 27–48.

——, *These Things Have Been Written: Studies on the Fourth Gospel*, LTPNZ, Louvain/Grand Rapids, 1990.

Conzelmann, H., *An Outline of the Theology of the New Testament*, E.t., J. Bowden, London, 1969, pp. 321–358.

Coppens, J., 'Les logia johanniques du Fils de l'homme', in de Jonge's *L 'Evangile de Jean*, 1977, pp. 311–315.

Crawford, R.G., 'The Relation of the Divinity and the Humanity in Christ', *EQ* 53, 1981, pp. 237–240.

Creutzig, H.E., 'Zur johanneischen Christologie', *NKZ* 49, 1938, pp. 214–222.

Cross, F.L., *Studies in the Fourth Gospel*, London, 1957.

Culpepper, R.A., 'The Pivot of John's Prologue', *NTS* 27, 1980, pp. 1–31.

——, *The Anatomy of the Fourth Gospel*, Philadelphia, 1983.

Dahms, J.V., 'The Johannine Use of Monogenēs Reconsidered', *NTS* 29, 1982, pp. 222–232.

Davey, J.E., *The Jesus of St. John; Historical and Christological Studies in the Fourth Gospel*, London, 1958.

Davis, G.M., 'The Humanity of Jesus in John', *JBL* 70, 1951, pp. 105–112.

Deeks, D., 'The Prologue of St. John's Gospel', *BTB* 6, 1976, pp. 62–78.

——, 'The Structure of the Fourth Gospel', *NTS* 15, 1968, pp. 107–129.

Dekker, C., 'Grundschrift und Redaktion im Johannesevangelium', *NTS* 13, 1966/7, pp. 66–80.

Delling, G., *Wort und Werk Jesu im Johannes-Evangelium*, Berlin, 1966.

Dion, H.-M., 'Quelque traits originaux de la conception johannique du Fils de l'Homme', *Sciences ecclésiastiques* 19, 1967, pp. 49–65.

Dodd, C.H., *Historical Tradition in the Fourth Gospel*, Cambridge, 1965.

Dunn, J.D.G., 'Let John be John; A Gospel for Its Time' in *Das Evangelium und die Evangelien* WUNT 28, ed. by Stuhlmacher, Tübingen, 1983, pp. 309–339.

Dupont, J., *Essais sur la christologie de saint Jean; Le Christ, parole. lumiére et vie, la gloire du Christ*, Brugge, 1951.

Du Rand, J.A., 'The Characterization of Jesus as Depicted in the Narrative of the Fourth Gospel', *Neot* 19, 1985, pp. 18–35.

——, *Johanine Perspectives; Introduction to the Johannine Writings* Part 1, Doornfontein, 1991.

Du Toit, A.B., 'The Incarnate Word — A Study of John 1:14', *Neot* 2, 1968, pp. 9–21.

Easton, B.S., 'Bultmann's RQ Source', *JBL* 65, 1946, pp. 143–156.

Evans, C.F., review of Bultmann's *The Gospel of John: A Commentary*, SJT 26, 1973, pp. 341–349.

Fennema, D.A., 'Jesus and God According to John. An Analysis of the Fourth Gospel's Father/ Son Christology', Dissertation, Duke University, 1979.

——, 'John 1:18: "God the Only Son" ', *NTS* 31, 1985, pp. 124–135.

Fenton, J.C., 'Towards an Understanding of John', SE IV, Berlin, 1968, pp. 28–37.

Feulliet, A., 'Les *Ego Eimi* christologiques du quatrième évangile', *RSR* 54, 1966, pp. 5–22, 213–240.

——, *Etudes Johanniques*, Paris, 1962.

Floor, L., 'The Lord and the Holy Spirit in the Fourth Gospel', *Neot* 2, 1968, pp. 122–130.

Flores, J., *Cristologia de Juan*, Barcelona, 1975.

Forestell, J.T., *The Word of the Cross; Salvation as Revelation in the Fourth Gospel*, Rome, 1974.

Fortna, R.T., 'Christology in the Fourth Gospel: Redaction-Critical Perspectives', *NTS* 21, 1975, pp. 489–504.

——, 'From Christology to Soteriology; A Redaction-Critical Study of Salvation in the Fourth Gospel', *Int* 27, 1973, pp. 31–47.

——, 'Source and Redaction in the Fourth Gospel's Portrayal of Jesus' Signs', *JBL* 89, 1970, pp. 151–166.

——, *The Gospel of Signs; A Reconstruction of the Narrative Source Underlying the Fourth Gospel*, SNTSMS 11, Cambridge, 1970.

——, *The Fourth Gospel and its Predecessor*, Philadelphia/Edinburgh, 1988.

Freed, E.D., '*Egō Eimi* in John 1:20 and 4:25', *CBQ* 41, 1979, pp. 288–291.

——, *Old Testament Quotations in the Gospel of John*, Leiden, 1965.

——, 'The Son of Man in the Fourth Gospel', *JBL* 86, 1967, pp. 402–409.

——, 'Who or What Was Before Adam in John 8:58?', *JSNT* 17, 1983, pp. 52–59.

——, 'Variations in the Language and Thought of John', *ZNW* 55, London, 1964, pp. 167–197.

Fuller, R.H., 'Incarnation and Historical Perspective', *ATR* Supplement Series, No. 7, Nov., 1976, pp. 57–66.

——, *The Foundations of New Testament Christology*, London, 1965.

Garvie, A.E., 'Jesus in the Fourth Gospel', *Expositor*, 8:17, 1919, pp. 312–320.

Giblin, C.H., 'Suggestion, Negative Response, and Positive Action in St. John's Portrayal of Jesus (John 2:1–11; 4:46–54; 7:2–14; 11:1–44)', *NTS* 26, 1980, pp. 197–211.

Glasson, T.F., *Moses in the Fourth Gospel*, London, 1963.

Groenwald, E.P., 'The Christological Meaning of John 20:31', *Neot* 2, 1968, pp. 131–140.

Haenchen, E., ' "Der Vater, der mich gesandt hat" ', *NTS* 9, 1963, pp. 208–216.

——, 'Vom Wandel des Jesusbildes in der frühen Gemeinde', in *Verborum Veritas; Festschrift für Gustav Stählin zum 70. Geburtstag*, ed. O. Böcher and K. Hacker, Wuppertal, 1970, pp. 3–14.

Hanson, A.A., 'The Jesus of the Fourth Gospel', *New Divinity* 5, 1974, pp. 20–24.

Harnack, A. von, 'Zur Textkritik und Christologie der Schriften des Johannes. Zugleich ein Beitrag zur Würdigung der ältesten lateinische Überlieferung und der Vulgata', *SPAW* 5, 2, Berlin, 1915, pp. 534–573.

Harner, P.B., *The 'I Am' of the Fourth Gospel*, Facet Books, Biblical Series 26, Philadelphia, 1970.

Hayward, C.T.R., 'The Holy Name of the God of Moses and the Prologue of St. John's Gospel', NTS 25, 1978/1979, pp. 16–32.

——, 'The Interpretation of the Wine Miracle at Cana: John 2:1–11', in *Glory*, pp. 83–112.

Hegermann, H., ' "Er kam in sein Eigentum." Zur Bedeutung des Erdenwirkens Jesu im vierten Evangelium', in *Der Ruf Jesu und die Antwort der Gemeinde*; Exegetische Untersuchungen Joachim Jeremias zum 70. Geburtstag gewidmet von seinem Schülern, ed. E. Lohse et al., Göttingen, 1970, pp. 112–131.

Hengel, M., *The Johannine Question*, London/Philadelphia, 1989.

Higgins, A.J.B., 'The Words of Jesus According to St. John', *BJRL* 49, 1966/7, pp. 363–386.

Hill, D., 'The Request of Zebedee's Sons and the Johannine *doxa*-theme', NTS 13, 1973, pp. 281–285.

——, 'The Relevance of the Logos Christology', *ExpT* 78, 1967, pp. 136–139.

Holladay, C., *Theios Anēr in Hellenistic Judaism: A Critique of the Use of this Category in New Testament Christology*, Missoula, 1977.

Howard, W.F., *The Fourth Gospel in Recent Criticism and Interpretation*, London, 1931.

Howton, D.J., ' "Son of God" in the Fourth Gospel', *NTS* 10, 1964, pp. 227–237.

Jervell, J., *Jesus in the Gospel of John*, E.t., H.T. Cleven, Minneapolis, 1984.

Johnson, S.E., 'Notes on the Prophet-King in John', *ATR* 51, 1969, pp. 35–37.

Johnston, G., '*Ecce Homo*! Irony in the Christology of the Fourth Evangelist', in *The Glory of Christ in the New Testament*, 1987, pp. 125–138.

——, *The Spirit-Paraclete in the Gospel of John*, SNTSM 12, Cambridge, 1970.

de Jonge, M., 'The Fourth Gospel: The Book of the Disciples', in *Jesus: Stranger from Heaven and Son of God*, SBLSBS 11, Missoula, 1977, pp. 1–27.

——, 'Variety and Development in Johannine Christology', in *Jesus: Stranger from Heaven and Son of God*, SBLSBS 11, Missoula, 1977, pp. 193–222.

——, 'Jewish Expectations about the "Messiah" According to the Fourth Gospel', *NTS* 19, 1972, pp. 246–270.

——, 'The Son of God and the Children of God in the Fourth Gospel', in *Saved by Hope; Essays in Honor of Richard C. Oudersluys*, ed. J.I. Cook, Grand Rapids, 1978, pp. 44–63.

——, 'Jesus as Prophet and King in the Fourth Gospel', *EphThL* 49:1, 1973, pp. 160–177.

Joubert, H.L.N., ' "The Holy One of God" (John 6:69)', *Neot* 2, 1968, pp. 57–69.

Käsemann, E., *The Testament of Jesus*, E.t. G. Krodel, London, 1968.

——, 'The Structure and Purpose of the Prologue to John's Gospel', in his *New Testament Questions of Today*, pp. 138–167.

Kealy, S.P., *That You May Believe; The Gospel of John*, Slough, G.B., 1978.

Kinniburg, E., 'The Johannine "Son of Man" ', SE IV, Berlin, 1968, pp. 64–71.

Kooy, V.H., 'The Transfiguration Motif in the Gospel of John', in *Saved by Hope; Essays in Honor of Richard C. Oudersluys*, ed. J.I. Cook, Grand Rapids, 1978.

Kuhl, J., *Die Sendung Jesu Christi: und der Kirche nach dem Johannesevangelium*, Siegburg, 1967.

Kysar, R., 'Christology and Controversy', *CTM* 5, 1978, pp. 350–364.

——, 'The Father's Son—Johannine Christology', in *John, the Maverick Gospel*, Atlanta, 1976, pp. 22–46.

——, *The Fourth Evangelist and His Gospel*, Minneapolis, 1975.

——, 'Rudolph Bultmann's Interpretation of the Concept of Creation in John 1:3–4', *CBQ* 32, 1970, pp. 77–85.

——, 'The Fourth Gospel: A Report on Recent Research', ANRW ii 25.3, Berlin, 1985, pp. 2389–2480.

Lampe, G.W.H., 'The Holy Spirit and the Person of Christ', in *Christ in Faith and History*, 1972, pp. 111–130.

Lattke, M., 'Sammlung durch das Wort. Erlöser, Erlösung, und Erlöste in Johannesevangelium', *BK* 30, 1975, pp. 118–122.

Leroy, H., 'Jesusverkündingung im Johannesevangelium', in *Jesus in den Evangelien*, ed. J. Binzler, et al., Stuttgart, 1970, pp. 148–170.

Liebert, E., 'That You May Believe: The Fourth Gospel and Structural Development Theory', *BTB* 14:2, 1984, pp. 67–73.

Lieu, J., *The Second and Third Epistles of John*, Edinburgh, 1988.

Lindars, B., 'The Son of Man in the Johannine Christology', in *Christ and Spirit in the New*

Testament; Festschrift for C.F.D. Moule, ed. B. Lindars and S.S. Smalley, Cambridge, 1970, pp. 43–60.

——, 'The Fourth Gospel: an Act of Contemplation', in *Studies in the Fourth Gospel*, ed. F.L. Cross, London, 1961, pp. 23–35.

Loader, W.R.G., 'The Central Structure of Johannine Christology', *NTS* 30, 1984, pp. 188–216.

——, *The Christology of the Fourth Gospel; Structure and Issues* BBET 23, Frankfurt, 1989.

Lofthouse, W.F., 'Fatherhood and Sonship in the Fourth Gospel', *ET* 43, p. 442.

Macaulay, W.M., 'The Nature of Christ in Origen's *Commentary on John*', *SJT* 19, 1966, pp. 176–187.

MacRae, G.W., 'The Jewish Background of the Gnostic Sophia Myth', *NovT* 12, 1970, pp. 86–101.

——, 'The Fourth Gospel and *Religionsgeschichte*', *CBQ* 32, 1970, pp. 13–24.

McNamara, M., '*Logos* of the Fourth Gospel and *Memra* of the Palestinian Targum (Ex. 12:42)', *ET* 79, 1968, pp. 115–117.

McPolin, J., 'The "Name" of the Father and of the Son in the Johannine Writings', Dissertation, Rome, 1971.

Maddox, R., 'The Function of the Son of Man in the Gospel of John', in *Reconciliation and Hope*, 1974, pp. 186–204.

Mastin, B.A., 'A Neglected Feature of the Christology of the Fourth Gospel', *NTS* 22, 1975, pp. 32–51.

Mateos, J. and J. Barretos, 'Excursus II; El Hombre/Hijo del Hombre', *El Evangelio de Juan; Analisis linguistico y Comentario exegetico*, Madrid, 1982, pp. 930–935.

Matsunaga, K., 'The "Theos" Christology as the Ultimate Confession of the 4th Gospel', *Annual of the Japanese Biblical Institute* 7, p. 124.

Maurer, C., 'Der Exklusivanspruch des Christus nach dem Johannesevangelium', in *Studies in John Presented to Professor J.N. Sevenster on the Occasion of his Seventieth Birthday*, Leiden, 1970, pp. 143–160.

Mealand, D.L., 'The Christology of the Fourth Gospel', *SJT* 31, 1978, pp. 449–467.

——, 'The Language of Mystical Union in the Johannine Writings', *DownR* 95, 1977, pp. 19–34.

Meagher, J.C., 'John 1:14 and the New Temple', *JBL* 88, 1969, pp. 57–68.

Meeks, W.A., 'The Man from Heaven in Johannine Sectarianism', *JBL* 91, 1972, pp. 44–72.

——, *The Prophet-King; Moses Traditions and the Johannine Christology*, Leiden, 1967.

Menoud, P.-H., *L' évangile de Jean. Les études johanniques de Bultmann a Barrett*, Brugges, 1958.

Meye Thompson, M., *The Humanity of Jesus in the Fourth Gospel*, Philadelphia, 1988.

Miller, E.L., 'The Christology of John 8:25', *TZ* 36, 1980, pp. 257–261.

——, 'The Logic of the Logos Hymn: A New View', *NTS* 29, 1983, pp. 552–561.

——, 'The Logos was God', *EQ* 53, 1981, pp. 65–77.

——, 'The Logos of Heraclitus: Updating the Report', *HTR* 74, 1981, pp. 161–176.

Miranda, J.P., *Being and Messiah; The Message of St. John*, E.t. J. Eagleson, Maryknoll, New York, 1977.

——, *Der Vater, der mich gesandt hat; Religionsgeschichtliche Untersuchungen zu den johanneischen Sendungsformeln; Zugleich ein Beitrag zur johanneischen Christologie und Ekklesiologie*, Frankfurt, 1972.

——, *Die Sendung Jesu im Vierten Evangelium; Religions- und theologiegeschichtliche Untersuchungen zu den Sendungsformeln*, Stuttgart, 1977.

Mlakuzhyil, G., *The Christocentric Literary Structure of the Fourth Gospel*, Rome, 1987.

Moloney, F.J., 'The Fourth Gospel's Presentation of Jesus as "The Christ" and J.A.T. Robinson's *Redating*', *DownR* 95, 1977, pp. 239–253.

——, *The Johannine Son of Man*, Rome, (2nd ed.) 1979.

——,'The Johannine Son of Man', *BTB* 6, 1976, pp. 177–189.

——, 'John 1:18: "In the Bosom of" or "Turned Towards" the Father?', *AustBR* 31, 1983, pp. 63–71.

——, *The Word Became Flesh*, Theology Today Series 14, 1977.

Monaldo, L., *La "Exaltación" de Jesus en la Cruz Según el Cuarto Evangelio*, Quito, 1979.

Müller, U.B., *Die Geschichte der Christologie in der johanneischen Gemeinde*, SBS 77, Stuttgart, 1975.

——, 'Die Beteutung des Kreuzestodes Jesu im Johannesevangelium', *KD* 21, 1975, pp. 49–71.

Murray, J.O.F., *Jesus According to St. John,* London, 1936.

Mussner, F., 'Der Charakter Jesu nach dem Johannesevangelium', *TTZ* 62, 1953, pp. 321–332.

——, *The Historical Jesus in the Gospel of St John*, E.t., W.J. O'Hara, Freiburg/London, 1967.

——, 'Liturgical Aspects of John's Gospel', *ThD* 14, 1966. pp. 18–22; in his *Praesentia Salutis. Gesammelte Studien zu Fragen und Themen des Neuen Testamentes*, Düsseldorf, 1967, pp. 133–145.

Neyrey, J.H., 'John III — A Debate over Johannine Epistemology and Christology', *NovT* 23, 1981, pp. 115–127.

——, *An Ideology of Revolt; John's Christology in Social-Science Perspective*, Philadelphia, 1988.

——, ' "My Lord and My God": The Divinity of Jesus in John's Gospel', SBL 1986 Seminar Paper Series 25, Atlanta, pp. 152–171.

Nicholson, G.C., *Death as Departure*, Chico, 1983.

Nicol, G.G., 'Jesus' Washing the Feet of the Disciples: a Model for Johannine Christology [Jn. 13:3–12]', *ET* 91, 1979, pp. 20–21.

O'Day, G.R., *Revelation in the Fourth Gospel*, Philadelphia, 1986.

O'Grady, J.F., *Individual and Community in John*, Rome, 1978 (esp. pp. 26–36).

——, 'The Human Jesus in the Fourth Gospel', *BTB* 14, 1984, pp. 63–66.

Osborn, E., 'Negative and Positive Theology in John', *AustBR* 31, 1983, pp. 72–80.

Painter, J., 'Christology and the Fourth Gospel; A Study of the Prologue', *AustBR* 31, 1983, pp. 45–62.

——, 'Christology and the History of the Johannine Community in the Prologue of the Fourth Gospel', *NTS* 30, 1984, pp. 460–474.

——, *John: Witness and Theologian*, London, 1975.

Pamment, M., 'The Son of Man in the Fourth Gospel', *JTS* 36, 1985, pp. 56–66.

——, 'Eschatology and the Fourth Gospel', *JSNT* 15, 1982, pp. 81–85.

Pfitzner, V.C., 'The Coronation of the King — The Passion in the Gospel of John', *CTM* 4, 1977, pp. 10–21.

Pietrantonio, R., 'El Mesias Asesinado: El Mesias ben Efraim en el Evangelio de Juan', *Revista Biblica* 44, 1982, pp. 1–64.

——, ' "El Mesias permanece para siempre": Juan 12:12–36', *Revista Biblica* 47:3, 1985, pp. 121–142.

Pokorny, P., 'Der irdische Jesus im Johannesevangelium', *NTS* 30, 1984.

Pollard, T.E., 'The Father-Son and God-Believer Relationships according to St. John: a Brief Study of John's Use of Prepositions', in de Jonge's *L'Evangile de Jean*, pp. 363–369.

——, *Johannine Christology and the Early Church*, SNTSMS 13, London/New York, 1970.

Potterie, I. de la, 'L'Exaltation du Fils de l'homme (Jn. 12:31–36)', *Greg* 49, 1968, pp. 460–478.

Prete, B., 'La missione rivelatrice di Cristo secondo il quarto Evangelista', *Atti della settimana biblica* 20, 1970, pp. 133–150.

Price, J.L., 'The Search for the Theology of the Fourth Gospel', in *New Testament Issues*, ed. R. Batey, London, 1970, pp. 226–241.

Reim, G., 'Jesus as God in the Fourth Gospel: The Old Testament Background', *NTS* 30, 1984, pp. 158–160.

Richter, G., 'Die Fleischwerdung des Logos im Johannesevangelium', *NovT* 13, 1971, pp. 81–126; *NovT* 14, 1972, pp. 257–276.

Ridderbos, H., 'The Christology of the Fourth Gospel: History and Interpretation', in *Saved by Hope; Essays in Honor of Richard C. Oudersluys,* ed. J.I. Cook, Grand Rapids, 1978, pp. 15–26.

——, 'The Structure and Scope of the Prologue to the Gospel of John', *NovT* 8, 1966, pp. 180–201.

Riches, J.K., *Jesus and the Transformation of Judaism,* London, 1980.

——, 'What is "Christocentric Theology"?', in *Christ, Faith and History,* eds. Sykes and Clayton, Cambridge, pp. 223–238.

Riedl, J., *Das Heilswerk Jesu nach Johannes,* Freiburg, 1973.

Roberts, J.H., 'The Lamb of God', *Neot* 2, 1968, pp. 41–55.

Robertson, A.T., *The Divinity of Christ in the Gospel of John,* New York, 1916.

Robinson, J.A.T., *The Priority of John,* London, 1985.

——, 'The Relation of the Prologue to the Gospel of St. John', *NTS* 9, 1962, pp. 120–129.

——, 'The Use of the Fourth Gospel in Christology Today', in his *Twelve More New Testament Studies,* pp. 138–154.

——, 'The Destination and Purpose of St. John's Gospel', NTS 6, 1959, pp. 117–131.

——, 'The Most Primitive Christology of All?', in his *Twelve New Testament Studies,* pp. 139–153.

Robinson, J.M., 'The Johannine Trajectory', in *Trajectories Through Early Christianity,* by J.M. Robinson and H. Koester, Philadelphia, 1971, pp. 232–268.

Ruckstuhl, E., 'Abstieg und Erhöhung des johanneischen Menschensohns', in *Jesus und der Menschensohn; für Anton Vögtle,* ed. R. Pesch and R. Schnackenburg, Freiburg, 1975, pp. 314–341.

——, 'Die johanneische Menschensohnforschung', in *Theologische Berichte* 1, Zurich/Cologne, 1972, pp. 171–284.

Sabugal, S., *Christos: Investigación exegética sobre la cristologia juannea,* Barcelona, 1972.

——, 'Una contribución a la cristología juannea', *Augustinianum* 12, 1972, pp. 565–572.

Schlier, H., 'Zur Christologie des Johannesevangelium', in his *Das Ende der Zeit; Exegetische Aufsätze und Vorträge,* Freiburg, 1971, pp. 85–88.

Schnackenburg, R., *The Gospel According to St. John I,* New York, 1980, pp. 154–155, 481–575.

——, 'Der Menschensohn im Johannesevangelium', *NTS* 11, 1965, pp. 123–137.

——, 'On the Origin of the Fourth Gospel', in *Jesus and Man's Hope* I, ed. D.G. Buttrick, Pittsburgh, 1970, pp. 223–246.

Schneider, H., ' "The Word Was Made Flesh" (An Analysis of the Theology of Revelation in the Fourth Gospel)', *CBQ* 31, 1969, pp. 344–356.

Schneider, J., *Die Christusschau des Johannesevangeliums,* Berlin, 1935.

Schnelle, U., *Antidoketische Christologie im Johannesevangelium,* Göttingen, 1987.

Schulz, S., *Untersuchungen zur Menschensohn-Christologie im Johannesevangelium; zugleich ein Beitrag zur Methodengeschichte der Auslegung des 4. Evangeliums,* Göttingen, 1957.

Schweizer, E., *Egō Eimi,* Göttingen, 1939.

Scroggs, R., *Christology in Paul and John; The Reality and Revelation of God,* Philadelphia, 1988.

Segalla, G., 'Preesistenza, incarnazione e divinitá di Christo in Giovanni (Vge 1 Gv)', *RivB* 22, 1974, pp. 155–181.

——, 'Rassengna di cristologia giovannea', *Studia Patavina* 18, 1972, pp. 693–732.

Sidebottom, E.M., 'The Ascent and Descent of the Son of Man in the Gospel of St. John', *ATR* 39, 1957, pp. 115–122.

——, *The Christ of the Fourth Gospel in the Light of First-Century Thought*, London, 1961.

——, 'The Son of Man as Man in the Fourth Gospel', *ET* 68, 1956/7, pp. 231–234, 280–283.

——, *The Theology of the Gospel of John*, Cambridge, 1995.

Smalley, S.S., 'The Johannine Son of Man Sayings', *NTS* 15, 1968/9, pp. 278–301.

——, *John: Evangelist and Interpreter*, Exeter, 1978.

Smith, D.M., 'The Presentation of Jesus in the Fourth Gospel', *Int* 31, 1977, pp. 367–378.

——, *The Composition and Order of the Fourth Gospel; Bultmann's Literary Theory*, New Haven/London, 1965.

——, *The Theology of the Gospel of John*, Cambridge, 1995.

Smith, R.H., 'Exodus Typology in the Fourth Gospel', *JBL* 81, 1962, pp. 329–342.

Smith, T.C., 'The Christology of the Fourth Gospel', *Review and Expositor* 71, 1974, pp. 19–30.

——, *Jesus in the Fourth Gospel*, Nashville, 1959.

Sproston, W.E., ' "Is Not This Jesus, the Son of Joseph ... ?" (John 6:42); Johannine Christology as a Challenge to Faith', *JSNT* 24, 1985, pp. 77–97.

Staley, J.L., *The Print's First Kiss: A Rhetorical Investigation of the Implied Reader in the Fourth Gospel* SBLDS 82, Atlanta, 1988.

——, 'The Structure of John's Prologue: Its Implications for the Gospel's Narrative Structure', *CBQ* 48, 1986, pp. 241–263.

Stevens, C.T., 'The "I Am" Formula in the Gospel of John', Studia Biblica et Theologica 7, 1977, pp. 19–30.

Sturch, R.L., 'The Replacement of "Son of Man" by a Pronoun', *ET* 94, 1982/3, p. 333.

Suggit, J., 'John 19:5: "Behold the Man" ', *ET* 94, 1982/3, p. 333f.

Summers, R., 'The Christ of John's Gospel', *Southwestern Journal of Theology* 8, 1965, pp. 35–43.

Sundberg, A.C., 'Christology in the Fourth Gospel', *BR* 21, 1976, pp. 29–37.

——, '*Isos tō Theō* Christology in John 5:17–30', *BR* 15, 1970, pp. 19–31.

Sweeny, T.A., 'Jesus in the Fourth Gospel', Dissertation, Graduate Theological Union, 1974.

Sykes, S.W., 'The Theology of the Humanity of Christ', *Christ in Faith and History*, 1972, pp. 53–72.

Talbert, C.H., 'The Myth of a Descending-Ascending Redeemer in Mediterranean Antiquity', *NTS* 22, 1976, pp. 418–439.

Temples, S., *The Core of the Fourth Gospel*, London/Oxford, 1975.

Thüssing, W., *Erhöhung und Verherrlichung Jesu in Johannesevangelium,* Münster, 1966.

Tilborg, S. van, ' "Neerdaling" en incarnatie: de christologie van Johannes', *Tijdschrift voor Theologie* 13, 1973, pp. 20–33.

Treats, C., *Voir Jésus et le Pére en lui selon l'Evangile de Saint Jean*, Rome, 1967.

Tremel, Y.-B., 'Le Fils de l'homme selon Saint Jean', *LV* 12, 1963, pp. 65–92.

Vawter, B., 'Ezekiel and John', *CBQ* 26, 1964, pp. 450–458.

Via, D.O., 'Darkness, Christ, and the Church in the Fourth Gospel', *SJT* 14, 1961, pp. 172–193.

Watson, F., 'Is John's Christology Adoptionist?', in *The Glory of Christ in the New Testament*, Caird Festschrift, Oxford, 1987, pp. 113–124.

Watson, N.M., 'Risen Christ and Spirit/Paraclete in the Fourth Gospel', *AustBR* 31, 1983, pp. 81–85.

Wiles, M., *The Spiritual Gospel; The Interpretation of the Fourth Gospel in the Early Church*, Cambridge, 1960.

——, 'Does Christology Rest on a Mistake?', in *Christ, Faith and History*, 1972, pp. 3–12.

Zimmermann, H., 'Das absolute *Egō Eimi* als die neutestamentliche Offenbarungsformel', *BZ* 4, 1960, pp. 54–69, 266–276.

II. John 6

Anderson, P.N., ' "You (Alone) Have the Words of Eternal Life!" Is Peter Portrayed as *Returning* the "Keys of the Kingdom" to Jesus in John 6:68f.?' (unpublished paper presented at the Johannine Seminar, National AAR/SBL Meeting, Nov. 1989).

Balague, R.P., *Jesucristo, Vida y Luz*, Madrid, 1963.

Barnett, 'The Feeding of the Multitude in Mark 6/John 6; in *The Miracles of Jesus*, Gospel Perspectives 6, Sheffield, 1986, pp. 273–293.

Barrett, C.K., 'The Dialectical Theology of St. John', in *New Testament Essays,* London, 1972, pp. 49–69.

——, 'The Flesh of the Son of Man; John 6:53', in his *Essays of John*, London, 1982, pp. 37–49.

——, 'John and the Synoptic Gospels', *ET* 85, 1973/4, pp. 228–233.

Beasley-Murray, G.R., *John*, Waco, 1987, pp. 81–99.

Becker, H., *Die Reden des Johannesevangeliums und der Stil der gnostischen Offenbarungsreden*, Göttingen, 1956, (esp. pp. 67–70, 117).

Becker, J., *Das Evangelium nach Johannes* I, Gütersloh, 1979, pp. 188–206.

Blank, J., 'Die johanneische Brotrede. Einführung: Brotvermehrung und Seewandel Jesu: Jo. 6:1–21', *Bib Leb* 7, 1966, pp. 193–207.

——, ' "Ich bin das Lebensbrot" Jo. 6:22–50', *BibLeb* 7, 1966, pp. 255–270.

Bligh, J., 'Jesus in Galilee', *HeyJ* 5, 1984, pp. 3–26.

Borgen, P., *Bread from Heaven; An Exegetical Study of the Concept of Manna in the Gospel of John and the Writings of Philo*, NovTSup 11, Leiden, 1965.

——, '*Bread from Heaven*; Aspects of Debates on Expository Method and Form', in his *Logos Was the True Light — and Other Essays on the Gospel of John*, Trondheim, 1983, pp. 32–45.

——, 'Observations on the Midrashic Character of John 6', *ZNW* 54, 1963, pp. 232–240 (also in *Logos*, pp. 23–31).

——, 'The Unity of the Discourse in John 6', *ZNW* 50, 1959, pp. 277f. (also in *Logos* pp. 21f.).

Bornkamm, G., 'Vorjohanneische Tradition oder nachjohanneische Bearbeitung in der eucharistischen Rede Joh. 6?'; in his *Geschichte und Glauben* II, Munich, 1971, pp. 51–64.

Bowman, J., *The Fourth Gospel and the Jews*, Pittsburgh, PTMS 8, 1975, pp. 205–211.

Braun, F.-M., 'Quatre "signes" johanniques de l'unité chrétienne', *NTS* 9, 1962/3, pp. 147–155.

Carson, D.A., 'Current Source Criticism of the Fourth Gospel: Some Methodological Questions', *JBL* 97, 1978, pp. 411–429.

Charlier, J., 'La multiplication des pains', *As Seign* 32, 1967, pp. 31–45.

Conti, M., *Il Discorso del Pane de Vita Nella Tradizione Sapienziale*, Levanto, 1967.

Corbin, M., 'Le Pain de la Vie; La lecture de Jean 6 per S. Tomas d'Aquin', *RSR* 65, 1977, pp. 107–138.

Crane, T.E., *The Message of St. John; The Spiritual Teaching of the Beloved Disciple*, New York, 1980, pp. 59–64.

Cribbs, F.L., 'A Study of the Contacts that Exist between St. Luke and St. John', SBLASP 2, Missoula, 1973, pp. 1–93.

Crossan, J.D., 'It is Written: A Structuralist Analysis of John 6', SBLASP 1, 1979, pp. 197–214 (also in *Semeia* 26, 1983, pp. 3–21).

Dodd, C.H., *The Interpretation of the Fourth Gospel*, Cambridge, 1953.

Doorman, D.A., 'The Son of Man in John: A Fresh Approach Through Chapter 6', *SBT* 8, 1983, pp. 121–142.

Dunkerly, R., 'The Sign of the Meal (Jn. 6)', *London Quarterly and Holborn Review* 32, 1963, pp. 61–66.

Dunn, J.D.G., 'John VI — A Eucharistic Discourse?', *NTS* 17, 1971, pp. 328–338.

Durkin, K., 'A Eucharistic Hymn in John 6?' *ET* 98, 1987, pp. 168–170.

Ellis, P., *The Genius of John: a Composition-Critical Commentary on the Fourth Gospel*, Collegeville, Minn., 1984, pp. 100–134.

Ferraro, G., 'Giovanni 6:60–71. Osservazioni sulla struttura letteraria e il valore della pericope nel quarto vangelo', *RivB* 26, 1978, pp. 33–69.

Feuillet, A., 'Les thèmes bibliques majeurs du discours sur le pain de vie (Jn. 6). Contribution à l'étude des sources de la pensée johannique', *NRT* 82, 1960, pp. 803–822, 918–939, 1040–1062 (also in his *Johannine Studies*, E.t. T.E. Crane, New York, 1964, pp. 53–128).

——, 'Note sur la traduction de Jér xxxi 3c', *VT* 12, 1962, pp. 122–124.

——, *Le discours sur le pain de vie*, Paris, 1967.

Finkel, A., *The Pharisees and the Teacher of Nazareth; A Study of their Background, their Halachic and Midrashic Teachings, the Similarities and Differences*, Leiden, 1964 (esp. pp. 149ff.).

Fortna, R.T., *The Gospel of Signs; A Reconstruction of the Narrative Source Underlying the Fourth Gospel*, SNTSMS 11, Cambridge, 1970, pp. 55–70.

——, 'Source and Redaction Criticism in the Fourth Gospel's Portrayal of Jesus' Signs', *JBL* 89, 1970, pp. 151–166.

——, *The Fourth Gospel and its Predecessor; From Narrative Source to Present Gospel*, Philadelphia, 1988, pp. 79–94.

Freed, E.D., *Old Testament Quotations in the Gospel of John*, Leiden, 1965, pp. 11–20.

Gambino, G., 'Struttura, composizione et analisi letterarioteologica di Gv. 6:26–51b', *RivB* 24, 1976, pp. 337–358.

Gardner-Smith, P., *Saint John and the Synoptic Gospels*, Cambridge, 1938.

Gärtner, B., *John 6 and the Jewish Passover*, Lund, 1959.

Geiger, G., 'Aufruf an Rückkehrende; zum Sinn des Zitats von Ps. 78:24b in Joh. 6:31', *Biblica* 65, 1984, pp. 449–464.

Ghiberti, G., 'Il c. 6 di Giovanni e la presenza dell' Eucharestia nel 4'o Vangelo', *Parole de Vita* 14, 1969, pp. 105–125.

Giblin, C.H., 'The Miraculous Crossing of the Sea (John 6:16–21)', *NTS* 29, 1983, pp. 96–103.

Gourges, M., 'Section Christologique et section Eucharistique en Jean VI; Une Proposition', *RB* 88, 1981, pp. 515–527.

Grassi, J.A., 'Eating Jesus' Flesh and Drinking his Blood: the Centrality and Meaning of John 6:51–58', *BTB* 17, 1987, pp. 24–30.

Grigsby, B., 'The Reworking of the Lake-Walking Account in the Johannine Tradition', *ET* 100, 1989, pp. 295–297.

Gruenler, R.G., *The Trinity in the Gospel of John (A Thematic Commentary on the Fourth Gospel)*, Grand Rapids, 1986, pp. 43–51.

Haenchen, E., 'Johanneische Probleme', *ZTK* 56, 1959, pp. 19–54.

——, A Commentary on the Gospel of John Vol. 1, E.t., R. Funk, Philadelphia, 1984.

Heil, J.P., *Jesus Walking on the Sea; Meaning and Gospel Functions of Matt. 14:22–23, Mark 6:45–52 and John 6:15b–21*, Rome, 1981.

Hofius, O., 'Erwählung und Bewahrung. Zur Auslegung von Joh. 6:37', Theologische Beiträge 8, 1977, pp. 24–29.

Hoskyns, E., 'The Unbelief of the Galileans', *The Fourth Gospel*, ed. F.N. Davey, London, 1947 (2) pp. 277–288.

——, 'The Interpretation of the Sixth Chapter', *The Fourth Gospel*, pp. 304–307.

Jeremias, J., 'Joh. 6:51c–58 — redaktionell?', *ZNW* 44, 1952/3, pp. 256–257.

Johnston, E.D., 'The Johannine Version of the Feeding of the Five Thousand — an Independent Tradition?', *NTS* 8, 1961/2, pp. 151–154.

Joubert, H.L.N., ' "The Holy One of God" (John 6:69)', *Neot* 2, 1968, pp. 57–69.

Kealy, S.P., *That You May Believe; The Gospel According to John*, Northampton, 1978, pp. 81–89.

Kieffer, R., *Au delà des recensions? L'évolution de la tradition textuelle dans Jean VI, 52–71*, Lund, 1968.

Kilmartin, E.J., 'Liturgical Influence on John VI', *CBQ* 22, 1960, pp. 183–191.

Köster, H., 'Geschichte und Kultus im Johannesevangelium und bei Ignatius von Antiochien', *ZTK* 54, 1957, pp. 56–69.

Krodel, G., 'John 6:33', *Int* 37, 1983, pp. 283–288.

Kuzenzama, K.P.M., 'La préhistorie de l'expresion "pain de vie" (Jn. 6:35b, 48)', *Rev.Af.Th.* 4, 1980, pp. 65–83.

Kysar, R., *John*, Minneapolis, 1986, pp. 89ff.

——, 'The Source Analysis of the Fourth Gospel — A Growing Consensus?', *NovT* 15, 1973, pp. 134–152.

Lee, E.K., 'St. Mark and the Fourth Gospel', *NTS* 3, 1956/7, pp. 50–58.

Leenhardt, F.J., 'La structure du chapitre 6 de l'évangile de Jean', *RHPR* 39, 1959, pp. 1–13.

Léon-Dufour, X., 'Trois chiasmes johanniques', *NTS* 7, 1960/1, pp. 249–255.

Léonard, J.-M., '2 Rois 4:42–44 et Jean 6:1–13', *ETR* 55, 1980, pp. 265–270.

Lightfoot, R.H., *St. John's Gospel; A Commentary*, ed. C.F. Evans, Oxford, 1956, pp. 251–271.

Maier, G., *Johannes-Evangelium*, Stuttgart, 1984.

Malina, B.J., *The Palestinian Manna Tradition; The Manna Tradition in the Palestinian Targums and its Relationship to the New Testament Writings*, AGSU 7, Leiden, 1968.

Martyn, J.L., *History and Theology in the Fourth Gospel*, revised ed., Nashville, 1979.

——, 'Source Criticism and Religionsgeschichte in the Fourth Gospel', in *Jesus and Man's Hope*, Pittsburgh, 1970, pp. 247–273.

——, 'We Have Found Elijah', in *Jews, Greeks, and Christians; Religious Cultures in Late Antiquity; Essays in Honor of William David Davies*, ed. R. Hamerton-Kelly and R. Scroggs, Leiden, 1976, pp. 181–219; also in Martyn, *Gospel*, pp. 9–54.

Mateos, J., and Juan Barretos, *El Evangelio de Juan; Analisis Linguistico y Commentario Exegetico*, Madrid, 1982, pp. 303–355.

McPolin, J., 'Bultmanni theoria litteraria ad Jo 6:51c–58c', *VD* 44, 1966, pp. 243–258.

Mees, M., 'Sinn und Bedeutung westlicher Textvarianten in Joh 6', *BZ* 13, 1969, pp. 244–251.

Menoud, P.-H., ' "Le fils de Joseph." Etude sur Jean 1:45 et 6:42', *RTP* 8, 1930, pp. 275–288.

Michael, J.H., 'The Actual Saying behind St. John vi. 62', *ET* 43, 1931/2, pp. 427–428.

Mollat, D., 'Le chapitre VI de Saint Jean', *LV* 31, 1957, pp. 107–119.

Moloney, F.J., 'John 6 and the Celebration of the Eucharist', *Down R* 93, 1975, pp. 243–251.

Mondula, N., *La puissance vivificatrice de la chair du Christ selon l'évangile de S. Jean*, Rome, 1978.

Moore, F.J., 'Eating the Flesh and Drinking the Blood: A Reconsideration', *ATR* 48, 1966, pp. 70–75.

Morris, L., *The Gospel According to St. John*, Grand Rapids, 1971.

Moule, C.F.D., 'A Note on Didache IX.4', *JTS* 6, 1955, pp. 240–243.

Nicol, W., *The Sëmeia in the Fourth Gospel; Tradition and Redaction*, NovTSup 32, Leiden, 1972, pp. 32–35.

Odeberg, H., *The Fourth Gospel; Interpreted in its Relation to Contemporaneous Religious Currents in Palestine and in the Hellenistic-Oriental World*, (1929) E.t. 1974, Chicago, pp. 235–269.

Pahk, S.S., 'The Meaning of Bread: A Structuralist Analysis of John VI, 1–58', Dissertation, Vanderbilt University, 1980.

Pancaro, S., *The Law in the Fourth Gospel*, Leiden, 1972, pp. 281–287, 454–472.

Phillips, G., 'This is a Hard Saying: Who Can be a Listener to It?', *SBLASP* 1, Missoula, 1979, pp. 185–196.

Preiss, T., 'Etude sur le chapitre 6 de l'Evangile de Jean', *ETR* 46, 1971, pp. 143–167.

Quiévreux, F., 'Le récit de la multiplication des pains dans le quatrième Evangile', *RSR* 41, 1967, pp. 97–108.

Richter, G., 'Die Alttestamentlichen Zitate in der Rede vom Himmelsbrot: Joh 6:26–51a', in his *Studien*, 1977, pp. 199–265.

——, 'Zur Formgeschichte und literarischen Einheit von Joh 6:31–58', in his *Studien*, pp. 88–119; also in *ZNW* 60, 1969, pp. 21–55.

Roberge, M., 'Jean 6:22–24: Un problème de critique littéraire', *LThPh* 35, 1979, pp. 139–151

——, 'Jean 6:22–24: Un problème de critique textuelle', *LThPh* 34, 1978, pp. 275–289.

——, 'Le discours sur le pain de vie (Jean 6:22–59), Problemes d'interprétation', *LThPh* 38, 1982, pp. 265–300.

Ruager, S., 'Johannes 6 og nadveren', *TTki* 50, 1979, pp. 81–92.

Ruckstuhl, E., *Die literarische Einheit des Johannesevangeliums*, Freiburg, 1951, pp. 243–271.

——, 'Literarkritik am Johannesevangelium und eucharistische Rede (Jo. 6:51c–58)', *DivT* 23, 1945, pp. 153–190, 301–333.

Ruddick Jr., C.T., 'Feeding and Sacrifice — The Old Testament Background of the Fourth Gospel', *ET* 79, 1967/8, p. 340f.

Rusch, F.A., 'The Signs and the Discourses — The Rich Theology of John 6', *CTM* 5, 1978, pp. 386–390.

Schenke, L., 'Die formale und gedankliche Struktur von Joh 6:26–58', *BZ* n.f. 24, 1980, pp. 21–41.

——, 'Die literarische Vorgeschichte von Joh. 6:26–58', *BZ* n.f. 29, 1985, pp. 68–89.

——, *Die wunderbare Brotvermehrung*, Würtzburg, 1983, pp. 81–89, 119–128, 152–157.

Schlier, H., 'Joh 6 und das johanneische Verständnis der Eucharistie', in his *Das Ende der Zeit; Exegetische Aufsätze und Vorträge*, 2, Freiburg/Vienna, 1971, pp. 102–123.

Schnackenburg, R., 'Zur Rede vom Brot aus dem Himmel: Eine Beobachtung zu Joh 6:52', *BZ* 12, 1968, pp. 248–252.

——, 'Das Brot des Lebens', in *Tradition und Glaube; Das frühe Christentum in seiner Umwelt; Festgabe für Karl Georg Kuhn zum 65. Geburtstag*, ed. J. Jeremias, H.-W. Kuhn, and H. Stegmann, Göttingen, 1971, pp. 328–342.

Schneider, J. 'Zur Frage der Komposition von Jo 6:27–58', in *In Memoriam Ernst Lohmeyer*, ed. W. Schmauch, Stuttgart, 1951, pp. 132–142.

Schnelle, U., *Antidoketische Christologie im Johannesevangelium: Eine Untersuchung zur Stellung des vierten Evangeliums in der johanneischen Schule*, Göttingen, 1987, pp. 114ff., 216–228.

Schulz, S., *Untersuchungen zur Menschensohn-Christologie im Johannesevangelium*, Göttingen, 1957, pp. 115–118.

Schürmann, H., 'Die Eucharistie als Repräsentation und Applikation des Heilsgeschehens nach Joh 6:53–58', in *Ursprung*, pp. 167–184; also in *TTZ* 68, 1959, pp. 30–45, 108–118.

——, 'Joh 6:51c — ein Schlüssel zur grossen Johanneischen Brotrede', in *Ursprung*, pp. 151–166; also in *BZ* 2, 1958, pp. 244–262.

Schweizer, E., 'Das johanneische Zeugnis vom Herrenmahl', *EvTh* 12, 1952/3, pp. 341–363.

Segalla, G., *Gesu' Pane del Cielo per la Vita del Mondo; Cristologia ed Eucaristia in Giovani*, Pavoda, 1976.

——, 'La struttura circolare-chiasmatica di Gv 6:26–58 e il significato teologico', *BeO* 13, 1971, pp. 191–198.

Shorter, M., 'The Position of Chapter VI in the Fourth Gospel', *ET* 84, 1973, pp. 181–183.

Siedlecki, E.J., *A Patristic Synthesis of John VI, 54–55*, Mundelein, Illinois, 1956.

Skrinjar, A., 'De terminologia sacrificiali in J 6:51–56', *Divus Thomas*, Piacenza, 1971, pp. 189–197.

Smith, M., 'Collected Fragments: On the Priority of John 6 to Mark 6–8', SBLASP 1, Missoula, 1979, pp. 105–108.

——, 'Mark 6:32–15:47 and John 6:1–19:43', SBLASP 2, Missoula, 1978, pp. 281–282.

Springer, E., 'Die Einheit der Rede von Kaphernaum (Jo. 6)', *BZ* 15, 1918–21, pp. 319–334.

Stanley, D.M., 'The Bread of Life', *Worship* 32, 1957–8, pp. 477–488.

Teeple, H.M., *The Literary Origin of the Gospel of John*, Evanston, 1974.

Temple, P.J., 'The Eucharist in St. John 6', *CBQ* 9, 1947, pp. 442–452.

Temple, S., 'A Key to the Composition of the Fourth Gospel', *JBL* 80, 1961, pp. 220–232.

Tenney, M.C., *John: The Gospel of Belief; An Analytical Study of the Text*, London/Edinburgh, 1948/54.

Thomas, J., 'Le discours dans la synagogue de Capharnaum. Note sur Jean 6:22–59', *Christus* 29, 1982, pp. 218–222.

Thompson, J.M., 'The Interpretation of John VI', *Expositor* 8th ser., 11, 1916, pp. 337–348.

Thyen, H., 'Aus der Literatur zum Johannesevangelium', *TRu* 43, 1978, pp. 328–359.

Vannestre, A., 'Le pain de vie descendu du ciel (Jn. 6:55–58)', *AsSeign* 54, 1966, pp. 41–53.

Wahlde, V.C. von, 'Faith and Works in Jn. 6:28–29; Exegesis or Eisegesis?', *NovT* 22, 1980, pp. 304–315.

——, 'A Redactional Technique in the Fourth Gospel', *CBQ* 38, 1976, pp. 520–533.

——, 'Literary Structure and Theological Argument in Three Discourses with the Jews in the Fourth Gospel', *JBL* 103, 1984, pp. 575–584.

——, '*Wiederaufnahme* as a Marker of Redaction in Jn. 6:51–58', *Bib* 64, 1983, pp. 542–549.

Weiss, B., *Das Johannes-Evangelium*, Göttingen, (1834) 1902.

Wellhausen, J., *Das Evangelium Johannis*, Berlin, 1908.

Wendt, H.H., *The Gospel According to St. John* (An Inquiry into Its Genesis and Historical Value), 1900, E.t. by E. Lummis, Edinburgh, 1902.

Wilckens, U., 'Der eucharistische Abschnitt der johanneischen Rede vom Lebensbrot (Joh 6:51c–58)', in *Neues Testament und Kirche*; Für Rudolph Schnackenburg, ed. J. Gnilka, Freiburg/Vienna, 1974, pp. 220–248.

Wilkens, W., 'Das Abendmahlszeugnis im vierten Evangelium', *EvTh* 18, 1958, pp. 354–370.

——, 'Evangelist und Tradition im Johannesevangelium', *TZ* 16, 1960, pp. 81–90.

Worden, T., ' "Seigneur, à qui irions-nous?" ', *Concilium* 50, Paris, 1969, pp. 105–181.

Zarella, P., 'Gesú cammina sulle acque; Significato teologico de Giov. 6:16–21', *Scuola Cattolica* 95, 1967, pp. 146–160.

III. The Sacraments in John

Anderson, P.N., 'The "Medicine of Immortality" in Ignatius and John 6' (unpublished paper presented at the Johannine Seminar, National AAR/SBL Meeting, Nov. 1990).

Aune, D.E., 'The Phenomenon of Early Christian "Anti-Sacramentalism" ', in *Studies in New Testament and Early Christian Literature; Essays in Honor of Allen P. Wikgren*, ed. D. Aune, Leiden, 1972, pp. 194–214.

Bahr, G.J., 'The Seder of Passover and the Eucharistic Words', *NovT* 12, 1970, pp. 181–202.

Baker, J.A., 'The "Institution" Narratives and the Christian Eucharist', in *Thinking about the Eucharist; Essays by Members of the Archbishop's Commission on Christian Doctrine*, preface by I.T. Ramsey, London, 1972, pp. 38–58.

Ball, R.M., 'S. John and the Institution of the Eucharist', *JSNT* 23, 1985, pp. 59–68.

Barrett, C.K., 'Sacraments', in *Essays on John*, pp. 80–97.

Beasley-Murray, G.R., 'John 3:3, 5: Baptism, Spirit and the Kingdom', *ET* 97, 1985/6, pp. 167–170.

Bornkamm, G., 'Die eucharistische Rede im Johannes-Evangelium', *ZNW* 47, 1956, pp. 161–169; in his *Geschichte und Glauben* III, Munich, 1968, pp. 60–67.

Braun, F.-M., 'Le baptême d'après le quatrième Evangile', *RevTom* 48, 1948, pp. 347–393.

——, 'L'eucharistie selon saint Jean', *RevTom* 70, 1970, pp. 5–29.

Brooks, O.S., 'The Johannine Eucharist; Another Interpretation', *JBL* 82, 1963, pp. 293–300.

Brown, R.E., 'The Eucharist and Baptism in John', in his *New Testament Essays*, pp. 108–131.

——, 'The Johannine Sacramentary', in his *New Testament Essays*, pp. 77–107.

Costa, M., 'Nota sul simbolismo sacramentale del IV Vangelo', *RivB* 13, 1965, pp. 239–254.

Craig, C.T., 'Sacramental Interest in the Fourth Gospel', *JBL* 58, 1939, pp. 31–41.

Cullman, O., *Early Christian Worship*, E.t. A.S. Todd and J.B. Torrence, London, (Gr. 1950) 1953.

Evans, C.F., 'The Eucharist and Symbolism in the New Testament', in *Thinking about the Eucharist; Essays by Members of the Archbishop's Commission on Christian Doctrine*, preface by I.T. Ramsey, London, 1972, pp. 59–66.

Feuillet, A., *Le sacerdoce du Christ et de ses ministres d'après la prière sacerdotale du quatrième évangile et plusieurs données parallèles du Noveau Testament*, Paris, 1972.

Ford, J.M., ' "Mingled Blood" From the Side of Christ (John 19:34)', *NTS* 15, 1969, pp. 337f.

Fritschel, T.C., 'The Relationship between the Word and the Sacraments in John and in Ignatius', Dissertation, Hamburg, 1962/3.

Ghiberti, G., 'Il c[ap] 6 di Giovanni e la presenza dell' Eucharistia nel 4'o Vangelo', *Parole di Vita* 14, 1969, pp. 105–125.

Grigsby, B., 'Washing in the Pool of Siloam — A Thematic Anticipation of the Johannine Cross', *NovT* 27, 1985, pp. 227–235.

Howard, J.K., 'Passover and Eucharist in the Fourth Gospel', *SJT* 20, 1967, pp. 329–337.

Hultgren, A.T., 'The Johannine Footwashing (13:1–11) as Symbol of Eschatological Hospitality', *NTS* 28, 1982, pp. 539–546.

Klos, H., *Die Sakramente im Johannesevangelium; Vorkommen und Bedeutung von Taufe, Eucharistie und Buße im vierten Evangelium*, SBS 46, Stuttgart, 1970.

Koehler, T., 'The Sacramental Theory in John 19:26f.', *University of Dayton Review* 5, 1968, pp. 49–58.

Köster, H., 'Geschichte und Kultus im Johannesevangelium und bei Ignatius von Antiochien', *ZTK* 54, 1957, pp. 56–59.

Kysar, R., 'The Sacraments', in his *The Fourth Evangelist and his Gospel*, 1975, pp. 249–263.

Lilly, J.L., 'The Eucharistic Discourse of John 6', CBQ 12, 1950, pp. 48–51.

Lindars, B., 'Word and Sacrament in the Fourth Gospel', *SJT* 29, 1976, pp. 49–63.

Lohse, E., 'Wort und Sakrament im Johannesevangelium', *NTS* 7, 1960/1, p. 110–125.

MacGregor, G.H.C., 'The Eucharist in the Fourth Gospel', *NTS* 9, 1962/3, pp. 111–119.

Marxsen, W., *The Lord's Supper as a Christological Problem*, E.t. by L. Nieting, Philadelphia, 1970.

Matsunaga, K., 'Is John's Gospel Anti-Sacramental? — A New Solution in the Light of the Evangelist's *Milieu*', NTS 27, 1981, pp. 516–525.

Menken, M.J.J., 'John 6:51c–58: Eucharist or Christology?', *Bib* 74, 1993, pp. 1–26.

Menoud, P.-H., 'The Preaching of the Gospel and the Celebration of the Sacraments in the Infant Church', in his *Jesus Christ and Faith*, Pittsburg, 1978, pp. 551–563.

Michaelis, W., *Die Sakramente im Johannesevangelium*, Bern, 1946.

Moloney, F.J., 'When is John Talking about the Sacraments?', *AustBR* 30, 1982, pp. 10–33.

——, 'John 6 and the Celebration of the Eucharist', *DownR* 93, 1975, pp. 243–251.

Moore, F.J., 'Eating the Flesh and Drinking the Blood; A Reconsideration', *ATR* 48, 1966, pp. 70–75.

Naish, J.B., 'The Fourth Gospel and the Sacraments', *Expositor* 8th ser., 23, 1922, pp. 53–68.

Niewalda, P., *Sakramentssymbolik im Johannesevangelium? Eine exegetisch-historische Studie*, Limburg, 1958.

Paschal, R.W., 'Sacramental Symbolism and Physical Imagery in the Gospel of John', *TB* 32, 1981, pp. 151–176.

Perry, J.M., 'The Evolution of the Johannine Eucharist', *NTS* 39, 1993, pp. 22–35.

Philips, T., *Die Verheissung der heiligen Eucharistie nach Johannes; eine exegetische Studie*, Paderborn, 1922.

Proudman, C.L.J., 'The Eucharist in the Fourth Gospel', *CJT* 12, 1966, pp. 212–216.

Raney, W.H., *The Relation of the Fourth Gospel to the Christian Cultus*, Giessen, 1933.

Ruckstuhl, E., 'Wesen und Kraft der Eucharistie in der Sicht des Johannesevangeliums', in *Das Opfer der Kirche; Exegetische, dogmatische und pastoraltheologische Studien zum Verständnis der Messe*, ed. R. Erni, Lucerne, 1954, pp. 47–90.

Ruland, V., 'Sign and Sacrament; John's Bread of Life Discourse (Chapter 6)', *Int* 18, 1964, pp. 450–462.

Schnackenburg, R., 'Die Sakramente im Johannesevangelium', in *Sacra Pagina; Miscellanea biblical congressus internationalis catholici de re biblica*, 2 vols., ed. J. Coppens, A. Descamps, and E. Massaux, Paris, 1959, vol. 2, pp. 235–254.

Schnelle, U., 'Der gegenwärtige Christus: Sakramente und Johanneische Christologie', in *Antidoketische*, pp. 195–230.

Schweizer, E., 'Das johanneische Zeugnis vom Herrenmahl', *EvT* 12, 1952/3, pp. 341–363.

Shaw, A., 'The Breakfast by the Shore and the Mary Magdalene Encounter as Eucharistic Narratives', *JTS* 25, 1974, pp. 12–26.

Smalley, S.S., 'Liturgy and Sacrament in the Fourth Gospel', *EvQ* 29, 1957, pp. 159–170.

Temple, P.J., 'The Eucharist in St. John 6', *CBQ* 9, 1947, pp. 442–452.

Tragan, P.R., ed., *Segni e sacramenti nel Vangelo di Giovanni, Sacramentum* 3, Rome, 1977.

Vawter, B., 'The Johannine Sacramentary', *TS* 17, 1956, pp. 151–166.

Ward, R.A., 'The Semantics of Sacramental Language; With Special Reference to Baptism', *TB* 17, 1966, pp, 99–108.

Worden, T., 'The Holy Eucharist in St. John — I', *Scr* 15, 1963, pp. 97–103.

——, 'The Holy Eucharist in St. John — II', *Scr* 16, 1964, pp. 5–16.

Zizioulas, J.D., *Being as Communion; Studies in Personhood and the Church*, London, 1985.

IV. Johannine Christianity

Agourides, S., 'Peter and John in the Fourth Gospel', StEv IV, ed. by F.L. Cross, Berlin, 1968, pp. 3–7.

Anderson, P.N., 'Was the Fourth Evangelist a Quaker?', *QRT* 76, 1991, pp. 27–43.

——, 'The *Sitz im Leben* of the Johannine Bread of Life Discourse and its Evolving Context', paper presented at the 1993 SNTS Johannine Literature Seminar.

Barrett, C.K., 'Johanneisches Christentum', in J. Becker's *Die Anfänge des Christentums*, Stuttgart, 1987, pp. 255–278.

Brown, R.E., *The Churches the Apostles Left Behind*, New York, 1984, pp. 84–123.

——, *The Community of The Beloved Disciple*, New York, 1979.

——, 'Johannine Ecclesiology — The Community's Origins', *Interpreting the Gospels*, ed. by J.L. Mays, Philadelphia, 1981, pp. 291–307 (originally in *Int* 31, 1977, pp. 379–393).

——, ' "Other Sheep Not of this Fold": the Johannine Perspective on Christian Diversity in the Late First Century', *JBL* 97, 1978, pp. 5–22.

——, 'The Relationship to the Fourth Gospel Shared by the Author of 1 John and by his Opponents', in *Text and Interpretation*, ed. by E. Best and R. McL. Wilson, Cambridge, 1979, pp. 57–68.

Bultmann, R., *Theology of the New Testament* Vol. II, New York, 1955, pp. 3–14.

Burge, G.M., *The Anointed Community; The Holy Spirit in the Johannine Tradition*, Grand Rapids, 1987.

Byrne, B., 'The Faith of the Beloved Disciple and the Community in John 20', *JSNT* 23, (1985), pp. 83–97.

Cullmann, O., *The Johannine Circle*, E.t. J. Bowden, London, 1976.

Culpepper, A., *The Johannine School*, SBLDS 26, Missoula, 1975.

Dahl, N.A., 'The Johannine Church and History', in Ashton's *Interpretation*, pp. 122–140 (repr. from *Current Issues in New Testament Interpretation*, 1962).

Dodd, C.H., *The Interpretation of the Fourth Gospel*, Cambridge, 1953, pp. 3–9.

Dunn, J.D.G., *Unity and Diversity in the New Testament*, London/Philadelphia (1977) 1990.

Grayston, K., 'Jesus and the Church in St. John's Gospel', *London Quarterly and Holborn Review* 35, 1967, pp. 106–115.

Haacker, K., 'Jesus und die Kirche nach Johannes', *TZ* 29, 1973, pp. 179–201.

Howard, W.F., *Christianity According to St. John*, London, 1943.

Jonge, M. de, 'The Beloved Disciple and the Date of the Gospel of John', in *Text and Interpretation*, pp. 99–114.

Käsemann, E., *The Testament of Jesus*, E.t. G. Krodel, Philadelphia (Gr. 1966) 1968.

Kysar, R., 'Community and Gospel: Vectors in Fourth Gospel Criticism' in *Interpreting the Gospels*, 1981, pp. 265–277 (originally in *Int* 31, 1977, pp. 355–366).

Lieu, J., *The Second and Third Epistles of John*, SNTW, Edinburgh, 1986.

Martyn, J.L., *The Gospel of John in Christian History*, (three previously published essays, etc.) New York, 1978.

Maynard, A.H., 'The Role of Peter in the Fourth Gospel', *NTS* 30, 1984, pp. 531–548.

Meeks, W.A., 'The Man from Heaven in Johannine Sectarianism', repr. in Ashton's *Interpretation*, pp. 141–173 (originally in *JBL* 91, 1972, pp. 44–72).

Minear, P.S., 'The Audience of the Fourth Evangelist', in *Interpreting the Gospels*, 1981, pp. 247–264.

Painter, J., 'The Church and Israel in the Gospel of John: A Response', *NTS* 25, 1978, pp. 103–112.

——, 'The Farewell Discourses and the History of Johannine Christianity', *NTS* 27, 1981, pp. 525–543.

——, *The Quest for the Messiah; The History, Literature and Theology of the Johannine Community*, Edinburgh, 1991.

Pancaro, S., ' "People of God" in St. John's Gospel?', *NTS* 16, 1969, pp. 114–129.

Peterson, N.R., *The Gospel of John and the Sociology of Light*, Valley Forge, 1993.

Quast, K., *Peter and the Beloved Disciple; Figures for a Community in Crisis*, JSNTS 32, Sheffield, 1989.

Rensberger, D., *Johannine Faith and Liberating Community*, Philadelphia, 1988.

Segovia, F.F., *Love Relationships in the Johannine Tradition*, SBLDS 58, Chico, 1982.

Smith, D.M., 'Johannine Christianity: Some Reflections on its Character and Delineation', *NTS* 21, 1975, pp. 222–248.

Smith, T.V., *Petrine Controversies in Early Christianity; Attitudes towards Peter in Christian Writings of the First Two Centuries* WUNT 2 #15, Tübingen, 1985, esp. pp. 143–190.

Snyder, G.F., 'John 13:16 and the Anti-Petrinism of the Johannine Tradition', *BR* 16, 1971, pp. 5–15.

Staley, J.L., *The Print's First Kiss; A Rhetorical Investigation of the Implied Reader in the Fourth Gospel* SBLDS 82, Atlanta, 1988.

Wahlde, Urban C., *The Johannine Commandments*, New York/Mahwah, 1990.

Whitacre, R.A., *Johannine Polemic: The Role of Tradition and Theology*, SBLDS 67, Chico, 1982.

Woll, B.D., *Johannine Christianity in Conflict: Authority, Rank and Succession in the First Farewell Discourse* SBLDS 60, Chico, 1981.

Yarboro Collins, A., 'Crisis and Community in the Gospel of John', *CTM* 7, 1980, pp. 196–204.

V. Interdisciplinary Resources

Anderson, P.N., 'Peter and John: From Personalities to Prototypes' (unpublished; a five-session course taught for the Center for Christian Studies, Portland, OR, 1989).

——, 'Primitive Christology: From Personal Experience to Orthodox Creed ... *and Back Again*' (unpublished; an eight-session course taught for the Center for Christian Studies, Portland, OR, 1992).

——, 'Bakhtin's Dialogism and the Corrective Rhetoric of the Johannine Misunderstanding Dialogue' (unpublished paper presented at the 1994 National AAR/SBL Meeting in the Rhetoric and the New Testament Section).

Bakhtin, M., *The Dialogic Imagination*, ed. M. Holquist, Austin/London, 1981.

——, *Bakhtin School Papers,* E.t., N. Owen, Russian Poetics in Translation 10, 1983.

Berger, P., '*The Sacred Canopy'; Elements of a Sociological Theory of Religion*, New York, 1967.

Browning, R., 'A Death in the Desert', *The Poems of Robert Browning* II, Everyman's Library, London/New York, 1914 ed., pp. 486–503.

Bultmann, R., 'The Significance of "Dialectical Theology" for the Scientific Study of the New Testament', in his *Faith and Understanding*, London, pp. 145–164.

Chernus, I., *Mysticism in Rabbinnic Judaism*, Berlin/New York, 1982.

Ciholas, P., 'The Socratic and Johannine *Sēmeion* as Divine Manifestation', *Per.Rel.St.* 9, 1982, pp. 251–265.

Clark, K. and M. Holquist, *Mikhail Bakhtin*, Cambridge Mass./London, 1984.

Cumming, R.D., *Starting Point; An Introduction to the Dialectic of Existence*, Chicago, 1979.

Diefenbeck, J.A., 'Dialectic as the Relation of Absolute Assertions', in his *A Celebration of Subjective Thought*, Illinois University Press, 1984, pp. 155–168.

Duke, P.D., *Irony in the Fourth Gospel*, Atlanta, 1985.

Dulles, A., *Models of Revelation*, Garden City, NY, 1983.

Dunning, S.N., 'The Dialectic of Contradiction of Kierkegaard's Aesthetic Stage', *Journal for the American Academy of Religion* 49:3, pp. 382–408.

Dykstra, C. and S. Parks, *Faith Development and Fowler*, Birmingham, AL, 1986.

Fowler, J., *Stages of Faith: The Psychology of Human Development and the Quest for Meaning*, San Francisco, 1981.

——, *Becoming Adult, Becoming Christian; Adult Development and the Christian Faith*, San Francisco, 1984.

Grollenberg, L., *Unexpected Messiah; or, How the Bible Can be Misleading*, E.t. J. Bowden, London, 1988.

Lessing, G.E., 'Eine Duplik' (1778), in his *Werke* Bd. 6, Zürich, 1965, pp. 294ff.

Loder, J., *The Transforming Moment; Understanding Convictional Experiences,* San Francisco, 1981.

Malina, B.J., *The New Testament World; Insights from Cultural Anthropology*, Louisville, 1981.

Palmer, P., *To Know as We Are Known; A Spirituality of Education*, San Francisco, 1983.

Plato, *Theatetus*, translation and essay by R.A.H. Waterfield, Penguin Classics, 1987.

Polanyi, M., *Personal Knowledge*, Chicago, 1958.

Riches, J. and A. Millar, 'Conceptual Change in the Synoptic Tradition', in *Alternative Approaches to New Testament Study*, ed., A.E. Harvey, London, 1985, pp. 37–60.

Ricoeur, P., 'Toward a Hermeneutic of Revelation', in his *Essays on Biblical Interpretation*, Philadelphia/London, 1981, pp. 73–118.

Robinson, R., *Plato's Earlier Dialectic*, New York/London, 1980, esp. pp. 61–92.

Shaw, G., *The Cost of Authority; Manipulation and Freedom in the New Testament*, London, 1983, pp. 190–292.

Theissen, G., *Psychological Aspects of Pauline Theology*, SNTW, E.t. (of 1983) by J.P. Galvin, Edinburgh, 1987.

Wallis, R., *Sectarianism; Analyses of Religious and Non-Religious Sects*, London, 1975.

Weber, M., *The Sociology of Religion*, E.t., E. Fischoff (Ger. 1922, rev. 1956) London, 1963.

Wells, G.J., and E.L. Loftus, (eds.) *Eyewitness Testimony: Psychological Perspectives*, Cambridge, 1984.

Yamauchi, E.M., 'Magic in the Biblical World', *TynB* 34, 1983, pp. 169–200.

——, 'The Descent of Ishtar, the Fall of Sophia, and the Jewish Roots of Gnosticism', *TynB* 29, 1978, pp. 143–175.

Yarmey, A.D. "Age as a Factor in Eyewitness Memory", in *Eyewitness Testimony; Psychological Perspectives*, ed. G.L. Wells and E.L. Loftus, Cambridge, 1984, pp. 142–154.

Indexes

I: Scripture and Ancient Texts

1. *Old Testament*

2. *New Testament*

3. Other Ancient Literature

II: Names

III: Thematic Index